Schilpp, Paul Ar-
thur

The philosophy of
Sarvepalli Ra-
dhakrishnan

DATE DUE

THE PHILOSOPHY OF
SARVEPALLI RADHAKRISHNAN

THE LIBRARY OF LIVING PHILOSOPHERS

PAUL ARTHUR SCHILPP, *Editor*

Already Published:

THE PHILOSOPHY OF JOHN DEWEY (1939)

THE PHILOSOPHY OF GEORGE SANTAYANA (1940)

THE PHILOSOPHY OF ALFRED NORTH WHITEHEAD (1941)

*THE PHILOSOPHY OF G. E. MOORE (1942)

THE PHILOSOPHY OF BERTRAND RUSSELL (1944)

THE PHILOSOPHY OF ERNST CASSIRER (1949)

ALBERT EINSTEIN: PHILOSOPHER-SCIENTIST (1949)

THE PHILOSOPHY OF SARVEPALLI RADHAKRISHNAN (1952)

In Preparation:

THE PHILOSOPHY OF KARL JASPERS

THE PHILOSOPHY OF JACQUES MARITAIN

Other volumes to be announced later

*Starred volume above is temporarily out of print. See last paragraph of the General Introduction.

SIR SARVEPALLI RADHAKRISHNAN

THE PHILOSOPHY OF
SARVEPALLI
RADHAKRISHNAN

Edited by

PAUL ARTHUR SCHILPP

NORTHWESTERN UNIVERSITY

NEW YORK

TUDOR PUBLISHING COMPANY

THE PHILOSOPHY OF SARVEPALLI RADHAKRISHNAN

Copyright 1952
by The Library of Living Philosophers, Inc.

GENERAL INTRODUCTION *

TO

"THE LIBRARY OF LIVING PHILOSOPHERS"

ACCORDING to the late F. C. S. Schiller, the greatest obstacle to fruitful discussion in philosophy is "the curious etiquette which apparently taboos the asking of questions about a philosopher's meaning while he is alive." The "interminable controversies which fill the histories of philosophy," he goes on to say, "could have been ended at once by asking the living philosophers a few searching questions."

The confident optimism of this last remark undoubtedly goes too far. Living thinkers have often been asked "a few searching questions," but their answers have not stopped "interminable controversies" about their real meaning. It is none the less true that there would be far greater clarity of understanding than is now often the case, if more such searching questions had been directed to great thinkers while they were still alive.

This, at any rate, is the basic thought behind the present undertaking. The volumes of *The Library of Living Philosophers* can in no sense take the place of the major writings of great and original thinkers. Students who would know the philosophies of such men as John Dewey, George Santayana, Alfred North Whitehead, Benedetto Croce, G. E. Moore, Bertrand Russell, Ernst Cassirer, Karl Jaspers, *et al.,* will still need to read the writings of these men. There is no substitute for first-hand contact with the original thought of the philosopher himself. Least of all does this *Library* pretend to be such a substitute. The *Library* in fact will spare neither effort nor expense in offering to the student the best possible guide to the published writings of a given thinker. We shall attempt to meet this aim by providing at the end of each volume in our series a complete bibliography of the published work of the philosopher in question. Nor should one overlook the fact that the essays in each volume cannot but finally lead to this same goal. The interpretative and critical discussions of the various phases of

* This *General Introduction,* setting forth the underlying conception of this *Library,* is purposely reprinted in each volume (with only very minor changes).

v

a greater thinker's work and, most of all, the reply of the thinker himself, are bound to lead the reader to the works of the philosopher himself.

At the same time, there is no denying the fact that different experts find different ideas in the writings of the same philosopher. This is as true of the appreciative interpreter and grateful disciple as it is of the critical opponent. Nor can it be denied that such differences of reading and of interpretation on the part of other experts often leave the neophyte aghast before the whole maze of widely varying and even opposing interpretations. Who is right and whose interpretation shall he accept? When the doctors disagree among themselves, what is the poor student to do? If, finally, in desperation, he decides that all of the interpreters are probably wrong and that the only thing for him to do is to go back to the original writings of the philosopher himself and then make his own decision—uninfluenced (as if this were possible!) by the interpretation of any one else—the result is not that he has actually come to the meaning of the original philosopher himself, but rather that he has set up one more interpretation, which may differ to a greater or lesser degree from the interpretations already existing. It is clear that in this direction lies chaos, just the kind of chaos which Schiller has so graphically and inimitably described.[1]

It is curious that until now no way of escaping this difficulty has been seriously considered. It has not occurred to students of philosophy that one effective way of meeting the problem at least partially is to put these varying interpretations and critiques before the philosopher while he is still alive and to ask him to act at one and the same time as both defendant and judge. If the world's great living philosophers can be induced to co-operate in an enterprise whereby their own work can, at least to some extent, be saved from becoming merely "dessicated lecture-fodder," which on the one hand "provides innocuous sustenance for ruminant professors," and, on the other hand, gives an opportunity to such ruminants and their understudies to "speculate safely, endlessly, and fruitlessly, about what a philosopher must have meant" (Schiller), they will have taken a long step toward making their intentions clearly comprehensible.

With this in mind, *The Library of Living Philosophers* expects to publish at more or less regular intervals a volume on each of the greater among the world's living philosophers. In each case it will

---

[1] In his essay on "Must Philosophers Disagree?" in the volume by the same title (Macmillan, London, 1934), from which the above quotations were taken.

be the purpose of the editor of *The Library* to bring together in the volume the interpretations and criticisms of a wide range of that particular thinker's scholarly contemporaries, each of whom will be given a free hand to discuss the specific phase of the thinker's work which has been assigned to him. All contributed essays will finally be submitted to the philosopher with whose work and thought they are concerned, for his careful perusal and reply. And, although it would be expecting too much to imagine that the philosopher's reply will be able to stop all differences of interpretation and of critique, this should at least serve the purpose of stopping certain of the grosser and more general kinds of misinterpretations. If no further gain than this were to come from the present and projected volumes of this *Library*, it would seem to be fully justified.

In carrying out this principal purpose of the *Library*, the editor announces that (in so far as humanly possible) each volume will conform to the following pattern:

First, a series of expository and critical articles written by the leading exponents and opponents of the philosopher's thought;

Second, the reply to the critics and commentators by the philosopher himself;

Third, an intellectual autobiography of the thinker whenever this can be secured; in any case an authoritative and authorized biography; and

Fourth, a bibliography of the writings of the philosopher to provide a ready instrument to give access to his writings and thought.

The editor has deemed it desirable to secure the services of an Advisory Board of philosophers to aid him in the selection of the subjects of future volumes. The names of the six prominent American philosophers who have consented to serve appear below. To each of them the editor expresses his sincere gratitude.

Future volumes in this series will appear in as rapid succession as is feasible in view of the scholarly nature of this *Library*. The next two volumes in this series should be those of Karl Jaspers and Jacques Maritain.

As many would-be purchasers of earlier volumes in this series have known to their discomfort, the first four volumes of our *Library* had been out of print for a number of years. The editor is happy to report that, owing to the fact that a new publisher, the

Tudor Publishing Company of New York City, has taken over the publication of our *Library*, seven of the present eight volumes in our series are again in print. At the time of this writing, only Volume IV, on *The Philosophy of G. E. Moore*, is still out of print. However, the entire project of *The Library of Living Philosophers* still is not on a sound financial foundation, owing to the lack of necessary funds. The *Library* would be deeply grateful, therefore, for gifts and donations. Moreover, since November 6th, 1947, any gifts or donations made to The Library of Living Philosophers, Inc., are deductible by the donors in arriving at their taxable net income in conformity with the Internal Revenue Code of the Treasury Department of the United States of America.

P. A. S.
Editor

DEPARTMENT OF PHILOSOPHY
NORTHWESTERN UNIVERSITY
EVANSTON, ILLINOIS

ADVISORY BOARD

TABLE OF CONTENTS

ix

PREFACE

FROM its inception, now twelve years ago, this series has been called, *The Library of Living Philosophers,* NOT "The Library of American Philosophers" NOR "The Library of Western Philosophers." Which is to say that this series was never conceived in a narrow, national, racial, religious, or in any other provincial fashion. As John Wesley had "the world" as his "parish," so *The Library of Living Philosophers* was meant to include the *living* philosophers of the world, with regard only for their influence upon the philosophical thinking of this century.

It was inevitable, therefore, that an Oriental philosopher of such world-wide reputation as Sir Sarvepalli Radhakrishnan should become the subject of a volume in this series. And this perhaps all the more so because he also is one of the foremost living Absolute Idealists, representing the Great Tradition in philosophy, which, thus far, has had no representation in our *Library.*

If, in addition, a volume on *The Philosophy of Sarvepalli Radhakrishnan* should be of aid in bringing Oriental thought and Occidental philosophy a little closer together, such a result is certainly greatly to be welcomed. Nor would it be possible to find a more excellent example of a living "bridge" between East and West than Professor Radhakrishnan. Steeped, as Radhakrishnan has been since his childhood, in the life, traditions, and philosophical heritage of his native India, he has also struck deep roots in Western philosophy, which he has been studying tirelessly ever since his undergraduate college-days in Madras Christian College, and in which he is as thoroughly at home as any Western philosopher. Beyond this: more than any living philosopher of East or West, Radhakrishnan has been devoting the major portion of his academic career as well as of his voluminous writings to what has almost become the passion of his life, namely that of bringing East and West together: by interpreting the great cultural tradition and spiritual insight of the East to the West, on the one hand, and by helping the East, on the other hand, to realize that—not merely in science and technology, but also—in philosophical thought and speculation the East can still learn some important lessons from the

xi

West. As leader of his country's delegation in UNESCO, Radhakrishnan has been doing additional important yeoman's service in the cause of international peace, understanding, good will, and co-operation.

In the preparation of this volume the editor owes Radhakrishnan an inestimable debt of gratitude. Throughout the twelve years of the existence of this *Library,* no other philosopher has given of his time more unstintedly to this project than has Professor Radhakrishnan. His advice and helpful co-operation have been available to the editor at all times. Not merely the editor's gratitude but that of all readers who will profit from a perusal of this volume is, therefore, due him.

There are bound to be some readers who, like the editor himself, could have wished that Radhakrishnan's ostensible "autobiography," written for this volume, might have contained a bit more of the details of his life. However, Radhakrishnan himself has justified his procedure in the letter which the reader will find included here in facsimile reproduction of Radhakrishnan's handwriting. One reason for his procedure, which our philosopher does not mention in this letter, would seem to lie in the fact that, for the volume, *Religion in Transition* (edited by Vergilius Ferm, and published in 1937), Radhakrishnan had already written a philosophical autobiography, under the revealingly accurate title, "My Search for Truth." That essay is a veritable gem, in any case, which no reader of the present volume should fail to read. (Fortunately for readers who do not possess the larger symposium, Shiva Lal Agarwala & Co., Ltd., Publishers, in Agra, U.P., India, have brought out a reasonably priced reprint of the 49 pages of this essay.)

The editor is also deeply obligated to the other contributors of this volume, who, by their kind co-operation, have not merely helped to make this book possible but made the work on it a labor of love. True enough, it is difficult to escape the impression that, owing to the universal Oriental spirit of kindness and courtesy as well as owing to the very high esteem in which Radhakrishnan is held everywhere, particularly in his native India, a larger number of essays in this volume (than was the case in former volumes) are perhaps more eulogistic in character than critical or philosophically objective. On the other hand, it is noteworthy that some of the most sympathetic treatments of Radhakrishnan's thought come from the pens of European and American writers, whereas at least two of the most negatively critical appraisals are written by Indian contributors. This fact in itself may be one of the most hopeful signs of the growing *rapprochement* between Eastern and Western philosophy.

It is to be regretted that one essay reached Professor Radhakrishnan's hands after his formal "Reply to Critics" had, in essence, already been completed. This regret is the more profound because the essay (Professor Browning's "Reason and Types of Intuition in Radhakrishnan's Philosophy"), perhaps more than any other essay in the entire volume, would seem to raise the most fundamental problems and crucial questions for such a philosophical position as that held by Radhakrishnan. If the problems discussed and the questions raised by Browning could have had sufficiently detailed discussion and pointed answers from the pen and mind of Radhakrishnan himself, the permanent value of the present volume could have been greatly enhanced. However, by the time Browning's paper reached Professor Radhakrishnan, the entire manuscript of the volume was almost on its way to the printer.

One of the greatest debts of gratitude the editor owes to the Watumull Foundation of Los Angeles and Honolulu. Without a grant-in-aid for research in India, which the Watumull Foundation kindly awarded to the editor for the purpose of completing the work of this volume, the editor would never have had the privilege of seeing and studying Indian thought and life at first hand. The privilege of such observation and study, for the past six months, has not merely been of tremendous aid to the editor in better understanding and appreciating India's philosophical heritage and spiritual outlook on life, but has, at the same time, greatly enriched his own life and work by direct personal contact with some of the foremost of living Indian philosophers and other scholars. His visits to and lectures before audiences of fifteen Indian (and Ceylonese and Kashmiri) universities have provided opportunities of inestimable value and of unforgettable character to him. Nor can he let this opportunity go by without expressing publicly his deep-felt gratitude and appreciation to the many Vice-Chancellors of and scholars in Indian universities, as well as to Governors of some of India's States and to their Prime Ministers for their almost uniform kindness, hospitality, and generosity with which he was met almost everywhere in India, Ceylon, and Kashmir. He can only express the hope that all of these persons will feel at least partly repaid for their kindness by the contents of the present volume, which certainly should be better than it possibly could have been without the deepened understanding of and insight into Indian life and thought which the travels and experiences of the past six months have made possible.

To the administration of Northwestern University the editor is indebted for the kindly and generously granted sabbatical leave during the academic year 1950/51 as well as for a small grant-in-aid from the Social Science Research Council of the Graduate School of the University.

Mr. Surindar Singh Suri, graduate student in the department of philosophy of Northwestern University, has kindly provided this volume with its valuable index. The editor's thanks are due to him as also to the Studio Everest in Calcutta, who have granted us the privilege of using their portrait-study of Professor Radhakrishnan as our frontispiece.

As will be noted by all who have been familiar with the first seven volumes in this series, the present one is the first volume to appear under the imprint of a new publisher. As of September 1st, 1950, the actual publication of the volumes in *The Library of Living Philosophers* has been taken over by the Tudor Publishing Company of New York.

The reader's attention should, finally, be called to the fact that uniform abbreviations have been used throughout this volume in all citations from Radhakrishnan's major works. A complete listing of these abbreviations will be found on p. 1. On the next page will be found a Note on the Transliteration of Sanskrit Words used in this volume.

Perhaps Professor Radhakrishnan will permit the editor to send this book out into the world of both East and West with a quotation from Radhakrishnan's own opening essay. On an early page of that essay, "The Religion of the Spirit and the World's Need," there occurs the following sentence, which expresses the spirit and intent of the present volume perhaps better than anything the editor could say:

"The prominent feature of our time is not so much the wars and the dictatorships which have disfigured it, but the impact of different cultures on one another, their interaction, and the emergence of a new civilisation based on the truths of spirit and the unity of mankind."

PAUL ARTHUR SCHILPP

"PRINCE OF KASHMIR" HOUSE-BOAT
NAGHIN BAGH (NEAR SRINAGAR)
KASHMIR, INDIA
MAY 31, 1951

ACKNOWLEDGMENTS

GRATEFUL acknowledgment is hereby made to the editors and publishers of all of Professor Radhakrishnan's works, and more particularly to Messrs. George Allen & Unwin, Ltd., London, the firm which has published most of Radhakrishnan's works; also to the authors, editors, and publishers of any other books or articles, quotations from which appear in this volume. We are especially grateful to them for the fact that they have not required us to make separate acknowledgment in the case of each separate quotation. It goes, of course, without saying that full bibliographical details are given.

ABBREVIATIONS USED FOR RADHAKRISHNAN'S PRINCIPAL WORKS

The principal works of Professor Radhakrishnan will be referred to in this volume by the use of the following *abbreviations*. Full bibliographical details for each of these works will be found in Part IV of this volume, entitled, BIBLIOGRAPHY, where each work is listed under the date of publication.

BG   The Bhagavadgita (1948)
D   Dhammapada (1950)
EPW   Education, Politics, and War (1944)
ER   Eastern Religions and Western Thought (1939)
EWR   East and West in Religion (1933)
FC   Freedom and Culture (1936)
GB   Gautama—the Buddha (1938)
GI   Great Indians (1949)
HH   The Heart of Hindusthan (1936)
HVL   The Hindu View of Life (1927)
IC   India and China (1947)
Ind P   Indian Philosophy (2 vols., 1923 & 1927, resp.)
ITP   Is This Peace? (1946)
IVL   The Idealist View of Life (1932)
K   Kalki, or: The Future of Civilization (1929)
MG   Mahatma Gandhi (1939)
MST   My Search for Truth (1937, in Religion in Transition; sep. offprint, 1948)
PRT   The Philosophy of Rabindranath Tagore (1918)
RR   The Reign of Religion in Contemporary Philosophy (1920)
RS   Religion and Society (1947)
RWN   The Religion We Need (1928)
SM   The Spirit in Man (1936, in Contemporary Indian Philosophy)
TB   The Teaching of Buddha (1933)

NOTE ON THE TRANSLITERATION
OF SANSKRIT WORDS

In so far as it has seemed necessary, the Sanskrit alphabet in this volume is transliterated as follows (following the s-called "Geneva System"):

(A) Vowels: a ā (â) i ī (î) u ū (û) ṛ ṝ ḷ e ai o au.
(B) Consonants: (1) Stops, Aspirated Stops, and Nasals:

    (a) Gutturals or Velars: k kh g gh ṅ
    (b) Palatals: c ch j jh ñ
    (c) Cerebrals or Retroflex Sounds: ṭ ṭh ḍ ḍh ṇ
    (d) Dentals: t th d dh n
    (e) Labials: p ph b bh m

(2) Semi-Vowels and Liquids: y r l v
(3) Spirants (Sibilants) and Spiritus Asper: ś (or ç) ṣ s h.

(C) Anusvara: ṃ (ṁ); Visarga: ḥ.

Sarvepalli Radhakrishnan

THE RELIGION OF THE SPIRIT
AND THE WORLD'S NEED
"Fragments of a Confession"

SYNOPSIS BY CHAPTER-TITLES

EMBASSY OF INDIA,
MOSCOW.

24ᵗʰ December 1950

My dear professor Schilpp,

I have your letter in which you ask me to make my introductory account a little more autobiographical than it is at present. I have added a few details but I do not think that you will be satisfied. Kindly forgive me.

I am not persuaded that the events of my life are of much interest to the readers of this volume. Besides, there is a sense in which our writings, though born out of ourselves, are worth more than what we are. We take much trouble about them even as devoted parents do with their children. As for the emotions and desires, which make life so intense and interesting, how many of us look straight into our souls?

I am now at work on the Reply to Critics and shall send it to you when all the papers reach me.

With admiring and grateful regards,

S. Radhakrishnan

FACSIMILE REPRODUCTION OF RADHAKRISHNAN'S LETTER TO THE EDITOR, EXPLAINING THE UNIQUE NATURE OF HIS "FRAGMENTS OF A CONFESSION"

THE RELIGION OF THE SPIRIT AND THE WORLD'S NEED: FRAGMENTS OF A CONFESSION

I. How I Came to the Study of Philosophy

LIFE and Writings. No man's story of his own life can fail to be of interest to others, if it is written in sincerity. Even if the stage be small and the rôle of the participant a minor one, the interactions of chance and circumstance with human desires and ideals that shape the destinies of any individual are of some interest to his fellows. But of all writing, autobiographical writing is the most delicate. We do not wish to confess our deeds and misdeeds in public. We are inclined to show to the world more of our successes than of our set-backs, more of our gains than of our losses. Robert Browning tells us that the meanest of mankind has two sides to his life, one to face the world with and the other to show the woman he loves. We have two sides, one in ordinary life and the other when we write about ourselves for the public. We want to live an imaginary life in other people's ideas of us. We then direct our efforts to seeming what we are not. Besides, any sensitive man who takes life seriously is somewhat inaccessible to the public. If he happens to be a writer, he does not generally reveal himself except through his writings, where he recreates his personal experiences by clothing them with general significance. Through his writings, which constitute his main life work, he tries to communicate the vital ideas which have shaped his life. My writings are no more than fragments of a confession.

In the present account it is not my intention to speak of my personal life, my parents and ancestry, my marriage and family, my likes and dislikes, my struggles and disappointments. No particular good fortune has lifted me above the sphere in which our common humanity struggles along, and I have had my own share of the burdens and anxieties of life. Although these are of immense importance to me, discretion forbids me to speak of them. Besides, they are of no particular interest to the philosophical public, who may wish to know my ideas and the processes of thought which led up to them.

5

Choice of Philosophy. There are some who make up their mind early what they are going to be and plan carefully from their early years to reach their goal. They find out what they wish to do and try to do it with all their might. I cannot say that I came to the study of philosophy as one dedicated from childhood to the service of the altar. I am not a philosopher because I could not help being one. "Life," says Dilthey, "is a mysterious fabric, woven of chance, fate and character." That philosophy became the subject of my special study, was it a part of my destiny, was it the result of my character or was it mere chance?

When I was a young student of seventeen in the Madras Christian College, and was vacillating about the choice of a subject from out of the five options of mathematics, physics, biology, philosophy and history, a cousin of mine, who took his degree that year, passed on his textbooks in philosophy to me, G. F. Stout's *Manual of Psychology;* J. Welton's *Logic* (two volumes) and J. S. Mackenzie's *Manual of Ethics;* and that decided my future interest. To all appearance this is a mere accident. But when I look at the series of accidents that have shaped my life, I am persuaded that there is more in this life than meets the eye. Life is not a mere chain of physical causes and effects. Chance seems to form the surface of reality, but deep down other forces are at work. If the universe is a living one, if it is spiritually alive, nothing in it is merely accidental. 'The moving finger writes and having writ moves on.'

When, however, the study of philosophy became my life's work, I entered a domain which sustained me both intellectually and spiritually all these years. My conception of a philosopher was in some ways similar to that of Marx, who proclaimed in his famous *Theses on Feuerbach* that philosophy had hitherto been concerned with *interpreting* life, but that the time had come for it to *change* life. Philosophy is committed to a creative task. Although in one sense philosophy is a lonely pilgrimage of the spirit, in another sense it is a function of life.

Contemporary History and India's Rôle. I spent the first eight years of my life (1888-1896) in a small town in South India, Tirutani, which is even today a great centre of religious pilgrimage. My parents were religious in the traditional sense of the term. I studied in Christian Missionary institutions for twelve years, Lutheran Mission High School, Tirupati (1896-1900), Voorhees' College, Vellore (1900-1904), and the Madras Christian College (1904-1908). Thus I grew up in an atmosphere where the unseen was a living reality. My approach to the problems of philosophy from the angle

of religion as distinct from that of science or of history was determined by my early training. I was not able to confine philosophy
to logic and epistemology.

There are tasks and responsibilities open to an Indian student
of philosophic thought, living in this profoundly meaningful
period of history. The prominent feature of our time is not so
much the wars and the dictatorships which have disfigured it, but
the impact of different cultures on one another, their interaction,
and the emergence of a new civilisation based on the truths of
spirit and the unity of mankind. The tragedies and catastrophies
which occupy so much of the foreground of our consciousness are
symbolic of the breakdown of the separatist tendencies and the
movement towards the integration of national societies in a world
whole. In the confusions of the contemporary scene, this fallible,
long-suffering and apparently helpless generation should not overlook the great movement towards integration in which it is par-
ticipating.

Through her connection with Great Britain, India is once again
brought into relationship with the Western world. The interpenetration of the two great currents of human effort at such a
crisis in the history of the human race is not without meaning for
the future. With its profound sense of spiritual reality brooding
over the world of our ordinary experience, with its lofty insights
and immortal aspirations, Indian thought may perhaps wean us
moderns from a too exclusive occupation with secular life or with
the temporary formulations in which logical thought has too often
sought to imprison spiritual aspiration. We do not seem to be
mentally or spiritually prepared for the increasing intimacy into
which remote peoples are drawn by the force of physical and economic circumstances. The world which has found itself as a single
body is feeling for its soul. May we not prepare for the truth of
the world's yet unborn soul by a free interchange of ideas and the
development of a philosophy which will combine the best of European humanism and Asiatic Religion, a philosophy profounder and
more living than either, endowed with greater spiritual and ethical
force, which will conquer the hearts of men and compel peoples
to acknowledge its sway? [1] Such a view of the function of philosophy
in modern life is born out of a necessity of thought and an Indian
student may perhaps make a little contribution to the development
of a world perspective in philosophy.

[1] ER, 259.

II. The Philosophical Situation

Tradition and Experiment. The danger of all human occupation is present also in philosophy, the danger of accepting standard solutions and performing mechanically, through sheer laziness and inertia, the established modes of thinking. If we teach ready-made doctrines and see in any system of thought perfection and completeness, we miss the true spirit of inquiry. There cannot be an authentic philosophical situation unless there is uneasiness about prevalent opinions. If we lose the capacity to doubt we cannot get into the mood of philosophic thought. Whitehead's observation that 'life is an offensive against the repetitive mechanism of the universe' is true of the philosophic life also.

If we take any philosopher as a *guru,* if we treat his works as gospel, if we make of his teaching a religion complete with dogma and exegesis, we may become members of the congregation of the faithful, but will not possess the openness of mind essential for a critical understanding of the master's views. The true teachers help us to think for ourselves in the new situations which arise. We would be unworthy disciples if we do not question and criticise them. They try to widen our knowledge and help us to see clearly. The true teacher is like *Kṛṣṇa* in the *Bhagavadgītā,* who advises Arjuna to think for himself and do as he chooses, *yathā icchasi tathā kuru.*[2]

There is, however, a longing in the human mind for eternal truths embodied in fixed formulas which we need not discuss, modify or correct. We do crave for a constant rule of life, a sure guide to heaven. Devotion to a master who lays down the law gives us rest, confidence and security. To minds wearied and worried by doubt, authoritarian religions give a sense of release and purpose. We cannot, however, expect rational criticism from those who have too much reverence for authority.

Again, tradition in human life takes the place of instinct in animals. It makes a man think, feel and desire in forms that have prevailed in the human environment for centuries and about whose validity he feels no misgivings whatsoever. We are all born to our traditions. In regard to them there is a certain degree of inevitability. We are as little free in choosing our cultural ancestors as we are in choosing our physical ancestors. Insofar as a person lives according to tradition and obeys it instinctively, he leads

[2] BG, xviii, 63.

a life of faith, of a believer. The need for philosophy arises when faith in tradition is shaken.

In the matter of tradition the Americans are in a fortunate position because they have no ancestors and no classic soil. Goethe, in a little poem, *Amerika, du hast es besser,* writes 'your fate is happier than that of our old continent. You have no ruined chateaux . . . you are not troubled by vain memories and useless quarrels.' India, however, has had a long tradition and I grew up in it. I started therefore with a prejudice in its favour.

The Undermining of Tradition. My teachers in Christian missionary institutions cured me of this faith and restored for me the primordial situation in which all philosophy is born. They were teachers of philosophy, commentators, interpreters, apologists for the Christian way of thought and life, but were not, in the strict sense of the term, seekers of truth. By their criticism of Indian thought they disturbed my faith and shook the traditional props on which I leaned.

While the undogmatic apprehensions and the discipline of mind which Hinduism provides as the essential means for the discovery of truth are established in a rigorously logical manner, while the great insights, fundamental motives and patterns of thought of Hindu religion have meaning for us even today, it has taken on in its long history many arbitrary and fanciful theories and is full of shackles which constrict the free life of the spirit. Besides, we live in a time when we have become the inheritors of the world's thought. We have accumulated much historical knowledge about religions and philosophies. We find that innumerable people before us have raised these questions about the nature of the universe, the principle of being and have given answers which they treated as final and absolute. The very multiplicity of these absolutisms makes it difficult for us to assume, if we are honest, that our absolutism is the true one and all others false. Faced by these conflicting and competing absolutisms, we become either traditionalists or sceptics. A critical study of the Hindu religion was thus forced on me.

I started my professional life as a teacher of philosophy in the Madras Presidency College in April 1909, where I worked for the next seven years. During that period I studied the classics of Hinduism, the *Upaniṣads,* the *Bhagavadgītā* and the commentaries on the *Brahma Sūtra* by the chief ācāryas, Śaṁkara, Rāmānuja, Madhva, Nimbārka and others, the Dialogues of the Buddha as well as the scholastic works of Hinduism, Buddhism and Jainism.

Among the Western thinkers, the writings of Plato, Plotinus and Kant, and those of Bradley and Bergson influenced me a great deal. My relations with my great Indian contemporaries, Tagore and Gandhi, were most friendly for nearly thirty years, and I realise the tremendous significance they had for me.

Although I admire the great masters of thought, ancient and modern, Eastern and Western, I cannot say that I am a follower of any, accepting his teaching in its entirety. I do not suggest that I refused to learn from others or that I was not influenced by them. While I was greatly stimulated by the minds of all those whom I have studied, my thought does not comply with any fixed traditional pattern. For my thinking had another source and proceeded from my own experience, which is not quite the same as what is acquired by mere study and reading. It is born of spiritual experience rather than deduced from logically ascertained premises. Philosophy is produced more by our encounter with reality than by the historical study of such encounters. In my writings I have tried to communicate my insight into the meaning of life. I am not sure, however, that I have succeeded in conveying my inmost ideas. I tried to show that my general position provides a valid interpretation of the world, which seems to me to be consistent with itself, to accord with the facts as we know them, and to foster the life of spirit.

III. INDIAN PHILOSOPHY

Continuity with the Past.   Human minds do not throw up sudden stray thoughts without precedents or ancestors. History is continuity and advance. There is no such thing as utterly spontaneous generation. Philosophic experiments of the past have entered into the living mind of the present. Tradition links generations one with another and all progress is animated by ideas which it seems to supersede. The debt we owe to our spiritual ancestors is to study them. Traditional continuity is not mechanical reproduction; it is creative transformation, an increasing approximation to the ideal of truth. Life goes on not by repudiating the past but by accepting it and weaving it into the future in which the past undergoes a rebirth. The main thing is to remember and create anew. Confucius said: "He who by reanimating the Old can gain knowledge of the New is fit to be a teacher." [3]

Indian people have concentrated for centuries on the problems of divine reality, human life and destiny. Philosophic wisdom has

[3] *Analects.* II. 10. Arthur Waley's English Tr.

been the drive and inspiration of their culture. We today think with our past and from the level to which the past has taken us. *Influence of Indian Culture.* Indian wisdom has also contributed effectively to the cultural developments of the regions of South East Asia, which till yesterday were called Further India. The characteristic features of Indian culture can still be discerned from "Ayuthia and Angkor to Borobudur and Bali." India's historic influence spread through the arts of peace and not the weapons of war, through moral leadership and not political domination. Her influence could be discerned in the development of European thought from the time of the Orphic mysteries. Today Indian wisdom is essential not only for the revival of the Indian nation but also for the re-education of the human race.

Difficulties of Historical Interpretation. When that noble and generous thinker, Professor J. H. Muirhead, invited me in 1917 to write an account of Indian Philosophy for his Library of Philosophy, I accepted his call, though not without considerable doubt.

To outline the history of Indian philosophic thought, which has had a long span of development of over three thousand years, on a cautious estimate, is indeed a prodigious task and I was aware that it was beyond the capacity of any single person. It might be done by a band of scholars in a co-operative undertaking, spread over a number of years, with the assistance of many research workers. The result of such an undertaking will be, not a book but an encyclopaedia, careful and comprehensive. Again, no scholar, however learned, can know everything on so vast a field. There will be gaps and mistakes. Besides, history is not only seeing but also thinking. Thinking is always constructive, if not creative. Historical writing is a creative activity. It is different from historical research. By the latter we acquire a knowledge of the facts in their proper succession, the raw material. It is the task of historical writing to understand these facts and give us a feel of the past, communicate to us the vibration of life. This requires knowledge as well as sensibility. The writer may at times allow his personal bias to determine his presentation. His sense of proportion and relevance may not be shared by others. His work at best will be a personal interpretation and not an impersonal survey.

There is also the danger that we are inclined to interpret ancient systems in a manner acceptable to modern minds. Such efforts sometimes overstep the mark and make ancient thinkers look very much like contemporaries of ours. Often a sense of hero-worship exalts the classical thinkers above the level of history. Instead of trying to understand them, as they are, as human beings, however great in mind and spirit they may be, we give to them imaginary perfections and treat their writings as sacred texts which contain solutions for our present problems.

My Limited Aim. I was aware of the dangers and difficulties involved in an adequate historical interpretation of Indian thought as well as of my own limitations, philosophical and linguistic. I, therefore, assumed a modest task, to produce an introduction to a vast, varied, and complex process of development, a book which will arouse the interest of the readers in the insights and inspirations of the Indian genius. I tried to unroll a great panorama in which every element has some charm or interest. I tried not to overstate any case or indulge in personal dislike for its own sake.

History of philosophy should not be reduced to a mere statement of doctrines in chronological order. These doctrines are propositions, sentences with a meaning. Meanings are not absolute. They have no sense apart from when and by whom and for whom they were meant. The formulators of philosophical systems are not abstract thinkers or anonymous beings without birthdate or dwelling place. The date of a thinker and the place of the origin and growth of his thought are not external labels tacked on to systems, merely for placing them in their proper chronological order. Like all thought, philosophical thought belongs to the context of life. Its exponents belong to their age with its living beliefs and traditions, its scientific notions and myths. If we are to gain insight from the study of past writers, we must remove them from us, emphasise their distance in time and realise how different in many ways they are from us. To understand their thought we must learn to feel and understand their world even as they felt and understood it, never approaching them with condescension or contempt. Only in that way can we understand their living effective communication with us.

Need for Humility. There have been historians of Indian philosophy in our country who looked upon India's philosophic thought as a continuity in which it progressed rationally from one conception to another, where systems succeeded each other in intelligible order until it culminated in their own thought. All that was past was a progress towards their own present thinking. Mādhava's *Sarvadarśanasaṁgraha* is a well-known instance of the treatment of the history of thought as a continuous progress to *Advaita Vedānta*. In the West, Hegel related the past history of thought as a collection of errors over against which stood out his own idealism as the truth. Intellectual unselfishness or humility is the mother of all writing, even though that writing may relate to the history of philosophy.

Though we cannot say that systems succeed each other in an ordered progression, there is no arbitrariness. Changes of life have brought about changes in thought and *vice versa*. The past philosophical development in East and in West has an integral reality. It is not a bewildering maze of clashing opinions, utterly irrational. We can discern an order in the dynamic interplay of ideas.

In all philosophical interpretation, the right method is to interpret thinkers at their best, in the light of what they say in the moments of their clearest insight. There is no reason why philosophical writers should not be judged as other creative artists are, at least in the main, on the basis of their finest inspirations.

Ancient Indians do not belong to a different species from ourselves. An actual study of their views shows that they ask questions and find answers analogous in their diversity to some of the more important currents in modern thought. The systems of Nāgārjuna and Śaṁkara, for example, are marvels of precision and penetration, comparable to the very best of Western thought.

Comparative Method. In re-thinking the systems of the past, I sometimes employ terms with which the Western readers are familiar. I am aware of the limitations of the comparative method which can be either a bane or a blessing. We cannot overlook the different emphases, not only between East and West, but in the different systems of the East as well as in those of the West. These differences, when valid, are complementary, not contradictory. In many detailed investigations there is agreement between the thinkers of the East and the West.

The comparative method is relevant in the present context, when the stage is set, if not for the development of a world philosophy, at least for that of a world outlook. The different parts of the world cannot anymore develop separately and in independence of each other. Even as our political problem is to bring East and West together in a common brotherhood which transcends racial differences, so in the world of philosophy we have to bring about a cross-fertilisation of ideas. If systems of philosophy are themselves determined by historical circumstances, there is no reason why the methods adopted in historical interpretation should not take into account the needs and conditions of the age. Each interpreter appeals to his own generation. He is wise to let the generation that succeeds him choose its own exponents. It will do so whether he likes it or not. His work is fulfilled if he keeps the thought alive in his generation, helps to some extent his successors, and attempts to answer, so far as he can, the desire of his age.

IV. SCIENTIFIC OUTLOOK

The Contemporary Scene. Though I have not had a sense of vocation, a sense that I was born to do what I am now carrying out, my travels and engagements in different parts of the world for over a generation gave me a purpose in life. My one supreme interest has been to try to restore a sense of spiritual values to the millions of religiously displaced persons, who have been struggling to find precarious refuges in the emergency camps of Art and Science, of Fascism and Nazism, of Humanism and Communism. The first step to recovery is to understand the nature of the confusion of thought which absorbs the allegiance of millions of men. Among the major influences which foster a spirit of scepticism in regard to religious truth are the growth of the scientific spirit, the development of a technological civilisation, a formal or artificial religion which finds itself in conflict with an awakened social conscience, and a comparative study of religions.

Achievements of Science : Physics. The victories of science have been so dazzling and its progress so rapid that our minds are filled with scientific conceptions and habits of life. From the time Copernicus removed the earth from the centre of the universe, the primacy of man in the universe has disappeared. Till Galileo founded modern mathematical physics, the mathematically exact movements of the heavenly bodies were traced to psychic forces, supernatural agents, a vast hierarchy of angelic beings who inhabit the stars and control our destiny. The two centuries after Newton witnessed wide developments in astronomy, physics and chemistry, especially in increasing knowledge of the dimensions of the universe and of the nature and workings of matter. Sir James Jeans writes,

The last hundred years have seen more change than a thousand years of the Roman Empire, more than a hundred thousand years of the Stone Age. This change has resulted in large part from the applications of physical science, which, through the use of steam, electricity and petrol, and by way of the various industrial arts, now affects almost every moment of our existences. Its use in medicine and surgery may save our lives; its use in warfare may involve us in utter ruination. In its more abstract aspects it has exerted a powerful influence on our philosophies, our religions and our general outlook of life.[4]

Biology. Organic life is sought to be explained in accordance with clearly perceptible natural laws. Man himself is no exception to the general laws which govern organic processes. He should see himself as a part of an irrefragable web of cause and effect, of inviolable law. He is not a free being, capable of choice, able to decide whether he shall write classics of wisdom or advertisements for cosmetics. Heracleitus said long ago, 'Man's character is his fate.' [5]

Psychology. According to modern psychology, man is not master of himself even in his conscious ego. The conscious life of the soul is governed by animal instincts hidden and embedded in the unconscious. Freud writes:

Humanity has in the course of time had to endure from the hands of science two great outrages upon its naive self-love. The first was when it realised that our earth was not the centre of the universe, but only a tiny speck in the world-system. . . . That is associated in our minds with the name of Copernicus. . . . The second was when biological research robbed man of his peculiar privilege of having been specially created, and relegated him to a descent from the animal world, implying an ineradicable animal nature in him; this transvaluation has been accomplished in our time upon the instigation of Charles Darwin, Wallace and their predecessors. . . . But man's craving for grandiosity is now suffering the third and most bitter blow from the present day psychological research, which is endeavouring to prove to the 'ego' of each one of us that he is not even master in his own house but that he must remain content with the veriest scraps of information about what is going on unconsciously in his own mind.[6]

Freedom of the will is an egotistic delusion. Descartes said, "I regard the human body as a machine so built and put together that, still, although it had no mind, it would not fail to move in all the same ways as at present, since it does not move by the direction of its will." Sir Charles Sherrington writes:

Descartes' conception of the doings of man still finds its echo in official Russia. The citizen there taken *en gros,* seems to be viewed as a system of reflexes. The State can 'condition' and use these systems of reflexes. 'Reflexology,' as it is there called, becomes a science of Man on which the State leans. In 'reflexology' Descartes would find Ivan Pavlov of Petrograd his greatest successor; and the successor was an experimentalist as Descartes was not.[7]

---

[4] James Jeans, *The Growth of Physical Science* (1947).   [5] *Fragment* 121.

[6] Sigmund Freud, *Introductory Lectures on Psychoanalysis.* (English Tr. G. I. Riviere, 1922), 240.

[7] Charles Sherrington, *The Integrative Action of the Nervous System* (1926).

Human personality is determined by the external environment by which it is surrounded. It has no principle in it by which it can resist the environment. Such a view makes short work of miracles, of effective prayer and reduces man, dressed in a little brief rationality, to the level of circles and stones. What we call the soul of man is but an empty word. A highly developed cerebral animal, that is what man is.

Ethics. Human values are determined by the chance situation in which man finds himself and to which he has to adjust his way of living. Professor John Dewey writes, "Life is a process of experimented adjustment in a precarious world. Problems are solved when they arise, namely in action, in the adjustment of behaviour." [8] From such a view it follows that moral standards are subject to change. Professor Dewey says, "Values are as unstable as the forms of clouds. The things that possess them are exposed to all the contingencies of existence, and they are indifferent to our likings and tastes." [9]

History. Philosophers claim to establish history as a realm in which the freedom of man may be demonstrated as against the autocracy of nature. Professor Collingwood argues that historical thought is the discovery of individuality which is freedom. [10] Modern historical investigation, however, has discovered in increasing measure the predominance of geographical, economic, social, and other causes even in the most outstanding of human achievements. It is argued that man and his civilization are merely the products of natural and material forces. [11] This view is not peculiar to Marx.

Metaphysics. It is the contention of the Logical Positivists that nothing that is not evident to the senses or to the extension of the senses provided by scientific instruments has any claim to truth. Metaphysics which discusses problems of God and soul are idle speculation. Religion is an emotional reaction. Religion and metaphysics are no doubt facts of human life, like poetry and fiction. They are an outlet for the gratification of our emotions, but do

8 John Dewey, *Influence of Darwin on Philosophy* (1910), 44.

9 Cp. *Jean-Paul Sartre:* "My freedom is the unique foundation of values. And since I am the being by virtue of whom values exist, nothing, absolutely nothing can justify me in adopting this or that value or scale of values. As the unique basis of the existence of values, I am totally unjustifiable. And my freedom is in anguish at finding that it is the baseless basis of values." Quoted in G. Marcel's *The Philosophy of Existence* (1948), 63.

10 James Collingwood, *Human Nature and Human History* (1937). *Speculum Mentis* (1924), VI.

11 Cp. *Bury:* "A historian may be a theist, but so far as his work is concerned this particular belief is otiose." "Darwinism and History," in *Selected Essays* (1930), 33.

not satisfy the desire for knowledge. Only those statements are true which admit of empirical verification by an appeal to sense data or the data of introspection. But propositions dealing with religion, relating to God's existence, attributes and activities, like all judgments of value, fall outside these limits. They cannot be empirically verified. They are merely the expression of emotions, admitting neither of truth nor of falsehood.

The fear of metaphysics is unreal. But the metaphysical nature of man will not remain vacant. It will have a content. Metaphysical emptiness does not exist, for it is itself a metaphysics, a sceptical metaphysics. To refuse to philosophise is in itself a kind of philosophy. "The malady of contemporary empiricistic philosophising," as Einstein calls it (in Paul A. Schilpp's *The Philosophy of Bertrand Russell*, LLP, Vol. V, 289), will not last long.

The Doom of the Universe. To crown it all, science presents a gloomy picture of the future of the universe. The inorganic irreversible evolution imposed by Carnot-Clausius' law, also called the second law of thermodynamics, corresponds to an evolution toward more and more "probable" states, characterised by an ever increasing symmetry, a levelling of energy. The universe tends towards an equilibrium where all the dissymetries will be flattened out, where all motion will have stopped, where absolute cold will reign.

All that remains for man to do is to be born, to grow up, to earn and to spend, to mate, to produce offspring, to grow old, and at last to sleep forever, safe in the belief that there is no purpose to be served in life except the fulfilment of the needs of man set in a vast and impersonal framework of mechanical processes. The earth turns, the stars blaze and die, and man need not waste his thought on seeking a different destiny.

Universality. The most remarkable feature of the scientific culture is its universality. It is one, though its achievements may be in different places and by different persons. There are no competing scientific cultures as there are competing religions or competing codes of law. In the geographical sense also it is universal, in that it has penetrated all parts of the world. Nature is one, and therefore science is one. A universal human community is the social aspiration of science.

The barriers which restrict the free flow of scientific information for reasons of security are against our conceptions of the universality of science. They increase distrust and anxiety and hamper international co-operation. Nations, instead of co-operating with one another for improving the material conditions of human life, are competing with one another about the possession of the means for annihilating vast populations and even making parts of the earth temporarily uninhabitable. Many famous scientists who are still animated by the true spirit of science call for an open exchange of information about all aspects of science, atomic science included. If it is done under international auspices and with proper safeguards, it will relieve tension, restore confidence, and result in a radical readjustment in international relationships.

A scientific frame of mind has become a part of the mental outfit of even ordinary men and women. The respect hitherto given to poets, priests and philosophers is now transferred to scientists and technicians. The more they lay bare the hidden springs of the universe, the more they master the secrets of the atom, the less significant do we become and the more dwarfed by power.

Effects on Religion. A scientific view of the world has shaken the foundations of many of the ancient creeds. Their authoritarian formulas do not carry conviction to the inquiring mind. Myths of creation are repudiated by geology. Conceptions of mind and soul are revolutionised by biology and psychology. Supernatural events on which religions are based are explained in a naturalistic way by anthropology and history. Though belief in miracles occurs in certain circumstances and in certain epochs, they never happened in fact; for the world is bound by invariable laws working through nature and history in an unbroken chain of cause and effect. Once upon a time, perhaps, religion helped men to liberate themselves from primitive superstitions and crude beliefs. This very process of emancipation demands the supersession of religion, its myths and legends, its obsolete theories and antiquated muddles. No religion which tolerates these superstitions can be accepted by mankind today. As we are now advancing to a new stage of civilisation, it is argued, we have to discard religion as an outworn instrument of a dead past. "When we become men we put away childish things," said St. Paul. We are no longer young; we have outgrown our toys. The exploitation of human infantilism should now disappear.[12]

12 Bormann wrote in 1941: "No human being would know anything of Christianity, if it had not been drilled into him in his childhood by pastors. The so-called God-Almighty in no wise gives any knowledge of his existence to young people in advance, but in an astonishing manner, in spite of his omnipotence, leaves this to the efforts of the pastors. If, therefore, in the future your youth learns nothing more of Christianity, whose doctrines are far below ours, Christ will disappear automatically." *Germany's Underground,* by A. W. Dulles (1947), 115.

Empirical Science and Dogmatic Religion. The whole spirit of science is opposed to that of religion as ordinarily understood.[13] Its attitude is frankly empirical, whereas the religious temper tends to be dogmatic. While scientific hypotheses are provisional, religious creeds profess finality. The former induce an attitude of humility and tolerance, the latter breed intolerance and fanaticism. The authoritarian attitude of religions and the incredible beliefs accepted by them have made it difficult for honest men to accept religious creeds. We cannot say with Dostoevsky "If any one could prove to me that Christ is outside the truth, I would prefer to stay with Christ and not with truth." For us nothing can be true by faith if it is not true by reason. The temper of science combines scepticism with openness to new facts. If life is languishing from religion, it is due to dogmatic religion as much as to mechanistic science.

V. TECHNOLOGICAL CIVILISATION

Technology and Life. Technology is the manipulation of the environment in the interests of human life. It has been with us from the beginning of our history. The creation and use of artificial tools has distinguished man's life from that of the animals. The epochs of human history are distinguished by the character of their technology, stone age, bronze age, iron age. If man does not use artificial means, he will remain completely at the mercy of nature and its hazards. By the invention of technical appliances he emancipates himself to some extent from his bondage to nature. He defies the weather by building huts and houses and living in them. He becomes independent of fig leaves and animal skins by the use of the spinning wheel and the loom. He produces what he wants by agriculture. From that dim and distant date when the human creature struck out the first flint instrument, through all the ages until now, when man belts the globe with the radio and annihilates whole cities with atom bombs from the sky, the course of human life has been a career of material conquest and mechanical achievement. The pen, the brush, the spade, the lever, the pulley, the loco-

---

[13] Cp. *Stalin,* "The party [the Communist party] cannot be neutral regarding religion, and it conducts anti-religious propaganda against all religious prejudices because it stands for science, and religious prejudices are opposed to science since any religion is contrary to science." *Moscow Correspondent,* by Ralph Parker (1949, 176. "By its very essence, every religion is a conservative, reactionary, anti-scientific force which has always resisted the birth of new ideas, has always fought and is always fighting against new progressive and revolutionary ideas." F. N. Cleschuk: *On Scientific-Atheistic Propaganda.*

motive and the internal combustion engine form a continuous ascent. Yet we never considered the previous civilisations to be technological in character. Man, not the machine, was still the master. Today the machine has become the dominating factor of civilisation.

Industrial Revolution. The first great triumph of the machine was the industrial revolution, a product of science, of the spirit of invention, and of the large scale organisation of labour. The steam engine, electric power, and the development of chemistry helped the technological revolution. The application of machines to agriculture and industry has revolutionised the conditions of life. If we have the will, it is possible for us to eliminate from the world, hunger, want, poverty, disease, ignorance. We are capable of nourishing, clothing and housing every inhabitant of the earth. The techniques of medicine and surgery, hygiene and sanitation are sufficient to produce everywhere conditions of life which would guarantee to a high degree long life and healthy development for all. The cinema and the radio allow an almost unlimited spread of fundamental education. We have at our disposal means which would safeguard a high standard of life, material and cultural, for all mankind.

If hunger and disease, poverty and ignorance, which are no more inevitable, are still to be found in large parts of the earth, it is because we are abusing the technical possibilities in the interests of wrong social, political and international power relations. What is wrong is not technology but the social and cultural life of man, its purely industrial and utilitarian view of life, its cult of power and comfort.

Effects on Human Relations. Technology has changed not only man's relations to nature but man's relations to man. So long as the technical appliances were controlled by human elements, so long as society was able to assimilate them, the social equilibrium was maintained; but, unfortunately for us, the greatest advances in technology happened in an age of ethical confusion and social chaos. A society spiritually and ethically enfeebled allowed the development of great industries without proper safeguards.[14] The

---

[14] Professor F. York Powell, Regius Professor of Modern History at the University of Oxford, in the Introduction which he wrote to Charles Austin Beard's book on *The Industrial Revolution* (1901), observed: "The English people, never by any plague, or famine, or war, suffered such a deadly blow at its vitality as by the establishment of the factory system without the proper safeguards."

natural community of life was broken up. Cottage industries, where the craftsmen owned the means of production, have been displaced by large concerns, where the means of production are owned by men of wealth. As a result all the evils of class distinctions of rich and poor, advanced and backward nations, have sprung up. There is concentration of productive power and wealth in a few hands or their monopolization by a State bureaucracy. The means have become more important than the ends. Men are being used for the production of material goods at the expense of their mental and physical health. The machine invented by man now controls his will. The farmers and craftsmen have become technicians; and cultures have become standardised with the result that we have the same films, the same magazines, and the same dance-tunes all over the world. In previous ages we also had tools for destructive purposes. We had weapons of war; but these weapons have today become dangerous. The war industries are controlled by the State, and in this way modern totalitarian States developed. The new developments have produced instability and confusion, political strains and economic stresses. We cannot overlook the obvious fact that human society is changed as much by a revolution in the methods of production as by a revolution in the forms of government.

In the highly industrialised countries we have colossal systems of power dealing with huge numbers of men and women and vast masses of material. Men and women in large numbers are taken out of their natural context, cut adrift from their moorings and brought under a different system of life. They have ceased to be persons, subjects with inward life and personal choice, and have become objects, things, instruments. Men need to be rooted in a place, custom and habit. These children of the machine are uprooted, displaced persons, immigrants. An organic society, through large scale industrialisation, has become an amorphous inorganic mass. There is a complete distortion of the basic conditions of normal human life. Man is handed over to the organisation where efficiency is treated as the supreme end. Inefficiency is punished by unemployment in democratic societies or by the more severe penalties of slavery or liquidation in non-democratic ones.

In an industrial civilisation we strive for the kind of success which is measured by bank balances. This ambition leads to aggressiveness which takes many forms: envy, rivalry, conflict. Competition for success creates tensions and makes human beings unbalanced and neurotic. As our enslavement to the economic machine is rising, human values are declining. We are at war with others because we are at war with ourselves. The uprooted individual, mindless, traditionless, believes in nothing or anything. Scepticism and superstition hold the field. As he has no inward being, his surface nature is moulded by widespread and insistent propaganda. Any self-constituted saviour of society, who promises to provide food and shelter at the price of subjection to his leadership, wins a following. The omnipotent State rushes into the void caused by the disappearance of traditional values, and lays claim to the overriding loyalty of all that come within its orbit. The establishment of dictatorships and the increasing supremacy of the State even in democracies are characteristic features of our time. With its ever growing reliance on objective criteria of thought and ever deepening ignorance of the real nature of human life, contemporary technological civilisation has become a social disease. We see on all sides the apotheosis of power and the withering of man who has been cut off from the sources of self-renewal. Having lost his sense of responsibility he is capable of almost limitless self-deception. New superstitions have sprung up which inspire millions of men and women with the fervour, the sanctions and the inhibitions of great religions. We seem to be caught up in a momentum of evil which is dragging us down to disaster. Mr. George Orwell thought that we shall all be living under totalitarian tyrannies by *1984*.

VI. RELIGION AND SOCIAL CONSCIENCE

Practical Atheism. The two wars have revealed, apart from the destruction, human and material, unparalled in recorded history, the enormous capacity for cruelty and evil of which human nature is capable. The fact that it has been possible for us to fall so easily into barbarism shows how frail our religious culture has been. Macaulay's words to the Wilberforces, that there were not two hundred men in London who believed in the Bible, may be a gross exaggeration; but they indicate that many of the leading men were unbelievers. Almost all of us are atheists in practice, though we may profess belief in God. We may visit temples, attend services, repeat prayers; but we do all this with a kind of reverent inattention, or sacred negligence. We deny God's existence in everything that we do. We bow down before the world, flesh and power. Fenelon writes in his *Letters:* "There is practically nothing that men do not prefer to God. A tiresome detail of business, an occupation utterly pernicious to health, the employment of time in ways one does not dare to mention. Anything rather than God." If we are religious, we must live our religion. If we do not live our religion, our religion is a phantasy or a doctrine. If our actions are opposed to those which are demanded by our religion, we cannot say that we are religious. We are really unbelievers, because we not only fail to carry out the demands of our religion but do not even think that these demands are to be carried out. If any one tells us that we should adopt the precepts of Jesus in our daily life, we laugh at him and advise him to substitute for them some inventions of our own.

Escapism. For a few earnest spirits, religion has been an escapism. The Psalmist cries: "Man walketh in a vain shadow and disquieteth himself in vain." "Oh, that I had wings like a dove, for then would I flee away and be at rest." We divide the world into God and creation, absolute unity and purity on one side, and a realm of discord and hostility on the other. We strive to escape from the unbearable sadness of the actual into an ideal world where we satisfy our lonely self in the silent spaces of speculation.

Defence of Reaction. If we do not interpret religion as a way of escape, we make it a defence of the established order. It comes to terms with the civilisation in which it is placed, by justifying its judgments. The Erastian view of Christianity believes that the Church exists for enforcing obedience to social laws by means of supernatural sanctions which control those details of personal conduct that are beyond the reach of state laws. There does not seem to be any essential difference between a religious man and a nonreligious one, in regard to individual and social life. They both live by the law of the world. Jesus rejected the temptation of the kingdom of this world; but his followers adopt a compromising conformist attitude to the state, to the kingdom of Caesar, by employing the distinction between Caesar's things and God's things.[15] Even the founders of religions accept the sufferings of the majority of human beings as part of their necessary lot in life, if not as a penance for some heavy guilt which they had incurred in their previous lives. They treat existing institutions as part of an eter-

---

[15] "Be not conformed to this world, but be ye transformed by the renewing of your mind." Cp. *Middleton Murry:* "The Church knows its function; which is that of a good wife to the State. Like a good wife it never advises and never criticises, and, when there is a row, it always stands up for its husband. And it insists on one thing, as far as it may—that the husband shall keep out of the kitchen." *The Betrayal of Christ by the Churches* (1940), 15.

nal divine order. Poverty, disease, slavery, and war have all been justified and sanctioned by religion. Future happiness is promised as a recompense for present suffering.

Even those who do not themselves take religion seriously adopt it as a device to reconcile suffering men to their condition. That realistic, if not devout psychologist, Napoleon, made the well known comment:

What is it that makes the poor man think it quite natural that there are fires in my parlour while he is dying of cold? That I have ten coats in my wardrobe while he goes naked? That at each of my meals enough is served to feed his family for a week? It is simply religion which tells him that in another life I shall be only his equal and that he actually has more chances of being happy there than I. Yes, we must see to it that the floors of the churches are open to all, and that it does not cost the poor man much to have prayers said on his tomb.

Protest Against Religion. Social idealists with their love of equality and hatred of sham, who burn with a passion to create tolerable conditions of good life for the weltering mass of men, find religion to be worthless at its best and vicious at less than best. "Heaven help us, said the old religion; the new one from the very lack of that faith will teach us all the more to help one another." [16] Militant atheism is the answer to dishonest religion.[17]

Religions cannot claim to be the great civilising agencies of the world. Although it is true that they, to some extent, inspired spiritual life, encouraged the arts, disciplined the mind and fostered the virtues of charity and peace, they have also filled the world with wars and tortured the souls and burnt the bodies of men. When we note the magnificent achievements of religion we should not fail to note the incredible corruption and degradation in its record. It has given its sanction to many forms of exploitation and violence. On the supreme issue which faces mankind today, peace or war, religions have been hesitant and complacent, if not militant and reactionary.

Rivalries of Religions. Since 1500 mankind has been steadily marching towards the formation of a single society. The two wars

[16] George Eliot.

[17] "The militant godlessness of the Communist revolution is to be explained, not only by the state of mind of the Communists which was very narrow and dependent upon various kinds of *ressentiment,* but also by the historical sins of orthodoxy which had failed to carry out its mission of the transfiguration of life, which had been a support of an order which was based upon wrong and oppression." Nicholas Berdyaev, *The Russian Idea* (English Tr., 1947), 247.

have led to a shrinkage of space and contraction of the world. The physical unity of the world requires to sustain it a psychological oneness. The barriers of dogmatic religions are sterilising men's efforts to co-ordinate their forces to shape the future. Each religion is a rival to others. There are some things which are more important than our particularist allegiances: truth and humanity and that universal religious consciousness which is the common possession of all human beings by virtue of their spiritual endowment. So long as our group loyalties are strong and overriding we cannot belong to the general human society.

Incoherence in Thought and Life. Religion, as it has been functioning, is unscientific and unsocial. On account of these features of traditional religion large sections of humanity are the victims of unwilling disbelief. It is an age of incoherence in thought and indecision in action. Our values are blurred, our thought is confused, our aims are wavering, and our future is uncertain. There are bits of knowledge here and there but no visible pattern. W. B. Yeats refers to our condition in memorable words which we may well ponder:

> Things fall apart; the centre cannot hold.
> Mere anarchy is loosed upon the world,
> The blood-dimmed tide is loosed, and everywhere
> The ceremony of innocence is drowned;
> The best lack all conviction, while the worst
> are full of passionate intensity.[18]

If we are to overcome the dangers that threaten us, we must confront them fearlessly and take the measure of their power to injure us. The issue for religion in our day is not in regard to doctrinal differences or ritual disagreements, but it concerns the very existence of religion. The state of coldness or indifference which ignores religion is more deadly than open rejection. Even Marx looks upon religion, not as insignificant but as pernicious. Our modern intellectuals sum up the situation thus: some think God exists, some think not, it is impossible to tell, but it does not matter.

The Need for Integration. The mind of the world requires to be pulled together and the present aimless stare of dementia replaced by a collective rational purpose. We need a philosophy, a direction and a hope, if the present state of indecision is not to lead us to despair. Belief may be difficult, but the need for believing is inescapable. We are in search of a spiritual religion, that is uni-

18 W. B. Yeats, *Collected Poems* (1933), "The Second Coming."

versally valid, vital, clear-cut, one that has an understanding of the fresh sense of truth and the awakened social passion which are the prominent characteristics of the religious situation today. The severe intellectual honesty and the burning passion for social justice are not to be slighted. They are expressions of spiritual sincerity. Our religion must give us an energy of thought which does not try to use evasions with itself, which dares to be sincere, an energy of will which gives us the strength to say what we believe and do what we say. If the world is today passing through a mood of atheism, it is because a higher religion is in process of emergence. Doubt and denial of God have often proved dialectical moments in the history of religions, ways by which mankind has increased its knowledge of God and emancipated itself from imperfect conceptions of religion.

The opposite of religion is not irreligion but a counter-religion.[19] When the Buddha denied the Vedic gods, he did so in the name of a higher religion. When Socrates was put to death on the charge of atheism, his offence was the repudiation of an imperfect religion. When Christians were brought into the Roman amphitheatre to undergo martyrdom for their convictions, the pagan mob shouted "The atheists to the lions." Atheism has often been the expression of the vitality of religion, its quest for reality in religion. The fact that man is unable or unwilling to acknowledge God means only that he cannot accept the ideas and beliefs about God framed by men, the false gods which obscure the living and ineffable God. Today the world is very sick, for it is passing through a crisis of the birth of a new religion.

VII. Saṁsāra or the World of Change

Philosophical Explanation. Whereas the scientific mind is satisfied with secondary causes, the philosophic mind demands final causes. Philosophy is an attempt to explain the world to which we belong. It is experience come to an understanding with itself. Experience relates to the world of objects, of things, of nature studied by the natural sciences; the world of individual subjects, their thoughts and feelings, their desires and decisions, studied by the social sciences, like psychology and history; the world of values, studied by literature, philosophy and religion. We must weave into a consistent pattern the different sides of our experience. There

19 Cp. *Amiel:* "Men think they can do without religion; they do not know that religion is indestructible, and that the question simply is, which will you have?"

can be no bifurcation between them. We must endeavour to frame a coherent system of general ideas in terms of which the different types of experience can be interpreted. Even if we may not be able to reach a final and adequate answer, it is useful to make the attempt. After all, the wisest of us, like Socrates, are ignorant men thinking aloud, faced by the infinitude and complexity of the world.

A spiritual interpretation of the universe is based on a number of arguments, which may not be separately infallible, but they do strengthen one another. We may indicate them by looking at the question from the three different angles of the object, the subject and the spirit.

The World as Saṁsāra. It is interesting to know that the Indian thinkers, Hindu and Buddhist, viewed the world as a stream of happenings, a perpetual flow of events. Change is the essence of existence. The ultimate units of the concrete flow of experience are neither points of space nor instants of time nor particles of matter. They are events which have a three-dimensional character, a concrete content occupying a point of space at an instant of time. Śivāditya (eleventh century) in his *Saptapadārthi* observes that the concrete filling, space and time are in reality one only.[20] Space, time, matter or life are abstractions from a happening with a qualitative character and a spatio-temporal setting. This world or saṁsāra is a process consisting of events, to use Whitehead's expressions.

Cosmic Evolution. The world process is not an incessant fluctuation comparable to a surging sea. It is a movement with a direction and a goal. Aristotle said that, if nothing depended on time for its realisation, everything would already have happened. If time is a necessary element in the structure of the cosmic process then nature is a creative advance. The idea of evolution is not unknown to Indian thinkers, though they conceived it as a metaphysical hypothesis rather than as an empirically verified theory.

If the cosmos is a process, what is it that proceeds, and what is its destination? In the ancient Upaniṣad, the *Taittirīya* (eighth century B.C.), cosmic evolution is represented by the five stages of matter (anna), life (prāṇa), perceptual-instinctive consciousness (manas), reflective consciousness (vijñāna), and spiritual or creative consciousness (ānanda). In the cosmic process we have the successive emergence of the material, the organic, the animal, the human and the spiritual orders of existence.

---

20 *ākāsāditrayaṁ tu vastuta ekam eva.* 27.

Matter and Life. Materiality is the first manifested form of cosmic existence. From unmanifested being we get the material manifestation. If matter grows into life, is there anything in matter compelling it to grow into life? Can the emergence of life be traced to the working of the principle of matter? It is assumed that it is the work of life itself energising in and on the conditions of matter and applying to it its own laws and principles. Life exhibits characteristics which go beyond the general laws of inorganic processes. Living organisms respond to situations in a way that they preserve and perpetuate themselves. Their nutritive, reparatory and reproductive functions are 'intelligent,' though not guided by intelligence. They are full of "prospective adaptations." Their actions tend to produce results which are beneficial to the individual and the species. Such actions, on the part of human individuals, are due to foresight. We need not postulate any mysterious vital force; but we must recognise that life is a unique kind of activity for which the formulas of matter and energy are not adequate.

Life and Mind. Similarly when mind emerges out of life, it is due to the principle of mind working with its own impulses and necessities in life. Mind is not a kind of ghost introduced into the living organism. The principles of life and mind are not to be treated as working on independent lines in the conscious being. The unity of the living whole is preserved when the quality of mind arises.

Mind and Intelligence. Animals are conscious; men are self-conscious, and so have greater dignity than stones, or plants or animals. By overlooking the distinction between men and animals, Hitler, for example, argued that the individual is nothing, it is the group that counts. Nature, he argued in his *Mein Kampf,* is ruthless in regard to individual lives and considerate only for the development of the species. He thought of man as merely the highest of the animals. "It is not necessary that any of us should live," he said. "It is only necessary that Germany should live." Even John Dewey argues in a similar vein:

Within the flickering inconsequential acts of separate selves dwells a sense of the whole which claims and dignifies them. In its presence we put off mortality and live in the universal. The life of the community in which we live and have our being is the fit symbol of this relationship. The acts in which we express the perception of ties which bind us to others are its only rites and ceremonies.[21]

21 John Dewey, *Human Nature and Conduct,* 332.

History is not a branch of biology. The drama of human personalities is distinct from life in the animal kingdom. Social sciences
which deal with the story of man in society are a separate category
from natural sciences.

Men have a restless reaching out for ideals. The human individual has to work his evolution consciously and deliberately. His
growth is not effected fortuitously or automatically. He has to act
responsibly and co-operate willingly with the purpose of evolution.
If he falls into the external sphere, if he does not recognise his own
dignity, the law of Karma rules. If he withdraws from the external,
he can participate creatively in the cosmic development.

Intelligence and Spirit. Looking back on the millions of years of
the steady climb of life on the path of evolution, it seems presumptuous for us to imagine that with thinking man evolution has come
to an end. The Upaniṣad affirms that there is a further step to be
taken. Animal cunning has become human foresight; human self-
consciousness must grow into comprehensive vision, into illumined
consciousness.[22] We must pass beyond the dualities and discords
of intellect and possess truth as our inherent right. Ānanda, or joy,
which is, according to St. Paul, one of the fruits of the spirit, is the
stage we have to reach. The new spiritual man differs from the
present intellectual man as much as the latter differs from the animal and the animal from the plant. Every human individual is a
historical becoming. What we are here and now is the result of
what we were, what we thought, what we felt and willed, what we
did during earlier periods of our personal history. We cannot understand a human individual except as a process in time. There is
no such thing as an I-substance. When we speak of the essence of
the human individual, we refer not to his existence or the series of
changes through which he passes, but to the plan or pattern of behaviour which he is attempting to realise. Human life presses forward through blood and tears to realise its form. As progress at the
human level is willed, not determined, we are participants in history, not mere spectators of it. We can do much to determine our
own future. If we follow false lights and seek for finite and relative
progress, which is often precarious and disappointing, we do not
further our own evolution. If, on the other hand, we overcome the
narrowness of our ego, open out to others, overflow and communi-

---

22 Cp. *Jalālu'd Dīn Rūmī:* "First came he from the realm of the inorganic,
long years dwelt he in the vegetable state, passed into the animal condition, thence
towards humanity; whence again, there is another migration to be made." *Mathnawī*
4.3637f.

cate love and joy, we foster our growth. By our freely chosen activities we may retard or further the march of the world to its consummation. We are living our lives in the process of a great gestation. The slowness of the process, the occasional backslidings in any historical period do not disprove the possibility of development. History is neither a chapter of accidents, nor a determined drift. It is a pattern of absolute significance.

There is as much discontinuity between the human and the spiritual as there is between the human and the animal. Spiritual life is not only the negation but the fulfilment of the human life. We sometimes stress the continuity, sometimes the newness of it. "Behold, I make all things new."

The Goal of the Cosmic Process. The meaning of history is to make all men prophets, to establish a kingdom of free spirits. The infinitely rich and spiritually impregnated future, this drama of the gradual transmutation of intellect into spirit, of the son of man into the son of God, is the goal of history. When death is overcome, when time is conquered, the kingdom of the eternal spirit is established.

Ānanda, spirit, which is the goal of evolution, comprises all the rest. It is not unrelated to the others which it has superseded and resolved into itself. All of them are activities of the Spirit. Each of them in its operation in the whole presupposes the others. Since all are necessary to the whole, no one can claim a primacy which belongs to the whole or the Spirit itself. We cannot unify the categories by annihilating them. Matter and life are different. The different levels of existence are not to be treated as inferior or degraded. In its place everything has value. The world is of one piece, though it has different stages which cannot be partitioned.

In the cosmic evolution, the different stages are not opposed as good and evil. It is an evolution from one stage to another and the different stages are distinguishable only within a unity. The one Spirit is manifesting itself in its various activities which are all partial and therefore inadequate. Wholeness belongs to the Spirit itself.

Spirit and Body. It follows that we should not assume that body is the lower element out of which evil arises. The whole man, body, mind and spirit, is one; Spirit is not to be delivered out of entanglement with the body. In the Rabbinical phrase the body is the "scabbard of the soul." It is "the temple of the Holy Spirit." [23] It is, according to Hindu thought, the instrument of ethical life,

[23] 1. *Corinthians.* III. 6, 18; VI. 19.

dharma-sādhanam. Even the lowest form of manifestation is an expression of the Divine, *annaṁ brahmeti vyajānāt.*

Philosophy as Criticism of the Categories. There is a tendency to apply categories, which have proved helpful and even necessary in certain areas, to others by the sheer impetus of the search for a comprehensive theory of being. In the eighteenth century Laplace conceived a theory of world mechanics. In the nineteenth century the Darwinian principle of natural selection was extended to all phenomena, living, minded and purposive. We can explain the lower by the higher, not *vice versa.* There is not a single type of law to which all existence conforms.

Spirit, the Explanation. The Upaniṣads believe that the principle of Spirit is at work at all levels of existence, moulding the lower forms into expressions of the higher. The splendour of Spirit, which in Greek philosophy was identified with the transcendental and timeless world of Ideas, or in Christian thought is reserved for the divine supernatural sphere, is making use of natural forces in the historical world. The highest product of cosmic evolution, ānanda or spiritual freedom, must also be the hidden principle at work, slowly disclosing itself. Spirit creates the world and controls its history by a process of perpetual incarnation. Spirit is working in matter that matter may serve the Spirit.

Puruṣa and Prakṛti. To account for the world of change, which is a progressive manifestation of the values of spirit, we assume not only the principle of spirit but also the principle of non-being which is being gradually overcome. We struggle with chaos, we mould crude primordial being into forms expressive of spirit. Spirit represents all that is positive in becoming. The things of the world are struggling to reach the spirit by overcoming their inner void, the interval between what they are and what they aim to be. This negative principle measures the distance between being and becoming. The world process can only be conceived as a struggle between two antagonistic but indispensable principles of being and non-being. What is called non-being is the limiting concept on the object side, the name for the unknown, the hypothetical cause of the object world. This non-being is an abstraction, that which remains when we abstract from the world all that gives it existence, form and meaning. It is the unmanifested, imperceptible, all but nothing, capable of receiving, though not without resistance, existence, form and meaning. It is a demand of thought more than a fact of existence, the limit of the downward movement, the lowest form which is all but nonexistent. It is the absence of form, though there is nothing in the actual world which is completely devoid of form. In Indian thought it is called *prakṛti*, the *avyakta*, the unmanifested, the formless substrate of things. It is potentially all things. The two, spirit and nature, puruṣa and prakṛti, are not two ultimate principles. They are parts of one World-Spirit, which divided into two, *dvedhā apātayat*, for the sake of cosmic development.[24] The two are opposite, yet complementary poles of all existence. They are not altogether independent of each other. The principle of non-being is dependent on being. It is that without which no effort would be possible or necessary. It is essential for the unfolding of the divine possibility. It is the material through which ideals are actualised. Proclus says that matter is a "child of God." So it is able to reveal spirit.

Prakṛti is not absolute non-being. It is unformed non-being which is powerless to form itself into being without the guidance of puruṣa, or the self. The existential development is not out of utter nothing or the absolute absence of all being. Nothing is the conceptual opposite of what truly and authentically is. If God creates out of nothing, he must be able to relate himself to nothing. But he cannot know nothing, for Pure Being excludes from itself all nullity. There is an inconscient world of being from out of which different worlds form themselves under the guidance of spirit. The dualism of puruṣa and prakṛti cannot be ultimate. The World-Spirit confronted by chaos or the waters over which the Spirit broods are both the expressions of the Supreme Being.

Inadequacy of Naturalist Theories. The theory of the Upaniṣads seems to receive confirmation in the attempts made by scientific metaphysicians to account for the nature of the cosmic process. Naturalist philosophers attempt to explain the cosmic process on strictly mechanical principles. They confuse a descriptive method for the creative cause. They argue that neither man nor animal was created by divine power within a period of a week, but that they both developed over millions of years by exceedingly slow processes of organic change. No intelligence operates as a cause in material or organic events. The expressions of intelligence we have in the world are themselves effects or results of physical activity, produced by the causes of matter and motion, known or unknown.

If, however, we are obliged to assume a controlling or directing intelligence at any part of the cosmic process, naturalism is repudiated. The central issue is, whether we can account for the whole range of natural phenomena in terms of the composition of forces,

24 *Bṛhad-āraṇyaka Upaniṣad.* I. 4. 3.

whether we can, for example, account for life on principles which govern inorganic phenomena or for mind on principles which govern inorganic and organic processes. When naturalist metaphysicians speak of evolution as self-sufficient and self-explanatory, they confuse a descriptive statement with a metaphysical explanation. They speak of forms of change, and not of origins and causes. They attribute all changes to external influences and fail to recognise the need for creative acts.

Greek naturalism regarded natural causation as a sufficient principle of explanation, but the representative Greek thinkers did not look upon the world as intelligible in and of itself. They attempted to explain the temporal world by relation to the world of eternal forms. *Nous* or *Logos* forms chaos into order and gives the unformed matter or *Hyle* its form. The question of the origin of the stuff which is shaped by *Nous* is not clearly answered.

Dialectical Materialism. Dialectical materialism admits self-movement, within matter and uses the word 'matter' in a vague and wavering sense, by attributing to it qualities of spirit, creative activity and intelligence. Material forces in a given correlation act uniformly as regards their results. If there is a change in the direction of the forces there will be a change in the results. We are not told how the changes in the forces and their direction are brought about. The way in which matter behaves is "objective dialectic" and its reflection in consciousness is "subjective dialectic." Marx identifies the two without offering any proofs for it. Dialectic may be an account of development in nature and social reality; but it is not its explanation. It is a method of interpretation, not a philosophy of history.[25]

Engels observes that our mastery of nature is due to our knowledge of it.

At every step we are reminded that we by no means rule over nature like a conqueror over a foreign people, like something standing outside nature. Our mastery of it consists in the fact that we have the advantage over all other beings of being able to know and correctly apply its laws.[26]

This knowledge gives us our superiority to material nature which is unconscious of its possibilities. It also illustrates the kinship between man and nature which implies a source of unity. The dualism between the two cannot be abolished by making nature a form of spirit as in Hegel or spirit a form of nature as in Marx.

[25] See RS (1947), 24ff.   [26] Friedrich Engels, *Dialectic of Nature.*

In his notes on Hegel's logic, Lenin abandoned the grosser elements of Marx's materialism and emphasised the reality of the perceived world rather than its materiality. He did not, however, develop the implications of the realist doctrine.

Bergson's Creative Evolution. Bergson is definite that even organic developments cannot be explained on principles of natural selection, adaptation to environment and variations. He argues that evolution would have stopped long ago if perfect adaptation to environment were its goal. He postulates an *elan vital* which governs the life-movement, urging it onwards to the creation of new species. With a wealth of detail Bergson shows up the insufficiency of the mechanistic theory. For Bergson, "duration means the invention and creation of forms, the continual elaboration of the absolutely new." [27] Only he assumes that this creative adventure is without a preconceived end or plan. Bergson exalts duration to the position of God. Duration is the clue to the mystery of existence. What is the origin of creative evolution? Bergson speaks of an interruption in the forward progress of the spiritual principle, a falling away in the opposite direction which is matter. There is no satisfactory account in Bergson of the rise of matter, of the accident of interruption. In the organic world the vital impulse makes use of matter and moulds it for its own purposes. For Bergson, reality is spirit and matter is the lapse from it.

Lloyd Morgan's Emergent Evolution. Lloyd Morgan makes a distinction between resultants and emergents. The former are continuations of the old while the latter refer to the new and unpredictable developments which take place at critical stages in the process of nature. Life is not a resultant of matter; nor is mind a resultant of life. Neither could have been anticipated before the event, even with a complete knowledge of the conditions preceding their emergence. They are absolutely new. Lloyd Morgan gives us a description of the processes of nature, but does not offer any explanation of them. He gives a phenomenological account and not a metaphysical theory. What gives to events their initial impetus, their structural pattern? Lloyd Morgan accounts for the complex process of evolution with its continuities and advances, resultants and emergents by an operative divine principle and activity. The creative activity of God is the only explanation for the cosmic evolution. Lloyd Morgan does not give an adequate account of the relation of the timeless divine purpose and the temporal unfolding.

[27] Henri Bergson, *Creative Evolution* (English Tr. 1911), 11.

Alexander's View of Deity. Samuel Alexander, in his *Space, Time and Deity,* holds that the universe has evolved out of the matrix of space-time. The characteristic of the world as movement is stressed by the adoption of time as basic to reality. Change is the universal characteristic of all things that have sprung out of the primal matrix. Reality is, for Alexander, a continuance of point-instants. From out of the matrix of space-time, different stages of being endowed with special characteristics develop, motion, matter, life, mind and its values, and deity. "The higher quality emerges from the lower plane of existence and has its roots in it, yet it raises itself above it and no longer belongs to it; it arranges its possessor in a new order of being." Life rises out of materiality and gives rise to mind. Values emerge next on the scale of evolution and the highest being to emerge out of the space-time matrix is God.

Deity is the next higher empirical quality to mind which the universe is engaged in bringing to birth. Deity is the quality which attends upon or more strictly, is equivalent to, previous or lower existences of the order of mind, which itself rests upon a lower basis of qualities and emerges when certain complexities and refinements and arrangements have been reached.[28]

God is not behind us. He is the supreme goal toward which the cosmic process tends in time. For Alexander, God is not the creator of the world, but, like matter and mind, a creature in the space-time universe. God is not a finished being but an eternal becoming. "He can never realise the idea of Himself, but finds Himself continually on the way towards this idea." In other words, cosmic existences are striving for ever more perfect forms of life. Man is evolving towards godhead. The universe seems to be a god-making one. Alexander cannot reduce new stages of being into special groupings of the old processes. There is the creativity of evolution which we have to accept with 'natural piety.' "The continual change and movement of things through the divine nisus moves ever upwards, towards ever higher, richer and more perfect forms." This nisus is the driving force of the whole process.

We cannot account for cosmic evolution by space-time and motion. To say that the future emerges from the past is a statement of fact. It is not an explanation. Does it emerge from the past because it is already present in a more or less latent form in the past? Unless we posit an Absolute, perfect and changeless and outside time and so outside the evolutionary process, we cannot be sure of the direc-

28 Samuel Alexander, *Space, Time and Deity,* II, 347.

tion of the evolution or the accomplishment of its purpose. If what Alexander says is true that God is the end of the evolutionary process, He is also the beginning. God cannot be the end if He were not also the beginning. God the consequent is also God the antecedent. There is, however, some point in Alexander's contention that God is a quality which in its completeness has yet to be achieved.

Whitehead's Ingressive Evolution. In Whitehead's philosophy the space-time of Alexander is replaced by space-time-matter. Space-time by itself is abstract and formal. The most elementary concrete unit is the *event* which has the formal characteristics of space-time and a material content or filling. When we wish to specify the character of events, we refer to objects. Objects are not events or complexes of events but qualify or are situated in events. "The structure of events provides the framework of the externality of nature within which objects are located." [29] Whitehead rejects the dualisms and bifurcations and emphasises the pervasive characters of organism, self-enjoyment and creativeness. To the question, why do some material forms become living ones, Whitehead's answer is, "All such connections are formed by the creative process which is the world itself." Nature is organic as a whole and in its parts. An electron has this organic structure even as a human being. The organic character of events is derived from their filling by organised objects. There is an ingression of eternal objects into nature. The two together are "intrinsically inherent in the total metaphysical situation." [30] Whitehead warns us against viewing the eternal objects and the passage as abstractions from the real. "Actual occasions," he says, "are only selections from the realm of possibilities." [31] The possible is eternal in which nothing can happen or pass and the actual is of the nature of passage and it is difficult to know how the actual passage can be contained in the eternal possible. The actual is external to the possible. There is nothing in the world of the possible answering to the passage of the actual. What is the status of eternal objects? If they are real, we have a bifurcation: if unreal, they have no metaphysical significance. The possible, which is the ultimate reality, contains the actual *eminenter,* says Whitehead. The actual event is divisible, whereas the object is organic and indivisible. While the world of events is characterised by change and diversity, the world of objects is characterised by unity and permanence. When objects become ingredi-

29 *Principles of Natural Knowledge,* 80.
30 *Science and the Modern World* (1926), 228.   31 *Ibid.,* 235.

ent to the framework of events, they impose unity and permanence and thus distort the nature of the framework.

Being organic, nature has scope for development, for the production of the new. The flow of events is a process in which all the past is gathered up and borne along by the current into the present and the future. The creative advance into novelty is explained by the divine creative thrust which informs and drives forward the becoming of the world. What is before all creation is the Absolute. God is with all creation. God is not an exception to the nature of the empirical world but is its central illustration. The primordial God of Whitehead is "the unlimited conceptual realisation of the absolute wealth of potentiality," [32] but he is deficient in actuality. "The consequent nature of God . . . is the realisation of the actual world in the unity of his nature and through the transformation of his wisdom. The primordial nature is conceptual, the consequent nature is the weaving of God's physical feelings upon his primordial concepts." [33] The concretisation of the conceptual plan requires a fulness of existence, an objectification in the medium of potential matter. The actual world presupposes both the ideal plan and the concrete setting: "In God's nature permanence is primordial and flux is derivative from the world; in the world's nature, flux is primordial and permanence is derivative from God." While God is seeking existence, the world is seeking unity and perfection. The end of the world is reached when the ultimate unity of the multiplicity of actual fact with the primordial conceptual fact is realised. For Whitehead, the world process has its origin in God, is sustained by him and returns into him. God is not merely a future possibility but the creative source and final goal of the universal. "He is the beginning and the end, the alpha and the omega." For Whitehead, God and the world are both expressions of the original creativity which is the Absolute. They are essential to and interact with each other in subordination to the original creativity which manifests itself in both. We seem to be near the concept of the spirit of God brooding over the waters.

These various interpretations of the cosmic process, dominated by the scientific spirit, are agreed in thinking that the temporal process gives meaning to our existence. They also feel that it is not easy to account for the complex world of perpetual change on strictly scientific principles. If there is the emergence of what is genuinely new in the cosmic process, then the cosmic series is not self-explanatory. Our search for the reality of the world, for the

[32] *Process and Reality* (1929), 486.   [33] *Process and Reality* (1929), 488.

structure of the cosmos, reveals the presence of something invisible and eternal which is working within the visible and temporal world. An element of mystery which refuses to reduce the meaning of the process to rational intelligibility is assumed by the scientific metaphysicians. Within the temporal process itself, science offers explanations for particular events, but it cannot deal with the why of the temporal process as a whole. It does not contain its origin or meaning within itself. It is not self-explanatory. The meaning of the mystery, the origin and the end of the world, cannot be scientifically apprehended. They require to be investigated metaphysically.[34]

Metaphysical Implications. Philosophy is a quest of truth which underlies existence. The very name *metaphysics* characterises the type of inquiry which goes beyond what is given to us. Whereas science deals with existent objects, philosophy tries to envisage the hidden structure, discover and analyse the guiding concepts of ontological reality. Why is there something rather than nothing? Why is there this world rather than another?

The Primacy of Being. The very existence of this world implies the existence of Being from which the world derives. Being is the foundation of all existence, though it is not itself anything existent. It is not something like a stone or a plant, an animal or a human individual. Whenever we say that anything is, we make use of the concept of Being. It is therefore the most universal and the most comprehensive concept. We unfold the nature of Being by the study of existences, though we cannot prove it. It is self-evident. If Being were not, nothing can possibly exist. Being is in all that exists. We live in the world of existence, we think of some kind of existence or other, but in metaphysics we get beyond the sphere of daily life, the objects of science, and rise to the transcendent conception of Being itself. Being posits everything but is not itself posited. It is not an object of thought, it is not the result of production. It forms an absolute contrast to and is fundamentally different from all that is. If anything exists, then Being is. As this world exists, Being is. *Aseitas* means the power of Being to exist absolutely in virtue of itself, requiring no cause, no other justification for its existence except that its very nature is to be. There can be only one such Being and that is the Divine Spirit. To say that God exists

---

[34] Cp. *Whitehead:* "We must provide a ground for the limitation which stands among the attributes of substantial activity. This attribute provides the limitation for which no reason can be given, for all reasons flow from it. God is the ultimate limitation and His existence the ultimate irrationality." *Science and the Modern World* (1926), 249.

a se, of and by reason of Himself, is to say that God is Being itself. This is the concept of Brahman as it is formulated in the Upaniṣads. It is the *I am that I am* of the Christian Scripture. It is also the central doctrine of Catholic Christianity. St. Thomas Aquinas describes God as *Esse* or Being, pure and simple. In Him there is no distinction whatever. Even the distinction between the knowing subject and the known object is lost. God knows Himself, not through representations of Himself, but without mediation, through His own being. God is absolute as distinct from dependent or conditioned being. As the ground of an ordered multiplicity He is one and not multiple. That which is to make all conditions possible cannot itself be subject to conditions.

Being and Freedom. Why has evolution taken this direction and not another? Why has the world this character and not any other? In other words, why is the world what it is and not another? Being which is the ultimate basis of all existence, which is independent and has nothing outside it to control it, has freely willed to realise this world, to actualise this possibility. Absolute Being is also absolute freedom. To the question, why should such an order exist at all, the only answer is because the Absolute is both Being and Freedom. He is *actus purus*, unconditional activity. All the worlds would collapse into nothingness if He were not active. His will prevents Being from being the abyss of nothingness. The 'given' fact of the world in which we are all involved is a mystery. The genesis of the universe with its specific character is traced to Being-Activity. As to why this possibility and not another is selected, is intelligible solely as mystery which we have only to acknowledge. It is the will of God. There are two sides of the Supreme, Essential Transcendent Being which we call Brahman; free activity which we call Īśvara: the timeless, spaceless reality and the conscious active delight creatively pouring out its powers and qualities, the timeless calm and peace and the timeful joy of activity freely, infinitely expressing itself without any lapse into unrest or bondage. When we refer to the free choice of this specific possibility, we deal with the Īśvara side of the Absolute. Pure Being without any expression or variation moves out of its primal poise so that worlds may spring into existence. Pure Being is not locked up in its own transcendence. Īśvara is the Absolute in action as Lord and Creator.[35] The created world is contingent be-

---

[35] Cp. *Origen's* account of the coeternity of the Son with the Father, "There never can have been a time when He was not. For when was the Divine Light destitute of its effulgence?" *De Principiis*, IV, 28.

cause it depends on the free will of the Supreme. Possible realities have potential being in the Absolute, existent realities have actual being though they are contingent. The Supreme has necessary being or, more accurately, it is its own being (svayambhu) and it is infinite because it possesses infinite possibilities. The mystery of the world abides in freedom. Freedom is the primordial source and condition of all existence. It precedes all determination.

Infinite Possibility and the Actual World. This world, we have seen, is not a machine. It is an act of worship. It is in love with God, as Aristotle said, and is working towards Him. Its possibility, the eternal idea which it is accomplishing, is conceived by the Greeks as an abstract principle, the timeless Logos. The words of the Prologue to St. John's Gospel make out that it is a personal being who is the moving dynamism of history. "In the beginning was the Logos, and the Logos was with God and the Logos was God. The same was in the beginning with God. All things were made by Him. . . . In Him was life; and the life was the light of men." It is a definite manifestation of that which in the end of time brings with it the victory of the divine will over the powers that threaten the meaning of life. It perfects the historical revelation and completes the meaning of earthly existence. It is the Divine Logos which permeates the world and forms it into a cosmos. According to Hindu thought, the God who is shaping the universe is not the Absolute, free from all relativity, but the active personal being who shares in the life of his finite creatures. He bears in them and with them the whole burden of their finitude. The Spirit has entered into the world of non-spirit to realise one of the infinite possibilities that exist potentially in Spirit. Unconditioned Being becomes conditioned by the assumption of the creation of a specific possibility. A further definition of the Supreme Being's relation to the world is given by stating that the World Spirit creates, sustains and ultimately resolves the universe. These three aspects are brought out by the names, Brahmā, Viṣṇu and Śiva.

They represent the three sides of God's activity in regard to the world. These three represent different functions of the one Supreme and are not, except figuratively, to be regarded as different persons. God the conceptual is logically prior to God the cosmic, who is logically prior to God the consequent or the final perfection. The Ideas of Brahmā are seeking concrete expression and Viṣṇu is assisting the world's striving for perfection.[36] During the process all his qualities of wisdom, love and patience find expression and help the fluent world to reach its end. God is spiritual Reality, unconditioned freedom and absolute love.

In the Upaniṣads, a fourfold distinction of the Supreme Being is set forth.[37] (1) Brahman, the Absolute Being (2) Īśvara, the unconditioned free activity (3) Hiraṇya-garbha, Prajā-pati, Brahmā, the World-Spirit in its subtle form and (4) Virāj, the World-Spirit in its gross form.

These bring out different aspects of the Supreme. There is a tendency to regard the Supreme as Īśvara or God as subordinate to the Supreme as Brahman or Godhead. For Eckhart God is secondary, not primary, for it assumes the distinction of subject and object while Godhead transcends this distinction. A being is different from what he does. I feel that these disclose great depths in the Supreme Being and only logically can we distinguish them. They are all united in the Supreme.

The Status of the World. This world is not an illusion; it is not nothingness, for it is willed by God and therefore is real. Its reality is radically different from the being of Absolute-God. The Absolute alone has non-created divine reality; all else is dependent, created reality. This is the significance of the doctrine of māyā. It does not mean that the temporal process is a tragedy or an aberration. The reality of the world is not in itself but it is in the thought and being of the Creator. It is what God thought and willed it to be before it was.

There is a beginning to time as well as an end. When we say that time is infinite, all that we mean is that its future is indefinite or incalculable. Between these two points, the beginning and the end, between the start and the finish, what happens is real and significant, not only for us but for the World-Spirit. God is so intensely concerned with this history that He not only looks on the human life as an interested spectator but He actively inter-

---

[36] Cp. *Whitehead:* "One side of God's nature is constituted by his conceptual experience. This experience is the primordial fact in the world, limited by no actuality which it presupposes. It is therefore infinite, devoid of all negative prehensions. This side of his nature is free, completely primordial, eternal, actually deficient and unconscious. The other side originates with physical experience, derived from the temporal world and then acquires integration with the primordial side. It is determined, incomplete, consequent, everlasting, fully actual and conscious." *Process and Reality* (1929), 488f.

[37] See *Ind P,* I (1923), 169-173. *Māṇḍūkya Upaniṣad* gives us a two-fold dialectic, relating not only to Reality but also to the being who apprehends it.

venes in it. It is not correct to say that this intervention took place only once. Every moment in the temporal process is a moment of decision. It is charged with an extreme tension. History is not a cyclic movement. It is full of new things, because God works in it and reveals Himself in it. The end of the time process is the triumph of the World-Spirit, or to use the phrases of Greek classical thought, the triumph of *Nous* over chaos.

Laws of Nature. There are laws of nature, physical, biological and psychological. These laws are comprehensively designated Karma. The Creator does not use the forces of nature to reward virtue or punish sin. Jesus said: "Think you that the eighteen upon whom the Tower in Siloam fell were sinners above all that dwelt in Jerusalem? I tell you nay. He maketh his sun to rise on the evil and on the good and sendeth rain on the just and on the unjust." [38] In this world there are no rewards or punishments but only consequences. There is no arbitrariness in the world. The laws of nature are the expression of the divine mind. The *Śvetāśvatara Upaniṣad* states that God is the ordainer or overlord of Karma, *karmādhyakṣaḥ*. Karma is not ultimate or absolute. It is the expression of God's will and purpose. It has an important and indispensable function in the divine economy. It belongs to the created world. If God is bound up to the order of nature, if He is responsible for the world without the power of redeeming it, if His will is inflexible that no prayer can reach, if He sanctions all the evil as well as the good in the world, if He treats the tears of the children and the agony of the innocents as just ingredients in a world of sacred necessity, the world becomes meaningless. The Supreme is love and knowledge, goodness and power. He is related to everything and every one in the universe. He responds to everything and to everything's response to Him.

Human Freedom. God is not fate, nor an impersonal, abstract determining power. We are not puppets moved hither and thither by the blind impersonal necessity of omnipotent matter or the sovereignty of divine providence. We cannot say that everything is finished before it starts and the last day of reckoning will read what the first day of creation wrote. In that case nothing new can happen and there is no room for contingency. The future has yet to be made. Our present choices give a new form even to the past so that what it means depends on what we do now.

The freedom of will possessed by self-conscious individuals makes possible sin and discord. They are not willed by the Divine,

[38] *Matthew* V, 45.

though they fall within His purpose. When we are self-willed we surrender to the restraint exercised by the play of mechanical forces. We are then the victims of Karma. We are free to do differently. We can turn our eyes towards the Light in prayer, make an effort of genuine attention to empty our mind of selfish desires and let the thought of the Eternal fill it. We will then bear within us the very power to which necessity or Karma is in subjection. It is our community with the Eternal that endows us with creative quality. It helps us to remake our environment and realise new types of achievement which will enrich the experience of the human race. Keats spoke of the world as the 'vale of soul-making' and declared in the same letter [39] that "as various as the lives of men are—so various become their souls and thus does God make individual beings, Souls, Identical Souls, of the sparks of his own essence."

Meaning of Liberation. An individual is free when he attains universality of spirit, but his liberated self retains its individuality as a centre of action so long as the cosmic process lasts. For complete liberation implies not only harmony within the self but also harmony with the environment. Complete freedom is therefore impossible in an imperfect world. Those who have attained to the consciousness of the Eternal work within the world to set other men forward in their journey toward the goal. In a true sense the ideal individual and the perfect society arise together.[40]

The redemption of the world is not to be treated completely *sub specie historiae.* It is an eternal operation. There is a steady advance in our apprehension of the ideal which belongs to the eternal world. Nicolas of Cusa says:

To be able to know ever more and more without end, this is our likeness to the eternal wisdom. Man always desires to know better what he knows and to love more what he loves; and the whole world is not sufficient for him because it does not satisfy his craving for knowledge.

Our ultimate aim is to live in the knowledge and enjoyment of the absolute values. When this aim is reached, the mortal becomes the immortal and time is taken over into eternity. Temporal life, is treated as contingent, transient, perishable, non-eternal, as its end is to be transfigured. Human life, on this planet, is a brief episode and its eternal value is however preserved in the abode of all eternal values, the Absolute-God.

[39] April 28th 1819. *Colvin's ed.,* 256.   [40] IVL (1932), 307.

The actual fabric of the world with its loves and hates, with its jealousies and competitions, with its unasked helpfulness, sustained intellectual effort and intense moral struggle, are no more than existences dancing on the stillness of Pure Being. They are not final and fundamental. They are not by any means illusory, a evil dream from which we have to wake up as soon as possible. It is wrong to think that the universe exists for us only to escape from it. Existence, rather, is here to be redeemed. If the Supreme is one and many, if He is Being and Activity, if He is transcendent and immanent, then the Spirit lives in the world, Being is in existence. The aim of the cosmic evolution is to reveal the Spirit.

God and the World. In his book on *God and the Astronomers* (1933) Dr. W. R. Inge refers to my view and points out that, if God is bound up with and immanent in the evolving universe, He must share the fate of the universe. If the second law of thermodynamics is true, that the universe is running down like a clock and a time will come when there will be no life or consciousness, the universe will reach a state of static eventlessness which is another name for extinction. If God is the soul of the universe, He is the soul of a doomed universe. If the world is as necessary to God as God is to the world, a time will come when God will be no more. A god under the sentence of death is no god at all.

This objection is not fatal to the view I have indicated. This world is the accomplishment of a specific possibility from the infinite possibilities whose ideal home is the Absolute. From the primary reality of Absolute-God, the derived reality of the world ensues. This world is creaturely being. It exists because and so long as God wills it to be.

While God is distinct from the world He is not separate from it. The world exists by the sustaining presence and activity of God. Without this presence and activity, it would collapse into nothingness. In this world one possibility of the divine is being accomplished in space and time. There is the operation of the divine in it. From this it does not follow that the world is organic to God. If anything, it is organic to this specific divine possibility which is in process of accomplishment. This possibility is regarded as the soul or the entelechy of the world; we may call it the World-Spirit. The soul of this particular world is a manifestation of the Absolute-God. When this possibility is realised, when the plan of the universe is fulfilled, there is an end to this world. Its disappearance is consistent with its created character.

Kant's Antinomy. The whole question of the status of time was raised by Kant in his Antinomies of Pure Reason. *"Thesis:* The world has a beginning in time and is confined within the limits of space. *Antithesis:* The world has neither beginning in time nor bounds in space but is infinite, as in space so also in time." This antinomy cannot be solved, for, according to Kant, reason finds itself in the power of transcendental appearance. Within the limits of the phenomenal world, the contradiction cannot be overcome. We cannot think that time will come to an end in time or that it will go on endlessly. How can the end of time occur within time? When the end of the cosmic history is reached, we have passed beyond the limits of history. We have transcended time. It is not a question of an end in time but an end of time.

Brahmaloka or the Kingdom of God. So long as there is the struggle, the process of becoming, the overcoming of non-being by being, we have the time process. But when all individuals have escaped from their alienation, from their slavery to the world, when all externality is overcome, there is the awakening of the Spirit in them all. When the Kingdom of Spirit is established on earth as it is in heaven above, God the antecedent becomes God the consequent. There is a coincidence of the beginning and the end. If it is held that the end will never be accomplished, that there will be perpetual singing and no completion in a song, that it is always a journeying without any journey's end, then the cosmic process will have no meaning at all. "Thy kingdom come" is the meaning of history, and the coming of the kingdom is the triumph of meaning. The truth about the earth is the *brahmaloka,* the transfiguration of the cosmos, the revolutionary change in men's consciousness, a new relationship among them, an assimilation to God. It is the attainment of wholeness, the overcoming of disruption, the surmounting of all false antinomies, the transcending of time in eternity, which we objectify as *brahmaloka.*

Universal Salvation. The attainment of spiritual freedom by all, universal salvation or *sarvamukti* is not inconsistent with the law of entropy. When we are all liberated, time is transcended, samsāra becomes mokṣa or nirvāṇa. According to the Mahāyāna Buddhism, universal redemption is the aim of the Buddha. St. Paul extends his hope of "redemption into the glorious liberty of the children of God" to the "whole creation." This cosmic deliverance, which is the close of the world, cannot be accurately described as a terrestrial future for it is a supramundane present.

When everyone achieves his fulfilment, the cosmic purpose is fulfilled. Pure undistorted truth of eternity burns up the world. The end of the process is in continuity with the beginning and when the two coincide, cosmic existence lapses into Absolute Being.

The End of the World. The possibility of the passing away of the present order of things is not only admitted but demanded by the view here set forth. When humanity, still captive in its germ, reaches its full stature of which we can not now imagine the greatness and the majesty, it unites with its source in the past. The World-Spirit, called Brahmā, Hiraṇya-garbha, is admitted to be finite, mortal, though he creates beings who gain immortality.[41] He is said to be the first-born, the first embodied being.[42] "Death is his body." [43] He strives to express his spirit through the body of non-being, the principle of objectivity. He is *tamaś śarīraka paramātmā.*

The meaning of time is beyond the confines of time. Time has meaning because it comes to an end. If it is unending, it is meaningless. Time process can be understood only in the light of the end it aims at; the victory over time, the victory over this disrupted, fallen condition, victory over alienation, estrangement, enslavement by the objective. We conceive the end itself as taking place in historical time, though it is illogical to relate to history in simply historical terms what is beyond history. Though it may not be possible for us to think of the end of time except in terms of time, yet the end is not a term in the time series. It belongs to another order of existence, inasmuch as it marks the end of time itself. It is victory over time. It is life eternal.

Though the present order of things must pass away, there will be other world orders in an endless series; for God is infinite possibility. We do not equate God with this evolutionary process. The dissolution of the world does not in any way affect the Absolute-God; for its knowledge of all possibilities is free from relativity. God is not merely the past, the present, and the future of this world, he is the transcendental principle of this and all possible worlds, whether they are to be realised or not. Even from the strictly scientific point of view the process of gradual degradation of energy must have had a beginning. If the whole universe is running down like a clock, it must have been wound up at the beginning. If it was wound up once, what prevents it from being wound up again, if

---

41 atha yan martyaḥ sann amṛtān asṛjata. *Bṛhad-āraṇyaka Upaniṣad.* Again, hiraṇyagarbhaṁ paśyata jāyamānam. Behold the World-Spirit, as he is being born. *Śvetāśvatara Upaniṣad* IV, 12.
    42 *Śiva Purāṇa.* V.1.8.22.   43 yasya mṛtyuś śarīram. *Subāla Upaniṣad.*

another possibility requiring this type of structure is to be started? [44]

VIII. The Human Condition and the Quest for Being

Psychological Approach. The religious implications of the terraced view of nature given in the *Taittirīya Upaniṣad* are confirmed by an analysis of human nature and its concrete manifestations. For the modern mind, philosophy is not speculative idealism; it is positive knowledge of actuality. Actuality is not only cosmic but individual. *ātmānaṁ viddhi.* Know the self, has been the direction to the seeker from very early times.

The study of the nature of the human individual started in that crucial period of human history, 800 to 200 B.C. The spiritual leaders of all subsequent history emerged in it, Lao-Tse, Confucius, the writers of the Upaniṣads and Gautama the Buddha, Zoroaster and the Prophets of Israel, Socrates and the Greek philosophers.

Resemblance to Existentialism. The novelty of the existentialist approach is greatly exaggerated. In the Upaniṣads we find frequent psychological analyses of the human individual, which have a certain resemblance to the existentialist approach. For the Indian thinkers including the Buddha, human life is a transitional stage from which we have to advance to a new conception of reality. The human being is a saṁsārin, a perpetual wanderer, a tramp on the road. His life is incessant metamorphosis. The wheel of life *saṁsāra-cakra* turns ceaselessly. This change will continue until man

---

[44] In a review of C. E. M. Joad's *Counter-Attack from the East,* which deals with my views, the *Times Literary Supplement* (London) of May 3, 1934, observed: "The metaphysics of Radhakrishnan's Absolute Idealism represents a real fusion of East and West in so far as it boldly confronts the problem which haunted Bradley— that of the relation between the Absolute and the God of religious experience—and answers it in the form of an eschatology at which Bradley may have hinted in his denial of ultimate reality to the finite self, but which he never made fully explicit. Radhakrishnan suggests a solution of the problem which is, in essentials, derived from Indian Idealism, endorsing the hypotheses of pre-existence and palingenesis, and envisaging a consummation wherein, all spirits being perfected at last and set free from the cycle of Karma, the purpose of God will be achieved and God Himself will relapse into the Absolute, creation being thus at once ransomed and annulled by the cessation of the impulse to individuate. This is no place to discuss the case for and against a subtle and elevated philosophical system; but it at least behoves every inquirer to ask himself whether the gulf between this eschatology and that which asserts the 'value and destiny of the individual' is or is not one which is ultimately bridgeable. Those who feel able to reply in the affirmative may well accept Radhakrishnan, not merely as the distinguished exponent of a lofty spiritual philosophy (as he assuredly is), but as the initiator of a new synthesis."

reaches his fulfilment. Indian thinkers will not view with sympathy the tendency which we find among a few existentialists to accept the human predicament of distress and crisis as final and even find satisfaction in it. The delight of some existentialists in anguish, their acceptance of anarchy as destiny, their contented contemplation of man's disaster and nothingness, their pre-occupation with the morbid and the perverse, their rejection of absolute and universal values—will not find much support in the writings of the ancient Indian thinkers or for that matter of the modern existentialists who are religiously inclined like Karl Jaspers and Gabriel Marcel. The problem of religion is bound up with man's intellectual nature, his distinctive way of knowing himself and the world in which he lives.

The Upaniṣads. Hindu thought looks upon man as the victim of ignorance, *avidyā,* which gives rise to selfish desire, *kāma.* The Upaniṣads speak to us of the agony of finite creatures living in time, the world of karma, the agony of feeling that we are at the mercy of time. This feeling of distress is universal. But they affirm the reality of another life, where we are liberated from the rule of time, from the bonds of karma. The reality of mokṣa or liberation inspires us with hope that we can triumph over time. It is a hope and a faith until the transcension of time occurs.

Gautama the Buddha. Legend or history tells us that the Buddha had everything he wanted materially and culturally and was yet haunted by vague dissatisfactions. From wanderings in the city he learnt that disease and death were regarded as inescapable evils. His discovery of the fact of human suffering led him to a psychological investigation of the causes of pain. He started out by trying all the methods for reaching knowledge currently accepted. He consulted hermits, practised austerities, went without food. It seemed silly to weaken and torture the body. He was not getting any the wiser. He withdrew into solitary meditation and tried to think things out. He declared that all suffering is due to ignorance of the impermanent nature of things and selfish craving. When we are the victims of ignorance, we absolutise our own ego, oppose it to society and miss our moral vocation. Ignorance is not something outside of man. He lives in it, for it is that in which historical man is involved. So long as he lives his unregenerate life in time, the life of craving and aversion, suffering will be his lot. A sense of blankness overtakes the seeking spirit, which makes the world a waste and life a vain show. But he can free himself from suffering, by the awareness of eternity, by the enlightenment that liberates the ego and transfigures its temporal experience.

The Doctrine of the Fall. The symbolism of the second chapter of *Genesis* expresses the same truth. We have tasted the fruit of the tree of knowledge and the fall of man is the result. This intellectual knowledge is a leap forward in man's awareness. It is said to be a fall because it produces a fissure or a cleavage in man's life, a break in the natural order of things. Animals do no evil for they do not know the distinction between good and evil. Even if man is an animal, he is the only animal that knows that he is an animal. The development of self-consciousness is, according to Hegel, the development of unhappy consciousness, for all divided consciousness is unhappy consciousness. Adam and Eve were smitten with fear the moment they became aware of the new relationship with reality into which they entered by eating of the fruit of the "tree of knowledge of good and evil." They are smitten with fear because of their anxiety that they may not rise equal to the sense of obligation which that awareness conveys. Adam in his temptation and fall is not an individual at the beginning of history but is man at every stage in that history. The fall is a logical way of representing the need for getting out of the fallen condition. The withdrawal of integration with the environment is not purposeless; for it opens out an immense vista of self-development until we recover integration at a higher level. This view is indicated in the Orphic myth concerning the origin of the human soul, which speaks of a fall of man's spirit from a higher to a lower world.

Existentialist Emphasis. Existentialists are firm in their view that man is not a mere biological urge or an embodied social function. He is not to be treated on the pattern of an object, which is non-existential. There is a certain degree of unintelligibility in regard to existential facts. They are not completely thinkable. They are resistant to thought. Existence in this sense is experienced but not explained. The human self is not an object of scientific knowledge. It is immersed in being; it participates in the creative intention of the cosmos. Man is essentially the possessor of freedom, not a mere thing which is a product of physical processes or an unreal appearance of the Absolute. Existentialism is a protest against the tendency to reduce the reality of the individual to forms of thought or universal relations. Man has an incommunicable uniqueness about him. He is not the Platonic universal differentiated by the presence of accidental forms. Individuals differ from each other

not only in their accidental properties but in their essential natures, in the forms or patterns which they are attempting to realise.
Being self-conscious, man is essentially free. In the interests of human freedom the existentialists even deny the reality of the transcendent. Marx says: "Man is free only if he owes his existence to himself." Nicolai Hartmann adopts the theory of postulatory atheism. We postulate the non-existence of God for the sake of human independence. Nietzsche's Zarathustra exclaims: "If there are gods, who could bear not to be a god? Therefore there are no gods." In different ways the two characteristics of the human being are brought out, his self-consciousness and moral freedom.

The Sense of Insecurity. Unsophisticated minds may take life as they find it and may not vex themselves about its limitations. But even they cannot for all time be immune to the questionings of fate. The events of the world seem to be essentially unstable and fleeting, energising and vanishing never to return. There is nothing that we can grasp, nothing that we can keep. The day of life sinks inevitably into the night of death, *maraṇāntaṁ hi jīvitam.* The dread of something impending, the uncanny apprehension of something evil that is to happen, makes the thinking man feel that there is nothing to live for. The sense of the impermanence of things is a recurring theme in all religious literature. Akbar carved a beautiful saying over the gate of the city which he deserted as soon as it was built. "Said Jesus, may his name be blessed, 'This world is a bridge, pass over it, but build no house upon it.'"

For Heidegger, all existence is infected with the character of time, of historicity. Nothing can escape the fate of history. All existence is threatened with two dreadful convictions, that of death and transitoriness and the dread of death. Man, Heidegger says, is aware of the intense actuality of life at the moment life is ebbing away. That drawing of the lonely Nietzsche with deep eyes and musical fingertips following the sinking sun on his deathbed sums up the meaning of life. Is it possible, asks Heidegger, that time, despite its ontological nature and of all the consequences that follow from it, offers us a ground for our existence and a certainty that will permit us to gain a fundamental tranquility of soul? "Temporality discloses itself as the meaning of real dread (*Sorge*)." In the exciting moments of fear, in the devastating experience of being thrown into the world of space and time, man finds that he stands on the obscure ground of a mysterious nothing, which is not a mere mathematical zero but something more positive than that. When man experiences this "nothingness" in all its existential weight he suffers from a feeling of profound unrest and care, a 'radical insecurity of being.' This sense of nothingness is not so much a metaphysical concept as a psychological state, an inner condition which provokes the sense of dread and starts the religious quest.

The Sense of Anxiety. Unless man is free to disobey the commands, he will not have the opportunity to conform to them freely and deliberately. Man's creative will is the source of selfish ambition as well as disinterested love. Although the true law of man's being is love, a harmonious relation among all living things, he rebels against this law when he imagines himself, not a single individual in the whole but the whole itself. A defiant self-affirmation which leads to enslavement, a false freedom which destroys itself, overtakes him. There is a complete sundering of that sense of compassion which is the intuitive sense of kinship and union with life, which was found in the earlier stages at an instinctive level. The possibility of the misuse of freedom becomes an actuality. Freedom passes into wilfulness and wilfulness gives rise to evil. The fact of moral freedom produces sin, though sin is not a necessary consequence of it. The abuse of freedom results in sins. To be good is to be capable of all evil and yet commit none. Sin is the refusal to grow, to evolve. It is to defy the cosmic destiny.

Jesus asks us to be delivered, not from temptation but, from evil. He knows that temptations come. Even the greatest of us are not free from them. We have to face them, though we need not go out of our way to find them. At no stage on earth can we be sure that we can be free from temptations. St. Paul says: "let him that thinketh he standeth take heed lest he fall." [45] Temptations are as inescapable as the air we breathe; but it is no less human to withstand them than it is to be tempted. When we are tempted we need not assume that the battle is lost. We can hold our ground as long as life lasts. The purpose of the trials and temptations is not that we may fall but that we may rise.

Kierkegaard, to whom the existentialist philosophers trace their descent, asserts that man is not an object to be known but a subject with a self to acquire. Man exists because he has freedom. It is freedom that helps him to reintegrate his personality. So far as man is human he must do either good or evil. If he drifts, he is forfeiting his humanity. It is better to do evil than surrender to automatism; for then we exist at least.

The fact of freedom, according to Kierkegaard, produces anxiety,

[45] I. *Corinthians* X.

the fear that we may abuse our freedom. He says, "Anxiety is the psychological condition which precedes sin. It is so near, so fearfully near to sin, and yet it is not the explanation for sin." [46] Anxiety is the precondition of sin, the fear that we may sin. It is a basic constituent of human freedom. Sin is not a psychological problem, but dread or anxiety-neurosis is. It is a redeeming quality that we are anxious, for under the stress of passion or fear, starvation, or religious frenzy, we are likely to do the most terrific deeds.

Kierkegaard defines self as spirit, "a relationship which relates itself to itself." It does not create itself but is created by another power and is therefore a "derived, constituted relationship," a relationship which relates itself to its own self and in doing so relates itself to this power. In this cycle of relationships there is in man's very nature dis-relationship leading to despair, to sickness unto death of which Christ spoke, according to Kierkegaard, when he raised Lazarus from the dead.[47] "This illness is not unto death, but for the glory of God, that the son of God might be glorified thereby." This despair is integral to man's existential inwardness, to his relationship to the eternal.

Inward Discord. When man looks at himself, the disorders of the flesh, the unendurable error of the senses, the fearful perversions of the heart, the debased instincts of nature, he stands aghast. His self-respect as a human being is hurt, and he feels himself degraded. He detects and beholds sin as an incomprehensible necessity, something older and deeper than his will for good. The fact of sin is an empirical discovery, not a theological dogma. Man is afraid of the unintelligible forces that control him. To gain security he strives all the time to enslave nature, enslave man. Man is a paradox. He desires things which are seemingly incompatible. He is the rival of his fellows and yet seeks peace and unity with them. He is in love with life and yet on occasions is prepared for death. In moments of self-analysis he examines his past, feels unsure of himself, pulled this way and that, feels distressed in spirit and sick unto death. Unhappiness is essentially a state of disruption and division. Man is haunted by doubts, What am I? From what causes do I derive my being? To what conditions shall I return?

The Need for Resolving the Discords. The tension in human nature is what makes man interesting. Without it he would not become aware of his utter nothingness, his forlornness, his insufficiency, his dependence, his weakness, his emptiness. His anguish and suffering have a dialectical necessity. The roots of religion are

---

[46] S. Kierkegaard, *Der Begriff der Angst*, 89.   [47] *John* XI, 4.

in this inner torment which has to be resolved. He must strive after unity with nature, with man, with himself. Only when he is victorious in his struggle does he attain human dignity. We are seekers, pilgrims on the march for the city that is to be, for we have no abiding city on earth. We must reach out beyond the frontiers of our dual, divided consciousness. We cannot remain content within an impermeable solitude of our own anguished desires. We cannot remain for ever in a state of unfulfilment. Even the lowest forms of life strive after adjustment.

The ancestors of man played an important part in this great drama of cosmic evolution, though they did not understand either the play or their part in it. Man has also to play his part, but with a knowledge of the structure and meaning of the play. By his intelligence he must comprehend the cosmic plan and by his will further it. Human progress does not depend on the slow action of physical or biological laws. It can be speeded up by our effort, if we liberate ourselves from bondage, if we escape from the life that is in part and enter into the life which is whole. The prayer of the Upaniṣads,[48] "Lead me from the unreal to the real, lead me from darkness to light, lead me from death to immortality," assumes that we live in a world of fear, of care, of abandonment, of death, of nothingness, and we seek a world of being, of fearlessness, of freedom, of spirit, of eternity. We seek to transcend the finitude of human existence and gain life eternal.

Escapist Solutions: Reversion to Non-Rational Life. Sometimes we are tempted to go back, become unthinking and unreflective, sink into the simplicity of biological existence, submerge in the elemental animal. This would be a deliberate sacrifice of our wholeness, an abandonment of the attempt to achieve integrity. We cannot reverse the process and throw away our heritage. Self-conscious man cannot become the instinctive animal. Even if he refuses to employ his intellectual consciousness he cannot get back the original integration with the environment. Memory and expectancy will interfere. Job seeks his asylum in sleep but does not succeed. "When I say, my bed shall comfort me, my couch shall ease my complaint, then thou scarest me with dreams and terrifiest me through visions." [49] We cannot shake off our rationality. We cannot get away from the strains of our self-consciousness. The cure for our unrest is not a relapse into the womb of the unconscious,

---

[48] *asato mā sad gamaya, tamaso mā mṛtyur gamaya mṛtyor mā amṛtaṁ gamaya.* *Bṛhad-āraṇyaka Upaniṣad* I.3.28.
[49] *Job* VII, 13-14.

but a rise into creative consciousness. What we aim at is the enlightenment of the sage and not the inexperience of the new-born babe.

Dogmas of Religion or Politics. We cannot cure the affliction caused by intellect, the loneliness, the insecurity and the anguish by drugs, by the myths of religion or the dogmas of politics. These plans of escape from the prison of our life may help a few for a little time. If we take opium we may find a few moments beautiful and calm in contrast to the jarring world outside; but they will not last. The unscientific dogmas, the crude superstitions tell us more about the mind of man than about the structure of reality, and cannot save man from scepticism.

If the lonely individual clings to something outside of him, he may gain security, but he does so at the expense of his integrity as an individual. We may renounce freedom of inquiry and bind our eyes from further seeking with the bandage of a final creed. We may thus be saved from making decisions or assuming responsibility for the future. But we will be disturbed and dissatisfied at the root, for the emergence of the individual self cannot be stifled. Happiness is in freedom, and freedom is in greatness of spirit.

Scientific Enlightenment. It is argued that scientific progress will destroy the feeling of loneliness with which we regard the alien world and terminate the inability of men to determine their own destiny.

We may grant that we can anticipate the course of natural phenomena and even to some extent control it. But nature can never be tamed to do man's will. Her blind caprices, her storms and tempests, her cyclones and earthquakes will continue to shatter his work and dash his dreams. Man cannot alter the limits of his life or his body. "Thou fool, this night shall thy soul be required of thee." Increasing knowledge of science without a corresponding growth of religious wisdom only increases our fear of death. Our scientific culture is unparalleled in human history. We have dominated the forces of nature, controlled the seas and conquered the air. We have increased production, combated disease, organised commerce, and made man master of his environment; and yet the lord of the earth cannot live in safety. He has to hide under the earth, wear gas masks. He is haunted by the fears of wars and lives in the company of uncertainties. This war-haunted, machine-driven civilisation cannot be the last word of human striving. Unless we are blind idiots or self-satisfied morons, we will know that scientific organisation is not the fulfilment of the spirit of man.

Science can do little in that region in which human disorder has been most striking, the sphere of human relationships.

Social Progress. The fear which is the expression of man's rationality cannot be removed by any change in outer circumstances. We may abolish the horrors of the industrial age, clean up the slums and diminish drunkenness; yet the spirit of man cannot by these measures alone gain anything in security. In the most prosperous circumstances, our heart will still suffer from the torment of the infinite, from the anguish of beatitude. There are sufferings which can be overcome by changes in the social order, and it is our duty to achieve a social revolution and remove these social wrongs of hunger, cold, illiteracy, sickness, unemployment. But we have to recognise that there are certain evils which are organic to the spiritual condition of man and so cannot be removed by social changes. Dr. Johnson wrote two centuries ago:

> How small of all that human hearts endure
> That part which Kings or laws can cause or cure?

While we should liberate the spirit of man from the distorting influences of social slavery and cruelty, we must admit that the slavery of the mind and the cruelty of the heart can be removed only by another discipline.

Creative Consciousness. Intellectual consciousness has inflicted the wounds, has brought about the fall; full, free, creative consciousness must heal the wounds and secure redemption. If we remain at the level of intellectual consciousness, if we are satisfied with ourselves and the world, we are once-born. Our lives would be facile, unintentional and unpurposive. The twice-born are those whose complex and ardent personalities are broken on the wheel of doubt and spiritual crisis and then reassembled, reanimated and reintegrated.

Through the exercise of the intellectual consciousness man is able to discriminate between subject and object. Man, a product of nature, subject to its necessities, compelled by its laws, driven by its impulses, is yet a non-nature, a spirit who stands outside of nature, outside of his 'given' nature. He has the capacity for self-transcendence, the ability to make himself an object. Man therefore has affinities with a world of nature and with a world outside of nature. The Buddha, for example, distinguishes between Karma and nirvāṇa. Karma is the principle which governs the world of objects, of cause and effect, nirvāṇa is the principle of subject which transcends the object, the centre of being.

Existence and Being. In his book on *Being and Time* (*Sein und Zeit,* 1927, Pt. I), Heidegger draws a distinction between being and existence. The important fact about man is not that he exists but that he knows that he exists; he has the power to perceive the meaning of existence. Sub-human entities like stones, plants, and animals exist and pass out without a consciousness of their existence. They are incapable of either doubt or illumination. Man's existence includes the power, the determination to stand out of existence and in the truth of being. If man fails to transcend his existential limits, he too would be condemned to death and nothingness. He must first experience the void, the nothingness, the śūnya of the Mādhyamaka Buddhist, not for its own sake but for transcending it, for getting beyond the world of saṁsāra to the other shore of being. The experience of dread is the experience of the problem whether man shall attain to being or shall not, whether he shall annihilate nothingness and get beyond it or whether nothingness shall annihilate him. The self in man enables him to overcome the void, experience it, and then transcend it. We become conscious of reality through the disappointment with existence. Man's uneasiness and bewilderment arise from the fact of the absence of reality in the things of the world. We must get beyond the things of the world. "If any man came to me and hate not his father and mother and wife and children, and brethren and sisters yea and his own life also, he cannot be my disciple." [50] To stand out of existence there must come upon the individual a sense of crucifixion, a sense of the agonising annihilation, a sense of the utter nothingness of all this empirical existence which is subject to the law of change, death. Only through loneliness can nearness to reality be achieved. We must endure the terrible awakening summed up in Jesus' words, "My God, my God, why hast thou forsaken me?" When the individual withdraws from the empirical, when he penetrates to the centre, when the objective world falls away, he affirms the reality of spirit, which is not an object, which is not a temporal existent, which, though in time, is not of it. He then realises that time is not all, that death is not all, that it is possible to circumvent the time process and say with the Buddha or the Christ, "I have overcome the world." Faith in such a non-object principle is the defeat of death, and the renewal of life. When the spirit is affirmed, dread is annulled. Existentialist philosophers emphasise this essential phase of spiritual life, what the mystics call "the dark night of the soul."

[50] *Luke* XIV, 26.

If anguish were the permanent condition of human life, there is no escape from the apotheosis of nihilism, which would deny any purpose in the world and reduce it to futility, negation, death. The one and only meaning of reality would be nothingness. The teaching of the Buddha has been misinterpreted as a nihilism, forgetting that the Buddha's emphasis is on man's power to overcome the void and attain nirvāṇa.[51] If existence were all, if the objective time series were all, if saṁsāra were all, there would be no escape from fear. If we are to avert the common doom of death, we must take the aid of everlasting hope that death is not all, that all-devouring time is not all. When the Indian thinkers affirm that the world is māyā, that it is not real, though existent, that we can escape from it, that it is possible for us to circumvent the time process, they affirm the reality of spirit which is not objective, which is not (merely) existent. When we attempt to modify the world in accordance with our hearts' desires we affirm the existence of our own spiritual centre which is transcendent to the world of time. There is a reality which is different from existence, there is a subject which is non-object, there is a time-transcending element. Faith in such a non-object spirit means the defeat of death, and the renewal of life.[52] Man's awareness of his finiteness and temporality means his consciousness of eternity. It is the consciousness of infinitude that produces in us the consciousness of the finitude. In the uncertainty of life we feel a distant certainty through which alone this uncertainty is made possible. Being as such contains the possibility of God and of man's dignity. If there were no Being, there would be no God, all would be perishing existence. If man's existence is not a mere void or pure nothingness, there is Being in existence. We can attain illumination of Being by facing bitterly the ultimate meaning of nothingness.

The act by which we become conscious of our existence, by which we affirm that things exist and individuals exist, transcends concepts and ideas. It is a mystery for the intellect, but we do have an intuition of it. The subject matter of this intuition is Being itself. This Being is not a Platonic essence or a pale abstraction but Being as the very structure of reality in which the act of existence is immersed. It is Being at its supreme plenitude informing the entire dynamism of existence. In perceiving Being we perceive the divine reality. The created realm is not outside Being. We confront

---

[51] See my *Introduction to the Dhammapada* (1950).

[52] The fourth verse of the twenty-third Psalm is: "Yea, though I walk through the valley of the shadow of death, I will fear no evil."

Being in the world of existence, otherwise we will not be able to say that things exist, individuals exist. The order of existence implies an absolute irrefragable Being completely free from nothingness and death. An individual existence liable to death belongs to the totality of nature, the universal whole, the order of time of which we are all parts. Being with existence or nothingness implies Being without nothingness. This absolute Being is involved in our primordial intuition of existence. The universal whole whose part I am, this cosmic order is Being with nothingness from the very fact that we are all parts of it. Since the universal whole does not exist by itself there is another Being, transcendent and self-sufficient and unknown in itself, actuating all existents. This is Being without nothingness, Being by itself, Being which transcends the time order, the totality of nature. Existence is in Being. Saṁsāra is in nirvāṇa. Eternity is centred in time. That art thou. St. Paul says: "Know you not that you are the temple of God and the Spirit of God dwelleth in you?" [53] When the Quakers tell us that the Christ Light shines in the hearts of men, and if we would but heed the light, we would come to experience His life and power within us, they are referring to this element of non-nature or spirit in us.

The Moral Struggle. Whereas Heidegger takes us to being from existence from the logical side, Kierkegaard approaches the same problem from the moral side. According to the *Bhagavadgītā,* on the battleground of the human soul is waged the most desperate of all conflicts, that between the forces of good and of evil. The moral struggle is one between self and self, the locked and desperate encounter between the spirit and the flesh, between, what the Christians call, the spirit of Christ and the flesh of Adam. When we have the torment of the struggle in moral life, the self feels itself divided against itself. The struggle itself is not possible unless we look upon the longing for the good and the rebellion against it as belonging to the same individual. The felt contradiction is possible only through the reality which is above the discord. The awareness of the antithesis between what we are and what we wish to be is implicitly the work of the unity which dwells in every creature. We strive to give spirit existence, make the spiritual actual and thus harmonise our whole nature. The perfection of man, the capacity to reach his fulfilment through freedom is contained in the state of care or anxiety. This feeling indicates man's subjection to an alien world, his contingency. The possibility of the misuse of freedom which is the cause of anxiety, according to

[53] I. *Corinthians* III, 18.

Kierkegaard, shows the dis-relationship of the self to its own self. The anxiety can be allayed only by reintegration, by "relating itself to its own self," and by willing to be itself. The self then becomes grounded in its own real being. It is then that we are truly free. The creative act of freedom is possible only on the part of one who has broken through the necessity of the natural world. The law of Karma, viz., of necessity, reigns in the object world. Man with his creative acts can mould the closed circle of nature and disclose its possibilities. Man can continue the creative process in it by the exercise of freedom. By endowing man with self-conscious-ness, by making him in the image of God, the task is set to him, to continue the creation of the world. The human self incorporates in itself existence and value and is therefore capable of salvation.

Existentialism, a Transitional Phase of Individual Development. In this quest for Being every man is alone. It begins in man him-self, for inwards leads the mysterious path. It starts with a certain anguish of mind, the anguish which consists in a knowledge that a man can neither escape his own destiny nor the approach of death and the bewilderment of finding himself alone in the midst of an unfathomable universe.

The whole plan of evolution suggests that man has another des-tiny. It is the pressure of Reality which provokes the quest and the discontent. Unhappiness, consequent on avidyā or ignorance, is a metaphysical necessity which prepares for the restoration, for the attainment of vidyā or wisdom. The sense of the Beyond gives us soaring power. The ontological argument may not prove the exis-tence of God, but it does prove the human predicament and its need for an Absolute.

Thus, through an analysis of the finite and contingent character of human existence, through logic and morality, we apprehend the reality of a Being which is not existence, of a Self which is not ob-ject, of a Spirit which is not actual. This Being, Subject, Spirit is not an object presented to thought. It is the basis and source of thought. The self-knowledge is not a psychological awareness of phenomena, a collection of images and memories. It is not an awareness of the ego. It is the intuition of Being, knowledge of the ontological self, the living depth of human existence. Existential-ism is a stage in man's pilgrimage through life. It has to transcend itself; for an analysis of the human predicament reveals the fact of God as Being and God as Perfection.

IX. The Religion of the Spirit

Direct Experience of Eternal Being. When rational thought is applied to the empirical data of the world and of the human self, the conclusion of a Supreme who is Pure Being and Free Activity is reached; but it may be argued that it is only a necessity of thought, a hypothesis, however valid it may be. There is also an ancient and widespread tradition that we can apprehend the Eternal Being with directness and immediacy. When the Upaniṣads speak of jñāna or gnosis, when the Buddha speaks of bodhi or enlightenment, when Jesus speaks of the truth that will make us free, they refer to the mode of direct spiritual apprehension of the Supreme, in which the gap between truth and Being is closed. Their religion rests on the testimony of the Holy Spirit, on personal experience, on mysticism as defined by St. Thomas Aquinas, *cognitio dei experimentalis.* From the affirmations of spiritual experience, we find that it is possible to reconcile the conclusions of logical understanding with the apprehensions of integral insight.

Different Types of Knowledge. There are different types of knowledge: perceptual, conceptual, and intuitive and they are suited to different kinds of objects. Plotinus tells us that sense perceptions are below us, logical reasonings are with us, and spiritual apprehensions are above us.

Integral Insight and Logical Thought. The last type of knowledge may be called integral insight, for it brings into activity not merely a portion of our conscious being, sense or reason, but the whole. It also reveals to us not abstractions but the reality in its integrity. Existentialists dispute the priority of essence to existence. Whereas the possible is prior to the actual insofar as the genesis of the universe is concerned, in the world itself thought works on and in existence and abstracts from it. Thought reaches its end of knowledge in so far as it returns to being. Thought is essentially self-transcendent. It deals with an other than thought and so is only symbolic of it. Thinking deals with essences, and existences are unattainable to it. Existence is one way of being, though it is not the only way. Knowledge is reflection on the experience of existence. It is within being. The inadequacy of knowledge to being is stressed by Bradley in his distinction between *what* and *that,* between a logical category and actual being. In integral insight we have knowledge by identity. Although logical knowledge is mediate and symbolic, it is not false. Its construction is not an imaginative synthesis. It falls short of complete knowledge, because it gives the structure of being, not being itself. In integral insight we are put in touch with actual being. This highest knowledge transcends the distinction of subject and object. Even logical knowledge is possible because this highest knowledge is ever present. It can only be accepted as foundational. Being is Truth. *Sat* is *cit*.

We use the direct mode of apprehension, which is deeper than logical understanding, when we contemplate a work of art, when we enjoy great music, when we acquire an understanding of another human being in the supreme achievement of love. In this kind of knowledge the subject is not opposed to the object but is intimately united with it. By calling this kind of knowledge integral insight, we bring out that it does not contradict logical reason, though the insight exceeds the reason. Intellect cannot repudiate instinct any more than intuition can deny logical reason. Intellectual preparation is an instrument for attaining to the truth of the spirit, but the inward realisation of the truth of spirit transcends all intellectual verification, since it exists in an immediacy beyond all conceivable mediation.

Spiritual Experience, a Mode of Integral Insight. The Supreme is not an object but the absolute subject, and we cannot apprehend it by either sense-perception or logical inference. Kant was right in denying that being was a predicate. We are immersed in being. When the Upaniṣads ask us to grow from intellectual to spiritual consciousness, they ask us to effect an enlargement of our awareness by which the difficulties of insecurity, isolation, and death are overcome. We are called upon to grow from division and conflict into freedom and love, from ignorance to wisdom. Such wisdom cannot come except to those who are pure not only in heart but also in the intellect, which has to rid itself of all preconceptions. Unmediated apprehension of the primordial Spirit is the knowledge of God. It is achieved by a change of consciousness, the experience of a new birth. It means an illumined mind, a changed heart, and a transformed will. Wisdom composes the various elements of our mental life, modifies our being, restores our community with nature and society, and makes living significant. Wisdom is freedom from fear, for fear is the result of a lack of correspondence between the nature of the individual and his environment, the clash of the ego and the non-ego which is alien and indifferent to it. The struggle against the alien is the source of suffering. Man is a being who is straining towards infinity, in quest of eternity; but the condition of his existence, finite and limited, temporal and mortal, causes the suffering. When he attains 'integrality,' there is harmony in his life and its expression is joy.

Through wisdom we grow into likeness with the Spirit. St. Thomas Aquinas observes: "By this light the blessed are made deiform, that is like God, according to the scriptural saying 'When he shall appear, we shall be like him and we shall see him as he is.' " [54]

Universality of the Tradition of Direct Experience of God. There is a tradition of direct apprehension of the Supreme in all lands, in all ages and in all creeds.[55] The seers describe their experiences with an impressive unanimity. They are "near to one another on mountains farthest apart." They certify, in words which ring both true and clear, of a world of spirit alive and waiting for us to penetrate. Indian religions take their stand on spiritual experience, on divine-human encounter, *kṛṣṇārjunasaṁvāda*, and so do the prophets and saints of other religions. Augustine writes: "I entered and beheld with the eye of my soul above the same eye of my soul, above my mind, the Light unchangeable." [56] St. Bernard wrote that happy and blessed was he "who once or twice—or even once only—in this mortal life for the space of a moment has lost himself in God." St. John of the Cross speaks of that steady and established certitude of essential creative union which alone he considers worthy to be called the "spiritual marriage" of the soul.

What God communicates to the soul in this intimate union is utterly ineffable, beyond the reach of all possible words . . . in this state God and the soul are united as the window is with the light or the coal with the fire . . . this communication of God diffuses itself substantially in the whole soul or rather the soul is transformed in God. In this transformation the soul drinks of God in its very substance and its spiritual powers.

[54] I. John III, 2, quoted in *Summa Theologica* 1, q, 12, a, 5, C.

[55] "The close agreement which we find in these records (of mystic life), written in different countries, in different ages, and even by adherents of different creeds (for Asia has here its own important contribution to make) can only be accounted for, if we hold that the mystical experience is a genuine part of human nature, which may be developed, like the arts, by concentrated attention and assiduous labour, and which assumes the same general forms whenever and wherever it is earnestly sought." W. R. Inge: *The Philosophy of Plotinus.* (1918), I, 2. Rudolf Otto, in the Introduction to his book on *Mysticism: East and West,* observes: "We maintain that, in mysticism, there are wide and strong primal impulses working in the human soul which as such are completely unaffected by differences of climate, of geographical position or of race. These show, in their similarity, an inner relationship of types of human experience and spiritual life which is truly astonishing." (English translation, 1932), XVI.

[56] *Confessions* VII, 16.

Nature of Spiritual Experience. Spiritual experience, as distinct from religious feeling of dependence or worship or awe, engages our whole person. It is a state of ecstasy or complete absorption of our being. When the flash of absolute reality breaks through the normal barriers of the conscious mind it leaves a trail of illumination in its wake. The excitement of illumination is distinct from the serene radiance of enlightenment. The experience is not of a subjective psychic condition. The contemplative insight into the source of all life is not an escape into the subjective. The human individual can strip himself one after the other of the outer sheaths of consciousness, penetrate to the nerve and quick of his life until all else fades away into illimitable darkness, until he is alone in the white radiance of a central and unique ecstasy. This is the fulfilment of man. This is to be with God. This is to be of God. During our hurried passage through life there may come to us a few moments of transcendent joy, when we seem to stand literally outside our narrow selves and attain a higher state of being and understanding. All religions call upon us to renew those great moments and make the experience of spirit the centre of our lives.

The Absolute as Transcendent and Immanent. When the vision fades, the habitual awareness of this world returns. The so-called proofs of the existence of God are the results of critical reflection on the spiritual intuitions of the ultimate Fact of Spirit. These intuitions inspire the acts of reflection, which only confirm what has been apprehended in another way. The reflections are pure and true to the extent that they refer to the intuited facts. There is a perpetual disquiet because ultimate Being is not an object. Reflective accounts are thus only approximations.

Being as such is uncharacterisable and our descriptions and translations are in forms of objects which are less than Being and consequently are inadequate. Abstract ideals and intellectualisations do not deal justly with Being which is given to us as Absolute Presence in adoration and worship. It is through religious contemplation that we realise the Holy. It is not simple apprehension. It is the surrender of the self, its opening to the Supreme.

The experience of a pure and unitary consciousness in a world divided gives rise to the twofold conception of the Absolute as Pure Transcendent Being lifted above all relativities, and the Free Active God functioning in the world. Some emphasise the transcendent aspect, the fulness of being, the sublime presence, the sovereignly subsistent 'other,' above all names and thought; others the immanent aspect, the fulness of life, the living personal God of love who made the world, gave us freedom, and wishes us to participate in the riches of life. St. John of the Cross says:

Beyond all sensual images, and all conceptual determination, God offers Himself as the absolute act of being in its pure actuality. Our concept of God, a mere feeble analogue of a reality which overflows it in every direction, can be made explicit only in the judgment: Being is Being, an absolute positing of that which, lying beyond every object, contains in itself the sufficient reason of objects. And that is why we can rightly say that the very excess of positivity which hides the divine being from our eyes is nevertheless the light which lights up all the rest: *ipsa caligo summa est mentis illuminatio.*

We have here the two aspects of supracosmic transcendence and cosmic universality, the divine mystery which is inexpressible, Eckhart's Godhead, and the mystery which is directed towards the world, Eckhart's God. The God who reveals Himself to the world and to man is not the Absolute which is inexpressible, relationless mystery.

Attempts to rationalise the mystery, to translate into the language of concepts that which is inexpressible in concepts, have resulted in different versions. We may use the trinitarian conception to unfold the nature of the Supreme Being; the Brahman, the Absolute, is the first person, the second is Īśvara, and the third is the World-Spirit. The three persons are different sides of the one Supreme. They are not three different persons but are the one God who hides himself [57] and reveals himself in various degrees. In communicating their experiences the seers use words and symbols current in their world.

Free Spirits. The liberated souls have overcome the power of time, the force of Karma. There is something in common between the wisdom of the sage and the simplicity of the child, serene trust and innocent delight in existence. The happy state of childhood is almost the lost paradise of the human mind. The free spirits are the rays of light that shine from the future, attracting us all who still dwell in darkness. They do not separate themselves from the world but accept the responsibility for perfecting all life. There is no such thing as individual salvation, for it presupposes the salvation of others, universal salvation, the transfiguration of the world.[58] No man, however enlightened and holy he may be, can ever really be saved until all the others are saved. Those individ-

---

[57] "Verily Thou art a God that hidest Thyself." *Psalm* 103.
[58] See IVL (1932), 123ff.

uals who have realised their true being are the integrated ones who have attained personal integrity. Their reason is turned into light, their heart into love, and their will into service. Their demeanour is disciplined and their singleness of spirit is established. Selfish action is not possible for them. Ignorance and craving have lost their hold. They are dead to pride, envy, and uncharitableness. The world in which they live is no more alien to them. It is hospitable, not harsh. It becomes alive, quakes, and sends forth its greetings. Human society becomes charged with the grace and grandeur of the eternal. These free spirits reach out their hands towards the warmth in all things. They have that rarest quality in the world, simple goodness, beside which all the intellectual gifts seem a little trivial. They are meek, patient, long-suffering. They do not judge others because they do not pretend to understand them. Because of their eager selfless love they have the power to soothe the troubled heart. To those in pain their presence is like the cool soft hand of some one they love, when their head is hot with fever. The released individuals are artists in creative living. With an awareness of the Eternal, they participate in the work of the world. Even as the Supreme has two sides of pure being and free activity, these liberated souls, who are the vehicles of divine life,[59] have also two sides: the contemplative and the active.

Contemplation and Action. Their life is socially minded. We are members of a whole, parts of brahmāṇḍa (the cosmic egg), which is one, which is perpetually in transition until its final purpose is achieved. "No man liveth unto himself and no man dieth unto himself" (St. Paul). Their attitude is not one of lofty condescension or patronising pity to lift a debased creature out of mire. But it is a conviction of the solidarity of the world *loka-saṁgraha* and a recognition that the low and the high are bound together in one spirit. Vicarious suffering, not vicarious punishment, is a law of spiritual life. The free spirits bend to the very level of the enslaved to emancipate their minds and hearts. They inspire, revive and strengthen the life of their generation.

The Charge of World-Negation. From the time I was a student, I have heard criticisms made against Indian religions that they are world-negating and that the attitude of our religious men is one of withdrawal from the world. Though the supreme quest is for the freedom of the spirit, for the vision of God, there is also the realisation of the ever present need of the world for the light and guidance of free spirits. A life of service and sacrifice is the natural

[59] "Grace makes us participants of the divine nature." II. *Peter* I, 4.

and inevitable expression and the proof of the validity of spiritual experience. After years of solitary contemplation the Buddha attained enlightenment. The rest of his life was devoted to intense social and cultural work. According to Mahāyāna Buddhism, the released spirits retain their compassion for suffering humanity. Even those whose activities are limited to the instruction of their disciples participate in social leadership in so far as they aim at refashioning human society. Gandhi, well known as a religious man, did not strive to escape from the human scene to forge a solitary destiny. He said: "I am striving for the kingdom of salvation which is spiritual deliverance. For me the road to salvation is through incessant toil in the service of my country and of humanity. I want to identify myself with everything that lives. I want to live at peace with both friend and foe." He reckoned social reform and political action among his religious duties. He founded not a monastic order but a revolutionary party. Gandhi brought home to us the lessons of the saints of old, that no one who believes in spiritual values can abandon to their fate the millions of people whom misery and impossible conditions of life have condemned to a hell on earth. Active service is a part of spiritual life.

Although the unitive knowledge of God here and now is the final end of man, it remains true that some forms of social and cultural life put more obstacles in the way of individual development than others. It is our duty to create and maintain forms of social organisation which offer the fewest possible impediments to the development of the truly human life. By improving the conditions of social life we remove powerful temptations to ignorance and irresponsibility and encourage individual enlightenment. Every man, whatever may be his racial or social origin, is potentially a son of God, made in his image. Human personality is sacred. The human person has a claim to be treated as an end in himself and is therefore entitled to the rights to life, freedom, and security. Freedom to be himself is the right of personality. These rights involve duties. Our legal and political systems must help the realisation of our rights and the acceptance of our obligations. Our civilisation has failed to the extent to which these ideals are denied or betrayed. We must work for the achievement of these ideals in accordance with the principles of freedom, truth, and justice. This is not to reduce religion to a sublimated social engineering.

Tendency to Other-Worldliness. There is a tendency in all religions, Eastern or Western, to neglect the practical side. Any one who approaches the New Testament will find that the emphasis is on other-worldliness. Jesus' teaching about the Kingdom of God and its righteousness, of its coming and of the conditions of our partaking in it, does not betray any interest in the structures of our temporal life. The letters of the Apostles are concerned with the preaching of salvation, the proclamation of Resurrection, of the divine judgment, of the restoration and perfection of all things beyond their historical existence. The few brief comments on the state, on marriage and family life, on the relations between masters and slaves, do not take away the essentially other-worldly character of the teaching of Jesus and his disciples. In the last century his teaching has been interpreted in a manner that shows its kinship with our social and cultural problems.[60]

Religion as the Inspiration of Life. Religion is not a particular way of life but is the way of all life. Jesus said: "I am the Way, the Truth and the Life." Religious life is neither ascetic nor legalistic. It condemns mere externalism and does not insist on obedience to laws and ordinances. "Where the spirit of the Lord is there is liberty." Liberty is freedom from all taboos and restrictions. We are not called upon to hate the world because it is the creation of a hostile demiurge. To look upon the world as undivine is a speculative aberration. God is not jealous of his own works. The world is an abyss of nothingness, if we take away its roots in the Divine. What the Indian thinkers aim at is action without attachment. It is action of an individual who is no more a victim of selfishness, who has identified himself with the divine centre which is in him and in all things. Since he is not emotionally involved in the 'fruits of action,' he is able to act effectively. True religion has elements in it of withdrawal from the world and of return to it. Its aim is the control of life by the power of spirit.

Our social conscience has been anaesthetised by a formal religion and it has now to be roused. In recent times, it is the atheists and not the saints that have taken the lead in the work of social enlightenment and justice. In the history of religions, however, the rôle of the religious leader has been important. Though dedicated to a life of contemplation he is led to act like a ferment of renewal in

---

[60] "All New Testament scholars nowadays would admit that this nineteenth century interpretation, whether we like it or not, was a falsification of the historical facts. Whether you understand the Kingdom of God more as a present reality or as something to come, in either case it is a reality which entirely transcends the sphere of civilisation." Emil Brunner, *Christianity and Civilisation*, First Part (1948), 7.

the structure of society. That great tradition of which Gandhi is the latest example, requires to be renewed.[61] The integrated individuals are the rare privileged beings who are in advance of their time. They are the forerunners of the future race,[62] who set to us the path we have to take, to rise from fallen to transfigured nature. They are not, however, to be regarded as unique and absolute manifestations of the Absolute. There cannot be a complete manifestation of the Absolute in the world of relativity. Each limited manifestation may be perfect in its own way, but is not the Absolute which is within all and above all. The life of a Buddha or a Jesus tells us how we can achieve the same unity with the Absolute to which they had attained and how we can live at peace in the world of manifested being. The light that lighteth everyone that cometh into the world shone in those liberated spirits with great radiance and intensity. The Kingdom of God is the Kingdom of persons who are spiritually free, who have overcome fear and loneliness. Every one has in him the possibility of this spiritual freedom, the essence of enlightenment, is a *bodhisattva*. The divine sonship of Christ is at the same time the divine sonship of every man. The end of the cosmic process is the achievement of universal resurrection, redemption of all persons who continue to live as individuals till the end of history.

The Discipline of Religion. The function of the discipline of religion is to further the evolution of man into his divine stature, develop increased awareness and intensity of understanding. It is to bring about a better, deeper and more enduring adjustment in life. All belief and practice, song and prayer, meditation and contemplation, are means to this development of direct experience, an inner frame of mind, a sense of freedom and fearlessness, strength and security. Religion is the way in which the individual organises his inward being and responds to what is envisaged by him as the ultimate Reality. It is essentially intensification of experience, the displacement of triviality by intensity.

Religion a Personal Achievement. Each individual is a mem-

---

[61] God enquires of Israel: "Is this such a fast that I have chosen? a day for a man to afflict his soul? is it to bow down his head as a bulrush, and to spread sackcloth and ashes under him? Wilt thou call this a fast, and an acceptable day to the Lord? Is not this the fast that I have chosen; to loose the bonds of wickedness, to undo the heavy burdens, and to let the oppressed go free, and that ye break every yoke?" *Isaiah* LVIII, 5, 6.

[62] Christ, said St. Paul, was to be the first born of a great brotherhood. *Romans* VIII, 29.

ber of a community where he shares work with others; but he is also an individual with his senses and emotions, desires and affections, interests and ideals. There is a solitary side to his being as distinct from the social, where he cherishes thoughts unspoken, dreams unshared, reticences unbroken. It is there that he shelters the questionings of fate, the yearning for peace, the voice of hope and the cry of anguish. When the Indian thinkers ask us to possess our souls, to be ātmavantam, not to get lost in the collective currents, not to get merged in the crowd of those who have emptied and crucified their souls, ātmahano janāh, who have got their souls bleached in the terrible unmercy of things, they are asking us to open out our inward being to the call of the transcendent. Religion is not a movement stretching out to grasp something, external, tangible and good, and to possess it. It is a form of being, not having, a mode of life. Spiritual life is not a problem to be solved but a reality to be experienced. It is new birth into enlightenment.

Three Stages of Religious Life. The Upaniṣads speak to us of three stages of religious life, śravaṇa, hearing, manana, reflection, nididhyāsana or disciplined meditation. We rise from one stage to another. Joachim of Floris in the twelfth century sees the story of man in three stages. The first is of the 'Father' of the Letter, of the Law, where we have to listen and obey. The second is of the 'Son;' here we have argument and criticism. Tradition is explained, authority is explicated. The third stage is of the Spirit, where we have 'prayer and song,' meditation and inspiration.[63] Through these, the tradition becomes a vital and transforming experience. The life of Jesus, the witness of St. Paul, of the three apostles on the Mount of Transfiguration, of Ezekiel, and of scores of others are an impressive testimony to the fact of religion as experience. Muhammad is said to have received his messages in ecstatic states. St. Thomas, in the beginning of the Fourth book of his *Summa Contra Gentiles,* speaks of three kinds of human knowledge of divine things. "The first of these is the knowledge that comes by the natural light of reason," when the reason ascends by means of creatures to God. The second "descends to us by way of revelation." The third is possible only to the human mind "elevated to the perfect intuition of the things that are revealed." Dante symbolised the first by Virgil, the second by Beatrice, the third by St. Bernard.

Religion as Self-Knowledge. Though God is everywhere, he is found more easily in the soul. The inward light is never darkened

[63] See Gerald Heard: *The Eternal Gospel* (1948), 6.

and it enlightens with understanding the minds of those who turn to it. Our self is a holy temple of the Spirit into which we may not enter without a sense of awe and reverence.

Behold Thou wert within and I abroad, and there I searched for Thee. Thou wert with me but I was not with Thee. Thou calledst and shoutedst, burstedst my deafness. Thou flashedst, shonedst, and scatteredst my blindness. Thou breathedst odours, and I drew in breath, and pant for Thee. I tasted and hunger and thirst. Thou touchedst me, and I was on fire for Thy peace.[64]

"Thou wert more inward to me than my most inward part, and higher than my highest." [65] Bishop Ullathorne says:

Let it be plainly understood that we cannot return to God unless we enter first into ourselves. God is everywhere, but not everywhere to us. There is but one point in the universe where God communicates with us, and that is the centre of our own soul. There He waits for us; there He meets us; there He speaks to us. To seek Him, therefore, we must enter into our own interior.[66]

When Kierkegaard tells us that truth is identical with subjectivity, he means that if it is objectified, it becomes relative. He does not mean that the truth is peculiar to and private to the individual. He makes out that we must go deep down into the subject to attain the experience of Universal Spirit. Professor A. N. Whitehead says that "religion is what the individual does with his solitariness." [67] Each individual must unfold his own awareness of life, witness his own relation to the source or sources of his being and, in the light of his experience, resolve the tragedies and contradictions of his inward life. "If you are never solitary, then you are never religious." [68] It is in solitude that we prepare the human candle for the divine flame. This does not mean a facile commensurability between God and man. It means that man can transcend himself, can exceed his limits. To get at the transcendent within oneself, one must break through one's normal self. The revelation of the divine in man is of the character of an interruption of our routine self. We must impose silence on our familiar self, if the spirit of God is to become manifest in us. The divine is more deeply in us than we are ourselves. We attain to spirit by passing beyond the frontiers of the familiar self. If we do not mechanise the doctrine of Incarnation, of 'God manifest in the flesh,' we make out that

---

64 St. Augustine, *Confessions* X, 38. 65 *Confessions* III, 11.
66 *Groundwork of Christian Virtues*, 74. 67 *Religion in the Making* (1926), 16.
68 *Religion in the Making* (1926), 16.

man has access to the inmost being of the divine, in these moments of highest spiritual insight. The highest human life is life in God. In the words of Eckhart, "God in the fulness of his Godhead dwells eternally in His Image, the soul."

Religions prescribe certain conditions to which we have to submit if we are to gain religious illumination. Discipline of the intellect, emotions and will is a prerequisite for spiritual perception. Religious spirits use the catastrophes of the world as opportunities for creative work. The world is the field for moral striving. The purpose of life is not the enjoyment of the world but the education of the soul.

Increasing Emphasis on Religion as Conversion. In the middle of January 1946 was published the Report of the Commission appointed by the Archbishop of Canterbury "to survey the whole problem of modern evangelism with special reference to the spiritual needs and the prevailing intellectual outlook of the non-worshipping members of the community and to report on the organisation and methods by which the needs can most effectively be met." This Report, entitled *The Conversion of England,* points out that religion has become a waning influence in the national life of the country and calls for a strengthening and quickening of spiritual life. Religion, it urges, is a conversion, a mental and spiritual revolution, a change from a self-centred to a God-centred life. It is a call to a new vision and understanding of life. The Report asks for the assertion of the primacy of spirit over the long dominant external forms of religion, submission to authority, subscription to a formula. The discipline of religion consists in turning inwards, deepening our awareness and developing a more meaningful attitude to life which frees us from bondage and hardening of the spirit. "Except ye be converted and become as little children, ye shall not enter into the kingdom of heaven."

Yoga. There are different ways which are prescribed by religions to achieve this inward change. *Yoga* is used in Indian religions for the methods of drawing near to the Supreme. *Yoga* is a path, a praxis, and training by which the individual man, bleeding from the split caused by intelligence, becomes whole. Intellectual concentration *jñāna,* emotional detachment, *bhakti,* ethical dedication, *karma,* are all types of *Yoga.* In Patañjali's *Yoga Sūtra,* we have a development of what Plato calls recollection, the way by which we steadily withdraw from externality, from our functions which are at the mercy of life and enter into our essential being, which is not the individual ego but the Universal Spirit. It is the act of recollection by which the recollecting self distinguishes its primal being from all that is confused with it, its material, vital, psychological and logical expressions. By recollection the self is assured of its participation in ultimate being, the principle of all positivity, the ontological mystery. We have power over the outer expressions. We may submit ourselves to despair, deny physical being by resorting to suicide, surpass all expressions and discover that deep down there is something other than these empirical manifestations. Even the thinking subject is only in relation to an object, but the spirit in us is not the subject of epistemology. It is primordial being.

When we are anchored in the mystery which is the foundation of our very being, our activities express "Thy will and not mine." When we are in Being we are beyond the moral world of freedom. Our deeds flow out of the heart of reality and our desires are swallowed up in love. Spiritual freedom is different from moral autonomy. The inward hold we get makes us the masters of life. Religion then is experience turning inwards towards the realisation of itself.

X. Religion and Religions

Sectarian Divisions. The Report on the *Conversion of England* deplores the unhappy divisions, the lack of charity among particular congregations, which obscure the fellowship of the Christian Church and calls upon the different Christian sects to continue and co-operate in the task of the conversion of England. It asks us to adopt the principle of unity in variety, which is not only a profound spiritual truth but the most obvious common sense.

The Need for Comprehension. If we accept this principle seriously we cannot stop at the frontiers of Christianity. We must move along a path which shall pass beyond all the differences of the historical past and eventually be shared in common by all mankind. Belief in exclusive claims and monopolies of religious truth has been a frequent source of pride, fanaticism and strife. The vehemence with which religions were preached and the savagery with which they were enforced are some of the disgraces of human history. Secularism and paganism point to the rivalries of religions for a proof of the futility of religion. A little less missionary ardour, a little more enlightened scepticism will do good to us all. Our attitude to other religions should be defined in the spirit of that great saying in a play of Sophocles, where Antigone says, "I was not born to share men's hatred, but their love." We must learn the basic principles of the great world religions as the essential means of promoting international understanding.

Besides, Whitehead observes that "the decay of Christianity and Buddhism as determinative influences in modern thought is partly due to the fact that each religion has unduly sheltered itself from the other. They have remained self-satisfied and unfertilised." [69] A study of other living religions helps and enhances the appreciation of our own faith. If we adopt a wider historical view we obtain a more comprehensive vision and understanding of spiritual truth. Christian thinkers like St. Thomas Aquinas were willing to find confirmation of the truths of Christianity in the works of pagan philosophers. We live in a world which is neither Eastern nor Western, where everyone of us is the heir to all civilisation. The past of China, Japan, and India is as much our past as is that of Israel, Greece, and Rome. It is our duty and privilege to enlarge our faculties of curiosity, of understanding, and realise the spaciousness of our common ground. No way of life is uninteresting so long as it is natural and satisfying to those who live it. We may measure true spiritual culture by the comprehension and veneration we are able to give to all forms of thought and feeling which have influenced masses of mankind. We must understand the experience of people whose thought eludes our categories. We must widen our religious perspective and obtain a world wisdom worthy of our time and place.

Religious provincialism stands in the way of a unitary world culture which is the only enduring basis for a world community. "Shall two walk together except they have agreed?" To neglect the spiritual unity of the world and underline the religious diversity would be philosophically unjustifiable, morally indefensible, and socially dangerous.

The arrogant dislike of other religions has today given place to respectful incomprehension. It is time that we accustom ourselves to fresh ways of thinking and feeling. The interpenetration of obstinate cultural traditions is taking place before our eyes. If we have a sense of history we will find that human societies are by nature unstable. They are ever on the move giving place to new ones. Mankind is still in the making. The new world society requires a new world outlook based on respect for and understanding of other cultural traditions.

Religious Education. The procedure suggested here provides us with a basis for inter-religious understanding and co-operation.

[69] Quoted in Inge: *Mysticism and Religion* (1947), 40.

It involves an abandonment of missionary enterprises such as they are now. The "compassing of sea and land to make one proselyte" [70] is not possible when our ignorance of other peoples' faiths is removed. The main purpose of religious education is not to train others in our way of thinking and living, not to substitute one form of belief for another, but to find out what others have been doing and help them to do it better. We are all alike in need of humility and charity, of repentance and conversion, of a change of mind, of a turning round. The missionary motives are derived from the conviction of the absolute superiority of our own religion and of supreme contempt for other religions. They are akin to the political motives of imperialist countries to impose their culture and civilisation on the rest of the world. If missionary activities such as they are now are persisted in, they will become a prime factor in the spiritual impoverishment of the world. They are treason against Him who "never left himself without a witness." St. Justin said: "God is the word of whom the whole human race are partakers, and those who lived according to Reason are Christians even though accounted atheists . . . Socrates and Heracleitus, and of the barbarians, Abraham and many others." St. Ambrose's well-known gloss on *I Corinthians* XII.3, "all that is true, by whomsoever it has been said, is from the Holy Ghost," is in conformity with the ancient tradition of India on this matter. "As men approach me, so I do accept them, men on all sides follow my path" says the *Bhagavadgītā*.[71] "If the follower of any particular religion understood the saying of Junayd, 'The colour of the water is the colour of the vessel containing it,' he would not interfere with the beliefs of others, but would perceive God in every form and in every belief," says ibn-ul-'Arabi.[72] Our aim should be not to make converts, Christians into Buddhists or Buddhists into Christians, but enable both Buddhists and Christians to rediscover the basic principles of their own religions and live up to them.

Progress in Religions. Every religion is attempting to reformulate its faith in accordance with modern thought and criticism.

[70] *Matthew* XXIII, 15. Cp. C. S. Lewis: "Democrats by birth and education, we should prefer to think that all nations and individuals start level in the search for God, or even that all religions are equally true. It must be admitted at once that Christianity makes no concessions to this point of view."! *Miracles* (1947), 140.

[71] BG, 1. IV. 11.

[72] R. A. Nicholson: *Studies in Islamic Mysticism* (1921), 159. Cp.: Faridu'd Din Attar in *Manṭiqu't Tayr:* "Since then there are different ways of making the journey, no two (soul) birds will fly alike. Each finds a way of his own, on this road of mystic knowledge, one by means of the Mihrab and another through the Idol." See Ananda K. Coomaraswamy. *The Bugbear of Literacy* (1947), Ch. III.

Stagnant and stereotyped religions are at variance with the psychology of modern life. If, in the name of religion, we insist on teaching much that modern knowledge has proved to be untrue, large numbers will refuse to accept devitalised doctrines. Aware of this danger, religions are emphasising the essential principles and ideals rather than the dogmatic schemes. For example, the moral and spiritual truths of Christianity, faith in the Divine Being, in the manifestation of the spiritual and moral nature of the Divine in the personality of Jesus, one of the eldest of many brothers, faith that we can receive strength and guidance by communion with the Divine, are regarded as more important than beliefs in the miraculous birth, resurrection, ascension and the return of Jesus as the judge of mankind at the end of human history. The *Report of the Commission on Christian Doctrine* [73] appointed by the Archbishops of Canterbury and York, made it permissible for the English Churchmen to hold and to teach the Christian faith in accordance with the verified results of modern scientific, historical, and literary criticism. Other religions are also attempting to cast off the unessentials and return to the basic truths. Whereas the principles of religions are eternal, their expressions require continual development. The living faiths of mankind carry not only the inspiration of centuries but also the encrustations of error. Religion is a "treasure in earthen vessels" (St. Paul). These vessels are capable of infinite refashioning and the treasure itself of renewed application in each succeeding age of human history. The profound intuitions of religions require to be presented in fresh terms more relevant to our own experience, to our own predicament. If religion is to recover its power, if we are to help those who are feeling their way and are longing to believe, a restatement is essential. It is a necessity of the time. "I have many things to say unto you, but ye cannot bear them now; when he, the Spirit of Truth, is come, he will guide you into all the truth." [74] Every religion is growing under the inspiration of the Divine Spirit of Truth in order to meet the moral and spiritual ordeal of the modern mind. This process of growth is securing for our civilisation a synthesis on the highest level of the forces of religion and culture and enabling their followers to co-operate as members of one great fellowship.

Fellowship, not Fusion. The world is seeking not so much a fusion of religions as a fellowship of religions, based on the realisation of the foundational character of man's religious experience.

[73] 1938, Society for Promoting Christian Knowledge.   [74] *John* XVI, 12f.

William Blake says: "As all men are alike (though infinitely various), so all Religions, as all similars, have one source." The different religions may retain their individualities, their distinctive doctrines and characteristic pieties, so long as they do not impair the sense of spiritual fellowship. The light of eternity would blind us if it came full in the face. It is broken into colours so that our eyes can make something of it. The different religious traditions clothe the one Reality in various images and their visions could embrace and fertilise each other so as to give mankind a many-sided perfection, the spiritual radiance of Hinduism, the faithful obedience of Judaism, the life of beauty of Greek Paganism, the noble compassion of Buddhism, the vision of divine love of Christianity, and the spirit of resignation to the sovereign lord of Islam. All these represent different aspects of the inward spiritual life, projections on the intellectual plane of the ineffable experiences of the human spirit.

If religion is the awareness of our real nature in God, it makes for a union of all mankind based on communion with the Eternal. It sees in all the same vast universal need it has felt in itself. The different religions take their source in the aspiration of man towards an unseen world, though the forms in which this aspiration is couched are determined by the environment and climate of thought.[75] The unity of religions is to be found in that which is divine or universal in them and not in what is temporary and local. Where there is the spirit of truth there is unity. As in other matters, so in the sphere of religion there is room for diversity and no need for discord. To claim that any one religious tradition bears unique witness to the truth and reveals the presence of the true God is inconsistent with belief in a living God who has spoken to men "by diverse portions and in diverse manners." [76] God is essentially self-communicative [77] and is of ungrudging goodness, as Plato taught.[78] There is no such thing as a faith once for all delivered to the saints. Revelation is divine-human. As God does not reveal His Being to a stone or a tree, but only to men, His revelation is attuned to the state of the human mind. The

[75] Plutarch observes: "Nor do we speak of the 'different Gods' of different peoples, or of the Gods as 'Barbarian' and 'Greek,' but as common to all, though differently named by different peoples, so that for the One Reason (Logos) that orders all these things, and the One Providence that oversees them, and for the minor powers (i.e. gods, angels) that are appointed to care for all things, there have arisen among different peoples different epithets and services, according to their different manners and customs." *Isis and Osiris*, 67.

[76] *Epistle to the Hebrews* I, 1.   [77] *Bhagavadgītā*, IV, 3.   [78] *Timaeus*, 29B.

Creative Spirit is ever ready to reveal Himself to the seeking soul provided the search is genuine and the effort intense. The authority for revelation is not an Infallible book or an Infallible Church but the witness of the inner light. What is needed is not submission to an external authority but inward illumination which, of course, is tested by tradition and logic. If we reflect on the matter deeply we will perceive the unity of spiritual aspiration and endeavour underlying the varied upward paths indicated in the different world faiths. The diversity in the traditional formulations tends to diminish as we climb up the scale of spiritual perfection. All the paths of ascent lead to the mountain top. This convergent tendency and the remarkable degree of agreement in the witness of those who reach the mountain top are the strongest proof of the truth of religion.

Different Traditions of Religion. Religious life belongs to the realm of inward spiritual revelation; when exteriorised it loses its authentic character. It is misleading to speak of different religions. We have different religious traditions which can be used for correction and enrichment. The traditions do not create the truth but clothe it in language and symbol for the help of those who do not see it themselves. They symbolise the mystery of the spirit and urge us to move from external significations, which reflect the imperfect state of our consciousness and social environment, to the thing signified. The symbolic character of tradition is not to be mistaken for reality. These are second-hand notions which fortify and console us so long as we do not have direct experience. Our different traditions are versions in a series, part of the historical and relative world in which we live and move. If we cling to these historically conditioned forms as absolute they will not rescue us from slavery to the momentary and the contingent. They leave us completely immersed in the relative. It does not mean that there is nothing central or absolute in religion. The unchanging substance of religion is the evolution of man's consciousness. The traditions help to take us to the truth above all traditions and of which the traditions are imperfect, halting expressions. If we love truth as such and not our opinions, if we desire nothing except what is true and acceptable to God, the present religious snobbery and unfriendliness will disappear. If we open ourselves up unreservedly to the inspirations of our age, we will get to the experience of the one Spirit which takes us beyond the historical formulations. Averroes, the Arab philosopher, distinguished between philosophic truth (*secundum ra-*

tionem) [79] and religious views (*secundum fidem*).[80] No single religion possesses truth compared with philosophic knowledge, though each religious view may claim to possess a fragment of the truth. "Yet every priest values his own creed as the fool his cap and bells." Our quarrels will cease if we know that the one truth is darkened and diversified in the different religions. If we are to remove the present disordered, divided state of the world, we have to adopt what William Law called

a catholic spirit, a communion of saints in the love of God and all goodness, which no one can learn from that which is called orthodoxy in particular churches, but is only to be had by a total dying to all worldly views, by a pure love of God and by such an unction from above as delivers the mind from all selfishness and makes it love truth and goodness with an equality of affection in every man, whether he is Christian, Jew or Gentile.

William Law says also:

The chief hurt of a sect is this, that it takes itself to be necessary to the truth, whereas the truth is only then found when it is known to be of no sect but as free and universal as the goodness of God and as common to all names and nations as the air and light of this world.

Maitrī Upaniṣad says:

Some contemplate one name and some another. Which of these is the best? All are eminent clues to the transcendent, immortal, unembodied Brahman; these names are to be contemplated, lauded and at last denied. For by them one rises higher and higher in these worlds; but where all comes to its end, there he attains to the unity of the Person.

In the midst of the travail in which we are living we discern the emergence of the religion of the Spirit, which will be the crown of the different religions, devoted to the perfecting of humanity in the life of the spirit, that is, in the life of God in the soul. When God is our teacher, we come to think alike.

Freedom from Dogma. The thought of the Upaniṣads, the humanism of Confucius, the teaching of the Buddha are marked by the comparative absence of dogma, and their followers are, therefore, relatively free from the evils of obscurantism and casuistry. This is due to the fact that there is greater emphasis in them on the experience of Spirit. Those whose experience is deepest do not speak of it because they feel that it is inexpressible. They feel that they are breaking, dividing, and betraying the

79 tattvam.   80 matam.

experience by giving utterance to it. By their attitude of silence they affirm the primacy of Being over knowledge with the latter's distinction of subject and object. In the deepest spiritual experience we are not self-conscious. When we describe it, it is by way of second reflection, in which we turn the inward presence into an object of thought. We take care to observe that the truth goes beyond the traditional forms. Ruysbroeck says about the reality known by the seer: "We can speak no more of Father, Son and Holy Spirit, nor of any creature, but only of one Being, which is the very substance of the Divine Persons. There were we all one before our creation, for this is our super-essence. There the Godhead is in simple essence without activity." A devout Catholic of the Counter-Reformation period, J. J. Olier, observes: "The holy light of faith is so pure, that compared with it, particular lights are but impurities: and even ideas of the saints, of the Blessed Virgin and the sight of Jesus Christ in his humanity are impediments in the way of the sight of God in His purity." When the seers try to communicate their vision in greater detail they use the tools put into their hands by their cultural milieu. Jesus interprets his experience in terms of notions current in contemporary Jewish thought. We perhaps owe the doctrine of the world's imminent dissolution to the Jewish circle of ideas. So long as we are on earth we cannot shake off the historical altogether.

The Mystery of Spiritual Life. Sometimes we exteriorise the mystery of spiritual life. Religions which believe in the reality of spiritual life interpret the dogmas with reference to it. Religious views are not so much attempts to solve the riddle of the universe as efforts to describe the experience of sages. The concepts are verbalisations of intense emotional experience. They are lifted out of their true empiricism and made historical rather than experimental, objective instead of profound inward realisation. Christ is born in the depths of spirit. We say that he passes through life, dies on the Cross and rises again. These are not so much historical events which occurred once upon a time as universal processes of spiritual life, which are being continually accomplished in the souls of men. Those who are familiar with the way in which the Kṛṣṇa story is interpreted will feel inclined to regard Christhood as an attainment of the soul; a state of inward glorious illumination in which the divine wisdom has become the heritage of the soul. The annunciation is a beautiful experience of the soul. It relates to the birth of Christhood in the soul, "the holy thing begotten within." The human soul from the Holy Breath, *Devakī* or *daivī prakṛti,* divine nature is said to be the mother of Kṛṣṇa. Mary, the mother of the Christ child, is the soul in her innermost divine nature. Whatever is conceived in the womb of the human soul is always of the Holy Spirit.

Universal Religion. The mandate of religion is that man must make the change in his own nature in order to let the divine in him manifest itself. It speaks of the death of man as we know him with all his worldly desires and the emergence of the new man. This is the teaching not only of the Upaniṣads and Buddhism but also of the Greek mysteries and Platonism, of the Gospels and the schools of Gnosticism. This is the wisdom to which Plotinus refers, when he says, "This doctrine is not new; it was professed from the most ancient times though without being developed explicitly; we wish only to be interpreters of the ancient sages, and to show by the evidence of Plato himself that they had the same opinions as ourselves." [81] This is the religion which Augustine mentions in his well-known statement: "That which is called the Christian Religion existed among the Ancients, and never did not exist, from the beginning of the human race until Christ came in the flesh, at which time the true religion, which already existed, began to be called Christianity." [82] This truth speaks to us in varying dialects across far continents and over centuries of history. Those who overlook this perennial wisdom, the eternal religion behind all religions, this *sanātana dharma,* this timeless tradition, "wisdom uncreate, the same now that it ever was, and the same to be forevermore," [83] and cling to the outward forms and quarrel among themselves, are responsible for the civilized chaos in which we live. It is our duty to get back to this central core of religion, this fundamental wisdom which has been obscured and distorted in the course of history by dogmatic and sectarian developments.

At the level of body and mind, physique and temperament, talents and tastes, we are profoundly unlike one another; but at the deepest level of all, that of the spirit which is the true ground of our being, we are like one another. If religion is to become an effective force in human affairs, if it is to serve as the basis for the new world order, it must become more inward and more universal, a flame which cleanses our inward being and so cleanses the world. For such a religion the historical expressions of spiritual truth and the psychological idioms employed by religions to convey the universal truth cease to be rocks of offence. The barriers dividing

81 *Enneads* V, 1.8.   82 *Librum de vera religione:* Chapter 10.   83 *St. Augustine.*

men will break down and the reunion and integration of all, what the Russians call *sobornost,* an altogetherness in which we walk together creatively and to which we all contribute, a universal church will be established. Then will the cry of St. Joan in Bernard Shaw's epilogue to that play be fulfilled: "O God that madest this beautiful earth, when will it be ready to receive thy saints?" Then will come a time when the world will be inhabited by a race of men, with no flaw of flesh or error of mind, freed from the yoke not only of disease and privation but of lying words and of love turned into hate. When human beings grow into completeness, into that invisible world which is the kingdom of heaven, then will they manifest in the outer world the Kingdom which is within them. That day we shall cease to set forth God dogmatically or dispute about his nature but leave each man to worship God in the sanctuary of his heart, to feel after him and to possess him.

While I never felt attracted to travelling for its own sake, I have travelled a great deal and lived in places far from home, in England and France, America and Russia. For some years, I have spent long periods in England and the qualities of the English people such as their love of justice, their hatred of doctrinairism, their sympathy for the underdog, made an impression on me. All Souls College, which has provided a second home for me all these years, has given me an insight into English intellectual life with its caution and stability, confidence and adventure. Whatever one may feel about the character of the Russian Government, the people there are kindly and human and their lives are filled as anywhere else with jokes and jealousies, loves and hates. Though I have not been able to take root in any of these foreign countries, I have met many, high and low, and learned to feel the human in them. There are no fundamental differences among the peoples of the world. They have all the deep human feelings, the craving for justice above all class interests, horror of bloodshed and violence. They are working for a religion which teaches the possibility and the necessity of man's union with himself, with nature, with his fellowmen, and with the Eternal Spirit of which the visible universe is but a manifestation and upholds the emergence of a complete consciousness as the destiny of man. Our historical religions will have to transform themselves into the universal faith or they will fade away. This prospect may appear strange and unwelcome to some, but it has a truth and beauty of its own. It is working in the minds of men and will soon be a realised fact. Human unity depends not on past origins but on future goal and direction, on what we are becoming and whither we are tending. Compared with the civilisation that is now spreading over the earth's surface, thanks to science and technology, the previous civilisations were restricted in scope and resources. Scientists claim that organic life originated on this planet some 1200 million years ago, but man has come into existence on earth during the last half million years. His civilisation has been here only for the last 10,000 years. Man is yet in his infancy and has a long period ahead of him on this planet. He will work out a higher integration and produce world-minded men and women.

The eternal religion, outlined in these pages, is not irrational or unscientific, is not escapist or a-social. Its acceptance will solve many of our desperate problems and will bring peace to men of good will.

This is the personal philosophy which by different paths I have attained, a philosophy which has served me in the severest tests, in sickness and in health, in triumph and in defeat. It may not be given to us to see that the faith prevails; but it is given to us to strive that it should.

S. Radhakrishnan

EMBASSY OF INDIA
MOSCOW, U.S.S.R.

1

George P. Conger

RADHAKRISHNAN'S WORLD

1

RADHAKRISHNAN'S WORLD

sa mahātmā sudurlabhaḥ *
—*Bhagavadgītā*, vii, 19

FOR any one who thinks of drive, energy, and manifold activity as peculiarly characteristic of the West, it may be surprising to find that among the philosophers of our time no one has achieved so much in so many fields as has Sarvepalli Radhakrishnan of India. His career, even thus far, can be matched only by drawing upon the careers of a group of his contemporaries. Any number of these have been teachers, authors, lecturers, translators, and editors. Some have been historians of philosophy. Some have had academic administrative greatness thrust upon them. A few, like W. E. Hocking, have travelled much in the realms of gold and taught in the universities of foreign lands. William James was influential in religion, and John Dewey has been a force in politics. One or two American philosophers have been legislators. Jacques Maritain has been an ambassador. Radhakrishnan, in a little more than thirty years of work, has done all these things and more.

In a philosophy which attempts to portray the world *sub specie aeternitatis* biographical details, however striking, seem incidental. Radhakrishnan was born in 1888, and educated at Madras Christian College. He has been professor of philosophy at Mysore, Calcutta, and Andhra Universities; member of the India Constituent Assembly; Vice-Chancellor of Banaras Hindu University; Spalding Professor of Eastern Religions and Ethics at Oxford; and prominent in the intellectual and cultural activities of both the League of Nations and the United Nations, particularly in U.N.E.S.C.O. At the time of writing he is India's Ambassador to the Soviet Union.

His extensive and impressive work merits attention for three reasons. First, it is a typical and at the same time somewhat distinctive statement, or restatement, of intuitional absolute idealism. In book after book, on pages that glow with conviction and

* "Such a great soul is very difficult to find."

85

gleam with shining phrases, Radhakrishnan has developed this portion of the great tradition in a fresh rendering of "the perennial philosophy." Less ponderous than Royce, less meticulous than Bradley, less involved than Hegel, he has made idealism flow from a deep spring. By comparison Eucken is provincial and Keyserling is trivial. Not since Fichte and Schelling has there been such a precipitate stream of inspiration. He has surpassed the personalists in his philosophy of spirit and rivalled the pragmatists in promulgating a philosophy of life.

In the second place, his philosophy, in spite of what look like some deviations, as well as a considerable partiality for the Vedānta system, is so thoroughly Indian, so comprehensive, and so widely oriented in the contemporary world that his work may almost stand as India's distinctive contribution, and in a culture which perforce is vastly more concerned with the question than it was in 1883, may answer Max Müller's query, "What Can India Teach Us?" For this reason alone, Radhakrishnan's thoughts find a welcome in every broad philosophic mind.

In the third place, never in the history of philosophy has there been quite such a world-figure. With his unique dual appointment at Banaras and Oxford, like a weaver's shuttle he has gone to and fro between East and West, carrying a thread of understanding, weaving it into the fabric of civilization. We hear him and hear of him in China and South Africa, in Chicago and Mexico City. Naturally he has been a shining figure in U.N.E.S.C.O. Lately his ancient but eager young mother-country has claimed him for one of its most important ambassadorships. Except for an occasional Marcus Aurelius, philosophers never will be kings, but sometimes a philosopher wields among his contemporaries an influence which any king might envy. Some of Radhakrishnan's interpretations of Western philosophies, and even of Indian schools themselves, look a bit strange; they are like valence electrons, which, however uncertain their original positions may be, no doubt are slightly displaced when they begin to bind their atoms in a molecule. One suspects that Radhakrishnan's enthusiasm occasionally causes him to make loose estimates; electrons, too, dance in a glow or flame.

I

His earlier books, quite appropriately, are interpretations and criticisms of the works of other men. When he writes of Indian thinkers, as in his *Philosophy of Rabindranath Tagore* and his well-known two-volume *Indian Philosophy*, it is often difficult to tell whether the views cited are those of the author under consideration or of the interpreter. This is of little consequence in the volume on Tagore ̖ because the younger man was so much under the influence of the̖older and both were̖ so imbued with the spirit of the Upaniṣads and the system of the Vedānta that the interpreter is all but̖transparent̖and there is no noticeable refraction. In his preface to his̖substantial *Indian Philosophy*, Radhakrishnan frankly admits that the judgments and sympathies of a writer can not long be hidden, and that it is not necessary to abstain from criticism in order to give fair and impartial statements.[1] His work, compared to other available histories of Indian thought and introductions to it, stands somewhat in the relation of a lifelike painting to a photograph. Radhakrishnan's painting shows not merely the face and form of its subject, Indian thought; it is touched up and set off by a play of lights and shadows from the West.

When in 1920 he begins more specifically to interpret the thought of the West, in his *Reign of Religion in Contemporary Philosophy*, the result appears to be not quite so happy. This is a relatively early book; the author afterward called it "ambitious." [2] In the scrutiny of others, every philosopher seems to be held accountable for his intellectual measles and wild oats. The book in question was well received by many who agreed with its thesis (that religious interest of the Western authors who are studied shatters what might and should be a monism into an implicit or explicit pluralism); but at this distance it seems more brittle and contentious than Radhakrishnan's later work. His treatment of Bergson, in particular, is rather surprising; it is strange that he who was to be a great champion of intuitionism in the East was not more cordial toward its great champion in the West. But, as Radhakrishnan says, we ought to interpret thinkers at their best,[3] and here we shall try to apply to him his own saying.

II

Throughout the earlier, the later, and the most recent works, there sounds over and over the call to an absolute idealism, based essentially on immediate intuition, founded in and issuing in the life of spirit. Like the Taoists in the ancient East and Dewey, for

[1] Ind P, Vol. I, 9.   [2] MST, 24.   [3] *Ibid.*, 25.

example, in the modern West, Radhakrishnan has the gift of expressing what is virtually the same teaching again and again, but of having been so moved by the teaching that each later expression seems fresh.

Several familiar idealist arguments are easily recognizable in their Indian dress; epistemology has little or no geography. Thus for Radhakrishnan knowledge is an ultimate fact, incapable of derivation from anything else.[4] All knowledge presupposes the knower, who is constant, whereas the known is unsteady.[5] It is stoutly maintained that, in spite of some inclination to regard it as such,[6] the world is not an illusion or deception; [7] still, it is obvious that nature is not self-existent.[8] Although persistent aspects of experience refuse to be reduced to mere sentience, and a stone is not a self,[9] matter reduces itself to certain feelings and to relations among them; it is experience and possible experience.[10] It is not a concrete actuality, but an abstract idea.[11] Matter, life, and consciousness are ideal constructions, grades of experience.[12]

The subject-object distinction is one within experience.[13] Selfhood comes in for some emphasis here, although it appears more essentially in its intuitional and moral functions. All existence is existence for selves.[14] Self-knowledge is the only true and direct knowledge we have.[15] The order of nature is a dependable unity because the self is a unity.[16]

In the familiar idealist vista, epistemology opens out into metaphysics. To know the self as limited is to know that there is something beyond the limit.[17] A felt necessity of thought compels us to admit an absolute reality.[18] The fact that we know shows that nature is akin to human consciousness; [19] the fact that reason attains its ends shows that there is a harmony between human intelligence and the structure of reality.[20] We could not have had the idea of an absolute reality without experiencing the corresponding object.[21] The argument grows more insistent in the statement that there can not be a world without an absolute consciousness.[22] The problem of other minds is met by the statement that individuals are able to have common experience, to know a

4 IVL, 263.
5 ER, 87.
6 BG, 38.
7 RS, 103; BG, 41.
8 RR, 334.
9 IVL, 246.
10 Ibid., 241.
11 Ibid., 16.
12 Ibid., 311.
13 RR, 333.
14 Ind P, Vol. I, 194.
15 IVL, 139.
16 Ibid., 154.
17 RR, 334; IVL, 302.
18 Ind P, Vol. II, 533.
19 PRT, 17.
20 RR, 234.
21 IVL, 220.
22 RR, 340.

real world as identical for all, because there is an ideal self operative in us.[23]

Somewhat less subjectively, it is said that if we are loyal to the spirit and achievements of science we are led to believe that there lies behind the cosmic process a spiritual reality, although this is difficult to grasp and impossible to define.[24] Somewhat more definitely, we find that the world's subjection to law and its tendency to perfection indicate that it is based on a spiritual reality;[25] there seems to be an ethical trend inherent in nature itself.[26] More pragmatically, faith is urged by its own needs to posit a transcendental reality.[27] From the eternal values we pass to a supporting mind in which they dwell;[28] without this sanction, art, science, and morality would lose their significance.[29] The religious consciousness, too, bears its weighty witness.[30] A sense of rest and fulfilment, of eternity and completeness requires the conception of a Being not limited by the cosmic process.[31] Even an argument from ignorance is pressed into service. We can not say that what our minds fail to grasp is unthinkable.[32] We have no right to deny what we do not understand;[33] our unconsciousness of the Supreme need not be conclusive proof of the non-existence of the Supreme.[34]

III

The idealist argument is crowned by the emphasis which, in the Upaniṣadic traditions, is accorded to intuitive experience. The rationality of the world is transparent to intellect, but its mysteriousness can be grasped only by intuition.[35] Intuition is direct knowledge;[36] compared with intellectual processes, it is another manifestation of spirit.[37] Besides consciousness and self-consciousness, we have spiritual or superconsciousness, a level of experience at which new aspects of reality reveal themselves.[38] In this experience there is an extension of perception to regions beyond sense,[39] an awareness of real values which are neither objects in space and time nor universals of thought.[40] Like Gerald Heard, Radhakrishnan holds

23 IVL, 271.
24 K, 43. (All quotations from *Kalki* in this essay are from the edition of 1948.)
25 HVL, 124.   26 K, 43.   27 HH, 60.
28 IVL, 200.   29 RR, 188.   30 IVL, 86f.
31 SM, 280.   32 IVL, 302.   33 Ind P, Vol. I, 170.
34 IVL, 323.   35 MST, 38.   36 IVL, 144.
37 RR, 196.   38 IVL, 301.   39 *Ibid.*, 143.
40 SM, 267.

that there is an expansion of consciousness.[41] Intuition is integral experience,[42] the exercise of consciousness as a whole,[43] the response of the whole man.[44] In this response the work of reason is included,[45] for awareness of one's true nature is not intellectual but integral,[46] and spirit is mind in its integrity.[47] Intuition is individual,[48] private, subjective, intimately personal; the world has its focus in the individual, not the herd,[49] so that if individuality is lost all is lost.[50]

Although we are cautioned that subjective certitude differs from logical certainty and is not necessarily truth,[51] that paradoxes are perhaps not discoveries,[52] and that bodily weakness sometimes produces hallucinations which are mistaken for spiritual visions,[53] Radhakrishnan declares that his is no appeal to a subjective whim or the morbid views of a psychopathic mind.[54] Intuition is not used as an apology for doctrines which could not or would not be justified on intellectual grounds.[55] A proof of intuition's validity, in fact, is that we can not think it away; it belongs to the structure of the mind.[56] Any sound rationalism will recognize the need for it;[57] the cosmic process, too, as the perfect creation of novelty, points to this need.[58] To say that spiritual intuition does not correspond to reality is a gratuitous assumption.[59] Pragmatically, the truth of the experience is due to the fact that it satisfies our wants, including those which are intellectual.[60] It is not error, because it is workable.[61]

Sometimes the experience is said to be rather in the form of an effortless insight;[62] to know the truth the heart of a child is needed,[63] and the saint's certainty is strange and simple.[64] Elsewhere it is urged that successful intuition requires previous study [65] and continuous creative effort.[66] To be spiritual is to think so hard that thinking becomes knowing or viewing.[67] Intellectual effort appears to mark here an intermediate stage. First there is the simple intuitive experience which is free from doubt; doubt arises only when reflection supervenes.[68] There is, however, no break between intuition and intellect, and the former is better off with the

41 IVL, 211; RS, 48; BG, 237.   42 IVL, 179.   43 RR, 188.
44 SM, 269.   45 Ibid., 269. 46 BG, 50.
47 SM, 267.   48 IVL, 144.   49 RS, 6off.
50 Ibid., 77.   51 SM, 270.   52 ER, 24.
53 BG, 344.   54 RR, 439.   55 SM, 269.
56 IVL, 156.   57 SM, 267.   58 MST, 38.
59 IVL, 85.   60 ER, 24.   61 IVL, 155; RR, 239; RS, 27.
62 IVL, 152.   63 MST, 21.   64 HH, 59.
65 IVL, 177.   66 BG, 193.   67 ER, 25.
68 IVL, 146.

latter than without it. Intuition, if not thus supported, will lapse into self-satisfied obscurantism,[69] but by making it, more intellectual we deepen its content.[70]

When intuitions arise, they can and should be logically demonstrated.[71] Sometimes it is maintained that logic supports this intuitionism;[72] the idealist logic is apparently accepted as final,[73] without much exposition and with practically no criticism. Occasionally logic is enlisted in a pragmatic way.[74] At other times logic is not so implicitly trusted;[75] in fact Western philosophy is criticized as a set of variations on one theme, the supremacy of the logical.[76]

In phrases recalling the Yōga sūtras and the Beatitudes it is said that the intuitive experience requires moral preparation. The mind must be set free from anxiety and desire;[77] the heart must be clean if it is to reflect God.[78] There must be absolute inward purity, self-mastery.[79] Moral ascesis shapes the soul into harmony with invisible realities.[80] An austere life turns knowledge into wisdom.[81] Extremes and aberrations, all too familiar in the history of asceticism, are not in question; this is the robust and joyous asceticism of the healthy-minded.[82] At least something of the experience is open to any one who will take the trouble necessary to attain it.[83]

Intuitive experience merges with mystical experience. Although it is admitted that some mystics are too emotional,[84] in the genuine experience the whole mind is said to leap forward in a quivering instant.[85] We read of the formless blaze of spiritual life; the mystic is said to tread on thin rare air.[86] Time stops short, and life is still as death,[87]—but again, the body is intense and urgent with vitality.[88] The mystic acquires a wonderful clarity of mind;[89] elsewhere it is a mysterious, unclear, inarticulate knowledge which brings us closest to reality.[90]

Although it is unverifiable and incommunicable to others, the mystical experience is not less valid.[91] It is self-establishing, self-evidencing, self-luminous;[92] reality is its own witness.[93] In the experience one has pure comprehension, entire significance, complete

69 MST, 38.
72 RR, vii, 23, 207; IVL, 181.
75 IVL, 55, 154, 158, 182; ER, 90.
78 BG, 194.
81 ER, 24.
84 ER, 297.
87 EPW, 160.
90 IVL, 311.
93 HH, 62; IVL. 102.

70 IVL, 153.
73 Ind P, Vol. I, 42.
76 EPW, 183.
79 IVL, 111.
82 RR, 428.
85 Ibid., 24.
88 RS, 44f.
91 Ind P, Vol. I, 178.

71 Ibid., 181.
74 HH, 60; IVL, 222
77 IVL, 157.
80 SM, 270.
83 SM, 276.
86 Ibid., 317.
89 Ibid., 44f.
92 IVL, 92.

validity.[94] Mysticism takes its stand on verifiable truth. It is not contingent on any events past or future. No scientific criticism can refute it. Its only apologetic is the test of spiritual experience.[95] "How can one contest the fact of another's possessing knowledge of Brahman, vouched as it is by his heart's convictions?"[96]

IV

The ultimate outcome of it all, intelligence and intuition together (again true to the Upaniṣadic and Vedantic tradition), is that the individual self becomes identical with the Absolute. The identity of subject and object is the necessary implication of all relevant thinking, feeling, and willing.[97] The individual self is invaded by the Universal Self, which the individual feels as his own.[98] In the process the difficulties of the empirical world are resolved.[99] As an organism gradually absorbs and remolds into itself the mechanical side of things, so the subject transfigures the object;[100] the subject becomes its own object, timeless and spaceless, and is aware of itself as the basis and reality of all experience.[101] The union of seer and seen is ineffable;[102] any other position would be illogical.[103] To know one's self is to know all we can know and all we need to know.[104] Radhakrishnan regards it as beyond question that on any view of its origin the world exists in order that we may apprehend ourselves.[105]

It should be made clear here that the self thus sought is not a mere object of knowledge but is rather the presupposition of knowledge.[106] It is the persistent substratum,[107] the self as *knower*, not the phenomenal self as known.[108] It is known as a *"that,"* not a "what."[109]

From this approach, also, epistemology opens out into metaphysics; mind in us is World-Mind, self is Cosmic Self, spirit is Absolute Spirit. Radhakrishnan says that the true subject is the simple self-subsistent universal spirit which can not be directly presented as object.[110] Brahman is the subsistent simplicity, its own object in an intuition which is its very being.[111] It is within this universal spirit that the distinction of subject and object arises.[112]

94 IVL, 92f.
97 Ind P, Vol. I, 170.
100 Ind P, Vol. I, 195.
103 Ind P, Vol. I, 195.
106 Ind P, Vol. I, 194.
109 IVL, 140.
112 IVL, 271.

95 ER, 294f.
98 IVL, 92.
101 IVL, 301f.
104 ER, 61.
107 IVL, 269.
110 *Ibid.,* 271.

96 Quoted, Ind P, Vol. II, 512.
99 *Ibid.,* 207.
102 RR, 188.
105 *Ibid.,* 351.
108 BG, 57.
111 BG, 20.

Sometimes this union of individual and Absolute looks like a lapse, or relapse, into an undifferentiated, or dedifferentiated, continuum.[113] Thus it is said that we may sink or swoon into the bosom of the Infinite in a thousand ways.[114] We rid the soul of every specific operation and image [115] in order to get at the abyss of subjectivity, the Absolute Self.[116] We are assured, however, that life eternal is not dissolution into the indefinable Absolute, but attainment of a universality and freedom of spirit which is lifted above empirical movement.[117] The relation between the Absolute and the finite individual is unimaginably intimate, though difficult to define and explain.[118]

Sometimes, indeed, the traditional identity is relaxed a bit. In a comment on a verse of the Gītā, it is said that if we do not attain identity we may be content with attaining similarity; life eternal is not identity with the Absolute, but similarity.[119]

V

It is admitted that "strictly speaking" we can not give any description of the Absolute Brahman;[120] if philosophy is bold and sincere it must say that the relation of the Absolute and the world can not be explained.[121] An austere reticence [122] or silence [123] is commended.

With all this admitted, however, we find many descriptive statements about the Absolute. Some of them, in addition to those noted above, are affirmations. The Absolute is said to be absolutely self-sufficient,[124] the whole of perfection.[125] The Real is a spirit;[126] its mind and thoughts are possibilities or ideal forms.[127] It develops in the antithesis of subject and object.[128] It returns into itself in the fulness of self-consciousness.[129] It transcends its infinite expressions.[130]

Other descriptive statements are couched in negatives. The Absolute is not capable of division or partition into fragments.[131] It is unconditioned reality, in which time and space and objects vanish.[132] It is independent of causal relations.[133] We can not call it

113 Cf. F.S.C. Northrop. The Meeting of East and West (1945).
114 IVL, 215.   115 BG, 200.   116 Ibid., 58.
117 Ibid., 314.   118 Ibid., 33.   119 Ibid., 314.
120 Ibid., 21.   121 Ind P, Vol. I, 186.   122 ER, 28.
123 BG, 21.   124 Ind P, Vol. I, 184.   125 PRT, 16.
126 Ind P, Vol. I, 176.   127 SM, 281f.   128 RR, 319; BG, 38.
129 RR, 165.   130 SM, 285.   131 BG, 328.
132 Ind P, Vol. I, 33.   133 Ibid., 175.

personal.[134] The *Gītā* says that it neither acts nor is tainted.[135] It is thought of as pure and passionless.[136]

Although, as above noted, we are once cautioned that paradoxes are perhaps not discoveries (*cf.* fn. 52), still other descriptions are paradoxical, using opposites and implicitly or explicitly combining affirmatives and negatives. The Absolute is the one in whom all is found and yet all is lost.[137] Some hard sayings come to light, especially when various passages are compared. The Real is neither true nor false;[138] it is, however, capable of accommodating all forms of truth.[139] There are "distincts," such as the true, the beautiful, etc., in the ultimate reality,[140] but there are no degrees in it.[141] There is, however, a graded scale of description from the most impersonal to the most personal.[142] It is changeless,[143] not subject to evolution, and incapable of increase;[144] still, it is not a static entity, but an ideal which works in human knowledge.[145] It is free and expansive,[146] and it is of its nature to grow into the world.[147]

With or without such difficulties of description, the Absolute is said to yield both a universe and a personal God.

As to the universe, we can not ask how the world is related to the relationless Brahman.[148] We can, however, say that this particular possibility arose as an expression of the freedom of the Absolute—not that the Absolute has to express any of its possibilities,[149] but that the universe is a manifestation of the Absolute's creative joy.[150] However, there is at least a presumption that Brahman is unaffected by the world;[151] the world of change does not disturb its perfection.[152] The radical novelty of each moment of evolution in time is not inconsistent with Divine Eternity.[153] The Absolute expresses itself in the world, which is a strife between being and non-being in the process of becoming.[154]

We can account for the world by recourse to the concept of *māyā*. This is said to be the fact of the inexplicable existence, the "why" of this world.[155] It is a delimitation distinct from the unmeasured and the immeasurable.[156] It is the interval between what the separate things are and what they ought to be,[157] in other

134 *Ibid.,* Vol. II, 536.   135 BG, 312.   136 IVL, 342.
137 *Ibid.,* 343.   138 Ind P, Vol. I, 176.   139 RR, 451.
140 *Ibid.,* 238.   141 Ind P, Vol. I, 199.   142 IVL, 100.
143 *Ibid.,* 107.   144 *Ibid.,* 343.   145 RR, 251.
146 *Ibid.,* 451.   147 *Ibid.,* 443.   148 Ind P, Vol. I, 184.
149 SM, 286.   150 RR, 164.   151 Ind P, Vol. I, 184.
152 SM, 285.   153 BG, 281.   154 *Ibid.,* 40.
155 Ind P, Vol. I, 34.   156 BG, 38.   157 Ind P, Vol. I, 35.

words, the immense potentiality of the world.[158] It denotes the fragility of the universe and (recalling the idealist metaphysics of the whole treatment) our tendency to identify ourselves with our apparent selves.[159] In fine, the relation of the Absolute and the world is logically inconceivable;[160] the question is irrelevant,[161] and has to do with a mystery which we reverently accept.[162]

In another of its dual expressions, the Absolute includes the personal God and the "object," bare space-time, the unfathomable night.[163] God, then, appears as another possibility of the Absolute which has been actualized.[164] The Absolute is supra-personal,[165] but (recalling now the essential place of the human mind in the world) at the stage of duality is conceived as a personal being;[166] God is the Absolute from the cosmic point of view, the Absolute as known by us.[167] This seems to be the highest representation for the logical mind;[168] God is conceived as the basis and goal of all that exists,[169] but lapses into the Absolute at the end.[170] In the meantime the assumption of human nature by the divine Reality does not take away or add to the integrity of the divine.[171] Even God for the time being accepts a certain amount of "the given," but his infinity reveals itself when the cosmic plan reaches its fulfilment.[172]

VI

When it comes to a metaphysic of ethics we should expect that the buoyant spirit of Radhakrishnan would not be bound by any cramping interpretation of *karma*. He declares that *karma* is not inconsistent with freedom;[173] it is a condition, not a destiny.[174] In the *Gītā* it is even a creative force, a principle of movement,[175] and there is real indeterminacy and contingency in the world.[176] This indeterminacy pertains to the human will. It is when a man attains unity that he has the right to say "I will;" free decisions seem to come of their own accord,[177] and in liberation the man becomes his own masterpiece.[178] In a world of such contingency we can not be sure of human progress [179]—still, any permanent breakdown of human values is unthinkable.[180]

[158] *Ibid.*, 36. [159] ER, 27. [160] *Cf.* Ind P, Vol. I, 184; BG, 138.
[161] RR, 443. [162] IVL, 344. [163] ER, 125.
[164] IVL, 343. [165] HVL, 31. [166] ER, 126.
[167] MST, 40. [168] IVL, 107. [169] *Ibid.*, 108.
[170] SM, 283. [171] BG, 32. [172] SM, 282.
[173] HVL, 75. [174] BG, 48. [175] *Ibid.*, 227.
[176] IVL, 336. [177] SM, 274. [178] BG, 76.
[179] RS, 33. [180] *Ibid.*, 20.

The Hindu *dharma* is a close combination of ethics and religion,[181] but, as in the case of *karma,* it must not be interpreted in any cramping fashion. It should not be identified with any specific institutions,[182] or blindly imposed upon a society where conditions are changing as they are at present.[183] The rules change from age to age,[184] and the only thing eternal about morality is man's desire for the better.[185]

A good deal of current morality is conventional and unsound.[186] Our laws and institutions exert a steady pressure on us to make us worse than we are.[187] Traditional asceticism is condemned; we should not save the soul at the risk of destroying the species.[188] It is good to be devoted to the moral code, but it is wicked to be fanatic about it.[189]

The Hindu code does not condemn all compromises.[190] For instance, although marriage is the normal preparation for quiet happiness[191] and monogamy is the ideal,[192] it is said that, if traditional taboos and institutional attitudes thwart love and happiness, they may be violated.[193] Non-marital relations may be countenanced in exceptional cases; we can not make men and women faithful by making it difficult for them to be unfaithful.[194] In this imperfect world we must choose not between good and bad, but between bad and worse.[195] We are like ships which are more likely to reach port if they compromise a little with wind and weather.[196] It must be noted, however, that taboos on personal conduct are justified in the interests of the weak and young.[197] The young can not be a law unto themselves.[198] Only those who are well disciplined and have developed a delicacy of apprehension which is conspicuous in saints have the right to go beyond the rules.[199] Primitive lusts are no novel form of advanced thought.[200]

The pattern of the good life begins to emerge. Happiness is virtue, refinement, charm.[201] Each of us longs for the simple and the living, for a little friendship, a little human happiness, for devotion to a cause to which we can give ourselves.[202] Personality is not alone physical manhood or economic well-being or sensitive conscience; without a spiritual center man's life has no integ-

181 HH, 17ff.
184 *Ibid.,* 113.
187 EPW, 52.
190 RS, 201.
193 RS, 191f.
196 *Ibid.,* 224.
199 RS, 196.
202 *Ibid.,* 62.

182 RS, 114.
185 *Ibid.,* 114.
188 RS, 149.
191 *Ibid.,* 159.
194 *Ibid.,* 195.
197 *Ibid.,* 195.
200 *Ibid.,* 197.

183 *Ibid.,* 115.
186 *Ibid.,* 191.
189 K, 57.
192 *Cf.* RS, 175.
195 *Ibid.,* 226.
198 K, 62.
201 *Ibid.,* 62.

rity.[203] Spiritual life is a functioning of the whole man.[204] The ego holds something not itself to which it should abandon itself. In this abandonment consists its transfiguration.[205] To be inspired in thought by divine knowledge, moved in will by divine purpose, mold an emotion into harmony with divine bliss, get at the great Self of true goodness and beauty to which we give the name God is the ultimate purpose and meaning of human living.[206] In the highest state a man is integral in being, perfect in knowledge, absolute in love, complete in will.[207]

Now come two touches which perhaps only a thinker reared in the Hindu traditions could contribute. First, the real sage, moving at ease in the world of spirit and of sense,[208] is free from temptation [209] and not worried about standardized conceptions of conduct.[210] He has passed beyond the dualities, and duty *as such* drops away.[211] And then, with all this shining picture of moral ideals, there is a dark line; it is said that for the majority of men the higher life is unspeakably gloomy.[212]

VII

In comparatively recent years Radhakrishnan has turned his attention increasingly to concrete social problems of the contemporary world. While the group exists only to secure the complete unfolding of individual personality,[213] between man and society there is a deep mysterious primordial relationship.[214] Traditional individualism does not deal adequately with the individual's social obligations.[215]

Any Hindu facing the Western world is sure to be asked about the caste system. Radhakrishnan says that we must distinguish between castes and classes,[216] and not so much classes of individuals as kinds of services.[217] Any society has a functional hierarchy; a classless society is impractical.[218] All men are equal as centers of absolute value; it is as regards instrumental value that they are unequal.[219] There is a kind of *noblesse oblige* about it. To prevent pride of power and abuse of privilege we must rely on good breeding, with active control by the religious conscience.[220] The higher

203 IVL, 65f.
204 *Ibid.,* 88.
205 BG, 31.
206 ER, 57.
207 BG, 222f.
208 ER, 109.
209 *Ibid.,* 103.
210 IVL, 118.
211 BG, 72f.
212 EPW, 44.
213 BG, 44.
214 EPW, 98.
215 RS, 94.
216 ER, 371ff.
217 EPW, 43.
218 RS, 97.
219 *Ibid.,* 91.
220 *Ibid.,* 97.

the man, the fewer are his rights and the more numerous are his duties.[221]

Radhakrishnan's academic distinctions give impact to that part of his social philosophy which is concerned with education. He decries an education which stimulates the mind without satisfying it.[222] He may be said to be partial to the "great books." When the young mind is brought into contact with the noblest classics of art and literature it absorbs their mellow lights, their sacred enthusiasms, their austere patterns.[223] In contemporary curricula the scattered elements of knowledge and detached specialism require the subtle alchemy of spirit to transform them into wisdom.[224] An intellectual opinion is not a spiritual experience.[225] The end of education is self-knowledge, in so far as the self is a calm discriminating spirit.[226] The aim of spiritual education is to make the outer and the inner man one;[227] if education does not teach us to live well it has failed of its purpose.[228]

A university should give an outlook on life reverent to the eternal values and responsive to temporal events.[229] Universities must keep the soul alive and be the nation thinking aloud; if they are to do this, they must have a few creative personalities, priests of learning, prophets of spirit.[230] Great minds convert us by the light they shed.[231] What matters in any system of education is the accent.[232]

Any worthy representative of India in these days must be concerned with the problems of politics. For Radhakrishnan, democracy is the political expression of the ethical principle that the true end of man is responsible freedom.[233] It is essentially recognition of human dignity;[234] and since the human individual is the highest and most concrete embodiment of the Spirit on earth, democracy is the highest religion.[235] The common man is not common.[236] Democracy is a habit of mind. It is easy to acquire its forms but not its spirit. Essentially a democrat is one who has the trait of humility, the power to put himself in second place, to believe that he may possibly be mistaken and his opponent probably right.[237] Democracy is not an attempt at uniformity, but at integrated variety.[238] A balance of liberties, an organized harmony of individual freedoms is ideal. Here as elsewhere, the truth lies in the union of

221 HVL, 119.   222 K, 36.   223 EPW, 79.
224 Ibid., 105.   225 Ibid., 106.   226 Ibid., 101.
227 Ibid., 106.   228 Ibid., 28.   229 Ibid., 175.
230 Ibid., 88.   231 IC, 62.   232 EPW, 102.
233 RS, 90.   234 MST, 31.   235 EPW, 8.
236 Ibid., 39.   237 Ibid., 16.   238 BG, 366.

opposites, a reconciling synthesis, socialized individualism.[239] There can not be an effective democracy if economics is defective.[240] Political liberty is of little value, as long as there is growing economic inequality.[241] Economic individualism means stratification.[242] Man is meant for happiness, but in the present state of things is everywhere unhappy.[243] The workers and peasants can not be satisfied with crumbs from the capitalist's table, or from capitalism's self-indulgent charity in the form of old age pensions, health and unemployment insurance, and minimum wages.[244] Writing in 1942, Radhakrishnan says that laws and institutions bind the wage earners with fetters as strong as those riveted to slaves. The laws define the rights of the strong and wealthy, but are indifferent to those of the poor and weak.[245] Prosperity without justice is like a house built on sand.[246] Under the profit motive other sides of human nature, like loyalty to the community and the desire to do a good job, tend to atrophy.[247]

Communism, although it need not be identified with violence, irreligion, tyranny, or individual suppression, is not the answer; in its theory there is no room for democracy.[248] The revolutionary conceives the problem in too simple, external terms.[249] The broad principles of Communism—that there shall be no exploitation, no private ownership of the means of production—are likely to be accepted in increasing measure by the democratic nations.[250] Confronted by revolutionary movements, it is the path of wisdom to bring about changes by peaceful and constitutional methods.[251] Even revolutionary changes can be brought about by persuasion,[252] but we must remember that only a faith can prevail against a faith.[253]

The faith that is necessary centers in the individual and his spiritual destiny. A non-capitalistic democracy takes away political power from property as such and vests it in the individual as such.[254] The hope of the future is, as usual, with the liberals.[255] We must not hastily sweep away the present order.[256] We can not expect to outgrow the profit motive completely,[257] but there must be great limitations and responsibility in the acquisition of wealth.[258] Huge profits ought to be unlawful and excessive incomes

239 EPW, 97.
240 *Ibid.*, 13.
241 RS, 39.
242 K, 18.
243 IC, 42.
244 RS, 95.
245 *Ibid.*, 95.
246 EPW, 53.
247 *Ibid.*, 41.
248 RS, 99.
249 *Ibid.*, 100.
250 IC, 29.
251 EPW, 42f.
252 *Ibid.*, 44.
253 RS, 80.
254 *Ibid.*, 99.
255 ER, 347.
256 RS, 63.
257 EPW, 41.
258 RS, 98.

ought to be curbed by high taxes.[259] There ought to be a proper distribution of wealth; equal distribution is another question.[260] There should be work and security for all adults, proper education for the young, widespread distribution of the necessities and amenities of life, full safeguards against unemployment and freedom of self development.[261] It is interesting to compare these words of 1942 with the ideals set forth in the Constitution of India in 1950; Radhakrishnan has exerted notable influence on at least one of the most outstanding leaders of the new government.

Some of Radhakrishnan's views incline toward socialism. There is nothing wrong with the ideal of a state's owning public utilities for the benefit of all.[262] Social ownership of large sources of wealth and power is less dangerous to ethical life and more helpful to social fellowship.[263] Regulated control is less tyrannical than blind competition.[264]

There is no blind allegiance or commitment to democratic institutions. The State should be a convenience, not at end,[265] and a nation should not be obliged to devote the best part of its time to political matters.[266] To be best governed is to be least governed.[267] Democracy rarely permits a country to be ruled by its ablest men;[268] benevolent despotisms, for brief periods, have done better.[269] If a dictator is democratic at heart it does not matter much if he appears to be a dictator.[270] Political wisdom can not be in advance of social maturity.[271]

VIII

A man of such world contacts as Radhakrishnan would be expected to have broad and enlightened internationalist views. He says, for instance, that in the World War of 1914-18 we passed through the fire but perished in the smoke.[272] The root cause of international troubles is that an interdependent world is being worked on a particularist basis.[273] Modern civilization exhibits all the features strangely similar to the symptoms which accompany the fall of civilizations—lack of tolerance and justice, love of ease and comfort, selfishness, the rise of strange cults, the unwillingness of man to use his intellectual powers.[274] No civilization, however

259 EPW, 42.   260 RS, 93.   261 Ibid., 96.
262 EPW, 13.   263 Ibid., 42.   264 Ibid., 367.
265 Ibid., 13.   266 Ibid., 12.   267 K, 65.
268 Ibid., 22.   269 Ibid., 66.   270 EPW, 8.
271 RS, 227.   272 EPW, 171.   273 Ibid., 33.
274 ER, 256.

brilliant, can stand up against social resentments and class conflicts which accompany a maladjustment of wealth, labor, and leisure.[275] Present day capitalism, militarism, and nationalism kill the spirit in man.[276] We can not sit on a powder magazine and smoke a pipe of peace.[277]

The influence of the never-to-be-forgotten Gandhi appears in Radhakrishnan's emphasis on non-violence. Non-violence is not a physical condition but a mental attitude of love.[278] If we are not ready for non-violent resistance it is better to resist evil by violence than not at all.[279] There are just wars, alternative to servitude, but the question is, what is just?[280] In the long run, however, a civilization in which the unspeakable fiendishness of war is possible is not worth saving.[281] We are kept in barbarism by artificial means.[282] If we believe absurdities, we shall commit atrocities.[283] War settles only which side is the stronger.[284] Spiritual numbness overtakes an entire people in the hour of victory;[285] we can not recover the virtues at peace time.[286]

As for the second World War, Radhakrishnan declares that the policy of requiring unconditional surrender was wrong,[287] and that the use of the atom bomb was against all the laws of international usage and morality.[288]

Although in a world of physical barriers nationalism had a place,[289] and although even now, for rich full life, national consciousness is essential,[290] nationalism is a step, an essential step toward internationalism.[291] Patriotism is ordinarily only hatred disguised in acceptable terms.[292] If a greedy individual is a nuisance, a greedy nation is a catastrophe.[293] Moral standards must apply to states;[294] nations, like individuals, are made not only by what they acquire but by what they resign.[295] The withering away of the state means the displacement of coercion by habit, discussion, and argument, and the building up of a system of law, liberty, and peace.[296] Wherever minds are sensitive, hearts generous, spirits free, there is your country.[297]

With all its imperfections, a civilization built on audacities of speculative doubt, moral impresssionism, and fierce racial and na-

275 *Ibid.*, 384. 276 RS, 16. 277 EPW, 11.
278 RS, 202. 279 *Ibid.*, 236. 280 *Ibid.*, 218f.
281 *Ibid.*, 222. 282 *Ibid.*, 211. 283 ER, 80.
284 RS, 218. 285 IC, 183f. 286 RS, 217.
287 IC, 183. 288 ITP, 21. 289 EPW, 69.
290 RS, 81. 291 EPW, 137. 292 RS, 228.
293 IC, 179. 294 RS, 214. 295 EPW, 11.
296 RS, 223. 297 EPW, 169.

tional antagonisms need not dishearten us.[298] We must dare to fail before we can hope to succeed.[299] Nations are to be judged by the dreams in their hearts.[300] Civilization is an act of spirit;[301] it is based on a vision.[302] If modern civilization can be tolerant, humane, understanding, and not self-seeking, it will be the greatest achievement of history.[303] We are about to make a new experiment in the art of life on a worldwide scale;[304] for it, we should have the attitude of acceptance and adventure.[305]

IX

Every civilization is the expression of a religion, for religion signifies faith in absolute values and a way of life to realize them.[306] Politics is the most effective means of rendering religion, with its faith in human brotherhood, in visible form.[307] Religious idealism is the most hopeful instrument for peace.[308] When, however, we look to the traditional and established religions, they fall far short of such ideals. The traditional faith in God is passing, whatever the theologians who have vested interests may say.[309] A wealth of superstitions and taboos, primitive myths and unhistorical traditions, unscientific dogmatisms and national idolatries constitute the practicing religion of the vast majority of mankind today.[310] Attempts to interpret ancient scriptures to suit modern demands may show reverence for the past but not intellectual honesty.[311] The days of external ceremonial religion which can coexist with a deceitful paganism are over.[312] A difficulty with all religions is their emphasis on the insignificant.[313]

Radhakrishnan's scholarly and important book, *Eastern Religions and Western Thought,* is incisively critical of historic Christianity. In this and other works, with the keen eye of an Oriental outsider, he excoriates historic Christian otherworldliness;[314] the "curious" Christian doctrine of vicarious sacrifice [315] (although much in Hinduism, too, suggests vicarious sacrifice);[316] the influences of other religions and cults;[317] the suggestion of eating the sacrificial animal that lingers in the doctrine of the real presence;[318] the trinitarian "jugglery of words" in order to retain be-

298 ER, 33.

301 MST, 34.

304 K, 10.

307 EPW, 2.

310 ER, 290.

313 EPW, 30.

316 HH, 119f.; IVL, 335; cf. RS, 211.

299 EPW, 135.

302 ER, 358.

305 Ibid., 58.

308 K, 72.

311 K, 13.

314 ER, 71f.

317 ER, Chaps. V, VI.

300 IC, 29.

303 Ibid., 258.

306 RS, 21.

309 Ibid., 12f.

312 MST, 35.

315 HH, 98.

318 Ibid., 226.

lief in the one God;[319] the difficulty of distinguishing the Madonna and the saints from minor deities as symbols;[320] Western asceticism,[321] with the Christian attitude on sex[322] and emphasis on negative virtues;[323] the corruption of Jesus' teaching of non-violence;[324] present day humanism;[325] and the use of the churches as a religious cloak for prejudice and passion.[326]

For Radhakrishnan, the problem is not the incredible dogmas of religion, but the place of the spiritual in the universe.[327] Underlying all diversity of dogmas is the undefined and indefinable conception of an ultimate reality.[328] We must devise fresh statements for universal truths which are in harmony with modern knowledge and criticism.[329] Real religion can exist without a definite conception of deity, but it must at least distinguish between the sacred and the profane.[330] For the self-conscious individual religion is faith in values; for the spiritual being it is contact with reality which is the source of all value.[331]

As might be expected from what has been said concerning Radhakrishnan's emphasis on intuition, an attempt to make religion absolutely rational would be to misconceive its essential character.[332] The integral intuition is our authority for religion;[333] the ultimate evidence of any religious faith is the evidence of the believer's heart.[334] All true religion is highly mystical.[335]

The fate of the human race hangs on the rapid assimilation of qualities associated with the mystic religions of the East.[336] We need a philosophy which will combine the best of European humanism with Asiatic religion.[337] On the other hand, a single religion for all all mankind would take away spiritual richness.[338] One religion can hardly replace another; the convert to a new religion is a stranger to himself.[339] As some men in China say, what we need is not so much a fellowship of beliefs as of believers.[340] Put the fire of spirit on any altar, and it blazes up to heaven.[341]

X

Such, in many of its author's own words, is the living philosophy which is to be scrutinized in the present volume. This essay is pri-

[319] Ibid., 343.
[320] Ibid., 343.
[321] Ibid., 72.
[322] RS, 148.
[323] ER, 108.
[324] RS, 207ff.
[325] ER, 75.
[326] EPW, 78.
[327] RS, 40.
[328] K, 45.
[329] Ibid., 42.
[330] ER, 21.
[331] IVL, 302.
[332] SM, 277.
[333] IVL, 89.
[334] BG, 343.
[335] Ind P, Vol. I, 236.
[336] ER, 259.
[337] Ibid., 259.
[338] K, 45.
[339] ER, 329.
[340] IC, 22.
[341] IVL, 206.

marily concerned with exposition rather than with criticism, but it may not be out of place to include a few words in answer to the question suggested at the beginning—What can Radhakrishnan, or for that matter, What can India teach us?

The answer, of course, involves consideration of intuitional absolute idealism. There is no question that this noble philosophy in recent years has lost ground in the West; neither idealism nor absolutism nor intuitionism has a status there today compared to their strength at the turn of the century. It appears that whatever of the philosophy we accept from Radhakrishnan or from India will be subject to discount on at least two accounts. One is neurological-psychological and the other psychological-epistemological-logical.

The Indians traditionally have been greatly concerned with psychology and have had centuries in which to develop their convictions. No one can say that they have not been empirical, for "empirical" can mean "experiential" as well as "experimental;" and if the Indians have been short on laboratories they have been long on life. Their empiricism, however, has been largely a rule-of-thumb procedure, and their introspections, because of their unique preoccupation with the inner life, the exaggerated reverence paid to their teachers and commentators, and perhaps because of the long continued virtual isolation of India, have shown a high degree of inbreeding and developed a kind of group auto-suggestion. Psychology has had its troubles in the West; but in the West its doctrines are more varied and at the same time more precise, as well as on the whole more ready to confront the problems presented by the nervous system.

Radhakrishnan, although he maintains that future attempts at philosophy must relate themselves to recent advances in the natural sciences "and psychology," [342] decries what he calls the cheap godless naturalism of the intellectuals,[343] and evidently regards as important the fact that consciousness can not be reduced to neurological happenings.[344] He is willing to grant that the human self is an emergent from the world process and not a substance different in kind from the process itself; [345] but he holds that self-conscious mind gradually achieves a degree of independence and reacts with increasing freedom.[346] He defines the soul as a region beyond the body and the intellect, and as a region in which the spirit finds its

---

342 HH, 137.   343 ER, 16f.   344 IVL, 25.
345 Ibid., 266.   346 Ibid., 290f.

aspiration.[347] He recognizes the unconscious,[348] but does not, for instance, use the results of psychoanalysis to throw any light on the dream state. Dreamless sleep is regarded as a source of knowledge.[349] We saw that for him, besides consciousness and self consciousness, there is superconsciousness; he is ultimately most concerned with the last named and its yield of intuitions.

We can not here engage in any long discussion of intuitionism, but must restrict ourselves to a few points. First, a critic of intuitionism can always be met by the statement that he is not good enough for the method, that it requires stern preparation, especially moral discipline, and sometimes even ascetic practices. Such an argument can go on forever; there is no answer to it, except perhaps to say that the intuitionist, instead of poisoning the wells, would disinfect them—and that the East, in all its glory, has no monopoly on moral excellence.

Radhakrishnan's doctrine of intuition as "integral experience" appears to offer important possibilities for Western thought. To be sure, if it were to be widely accepted, it would probably need to be freed from any implications of a superconsciousness, and rendered really integral, as a total reaction or total adjustment of the whole man, physiologically as well as psychologically and/or spiritually, to the total situation confronting him. We shall return to this point below.

XI

Another respect in which Western thought may well be cautious appears from psychological-epistemological data as these are brought to bear upon logic.[350] The presupposition for this criticism of Radhakrishnan is that our thinking, instead of being *sui generis* and independent of ordinary conditions, simply follows the pattern of our perception. It is commonplace to say that perception is selective; somewhat less frequently we find mention of the correlative fact, the fact of neglect. In the very act of perceiving any given thing, say A, we inevitably for the time being neglect its background or condition, *non-A*. Unless there is something about thinking which delivers it from this "horizon principle," we *think* of any given thing A by selecting it against its temporarily neglected *non-A*. At a later moment we may broaden the field of perception's field or of thinking's object; but there will still be an outlying,

[347] ER, 2.   [348] IVL, 216.   [349] ER, 125.
[350] For a discussion of the following points, see G. P. Conger, *The Horizons of Thought*, 1933, esp. 96.

temporarily unexplored *non-A*. This holds whether we perceive or think of an ordinary object, or of a group of objects, or of a self (the self as *known;* we consider the self as knower presently), or of the universe. We are dealing always with an *A* and a correlative *non-A;* since one is at least momentarily selected and the other for the given moment neglected, we must deal with them in somewhat different ways. Before considering the different ways, let us take account first of what we have just done in mentioning the two together. Each of them has been mentioned, indicated, denoted; let us say that either or both can be treated *denotatively,* but thereafter differences of treatment appear. Anything which we have selected we may proceed to describe, observing its qualities, stating its properties, indicating its relations with other actual or possible selected objects of perception or thinking. Let us call this connotation, and say that selected objects may be treated *connotatively.* But along with each selection goes its correlative neglect, neglect of the temporarily unexplored background. The neglected must for the time being simply be neglected. We can say *that* it is (at least that it is an object of reference) and that it is neglected, but we have no right to describe it, or to say either *what* it is or what it is not. We must leave the description open—that is, let us say, treat it *enotatively.* A descriptive statement about anything left enotative is like a football run out of bounds; in whichever direction, affirmative or negative, the ball is advanced, the play does not count. Finally, since none of the permitted connotative statements may be said to exhaust all the properties of an object or the relations of a term, we must allow at least for possible gaps within the selected, connotatively known field. There is not merely an external but an internal neglect. In other words, along with enotation we must recognize *innotation.*

Two or three special consequences should be noted. First, *non-A* differs from *not-A,* in that *non-A* may be either more *A* or may be *not-A,* entirely exclusive of *A. Not-A* is a negative of exclusion, whereas *non-A* is merely a negative of suspension. Many subtleties can be tracked down by recognizing and employing this distinction.[351]

Again, it should be admitted that the boundary between a selected perceived object *A* and its neglected background *non-A* can not be fixed with precision. In thinking, by virtue of the negative of exclusion and the principle of non-contradiction, the boundary zone is rendered more precise. It is commonly said that there is

351 *Cf.* Ind P, Vol. I, 178; Vol. II, 536; IVL, 101,

no *tertium quid* between A and *not-A;* it would be more in accord with the conditions of thinking to say that any *tertium quid* is left innotative. The notion of limit may be invoked here, but the notion of limit itself properly involves provision for intervals left innotative. When it is said that to know the self as limited is to know that there is something beyond the limit, the latter notion is likely to be misleading. (To know *that* there is something does not tell us *what* that something is.)

Once more, what of the elusive, and in some treatments all-but-illusory, self as knower, always involved in perception or thinking, but as Radhakrishnan holds, always distorted when made an object, a self as known? We must say, *that* it is, but the moment we try to say what it is, it becomes the self as known. If this is the case, we must be careful about attempting to describe the self as knower, or to say what it is or what it is not. Still more must we be cautious about statements that reality, or the universe, is essentially identical with the self as knower. Apart from the risky subjectivism, the notion of identity, too, needs provision for differences left innotative. The fact is that the self as knower and the universe alike elude our connotative thinking.

This account of the limitations of our thinking has profound bearing upon other key problems of metaphysics, especially those phrased in terms of infinites and absolutes. Anything infinite is somewhere non-finite or indefinite; the reference is usually enotative, but the rule may work the other way. When one attempts to "start" with the infinite or the unconditioned [352] (more properly the non-finite or the non-conditioned) as primary and derive the finite or the conditioned from it, some feature as regards the infinite must be left innotative.[353] Thinking is not rendered conclusive merely by exchanging enotative and innotative references. It is no wonder that Radhakrishnan speaks of the dizziness of inquiry into the infinite.[354]

Most pointedly in the present connection, these horizon principles apply to anything regarded as absolute or The Absolute and help to clarify the difficulties which, as we saw, are encountered by Radhakrishnan in his attempts to be descriptive. Our ordinary experience is surely qualified, limited, incomplete, imperfect; our A is subtended by our *non-A*. But we have no warrant for asserting categorically that *non-A* is either A or *not-A*, that the Absolute Ground is like us or is not like us.[355] If we try to make the Absolute

352 IVL, 169.   353 *Cf.* BG, 33.
354 HH, 140.   355 *Cf.* IVL, 99.

equal "the whole of things," a similar difficulty appears. The whole may be denoted by $(A + non\text{-}A)$, but the inclusion of $non\text{-}A$ requiries provision for enotative or innotative reference, or both, as regards A, and if the whole $(A + non\text{-}A)$ is described in other terms it is selected from the non-whole, or $non\text{-}(A + non\text{-}A)$.

Consequently, if we try to make the self, particularly the self as knower, equivalent to or identical with any Absolute, we are conceptually in deep water, with the essential provisions for innotative and enotative references complicating one another. The concept of "nothing" will not help. "Nothing" in such cases does not mean absence of everything; it means *presence* of something denoted but left enotative [356] or innotative.[357]

In spite of these limitations which leave no certain warrant for either affirmative or negative statements about the primary self and the ultimate absolute, as well as in cases of the other concepts noted, we are not quite without recourse. There is first the recourse of assumption, hypothesis, or postulate.

This is not merely the ordinary scientific postulation, which, if properly based, is at least quite likely to be confirmed, nor is it the mathematical postulation from which consistent consequences, whatever they are, may be deduced. Here, in the cosmic problems, postulation involves the acceptance and development of one possible alternative respecting the enotative $non\text{-}A$ and abandonment or disregard of the other alternative or alternatives. We may, for example, make the assumption that the $non\text{-}A$ is more A rather than $not\text{-}A$, as when Radhakrishnan assumes the trustworthiness of nature.[358] Often the assumption is pleasant. If the A may be regarded as any ground for an estimate of probabilities (this depending on what possibilities are left enotative or innotative), we may have in our assumption whatever confidence this ground warrants. On the other hand, it must be said that the way is open for an opponent to make the opposite assumption, and there is no authentic way of convincing him that he is wrong. One man takes the chance one way and the other the other. In the problem before us, Radhakrishnan boldly takes the chance, to the edge of dogmatism about it; the Western thinkers, who have seen the rise and decline of German-English-American idealism are likely to be more cautious. As introspection seems to them inbreeding, absolute idealism seems extravagance—in the root sense of the word, a wandering outside the proper bounds of descriptive thinking.

In the second place, it is also possible to appeal to the principle

356 *Cf. ibid.*, 271.   357 *Cf.* ER, 126.   358 IVL, 154f.

of growth. Radhakrishnan has emphasized that the root of the word Brahman is *brih*, to grow. This recourse helps with problems of time; the past, as fixed, and at least as far as it is known, can be treated connotatively. The future is, let us say, enotative. The present is the moving boundary between them; the familiar problem of time-span or specious present reveals the pertinence here of innotation. Recognition of growth, too, helps with the problem of being and non-being. Being, by becoming, grows out into what was formerly non-being, without, however, exhausting it. The same principle applies, only in reverse fashion, when the Absolute Ground is dignified by the term Being and the finite Universe is discounted as non-being.[359] Here again enotation is exchanged for innotation.

In another recourse, when thinking encounters the horizon limitations we may sometimes invoke a hierarchy of selections and correlative neglects, in a kind of theory of types, distinguishing various degrees or shells or levels of A and non-A. Thus, using subscripts, A_1 is subtended by non-A_1, and $(A_1 + non$-$A_1)$, which we may call A_2, is subtended by non-$(A_1 + non$-$A_1)$, which we may call non-A_2, and so on. Some apparent contradictions may be relieved, if not resolved, by recognizing these distinctions, but this difficult recourse, if adopted, serves only to postpone the problem by pushing thought's horizons further out, or down.

In short, all monisms, when the attempt is made to think them through, sooner or later fall foul of the horizons of thought, and to call one's monism absolute only complicates the difficulties. Thinking, even where it is not explicitly dual, is implicitly dual, and in any case the duality of thinking can not be resolved by thinking. In Hinduism, duality, thrust out through the door of argument, shines in through the window of *māyā*!

XII

There remains, however, the way of intuition. We must think of any A dualistically, by selecting it in contrast to its correlative non-A, but we have to live with the whole universe, with both A and non-A. Intuition, one might say, is the registry of the universe (whatever that term may denote) in the personality, and the personality's response. By comparison the distinction between A and non-A is secondary; the crystal of thought splits the unbroken beam.

[359] *Cf.* BG, 39.

The ultimate witness for intuitionism is life-experience—which is to say, personality. But an intuitionist can not on that ground argue conclusively that the universe is to be described as one Spirit, or one mechanism, or in any other way. He can, and often does, argue; but he can not argue conclusively, because every *A* of his argument must be conditioned at least by its enotative *non-A*. Radhakrishnan, like many others, in spite of his occasional admissions of the limitations of our reason, overreaches himself in extravagant descriptive statements, some of which have been cited above. Description of the universe, as far as we can think or speak, is the task of intellect, not of intuition.[360]

This is by no means to say that description, observation, reason, and argument are to be abandoned in favor of a blank or blanket intuitionism. To leap or plunge or swoon into the Absolute, the Infinite, Tao, Nirvāṇa, or a dedifferentiated continuum, is to go into spiritual reverse, and in one way or another to ignore or to relinquish the findings of the sciences and most of the fruits of Western culture.

Some more positive, constructive way there must be to combine intuition and reason and science. Radhakrishnan's integral experience points the way, even if it misconstrues the goal. It needs to be purged of its inconsistencies and shorn of its extravagances, and to become more genuinely integral, inclusive of more facts, more science, more naturalism. Sometimes he is vague and indefinite, or, in his attempts to be definitive, he is inconsistent. Again, sometimes he is otherworldly, or, in his attempts to be practical, he is too Oriental to serve planetary culture without further crystallization. But if, in any way, within the limitations proper to thinking, India

360 Without pressing the illustration too far, we may say that intuition and reason are related somewhat as a circle is related to its inscribed polygon. We must remember that the circle itself is an *A* in the midst of its *non-A*, but we may think of its circumference line as belonging to both. Let us suppose then that the universe, (A + non-A), presents itself in an intuition, represented by the circle. Ordinary observation and thinking is the attempt to build up chords and angles and polygons within the circle. The polygons of thought and language are incommensurable with the circle of intuition, no matter to what lengths the lines may be multiplied to approximate the area under the curve. The straight lines, as far as they go, render the area covered by the circle more thoroughly interrelated and more explorable, but only as more and more lines are added to build out the polygon without distortion or asymmetry. Many intuitionisms have disregarded too many facts and theories about the world. The attempt to express intuitions in sweeping thoughts may be likened to a shift from rectangular to polar co-ordinates. We still have to do with straight lines (in trigonometric functions); the formula for the area of the circle still involves the irrational π, and any application of the theorem of limits properly involves provision for residual areas left innotative.

can naturalize its spiritualism and the West can spiritualize its naturalism, there may be a profound and moving integration of philosophies.

Historically, the root of the whole matter is that the West has been more concerned to introduce sharp distinctions, both of method and content, in what might be world-philosophy. Western philosophy comes to us, passed, so to speak, through a doubly dualistic filter—first, as to method, through the keen mind of Greece, with its distinction of A and not-A, and then, as to content, through the devoted mind of Palestine, with its distinction between the supernatural and the natural. Both these distinctions Radhakrishnan would melt down in a monism. He is too wise and too practical to let his monism be empty; but in his attempt to fill it out, the monism becomes over-ambitious and paradoxical.

The conclusion of the whole matter is that Radhakrishnan *presents a type of life*, attractive and somehow essentially authentic. Notice how for him everything—psychology, epistemology, metaphysics, ethics, education, politics, economics, religion—converges and culminates in *spirit*. With brilliant mind and glowing heart he beckons us to an integral experience, an integrated life. He summons us all to seek it, even though some of us must seek it in ways other than his own.

GEORGE P. CONGER

DEPARTMENT OF PHILOSOPHY
UNIVERSITY OF MINNESOTA

2

Bernard *Phillips*

RADHAKRISHNAN'S CRITIQUE OF NATURALISM

RADHAKRISHNAN'S CRITIQUE OF NATURALISM

THE age-old dream of mankind united in the enterprise of building a world civilization has in this century assumed the proportions of an attainable goal. It is the glorious destiny of the present age to contribute at least to the beginnings of its eventual realization. The physical instrumentalities requisite to this unification already exist, and are daily being improved. The geographical barriers which formerly helped to produce the separation of peoples have been eliminated by the advances of technology. If the human race continues to be a house divided against itself, it is on account of politics and culture, not because of mountains and oceans. So far, it is the political and economic aspects of the problem which have largely captured the attention of those who are devoted to the idea of One World. The various proposals to alter or extend the powers of the United Nations Organization, the multitudinous schemes for world government, the programs of international aid and economic development are all indicative of the obsolescence of isolationism as a political concept.

The urgency which characterizes problems of international politics and economics makes it understandable that many persons of good will should feel bound to focus all efforts on their solution. At the same time, one cannot help but perceive that there is an all but fatal defect in a great deal of the thinking about these matters which is carried on in exclusively political and economic terms. For, generally, it tends to be negative and external; it seeks to free the world from fear of aggression and from poverty; but it is largely unconcerned with the problem of effecting a deep union of the minds and hearts of men. It pins its hopes on the devising of political techniques and strategies, and is inclined to forget that these are empty forms so long as they cannot presuppose a commensurate socio-cultural consciousness. Political ideals will take on flesh only as they are nourished by a truly global consciousness and a truly global culture; and the creation of the latter is not primarily the task of politics or economics. If so many political idealists are today on the verge of despair it is because they have been attempting to impose on provincial man a pattern of life designed for cosmopolitan man. The world community of the future will begin to emerge from the blueprint stage only as a new type of human being becomes dominant—the human being whose allegiance is to the human race and who has been nurtured in a common human heritage. When the cultural treasures of the earth are combined into a common trust fund for all peoples, when education comes to conceive of its function as the transmission and expansion of the heritage of humanity, then and only then will a world civilization have become a reality. As the civilization of Europe drew upon the cultural resources of Greece, Rome, and Palestine, and would be inconceivable without them, so the world civilization of the future will have to absorb and to integrate the contributions of all of its citizens. As the cultivated Westerner of today is conscious of his indebtedness to Plato, Cicero, and Isaiah, so will the world citizen of tomorrow acknowledge in addition to these, also Buddha, Śaṁkara, Confucius, and Lao-Tzu as his cultural forbears. Only such a genuinely cosmopolitan culture can hope to transcend the provincialisms and partialities which characterized all the great but limited cultures of the past. In former days it was possible to regard an individual as cultured though his perspective were limited to a portion of the earth's surface. In the future such a person must be judged provincial. In time to come, the scholar nurtured in the traditions of a single civilization will be as much of an anachronism as one would be in our own day who had been reared exclusively on a diet of Latin classics.

It is in some such terms as these that educators today ought to be thinking. They have a tremendous rôle to play, if they will but raise their sights to contemplate the new ideal of the world citizen, and give themselves wholeheartedly to the high task of raising a generation of men shaped in its image. There are not many persons in the world today who would qualify as exemplars for such a new educational enterprise, but any list which might be drawn up, however short it would be, would certainly have to include the name of Sir Sarvepalli Radhakrishnan. His life and thought provide a vivid demonstration of the meeting of East and West, and testify to the enrichment of experience which such a synthesis can effect. The future of mankind will be bright when this sort of person ceases to be the rare exception.

The creation and diffusion of a common cultural heritage as the foundation of a future common world order is an enterprise which lacks the glamour associated with political and economic panaceas. It is a slow and laborious project and is, therefore, not likely to make the headlines. Since its fruits will not be immediately evident, it will be sustained only by an unrelenting idealism founded on a deep understanding of what it is the world needs. The ideal is one which the teacher will have to hold constantly before himself as, enmeshed in the daily educational routine, he endeavors to awaken the minds of his charges. Dedication to the ideal will inspire and strengthen the scholar as he patiently completes his translations and commentaries, in order that the cultural possessions of one people may become the common property of all. The influence of the ideal is detectable in the increasing international exchanges of students and scholars, in such pioneering ventures as the East-West Philosophers' Conferences of the University of Hawaii, in the writings of such men as Radhakrishnan, Suzuki, Northrop and others who are dedicated to the crossing of cultural boundaries, and in such volumes as those comprising "The Library of Living Philosophers."

There are various levels of inter-cultural understanding. On its most superficial level, it signifies mere acquaintance with the salient external traits of another culture. Customs, beliefs, and artifacts are regarded purely descriptively as data which it behooves one to take account of if he would deal with or manipulate the people of whose culture they are the expression. In a deeper sense, understanding implies, in addition, some comprehension of the social and historic context from which the facts have emerged, and some sense of the scale of valuations which they embody. At its deepest, understanding involves some degree of identification and acceptance. The fullest degree of understanding comes only with the capacity to see the culture of another as an essentially human mode of response, and with the ability to accept it in some degree as valid for oneself. Each culture synthesizes in varying proportions the particular and the universal, the perennial and the provincial. To attain the level of understanding at which one can begin to perceive in a foreign culture truths and perspectives which are lacking in one's own heritage requires an uncommon amount of good will and a power to penetrate beneath externals and to distinguish the essential from the accidental. Until this kind of understanding is achieved, a member of another group will inevitably be regarded as "queer" or even as not quite fully human. Only to the deepest kind of understanding does the common nature of man become manifest, and only by devotion to this ideal of inter-cultural understanding can the foundations of a comprehensive and non-imperialistic world-order be laid.

The achievement of genuine understanding is hampered by the natural reluctance of men and of nations to own up to their deficiencies, and to depart from established patterns of thought and practice. Individuals and cultures, pretending to an absolute self-sufficiency, are loathe to admit their limitations, and will vigorously deny that they have anything to learn from others. Thus Eastern peoples, on the one hand, although conceding the technological superiority of the West, at the same time insist that in regard to the finally important arts of life it is the West which will have to sit at the feet of the East. America, on the other hand, rather satisfied with herself, is also in an exporting frame of mind. In her new rôle as material benefactor of mankind, she has poured forth money and materials to all parts of the world in unheard of quantities. If at the same time many Americans seem puzzled that the world does not react with the proper degree of gratitude, it is because they have forgotten that neither nations nor individuals can be happy in the position of poor relations receiving handouts. All the nations of the world feel, and rightfully, that there are values —not necessarily material resources—which they have to contribute, and which Americans should be willing to acknowledge. They would more eagerly applaud America's material generosity if this were accompanied by some measure of spiritual and cultural receptivity. Isolationism and national self-sufficiency are as obsolete as cultural ideals as they are as political concepts.

The willingness to expose oneself to the cultural achievements of others is, however, only a necessary but not a sufficient condition of world understanding. A world culture will not arise automatically through bringing into proximity with one another items drawn from divers cultures. Juxtaposition is not integration. Significant syntheses will emerge only from persistent efforts to transcend limited points of view and to integrate partial truths into richer and deeper insights. It is not a question of political trading in cultural treasures, or of "making deals" or effecting compromises so that all may be appeased. The pursuit of truth is not a species of international bartering; its only medium is creative thought. And it is here that the philosopher, concerned as he is with the analysis and validation of meanings and with the dialectical interrelations of ideas, has an enormously important rôle to play, if he will but rise to the task and exhibit the large-mindedness which it demands. For what is called for is the analytical ability to penetrate to the essential insights embedded in the various cultures of the world, and the synthetic power to fashion out of them more comprehensive perspectives. The task is not one which can be competently discharged by the philosopher whose familiarity is with one tradition or one culture only. He alone who is willing and able to adopt a world-perspective may be of help in this enterprise. If what Plato says of the philosopher is truly characteristic of him, namely, "that he is a lover, not of a part of wisdom only, but of the whole," then we cannot doubt but that the true philosopher will meet the challenge.

As an American philosopher turns in this spirit to examine the philosophical heritage of India, he is bound at first to stand amazed at the sheer abundance of ideas and arguments which it reveals, and to wonder that it is still so largely unknown in the West. Here is a philosophical tradition whose beginnings antedate the origins of Western philosophy by perhaps a millenium. It is filled with ingenious speculations and acute arguments. In ancient times it had already developed ideas which in Western thought are of relatively recent vintage; and it has fully explored bypaths which in the West have hardly been entered upon. The further one proceeds in the study of Indian thought, the less will he be inclined to disagree with Mr. T. S. Eliot's estimate of the Indian philosophers that "their subtleties make most of the great European philosophers look like schoolboys." [1] In any case, certain pervasive traits of Indian philosophy will begin to impress themselves on his mind. For example, he can hardly fail to notice the great concern which this tradition has for the inner life and the things of the spirit. As the West has devoted itself during the last four or five centuries to the understanding and mastery of nature, so it appears that through three or four thousand years India has concentrated on the achievement of self-understanding and self-mastery. And as Western science is now learning to tap the great reservoirs of energy in the heart of the atom, so perhaps the Indian philosophers may have long since discovered sources of psychic energy of whose existence the average Western philosopher does not yet dream. The spiritual-mindedness which he finds to be a generic trait of Indian philosophy will probably cause him some uneasiness, if he is a typical academic American philosopher. This intense concern with the soul and its salvation is hardly the fashion

[1] Eliot, T. S., *After Strange Gods* (New York, 1934), 43.

in Western philosophy today, save in those circles which are still attached to the medieval tradition. The Western philosopher will also wonder at the Indian conception of the function of philosophy, as a way of life, as a spiritual discipline which leads to salvation, and not merely as a theoretical pursuit for the satisfaction of curiosity. But, as he continues his survey of the Indian philosophical tradition, one fact above all will startle him, and that is the almost total absence in it of any lasting form of philosophic naturalism.* Of the three great heterodox schools of philosophy which in ancient India denied the authority of the Vedas and the Brahmin caste, namely Buddhism, Jainism, and Carvaka materialism, only the last-named has perished with hardly a trace. That the super-abundant philosophical literature of India should contain no first-hand expressions of naturalism, and that we should be totally unaware that the position had ever been assumed, except for references to it in the writings of its opponents, is an exceedingly odd circumstance. How is it to be explained? Is it merely the result of an historical accident, or does it have a deeper significance? Was the point of view eliminated from the heritage of India by those who saw in it a threat to their dominant position in Indian society? Why then did they not take similar steps to extirpate those other heresies whose presence constituted an even greater challenge to their position, and why have they tended throughout the course of Indian history to show the most exemplary tolerance towards the widest variety of creed and expression? Is India's age-old addiction to a spiritual point of view to be explained away genetically in terms of her enervating climate, for example, or in terms of her inability to cope with nature? Or is it that ultimately naturalism is found to be inherently defective by the mature philosophical consciousness, and that it is a mode of thought which recommends itself only to youthful peoples who have not yet fully grasped the human situation, but one which a mature culture is bound to set aside?

One's final answer to these questions, it goes without saying, would be in no slight degree influenced by one's general views as to the essential truth or falsity of the spiritual view of life; but whatever be the interpretation, the fact itself serves sharply to differentiate Indian philosophy from the history of philosophy in the West. It would hardly do, however, to view the contrast as illustrat-

* The reader of this essay should also consult the essay by M. N. Roy, entitled, "Radhakrishnan in the Perspective of Indian Philosophy," which attempts to disprove Mr. Phillips' assertion at this point. *Editor.*

ing the opposition between spirit and matter. No facile generalizations will adequately convey the varieties of Oriental or Occidental thought, and least of all those which forget to mention that there was a thousand year stretch of Western philosophy which in all essentials was at one with the spirit of Indian philosophy. In all such comparisons, the factor of time dare not be ignored. It is misleading, for example, to attempt to bring out the contrast between India and the West by pointing to the differences between the teachings of the Upaniṣads and the doctrines of American pragmatism. One might just as well adduce the resemblances between Śaṁkara and Meister Eckhardt as evidence of the fundamental concord of East and West. Let us also remember that the great creative period of Indian philosophizing came to an end with the Moslem invasions of India, and that it is impossible to say what the later course of Indian thought might have been had it continued to develop freely.

Nevertheless, and with these reservations in mind, the virtually unanimous repudiation of naturalism by the great Indian philosophers in the last two thousand years is in startling contrast to the fate of naturalism in the history of Western philosophy. For here, naturalism has had a history, it has had defenders, and they have been granted a serious hearing. From the earliest days of Greek philosophy, from the period of the Ionian nature philosophers, through the times of the Greek and Roman Epicureans, naturalism was a vigorous and vocal movement. During the Middle Ages, for evident reasons, its partisans, if any, were not heard from; but, with the Renaissance, it emerged again, and has since grown in strength and subtlety, so that today it may fairly be said to hold equal honors with any other school of thought in the West. Indeed, it would hardly be an exaggeration to say that in academic circles in America today, and particularly among younger philosophers, some type of empirico-naturalism is the philosophical position most widely held. Outside professional philosophical circles it enjoys a wide prestige among scientists; and on an unreflective level it is the actual working philosophy of life of countless numbers of people. Thus, although a comparative survey of the major trends of Indian and Western philosophy would reveal no over-all opposition between spiritualism and naturalism, it would disclose a significant contrast between one long tradition which has been anti-naturalistic almost throughout, and the other in which naturalism has often made a strong showing and has lately come to enjoy considerable prestige. What would have happened if Europe had been overrun by Islam, and India had been spared to develop on her own, no one can say. The subsequent course of events might perhaps have been exactly reversed. The West might now be emerging from a long period of medieval supernaturalism, eager to catch up with an India four or five centuries ahead in science and technology, and Western philosophers might now be reminding their Indian colleagues—absorbed in logical positivism, pragmatism, and evolutionary naturalism—that there were a few secrets of the interior life which the West had preserved and which India would do well to learn!

Is the confidence of the Western naturalist likely to be disturbed by the spectacle of this age long repudiation of his position by an acute philosophical tradition which has been perennially committed to some kind of spiritualism? Hardly. Any momentary doubts as to the soundness of his tenets would be quickly dispelled by the reflection that the persistence of this long tradition is due to its insulation from the method and spirit of science, and that now that science begins to permeate Indian culture, it will disintegrate the spiritual view of life as surely and as effectively as it exploded the prevailing *Weltanschauung* of the European Middle Ages. India is now committed to a program of modernization and industrialization, and as she is forced to pay more and more attention to this world and to nature, naturalistic modes of thought will become increasingly prevalent. As democratic ideas begin to take hold, the old caste system will crumble, and the power of the Brahmin will be broken. Democracy and technology will be followed by universal education and growing secularism. Humanitarian ideals will replace other-worldly goals. The energies now wasted on rite and ceremony will in the future be directed into constructive channels of social reform, and will bring about the elimination of disease and poverty. India is now emerging from her middle ages, and will, within a shorter time, retrace the essential course which the West has pursued since the Renaissance.

Although conceding that, in the abstract, all things are possible, most Indian philosophers would not regard this as a real possibility. The spiritual approach to life is too deeply rooted in India, they would argue, ever to be extirpated. The religious tradition in the West was not, as it was in India, a native growth, but a graft on a pagan stock. The graft never completely took, and the stock was not properly pruned, so that lately, the scion has been threatened by a lush growth of shoots from the stock. In India, they would claim, the spiritual life is an indigenous expression of the soul of the culture, and for that reason it will be able to assimilate what is true and good in the scientific approach without any jeopardy to its own integrity. Science in the West has got out of hand, because the West has all but lost the spiritual resources which alone can supply the proper controls. In the end, then, India will help to restore the lost balance and will bring salvation to the West, because she has preserved her ancient heritage of spirituality.

The naturalist may not be convinced by this reply, but he may well conclude that he had seriously underestimated the power which spiritualistic philosophies still retain in some areas of the world. What can hardly fail to cause him some wonder is the spectacle of so many eminent Indian thinkers, whom he is bound to respect on other grounds, somehow persisting in their ancient idealistic doctrines, though fully conversant with the recent thought of the West. Of these Radhakrishnan is one of the most distinguished examples. Though living in the modern world, and sensitive to its every phase, these Oriental scholars are yet not altogether of it, and they remain committed to a spiritualism which is not merely a matter of doctrine, but which permeates their entire being. The discerning naturalist will soon perceive that in such men as these he is confronted by a sort of adversary which he is not accustomed to encounter. For it had hardly occurred to him that spiritualism could still be a live alternative, and that it could be anything but a merely academic position held by a few rare members of a species rapidly becoming extinct, or else an unphilosophical dogma based on faith or derived from a supposed revelation. Yet, here in India, it seems far from dead, and it numbers among its representatives persons whose credentials entitle them to a respectful hearing. Under the circumstances, the conscientious naturalist may feel duty-bound to give it the most careful examination; for, not only would he want the reassurance that his own views will remain standing in the face of such worthy opposition, but he would also feel that unless the differences between the views are somehow composed, the ideal of world understanding will be difficult to realize.

In seeking among the current systems of Indian thought for a philosophy which will serve as a touchstone by which he may try the worth of his own views, he can hardly do better than to select for consideration the philosophy of Radhakrishnan. The challenge presented to Western naturalism by Radhakrishnan's philosophy derives its strength from several circumstances. It is founded on an immense learning, and a profound understanding of both the Indian and the Western traditions of thought. It is expressive of a largeness of mind unbounded by any narrow loyalties, and endowed with the ability to perceive the essential virtues of both Indian and Western civilization without being blind to the deficiencies of either one. Unlike so much of the academic idealism of the West, which so often is only a bloodless ballet of categories, Radhakrishnan's spiritualism has the existential orientation of a way of life. It stems from a background in which the evidence of things unseen is not regarded as tenuous, where the things of the spirit seem compelling realities, where saints and holy men are part of the landscape, where self-composure, inner strength and peace of mind are the visible fruits of spiritual discipline, where, in short, the idealistic view of life is not merely debated, but lived. Where philosophy is thus not merely a cerebral exercise but the pursuit of salvation, it is not sharply distinguished from religion. At the same time, Radhakrishnan speaks not as a propagandist for a creed, but as a philosopher to other philosophers. His appeal is neither to authority, faith, nor dogma, but to reason and experience. And he has often been an outspoken critic of orthodoxy and of institutionalism in religion, as is evidenced, for example, by the following remarks:

A spiritual as distinct from a dogmatic view of life remains unaffected by the advance of science and criticism of history. Religion generally refers to something external, a system of sanctions and consolations, while spirituality points to the need for knowing and living in the highest self and raising life in all its parts.[2]

Science cannot minister to the needs of the soul; dogmatism cannot meet the needs of the intellect. Atheism and dogmatism, scepticism and blind faith, are not the only alternatives.[3]

We cannot rest the case of religion any more on dogmatic supernaturalism. . . . Mysticism takes its stand on verifiable truth and not on the correct solution of credal puzzles. It is not opposed to science and reason. It is not contingent on any events past or future. No scientific criticism or historical discovery can refute it, as it is not dependent on any impossible miracles or unique historical revelations. Its only apologetic is the testimony of spiritual experience. It is not committed to the authenticity of any documents or the truth of any stories about the beginnings of the world or prophecies of its end. . . . It revolts against institutionalism and stereotyped forms of religious life. The mystics of all religions have at some point or other in their careers protested against outside authority, credal bonds, and spiritual dictatorships.[4]

[2] ER, 61.   [3] *Ibid.*, 293.   [4] *Ibid.*, 294-5.

What Radhakrishnan is committed to is no rigid creed, but a purely spriritual or mystical view of life; and he distils the essence of such a view of life and separates it from the externalities and relativities with which it is generally associated and by which it is so often concealed. Recent Western naturalism has hardly taken the opportunity to consider a purely spiritualistic view of life which speaks with profound conviction and yet is not firmly attached to any organized institution. One often has the suspicion that the *horror supernaturae* which naturalism so frequently evinces is in part, at least, inspired by the abuses of organized religion; but here, in the philosophy of Radhakrishnan, it has the opportunity of coming to grips with the spiritual view of life as such.

The expression "recent Western naturalism," does not, of course, designate any single point of view. Naturalism is rather a spectrum of attitudes, ranging from the crassest sort of materialism to what is all but an attenuated supernaturalism. It must not be defined so narrowly that only the most extreme forms of it are included in the definition; neither must it be defined so broadly that hardly any form of philosophy is excluded. A definition of naturalism which shall be both precise and comprehensive is not easily given. Thus, should one venture to assert that the common denominator of all naturalisms is the claim that nature alone exists, and that the natural order is self-sustaining, then one would have to face the problem of defining *nature,* in order that the original definition may have significance. If one equates "nature" with the realm of matter, then one has reduced naturalism to materialism. If, by "nature," one intends the causal order, then one eliminates teleology, and is unable to give an intelligible account of human life, which cannot be construed in purely causal terms. If "nature" signifies that which is set over against the human, then it hardly makes sense to go on and declare man to be a part of nature. And if "nature" is but a synonym for the totality of existence, then the thesis that nature alone exists is a tautology and is neither illuminating nor definitive of a philosophical position. In this case, nothing could be unnatural or supernatural, nothing could be above nature or outside it; for by definition whatever exists or occurs would be equally a part of nature.

Because of these and similar difficulties, some philosophers have urged that naturalism be defined in terms of method rather than as a metaphysic. This is the approach adopted by the authors of the recent co-operative volume, entitled *Naturalism and the Human Spirit*. Thus, Professor Hook, writing in this volume, asserts that

Despite the variety of specific doctrines which naturalists have professed from Democritus to Dewey, what unites them all is the wholehearted acceptance of scientific method as the only reliable way of reaching truths about the world of nature, society, and man. . . . The least common denominator of all historic naturalisms, therefore, is not so much a set of specific doctrines as the methods of scientific or rational empiricism.[5]

Such an approach accords with the strong tendency in much recent philosophy to substitute epistemological and semantic analyses for metaphysical concepts and distinctions. Naturalism, from this point of view, is essentially equivalent to empiricism, and empiricism is most adequately exemplified in what is called the method of science. The contributors to this volume are very anxious not to be confused with the logical positivists, whose view of science they regard as too limited and too physicalistic, and who claim that value judgments are unverifiable. They would also wish to be distinguished from the tough-minded materialist who will recognize nothing as ultimately real but the modes of matter. Nothing would more deeply offend the members of this group than to be labelled "materialists." They are not committed to maintaining the exclusive reality of the physical. Nature, they would claim, contains whatever experience reveals it to contain. Nature is the realm which is explored by scientific method, and science is the only reliable instrument of knowledge which man possesses.

On the other hand, we find another group of contemporary naturalists who show no aversion whatsoever to the title "materialists." They are prepared to enter a claim for a metaphysic as well as for a method. In the recently published manifesto of this group, we find the editors concerned to differentiate their own position from milder forms of naturalism:

In the recent volume *Naturalism and the Human Spirit* (edited by Y. H. Krikorian) the reader is informed that "contemporary naturalism recognizes much more clearly than did the tradition from which it stems that its distinction from other philosophical positions lies in the postulates and procedures which it criticizes and rejects rather than in any positive tenets of its own about the cosmos."

This passage will serve clearly to distinguish current naturalism from the frank materialism described above. Whereas this type of naturalism

[5] *Naturalism and the Human Spirit,* ed. by Y. H. Krikorian (New York, 1944), 45.

is reluctant to commit itself to a positive theory of the world, materialism endeavors to set forth a synoptic view of man and the universe
implicit in the sciences at their present stage of development.[6]

But though eschewing excessive timidity, these "frank" materialists
would still insist on being distinguished from "crude" materialists,
in that the former combine with a doctrine of the temporal primacy
of the realm of matter some account of emergent levels to which
the laws of the physical are not adequate:

The theory of integrative levels turns its back upon any crude mechanism. . . .[7]

Modern materialism, as we understand it, asserts the following: the
inorganic pattern of matter is prior to living, minded and purposive
organisms, which arise gradually and only as a result of a complex evolutionary development. With the advent of organic life, new, biological
laws begin to operate. The principles of physics and chemistry necessarily apply, but are not by themselves sufficient to the biological level.
Thus mechanism or the theory that physico-chemical explanation is
adequate to all levels, is emphatically rejected. . . . The one-floor plan
of the classical biological mechanism is thus superseded by a modern
structure displaying many diverse stories. The top stories, however, are
always supported by the lower floors; and all the floors rest upon the
ground floor studied by physics and chemistry. . . . Organized matter
reveals integrative levels of organization characterized by distinctive
laws.[8]

But, though naturalists are of many shades and hues, the differences between them are less important than certain essential resemblances; and the differences between them are as nothing
compared with the differences which any one of them would have
with such a position as Radhakrishnan's. And though they may
permit themselves the luxury in peaceful times of arguing their
differences, we may suppose that, when faced with the sort of
threat posed by the philosophy of Radhakrishnan, they would
quickly unite around some treaty of alliance. The terms of such
a document could not be too precisely drawn, and some differences
of interpretation would have to be allowed for; but still the area
of agreement would be a considerable one and sufficient to allow
for common concerted action. The essence of the agreement would,
however expressed, in some way cover the following four sets of
ideas:

[6] *Philosophy for the Future—the Quest of Modern Materialism*, ed. by R. W.
Sellars, V. J. McGill, and M. Farber (New York, 1949), ix.
[7] *Ibid.*, vii.   [8] *Ibid.*, vi.

1. Science is the only reliable mode of knowing available to man, and rests on the possibility of intersubjective confirmation. All human knowledge derives from experience and refers to actual or possible experience. Experience contains as an essential factor the data of the senses. Scientific verification always involves some sort of an appeal to the given, and it is only to the senses that anything is given. The senses alone intuit (which does not exclude the possibility that in all sense knowledge there may be an element of conceptualization or interpretation). Science is the search for uniformities in the behavior of things in space and time. Its aim is manipulative, not merely theoretical; and it seeks to discover patterns of relatedness in order that it may gain the power of predicting and controlling the occurrence of phenomena. Science knows of no absolutes either in knowledge or in being. Scientific truth is always provisional and ever liable to revision.

2. There exists a realm of the physical which is the ultimate matrix of all becoming. The precise nature of this realm is for the physicist and the chemist to discover. But, whether it is ultimately of the nature of energy or matter or both, it certainly is non-spiritual. It is the realm of causality, not of teleology, of facts, not of value. It is self-sustaining and utterly impersonal. Whatever else may exist has emerged from it. There is not a shred of warranted evidence for the existence of anything outside it or independent of it; i.e., there is no evidence for the existence of anything which is "supernatural" or purely spiritual. The universe exhibits no pervasive teleology; and, if teleology is admitted at all, it can only be in connection with the highest levels which have emerged.

In conformity with the findings of the biological sciences, purpose, intention, plan are confined to the top reaches of the phylogenetic scale. General teleology is therefore excluded. The modern materialist foregoes the comfort, unless it be in poetic reverie, of imagining that the order of nature is attuned to his purposes, or endowed with sensitivity and beneficence. Such longings have yielded myths in all ages, but are scarcely appropriate for a scientific era like our own. The materialist makes himself at home in the world, not by investing Nature with purpose, but by transforming it to meet his needs.[9]

Thus man stands alone and on his own in a changing world. He is a creature of time, and he can have no affiliations with any eternal order, since none such is known to exist. The real world, the only world of which we have knowledge, is characterized by temporality, not by eternity.

[9] Sellars, McGill, Farber, *op. cit.*, vii.

3. Selfhood, consciousness, personality refer to no independent substantial realities but to complex functions, associated with highly organized physico-chemical systems, which arise in and are conditioned by a social context. There are no disembodied souls or spirits of which we have any evidence. Science attests to the physico-chemical basis of life and the biological basis of mentality. Intelligence and the higher mental functions are contingent upon the possession of a highly developed nervous system. Most naturalists would find little to disagree with in the following account:

> Thought and symbolism have a strategic rôle in the material world at the human level, but always in close connection with brain events and brain traces. No mental process occurs without its appropriate neural patterns. In the behavior of the organism, the psychic and the biological are fused. . . . The study of behavior is the only scientific approach to the understanding of mind; but this does not rule out hypotheses as to the contents of other minds, that is, reconstruction of mental states of others, on the basis of behavior. . . . Introspection is, of course, a valid method, but the final test of it is behavioral. . . .
>
> The psycho-biological individual must be understood in his development and relations. Personality is conditioned by society and can only be comprehended in its historical context.[10]

Man is wholly a natural product, and he has no supernatural destiny. The belief in immortality is the expression of wishful thinking.

4. Since there is no evidence for a real world beyond the present one, man's goals and values ought to be wholly this-worldly and humanistic. There is no source of value other than man's needs, and these needs relate wholly to this world. Salvation is to be defined in terms of the elimination of disease and poverty, the spread of education and the widest distribution of material comforts, the elimination of war and strife. Man has no needs which in principle cannot be supplied by the exercise of intelligence in the form of theoretical and applied science. *Goodness* is a social and not an individual concept. Self-perfection is to be defined in terms of rendering oneself useful to society and developing the capacity for enjoying the goods which this world has to offer. Human nature contains within itself the possibilities of its own regeneration, and requires no help from superhuman sources. There is nothing warped in it which cannot be straightened out by intelligence. The science of man is yet in its infancy. The difficulties of our times are to be ascribed to the lag which exists between the sciences of na-

10 *Ibid.,* vii-viii.

ture and the sciences of human nature. Our powers over nature have outstripped our understanding of man; it is by applying ourselves assiduously to the cultivation of the science of man that we shall solve the problems of human adjustment which beset the present age. Once achieved, the knowledge of the mainsprings of human action will enable us to predict and control human behavior and to cope scientifically with war and aggression, with hatred and greed. It is by the knowledge of the truth that men will be set free, and the saving knowledge can and must be arrived at through the employment of the only reliable cognitive instrument yet devised, namely, scientific method.

Defined in some such terms as these, the naturalistic attitude toward life has come increasingly to pervade Western culture. As the science from which it draws its strength has grown in prestige, so has the naturalist attitude likewise gained followers. To the Oriental mind it stands out as the most striking feature of the Western spirit, and seems almost definitive of its essence. "Emphasis on logical reason," says Radhakrishnan,

humanist ideals, social solidarity and national efficiency are the characteristic marks of the Western attitude to life. The outstanding epochs of Western culture—the Greek age, the Roman world before Constantine, the period of the Renaissance, and our own times—bear witness to the great tradition founded on reason and science, on ordered knowledge of the powers and possibilities of physical nature, and of man conceived as a psycho-physical organism, on an ordered use of that knowledge for a progressive social efficiency and well-being which will make the brief life of man more easy and comfortable.[11]

There are some important exceptions to this generalization, to be sure, but we need not pause to itemize them, for its essential truth is irrefutable. It calls attention to the fact that the naturalistic and humanistic strain in Western culture has had and is having a far wider audience than it ever enjoyed in the East. Moreover, though there have been and are other important strands in Western culture, it is the persistence of naturalism and its latter day expansion which strike the Indian thinker as the diagnostic trait of Western civilization, and as the element in it which he finds hardest to reconcile with his own traditions. In respect of each of the four sets of ideas which constitute the characteristic claims of the naturalistic philosophy, he is forced to enter a protest; he can accept neither naturalism's epistemological foundation, nor its metaphysical

11 EWR, 57.

doctrine of the nature of the ultimately real, nor its psychological account of the being of man, nor finally its views of man's ultimate good and the mode of attaining to it.

1. All knowledge, Radhakrishnan would agree, does indeed arise out of experience and refer ultimately to it; but the delimitation of experience to scientific experience is not *empiricism* but *apriorism*. There is no first principle which permits of the deduction that only through the senses may the real be apprehended. There is no way of legislating in advance what the form or the content of experience must be. The "postulate of empirical thought" asserts that through the senses alone do we contact reality, that all data are in the last analysis sense data, that we see only with the eyes of the body. But, if this means anything more than the tautology that sense knowledge must be based on the senses, then it is a dogmatic and unproven circumscription of the scope of possible experience. The Indian tradition has throughout its history admitted non-sensuous modes of givenness. Deny the reality of super-sensory vision, and Radhakrishnan's case for spiritualism completely collapses. "If," he admits, "all knowledge were of the scientific type, the contemporary challenge to religion would seem to be conclusive. The problem thus narrows itself down to the reality of intuitive knowledge and the conditions of its validity." [12] On the other hand, once affirm the reality of non-sensuous types of immediacy, and empiricism is no longer a defensible position. For, as Kant recognized, all of empiricism as well as the whole of the Critical Philosophy rests on the axiom which cannot possibly be proven that "We are so constituted that our intuition must always be sensuous. . . . Without sensibility, objects would not be given to us." [13]

Radhakrishnan is in fullest sympathy with the essential import of the verifiability principle, but not with the particular interpretation of it which the logical positivist makes. It is quite true that all meaningful assertions must be capable of some verification, and it is no part of philosophy to accept faith, dogma or authority as evidence for any claim. But why insist that verification is necessarily of one sort only, and that it inexorably demands an ultimate reference to the data of the senses? The positivist's contention is not merely that all meaningful statements must be verifiable, but that they must be amenable to *verification in terms of sense ex-*

12 IVL, 127.
13 Kant, I., *Critique of Pure Reason*, tr. by F. M. Müller (New York, 1949), 41.

perience. The intent of positivism is to ground all meaning ultimately in sensation.

The spiritual view of life, Radhakrishnan would insist, most certainly does have the support of experience, but experience conceived of in broader terms than those which are acknowledged by the naturalist. The particular mode of experience on which the spiritual view rests claims to be of a uniquely self-authenticating sort, and for this reason the naturalist has refused to recognize it as a valid mode of knowing. Radhakrishnan generally employs the term *intuition* to designate this special form of cognition; but his usage in this matter is not altogether consistent, for sometimes he also uses it to signify any non-sensuous knowledge which comes with immediacy. But as indicating the foundational experience on which the spiritual view of life is erected, it refers to what has otherwise been called *the mystical experience, supreme enlightenment* or *bodhi, prajña* or *transcendental wisdom, scientia intuitiva, absolute knowledge,* the *beatific vision.* It is the highest level of consciousness to which man can attain; it is the supreme integral experience. It is not merely a mode of knowing but a mode of being. It claims to accomplish a union of the mind with that which is ultimate in the nature of things, and it involves a oneness between the knower and the known of a sort which never occurs in ordinary experience. It is absolute and indubitable, and utterly transcends the power of concepts to convey. As Spinoza, for instance, describes it, this supreme type of knowing does not consist in being persuaded by rational argument, but in an unmediated union with the thing known. ". . . this kind of knowledge does not result from something else but from a direct revelation of the object itself to the understanding." [14] "From this third kind of knowledge arises the highest possible peace of mind." [15]

The layman commonly recognizes only the conscious level of rational, discursive knowing. Lately, we have been compelled to acknowledge another portion of ourselves which is sub-rational and sub-conscious. What Radhakrishnan and the entire mystical tradition point to is a level of experience which is not antithetical to reason but is rather super-rational and super-conscious. As reason integrates and completes the data of the senses, so does intuition stand in relation to reason. Says Radhakrishnan:

---

[14] Spinoza, B., *Short Treatise on God, Man and his Well-Being,* Ch. XXII.
[15] Spinoza, B., *Ethics,* V, xxvii.

Intuition is only the higher stage of intelligence, intelligence rid of its separatist and discursive tendencies.[16] Intuition is not an appeal to the subjective whims of the individual, or a dogmatic faculty of conscience, or the uncritical morbid views of a psychopath. It is the most complete experience we can possibly have.[17] Though intuition lies beyond intellect, it is not contrary to it. It is called saṁyagjñāna, or perfect knowledge. Reflective knowledge is a preparation for this integral experience. . . . Intuition is not a-logical but supra-logical. It is the wisdom gained by the whole spirit which is above any mere fragment thereof, be it feeling or intellect.[18]

In other words, just as there is a level of immediate knowledge which is below the level of reason, so also, is there a higher mode of immediacy which is super-rational. Beyond scientific experience there is spiritual experience; and a genuine empiricism will take stock of all modes of experience and not confine itself to only one sort. Knowledge through concepts confirmed by sense-experience is the pattern of science, and in relation to its purposes this form of knowledge has by its eminent successes fully vindicated itself. But the success of the scientific method in relation to one area of experience implies nothing as to the possibility or feasibility of quite different approaches for totally different areas of experience. The spiritual view of life is founded on another sort of experience which is non-conceptual in its essence.

There is a knowledge which is different from the conceptual. . . . It is non-sensuous, immediate knowledge. Sense knowledge is not the only kind of immediate knowledge. As distinct from sense knowledge or pratyakṣa (literally presented to a sense), the Hindu thinkers use the term aparokṣa for the non-sensuous immediate knowledge. This intuitive knowledge arises from an intimate fusion of mind with reality. It is knowledge by being and not by senses or symbols. . . . In logical knowledge there is always the duality, the distinction between the knowledge of a thing and its being. . . . Knowing a thing and being it are different. So thought needs verification.[19]

Thought needs verification; but intuition as the highest mode of cognition is self-authenticating and free from the possibility of doubt. When, as in ordinary consciousness, thought and its object are two, then thought needs confirmation by reference to its object. But when, as in intuition, the subject and the object are one, then the experience has a self-containedness and refers to nothing be-

16 RR, 438.   17 Ibid., 439.
18 IVL, 147.   19 Ibid., 138.

yond itself. It does not require reference to the given for validation, because it is at one with the given.

It is of no use to try to conceive what this sort of experience is like in advance of actually having it. It can be known only by having it, not by conceiving of it. To insist that it must be capable of being conceived is to assume that all knowing is conceptual in character, and that precisely is the issue. Beyond noting that there is nothing inherently self-contradictory in such an experience and that it is therefore intrinsically possible, there is little one can do to demonstrate its actuality. If it does exist, its actuality can be known only by acquaintance and not by description. We cannot demonstrate to a congenitally blind person that there is such a thing as the experience of color; for the demonstration would not be intelligible to him unless he had a prior acquaintance with the nature of that whose existence was being proved, and this acquaintance, *ex hypothesi*, he does not have. It may be possible through surgery or otherwise to remove the impediments to his vision, and then he will come to see for himself. With the vision, no further demonstration will be necessary; without it, no demonstration is possible in the nature of the case. The analogy is not altogether apt, however; for there is this important difference to be noted. Opening the eyes of the body is not always possible and depends, among other requirements, also on the external knowledge and skill of a physician. The eyes of the soul, on the other hand, are opened through spiritual disciplines and exercises; whoever is willing honestly to submit himself to the experiment, therefore, may come to see for himself.

Implicit in all this is a quite different conception of the nature and function of philosophy from that which prevails in the West today. Philosophy here bases itself not merely on reason and sense, but culminates in a super-sensuous and super-rational spiritual experience. Philosophy eventuates in vision; and for the realization of this vision, certain discursive meditations as well as practical disciplines are necessary. Whether one would wish to limit philosophy to discursive thinking alone or to comprehend under it both rational thought and intuitive vision is of little moment. The important thing is that, for Radhakrishnan and the tradition which he represents, the ultimate goal is the beatific vision which is beyond words and concepts. Thus philosophy as discursive thinking is not merely an intellectual game, nor is it an end in itself; it is the pursuit of salvation, the striving for integral vision.

Philosophy as conceptual knowing is a preparation for intuitive insight, and an exposition of it when it arises. There is a need for logic and language; for the expression of all knowledge perceptual, conceptual, or intuitional requires the use of concepts. Only we have to remember that the rationalisation of experience is not its whole truth. The great truths of philosophy are not proved but seen. The philosophers convey to others visions by the machinery of logical proof.[20]

So, similarly, for Spinoza, the aim is to achieve the "third kind of knowledge" which leads to human freedom and bliss; the philosopher is not under obligation to explain everything, but to "consider those things only which may conduct us as it were by the hand to a knowledge of the human mind and its highest happiness."[21] Philosophy, for this tradition, is primarily *praxis,* and not merely *theoria.* In order that the eyes of the soul may be opened more is necessary than the development of cerebral virtuosity; a reorganization and reorientation of the whole being is necessary, and this cannot be accomplished without spiritual disciplines. The intellectual and the moral cannot be separated in the higher modes of knowing. This view is not, of course, unknown to the Western tradition; but in contemporary academic philosophy in the West it strikes a rather foreign note. Philosophical education is currently an enterprise which is wholly intellectual in character; its aim is to develop skill in manipulating concepts. That the higher reaches of philosophical insight are realized only in connection with a certain mode of life would hardly be agreed to by academic philosophers in the West today; but it has always been axiomatic in the tradition from which Radhakrishnan stems.

Because the objects are perceived only when our minds are trained, it does not follow that the objects are subjective. To see a rose we must turn our eyes in that direction. To realise the supreme spirit, a certain purifying of the mind is necessary. The reality of spirit is not invalidated simply because it is seen only by those who are pure in heart.[22]

In order to be informed in certain matters, it is first necessary to be transformed, and whoever is not willing to pay the price in terms of spiritual discipline must not expect to acquire the genuine article. In the impersonal study of objects, qualities of intellect alone are required, but in the higher matters, the state of the knower conditions what can be known. In fact, from Radhakrishnan's point of view, this is the chief significance of the ethical. The ethical is that which conduces to the unitive knowledge of ultimate

20 *Ibid.,* 152.   21 Spinoza, B., *Ethics,* Part II, Introduction.   22 IVL, 334.

reality. The immoral act is immoral because by its nature it makes for separateness and destroys the possibility of achieving the ultimate intuition.

The fundamental claim that there are degrees of knowledge, and that all knowing is not, as the naturalist has tended to claim, of one sort only, has been a perennial thesis of the so-called "great tradition" in the history of philosophy. In many different ways the attempt has been made by philosophers to give expression to this idea. It is not necessary to claim that the various classifications of the modes of knowing which have been proffered all agree in every detail, or that they are all accurate, or that the philosophers themselves have always had personal experience of the modes of knowing which they were attempting to describe;[23] but despite all, it is difficult to avoid being impressed by the amount of concurrence, and particularly by the widespread agreement with reference to the existence of a supreme mode of intuitive knowing. Add to the voices of the philosophers the claims of the mystics, and you are presented with a massive testimony which cannot be lightly dismissed. However unused to this sort of thing the empirico-naturalist may be, however little it answers to anything in his own personal experience, he must at the very least concede it as a possibility. And in view of the quality of the men who have claimed the experience, he must even allow that it may be more than a bare possibility. Referring to the mystical experience in his *Varieties of Religious Experience,* William James wrote:

The overcoming of all the usual barriers between the individual and the Absolute is the great mystic achievement. In mystic states we become one with the Absolute and we become aware of our oneness. This is the everlasting and triumphant mystical tradition, hardly altered by differences of clime and creed. In Hinduism, in Neoplatonism, in Sufism, in Christian mysticism, in Whitmanism, we have the same recurring note, so that there is about mystical utterance an eternal unanimity which ought to make a critic stop and think, and which brings it about that the mystic classics have, as has been said, neither birthday nor native land. Perpetually telling of the unity of man and God, their speech antedates language, nor do they grow old.[24]

As against the naturalistic epistemology, then, Radhakrishnan would contend that there is a super-conscious level of intuitive

---

[23] Thus it is extremely doubtful that Bergson, in his earlier discussions of intuition was directly acquainted with the type of experience for which he was arguing. In the later *Two Sources of Morality and Religion,* he in effect admits that the mystical experience is the supreme example of intuition.

[24] Quoted in IVL, 105f.

knowing in which the individual achieves union with ultimate reality. The content of this experience cannot be transcribed into the language of concepts, but it is a form of knowledge which is absolute and self-authenticating. It has been actually achieved by a relatively small number of human beings who made themselves pure in heart and poor in spirit, and it can be achieved by any who are willing and able to follow in their footsteps and accept the discipline which they have outlined.

2. The metaphysical account of things which is implicit or explicit in naturalism is also repudiated by Radhakrishnan on the grounds of the evidence provided by spiritual experience. Behind, within, over above the natural order there is the order of spiritual reality which is the presupposition and the completion of the natural. The relation between the Absolute and its appearances, the infinite and the finite, can never be rendered clear to the discursive understanding; it becomes intelligible only in the mystical experience. All attempts to construe it in precise terms are in the end futile, in that one of the terms of the relation transcends any categoreal description. The entire mystical tradition would be in perfect accord with Kant that the categories do not apply to the Unconditioned. In seeking to refer to the Absolute by means of ordinary discourse we can only stutter, or speak the language of myth, or tell a "likely story;" and when our analogies are pressed too hard, they will always break down. In the end we shall have to invite the questioner to look for himself. But, though impossible to delineate by means of conceptual language, the reality of a spiritual absolute is attested to by spiritual experience, and it has been the perennial theme of Indian philosophy. As Radhakrishnan says, "Throughout the history of Indian thought, the ideal of a world behind the ordinary world of human strivings, more real and more intangible, which is the true home of the human spirit has been haunting the Indian race." [25]

Philosophers and theologians have frequently attempted to establish by means of rational demonstration the existence of a spiritual absolute which underlies and sustains the natural order, and Radhakrishnan himself, on occasion, resorts to the arguments of natural theology. Thus he contends that,

The historical world of becoming is incapable of explanation from within itself. It is this fact that is brought out by the famous "proofs" for the existence of God. . . . The inadequacy of naturalism shows that

[25] Ind P, II, 766.

the world process with its order and creativity requires for its explanation a creative power.[26]

And again,

The view of mechanism that the world came into existence of its own and has come to be what it is, without any reason or purpose behind it all, does not seem to be quite satisfactory. Even if the world is a mechanism, the questions remain, what guides the mechanism? Who set it up? . . . The world process where everything depends on something else is not self-sufficient. Each event is what it is because of its relation to other events. We seek for something that is its own explanation, but we never get it. The world is an infinite series of conditioned events, but science cannot say why it is what it is. The value of the causal argument lies in that it insists that the finite universe demands a principle beyond itself to explain it. Science is a system of second causes which cannot describe the world adequately, much less account for it.[27]

But it is not at all clear to what extent Radhakrishnan would want to lean on arguments of this nature in view of his fundamental claim of the possibility of an intuitive vision of the ultimate spiritual reality. It does not seem that they are thrown in merely as a concession to Western philosophers addicted to rational argument, nor on the other hand does he seem to regard them as having an absolute logical cogency. But even if they are viewed as cogent, they are not completely sufficient for the real purpose which Radhakrishnan has in mind and which can be achieved only through the mystical experience. For the objective certainty that the Absolute exists is not the same thing as the beatific vision, nor does it have the same effects on the life of the individual. Radhakrishnan's intent may be to produce by means of logical arguments a degree of intellectual conviction sufficient to inspire the individual to take up the discipline which leads to the final realization.

Nevertheless, whether on the basis of intuition or argument or both, the idealistic view of life is committed to the primacy of spirit over matter. This does not mean *mentalism,* and Radhakrishnan is far from asserting that all things are of such stuff as ideas are made. The basic claim is merely that the universe is not a blind process, but a teleological one, and that the course of evolution is not accidental, but in some way the expression of purpose. That the realm of the physical is not self-sustaining, and that it is pervaded by purpose, and that it is the creation or manifestation of a spiritual order is the central tenet of his metaphysic.

---

26 IVL., 331.   27 *Ibid.,* 316.

3. Radhakrishnan's doctrine of the nature of the self, as his view of the nature of ultimate reality, takes its content and its validation ultimately from intuition. The self as knower, the ultimate subject of knowledge, cannot be known through the ordinary modes of knowing. In these, the subject of knowledge is ever in the invisible background, and only the object of knowledge is visible in the foreground. Here, too, Radhakrishnan would agree with Kant that the noumenal or transcendental ego cannot enter the field of ordinary consciousness or be known through the categories which define scientific experience. For Radhakrishnan metaphysics is ultimately a kind of autology; the culminating insight which is revealed in the nature of ultimate reality likewise discloses the ultimate nature of the self, as well as the relation of the self to the Self. Self-knowledge is not the beginning of wisdom but its final consummation, and it is the fruit of intuitive realization. However, it may be said that man is not merely a product of nature, and that his ultimate being is not merely the functioning of his body. There is that in him—a divine spark—which is the badge of his affiliation with the spiritual order. His task in life is to become awakened to what is divine in him and to come to know himself for what he really is. His ordinary conventional self is largely a husk which has been imposed on him; so far as his life is the product of stimuli and social forces, the behavioristic approach is applicable to him. But he has the possibility of awakening to his real inner nature and of growing into freedom and spiritual manhood. Just as nature conceals and symbolizes a deeper order, so there is a self deeper than the one which naturalistic psychology is aware of, and that which is deepest in man is of a piece with or akin to that which is ultimate in the nature of things. Salvation, liberation, enlightenment, spiritual freedom come from achieving union with ultimate reality, and the intuitive consciousness of this union is realized in the mystical experience. The ultimate subject is a reality in itself and not a natural product or an emergent from the social matrix. In the Indian tradition it is regarded as having neither beginning nor end. As Radhakrishnan puts the matter,

If there is one doctrine more than another which is characteristic of Hindu thought, it is the belief that there is an interior depth to the human soul, which, in its essence, is uncreated and deathless and absolutely real.[28]

28 ER, 83.

In all experience we have the duality between the subject experiencing and the object experienced. The subject of experience is said to be distinct from every moment of the experience. It is the persistent substratum which makes all knowledge, recognition and retention possible.[29]

The true subject or the self is not an object which we can find in knowledge for it is the very condition of knowledge. It is different from all objects, the body, the senses, the empirical self itself. We cannot make the subject the property of any substance or the effect of any cause, for it is the basis of all such relations. It is not the empirical self but the reality without which there could be no such thing as an empirical self. . . . To confuse the subject with the mind immersed in bodily experience prevents us from attaining complete comprehension of the object that appears to confront us. The true subject is the simple, self-subsistent, universal spirit which cannot be directly presented as the object. When Plato says that the mind in man is the offspring of the eternal world-mind, when Aristotle speaks of an 'active reason,' at the apex of the soul, which is divine and creative, when Kant distinguishes the synthetic principle from the merely empirical self, they are referring to the self as subject.[30]

Psychologically, then, Radhakrishnan is a dualist, and he regards the body not as the ultimate basis of the self but as its temporary habitation. The apparent dependence of the self on the body, and on the nervous system in particular, is only a *de facto* characteristic of the empirical self, and not a necessary characteristic of the metaphysical subject. The more immersed a person is in his empirical and conventional self and the less awakened he is to his real self, the more is he at the beck and call of his body. The more enlightened he becomes, the freer he becomes, the more is he able to transcend the brute laws of physiology by which he was enchained. He begins to control the body and make of it his instrument rather than allowing himself to be dragged about by it. There is no part of the body, not excluding the so-called involuntary muscles and organs, which cannot be brought under the control of his will. Even ordinary modes of knowing which rely on the nervous system and the receptor organs may be transcended by a super-sensuous form of cognition which operates apart from the nervous system. Man's subjection to his body is only the measure of his unenlightened state.

It follows from this that the disintegration of the body does not have as a necessary corollary the destruction of the real self,

[29] IVL, 269.　　　　[30] *Ibid.*, 270f.

The life of the human self does not centre in the body, though it uses the latter for the promotion of its purposes. . . . The death of the physical body does not mean dissipation of the self . . . an empirical conjunction is not a metaphysical necessity. If we require brains to think when we are embodied, it does not follow that we require brains to think even when we are disembodied.[31]

This life is but one stage in the growth of the self.

4. As the soul of man did not wholly originate out of nature or society so it cannot find complete fulfillment through nature or society. Man is called upon to adjust to the environment, to reality; but the total real environment includes the spiritual order as well as the natural and the social order, and so long as man has not made the supreme adjustment, his adjustment remains incomplete. Man's ultimate aim is to realize his union with God and/or the Absolute Reality. This is the *summum bonum;* it is the experience which dispels all doubts and dissipates all dissatisfaction; it brings consummate happiness and the peace that passeth understanding. At least a glimpse of it may be achieved in the present life through the mystical experience; alongside it, all the other satisfactions which life has to offer are temporary, and fragmentary; by means of it man is restored to wholeness and made free. Whether one speaks of salvation, liberation, enlightenment or the beatific vision, one intends to emphasize the fact that life is a training ground, in which man ought to be preparing himself for his last end—the achievement of super-consciousness. This is the aim of life, not the widest dispersal of creature comforts, or even the achievement of a social utopia, but the evocation of higher and intenser forms of consciousness. Life is a process of self-realization, of self-discovery and self-transformation. In Radhakrishnan's words,

The destiny of the human soul is to realize its oneness with the supreme. There is a difference between the substantial immanence and the conscious union which requires of the creature voluntary identification. If the substantial reality of the human soul abides in that quality which we call spirit, growth or spiritual life means conscious realization of the fundamental truth.[32]

Here as elsewhere, the final evidence for the validity of this claim comes only through the mystical intuition itself, but its truth is nevertheless hinted at by man's inquietude. The insatiability of human desire, man's inability to find ultimate happiness or peace in any finite circumstance or combination of circumstances, that he perpetually "looks before and after and pines for what is not"

[31] *Ibid.,* 291.   [32] ER, 96.

—how is this basic fact of human psychology to be understood? Are we to interpret it as a "divine discontent" which signifies his affinity with another order, or does it signify merely that he is one of nature's freaks? Is there anything at all which will still the residual restlessness of the human heart? ". . . thou has created us for thyself," says Augustine, "and our heart cannot be quieted till it may find repose in thee." With this interpretation of the fact of man's inquietude, Radhakrishnan agrees. "It is because the universal spirit which is higher than the self-conscious individual is present and operative in self-conscious mind that the latter is dissatisfied with any finite form it may assume." [33] Man's inability to achieve perfect contentment in the finite, his unquenchable longing for consummate happiness may be taken as indicative of his supernatural destiny. It is the seal of his creator and serves perpetually to remind him who he is.

If this be the nature of man, then it is naive to suppose that he will ever find lasting peace in the pursuit of purely humanistic and social ends. So far as they lead to an expansion of self, they are all to the good, but when they become ends in themselves then they are distractions which tempt man away from his true mission in life.

"It is one of the illusions of modern life," Radhakrishnan remarks,

to believe that the way to spiritual peace is through material goods, that we can win men's hearts by offering them material benefits. It is assumed that if everyone has complete material satisfaction, his desire for heaven and absolute values will be dissolved. . . . Even if the world becomes an earthly paradise dripping with milk and honey, even if cheap automobiles and radios are made accessible to all, we will not have peace of mind or true happiness. Men and women who have every comfort and convenience which a material civilization can give them are feeling frustrated as if they had been cheated out of something.[34]

That is not to say that the material or the social goals are to be ignored altogether, but merely that they cannot give the final meaning to man's life. It would be totally wrong to conclude that the aspirant for ultimate salvation may altogether overlook the affairs of this world and the needs of his fellowmen, as wrong as it would be for a beginner at the piano whose ultimate aim is to play Bach to conclude that he may as well skip the preliminary and intermediate exercises and begin at once to master Bach. This world is a training ground for the spirit, and life is a progression which passes

[33] IVL, 302.   [34] RS, 61.

through a series of stages. Concern for the welfare of others leads to a widening and deepening of the self, and is part of the process of growing out of selfishness which is one of the requisites for spiritual vision. Every mode of activity which leads us out of our narrow, constricted selves is all to the good. Devotion to a vocation, the rearing of a family, friendship, art, social intercourse, allegiance to a cause or to country, these may all further the process of self-naughting if they are rightly pursued. But, though instrumental, they cannot of themselves bring about the final peace which passeth understanding.

Only in this sense can Radhakrishnan be charged with otherworldliness and pessimism. Although this life supplies the opportunities for attaining to the ultimate goal, it is not itself the ultimate goal. But it is not on that account to be despised, nor are the satisfactions which this life has to offer to be spurned. They are positive goods, without being the ultimate goods; they are illusions only when they are mistaken for the highest satisfactions. When the finite pretends to absoluteness, then it is evil; but so long as it furthers the march towards the final goal and does not seek to restrain the pilgrim, it is good. With a fine sense for the *via media,* Radhakrishnan expresses the truly religious view of the significance of this life:

The distinctive feature of the Hindu view is that it does not look upon the development of mind, life, and body as the primary ends of life. Health and vigor of the body are essential for vital energy and mental satisfaction. As the expression of the spiritual, the perfection of the physical is an integral part of man's complete living. While it is desired to some extent for its own sake, it is desired more for its capacity to further human activity which has for its aim the discovery and expression of the divine in man. Similarly, we are not called upon to crush the natural impulses of human life or ignore the intellectual, emotional, and aesthetic sides of man's being, for they are a part of man's finer nature, and their development not only satisfies the individual but helps to express the spirit in him. The aim of ascetic discipline is the sanctification of the entire personality. Again, morality, individual and social, is not a mere rational ordering of man's relations with his fellows but is a means for his growing into the nature of spirit. . . . The power of the spiritual truth casts its light on the natural life of man and leads it to flower into its own profound spiritual significance. Such a view does not take away from the value of ordinary life, which becomes supremely important when it is felt to be instinct with the life of the spirit and a support for its expression.[35]

[35] ER, 99.

There are two false extremes into one or another of which it is very easy to fall: one is the view that this life is everything, the other is that this life is nothing. "Mysticism," as Radhakrishnan notes,

has its fanatics. . . . The theory of *māyā* has been interpreted in this negative sense so as to lend support to the doctrine that man's life has no real meaning, that it is a mistake of the soul. . . .

Such exaggerations are to be met with in mysticism, Eastern as well as Western. But Śaṁkara has nothing in common with people who will not accept the visible world any more than with those who will accept nothing else.[36]

If pessimism signifies the claim that this life and all it has to offer is a positive evil, a snare and a delusion, then Radhakrishnan can in no wise be accused of pessimism. But if it be pessimism to refuse *finally* to acquiesce in the satisfactions of the finite, and to continually press on in the search for that "real good having power to communicate itself, which would affect the mind singly, to the exclusion of all else; . . . the discovery and attainment of which would enable me to enjoy continuous, supreme, and unending happiness," [37] then Radhakrishnan and the entire religious tradition would have to own up to the charge of pessimism. It is not that they find life unsatisfactory, but that they fail to find it finally satisfactory. No stage short of the highest can serve as the final resting place, they claim, and every stage which is not the final stage must eventually be transcended. Less elegantly put, an egg is a fine thing, but it must not insist on remaining an egg too long.

In the last analysis, then, the moral life has an individualistic rather than a social orientation, or rather the latter is indirect and secondary. Self-perfection is the goal of life. The moral life is a process of self-perfecting and self-discovery and culminates in the beatific vision. The function of ethics is to fit us to see, and the seeing comes not in the nature of an external reward for good deeds, but as the natural result of the discipline itself—just as the ability to play a musical instrument with skill is the intrinsic result of long years of devoted practice. The ethical is not something superimposed on man from above by an arbitrary despot, by obeying which one pleases the despot and thus earns a reward in the hereafter; it is rather in the nature of an athletic exercising of the soul as a result of which its powers of vision are strengthened. Ethics is

[36] *Ibid.,* 99f.
[37] Spinoza, B., *On the Improvement of the Understanding.*

thus instrumental to the beatific vision, it is not an end in itself. One cannot attain spiritual stature without attending to the needs of his fellowmen and having genuine concern for them, but what ultimately constitutes the goodness of an act is that it makes man more fit for the final vision. That is good which promotes self-discovery, self-naughting and the realization of the true self; that is evil which intensifies separation, constricts man further in his finite individuality, and blinds him to ultimate reality. In Radhakrishnan's own words,

> The motive behind ethical practices is that of purging the soul of selfish impulses so that it may be fitted to receive the beatific vision. Spiritual strenuousness, meditation, the freeing of the mind from hatred, anger, and lust are emphasized. We must seek the eternal with all our power. . . . The perfecting of self is to pass from the narrow, constricted, individual life to the free, creative, spiritual life. It is to get our tangled lives into harmony with the great movement of reality. It is not to be unsociable or to despise the natural relationships of life or end in a type of self-centered spiritual megalomania.[38]

The concentration on self-perfection as man's highest task may seem to one who is accustomed to the naturalistic outlook as a species of subtle selfishness, and there is, of course, the danger that it may become this sort of thing. But properly understood, and properly pursued, it is the effort to achieve selflessness and union with the ultimate Self. On the one hand no progress can be made in this quest by selfishly ignoring the needs of others; the cultivation of love, understanding, and patience is indispensable for the realization of the highest goal; and these can be developed only in the context of a genuine concern for our fellowmen. At the same time, the Hindu would add that what the naturalist overlooks is that the significance of the help which we can render others is only in proportion to the stature we have ourselves attained. There are various forms of help which can be given; and the help given on the material level is not necessarily the most important or the most lasting. A man may be able to be of profound use to others in subtle ways, and may be able to bestow gifts of spiritual insight and regeneration without being outwardly active. One individual helps because of his deeds, another by his words, a third by his being.

If this task of perfecting oneself seems to a Western naturalist to be unworthy of so much thought and effort or as insufficient to occupy the whole of a person's life, it is only, Radhakrishnan would

[38] ER, 105.

say, because he has become so extraverted that he has lost awareness of the true dimensions of human life. He has come to believe that human nature can be regenerated by the behavioral experts; he has forgotten that the attainment of self-understanding and perfect integration is the most formidable task which any human being can set for himself. If our desire is merely to condition an individual to an average level of conventional goodness, we may perhaps feel safe in handing him over to the educationists and the psychologists. But if our aim is not merely to indoctrinate him with what Plato called "correct opinions," if it is our desire to bring him out of the cave and to accustom him to see the light, then "he must be required to take the longer circuit . . ." [39] Real selfhood and the deepest integration are not to be purchased cheaply. Self-knowledge is the most precious thing in life, but it can come finally only through the deepening of the self, and is not to be gleaned simply from the objective researches of the behavioral engineers. The nature of a subject is such that he must take a hand in his own making; he cannot simply be put together from without. The truth will indeed set him free; but it is a truth which can finally be won only through self-transformation.

It is only when we have this high goal in mind that we perceive the radical insufficiency of purely scientific or humanistic techniques for achieving it. We are aiming at the fullest development of man's highest potentialities. The man who has achieved spiritual liberation is almost of a new species. Humanism, to be sure, has produced fine and admirable human beings; but the difference between the finest fruit of humanistic cultivation and the saintly product of the religious life is so patent that it cannot be obscured by any argument. Between Confucius and Buddha, between Aristotle and St. Francis of Assisi, between Dewey and Gandhi, there is a difference not merely of degree but of kind. The people of one sort have an inner integration, a serenity, a spontaneity, a cosmic rootage which the people of the other sort lack altogether. The people of the one sort are "self-made men;" the people of the other sort seem to have tapped an unfailing reservoir from which they are constantly being refilled. As Radhakrishnan puts it,

Real love or will to good expresses itself in various forms, from sacrifice of oneself for one's neighbor to the acceptance of even those who offend us cruelly. All this is possible only if we do not sacrifice the mystical to the moral. The truly religious live out of a natural profundity

39 Plato, *Republic*, VI, 504d.

of soul; their effortless achievements are not primarily directed to a refashioning of this world. Their faith is essentially life-transcending, and as a result, life-transforming.[40]

It is only through spiritual discipline, and not through humanistic or scientific techniques that ultimate enlightenment can be obtained. The deficiency of humanism is observed not merely in its lack of motive power to attain the highest modes of consciousness, but in its very ignorance of their existence. Spiritual exercises alone create the awareness of the goal and provide the nourishment which enables the soul to grow towards it. And the liberated individual alone knows fully the secret of life and is enabled thereby to live in the world without being wholly of it. He is able to work with a detached attachment, to be concerned with the world without being wholly committed to it. He does not abandon the world, but strives perpetually to redeem it. Like the Buddha, he will not take the last step into Nirvana until all are ready to enter with him.

. . . the seer does not abstain from the work of the world but does it with his eyes fixed on the eternal. Religion is not a flight from the world, a taking refuge in the ordered serenity of heaven, in despair over the hopeless disorder of earth. Man belongs to both orders, and his religion is here or nowhere. Life eternal consists in another kind of life in the midst of time. Religious life is a rhythm with moments of contemplation, . . . and of action with a sense of mission in the world. Action of the seer is more efficient since it springs from conviction and depth and is carried out with poise and serenity.[41]

The lives of the liberated, then, are the visible fruits of their spiritual rootage, and in the end provide the most telling argument for the validity of the spiritual view of life. Not a rational argument to convince the intellect, perhaps, but an existential testimony which it is impossible to ignore and which may inspire the sceptic to follow their example. In their presence we cannot help but feel that "we are not whole men, real individuals, but wrecks of men, shells of individuals. Our responses are formal and our actions imitative. We are not souls but human automata. So our lives lack grace, depth and power." [42] Our lives, however, may begin to take on the qualities which characterize theirs as we become their practicing disciples, and, in the resulting process of spiritual growth, we may experience the increasing certainty that the spiritual view of life is no dream but rather the clue which helps us to find that which is most truly ours.

[40] IVL, 68.   [41] ER, 97.   [42] IVL, 211.

Such in briefest outline is the "idealist view of life" which Radhakrishnan offers. It will be recognized as falling within the tradition which has been called *philosophia perennis,* and its claim to fame is not based on the originality of its underlying ideas but on the manner in which they have been presented for our times. It was Charles Peirce who made the observation that in the matter of fundamental conceptions, originality is the least of recommendations, and the great propounders of the perennial philosophy have ever regarded themselves not as absolute innovators but as rediscovering the way which had been only temporarily lost. Radhakrishnan's high merit lies in his great ability to present this ancient doctrine in its essential purity, freed from the obscuring and partisan details which have so often attached themselves to it. Having thus been tendered the refined essence of the spiritual view, philosophers today will be the better able to assess its true worth.

The heart of the perennial philosophy, which beats in all of the great religions of the world and in many of its philosophical systems, consists of the claim that there is a spiritual Absolute, beyond the power of words to express, which is the ultimate reality underlying the visible world; that, in his inmost essence, man is akin to or an expression of this ultimate reality, and that man's final end lies in the realization of his union with the ultimate. Furthermore, this realization is itself partly the result and partly the cause of a radical transformation in the personality; it is the result and completion of a process of self-naughting in the course of which the self is slain in order that the Self may be found. The final realization comes in the form of an ineffable mystical experience, towards which words can point, but whose content they can in no wise capture, in which is achieved the unitive knowledge of the Unconditioned. At all times and in almost all places, there seem to have been at least a small number of persons who have had the mystical experience, and who have emerged from it strikingly transformed and endowed with an impressive inner strength and serenity.

In various ways, the religions of the world have attempted to give expression to this view of things. Rarely, if ever, have the historical institutionalized religions succeeded in maintaining the doctrine in its pure form; in their hands, it seems inevitably to revert to an ore-like state and to become overlaid by substances which are not of its essence. From this point of view, as Bergson has pointed out, organized religion is "the crystallization, brought about by a scientific process of cooling, of what mysticism had poured, while hot, into the soul of man. Through religion all men get a little of what a few privileged souls possessed in full." [43] Gradually the true worth and possibilities of the ore are forgotten, and some of the impurities contained therein are taken for the real metal which they obscure. Men begin to concern themselves with the exact nature of these impurities, erudite tomes are filled with their disputations, and prizes and honors are distributed to those who can discourse most learnedly about them. Rival schools are formed and indulge in fierce controversy. Meanwhile the real secret of the ore is forgotten, forgotten until such time as the ore is once again run through the melting pot and the impurities are burned out of it in the heat of a mystic's experience. Then, once more, men may get a glimpse of the precious metal itself.

Once grant the reality of the mystic experience, and both the sceptic and the believer are seen to be in the right. The one is certain that he has in his possession something which is of great worth, and yet he has no way of demonstrating its worth, since he has no idea how to refine the metal and to extract its essence. The sceptic is equally certain that what is being proffered him is no precious metal but only a form of earth, and he is inclined to ridicule the believer for cherishing it so highly. This is the tragi-comedy which is perpetually being re-enacted in the history of religion.

The history of philosophy, from this point of view, presents a similar spectacle. Suppose that an occasional philosopher realizes the intuitive vision. Fully aware of the limitations of conceptual language, he will often be loath to write of his deepest experiences, as Plato indicated in his Seventh Epistle, or as did Aquinas when he put down his pen and refused to complete the *Summa Theologica*, explaining that in comparison with what he had seen all that he had written was as straw. If he should attempt to give an indication of the content of his experience it would likely be couched in the language of metaphor and paradox. He will regard words as mere signposts which indicate the general direction of the goal, but which must never be confused with the goal. But the inheritors of his works become more and more interested in the signposts themselves. They discuss the shapes of the signposts, the wood out of which they are constructed, and before long, doctoral dissertations are being written on the comparative merits of different varieties of wood in the construction of signposts. The language of the signposts comes in for the most minute analysis, and enormously com-

[43] Bergson, H., *The Two Sources of Morality and Religion*, tr. by Audra, Brereton and Carter (New York, 1935), 227.

plicated systems of thought are squeezed out of the words written on the signposts, which in turn give rise to commentaries and to commentaries on commentaries. The real intent of the words, which was merely to convey a general sense of direction and to urge the traveller to be on his way, has been altogether lost, but the formulas themselves are regarded as having singular intrinsic significance. Until one fine day the logical positivist arrives on the scene and with a smile on his face asks, "Gentlemen, what are you talking about? You have words, myriads of words, but to what do they refer? You make assertions of all kinds—how do you propose to verify them?" And who is prepared to say that his demand for verification is an unjustifiable one?

If there is such a thing as the perennial philosophy, and if man is what he is declared to be in this philosophy, then the marches and countermarches in the history of philosophy take on meaning. The age-old controversy between the relativist and the absolutist, the sceptic and the dogmatist, the empiricist and the rationalist, the nominalist and the realist, the materialist and the idealist, the naturalist and the supernaturalist is exactly what one might have expected. Both sides to the controversy are partially right and partially wrong. The one side is correct in its claim that there is something to be had, but it does not know how to describe it. The other rightly insists that the treasure is not actually at hand, but it does not realize that it is to be had. This would account for the circumstance in the history of philosophy which so greatly puzzled Kant —the endless conflict between the two parties. Kant often refers to the strange paradox that human reason seems perpetually driven to seek that which by its nature it cannot attain. In the face of endless attack and refutation, the metaphysician presses on and seeks to give expression to the Unconditioned, and is oblivious of the fact that he is doomed in advance to failure. He can neither attain what he seeks nor can he give up the quest. From the standpoint of the perennial philosophy, both his striving and his lack of success can be accounted for. He strives because he feels the magnetic lure of the Absolute which is really there; he fails because he is seeking to reach by dialectical skill what can only become apparent to the purified spiritual consciousness. And the empiricist, the naturalist, the positivist are all within their rights in perpetually reminding the metaphysician of his lack of success; their mistake is in failing to realize that their arguments are telling merely against the metaphysician and not against that which is the object of his quest. They are in error in that they are totally unaware that the object itself is real, and that it may be possessed by those who are prepared to fulfill the conditions it imposes. They become dogmatic in their turn when they propose to exclude from the realm of the real whatever falls outside the limits of their own—perhaps all too limited—experience.

But all this is on the assumption that the perennial philosophy is in fact true; and since, in the end, its truth hinges on the testimony of the mystic, the validity of intuitive spiritual experience is the finally crucial question. As Radhakrishnan has clearly admitted, if scientific experience alone is reliable, if we see only with the eyes of the body, then no real validation of the perennial philosophy is possible. The issue between the naturalist and the spiritualist thus comes, in the last analysis, to revolve about the status of intuition.

What position is the naturalist to maintain *vis-a-vis* the mystic claim? Or, more generally, how is naturalism as a philosophical doctrine to be validated? This is a fundamental question which seems hardly to have received the attention it deserves. Is naturalism a credo or is it the result of reasoned argument—does it rest on faith or on reason? One must confess that in the writings of contemporary naturalists argument is conspicuous largely by its absence. It tends to be replaced by bold assertion or by appeals to the prestige of science. But, if naturalism is only a credo, then it can hardly afford to look down on other credos. If naturalism is only one of several possible ultimate frames of reference, the choice of any one of which is in the end an arbitrary matter, then it is in no secure position to attack its alternatives. The decision to limit oneself to sense-experience offers in itself no ruling as to the possibility of other kinds of experience. Moreover, what is somewhat disheartening in contemporary Western philosophy is the spectacle of the several schools unable and unwilling to come to grips with the fundamental issues which divide them. Each contents itself with deducing the implications of the fundamental position which it has already assumed; but none seems prepared to examine the fundamental issues themselves with a view to effecting a possible reconciliation between them.

When naturalism has attempted to present an argument, it has generally been negative rather than positive in form. The attempt has been to disqualify supernaturalism as an alternative rather than positively to demonstrate the truth of naturalism. Often, in place of argument, the naturalist is content to point to the tremendous successes of science. A large part of Professor Dewey's philosophy consists in constantly reiterating the claim that, from the spectacular results obtained by applying science to the realm of nature, we may infer that equally impressive victories will be gained by applying the method of science to human nature. The obsequious eulogizing of science which is characteristic of much contemporary naturalism is hardly salutary. It reflects a certain existential timidity, and seems to stem from the conviction that it is better, after all, to shine by the reflected glory of the established sciences, than to risk a venture into unfamiliar terrain. There are many philosophers who reveal a timorousness with respect to science which reminds one of the servility to theology exhibited by the degenerate scholastics of the late Middle Ages.

That supernaturalism is a gratuitous hypothesis as far as science is concerned will be readily granted. That it has no heuristic value in this area, and that it may easily discourage research and experimentation need not be denied. Only, by the same token, one must also allow for the possibility that the hypothesis of naturalism will not take one very far in the direction of things spiritual, that it similarly discourages research and experimentation in the realm of spirit by focussing its exclusive attention on objects and outwardness instead of on subjects and inwardness. As science tends to atrophy in an atmophere of exclusive devotion to the things of the spirit, so spiritual insight progressively diminishes in the context of sensory object-mindedness.

The uncautious naturalist may advance the contention that the intuitive mystical experience is an intrinsic impossibility, and that science is the only possible method of knowledge. But this would be merely a statement of his position and no argument for it. For, on what grounds is the possibility of the mystic's experience to be ruled out? There is nothing in the nature of scientific method as such which precludes the possibility of other methods, any more than there is anything in the nature of a microscope which rules out the possibility of a telescope. If one were in a position to see that the whole of reality consisted exclusively of the realm of experience which the sciences explore, then and only then could one rule out mysticism on the grounds that it made no contact with anything real. But such an all-embracing insight the naturalist does not have, and in its absence it is surely begging the question to contend that the mystical experience does not refer to anything real because it does not refer to the realm of scientific experience.

Or again, the claim may be entered that the mystic's assertions are meaningless. But here too, unless one is prepared to defend one's criterion of the meaningful, one is similarly assuming the very point at issue. That all cognitive meaning must be grounded in sensation is itself either a dogma or else an example of a self-authenticating non-sensuous intuition. Any philosopher, of course, is perfectly within his rights in avowing that for him, personally, the mystic claim is not intelligible. That is an understandable psychological fact; but it is of merely autobiographical interest and surely not a matter of philosophical principle. What such an individual should recognize, however, is that what disturbs him in the mystic experience, namely its ineffability, is in fact also characteristic of sense-experience itself, the possibility of which latter he never thought of disallowing, however. Givenness is always ineffable; it can be pointed to by words, but words cannot convey it directly. All discourse ultimately carries back to an ostensive step, and at that point we have merely to behold. In this respect the mystic's vision is in no whit different from any other kind of seeing; it is not being disqualified because it is a "seeing," but only because it is not a "seeing" *via* the organs of sense. The positivist cannot wish to exclude "seeing" as such; his desire is merely to rule out all extra-sensory perception, and this he does not by reasoned argument, but by *fiat* or *a priori*.

But the more sophisticated naturalist will content himself with the stand that the *onus probandi* is on the supernaturalist to exhibit the reality of the realm of spirit. The naturalist need not assume the burden of categorically denying the possibility that such a realm may exist; but in the absence of any convincing demonstration there is no need to affirm its existence. Philosophy consists not of bare possibilities, but of established truths. With this thesis, Radhakrishnan would in principle agree. The request for some kind of verification cannot be dismissed as unreasonable; in the absence of all verification the adoption of a philosophical position would be a purely arbitrary matter. However, though no one can object to the general intent of the request for verification, its usual detailed specifications serve to poison the wells of the spiritualist. For it soon turns out that the naturalist is insisting that the demonstration shall be in his own terms, and that there can be but one sort of significant demonstration. On the one hand the naturalist invites the spiritualist to play the game in order to decide who is the winner. But when the supernaturalist sits down at the table, he is informed that the game must be played in accordance with the rules set up by the naturalist, and he observes that these rules are such as to guarantee in advance his own defeat. This is apparent, for example, in the following remark, which is quite typical of contemporary naturalism:

As for decreeing what does or can *exist,* there is nothing in scientific method that *forbids* anything to exist. It concerns itself with the responsibility of the assertions that proclaim the existence of anything. It does not jeer at the mystical swoon of rapture; it only denies the mystic's retrospective cognitive claims for which no evidence is offered except the fact of trance.[44]

True it is that scientific method does not forbid anything to exist. Neither does a microscope forbid the nebula to exist; but the claim that all responsible statements must rest on microscopic evidence would rule out statements about the nebula, just as Hook's restriction of responsible statements to those subject to scientific confirmation would settle in advance the question of the significance of the mystical experience. To insist that "responsibility" is to be defined in terms of the canons of science, and to exclude *ab initio* whatever does not conform to those canons, is not to decide the matter of whether science is in fact the only reliable mode of knowing; it is merely to beg the whole issue. This is made even clearer when Hook goes on to say:

I do not see that anything is gained by blinking the fact that the naturalist denies the existence of supernatural powers. . . . Nor need he pass as an agnostic except in those situations in which the weight of evidence is equally balanced and he suspends judgment until such time as more evidence is available. But if he is faithful to his method, he must assert that for every traditional conception of God, the weight of evidence so far is decidedly in the negative. So long as no self-contradictory notions are advanced, he will not rule out the abstract possibility that angelic creatures push the planets any more than that there exists a gingerbread castle on the other side of the moon. . . . Here as elsewhere, the naturalist must follow the preponderance of scientific evidence. He therefore welcomes those who talk about the experiential evidence for religious beliefs as distinct from those who begin with mystery and end in mystery. He only asks to be given an opportunity to examine the evidence and to evaluate it by the same general canons which have led to the great triumphs of knowledge in the past. . . . Unfortunately for all their talk of appeal to experience, direct or indirect, religious experientialists dare not appeal to any experience of sufficiently determinate character. . . . There is a certain wisdom in this reluctance. For if experience can confirm a belief, it can also invalidate it. But to most supernaturalists this is an inadmissible possibility. We

44 Hook, S., in *Naturalism and the Human Spirit,* 42.

therefore find that the kind of experience to which reference is made is not only unique but also uniquely self-authenticating. Those who are not blessed by the experiences are regarded as blind or deaf or worse! But is it not odd that those who worship Zeus on the ground of a unique experience should deny to others the right to worship Odin on the ground of a different unique experience.[45]

The references to Odin and Zeus as well as to angelic creatures and gingerbread castles are hardly a significant contribution to the argument. It is no part of the spiritualistic view of life to claim that organized religions have in all their details adequately voiced the perennial philosophy. Radhakrishnan, in particular, is never committed to defending the enshrined dogmas of any historical creed; he recognizes full well, as any reasonable person must, that if there is a core in all religion which expresses the perennial philosophy, there is also generally a rind of considerable thickness. The only worthwhile question concerns the nature and validity of the central claim. Let us, then, have done with gingerbread castles, and let us not glory in the refutation of the worshippers of Odin. If we need witnesses, let us call rather on Buddha, Lao Tzu, Jesus, Plato, Socrates, Plotinus, Spinoza, Aquinas, Pascal, and others of this sort. Should we find that the genuine article is one of those "excellent things" which "are as difficult as they are rare" then we should not be astonished that it has inspired so many shoddy imitations.

But how may we determine if there is such a genuine article; how may we avoid the danger of being duped? Only, according to Hook, if we are given the "opportunity to examine the evidence and to evaluate it by the same general canons which have led to the great triumphs of knowledge in the past." By thus playing it safe, the naturalist seeks to assure himself that he will not be duped. In rejecting all claims which do not pass scientific inspection, he will never fall prey to delusion. But now suppose it to be the case in this area, as in others, that where nothing is risked nothing will be gained—except safety from danger. Suppose there is a great treasure to be discovered, but that it lies far from the well-travelled and familiar trails; how will it ever be found by those who refuse to venture away from the roads to which they are accustomed? Does it not require a stout heart and a dauntless spirit to pioneer in uncharted territories?

"So that is what you are getting at;" the naturalist breaks in, "you are presenting me with the argument of James' *Will to Believe*, and seeking to confront me with the terms of Pascal's wager.

[45] *Ibid.*, 45f.

But I would have you know that I do not regard wishful thinking or cosmic betting as philosophically compelling arguments."

"No, I am not exactly duplicating the argument of James or Pascal, because, although I believe they did have a similar point in mind, they obscured its real meaning by presenting it as though it were an argument. I am not calling upon you to accept any argument or to take anything on faith. I merely ask that you be willing to experiment, and that you exclude no mode of experience in advance of experiment, in other words, that you be a genuine empiricist."

"Well, then, you are agreeing to my terms after all, are you not? You propose to give me the 'opportunity to examine the evidence and to evaluate it by the same general canons which have led to the great triumphs of knowledge in the past.'"

"No, not exactly. I would have you see that experiments are not all of one sort, and that the type of experiment which is to be conducted is determined by the nature of the material being examined. You are acquainted with experiments of the objective variety, in which the experiment is conducted upon something external to the experimenter himself. He remains on the sidelines, unaffected by the process of the experiment; his judgment is suspended until the outcome of the experiment is objectively certain. This is the safe sort of experiment to which you are committed; it entails no risk for the experimenter and his being is not put into any jeopardy. What you call 'scientific method' involves this sort of experimentation, even when it is applied to such a field as psychology. So long as one is dealing with the objective or intersubjective order of things, this approach is feasible. But now suppose there is a realm which does not belong to the order of objects, and suppose it to be of such a character that it is to be apprehended by us only on condition that we have first undergone a radical subjective transformation. In other words, suppose that we are called upon to experiment on our inmost selves, and that unless we are prepared to undergo the experiment with its attendant risks we can in no wise make contact with the realities we are seeking. Suppose that the data can neither be obtained nor interpreted except by those who are willing to fulfill the conditions called for, and which all conduce to the noughting of the self. This requirement is after all not altogether strange to you; to a lesser degree you meet with it in the field of the sciences. When you hold that a scientific principle is objectively confirmable, you do not mean to imply that simply anyone whatsoever can confirm it with a passing glance, but only that person who has had the training, experience, and necessary scientific equipment to fit him to judge of the matter at hand. Likewise, in the matter of the mystic's claim, though the qualifications demanded are of another sort and involve much more than intellectual training, we are not dealing with anything which is *intrinsically* unverifiable, but only with something which cannot be verified by those who refuse to transform themselves into qualified judges. You cannot preclude this possibility simply by *fiat* or by definition. The mystic claim is that there are things to be known in addition to what can be known of the objective order; how can this claim be ruled out except by the dogmatic declaration that it cannot be? I am not accusing you of being 'blind or deaf or worse' because you do not immediately apprehend the truth, any more than I should accuse a person who had no introduction to music or painting of being deaf or blind because he did not at the first acquaintance perceive the beauties of a great symphony or a great painting. I merely assert that there is something to be known and that you must be rendered fit to know it, or as the medievals would have put it, that all knowing is according to the mode of the knower. Your blindness, if blindness it be, is only temporary, but not intrinsic to your nature. It can be removed by a certain kind of therapy—a radical psychotherapy by the side of which what ordinarily passes under that name is the most superficial of things— which will result in a deep reorganization of your being, evoke potentialities in you of whose existence you do not now dream, and give you an awareness of things which at the moment are completely outside your ken."

"Well, what you have been saying is most interesting, and I see that I cannot dismiss it as a possibility, but if you would only prove to me that it is actually so, then I should not be averse to putting myself in your hands and submitting to the experiment."

"By your question you show that you have not yet understood the mystic's existentialist claim, which is that in this area, the thing you want cannot be had in advance nor without the willingness to experiment with your entire life. The knowledge you seek can only be evolved from within with the deepening of subjectivity; it cannot be imposed from without in the manner of objective data. This has always been the fundamental thesis of religious existentialism, and one may see it clearly expressed in the teaching methods adopted by such pathfinders as Buddha and Jesus, Kierkegaard and Socrates. The attempt to communicate their insights is always 'indirect;' the aim is not to transmit objective information but to induce the disciple to undertake the discipline of self-transformation which will in the end enable him to see for himself and in the absence of which it would do no good to tell him anything. This is what Kierkegaard had in mind when he declared that *Truth is subjectivity.* In your present state, neither the experiences themselves nor their interpretation are available to you; they will begin to become available to you as you enter on and proceed along the Path. I must caution you, though, that the Path is not to be lightly entered upon. The undertaking is the most formidable task which any human being can set for himself. Do not be misled by the doctrines and methods of the organized creeds; for, as Dostoievsky said, they have 'corrected' the pure teaching in order to render it less formidable for the mass of men. Nevertheless, however difficult and whatever the risks, this is the way along which we must proceed, if we are really in earnest—the way indicated by the great expounders of the perennial philosophy." The whole idea has been well and clearly put by Huxley:

Of the significant and pleasurable experiences of life only the simplest are open indiscriminately to all. The rest cannot be had except by those who have undergone a suitable training. . . . A man who has trained himself in goodness comes to have certain direct intuitions about character, about the relations between human beings, about his own position in the world—intuitions that are quite different from the intuitions of the average sensual man. Knowledge is always a function of being. What we perceive and understand depends on what we are; and what we are depends partly on circumstances, partly, and more profoundly, on the nature of the efforts we have made to realize our ideal and the nature of the ideal we have tried to realize. . . . In view of the fact that knowing is conditioned by being and that being can be profoundly modified by training, we are justified in ignoring most of the arguments by which non-mystics have sought to discredit the experience of mystics. The being of a colour-blind man is such that he is not competent to pass judgment on a painting. The colour-blind man cannot be educated into seeing colours, and in this respect he is different from the Indian musician, who begins by finding European symphonies merely deafening and bewildering, but can be trained, if he so desires, to perceive the beauties of this kind of music. Similarly, the being of a non-mystical person is such that he cannot understand the nature of the mystic's intuitions. Like the Indian musician, however, he is at liberty, if he so chooses, to have some kind of direct experience of what at present he does not understand. This training is one which he will certainly find extremely tedious; for it involves, first, the leading of a life of constant awareness and unremitting moral effort, second, steady practice in the technique of meditation, which is probably about as difficult as the technique of violin-playing. But, however tedious, the training can be undertaken by anyone who wishes to do so. Those who have not undertaken the training can have no knowledge of the kind of experiences open to those who have undertaken it and are as little justified in denying the validity of those direct intuitions of an ultimate spiritual reality, at once transcendent and immanent, as were the Pisan professors who denied, on *a priori* grounds, the validity of Galileo's direct intuition (made possible by the telescope) of the fact that Jupiter has several moons.[46]

"It appears then, you see, that man is confronted by a most uncomfortable situation. The highest treasure may be his, but there is no way in which he can assure himself of its existence except by risking his life in the search for it. If what Plato, Buddha, and the others have been claiming is in fact true about the ultimate nature of reality and man's relation to it, then in not submitting oneself to the experiment one stands to lose all. If Plato and the others were the victims of a delusion, then by engaging in the experiment one stands to lose certain goods which are at hand. If you do not try, you will never find out how things stand; if you do try, you may fritter your life away pursuing a will-o-the-wisp. But this is man's lot. This is the existential situation.

"The mystic asserts that there are modes of experience which can be had only as man attains a certain spiritual stature. If you refuse to grow until you are first objectively convinced that these modes of experience exist, then in the nature of the case—if he is right— you will never come to know anything at all about them. It is as though a man insisted in knowing fully about a woman as a condition of marrying her, when in fact there are inevitably things about her which he (and she) can come to apprehend only in the course of the marriage. To take such an initial stand in this instance would merely be to rule out marriage as a possibility. Again, there are questions which a two-year-old child may ask concerning adult life. The adult to whom the questions are put may know that the child cannot possibly understand the true import of the question he asks, much less appreciate the true answer. There is no way around such a situation—the child will simply have to wait until he grows up. Meanwhile the adult may put him off with a likely story or a parable. Now suppose there are some human beings, who, in respect to the level of consciousness which they have attained, stand to the average adult as he in turn stands to the child.

[46] Huxley, Aldous, *Ends and Means*, cited in Phillips, Nixon, and Howe, *The Choice is Always Ours* (New York, 1948), 191f.

They would full well be able to communicate with each other, but they could not significantly communicate with those who are not yet of their stature. If, out of charity towards their fellowmen, they endeavor to speak, they must resort to the language of myth and symbol and paradox, and they will hardly succeed in conveying very much to their listeners."

"Suppose, suppose, suppose! But how do I know this supposition, on which your whole case rests, is a true one?"

"You cannot know except in the way I have indicated. I am not asking you to take the supposition as true on pure faith, nor am I attempting to demonstrate its truth to you objectively. I merely want you to see that, if it is true, you would never be enabled to find it out for yourself so long as you took the stand that it must be capable of being checked 'by the same general canons which have led to the great triumphs of knowledge in the past.' On the level of pure theory, it would matter not a whit whether you were a naturalist or a spiritualist, and I should have no interest in trying to convince you of the objective truth of the one as against the other. But we are not involved in pure theory, and the naturalistic stand which you have taken commits you solely to experiments of the objective type. If you persist in it, you will never come around to trying the other type of experiment.

"The choice is ultimately yours, and you cannot be compelled to experiment with your life. If you are not prepared to make the attempt, that is, of course, entirely your affair; only, I beg of you, do not seek to rationalize your decision by deprecatory references to Zeus and gingerbread castles. And further, you ought in any case not be under the illusion that thus you are playing it safe; for then you would once again be missing the point of the mystic's claim. The risk is equally great whether one ventures forth or whether one stays at home; as in the one case one may be seeking what is not to be had, so in the other case one may not be seeking what is to be had. There is no way of removing from human life the risk which is inherent in it."

In some such way as this one might seek to elaborate the full import of the position to which Radhakrishnan is committed with its ultimate reliance on mystical intuition. The existentialist point of view, which refuses to separate theory and practice, and which makes of philosophy not a conceptual doctrine but a mode of life— of living in the highest—has always been a part of the Indian mystical tradition and is at least as old as the *Upaniṣads*. The desire to know God by acquaintance and not merely by description, the concentration on inner realization rather than on objective argument have been its characteristic features. Once take the view that philosophy ultimately rests on and culminates in vision, and the concern of the philosopher is to achieve the vision rather than to engage endlessly in argument about it.

The modern mind is rooted in the objective point of view, and does not take with ease to the existentialist claim with its emphasis on subjectivity and its demand for a "leap" into the unknown. Is there nothing objective by which one may be guided? How distinguish what the mystic calls the ultimate vision from an ordinary illusion? These are the questions which the claim invariably provokes, and they reveal how little of the real meaning of the claim has been absorbed. By such questions as these, the naturalist reveals himself as wanting to comprehend the ultimate experience without actually undergoing it; he is anxious to get a preview of coming attractions that he may determine in advance whether the performance is worth attending. Without first becoming transformed himself, he seeks a glimpse into the mode of consciousness possessed by those who have been transformed; and this in the nature of the case he can never get. The question—by what signs may the ultimate experience be known and distinguished from a merely hallucinatory experience—shows not merely that the questioner has not yet had the experience, but that he has not so much as grasped what is the claim of the mystic with respect to this experience. He is still thinking of it as another experience of the same general sort as those to which he is already accustomed; else he would not ask the question about that experience which claims to be uniquely self-authenticating, and to be the ultimate cognitive experience involving an immediate union with the source of all cognition. He may, of course, deny that there is any such experience; but it is naive to ask that its actuality be demonstrated by reference to ordinary experience.

But, if there is no objectively binding proof of the reality of the mystic's experience, why, then, should one seek it? There is no objectively compelling reason for seeking it. Given an individual who is perfectly content with his life as it is, who is constantly in a state of ecstatic bliss, who finds himself in the continuous possession of everything his heart desires, who is not in the slightest degree concerned with sickness, old age, death, or the mystery of life—imagine such a person to exist and by no logical argument could he ever be induced to undertake the quest. And the naturalist who is firmly convinced that science will one day lift the burden of man's finitude will likewise hardly be moved by objective arguments. But the individual who in one way or another gazes upon the same three sights which so stirred the Buddha, and who is overcome with a sense of the mystery of this unintelligible world, may then be seized, as the Buddha was, by the burning need to solve the riddle, the more so, if, like the Buddha, he then encounters one of his fellowmen whose countenance radiates strength and serenity.

Here, then, are two facts which, although they provide no infallible guarantee of the truth of the mystic's claim, nonetheless seem to yield a probability sufficient for the purposes of practice. On the one hand, there is the profound sense of need, the deep uneasiness, the longing for perfect happiness and for a knowledge which will illuminate the great mystery. The existence of the yearning is itself no infallible assurance that its fulfillment is possible; but it may be felt with an intensity so great as to induce one to risk the quest. The naturalist, to be sure, may choose to sneer at what the existentialist calls "cosmic anxiety," and may regard it rather as a "failure of nerve." But it is certainly not impossible that the *Angst* which attends the contemplation of a universe devoid of meaning is no merely subjective phenomenon, but is rather diagnostic of man's deepest nature and indicative of his ultimate destiny.

On the other hand, there is the witness of the saints—of those individuals who claim to have seen and whose lives have been transformed in striking ways. One may perceive in them qualities of strength and composure, of insight and charity which one finds altogether lacking in oneself as well as in all those who are the products of a purely humanistic cultivation, and one may, as a result, aspire to emulate them. The naturalist, of course, may remain unimpressed, and may persist in his faith that a developed science of psychology will one day comprehend the mechanics of such personality transformations and will even be able to generate them. But historically, it has certainly been the case that many persons derived the courage to attempt the Way from the spectacle of others who seemed to them to be living testimony to its truth.

The mystical tradition, moreover, although not providing theoretical certainty, exhibits a testimony too massive to be lightly set aside. Though in the end, one must continually insist, there can be no substitute for personal realization of the truth, still, as a matter of probability the existence of this testimony is much more easily accounted for on the hypothesis of the essential truth of the spiritualist position than by the hypothesis of naturalism. For what is the naturalist, after all, to make of a testimony as universal and as perennial as that provided by the mystical tradition? His only recourse is to pronounce the mystics as mentally unbalanced and as victims of some form of self-delusion; and he must appeal for support to the psychology of religion. But is such support forthcoming?

We must note first of all that psychology is a sword which cuts both ways. If the saint has a psychology, so, it can hardly be denied, has the naturalist. If there is a psychology of religion, then there is also a psychology of irreligion. That such a field has thus far not been developed is but an indication of the naturalistic bias which infects the whole of modern psychology. Psychology, in any case, is in no position to rule on the validity of any claim; for all experience, the scientist's as well as the lunatic's, is grist for the psychologist's mill. To imagine otherwise is to fall victim to psychologism. The validity of a cognitive claim is determined not by psychology but by the nature of reality; and in the case of the mystic claim, it is the nature of reality which is precisely the point at issue. If the reality which the mystic claims to exist does in fact exist, then he is perfectly sane; if it does not exist, then he is deluded; but for this reason alone and not because psychology has it within its power to declare him insane. Moreover, if there is anything to the mystic's claim, then the psychologist is in no position to assess it, for the latter's knowledge has been gleaned from the examination of other persons of his own stature; until such time as he has been himself transformed, the content of the mystic's consciousness must remain utterly beyond his ken.

But, foregoing such considerations, it seems extremely unlikely that the mystics suffer from mental disease, unless one takes the very fact of the mystical claim itself as an indication. Bergson, who, in the effort to clarify and give content to his own doctrine of intuition, was led in his later years to recognize in the mystical experience the most complete fulfillment of a mode of knowing to which he had been trying to direct the attention of philosophers, has given us, in *The Two Sources of Morality and Religion,* a highly interesting discussion of the nature of the mystical experience and its implications for philosophy. He regards it as did Aquinas as a *cognitio dei experimentalis,* and states:

If mysticism is really what we have just said it is, it must furnish us with the means of approaching, as it were experimentally, the problem of the existence and the nature of God. Indeed we fail to see how philosophy could approach the problem in any other way . . .[47]

And to the contention that the mystic is a pathological personality, he replies as follows:

. . . they were then swept back into a vast current of life; from their increased vitality there radiated an extraordinary energy, daring, power of conception and realization. Just think of what was accomplished in the field of action by a St. Paul, a St. Teresa, a St. Catherine of Sienna, a St. Francis, a Joan of Arc, and how many others besides! . . . When we grasp that such is the culminating point of the inner evolution of the great mystics, we can but wonder how they could ever have been classed with the mentally diseased. True, we live in a condition of unstable equilibrium; normal health of mind, as indeed, of body, is not easily defined. Yet there is an exceptional deep-rooted mental healthiness, which is readily recognizable. It is expressed in the bent for action, the faculty of adapting and re-adapting oneself to circumstances, in firmness combined with suppleness, in the prophetic discernment of what is possible and what is not, in the spirit of simplicity which triumphs over complications, in a word, supreme good sense. Is not this exactly what we find in the above-named mystics? And might they not provide us with the very definition of intellectual vigor? [48]

The great mystics, the only ones that we are dealing with, have generally been men or women of action, endowed with superior common sense; it matters little that some of them had imitators who well deserved to be called "crazy," or that there are cases when they themselves felt the effect of extreme and prolonged strain of mind and will; many a man of genius has been in the same condition.[49]

It thus appears that the naturalist's attempt to dismiss mysticism as an abnormal phenomenon is not founded on any observable facts, but is in the nature of an *ad hoc* explanation to which he is driven in the effort to save his own position. By all visible signs, the personality of the mystic seems to have been integrated, broadened, deepened and strengthened by the experience. Those who have argued that the ecstatic consciousness can be duplicated by certain narcotics have hardly been able to claim, in addition, that the use of these narcotics generates such positive personality transformations.

Finally, there is the amazing unanimity of the mystic testimony. Whether they come from the East or from the West, whether from the sixth century B.C. or from the seventeenth century A.D., they

[47] Bergson, H., *The Two Sources of Morality and Religion,* tr. by Audra, Brereton, and Carter (New York, 1935), 229.
[48] *Ibid.*, 216f.   [49] *Ibid.*, 233.

strike a common note. The delusion, if delusion it be, must be a collective one. The differences between the reports pale into insignificance besides the amount of agreement which they display. The differences such as they are can be easily understood as due to differing levels of the experience itself, as resulting from the attempt to conceptualize the experience after it has been had, and from the employment of imagery and symbol which vary in varying cultural contexts. On this matter, Radhakrishnan has said all that needs to be said:

Conceptual substitutes for ineffable experiences are not adequate. They are products of rational thinking. All forms, according to Śaṁkara, contain an element of untruth and the real is beyond all forms. Any attempt to describe the experience falsifies it to an extent. In the experience itself the self is wholly integrated and is therefore both the knower and the known, but it is not so in any intellectual description of the experience. The profoundest being of man cannot be brought out by mental pictures or logical counters. . . .

And yet we cannot afford to be absolutely silent. Though the tools of sense and understanding cannot describe adequately, creative imagination with its symbols and suggestions may be of assistance. . . .

The symbols and suggestions employed are derived from the local and historical traditions. . . . In the utterances of the seers we have to distinguish the given and interpreted elements. . . . When we are told that the souls have felt in their lives the redeeming power of Kṛṣṇa or Buddha, Jesus or Mohammad, we must distinguish the immediate experience or intuition which might conceivably be infallible and the interpretation which is mixed up with it. . . . We must distinguish the simple facts of religion from the accounts which reach us through the depth of theological preconceptions. That the soul is in contact with a mighty spiritual power other than its normal self and yet within and that its contact means the beginning of the creation of a new self is the fact, while the identification of this power with the historic figures of Buddha or Christ, the confusion of the simple realisation of the universal self in us with a catastrophic revelation from without, is an interpretation, a personal confession and not necessarily an objective truth.[50]

The apparent differences between the reports of mystics, such as they are, are of no great significance, and cannot be used to rebut the mystical testimony. The differences would serve to confuse only the literalist whose mind is fixated on words and cannot get beyond them to their referents. The conceptualizations of the mystic must be regarded for what they are—as "metaphors mutely appealing for

[50] IVL, 96-99.

an imaginative leap." [51] They are not uttered primarily for the purpose of conveying exact information but as markers are on the way to the goal. It is the height of futility to subject the words themselves to exact analysis, as though by so doing the ultimate truth could somehow be squeezed out of them. Do not mistake the pointing finger for the thing pointed at, say the Zen Buddhists.

The mystics have no difficulty in achieving understanding with one another, despite the unintelligibility of their remarks to the non-mystic. Since they can presuppose a common experience, their words, which are merely pointers to this common experience, do make sense to them. The non-mystic has not got this common experience; he has only the conceptualizations and as Kant has told us, "*Gedanken ohne Inhalt sind leer . . .*" There is nothing unique or amazing about this circumstance; exactly the same sort of thing obtains in regard to the every day perception of color. People endowed with normal vision are in a position to make all sorts of significant statements to each other about the relations of colors which are meaningless to the blind person who has only the words but lacks the common experience of color. Words in themselves cannot convey the sense of color to one who lacks the sense; but they can be expressive to one who has it in that they refer him to his experience. No language is meaningful outside of a context of community; and this community the mystics seem to have. The outsider may note a certain consistency in their obscurities and paradoxes. They all point to the same object, which is visible to them, but which is as yet beyond the range of vision of the non-mystic.

All conception needs a context of perception: this is the enduring and irrefutable thesis of the tradition of philosophical empiricism. But the question still remains—is perception of one kind only, or is there more than one kind of givenness? From the standpoint of the mystical tradition, the great truth of empiricism as against all speculative philosophy is to be found in its insistence on the need for verification, for an ultimate ostensive step. Its fatal error lies in its limiting itself to only a single sort of immediacy, viz., sense-perception. As no one saw more clearly than Kant, there is about all metaphysical concepts and reasonings an emptiness which stems from the fact that they are free floating and not grounded in givenness. And the mystic would have no quarrel with Kant's claim that the ordinary categories do not apply to the Unconditioned and that they are but empty forms except for the

[51] Whitehead, A. N., *Process and Reality* (New York, 1930), 6.

content provided by sense-experience. They would also be perfectly in accord with Kant as regards his claim that the Ideas of Reason refer to objects which are never given in sense-experience. Metaphysic aspires to objects which are forever beyond its reach, Kant noted and went on to say that, though there is no experience which can give content to the Ideas of Reason, they may remain as postulates of the moral life. Whether in fact the moral argument is on any sounder ground than the other metaphysical arguments which Kant repudiates, and in what sense—even if its validity be granted —it serves to give content to the empty forms which are the Ideas of Reason, we need not at this point stop to consider. The important thing to note is this, namely, that Kant's entire case is built on the assumption that *only to the senses is anything given, that the senses alone provide content for our concepts.* This is the axiom which underlies the Critical Philosophy. Once it is granted, Kant's conclusions cannot possibly be evaded. The mystic refuses to grant it, and, if we allow any truth to the mystic claim that there are non-sensuous modes of givenness, then Kant may be by-passed. The mystic argues that the Unconditioned may be known; God and the noumenal self may be given in experience, not in sense-experience to be sure, but in the intuitive mystical experience. It is the super-conscious experience, normally unavailable, which provides the *Anschauungen* without which the Ideas of Reason *sind leer.* Mysticism, in other words, is the verification of metaphysics. Disallow the possibility of the mystical experience, confine yourself solely to sense-experience, and you will be an easy mark for the arguments of the empiricist and the logical positivist. From this point of view, what Kant and the empiricists have claimed is, then, true about the normal experience of the non-mystical person. But its truth is merely *de facto,* and not *de jure;* it merely describes this sort of experience, but cannot legitimately declare it to be the only possible sort. The Kantian philosophy reminds us of what follows if all intuition is sensuous, namely that speculative metaphysics is guilty of all the fallacies of the Transcendental Dialectic. But Kant has no way of showing that in the nature of things all intuition must be sensuous. Thus, as Huxley has pointed out,

. . . if Kant was right and the Thing-in-itself is unknowable . . . all the other masters of the spiritual life were engaged in a wild goose chase. But Kant was right only as regards minds that have not yet come to enlightenment and deliverance. To such minds Reality, whether material, psychic or spiritual, presents itself as darkened, tinged, and refracted by the medium of their own individual natures. But in those who are pure in heart and poor in spirit there is no distortion of Reality, because there is no separate selfhood to obscure or refract, no painted lantern slide of intellectual beliefs and hallowed imagery to give a personal and historical colouring to the "white radiance of Eternity." . . . The Thing-in-itself *can* be perceived—but only by one who, in himself, is no-thing.[52]

Philosophy must be based on experience, but the question is— whose experience? Is there any *a priori* reason to suppose that all experience must be of one sort and of one level? May there not be disciplines which will open up realms of experience undreamed of by the ordinary philosopher? This is the essential claim of the mystic, which philosophers of an open mind should be prepared to consider seriously, however uncongenial it may be to their accustomed modes of thinking about philosophy. As Huxley further says,

In regard to few professional philosophers and men of letters is there any evidence that they did very much in the way of fulfilling the necessary conditions of direct spiritual knowledge. When poets or metaphysicians talk about the subject matter of the Perennial Philosophy, it is generally at second hand. But in every age there have been some men and women who chose to fulfill the conditions upon which alone, as a matter of brute empirical fact, such immediate knowledge can be had; and of these a few have left accounts of the Reality they were thus enabled to apprehend. . . . To such first-hand exponents of the Perennial Philosophy those who knew them have generally given the name of 'saint' or 'prophet,' 'sage' or 'enlightened one.' [53]

Suppose the saints to have seen . . . May their reports be used as a foundation on which to erect a philosophy? May philosophy be based on reports of the findings of others? Would not this be to ground philosophy in faith and authority? In answer to these questions, Bergson replies that there can be nothing wrong in the appeal to the authority of those who have had experiences which we have not ourselves had. A good deal of science is derived from merely reported observations. Thus, he says,

. . . it is by no means certain that a scientific experiment, or more generally an observation recorded by science, can always be repeated or verified. In the days when Central Africa was a *terra incognita,* geography trusted to the account of a single explorer, if his honesty and competence seemed to be above suspicion. The route of Livingstone's journeys appeared for a long time on the maps and atlases. You may

52 Huxley, Aldous, *The Perennial Philosophy* (New York, 1945), 223.
53 *Ibid.,* ix.

object that verification was potentially, if not actually feasible, that other travellers could go and see if they liked, and that the map based on the indications of one traveller was a provisional one, waiting for subsequent exploration to make it definitive. I grant this: but the mystic too has gone on a journey that others can potentially, if not actually, undertake; . . . Along with the souls capable of following the mystic way to the end there are many who go at least part of the way. . . . William James used to say he had never experienced mystic states; but he added that if he heard them spoken of by a man who had experienced them "something within him echoed the call." [54]

But one may easily be misled here, unless he keeps constantly in mind that the orientation of the mystic is towards practice and not towards the construction of theory for its own sake. The mystic is not presenting us his testimony as a girder which we may fit into the theoretical structure which we are erecting, but as an inducement to a way of life. There is no question of accepting anything on faith or on authority, for in this case the truth is no truth unless one has got it for oneself. The mystic's words, as we have said, are but markers urging us on our way so that eventually we may behold for ourselves. We should have attained the height of foolishness, therefore, were we to try to construct a philosophical edifice out of these signposts. If there is any faith or trust called for, it is only initial and provisional; it is not by itself the key to the kingdom of heaven, but only a basis for getting under way. The mystic asks you to accept nothing merely because he says it is so; it is not that kind of truth in which he is interested, but only the truth which you can realize for yourself. And if the great mystics have often been impatient with the ordinary philosopher, it is because he strikes them as being like the man who is presented with a map which points the way to a great treasure and who, instead of setting out to find it, spends the rest of his days recopying the map, and probing into the etymological derivations of the place-names which are on it.

There is then at the heart of that tradition which we have been calling the *philosophia perennis* quite a different conception of the nature of philosophy from the one which is current in academic circles in America today. Philosophizing is not an end in itself, but culminates in vision and in personality transformation. Philosophy is not a purely cerebral activity but a way of life, a therapy of the soul which eventuates in a growth into new modes of being. Neither in science nor in philosophy ought there to be a divorce

[54] Bergson, H., *op. cit.*, 234.

between theory and practice. To this extent the pragmatists are perfectly right; though their conception of the "practical" is far too narrow and often is almost synonymous with the "socially benefi- cial." This too is the great message of Indian philosophy throughout its history; and it is everywhere present in the philosophy of Radha- krishnan. The function of philosophy is not primarily the elabora- tion of doctrine as an end in itself. Its rôle is to serve as the guide of life, and to help direct the pilgrim on his progress toward the ultimate.

More than two thousand years ago, Plato, in describing the philosophers of his day, said of them that

when they carry on the study, not only in youth, but as the pursuit of their maturer years, most of them become strange monsters, not to say utter rogues, and that those who may be considered to be the best of them are made useless to the world by the very study which they extol.[55]

It is embarrassing for the Western philosopher to read these words, so accurately do they describe the contemporary philosophical scene. He may well feel that, unless the situation changes and philosophy returns to its true mission, a new Justinian may again arise and declare the Schools closed. Why has philosophy in the West so little prestige and so little influence today? Is this not the result of the disastrous separation of theory and practice? Has it not come from the pursuit of philosophy as a purely logical activity rather than as an enterprise of the spirit? Philosophers dispute endlessly, yet their lives are hardly affected by their philosophis- ings. One would have great difficulty in determining the vintage of a philosopher from the mode of life he leads. His philosophy is a purely intellectual activity. Idealism in the West does not signify an "idealistic" mode of life, and the naturalist and even the ma- terialist may be quite a harmless fellow, a devoted father, and a worthy citizen. In the Hindu tradition, philosophy is not merely a doctrine but a manner of life; it therefore has a solidity and com- mands a respect which it everywhere lacks in the West. In India, no philosopher can hold an audience for long unless his life is the visible expression of his philosophy.

If one criticizes the naturalist, then, it is not to refute him on the logical level, but only to remove the impediments which have restrained him from undertaking the experiment. There is no way of logically convincing him that he ought to undertake the experi- ment; and he who seeks to demonstrate logically the reality of

55 Plato, *Republic*, 487c.

spirit will hardly accomplish the conversion of the naturalist. He had better attempt to do it existentially, that is by becoming a living witness to the reality of spirit. What the spiritualist philosophy needs in the end to give it effectiveness is not one more subtle argument, but a few exemplars. It has got to become known by its fruits. Anyone who takes it seriously had therefore better get on with this task.

BERNARD PHILLIPS

DEPARTMENT OF PHILOSOPHY
UNIVERSITY OF DELAWARE

3

Robert W. Browning

REASON AND TYPES OF INTUITION IN
RADHAKRISHNAN'S PHILOSOPHY

3

REASON AND TYPES OF INTUITION IN
RADHAKRISHNAN'S PHILOSOPHY

WERE one to assess Radhakrishnan's work as a whole, it would be incumbent upon one to acknowledge the very great contribution made by the subject of this volume to the unparalleled human problem of achieving understanding across cultural boundaries. Measured beside this world task, much of our philosophizing seems to be trivial,—lacking at once in sense of proportion and seriousness. Many of those who have disciplined habits of "facing facts" seem unable to take in the larger facts; or at least they despair of presently saying anything significant about the larger problems. Radhakrishnan has resolutely confronted himself with the macroscopic issues—both those of mankind's future and those of cosmic scope. And, for him, these two are intimately connected. Nothing should be said to minimize the proportions of the moral problem; but, in a sense, Radhakrishnan's convictions are such that this problem is not as irreducible as it may seem. Not only is he convinced of the unity of mankind, but he finds a core in Western religion and reflection that accords with the more profound—but now somewhat moribund [1]—heritage of the East. We can name no one in our time who has done more to elicit this common core into the explicitness which is required for fully conscious orientation. His endowment is auspicious for the performance of his task; he is truly, as Muirhead observed two decades ago, "a philosophical bilinguist" upon "the spiritual wisdom of the world." [2]

If the present essay seems to add a few more paragraphs to the

---

[1] Ind P, II, 773-781; SM, 258ff.; HVL, 52, 128-130.

[2] *Hibbert Journal*, XXXI: 149 (October, 1932). Perhaps the same claim cannot be made concerning his relation to that "new" East which denies any "spiritual wisdom" and whose prophet died in London in 1883. However, we may wish him and his countrymen every Godspeed in mediating understanding between "East" and "West," each of which, in accord with the supposed appointments of history, is with good intentions preparing the means of dehumanizing and obliterating millions of innocents under the necessities of "liberating" mankind.

trivia of contemporary discussions, it will try to excuse itself on the grounds that the patient cannot speak to the physician in medical idiom; he must use his own language. If he is overwrought or very ill—and perhaps Western man is very ill with the hypertrophy of certain capacities and a condition of hypotrophy of others —still he must express himself in accord with his own experience; even the directions of how to follow a prescription will have to come in his own vernacular. Radhakrishnan is one of those best equipped to speak to our condition. He has been doing it. And the present volume provides a unique opportunity to become a little clearer about some of the prescription on points concerning which we are still confused.

For three centuries the efforts of Western philosophy have been quite as much devoted to finding out how we know as to what is known (or as to what is real). The questions of the present writer will probably manifest this preoccupation. It is to be admitted that epistemological questions are not the most important. But, to communicate fully to Western thinkers, Radhakrishnan will do best to try to speak to us where we are, showing us just what he means by saying that certain capacities of intuition are ours, and indicating exactly how one should go about testing these deliverances.

We wish to direct attention to several kinds of "intuition" and to two or more rôles of "reason" as—it seems to us—these appear in areas of Radhakrishnan's philosophy. Using our own framework, we shall attempt to give the outlines of an exposition of our author's views. Above all, we wish to lay hold of the opportunity provided by this volume to ask questions. Though fettered by our capacity as well as by space, the discussion will naturally move toward metaphysics when we ask questions about any differences in cognitive apparatus that are to be correlated with different sorts of realities apprehended; it will naturally involve psychology when emphasis is placed upon the structure of the self and the nature of its powers of knowing.

Radhakrishnan is such a master of style that one asked to write in expository fashion upon our author's philosophy knows antecedently that any remarks of his own, taken as terminal, are fated to be pathetic anti-climax. In this volume, however, there is no danger that one's observation or criticisms will be taken as terminal; and perhaps there is something helpful that one can do.

Due not only to the looseness of popular speech but owing also to the very history of Western reflection itself, the word "intuition" and—to a somewhat lesser extent—the word "reason" are ex-

traordinarily ambiguous.[3] Radhakrishnan's discussions, with all
their erudition in European as well as Indian literature, have not
overcome these difficulties. He himself properly complains:

It is unfortunate that we are obliged to employ the single term 'intuition' to represent scientific genius, poetic insight, ethical conscience,
as well as religious faith. Though these diverse movements represent
the integrated activity of the mind, the activity is oriented towards
knowing in some cases, enjoyment or creation in others.[4]

Thus the initial slant of our discussion may be largely terminological. The broadness of Radhakrishnan's sweeps seems to leave
certain vaguenesses or ambiguities. How much this situation reflects
a paucity of the English idiom, we cannot say.[5] Again, how much
it may reflect the nature of Radhakrishnan's audiences, we cannot
say. A prophet wishes to get the burden of his message across, and
is not likely to commit the value distortions of pausing to settle
everything everywhere with all the niceties which would properly
titillate the intellectual sensualities of the respective breeds of us
sedentary "ruminant professors."

I

From our author's uses of "intuition" (and related terms)—when
considered primarily in a cognitive context—one receives the impression of various meanings: sometimes it refers to processes;
sometimes to products; sometimes to faculties, capacities, or
sources. Sometimes it intimates what cannot be known in other
ways; sometimes it names a fuller "realization" of what may be
already abstractly known in symbols; sometimes it is attached to
the dawning, in the mind of a discoverer, of what will be, after
confirmation, a powerful scientific generalization; sometimes it denotes a knowledge of individual things in their concreteness; sometimes it is referring to unitive knowledge of The One Real.
Sometimes it is accenting the dynamism of thinking as against the

---

[3] At a tardy moment we find that Miss Wild says of "intuition" that "it is often
used when 'instinct' would convey too much of the animal; when 'revelation' would
arouse suspicion; when 'perception' would be too vague or too technical, 'rapid
synthesis of judgment' too prosaic, the 'fruits of experience or observation' too
loose, 'innate or a priori knowledge' too disputable, or 'one with' too incomprehensible." *Intuition,* Cambridge, 1939, 2.

[4] IVL, 200fn.

[5] E.g., "In Hindu Philosophy, pratibhā denotes the creative intuition of the
genius, and ārṣajñāna is the name given to the religious intuitions of the sages . . ."
IVL, 200fn.

results; sometimes it is emphasizing a spontaneous dynamism as against movements which may be automatic or mechanical. Intuition, as a higher capacity than that of (discursive) thought, is on occasion represented as dependent upon the lower, as supervening after study and analysis. At the same time it is suggested that the dependence runs in the opposite direction, for intuition is immanent in (discursive) thought, and is related to the latter as a whole is to a part.[6] At places, the reader may receive the impression that intuition is cognitively incorrigible or infallible; in other contexts it is asserted that intuitions should be probed and evaluated. Intuition is said to be non-discursive and non-conceptual; and yet it is claimed that intuitive knowledge "is rational intuition in which both immediacy and mediacy are comprehended," and that every intuition "has an intellectual content."[7] Intuition is held to lie deeply in the self, as an endowment of the latter's fundamental nature; it is also subject to cultivation. Frequently intuition is not primarily an epistemological or cognitive term, but marks something much more than a cognition or a kind of cognition alone; it labels a response of one's whole being.

This catalogue is surely not surprising in view of the history of the term. And it is only fair to make two or three observations at once. Those who tend to believe that talk of intuition is nonsense, that at most the word has emotive meaning, useful for casting a little aura, had better note that the initial semantic difficulty is not with the absence of any referents but with the plethora of them. Secondly, Radhakrishnan's deployments of the term are normally clear for practical purposes in the actual contexts; it is foolish to lift the same mark out of various linguistic constellations and pretend that it is or ought to be the same in meaning. Further, the range of our author's usages is a tribute to his versatility in the

6 "Intuition is not independent but emphatically dependent upon thought and is immanent in the very nature of our thinking. It is dynamically continuous with thought and pierces through the conceptual context of knowledge to the living reality under it. It is the result of a long and arduous process of study and analysis and is therefore higher than the discursive process from which it issues and on which it supervenes." But: "It stands to intellect as a whole to a part, as the creative source of thought to the created categories which work more or less automatically." SM, 269.

7 IVL, 153. Further, if one gathered, or came with the antecedent supposition, that certain areas of knowledge belong peculiarly to sense, some peculiarly to rational apprehension, and some peculiarly to intuition, then he would (like us) be profoundly shocked to read: "We can see objects without the medium of the senses and discern relations spontaneously without building them up laboriously. . . . we can discern every kind of reality directly." *Ibid.,* 143.

artificially separated departments of human experience—cognitive, moral, aesthetic, religious.

In our author's own classification, there are basically three types of cognition. "While all varieties of cognitive experience result in a knowledge of the real," he writes, "it is produced in three ways which are sense experience, discursive reasoning and intuitive apprehension." [8] One notes that each of these is productive of knowledge of the real, but some deep insufficiency is held to characterize the first two. Sense experience and logical knowledge "are recognized as inadequate to the real which they attempt to apprehend." [9] Plato, Bergson, and Bradley are cited in their respective ways of supporting this proposition. It is undeniable, of course, that "Intellectual symbols are no substitutes for perceived realities." But one wonders in different contexts if the deficiency (quite apart from the cases of symbolizing what "isn't there") is conceived to be one of the incompleteness of any abstract language, or a failure adequately to possess the object, or even a failure to become the object. Apparently sensory experience and intuitive apprehension are non-conceptual. Sensuous and non-sensuous perception (*aparokṣa*) are two kinds of immediate knowledge. "Intuition is the extension of perception to regions beyond sense." [10] We presume that sense perception preserves a duality between object known and the knower (we do not think that it is restricted to bare sense data, but, if it is not so restricted, we shall suggest that it always contains conceptual elements). Intuition, in many of Radhakrishnan's usages, seems to allow for a duality. With intuition, "we see things as they are, as unique individuals." There is a "close communion between the knower and the known." To us, communion is a strong word, but it still implies a duality. However, sometimes Radhakrishnan uses stronger expressions, which seem to deny the duality. In the same context he writes that "intuitive knowledge arises from an intimate fusion of mind with reality. It is knowledge by being and not by senses or by symbols. It is awareness of the truth of things by identity. We become one with the truth, one with the object of knowledge." [11] With our antecedently associated connotations of the terms, we would reconcile these statements by saying that Radhakrishnan is using intuition both to name a kind of intimate complete knowing (*samādhi*, as some Yogins claim it) of a concrete thing among the apparently plural

---

8 IVL, 134. Cp., "the three stages of mental evolution, sense, reason, and intuition," ER (2nd ed.), 63.

9 IVL, 134.   10 *Ibid.*, 143.   11 IVL, 138; cf. 146.

entities of the realm of *māyā* [12] and to name the consummatory toti-metaphysical insight in which empirical pluralities are transcended and all is apprehended as one (*samādhi,* as our author normally uses the term). At least we have intuitive apprehension distinguished from logical or conceptual knowledge.[13] And we have it distinguished from sensory experience. Further, of course, it is not to be confused with instinct.[14]

Within the region of intuitive knowledge, however, we find that we need to recognize: aesthetic insight into individual structures, scientific penetration into complex relations, moral intuition, and the content of religious faith.

II

It will be convenient, we think, to set down a framework—in part to expound Radhakrishnan and in part to provide some orientation with which to direct questions. Exhaustiveness and completeness of articulation are assuredly not claimed; the outline is framed with an eye on our author's writings and with occasional glances ahead at some distinctions we wish to employ.[15] In turn, it may help Radhakrishnan to spot gross importations and misinterpretations, and to fill up lacunae in our account. A wide variety of "intuitions" may be placed in five ranges or categories.

1. Sensory intuition
2. Rational intuition

12 May such knowledge perchance be the contemplative enjoyment of an unusually full sensory perception of the object, together with a holding in abeyance of the pushings and pullings of the rest of our existence? May we assimilate it to the aesthetic, as we shall take for granted later on? Or is it to be given a distinct category of its own, neither sensory nor aesthetic?

13 However, the absence or the presence of conceptual elements may not be the differentiating condition but rather whether the essential character is non-conceptual or conceptual. For, "we have to distinguish between the immediacy which appears at the sub-intellectual level before practical necessities and intellectual analysis break up the unity and the immediacy which appears at the supra-intellectual level, at the end and to some extent as the result of discursive thinking. . . . Plato and Śaṁkara agree that this kind of intuitive certainty is reached after a long process of discursive analysis." IVL, 149.

14 *Ibid.,* 213, 262. Also ER, 63.

15 One is aware of great dangers in tearing apart what may be seamless. However, it does seem that some classification is in order and likely to prove helpful. For instance, if we discriminate a category of intuition which is corrigible by evidence independent of its source, and some other class which is not so corrigible, this may afford a reconciliation of statements which apparently point in the two opposed directions.

3. Descrying of complex structures of fact and possible fact (including connections between unarticulated logical structures)
4. Valuational intuition
5. Integral experience.

It is likely that Radhakrishnan never refers to the first two (possibly the first three) as "intuition;" but even then—in addition to our own ulterior purposes—these will be useful (as perhaps we have already seen) in the way of saying what our author's intuition is not. The third is in a doubtful status; perhaps it should be eliminated; on the other hand, we have been inclined to break it into two or three types, to separate intuitions of fact from intuitions of unarticulated logical connection and from intuitions of possible restructuralizations of fact (as the man of practice or the prophet may sense them). The fourth obviously contains several sub-classes. Since one of these species is religious insight, it may be asked why the fifth is not incorporated into it, instead of being given separate standing. Our answers are that continuity between personal religious devotion and mystic experience is at least questionable; an integral experience (if such exist) that is non-dual (*advaita*) is *prima facie* different from the common struggles of the religious consciousness and of the moral consciousness, as well as from the garden varieties of relatively complete perceptual intuition; lastly, *anubhava* (one supposes) is a temporally decisive step toward deliverance, and Indian thought has traditionally insisted upon a clear distinction between the moral attaining of good karma while one is still on the wheel of birth and death and, on the other hand, *mokṣa,* or deliverance from *saṁsāra* itself.

III

1. First, there is sensory intuition. This may include (a) a postulated pure sensory given, requisite to perception but innocent of interpretation. It does comprise the perception (b) of qualities and (c) of relations. It may include the recognition of (d) "things."

Radhakrishnan, we believe, tacitly recognized (a).[16] He is explicit in his acceptance of (b), although of course, he does not call it "intuition." "Sense experience helps us to know the outer characters of the external world. By means of it we obtain an acquain-

---

[16] This statement is largely based on reading between the lines of his explication and comment upon the Nyāya and the Sāṁkhya systems. Cf., *e.g.,* Ind P, II, 303.

tance with the sensible qualities of the objects. Its data are the subject-matter of natural science which builds up a conceptual structure to describe them." [17] The textual evidence which we have noticed has been quite indeterminate with respect to the question of perception of relations, but on vague grounds we would incline to give an affirmative answer. Again, we are unclear as to whether Radhakrishnan would want the perception of relative wholes to be placed under the present genus, or whether this phenomenon should be assigned to a different class of intuitions. And this apparently single question becomes two, if we make a distinction between the ordinary perception of physical objects and samādhi with respect to some empirical unity.

If one takes physical objects as objects of sensory intuition, then one must literally say that we sense "things" (physical bodies and complexes thereof). This fits with the Gestaltist's brand of introspection very well,[18] but it has the old awkwardnesses over errors. On the other hand, physical things, etc., can be viewed as scientific hypotheses; although, of course, ordinarily hypotheses of such familiarity and high degree of confirmation are not thought of as such. This alternative jars common sense a bit, but finds it easier to manage errors and illusions.

The four forms of sensory intuition that have been suggested, with the exception of the first, are capable of a cross-classification into: (A) conscious perception, and (B) unconscious perception. This is to be mentioned because sometimes one finds that particular weight is placed upon subliminal perception. The reader may feel that Radhakrishnan makes this emphasis, although probably in connection with intuitions of types (3) and (4) and (5), rather than (1). That there is any perception at all—subliminal or supra-

17 IVL, 134.
18 Not, of course, with the Titchnerian and older British associational introspection. An increasing number of thinkers seem to be doubting whether "sense data" exist. This is a plausible view if "exist" means "consciously exist"—especially plausible if the qualifying phrase is tacked on "in their purity, in splendid isolation." It does not necessarily touch the meaning of sensory intuition labelled (a) under (1) above, or the meaning assigned to the "given" by H. H. Price, early in his work on *Perception*. This is compatible with the idealistic criticism that there is no (conscious) immediacy without meaning. The functionalist, however, might go farther with a strictly functional view of all sense-functioning, were he not restrained by his physiological conceptions, upon which he cannot say that the sense organs and their physical and chemical reactions go out of existence when they are not in positive "use." We take it to be a fact established by functional psychologists and instrumental philosophers that our experience is considerably prospective and that our perceptions normally are performing some rôle of "signs." In adult life, at least, we seldom "perceive" sense data without reference to their "meaning."

liminal—is surely a fit object of philosophic wonder. And such facts as the mystery of consciousness are the refutation of the older forms of naturalism and the obvious hurdles for the newer non-reductionistic forms. But—whereas truistically we are more conscious of conscious perceptions—there is a sense in which the taking account of subliminal cues are no more marvellous than taking account of the supra-liminal: the former are the obverse side of the shield of which the phenomena of attention are the familiar side.

IV

2. Radhakrishnan may prefer to associate the next cluster of intuitions with some other category, such as the "logical" or rational. But we do wish to draw attention to the fact that there are intuitions (a) of meanings and (b) of the relations of meanings, *e.g.*, entailment, incompatibility, etc. Logical relations do not see to their own realization; for actual inference, or at least for the non-authoritarian checking of it, these relations must be intuited.

The common distinction here made between direct apprehension of a meaning and seeing its implications is subject to some question, and may at any rate be a relative one. It is difficult to see how one would apprehend a meaning and yet perceive absolutely none of its logical relations. On the other hand, presumably no human mind immediately intuits all that is involved in some idea. Certain contemporary analytic philosophers frequently observe, and always operate upon the assumption, that we can use a word correctly for most practical purposes without knowing its analysis. The so-called rationalists of modern European philosophy accepted degrees or levels of confusion in the ranges of ideas which fell short of clarity and distinctness.

Pythagoras, Heraclitus and Plato, one presumes, were among the uncoverers of rational intuition in the West. Despite the centuries of scholasticism, in which supposedly it was a prime organon, it was rediscovered with a great flourish by the modern proponents of geometric method, whose hopes rose to exaggerated proportions.[19] Hobbes was shocked into philosophy on being confronted by rigorous implication. Descartes got confident that the clash of mere opinion and the disorder of the schools could be ended. Cognitive error was a moral defect, in his account, for it indicated presumptuous haste—a failure patiently to inspect one's supposed

---

[19] In accord with empirical prejudice, we may have the gravest doubts of this sort of "knowledge" alone giving any knowledge of matters of existence.

logical transitions until they either dissolved or were seen, with all meanings clear and distinct, to be perfectly cogent.[20] Spinoza certainly recognized what we are calling rational intuition here,[21] although we are not at all sure that it exhausts what he means by *ratio intuitiva*, and we are sure that it does not include the love in the *amor intellectualis dei*.[22] There is a further tempering off in Leibniz, who realizes that only for an Infinite Intelligence is rationalism a wholly valid method; but, on the strength of what is possible to man, he is inspired at least to envision a universal algebra.

With respect at least to the relations of meanings, there is a cross-classification here, under (2), somewhat analagous to that above, under (1). There are results obtained (A) by the clearly conscious intuitions at each link of a cogent chain of inference, as against (B) the possible intuition of the result without explicit apprehension of the steps. There may be garden varieties of the latter in simple matters—but it is difficult to be sure that these are not rather the result of perfected habits.[23] We have heard of—we have not

[20] *Meditation*, V.

[21] Whatever Spinoza's "intuition" may be, it is plain that he insists upon distinguishing between some sort of insight, on the one hand, and either rote learning of calculative operations or inductive surmises from successful rules of thumb, on the other. (We shall include this latter under another form of intuition, species (3).) Spinoza is, of course, right that no sampling of a few instances proves a theorem in theory of number. Or, as we all learned in school, a diagram proves no theorem in geometry, for strictly it is not a geometric object (but only a psychological prop), and, even taken as a geometric triangle, let us say, it would represent a special case. Its special properties must not be used in the proof. Mathematical theorems are not inductions.

Miss Wild observes that, with the same mathematical example of proportion ("given three numbers, to find a fourth"), there are apparently differences in Spinoza's specifications of the rôle of intuition; in one place, intuition has no need of reasoning and sees the proportions in the calculations immediately; in another, again the reasoning is not a part of the intuition but intuition contributes the feeling of the proportion; in another, intuition apparently discerns the result as well as the ratio; and in still another, intuition occurs dependent on and following after reasoning. Cf., *Intuition*, 20-22, 27f.

[22] Radhakrishnan would bear this out. Cf., IVL, 160ff. *Prima facie*, the additional meanings are to be referred to categories (4) and (5) below. Following Höffding, Hallett, and perhaps Joachim, and although recognizing differences in mysticism, we feel that Spinoza is to be called a mystic. But see Wild, *Intuition*, 30ff., for an alternative rendering.

[23] This is a plausible theory in one way and an implausible one in another. It comes to mind when anyone (like Spinoza) suggests that we intuit simple mathematical results but not complicated ones. The argument against the habit theory is simply an appeal to the phenomenological difference between insight and knowing something without insight (which possibly marks the difference between the *a priori* and the learning of conventionalized symbols). The habit theory, of course, when squared up with a functional view of consciousness, fits well into the perennial

witnessed—child "wonders" in mathematics, whose prodigy took the form of allegedly being able to give the product of the multiplication of two numbers of several digits without the conscious carrying out of the operations or the applying of memorized short-cuts. If such exist, these would come under (B). Let it be observed, however, that any chain of reasoning, as plodding as one pleases, exhibits one kind of "intuition" (A), if only the reasoner has the patience to be sure he has an "insight" into the necessity of the connections he is traversing.

We believe that Radhakrishnan recognizes these sorts of intuition. He acknowledges (A), but he does not call it "intuition"; for it seems to him to be associated with mechanical and routine operations as against the spontaneous and creative insight of intuition. He appropriately labels it the "logic of proof." "We forget that we invent by intuition though we prove by logic." [24]

As for (B), however, we are very troubled—more troubled with our own classification than with the doubtfulness of its existence or with our author's failure to pigeon-hole it for us. For Radhakrishnan, we believe, would recognize it, and—unlike his disposition of (A)—would call it intuition. Perhaps it belongs under (3) later, which Radhakrishnan does regard as intuitive. We put it here. On the other hand, what is to be done with the quite common phenomenon of a vague sense of where one can get, or cannot get, by a certain line of proof before one has followed it out to make entirely sure? This has resemblances to (B) under (2) here, but we are inclined to place it under (3) below. We suppose ourselves to be making something of the following sort of distinction: an insight into the relations and the logical results of such relations, whether explicit or subconscious, belongs to (2); but the feeling that there is such a relation to be found, or a hunch that one has got it, or a sense that a certain line of transitions will deductively establish something, belong under (3) later. The dim sense that a certain proof can be made is an induction until it is accomplished, even though what it refers to is the possibility of making a deduction. Now all this may appear rather arbitrary; for our mental processes do seem to be continuous from fishing for an idea, to

doctrine that the difference between "reasoning" and "intuition" is basically one of the quickness of arrival at the result. If the apprehension, though mediated, is mediated so quickly as to hide the telescoped processes from conscious notice, it is called "intuition." If the transitions have to be consciously noted, the chain is called "reasoning." But it is difficult to see how direct apprehension at some point can be avoided.

[24] IVL, 177.

getting a hunch, and further to articulating and checking it. Are we not imposing a distinction between deduction and induction, between inferences which in principle are certain and inferences which run beyond the present data? Yes; but this seems to be a rather well established distinction.

V

Intuitions of meanings and of their connections account for the deductive rational component in science, but alone they suffice only for mathematics in the broad sense, i.e., for hypothetical deductive systems. Obviously, empirical science must include (1) above, sensory intuitions. It is not obvious—judging by much of the semi-popular and quasi-technical literature—that it includes more; and Radhakrishnan is quite right in drawing attention to the something more that will have to be recognized in an adequate version. "The strictest scientist who believes that he does not go beyond the facts is also intuitive without knowing it." [25]

3. Plainly science does not consist in gawking at some part of the world. Neither is it exhausted in the recording of observations, as some seem to say, no matter in what hard-headed fashion this work be done. Such a truncated version would neglect the structural features of the sciences, as these exist. This is essentially what Whitehead meant when he expressed his gratitude that our ancestors long ago were not "wise positivists." [26] Description and classification are the ground-work of a science, but the more advanced sciences search for causal laws and explanatory theories. It might be argued, moreover, that description cannot be totally innocent of connection with wider structure than is given, and that classification, in taxonomy, for instance, requires more than simply counting clusters of indices or characteristics. Even with a theory of nominal essence, there may be a sort of "intuition"—but perhaps

[25] Ibid., 181.
[26] Whitehead was not strictly confining positivistic science to the recording of observations; he was allowing it to frame formulae of succession. "But there is an absence of understandable causation to give a reason for that formula for that succession. . . . The weakness of this positivism is the way in which we all welcome the detached fragments of explanation attained in our present stage of civilization. Suppose that a hundred thousand years ago our ancestors had been wise positivists. . . . Civilization would never have developed. Our varied powers of detailed observation of the world would have remained dormant. For the peculiarity of a reason is that the intellectual development of its consequences suggests consequences beyond the topics already observed. The extension of observation waits upon some dim apprehension of reasonable connection." Nature and Life, 23f.

with its value component it as likely belongs to (4) later, as to (3) here—which discerns relevance to purpose.

Of course, one could make an heroic effort to reduce the sciences to the strictly empirical, to strip them of their extrapolations and purge them of their metaphysical ingredients. Though some may talk in a way suggestive of it, probably no one wishes to lay our "world" back into a heap of disconnected sensations; and, as long as we have consciousness of the sort we have, it could not be done, even if one wished. (Perhaps the dada-ist or the practitioner of some other form of ultra-modern art comes closest.) It has to be noted that the scientist does not engage in random observations. Operationalism is an attempt to carry out part of the program of purifying science without sacrificing its active experimental character. Experiments are directed; and operations have to be defined in some terms. Laudable as is the operationalist's aim to rid science of folklore and undiscerned prejudice, we do not suppose that the catharsis will remove all metaphysical elements. There will remain tacit metaphysical assumptions guiding the framing of experiments and defining the operations conceived to be relevant to desired discoveries.

Thus something of what we wish to do in having category (3) is at once to emphasize the presence of, and to ascribe a source for, explanatory hypotheses in science. The hypotheses may be called "intuitions," especially in their moment of crystallization in the mixed vague solution of distillates from the past and of the fluid pourings of the present; and the activity of getting the crystals, or of their happening, and perhaps the immediate matrix in which or from whence they come, can be labelled "intuition." (We shall speak of some difficulties later.)

This approximates, we trust, what Radhakrishnan is indicating in his discussion of "Intuition and Genius in Science." [27] But it does not sufficiently emphasize the range of what we would like to try to bring within category (3). We desire something that would serve as a common denominator between Poincaré, Wertheimer, Whitehead and our author. At the same time, as we try to scan its continuities, it runs in one direction toward the dim discernments of specific structures, and it stretches in the other direction toward the vague metaphysical frameworks operative behind and in our thinking. The extremes are seldom referred to as "hypotheses;" that term seems to be reserved usually for the middle stretches where we are most conscious of being engaged in inquiry, most

[27] IVL, 175-182.

conscious that we are uncertain and that we are looking for structures with certain qualifications, whether of a singular texture or of repeated patterns.

As we suggested under (d) of category (1) earlier, a belief in a physical object is an hypothesis; ordinarily one would only accept such usage when there is doubt as to what particular physical object or kind of object it is. Is this my grandfather's lever watch? Is this a time-bomb? The descrying such possibilities or hypotheses may be called "intuitive." So too for singular historical events. Did Julius Caesar cross the Rubicon, and was it in his mind to become head of the Roman state and to transform the Republic? Did this hand-cuffed man commit such-and-such a crime? One realizes that one had better not consider vague affirmative feelings as "knowledge." But they play an essential rôle in what becomes knowledge. And at times we place considerable weight on them, when we have nothing more solid available. Compared with what one has at some standpoint of assured truth, such intuitions may not seem to be worth much, for even the best of them cannot be said to be reliable until *ex post facto* they have proven to be reliable. (By the "best" of them, presumably one means those that occur in strength after a perusal of all available evidence, and in a mind that is disciplined against emotional bias. Sometimes this could exemplify a subconscious or implicit exemplification of Mill's canons of "agreement," "difference," etc., but prior to any overt testing.) However, much of the life of practice is—and, in view of ignorance and the limitations on time for research, even has to be—guided by such intuition. One skirts here the subject of value-discernment and the question of moral knowledge. Recognition of intrinsic values will be placed under category (4) to come later. But intimations of what a situation is, or a vague sense of what is likely to happen if a certain act is done or policy followed, belong here under (3). Perhaps, too, the sense of the artist as to what he can do by giving a certain turn to a medium belongs here; whereas both his own and some other spectator's appreciation of any resulting beauty will be assigned to (4). It has already been indicated that one's feeling for what can be proved by taking a certain course of logical transitions is to be put here under (3), whereas his intuition of the cogency of each step, when taken, was illustrative of type (2).

Toward the other end of the present spectrum—the end of intuitions of greatest scope and highest generality—will lie the descrying of metaphysical hypotheses. At any rate, some philosophic hypotheses are in principle the same sort of thing as we have in the sciences, and would be a continuation of science if the sciences were not specialized in the way they are. It does not seem too strange to call them hypotheses, for they have been under discussion and have been regarded as doubtful—if not by their authors, then by someone else. Perhaps the most general assumptions of all have been so widely shared or are so implicitly a part of our thinking that we have never consciously entertained them, not to mention having doubted them. This thought is suggested by Whitehead, and is a plausible extrapolation from the difficulties of becoming conscious of our presuppositions. It is characteristic of attention to focus upon what changes and what is at issue, and to neglect the background which is always there.

Now let us see if we can document some of these conceptions with textual illustrations from Radhakrishnan. There are a sufficient number of allusions to the rôle of (3) in mathematical thinking; there is a rich array of illustrations from the framing of scientific hypotheses; there are a plentitude of remarks upon intuition in philosophy, but most of them are problematic with respect to the present point. We hardly noticed any instances of intuition of singulars in the sense here at issue.

"In every logical proof," says Radhakrishnan, "there is a grasping of the intellectual togetherness as a whole, an intuition of the whole as sustained by the different steps. Not only creative insight but ordinary understanding of anything implies this process." [28] This seems to us unassailable. Again: "All dynamic acts of thinking, whether in a game of chess or a mathematical problem, are controlled by an intuitive grasp of the situation as a whole." [29] These citations are perhaps sufficient for the over-arching intuition which sees the relevance of the parts in some complicated logical or mathematical sequence. Our only argument might be over whether or not this grasp is characterized by certainty.[30] We should insist that one may be confident that he has seized a line of proof when actually there is a gap in it.

With respect to science, Radhakrishnan observes: "The art of discovery is confused with the logic of proof and an artificial simplification of the deeper movements of thought results. We forget that we invent by intuition though we prove by logic." [31] "The

---

[28] IVL, 181.   [29] *Ibid.*, 149.

[30] We are glad to note the phrasing of a remark: "Even in pure mathematics where the conclusion is not evident, until the data are brought together and set forth in logical sequence, there is an element of intuition." IVL, 153.

[31] IVL, 177.

canons of formal logic would be of excellent use, when all truths are discovered and nothing more remained to be known, but logic cannot dictate or set limits to the course of nature and progress of discovery." [32] Again: "The creative insight is not the final link in a chain of reasoning. If it were that, it would not strike us as 'inspired' in its origin." [33] Creative work "advances by leaps."

The great scientific discoveries are due to the inventive genius of the creative thinkers and not the plodding processes of the intellect. The latter might give us more precise measurements, more detailed demonstrations of well-established theories. . . . When we light upon the controlling idea, a wealth of unco-ordinated detail falls into proper order and becomes a perfect whole.[34]

Radhakrishnan has something to say about the nature of intuition which makes the inductive advances of the sciences; these remarks do not take us into his metaphysics of selfhood, so we may appropriately note them here. Scientific discovery is not reached by "conceptual synthesis," that is, by patching together abstract concepts. This mistaken supposition is to be accounted for on the basis of the following facts: first, familiarity with the materials is necessary for the emergence of the insight; second, when the discovery has been made, one can show *ex post facto* how the known facts almost pointed it out; and third, "for purposes of communication, the insight has to be set forth as a rational synthesis." [35] Perhaps he too easily discounts "imagination" which he associates with mere guessing, but he is quite right in saying: ". . . an illuminating hypothesis is not the work of mere uncontrolled imagination. Imagination unvivified by intuition, imagination which is day dreaming, fancy, reverie or guess work, will not help us to light upon the truth except by accident." [36] Plodding has already been denied effectiveness: "If the process of discovery were mere synthesis, any mechanical manipulator of prior partial concepts would have reached the insight and it would not have required a genius to arrive at it." [37] He takes note (as Poincaré and others have suggested) of the helpfulness, after much inquiry, of relaxation: "Archimedes solved his problem in his bath and not in his study." [38]

[32] *Ibid.*, 130.   [33] *Ibid.*, 178.   [34] *Ibid.*, 175.   [35] *Ibid.*, 177.   [36] *Ibid.*, 179.
[37] *Ibid.*, 178. "Apples had been falling to the ground a long time before Newton worked out the law of gravitation." *Ibid.*, 176. Radhakrishnan cites Needham: " 'There is without the least doubt an instinct for research, and often the most successful investigators of nature are quite unable to give an account of their reasons for doing such and such an experiment, or for placing side by side two apparently unrelated factors.' " *Ibid.*, 176: quoted from *The Sceptical Biologist*, 80.
[38] IVL, 180.

We wish to defer until later the consideration of certain questions concerning Radhakrishnan's conception of the relation of philosophy to various classes of intuitions. But here we may note that he—in addition to epitomizing the doctrines *about* intuition of a number of philosophers—positively affirms the rôle of intuition *in* philosophy, as though philosophy does not simply gather and relate truths from elsewhere but expresses truths that the soul already has. Roughly the reader is impressed that what Santayana gets by "animal faith," Radhakrishnan has by "spiritual faith." Nature constrained Hume, except in his sceptical moments, to suppose that fire will continue to burn and water to quench thirst; spiritual nature constrains Radhakrishnan to the "orderedness of the universe" which "is beyond mere logic."

For our senses and intellect the world is a multiplicity of more or less connected items external to themselves, and yet logic believes that this confused multiplicity is not final, and the world is an ordered whole. The synthetic activity of knowledge becomes impossible and unmeaning if we do not assume the rationality of the world. It is not arrived at by way of speculative construction; we have not searched the outermost bounds of nature or the innermost recesses of the soul to be able to say that the systematic unity of the world is a logical conclusion.[39]

It is not only the grounding of induction and deduction that is given this sort of *a priori* intuitive status. For "ethical endeavour assumes that life is worth living and will yield to the vision of the good. . . ." "We assume a spiritual imperative which urges us to seek not the safe and the expedient but the good, which is not to be confused with temporal well-being." [40] "The ethical soundness, the logical consistency and the aesthetic beauty of the universe are assumptions for science and logic, art and morality, but are not irrational assumptions." [41]

Radhakrishnan is surely dealing with fundamental matters here. It is no wonder, therefore, that there is some obscurity attending the profundity. He rightly says: "The deepest convictions by which we live and think, the root principles of all thought and life are not derived from perceptual experience or logical knowledge." [42] He traces these convictions to intuitive sources. One is not perfectly assured that there is no circularity here: men have some convictions, not explainable in certain ways, and hence there must be intuition to account for them; in turn, there is intuition, and it

39 *Ibid.*, 154.   40 *Ibid.*, 155.   41 *Ibid.*, 156.   42 *Ibid.*, 154.

tells us the truth of these convictions. The impression of a sort of circularity here may be wholly the reader's projection. And if there were a kind of elliptical construction, it may be of a species inevitable in metaphysics; we ourselves take it to be an illusion that the Cartesian program of linear deduction points the way to the "establishment" of everything in metaphysics. However, then, with respect to the way we have set up this supposed elliptical structure, it is at least possible to doubt whether our basic convictions are inexplicable in any other way than by intuition, that is, unless one is ready to call "intuition" whatever explains them. And, again, as we have—perhaps artificially—framed the thought, it is to be noted that the explanation of the existence of a conviction, a causal explanation, is not the same thing as the justification of a conviction.

Does Radhakrishnan regard these "deepest convictions" as true? As proven? He uses phrases suggestive of quite various alternatives, but we believe that, in large measure at least, this can be tidied up. In some places, the blunt words "faith," "assumption," or "postulate," are used. In one context, either a sort of inductive confirmation or a pragmatic justification is suggested. The word "fact" is used in another place; and in still another a sort of Kantian "proof" is asserted. Let us look carefully at some of the passages; perhaps they will disclose their own proper ordering.

The words "assume" or "assumption" have appeared five times in the quotations we have already given. Here are some others that suggest the same idea in different terms. "While thought cannot stir without faith in the consistency of the world, for thought itself it is only a postulate, a matter of faith." [43] "From the point of view of empirical understanding it is a mere hypothesis that the realms of nature and spirit, existence and value are not alien to one another;" however, then he continues, "but for intuition it is a fact." [44] The absence of proof but the pragmatic justification appears here: "If intuitive knowledge does not supply us with universal major premises, which we can neither question nor establish, our life will come to an end." [45] The suggestion of both inductive confirmation and pragmatic certification enters here: "Scientific experience increasingly confirms the venture of faith, but at no stage does the act of faith become a logically demonstrated proposition. Our whole logical life grows on the foundations of a deeper insight, which proves to be wisdom and not error, because it is workable." [46] In the following, both truth and proof are asserted, but the "proof"

43 *Ibid.*, 154.   44 *Ibid.*, 155.
45 *Ibid.*, 156.   46 *Ibid.*, 155.

may be pragmatic or it may be simply the self-certification of certain underived truths.

> They are the apprehensions of the soul. . . . Disbelief in them means complete scepticism. If all knowledge were of the type of perception or conception, disbelief would become inevitable. The proof of the validity of intuitive principles is somewhat similar to Kant's proof of *a priori* elements. We cannot think them away. Their opposites are inconceivable. We cannot disbelieve them and remain intellectual. They belong to the very structure of our mind. They are native to the soul. . . . If all knowledge depends for its validity on external criteria, then no knowledge is valid at all.[47]

Working backwards on the last lengthy quotation, it does seem to us that if any knowledge is to be certain, then some knowledge will have to be self-evident, as Russell at times and others have urged. If, however, one is content with only probability, then perhaps the self-certifying knowledge may be dispensed with.[48] As for the argument from inconceivability, it appears to us that the opposite of his ethical and aesthetic principles may be logically conceivable. We find ourselves unable, however, to conceive the opposite of deductive logical principles. We are unable to think up an absolute chaos, although we can easily conceive of a universe that would be so complicated that intelligence of the order of man's would fail to make any inductions (how he would live would be another question, excluded *per hypothesis*). Broad has argued that not only order but a degree of simplicity of order is a postulate of science. It is a nice question whether Kant's transcendental deduction, considered as a deduction, is not guilty of affirming the consequent. It would not do so if by some sort of insight the major premise is on the order of: "If and only if such-and-such categories, then such-and-such sort of knowledge (which the minor premise will exhibit) will be possible."

If it is needful to be explicit, we will go this far in interpreting the citations from Radhakrishnan. The "deepest convictions" to which he has referred are postulates, assumptions, or pieces of faith when viewed from the standpoint of what we have called intuition of type (2), rational or logical intuition; even though it is to be added that the assumption of the ontological validity of deduction is requisite for the application of the processes of this type. Radhakrishnan is surely right. Again, sense experience does not give these principles; Radhakrishnan is right. Further, there is pragmatic jus-

---

[47] *Ibid.*, 156f.   [48] Cf. e.g., Dewey, *Logic*, 142ff.

tification for acting on some such principles; again Radhakrishnan is right. It is always urged that inductive arguments in support of the principle of induction are circular; they seem to us to have a kind of pragmatic relevance that may be brought out by asking: "Suppose that induction never worked?" As for self-certification, ultimately discussion is irrelevant, but propaedeutically it may serve to facilitate inspection. When we conduct logical inspection, *i.e.*, test by throwing out anything whose contrary or contradictory is not self-contradictory, we think that we have left only logical "truths;" normative moral principles, for instance, are thrown out. However, as we admit in another connection, although we can conceive that total moral scepticism is true, we find that we cannot believe in it. Some moral convictions spring, as Radhakrishnan might say, from a deeper level of our being. If we call them postulates from the standpoint of deductive logic, their total status is not that of "postulates" which are "merely entertained" in order to see where they will inferentially lead; in our existential status we affirm them.[49]

With respect to philosophical intuitions of type (3) our author's position thus far has been somewhat problematic. He has plainly said that philosophy has or expresses intuitions; but his chief illustrations have been of fundamental sorts of principles that lie beyond or beneath what we usually regard as hypotheses. These dim intuitions are not those of a concrete emerging fact or of a particular connection between facts, but of an order that is presumed (or known) to be "there" all of the time. The "dimness" of their dawning (if this be a characteristic) is not due to the data having just recently been poured into consciousness, but rather is due in part to the absence of practical need for their being elicited into con-

---

[49] Miss Wodehouse sagely writes: "We can, in theory, cultivate as many hypothetical normative sciences as we like. . . . Now in ethics, as I conceive it, we seek finally to gather up, or to fall back upon, a full actuality. We have enriched our knowledge and extended our contacts by all these hypothetical studies, and now we link ourselves to our world not only through the one thing (knowledge) that we have supposed ourselves to care for, but through everything that we really care for. The uniting bonds will ramify in every direction; through the persons we are fond of, for instance, to the things that they in turn are fond of. Every interest discovers its touch with some other interest, and their mutual dependence. Finally, in conduct or in speech, we commit ourselves to some relevant part of a total assertion, momentous and substantial:—'This is the way that an integral fulfilling world-life, including our corner of it, must go. This is our way, our vocation, in a world-process which, for all its puzzles and tangles, has enough unity to earn the name of right living.' . . . The ethical judgment speaks for actuality *in excelsis*." In "Language and Moral Philosophy," *Mind* 47: 212.

REASON AND TYPES OF INTUITION   195

sciousness. They occur only in those minds that have got a compulsion or even a habit—quite abnormal on an animal basis—of examining their ideas and putting them in a logical framework. Radhakrishnan's account of self-knowledge is not such as to allow any touch of uncertainty.

The 'I' implicit in all knowledge is not something inferred from experience, but something immediately lived and known by experience. It is experienced as a fundamentally simple existent, and is not to be confused with the self as conceived. . . . The scepticism of Descartes reaches its limits and breaks against the intuitive certainty of self-consciousness. . . . Self-knowledge is far too primitive and simple to admit of an *ergo*.[50]

However, as a logical foundation for a superstructure, we find it (like Kant's "I think," which accompanies all representations) to be almost as empty as it is certain. True, it is eminently suggestive, for we feel the "mystery of the self." [51] (Confessionally speaking: why there should be anything at all is a mystery; it is even a mystery whether or not this is a mystery; why, if there was anything, it should rise to consciousness, is a mystery; why, among the things which are presumably conscious, there should be me—this is an awful mystery. It almost scares me back into transcendental morality and religion.) But theories about the self seem to be at best only probable, as are theories elsewhere. Perhaps Radhakrishnan would accept this for much of his discussion—where we suppose that he would say that he is really talking psychology.[52] We are disposed to affirm it where he is writing metaphysics also.[53]

When Radhakrishnan is discussing such subjects as matter,[54] order and progress, life, evolution, mind, self-consciousness, we find him usually discussing in a way which is in principle capable of connection with the special sciences. Whether or not his hypotheses be good, they are, on a high level of generality, structures of the same sort. We presume that such intuitions came into Radhakrishnan's mind and the minds of others in the manner of intuitions of type (3). With this, we may believe that one can reconcile the differing suggestions, some of which point, on the one hand, to an inductive confirmation of ranges of philosophical propositions, and some of which, on the other, indicate a sort of Kantian deduction.

50 IVL, 140.   51 Cf., *ibid.*, 206, 263, 273   52 E.g., *ibid.*, 262-269.
53 E.g., *ibid.*, 146, 269-311.   54 *Ibid.*, 226ff.

VI

4. With the discussion of philosophical intuitions under the last heading we touched upon the basis of ethics and aesthetics, but we explicitly come now to the first of those groups of intuitive powers which are most important—intrinsically "higher," we suppose, and urgently needed if man is to realize his capacities and perhaps if he is even to survive on his present lower levels of functioning. Contemporary man is doing well enough with intuitions of classes (1), (2), and much of (3).[55] He is miserably underdeveloped in (4) and (5)—so underdeveloped in Radhakrishnan's view that he does not know his need, though he feels it in vague dissatisfaction and sense of emptiness. "We must recapture the intuitive powers that have been allowed to go astray in the stress of life," says he.[56]

Precedent may be found in Radhakrishnan for following a not uncommon subdivision of intrinsic values into (A) Moral, (B) Aesthetic, and (C) Religious.[57]

In our own mind, a reminder is in order to the effect that here we are talking about discernment of intrinsic values. The finding of proximate goals and instrumental connections may perfectly well be the work of scientific intelligence—though we strongly suppose these involve the kind of functioning which we have signalized by giving it the distinctive category (3).[58] But, although discursive

[55] Western man, at any rate. Although it is said to be a matter of degree and emphasis rather than an absolute distinction, Radhakrishnan observes that: "While the dominant feature of Eastern thought is its insistence on creative intuition, the Western systems are generally characterised by a greater adherence to critical intelligence." IVL, 129. This is supported by citations of the logical achievements of Socrates and Aristotle, by notations of the influence of mathematics upon the Pythagoreans and Plato, by observation of the rôle of clear and distinct ideas in Descartes, Spinoza, Leibniz and recent symbolic logicians. It is found in the mentality of Kant's basic approach to philosophy (and, one might add, in the positivist's negations and affirmations); it is equally present in the reality-storming assault of the Hegelian dialectic. And so on. To be sure, Radhakrishnan's exceptions are quite as interesting—alluded to in the present context, and presented so richly in his various writings that a Western reader is ashamed of his religio-mystical illiteracy. Cf., IVL, 129-133.

[56] SM, 270.

[57] *Ibid.*, 270-286; IVL, 182-204.

[58] Whitehead apparently employs "intuition" to name both the discernment of possible structures with their lure and the taking account of the structures that are. Of the latter, the most pervasive features are raised into explicit consciousness with the greatest effort at metaphysical thought. With respect to the former, cultures and individuals exhibit special sensitivities to certain constellations of possibilities. (If one wishes to stretch the concept of intuition in Whitehead to be commensurate with his meaning of "feeling"—and there would be a certain legitimacy in doing this—then of course both of these meanings, as referring to conscious if not even intellectualistic perceptions, represent relatively highly restricted usages.)

knowledge sometimes results in a modification of our tastes and acceptances of intrinsic values, it seems impossible to us that the latter are thereby resolved into the former. This indirectly raises a question of classification, of course. If all intrinsic values are classed as aesthetic (in a comprehensive generic sense), then there will be no intrinsic moral values—unless these are a species of the former. More likely all moral values would be taken as instrumental—traffic codes to maximize the flow of intrinsic goods. There are the subtle points, however, that not only do we frequently come to enjoy good tools inherently, but we do admire certain sorts of act and disposition irrespective of their actual consequences in the circumstances of their enactment.

We are disposed to preserve (A), the moral, as distinctive, and not simply as a differentiated species of (B), the aesthetic; but it had best be broad enough to allow for three or more theories.

Then with (A) we have the conception of intuition as naming the capacity, or the content, or the processes, of apprehending intrinsic values (a) as goods which should exist as incarnating objective values; or of apprehending intrinsic values (b) which are inherent properties in certain acts, or attitudes, or characters in agents; or of apprehending intrinsic goods (c) as at once consummatory and filling the requirements for the integration of a system of goods. The first, (a), is meant to be wide enough to be instanced by such Western writers as G. E. Moore, Nicolai Hartmann, Hugo Münsterberg, B. M. Laing. The second, (b), could be given such elasticity as to cover, at the one side, Christian, Stoic, Kantian, and in general "formal" and "deontological" ethics, and at the other extreme, perhaps even theories which would say that all primary intrinsic values are generically aesthetic or non-moral, but that distinctively moral values somehow derive as emergents. The third, (c), is meant to take in such Gestaltists as Köhler and all those objective idealists who, of course, accept objective values, but who deny the finality of any value in isolation.

Moral intuition, for Radhakrishnan, is not what is found in routine, mechanical or formalized rational ethics.[59] In his discussion, emphasis is placed upon the phenomenon of the moral hero. (Nietzsche, Hartmann and James, in their respective ways, have drawn attention to the "creator," the "champion of ideas," the real "individual" with "brain born" ideas. Our staid Anglo-Saxon tradition has, for the most part, either levelled the prophets off into a sensible mediocrity or been a little ashamed of them. Poor St.

[59] SM, 273-275; IVL, 196-199.

Francis! If he didn't have the decent reserve not to go throwing himself at lepers, at least he should have been restrained by considerations of public health!) "Though morality commands conformity," notes Radhakrishnan, "all moral progress is due to nonconformists." [60] "In any critical situation the forward move is a creative act. . . . The moral hero follows an inner rhythm which goads him on and he has the satisfaction of obeying his destiny, fulfilling his self." [61] Socrates in prison and Jesus before Pilate did not behave at all like conventional good men. They quite failed to exhibit the common virtue of prudence.

Holiness is however different from vulgar prudence. . . . Those who have this chastity of mind and spirit which lies at the very heart and is the parent of all other good see at once what is good and hold to that and for its sake humble themselves even unto death. Well-being, comfort, luxury . . . leave them indifferent, if they are not felt as burdensome hindrances to the heroic life of creative love. This is true not only of the well-known sages of India and Greece, the prophets of Israel and the saints of Christendom, but also of the many obscure heroes of the moral life . . .[62]

There is no doubt about the phenomenon. There can be questions about the cause or source which our author ascribes to it. And we would like to ask questions about just what it is that the prophet intuits, and how certain it is. Is a prophet one who discerns and champions a value to which men have been blind, or which they have neglected? Is he one who makes a great effort toward, and great appeal for, a reorganization of structures to secure a wider realization of values which are already accepted? Or may he be both? Does an examination of the phenomena of moral heroes yield evidence that is best handled by theory (a) or (b) or (c), or, more likely, some other? In what respects are the intuitions of the prophet to be described as "discoveries" and in what respects as "creations"? Perhaps their creative character refers either to their non-deducibility from existing standards (and the "spontaneous" way in which the spirit blows them into consciousness) or to their far-reaching social effects. But their objective grounding in "spirit" —that they are distinct from idiosyncrasies—leads our author to call them "discoveries." When a man is integrated

he has the right to say 'I will.' His free decisions seem then to come of themselves and develop of their own accord, though they may be contrary to his interests and inclinations. They infringe on the ordinary

[60] IVL, 197.   [61] *Ibid.*, 196f.   [62] SM, 273.

routine of life and bring into it a new type of power. These creative decisions cannot be foreseen, though they may be accounted for in retrospect. Though they defy anticipation, they are thoroughly rational.[63]

Do the "creative decisions" fit what is called a formal or deontological ethics better than a teleological one? Do they register an objective fittingness to the total encompassing situation? Perhaps the view is close to that of Bradley. There is an appropriateness incarnate everywhere in the concrete universal. But it is at the same time teleological. Both phases are suggested by the terminology of Radhakrishnan. "Whether a plan of action is right or wrong . . . can be decided only by men whose conscience is educated. . . ." [64] And: "ethical certainty requires a highest end from which all other ends are derived, an end which flows from the very self and gives meaning and significance to the less general ethical ends." [65]

As for the certainty of moral judgments, there are several difficulties to be mentioned. Of course, if one has a view like G. E. Moore's, there is no claim of an intuition about what one should do; there are only intuitions of good, not of the content of "rightness" or "oughtness." Indeed, the Moore of the *Principia Ethica* was, with perfect consistency, highly sceptical as to whether we ever know what is right.[66] We think his analysis of "right" was mistaken (as he himself later inclined to believe), but, more importantly, the whole apparatus of utilitarianism—ideal as well as hedonic—does not seem to fit the consciousness of prophets or fanatics (whichever one may label them). Radhakrishnan may exaggerate in the other direction, but he seems closer to the phenomena when he says, "To one of ethical sensitiveness, the path of duty is as clear as any knowledge we possess." [67] This statement is interesting, in part because it attaches certainty to the concrete course of duty, and not just to the ends intended by it. It is interesting for other reasons, not the least of which is that it seems to us to be almost incredible, although we wish it to be true. We shall pretend to no significant degree of ethical sensitiveness, and thus our evidence from the moral kindergarten may be wholly irrelevant. But in our experience, at least, we find that as we increase our sensitivity a little our problems grow more complex.[68] When should we refuse the tacit

---

63 *Ibid.*, 274.   64 IVL, 142. Cp. Aristotle.   65 *Ibid.*, 158.
66 *Principia Ethica*, 149.   67 IVL, 198.

68 It is not that we have no practical certainties with respect to values or to the course of conduct. We have some practical certainties and some distressing uncertainties. I find myself referring to "knowledge" of intrinsic values. I can entertain the hypothesis that aesthetic and moral reactions are "only" reactions; I do not find that

obligations imposed upon us by the affection of our friends—friends whose agency, of course, is not really in our control? How far should we sacrifice the interests of those who are near and dear and dependent upon us by pouring their material basis into the seemingly bottomless hole of the world's abysmal corporeal need? Should we injure and kill men who are engaged in injuring and killing others? Perhaps a genuinely creative agent finds a positive solution which transcends all the antitheses and dilemmas which we conventional minds unimaginatively accept as ultimate. I hope so. But it is plausible that even some of the heroes have been troubled. Although we do not know the inner life of the prophet of Nazareth, for instance, it seems unlikely that all his nightly vigils were devoted to bringing his will into subjection to his ideal; probably some of them were struggles to become clear as to what he ought to do after he was resolved to do what he ought.

We do presume that Radhakrishnan's moral hero is one who intuits in specific situations what is the creatively appropriate thing for him to do. This obviates the supposition of a generalized intuition or a moral rule or universal law. In the Western philosophical context, such rules would apparently constitute synthetic propositions, and would be "rational" and a priori in nature. (To be sure, we may not have explored very far other sorts of a priori; N. Hartmann has advanced a sort of valuational or emotional a priori; possibly there are a priori symbolic forms for psycho-analysts, Mrs. Langer, and Gestaltists. Scheler and N. Hartmann have sought to apply their material a priori in ethics; but, with "strength" of value competing with its "height," and with differing degrees of involvement and with "personal values" also entering as factors, the supposed simple immediate intuition of location in a value scale is very far from solving specific moral problems.)

So far as we have noticed, Radhakrishnan seems to make no point of asserting any intuition in the realm of moral conformity. Inasmuch as even an extensive equipment of moral rules is not self-applying, we might have expected him to assign some low grade type of intuition as requisite for discerning relevance and,

---

I can believe it. Conceptually I can doubt whether acts manifesting cruelty are bad (this is not here an analytic statement); really I cannot doubt it. Conceptually I can entertain the idea that classics and comic strips "simply" appeal a bit differently to different people; but actually I cannot practically doubt a difference in inherent value, quite independent of—and at times inversely proportional to—their respective effects upon numbers of persons. But these practical certainties dissolve as I approach morally dilemmatic situations or questions of the comparison of two "high" values or two "low" values.

of course, for exercising any tailoring and adjustment with respect to the application of the multiplicity of *prima facie* imperatives. The foregoing constitutes no argument for it, but one does wonder whether our author's emphasis on the moral hero is not one which is engaged in transcending the moral point of view. It is not that we would confine the moral life to the realm of "claims and counterclaims" (at least if these be conceived in a legalistic way); but, like many other Westerners, we are unclear as to the relation of the saint to the moral realm (and, in the present context, we are presuming the moral hero is on the way to becoming a saint).

It is not our intent falsely to allege that the Hindu (in Radhakrishnan's interpretation) has no "social" obligations; plainly the "householder" has such responsibilities, and probably the system of caste was in considerable measure an institutionalized division of duties. It is not in our province to discuss whether the "forest dweller" and the "saṁnyāsin" are so individualistic that they disregard social ties, or whether they are heeding the call of a vocation which is intrinsically higher and thus given competitive priority among values, or whether they are to be conceived as still performing social functions of a most important sort, discharged through non-material media.[69] However, the scope of this paper does include such questions as the following. Is the teleological orientation toward salvation so basic that one speaks misleadingly if he refers (as we have done) to intrinsic good in the area of the moral? Rather does not the intrinsic good lie over the horizon from the moral, although—when in the moral realm—one should be marching toward that horizon? Is the moral at best in a sort of instrumental status,[70] a propaedeutic, a discipline? Strictly, is all intuition supra-moral, or is there a kind of intuition dealing with appropriateness at different levels of life? Is not the moral point of view bound up essentially with an ignorance that is to be done away with?[71] But how then does the insight come which shows that we

[69] Cf. HVL, 90ff.; ER, 43-57, 61-68, 77-110, 351-371, 378-383.

[70] Man "finds his goodness in what is more than himself. . . . Knowledge, art, morality and religion are the *devices* employed by man to realise his destiny as a member of a spiritual fellowship . . ." IVL, 273 (*Italics* mine). Here one notes, however, that plurality as well as unity seem inherent in the goal. "Again, morality, individual and social, is not a mere rational ordering of man's relations with his fellows but is a *means* for his growing into the nature of spirit." ER, 99. "The motive behind ethical practices is that of purging the soul of selfish impulses so that it may be fitted to receive the beatific vision." *Ibid.*, 105.

[71] "Hindu and Buddhist thinkers with a singular unanimity make out that *avidyā* or ignorance is the source of our anguish, and *vidyā* or wisdom, *bodhi* or enlightenment is our salvation. The former is intellectual knowledge which produces self-

must have a further insight to overcome present *avidyā*? (In the foregoing, we would not define the moral as necessarily exhausted in the duties between selves, but we would conceive it as necessarily related to finite selfhood.)[72] On the other hand, does not our author seem to refer to truth, beauty and goodness as absolutes for us?[73] (Perhaps they are absolutes for everything in the realm of plurality, from Īśvara on down.) He argues that Kant did not explicitly interpret his own mind, and boldly renders him: "The moral consciousness is the point where we touch absolute reality. Conscience is the call of reality within the individual mind." [74]

Radhakrishnan, of course, repeatedly denies that the doctrine of *māyā* is a doctrine of the unreality of the world, or that it makes all moral relations meaningless.[75] We feel that on this matter, he softens Śaṁkara considerably, and departs from him. He is liberalizing the thought of some in saying: "When the Hindu thinkers ask us to free ourselves from *māyā,* they are asking us to shake off our bondage to the unreal values which are dominating us. They do not ask us to treat life as an illusion or to be indifferent to the world's welfare." [76] Not only does he maintain that there is "no inconsistency between mysticism and the most exalted ethics," and that it is "a one-sided view of contemplation that makes it exclusive of moral activity," [77] but he seizes the nettle of the familiar Western charge that the ethics of Hindu mysticism, as well as of Buddhism, is world-negating. "If good will, pure love, and disinterestedness are our ideals," he declares, "then our ethics must be

---

consciousness and self-will." ER, 43. "While the human being belongs to a larger world . . . his self-consciousness sets up a dualism which is untrue to fact and opposed to his whole nature. . . . While this strong sense of individuality is necessary for action, it is confused with individualism. . . . His conscience is the sign of a divided life." IVL, 273. "Is the state of mokṣa, or release from saṁsāra, consistent with work for the world? Śaṁkara is inclined to answer this question in the negative, since all activity, with which we are familiar, presupposes a sense of duality . . ." Ind P, II, 643.

72 "Morality, in the modern world, is confused with social values, but the latter are not the whole of values." Ind P, II, 630.

73 "Truth, beauty and goodness are not subjective fancies but objective facts. They are not only ultimate values included in the purpose of the world but supreme realities." SM, 277. "They are the thoughts of God and we think after him. Truth, beauty and goodness are not existent objects like the things that are true, beautiful and good, and yet they are more real than the persons, things and relations to which they are ascribed." IVL, 199.

74 IVL, 164; cf. 70, 168ff.

75 HVL, 61ff.; ER, 27ff., 86, 88, 93, 99f.; cf. his remarks on Śaṁkara's ethics, Ind P, II, 621ff.

76 ER, 47.

77 *Ibid.,* 108.

rooted in other-worldliness." [78] And so he moves over to the counter-attack against naturalistic humanism.

We can report that in the West there are quite a number among us who think ourselves naturalists, but who do prefer co-operation, good-will, social betterment, etc., and not only because it seems prudent. We may even prefer these when they are disadvantageous to our own material interests.

Radhakrishnan may reply that such persons are in some sense "inconsistent" with their professed metaphysical basis, that they have not thought through their own views to coherence. [79] Either their sentiments are blinding them to the natural "consequences" of the position to which they really adhere, or else they genuinely have the moral commitment but wish to profess the naturalism which seems so popular and plausible.

It is to be admitted that naturalism in anything like its purity has not been tried in social life. In the main, we have been banking on education and sentiments which came from religious traditions, even when we have denied the cognitive claims made by the legacies. On the other hand, it is not fair to pick as examples those who have been in the forefront of reactions against our moral heritage. On the one side, there is a host typified by our Stuart Mills and our John Deweys who have been in the vanguard of movements of humane reform; on the other side, there are the Himmlers and Hitlers as well as the socially irresponsible Epicureans. Neither are representative.

Naturalism implies no transcendental ethics. But positively this does not imply no morals. It seems that the kind of morals that would be had would depend upon the men who had them. A most intricate psychological problem is constituted by attempting to forecast what this would be on the basis of the inherited nature of man; it is further complicated by the fact that any generation would have a cultural heritage. On top of this, the next several generations may be unpredictably distorted through the growth of psychological technology, which is perhaps more ominous than the recently opened Pandora's box of atomic energy.

Some Western naturalists (perhaps biased with a natural piety

---

[78] *Ibid.*, 83. Cf. IVL, 69ff., 82, 315, 333; also RR, 424-442.

[79] "An ethical theory must be grounded in metaphysics, in a philosophical conception of the relation between human conduct and ultimate reality. As we think ultimate reality to be, so we behave. Vision and action go together." ER, 80. Cf. also IVL, 52-74, 312ff.

which we admire) are confident that what we may for loose convenience call the "higher" capacities of man will assert themselves even when the metaphysical schema which was supposedly their root has been pulled up and completely dried out. Perhaps their faith exceeds their evidence, but they may plausibly argue that the supposed metaphysical roots were really at best only tendrils, put forth by vital processes seeking support of cultural formations in a certain environment. The "higher" as well as the "lower" expressions of these vital processes can be trusted to become manifest in a changed scene and climate.

For some of us the moral issue may not be simply the finding of a way that is viable. (Of course, at the present time in mankind's history, it looks as if this may—due to technological developments—become the issue.) Ordinarily one might think that there are a plurality of ways of life that are not, even in the long range, suicidal for men. But some of these we might conceivably pronounce to be the life of "well-adjusted animals" in contrast to what we might laud as "truly human" living. The determination of the source from which, or the basis on which, such evaluations are made is an interesting subject for inquiry, and particularly relevant for the naturalist to ask of himself. The life and arrangement disapproved as that of "well-adjusted animals" presumably frustrates or leaves undeveloped certain capacities that are regarded with esteem. If these are native, are they not weak enough that perhaps they can be neglected, perhaps they ought to be sacrificed, for the sake of the economy of satisfactions which, *per hypothesis*, can get along moderately well without them? If these "needs" and the taste for them are derived, artificial compounds, then may not the social arrangement which fails to generate them be perfectly justified in excusing itself from producing such exotic luxuries? But conceivably these are our so-called "higher" values which are being denied entry to existence or the right thereto. This may well be serious. To secure any decent standing for them in the order of relative priorities, we may have to resort to "intuitions" of their worth.

Naturalists are not happy with intuitions except those of types (1), (2) and (3), as we have labelled them in this essay. The intuition that x is accepted by Mr. Y. as a value can be drawn in as the matter of fact which it is. Likewise the observation that w is preferred to x by Mr. Y. But it is not easy to see how we get that v should be preferred to either w and x by Mr. Y and Mr. Z and others, save as a statement of individual or collective prudence.[80] Assuming that norms can be found in or legitimately derived from the realm of existence, it appears a little anomalous that some of us should be as confident as we are about the norms when we know as little as we do about the existences which are supposed to ground them. To some of us, perhaps the credibility of naturalism turns upon what can be justified from those structures in events of which we are now ignorant. (Presumably this will be true only of persons with very strong convictions of moral or aesthetic truths.)

Certain of Radhakrishnan's strictures on naturalism might strike some of us in a softer spot than they do, if these were urging and developing the considerations above, when making partially admissible pragmatic points:

> Moral enthusiasm is possible only if our motive includes the expectation of being able to contribute to the achievement of moral ideals. . . . We cannot help asking ourselves whether our ideals are mere private dreams of our own or bonds created by society, or even aspirations characteristic of the human species. . . . We need to be fortified by the conviction that the service of the ideals is what the cosmic scheme demands of us.[81]

These are important psychological considerations, but they do not touch the core of the matter for those who feel that all questions of existence, even the widest and deepest, are questions of fact. But he does move on the focus when he suggests that we should not rest content with Russell's "strange mystery" that " 'nature, omnipotent but blind . . . has brought forth at last a child, subject to her power, but gifted with sight and knowledge of good and evil, with the capacity of judging all the works of his unthinking mother.' " [82]

On Radhakrishnan's habit of treating naturalism as reductionistic, we wish to comment later. It may be remarked that apparently

[80] There is a shift of attention here, of course, from an "is" factor to an "ought" factor, but this focal transition is not the only one. It can be bridged to an imperative, a hypothetical imperative, by rendering explicit the conditions of prudence. That leaves the basic issue as to whether there are any categorical imperatives, but it also leaves two other questions: Whose interests are to be included in the reckoning of prudence, and how are comparative weightings of values to be determined, within the individual's life or as between all interested parties? Manifestly, concrete objects and events are frequently of positive value to one person or group and of negative value to another. And the conflicts of incomparable goods which the individual faces are intensified across the boundaries (whether these exist only in *māyā* or not) between persons.

[81] ER, 81f.

[82] Quoted in IVL, 56 from Bertrand Russell's *Mysticism and Logic*, 48.

some "insights" are so patent to him that, even if he be right, he does not seem to pause and progress patiently enough in getting to his idealism.[83] Here we will conclude by noting that he believes, as we interpret him, that if naturalism be true, or be accepted as true, there cannot be peace; but that really idealism is true, and it has scarcely entered men's minds what they can, indeed, will become; the great saints give an inkling of our present possibilities and our actual future.

These are in part assertions of fact that bear upon those areas which, as we have intimated, we need to know about but do not know much about. As speculative, comparison of Hobbes' psychology and Radhakrishnan's version of naturalism, and contrast of their respective estimates of the possibility of peace are relatively superficial because of the manifestly different degrees and levels of "peace." If by moral or institutional means we get over our habits of mass homicide, we may be very far from economic and social peace, from the elimination of group unrest and of intense friction between persons. Radhakrishnan probably includes triumph over these latter in his conception of peace.

Antecedent to inquiry, the empiricist would have to say that it is possible that individual man is, by inherited structures, given as an anarchy and fated to remain a relatively chaotic medley, and that mankind is by nature—not necessarily by the presence of a combative instinct—so endowed as to make the emergence of intense overt conflicts inevitable in collectivities. However, let us observe that some evidence is already in, and it is sufficient to render both suppositions unlikely. Some men are highly integrated, and some men have learned to live in peace with their fellows. It seems improbable that anything given in man absolutely precludes the formation of a peaceful world. If this be right, then, when and if he knows the truth, he "can" become "free." Though his future is far from assured, it may be that during coming millennia man can experiment along a wide variety of lines, rather than along just two or three, and approximate the realization of the socio-psychological truth. But, considering various ideological incubi and the fearsome rise of psychological technology, such secular optimism does not seem likely of confirmation in some early liberal future.

[83] It cannot be charged that Radhakrishnan is such an ingrained optimist that he has no inner grasp of pessimism; anyone who could interpret Gautama Buddha's problem so sympathetically or could compose such pages as 425-429 in RR has sounded the depths of despairing interrogations.

It is a pity that we cannot pause in our discussion to take note of Radhakrishnan's incisive discernment of the moral condition of man, especially Western man whose mechanical powers ill accord with his ethical infantilism. Few have ever stated it so eloquently or made such a sincere appeal to forsake our fevered morbidity. But Radhakrishnan observes, "The more sick, the less sensible." [84] He does not hesitate to prescribe for us, in terms of the truth as he sees it: "The way to growth lies through an increasing impersonality, through the unifying of the self with a greater than the self." [85]

VII

(B) We cannot here do an essay on Radhakrishnan's aesthetics; for we are not obliged to, and it would be too difficult for us. Although he does not write extensively on the subject, what he does say touches upon so many themes and remarks upon so many theories as to render simple statement impossible or unjust. A number of expressions and concepts (*e.g.,* fusion, oneness, absorption, vision, creation, inspiration, truth, reality, etc.) leave us quite uncertain as to how literally or how figuratively they are to be taken. At times, some of these and other terms seem to be employed in contexts of psychological description; in other places, they seem to be incorporated in metaphysical propositions. And Radhakrishnan's metaphysics of aesthetics is obscure. One cannot avoid it, however, if one tries to relate his view of the rôle of art to morality and religion. Very roughly, we suppose, the proximate and relevant portions may be put as follows. Aesthetic perception (whether in creation or appreciation) is done with the whole self,[86] or relatively so. And this self is at some stage of various possible levels of development; sensitiveness "is dependent on the degree of development of the self." [87] Such development may, in some sense, be equivalent to the degree of manifestation of, awareness of, submergence in—we do not know what characterization to use—the Absolute self. Artistic creations will be the natural vehicle of ex-

---

[84] ER, 44.

[85] And he spells out the discipline in three stages: "purification, concentration, and identification." *Ibid.,* 48ff.

[86] SM, 269; IVL, 136, 147, 153, 179ff., 196. With Bergson he seems to say that if we want to know the whole of a thing or the inner nature of reality, this does not mean that we should patiently use intellect upon all of it; instead it means that "we must resort to the whole personality of which intellect is only a part." IVL, 144.

[87] "Whether . . . an object presented is beautiful or ugly can be decided only by men . . . whose sensibility is trained." But: "Sensitiveness . . . is dependent on the degree of development of the self." IVL, 142. Cp. Aristotle.

pression of religious "truth" and of moral truth. With respect to the latter, we mean not only dressing morality in attractive garments but conveying the insight itself, in so far as it can be conveyed (presenting the "soul," to continue the figure of speech). Perhaps one should add that the richness of metaphysical truth will likewise require artistic symbols—and will overflow them all, though, presumably, this is not the way that philosophy is to set forth metaphysical propositions.[88] True morality is applied metaphysical truth; and religion is appropriated metaphysical reality.

On this assumed outline, there remain many questions. An immediate one relates to the themes of universality and individuality, which it may be felt that Bosanquet has already resolved in the Hegelian notion of the concrete universal. Radhakrishnan observes that ". . . great intuitions bear the stamp of personality . . . no two men can ever produce the same work of art, for art is the expression of the whole self . . ."[89] This must refer to our plural (empirical) spirits. But we also read: "Even if art is self-expression, the self that is expressed is not the narrow particular one."[90] Radhakrishnan is not purposely hiding anything from us; we run headlong into the statement: "The deeper we penetrate, the more unique we become, and the most unique is the most universal."[91]

His metaphysics of the "fact of the spiritual character of both subject and object"[92] lends a degree of plausibility to his acceptance of what we have regarded as the Yōgin's type of empirical samādhi. We must "transcend discursive thinking," he says, "if we want to know things in their uniqueness. . . . Direct perception or simple and steady looking upon an object is intuition. It is not a mystic process, but the most direct and penetrating examination possible to the human mind."[93] This account, however, whether or not it be complicated by doctrines of the possibility of such knowing without the senses, raises questions about the emphases upon creation (as against discovery), of remoulding as against receiving. It would take too much space to parade the passages which make one or other of these emphases. We will simply consider two suggestions as to how they might bear upon effecting a reconciliation.

First, certain passages may be sorted out on the basis of the distinction between the artist and the appreciator, who may represent respectively creation and beholding. This suggestion may serve in instances, but it does not go to the root of the matter. For Radha-

88 RR, 1, 4f., 15. 89 IVL., 147. 90 *Ibid.*, 193.
91 *Ibid.*, 146. 92 *Ibid.*, 146. 93 *Ibid.*, 146.

krishnan observes that appreciation itself is creative; [94] and, surely, in turn, the artist has to be his own appreciator in being his own critic while he works.[95]

Second, clarification may result from asking in what realm "creation" is conceived as taking place. This affords a possibly complete solution. If creation means bringing into the region of temporal discernment something which embodies a certain essence or frames it for contemplation, then there is creation. But no one creates the very possibilities, the very forms themselves; they only create the realizations. One may intuit but he does not create a Santayanan essence or a Whiteheadian eternal object. These have their non-existent sort of being, their status of possibilities, eternally in the Absolute.

However, we do have a classificatory concern which hinges on the distinction between the appreciator and the creator, or rather between factors in the complex activity of the "creator" who is carrying a rôle of doing in the same process as he is inspired by what he beholds.[96] Granting that both the immediate directing of his work and his vision of what he aims to consummate as a product are intuitive in nature, it may well be that they are not of the same species. Is his vision of what he aims to consummate an aesthetic intuition, while his discernment of how to do it is, perhaps, an intuition of our type (3), as discussed earlier, or, possibly, an intuition of type (4, A), a basically moral intuition of what he ought to do? We shall evade giving an answer; but at least a distinction of reason is possible between the rôles, with the consequences of possible different classification. In the testimony of artists one finds such varying reports that one supposes that, for instance, some sculptors envision the end-product almost in full detail long before the work is done if not even before it is commenced, whereas others do their thinking so much in the medium that nearly all their

94 *Ibid.*, 208.

95 Indeed, Radhakrishnan expressly notes that the working of genius in science and in art is not commanded, and cites the evidence or testimony of various scientists and poets. "A sort of intellectual passivity is demanded . . ." "Genius is not made with effort." IVL, 180; cf. 186, 346. These observations, however, are psychological references to the realm of consciousness; they would not preclude "creation" in the sub-conscious. To our author's impressive list, ranging from the Vedic authors to Housman, we beg to append the word of A. A. Milne, as disclosed in the quaint testimony of Pooh Bear. Making a poem isn't easy, says Pooh, "Because Poetry and Hums aren't things which you get, they're things which get *you*. All you can do is to go where they can find you." *The House at Pooh Corner*, N.Y., 1935, 146f.

96 Miss Wild not only makes a strong point of distinguishing knowledge (or appreciation) of beauty from the power to create it, but she argues by analogy that the latter had best be viewed as a skill. *Intuition*, 137f.

creative direction comes during the process.[97] The medium itself may make a difference. If one is working in marble, he had better get his inspiration clarified before proceeding; if one is working in clay, he might well differentiate it at work. Radhakrishnan's favorite illustrations are from poetry. He does distinguish the poetic "experience or the vision" (which "is the artist's counterpart to the scientific discovery of a principle of law") [98] from the work of composition or of translating into words and images.[99] "Even in the act of composition the poet is in a state in which the reflective elements are subordinated to the intuitive. . . . The spell of the experience is still on the poet and under its influence he employs intuitive words and images. . . . While poetry is not the vision itself, but only the image of it, still its quality depends on the degree with which it calls up the vision." [100] (Elsewhere it is clear that the quality also depends upon the worth of the vision.) [101] Although Radhakrishnan qualifies, if he does not deny, any division between intuition and expression, and even says that "The experience has its full shape in the words and phrases which clothe it," still he not only distinguishes the implicit presence of the expression from its explicit realization, but he observes that "inarticulateness stands between experience and expression for the average man." [102] And it is suggested that even when the poet has perfect awareness of his experience, "its verbal equivalent is not developed in it." [103] We would follow Radhakrishnan and Whitehead in distinguishing between, on the one hand, experience (yes, and intuition) and, on the other, capacity to express in symbolic objects or in extant literal language the content of the experience or intuition. The sermons of certain positivists with respect to the possibility of clear lin-

97 Dewey, a writer who loathes the word "intuition," recognized very acutely some of the phenomena named by it. On the present point, we recall him saying: "Whether a musician, painter, or architect works out his original emotional idea in terms of auditory or visual imagery or in the actual medium as he works is of relatively minor importance. For the imagery is of the objective medium undergoing development. The physical media may be ordered in imagination or in concrete material. . . . Only by progressive organization of 'inner' and 'outer' material in organic connection with each other can anything be produced that is not a learned document or an illustration of something familiar." *Art as Experience*, 75.

98 IVL, 184.   99 *Ibid.*, 187.   100 *Ibid.*, 188.
101 *Ibid.*, 188-192; cf. SM, 272.   102 IVL, 188.

103 *Ibid.*, 188. "But let it not be forgotten that the true work of art is charged with thought. It is not the expression of mere emotion. . . . A Beethoven symphony or a Shakespeare play has one indivisible inspiration but its expression involves elaborate labor on the intellectual plane." SM, 273. Radhakrishnan is nearer here to Matthew Arnold's "Austerity of Poetry" than in most of his references.

guistic statement of any idea at any time and the homilies of Croce with respect to the identity of intuition and expression may be healthy encouragements to efforts at clarity and to jestings at pretence, but they are ultimately false. There do seem to be pregnancies and gestation of what sometimes later becomes explicit cognition. And miscarriages, too.

The citation of the use of such a term as "experience" is a suitable place for raising the underlying question of the appropriateness of the word "intuition" or of any substitute which suggests cognitive content when one is speaking of the aesthetic. There is little doubt that Radhakrishnan claims a kind of cognitive content for it; but it is not clear what it is, and, in terms of the theory itself, it may be unfair or nonsensical to ask for a statement in literal language of what this content is.

We have no doubt of the apprehension of so-called eternal objects and we have small practical doubt (though considerable theoretical doubt) of an apprehension of beauty in beautiful things. Some ranges of the first of these have already been taken account of in intuition of type (2). Perhaps there are other ranges, *e.g.*, possible sense patterns, apprehended as intuitions of type (1), and possible patterns of (shall we say?) emotion, apprehended as intuitions of type (4B). These latter possibilities, or more likely some species of them, or some sub-species of both those of (4) and of (1), may be what we would need to discriminate in order to demarcate the beautiful.

As has already been evident, we are prepared to recognize as "knowledge" of certain sorts the discernments which do, or which might, issue in the following judgments: (a) "This is beautiful;" (b) "That would be beautiful;" [104] (c) "This is the thing to do next to make a certain object which would be beautiful." (We have suggested that the last may not belong to the same type as the first two.)

However, there is reason to think that all this would seem quite inadequate to Radhakrishnan. In explicitly discussing "artistic knowledge," he is obviously not treating of knowing how to do art, and he is apparently moving out into dimensions of "knowledge" which we would feel disposed to class as generically moral and

---

[104] "Imagination is the power of combining images or ideas, i.e. in finding between them a before unrecognized relationship, but intuition consists in the realization . . . of the presence of beauty brought about by the combination." Wild, *op. cit.*, 139.

perhaps metaphysical. Beauty of nature is not treated, but art is said to be a "form of knowledge," an "imitation . . . of inward reality." [105] Presumably this does not mean that works of art are material for knowledge by other persons who desire to become acquainted with the totally non-cognitive feelings of the artists; art productions are not just symptoms of the life of sentiment. Against Croce, Radhakrishnan urges that the viewing of poetry specifically as expression of personal mood would fail to account for its significance to other men.[106] The artist's mind "discerns within the visible world something more real than its outward appearance, some idea or form of the true, the good, or the beautiful. . . . Yet this idea or form, this meaning or value is . . . the very heart of the object itself. . . . Poetic truth is a discovery, not a creation." [107] Again, "Poetic truth is different from scientific truth since it reveals the real in its qualitative uniqueness . . ." [108]

Radhakrishnan does not seem simply to be saying that the arts increase our powers of perception and discrimination, and that they teach us to pause to attend to the qualitative aspects of experience. They do this. Even color photography is helping us to notice colors. Various arts, but perhaps especially the literary and dramatic arts, lure us from our rapt involvement in the practical routine.

There is a didactic aspect to almost all literature—often the more educative when it is not overt. Our emotions are unconsciously placed in tutelage. We learn something of what it is to be a human being. Our powers of social perception and life discernment are improved. In a balanced education, all of the humanities contribute to this. Especially in great novels and dramas we have exhibited for us—in a time range that is in our grasp and with the distracting unessentials pared away—some of the universal conditions to be taken into account in the administration of the human career. Indeed, this fact constituted until recently the core of one of the best theories of tragedy—and perhaps it still draws attention to a crucially important factor in accounting for how it is that we are deeply grateful for—and without any sense of gloating—a spectacle which portrays a course of happenings which is unpleasant, stark, pathetic, unrelieved by events though perhaps relieved by meaning and dignity.

Radhakrishnan, we think, in effect says all of this, and it is a saying of a great deal indeed. And we believe it is true.

105 IVL, 192.   106 *Ibid.*, 193.
107 *Ibid.*, 192.   108 *Ibid.*, 193.

However, it seems that Radhakrishnan is claiming still something more. This remainder is very important, if true, but of it we are quite doubtful. Our author is either conveying the idea that great art is an "argument" for idealistic philosophy, or he is holding that the idealistic philosophy is true and that the degree of its reflection in art is a criterion of the greatness of the work. It appears that Radhakrishnan would give a theory which would—with a universalized notion of the self—quite express the literal truth of Wordsworth's testimony: " '. . . I communed with all that I saw as something not apart from, but inherent in my own immaterial nature.' " "The endless variety of the sensible world," adds Radhakrishnan, "becomes the symbol of an invisible ideal world which is behind and within it, sustaining both it and the mind which perceives it." [109] Such statements, and further references to Platonic Ideas and Browning's "seeds of Creation," might be construed in a psychological descriptive sense, but what our author has asserted earlier makes such interpretation unlikely:

Strictly speaking, logical knowledge is non-knowledge, avidyā, valid only till intuition arises. The latter is reached when we break down the shell of our private, egoistic existence, and get back to the primeval spirit in us from which our intellect and our senses are derived. . . . The fact of the spiritual character of both subject and object is lost in our conventional life where we mistake our true self for the superficial one.[110]

The consequence of this is that what we have regarded as the moral effects and the tacit moral teachings of art are viewed as more than moral. They are, for Radhakrishnan, tied up with a metaphysic, and are not allowed a merely humanistic orientation. Every thoughtful person can agree that it is a function of the arts "to quicken the perceptions of wonder and surprise, of strangeness and beauty, of the mystery and miraculousness of the world that surrounds us," but Radhakrishnan will not let us go without the affirmation: "Man has the roots of his being struck deep into the nature of reality. On this bedrock are all his creative activities firmly based." [111] We all may admit that "The particular persons

109 *Ibid.*, 184.

110 *Ibid.*, 146. The explanation of Śaṁkara's distinction between the aesthetic attitude and saintly emancipation is stated thus by Professor Hiriyanna: "The elimination of Kāma and karma while their cause avidyā continues in a latent form marks the aesthetic attitude; the dismissal of avidyā even in this latent form marks the saintly attitude." Quoted by Radhakrishnan (presumably with approval), Ind P, II, 624fn. The points of analogy to Schopenhauer's teaching will impress the Western reader.

111 SM, 271.

and events in a play may not be existent and yet the play may have a meaning and a value which have a higher and more abiding reality than the existent things," but the subject of this volume will not let us take it in our own way. Although it is "not the function of art to give a detailed justification of particular events," still art "gives us a sense of the meaningfulness of life, evokes in us ideas of the larger beauty, justice and charity of the universe. . . . The universe is sound at the core." [112]

There is a plausibleness to this, and one might not refuse to assert it in a psychological context. Subjectively speaking, we are seldom so pessimistic about human existence as on encountering some forms of public amusement, including musical comedies. If this is all that life has to give it meaning, one says to oneself, then indeed it is a worthless show. How shoddy is the whole concatenation—that the groans and slaughterings of evolution were gone through to produce this! Great tragedy, on the other hand, can rend one's emotions, can depict a train of suffering without temporal salvation, and still leave one feeling that there is meaning. What man instances gives him a little nobility, whether or not there is a Cosmic Spectator. He is spared the greatest tragedy—that of being a farce.

It seems that Radhakrishnan is suggesting that all great art, regardless of medium, genre, or species, is essentially liturgy. That it frequently has liturgical effect, we have just iterated. That it has moral effects, we fully admit. But, unless stipulated by definition or legislated from a metaphysical point of view, it is doubtful whether the greatest art need be edifying, though we should have to concur that it must be profound. Remarks Radhakrishnan: "All great artists, who have the subtle, spiritual appeal, convey a stillness, a remoteness, a sense of the beyond, the far away." [113] One does not know whether the dependent clause is restrictive or appositive, although we assume the latter. The artist's representation of "new" eternal objects and new connections between the familiar can perhaps go far to explain the sense of "remoteness." [114] Swin-

---

[112] IVL, 194f. [113] SM, 272.

[114] Though we suppose the existent sets limits to human imagining and conceiving, we would suggest that knowledge of our existent world is not instanced when one is simply apprehending eternal objects. (Even rationalists did not maintain otherwise, save as these entities were ordered in a unique logical pattern.) However, entertaining essences can be called a kind of knowledge of possible worlds; and thus it is a way of putting our particular world and experience into perspective. Certainly some of art gives one a sense of "other worlds," and charges them with a glow of vividness. Such other worlds, of course, are not under necessity of being beautiful; men have imagined various hells which are not pleasant to contemplate. Whatever

burne and Housman, at their best, give one the sense of the "far away," but they would not, in the popular sense, be said to have "spiritual appeal." [115] Nor do the Lazaretto poets, who may be passed over as not great. But Dostoyevsky—he is great. It takes a very catholic conception of the "spiritual," rather thoroughly denuded of all connotations of uplift, to include Dostoyevsky in the characterization.[116]

If our interpretation of Radhakrishnan's metaphysics of aesthetics be correct, we should like to ask whether it has as a corollary the idea that the greatest spiritual leaders of mankind either were or could have been the greatest artists. Of course, there is no doubt of the pith of an Amos, of the superlative winsomeness of a Gautama, or of the power of the parables of Jesus; but art has been thought of in such a way that these figures are far from the greatest. That they did not put their greatest efforts into art, and that their artistic powers were placed in subservience to something else are perhaps factors; but we do not imagine that the introduction of these considerations can reverse the established estimate. If our author conceives that one or more of these figures were "enlightened," one wonders whether the removal of avidyā is supposed to have any effect on, or of resort to, artistic representation.

Works of art have moral effects. There is no denying this; censors from Plato on down have recognized it. But this is to say that the effects have been adjudged deleterious as well as beneficent. Of course, one can define art so that so-called "art" with bad conse-

---

the criteria of beauty are, they would constitute a set of restrictions to be imposed upon the infinite possibilities left open by the contemplation of eternal objects. The criteria of beauty may lie in existence in the sense of bearing some sort of congruence to basic organic structure and basic human structure. It is not plausible that the hypothetical congruence is entirely the product of culture; nor that beauty is determined by counting votes. Although Radhakrishnan says, "Deepest poetry has widest appeal" (IVL, 194), we suppose that the qualification "potentially" should be added, or some such phrase as, "if people have opportunity and sensitivity to apprehend it."

[115] In that recent pseudo-podium of mankind's life called "modern" Western civilization, the artists have typically been alienated from what is popularly called the "spiritual." For some, no doubt, this condition has been necessary as a symbol of autonomy—"Art for art's sake." For others, the reaction and struggle against conventional values has included everything that smacked of the religious heritage as well as of the Babbittry of the regnant commercial ends.

[116] We would not go as far as D. S. Mirsky in *A History of Russian Literature:* "But the truth is . . . that the tragedies of Dostoyevsky are irreducible tragedies that cannot be solved or pacified. His harmonies and his solutions are all on a lower or shallower level than his conflicts and his tragedies." (p. 354) And: ". . . the real Dostoyevsky is food that is easily assimilated only by a profoundly diseased spiritual organism." (p. 358)

quences is not art. Or, less severely, like Tolstoy, we can evaluate it on an ethical basis. But art, when accepted without such moral standards (whether these be definitive or matter of degree) does not seem to have any exact correlation with the moral, though admittedly when instances get "too bad" the supervening extra-artistic aspect will become dominant. (We assume the justifiability of the principle of censorship, although we think that it has been gravely misused. Totalitarian secular religions have now un-enviably succeeded to the office of attempting to ban whatever is not organic to their purposes.)

There are interesting questions as to how art produces its effects and as to whether these (or some of these) are to be considered part of its content. A wayfaring man sees the moral teaching sticking out in didactic literature—Aesop, *Proverbs,* Omar and much of Matthew Arnold—and finds it evident enough in propaganda art. Many critics would say that the cognitive and hortatory contents are no part of the aesthetic, and, in fact, detract from it. Radha-krishnan would probably concur. He does say that "Aesthetic creation and enjoyment are both non-intellectual actions." [117] And intuitive knowledge has been referred to as of a sort "which by its nature cannot be expressed in propositions." [118] Then the "form of knowledge" [119] which one receives in reading Hugo or Tolstoy (which we take to be great art but to some extent propaganda) is not to be found in any sentences of a character or analysis of a commentator. Somehow it springs from the whole. Yet, in literary art at least, plainly the content is relevant to the greatness of the art; the greatest works cannot be built out of perfect executions of trivia.

In representative or presentative art forms, should one say that what is represented or presented is somehow given as a truth about the world? If there is a normal reaction to this supposed true picture, is it no part of the content? However, can these be separated? And what, on the other hand, should be said of art that is so direct as apparently not to represent or present anything except itself, *e. g.,* music that is "pure," far removed from program music? Radha-krishnan declares: "The greatest gifts of art are peace and recon-ciliation. . . . Every beautiful statue has a certain air of repose, every great poem conveys a sense of peace." [120] Plausibly the best music does this also (celebrative oratorios and military overtures

---

[117] IVL, 194.　　　　[118] *Ibid.,* 127.
[119] *Ibid.,* 192.　　　[120] *Ibid.,* 194.

not coming in this category), but still the vehicle by which it "conveys" peace seems to be different.

It might be that the theme of human "reconciliation" with reality would enable one to harmonize the "spiritual appeal," which Radhakrishnan has insisted characterizes great art, with rather great pessimistic creations, which we supposed to constitute a difficulty for him. We quite had to agree that a powerful artist "gives a new meaning to our experience and organizes it in a different way due to his perception of subtler qualities in reality. He increases our understanding of life and gives us a heightened sense of reality. He bestows comprehension by bringing things into deeper accord." [121] But it seemed to us that the "new meaning" might be, in a vital sense, debilitating. Injunctions to "take the cash, and let the credit go," may be passed over, but not James Thompson's "City of Dreadful Night," which may be increasing "our understanding of life" and giving us "a heightened sense of reality." Or Housman:

> Stars, I have seen them fall,
>   But when they drop and die
> No star is lost at all
>   From all the star-sown sky.
> The toil of all that be
>   Helps not the primal fault;
> It rains into the sea
>   And still the sea is salt.[122]

We are afraid to cite Gautama, for he did have a way of deliverance, but with grace he awakened people to the emptiness and transiency of their existence, when these truths had been overlaid by pursuit of baubles or struggle for necessities. We wonder if Radhakrishnan will admit pessimistic artists to "greatness" on the grounds that they produce peace and reconciliation.

Such art does not seem to be "spiritual" in the sense of being edifying, constructive, or of tending toward attitudes of reverence and joy. Of course, all aesthetic reaction, whether in the appreciator or creator, is "spiritual" in the sense of being supra-animal, but this fact is one that includes pornography. We have had difficulty because we have believed that Radhakrishnan means that great art is edifying, and we have not thought that he would want to introduce a radical discontinuity between great art and ordi-

---

121 *Ibid.*, 194.   122 *More Poems,* VII.

nary art, or to restrict severely what he is willing to call "art." [123]

However, there is a correlative positive point with which to conclude this section. Much has been heard of a "problem of evil" from the massive optimistic traditions. Little has been made of a "problem of good." Yet some pessimistic naturalists have been, and should be, troubled by it. In simple human terms, heavenly music or anything exquisitely fine stir in one a nascent question, Why, in a naturalistic world, should such goods come forth? The interrogation arises as to the sureness of their fortuitousness. Browning's Bishop Bloughram could not settle down to the security of unbelief; he would encounter a "chorus ending from Euripides" or have "a fancy from a flowerbell," and these would reopen the possibilities of the "Grand Perhaps." [124]

VIII

(C) In turning to intuition in religion and to the content of religious values thus apprehended, it will be well to distinguish two views which Radhakrishnan rejects, but which, through familiarity, may impede understanding.

Many contemporary students of religion would hold that the unity of religion (as implied by the common noun) is doubtful and that the unity of a particular religion lies in the clustering of cognitive, moral, and aesthetic values in a traditional cultus; and that, consequently, when analyzed, nothing distinctive in the way of types of value ingredients is found in religions. Among others who hold that there are distinctively religious values, some would democratize these as a species of intrinsic values, lying without especial preëminence beside the moral and aesthetic species under their common genus.

Remarking upon the latter view first, it may be construed broadly enough to include considerable variety. Something approximating it has been given sophisticated statement in certain

---

123 Perhaps he does mean resolutely to affirm the last alternative, for he notes that "artists as a class" are not "patterns of morality," and adds: "Strictly speaking, an art independent of morality, which has no roots in our deepest ethical instincts, which does not draw towards the divine in things is not true art." IVL, 201.

124 Literally speaking, we do not see how anyone knows anything about the world from seeing a flowerbell except that the world is such as to produce a flowerbell and him who perceives it. One does not know that it was done on purpose. But it suggests such queries, of course, among the questions of what complexities give rise to this particular complexity with this particular quality.

German philosophers and even theologians.[125] A familiar attitude, untutored by tortuous epistemological considerations, may also illustrate this unmetaphysical and democratic sympathy for religious values among other values. Many of us, for instance, thoroughly approve of natural piety, although we are very vague about that to which the piety relates. A sense of dependence seems right, a feeling of gratitude for life feels appropriate, although we would have no confidence in personalizing that upon which one is dependent and to which he owes gratitude. One may quite believe in repentance without knowing to whom to repent. He may (like Matthew Arnold) see a beauty in holiness; or he may desire purity of heart, although he is quite agnostic about seeing God. Some pacifists have a religious reverence for life, not to be viewed as a tabu nor as a squeamishness about the unpleasant, but they may lack a metaphysic which makes their attitude mandatory. Of the phenomena, there is, we think, no doubt. Now perhaps all such phenomena are to be placed under the heading of the retention of sentiment during the decay of belief. But at least some of the agents can look this possibility squarely in the face and not adopt its tacit recommendation; instead, they in turn may view it as an instance of the over-intellectualism which has characterized both the dogmatists in religion and most philosophers outside.

Radhakrishnan, we suspect, would suggest that the democratization of religious values among other values is a mistake, and that the confusion over, agnosticism about, or even indifference to, the religious object is a most lamentable truncation. The phenomena cited cry out for completion in that which transcends and grounds them. Says he: ". . . the object of religion is not either the true or the good or the beautiful or a mere unity of them but God the universal consciousness who includes these values and yet transcends them." [126]

And this also is his denial of the first point of view, namely, that there are no essentially religious values, but only non-religious

[125] Religious values may be discriminated by reference to the attitude of the agent. That which is to be feared utterly and yet not hated, or loved utterly and yet not possessed, is sometimes employed as the criterion of the religious object or objects. The "holy," the "numinous," etc., figure in contemporary discussion. Perhaps most writers who start from this orientation wish to use the phenomena as evidences for the object toward which the taking of the described personal disposition is held to be appropriate. But some, following Ritschl, conceive the value as having its locus in the experience and not in the assumed object, and profess an agnosticism or an indifference concerning the referent's existence. This latter group of thinkers would safely illustrate the point of view mentioned,

[126] IVL, 199.

values, some of which have a religious aura attached to them and get called "religious" when they occur under the auspices of a religion. For it is the "object of religion" ("God the universal consciousness") which is for our author the guarantee that the religious consciousness "is an autonomous form of spiritual life." "Religious consciousness," he flatly states, "is not reducible to either intellectual or ethical or aesthetic activity or a sum of these." [127]

Now we fear that, if we arranged some of these matters in the form of an argument, a circularity would appear. However, presumably this would not bother our philosopher, for he has coherence in what he here asserts and he has "intuition or faith" to secure it.

The conception of "faith" has long been most recondite to us,[128] but, whatever it be positively, at least here we must not allow popular Western meanings [129] to lead us forthwith to dismiss the entire discussion. For we do think that Radhakrishnan intends to hold that there is a cognitive ingredient in it. He quotes with approval Wesley's saying that faith "is the vision of the soul, that power by which spiritual things are apprehended, just as material things are apprehended by the physical senses." Radhakrishnan continues: "We call it faith simply because spiritual perception, like other kinds of perception, is liable to error and requires the testing processes of logical thought." [130] The manner in which

[127] *Ibid.*, 199. Cp. 87f.; also: "It [religious experience] is unique and autonomous," SM, 275.

[128] We readily understand faith in the sense of loyalty or dogged adherence to cause, party or person. In this meaning, it is quite possible (though it is not characteristic, due to psychological reasons) to have faith in a cause and at the same time to make an impartial estimate that the odds are against it and that it will probably lose. Such a situation does not seem representative of religious faith; although, we suppose, it could be argued that this is due to the fact that religion has not acclimatized itself to an age of science in which one operates on probabilities. Are there any other meanings besides weak assent and strong intellectual perversity in the face of evidence? In religion, faith has not infrequently been held to be a way of knowledge: *Credo ut intelligam.* This can only be made plausible, as we see it, in two ways (since its offensive surface meaning seems to be a justification of begging the question): (a) it may refer, not really to knowledge, but to a condition of certain cognitive experiences, to putting oneself in a certain position so as to acquire the more relevant data, *e.g.,* being friendly to a person in order to understand him; or (b) it may boldly refer to knowledge, but to knowledge from a deeper source or wider effective environment than is currently accepted. We suspect that Radhakrishnan would accept both of these last meanings.

[129] "It is an unfortunate legacy of the course which Christian theology has followed in Europe that faith has come to connote a mechanical adherence to authority." HVL, 16.

[130] *Ibid.,* 16.

"spiritual" intuitions are tested will receive discussion later, but such testing assumes a content which can somehow be brought under question.

If he meant that there were no sort of apprehension or knowledge in religion, we should not discuss it here. And he does in one context remark that "Religion is not a form of knowledge. . . ." But the preceding sentences say: "Religion is not mere consciousness of value. There is in it a mystical element, an apprehension of the real and an enjoyment of it for its own sake which is absent in the moral consciousness." [131] A few pages earlier he observes: "The direct apprehension of God seems to be as real to some men as the consciousness of personality or the perception of the external world is to others." [132] Perhaps an intermediate passage is helpful for clarification: ". . . we may not know the ultimate meaning of God, though we may know something about God or what answers to God in reality through religious experience. The creeds of religion correspond to the theories of science." [133] This squares with such statements as, "Intuitions abide, while interpretations change." [134] But it is to be admitted that the comparison with science is not so clear, and the content of what gets tested becomes very obscure in some other passages. However, presenting them as dicta to be tested, Radhakrishnan finds these to be "affirmations of religious experience:" "There is a mode of consciousness which is distinct from the perceptual, imaginative or intellectual, and this carries with it self-evidence and completeness." "The larger environment is of the nature of one's own self. . . ." [135]

Many, many passages could and ought to be cited, some of which indicate the presentation of reality in religious experience, and others of which manifest a deep-rooted scepticism of any and all formulations of the content of the experience. These two trends may be related in summary statement by saying that apparently Radhakrishnan means to be very cautious in asserting for religion "knowledge about" its object, which is to be stated in discursive form, but wishes to insist upon a "knowledge by acquaintance" or knowledge by direct response. We find ourselves inclined to want to suggest that there is a kind of appropriateness to the religious response,[136] but it does not seem that this would exhaust our au-

---

131 IVL, 88.   132 Ibid., 83.   133 Ibid., 86.
134 Ibid., 90.   135 Ibid., 125.
136 Various critics would not concede the legitimacy of the concept of objective "appropriateness," and would regard it as a compromise, or as a sop to religion. Religion may be *expressing* something human, but the idea of its *apprehending* something—whether Divine, as Radhakrishnan affirms, or whether some relationship of

thor's intent. It appears that at any level of religious practice—
and he has true Hindu hospitality about these—there is always
some cognitive content.[137] The expressions may be myth and allegory, but they are representing something. We should like a literal
statement of what they are representing. Radhakrishnan, we suppose, would answer: You may have further statements, but those
also will be metaphors and figures, perhaps at a higher level; you
cannot have an adequate literal statement. If he were not so
courteous, he might add: A blind or perverse generation seeketh
after a literal statement. At least he does add: Some who have
wanted religion in a cheap and easy way wanted a formula to which
they could give assent; thus they sought to avoid paying the price
of genuine experience, which always must be first-hand.[138]

Without having discussed "integral experience" (or consummatory mystic experience, as we take it to be), it is awkward to say
anything further about such important questions as the relation
of symbols to religious intuition, or as the continuity or discontinuity between devotional religion and mysticism (with, it seems,
their intuitively given contents of God and the Absolute, respectively). Let us, accordingly, turn to "super-consciousness," and
then come back to a few questions of relationship to devotional
religion, poetic contents, and the consequent connection with
philosophy.

IX

5. Much orientation is given in a highly condensed statement
which we quote at length.

Besides consciousness in the animal world (perception and action),
and self-consciousness in the human (intelligence and will), we have
spiritual consciousness or super-consciousness, a level of experience at
which new aspects of reality reveal themselves. While in the first case
we have a psychological unity between the animal and the environment,
in the second we have a logical unity and in the third a spiritual unity.
At the spiritual level, the individual becomes aware of the substance of
spirit, not as an object of intellectual cognition but as an awareness in

---

man's nature to the enveloping environment (our minimal suggestion)—is to be dis-
allowed. With a safe subjective theory of value, a Santayana or a Western psychologist can acknowledge that persons at different levels are getting *values* out of religion,
but the values are not what they may think or pretend. To some extent they are
receiving mundane goods which their ideals or super-ego would prevent them from
seizing directly.

[137] Cf., *e.g.*, his beautiful statements, HVL, 31f.
[138] IVL, 203.

which the subject becomes its own object, in which the timeless and the spaceless is aware of itself as the basis and reality of all experience. The spirit which is inclusive of both self and object is self-subsistent and self-consistent. Nothing in our experience can be said to be real or individual without qualification except spirit. There is nothing within it to divide it, nothing outside to limit it. It alone satisfies our total desire and whole intelligence. It is all that there is, all being and all value.

It is because the universal spirit which is higher than the self-conscious individual is present and operative in self-conscious mind that the latter is dissatisfied with any finite form it may assume. When self-consciousness knows itself to be finite and limited, it is a greater than self that judges that which is less than itself in its wholeness. The reality of universal spirit is not an uncriticised intuition or a postulate of philosophy but the obvious implication of our daily life.[139]

Here we have the relation of consciousness, self-consciousness and spiritual consciousness set forth, with their metaphysic, which the last of the three discloses, but which also is argued for in a Roycean manner from the "implications" of the second level, if not the first. The One Real is the perfect fulfillment of everything; at the same time, these plural things are not real; for this One Real not only has "nothing outside to limit it," but even "nothing within to divide it."

The highly condensed passage cited does not make clear whether some distinctive experience of unity is referred to when "the subject becomes its own object," or whether the characterizations ascribed somehow belong in general to "the spiritual level." Of course, the critic might urge that even in "self-consciousness" the self makes itself an object in reflexively knowing itself, but the subsequent declarations made by our author certainly do not fit our ordinary waking assumptions. Perhaps Radhakrishnan means that these are truths which are implicitly present in all distinctively human activity, but which rise to explicitness only in religious consciousness. (Whether this consciousness rises in a gradual line of intensification, or whether chief attention is to be given to some radically novel higher discontinuous level in experience, of transcendent importance, is a question that will be amplified in a moment.) This interpretation implies that there are intuitions which do not include or are not accompanied by other explicit intuitions indicative of their status. This seems to accord well with certain statements of Radhakrishnan.

[139] *Ibid.*, 301f.

Creativity in cognitive, aesthetic, ethical or religious activity springs from thought which is intuitive or spiritually quickened. . . . The thinkers, the artists and the heroes, though they may not use, though they may often quarrel with the language of religion, are still religious in a true sense. For they have broken down the barriers between the individual and the universal.[140]

While art or beauty or goodness in isolation may not generate religious insight, in their intimate fusion they lead us to something greater than themselves.[141]

Inspiration in every one of its forms is a manifestation of the universal spirit in us; only the religious man is conscious of this fact.[142]

One presumes, however, that, not only is this religious awareness rather intermittent in many men, but that there are significant differences of intensity of its presence.

Somehow one feels that ordinary religious experience should be distinguished from the intuitive life of saints and seers. If for convenience we arbitrarily call the former "religious" and the latter "mystical," it will be easy to ask where the distinction lies, and if it is to be conceived as a difference in kind or a difference of degree. A *prima facie* possibility of the division is to say that self-consciousness may have religion while mysticism enjoys the intuitive. But if the distinctions are separations, this will not work. For if self-consciousness is the product of intellection,[143] and intuition is necessary to religion (even the less exalted forms of it), one runs into contradiction. However, it may well be that there is more of self-consciousness in ordinary religion, and it diminishes as it dissolves in the face of increasing spiritual insight.

There is much to suggest that ordinary religious life exhibits a pluralistic consciousness; it primarily takes the form of self-consciousness set over against other things; there is present a dualism of self and object or objects. In the more elementary forms, polytheistic worship of various "petty forces and spirits" appears; [144] above this is the devotion to various "incarnations;" the highest form of religious development, short of consummatory mystic union, is worship of the one God as a personal being.[145] In distinction from all of these, the highest integral or mystical experience is a "super-conscious" state which is non-plural and non-dual; [146] if

---

140 *Ibid.*, 205.　　　141 *Ibid.*, 201.　　　142 *Ibid.*, 206.

143 RR, 423.　　　144 Cf., HVL, 32.

145 Yet all of them, we presume, are to some extent enjoying "conscious union with the Divine . . . with love as the chief means," which he speaks of as constituting religion. IVL, 204. In established usage, these partake of personal mysticism, *bhakti.*

146 *E.g.*, ER, 50.

personality and personal relations imply a duality, then it is impersonal; if they imply finitude, it is super-personal.[147]

Our author writes: "While for the self-conscious individual, religion is only faith in values, for the spiritual being it is vital contact with reality which is the source of all values. So long as the human consciousness is on the pathway to reality, the spirit is an *other* to it." [148] Here one implicitly has three levels distinguished. The beginner in religion and the intellectual humanist, one presumes, are on the lowest of the three stages of ascent; they have intuitions of values but—whether or not they have any faith about gods or God—they do not have the faith in God which is characterized by direct perception and vital contact. This vital commerce is enjoyed at the next level, where progress is made until, thirdly, God no longer stands over in "otherness" as the opposing personal pole in religious communion, but "That art thou," "Brahman is ātman." (Admittedly, the citation quoted does not specify that the distinctions are to be taken only as matters of degree, although the word "pathways" does at least suggest that that which leads up to the consummatory experience is to be so understood.) As we see it, intuition is present at each level, but the representative focal object changes from level to level: for the first, value is the characteristic object of intuition; for the second, God for Whom the values are thoughts; for the third, the Absolute.

The common distinction between acquaintance with Another and merging in the One might also be used to indicate a difference between—in our arbitrary usage—ordinary religion and mysticism. The term "merging," however, is subject to question. Would not Radhakrishnan probably say that some such word as "awakening" would be much better, since "merging" falsely connotes a previous separation, which is not real but only apparent, due to *avidyā*? This in turn is complicated by the questions of whether any individuality is conceived to remain after deliverance (*mokṣa*) and whether it is held that there can be consummatory mystical experience spread out in a temporal span prior to such liberation from *saṁsāra*. Apparently the answer to the last question is affirmative.[149] But the former is much more complicated. Radhakrishnan, with care and

---

[147] *E.g.*, Ind P, II, 536; HVL, 30; SM, 283.   [148] IVL, 302.

[149] "In *samādhi* or ecstatic consciousness we have a sense of immediate contact with ultimate reality, of the unification of the different sides of our nature. It is a state of pure apprehension, in which the whole being is welded into one. To make this complete subjection of the whole personality to the divine a settled habit, a permanent condition, and not merely a fleeting and transitory episode, is the aim of religious discipline." ER, 51f. Cf. IVL, 94f.

candor, offers a few considerations which he labels "tentative and perhaps not quite self-consistent;" [150] to the Western reader he seems to be rash even at that. Our author takes note that theists generally wish to preserve individuality; and he boldly reinterprets Śaṁkara and denies that release spells immediate absorption. (One cannot avoid temporal terminology, and it seems that Radhakrishnan is challenging Śaṁkara's theory of time and the cosmic process, or rather the common interpretation thereof.) Apparently taking a realistic though not self-existent view of the cosmic process, he holds—on valuational or moral grounds, we suppose—that it continues until all souls are "saved;" and those who become freed individuals in the earlier stages keep on submitting to rebirth in order vicariously to assist their fellows (real or apparent).[151] Certain remarks seem profoundly social, for he holds perfect freedom of the individual to be impossible in an imperfect world; [152] but when the cosmic movement reaches fulfillment, individuals cease to exist as historical beings.[153] For all we know, another cosmic curtain is then drawn.[154] The "evidence" for these views, we repeat, seem to be value considerations. In this sense, some of the highest soarings of metaphysics are dependent upon some of the less exalted forms of intuition already reviewed. Although we once were surprisingly informed that "every kind of reality" can be discerned "directly," [155] possibly this was a declaration of faith in the power of intuition due to the unity of Spirit, but that it is practically relevant only to the greatest ṛṣis, if even to them.[156]

On the subject of the continuity or discontinuity between "religion" and "mysticism," as we arbitrarily labelled them—between personalistic, dualistic devotional mysticism and the beatific vision, as others may refer to them—there is a tremendous array of citations which scholarly patience could adduce to support either emphasis. One does not feel that the gulf is as great as, for instance,

---

150 IVL., 306. 151 *Ibid.*, 306. 152 *Ibid.*, 307.

153 *Ibid.*, 308. 154 *Ibid.*, 310. 155 *Ibid.*, 143.

156 No doubt we exhibit too many Western inhibitions and limitations in our approach to this point. Such striking remarks of our author may suggest the doctrine of the Jainas that knowledge through the senses is not immediate, for it is through a medium, whereas truly immediate knowledge is of spirit by spirit. Or, Patañjali comes to mind with his discipline of concentration, affording knowledge not only of other minds but of absent and subtle objects—the knowledge which we treated as empirical or pluralistic *samādhi*, and tried to append to the generically aesthetic intuitions. But perhaps it is soundest to follow the clue of our author's great affinity for the Advaita Vedānta; thus object and knower are really one; true knowledge is the dissolution of the cosmic illusion that they are different.

that between the "closed" and the "open" in Bergson's *Two Sources of Morality and Religion*. Radhakrishnan, to be sure, does not overlook the clash of the prophet with the priest, and he pronounces living religion to be "an eternal revolutionary." [157] In this sense, both *bhakti* and *Brahmānibhava* may belong on the side of the "open" religion, though there can be no doubt that the former especially is intimately nourished by the cultus and that it does not always rise to a universally hospitable attitude toward the devotees of other *avatars* or "incarnations." At least, Radhakrishnan has complete faith that what is in the soul will keep it on a journey until a certain destination is reached. In this sense, he is a proponent of continuity. He goes quite as far, or farther, than William James [158] or J. B. Pratt [159] in affirming that the "milder forms" of mysticism are in all "who feel an answering presence in deep devotion or share the spell which great works of art cast on us." [160] "The path to perfection is more a slope than a staircase," [161] he says. There is a continuity to maturity, even though the latter culminate in the ecstatic.[162]

> If the feeling for God were not in man, we could not implant it any more than we could squeeze blood from a stone. The heart of religion is that he truly belongs to another order. . . . His highest aim is release from the historical succession denoted by birth and death.[163]

Again:

> The rhythms of the poet find correspondence in the conditions of our soul; their words an authentic echo in our speech. The gleam haunting our whole life, the undiscovered spirit in us is suddenly recollected in Plato's sense. . . . We understand an object only when there is something in us akin to it.[164]

The continuity in Radhakrishnan's conception of the growth and unity of spirituality is reflected in his use of the word intuition to

---

[157] SM, 288.

[158] *Varieties of Religious Experience*, 379.

[159] *The Religious Consciousness*, 216.

[160] IVL, 93. Mysticism, our author says in one place, is "admission of mystery in the universe." ER, 61f. We certainly would not wish to minimize the significance of this, but we do believe it to be an over-simplification of his intent.

[161] ER, 48.

[162] *Ibid.*, 77.

[163] *Ibid.*, 83. But he rejects any idea of a special mystical faculty to account for mystical experience, "as there is a continuous development from sense perception to the vision of the real." *Ibid.*, 51.

[164] IVL, 207f.

cover such ranges of experience as are giving us a pedant's pleasure in attempting to distinguish and classify.[165]

If there is an underlying metaphysical unity of all spirit, and if there is a continuity of development in the soul's pilgrimage toward its realization, these do not prevent our philosopher from affirming qualitative novelty and distinctiveness.

. . . there is an ultimate goal which is beyond the conditions of progress . . .[166]

To seek for liberation from the wheel of births and deaths, is nothing more than to rise to the spiritual level from the merely ethical. The spiritual is not the extension of the ethical. It is a new dimension altogether . . .[167]

The moralistic individualism is based on an imperfect outlook . . . Though the pluralistic outlook is not a fiction framed by the individual self, but a grade of the growing universe, it has to be transcended.[168]

The seer, the sage and the saint all enter into direct communion with the heart of things. In that stage self and not-self are felt to be clasped in one.[169]

There is an experience which is the perfection of all imperfections in us. We are compelled to concede that man is but a transition stage, a rope, as Nietzsche puts it, between the beast and the superman of the future.[170]

The self has the consciousness that there is nothing else beside the Absolute.[171]

This religious or intuitional experience is the summit of the whole evolution.[172]

. . . the spasm of the human mind in contact with pure spirit, is the

[165] One has a similar, although lesser, problem with "integral experience." It may name the beautifully balanced life of a religious person who unites the cognitive, the aesthetic, and the moral, and who responsively traces them all to God. Such a man is —if we correctly remember a phrase of Carlyle's concerning his father—"religious with the consent of all his faculties." (Cf. IVL, 201.) On the other hand, "integral experience" may refer to the ineffable consummatory mystical experience. (Cf. Ind P, II, 510ff.) With a little extra emphasis upon the cognitive, the former could easily receive the support of Royce's conception of "insight." Insight is for Royce a species of knowledge "that unites a certain breadth of range, a certain wealth of acquaintance together with a certain unity and coherence of grasp, and with a certain closeness of intimacy whereby the one who has insight is brought into near touch with the objects of his insight." (*Sources of Religious Insight*, 5.) "Religious insight must be distinguished from other sorts of insight by its object, or by its various characteristic objects." (*Ibid.*, 7.) "What one pretends or at least hopes to know, when there is any question of religious insight, is something which has to do with the whole nature and destiny and duty and fate of man." (*Ibid.*, 24.)

[166] IVL, 303. [167] *Ibid.*, 304. [168] *Ibid.*, 305.
[169] RR, 435. [170] *Ibid.*, 432. [171] *Ibid.*, 436.
[172] *Ibid.*, 437.

supremely normal, though most of us are feeble-minded or more or less insane compared with this ideal of sanity.[173]

All experience of God when it becomes intense is ecstatic, though every ecstatic emotion is not an experience of God.[174]

The qualitative change marked by consummatory mystical experience is apparently not simply one of intensification; as we have indicated, it seems to give a different object—if one can still use the word, knowing that it is misused—than does devotion of the personal and dualistic sort.

X

For us, there are two conspicuous difficulties. To one of them, Radhakrishnan, like Śaṁkara and others before him, has given the most careful consideration. He has a theory to provide a solution. Let us give it a name: *perspectival intuitionism*. It is a way of avoiding illusionism with respect to one or other of apparently incompatible fundamental religious intuitions.

In the East, as in the West, some pious men have come to the Absolute; other pious men worship a personal God.

There are aspects in religious experience, such as the sense of rest and fulfilment, of eternity and completeness, which require the conception of a being whose nature is not exhausted by the cosmic process. . . . This side of religious experience demands the conception of the supreme as self-existence . . . absolute beatitude. On the other hand there are features of our religious experience which require us to look upon God as self-determining principle manifested in a temporal development, with wisdom, love and goodness as his attributes. From this point of view God is a personal being with whom we can enter into personal relationship.[175]

He observes that "Rationalistic logic and mystic contemplation favour as a rule the former conception, while ethical theism is disposed to the latter." [176] Most of us would feel that at least one alternative must be rejected, and possibly both. Not so Radhakrishnan. True, like Śaṁkara and like parts of the *Gītā* and unlike other parts of the *Gītā*, he does ascribe a higher truth or validity to the Absolutist version. But he does not then repudiate the other; he retains it, and seemingly in more than a "fictional" or "as if" status.

To some of us, to declare that the truth is the Absolute is to pro-

173 ER, 77. Cf. esp. *ibid.*, 49-51.   174 *Ibid.*, 77.   175 SM, 280.
176 HVL, 30.

nounce the idea of a personal God to be literally an illusion, although it may be a convenient symbol for certain values. For Radhakrishnan, this apparently is not the consequence. God is not the most ultimate of realities, but God is existent, "organic" to the world, or the "soul" of the world,[177] as Rāmānuja said; God is the prime concretion from the Absolute. "The Supreme, the Eternal, is the unity of all things finite and infinite. But when we consider the development of the Absolute, the distinction of self and not-self appears. The first existent or object in the Absolute is God, Īśvara or the world soul."[178] (We suppose it to have a "reality" which lesser "deities" and "incarnations" do not have, although one would feel more secure in this interpretation if there were a categorical statement saying that, while these forms serve as vehicles for mediating values, they are subjective fantasies. For possibly the avidyā of any dualistic view, even that remaining in monotheism, is of exactly the same sort as that manifested by the worshipper of stones or ancestors.)[179] Sometimes, indeed, Radhakrishnan's Absolute seems to take on a theistic or even deistic cast, the "Absolute" being the name of God in His (or Its) transcendental status;[180] one might incline not to give quite equal weight to the statements which reciprocally affirm God to be "the Absolute from the human end."[181] At least one might feel a textual tug in that direction due in part to Radhakrishnan's sometimes making positive affirmations about the Absolute as "pure consciousness and pure freedom" and as having "an infinite number of possibilities to choose from,"[182] and due in part to his sometimes evidentially founding the Absolute on certain religious needs

177 IVL., 338.   178 RR, 443f.

179 He does say definitely that the conception of incarnations or avatars is inconsistent, with "the continuous urge of spiritual life, the growing revelation of ends in which the divine life comes to its own, the immanent law which constitutes the unity of the world." IVL, 337. Perhaps something similar should be said for the cosmic God, but our author does not say it when he remarks that "God is conceived as a personal being . . ." Ibid., 342.

180 One feels this in scattered phrases, e.g., the Absolute "could have created a world different in every detail from that which is actual." Ibid., 344. One does not know whether Radhakrishnan's own views are strictly restrained in his superlative treatments of the Gītā, both in Ind P, I, Chap. IX, and in his recent volume, The Bhagavadgītā; but in these theism seems to emerge on top. Little weight should be placed on this consideration, because of the rectitude of Radhakrishnan's scholarship, with the consequent fact that the opposite argument could be made from his expositions of Śaṁkara.

181 IVL, 344. Also note: "We call the supreme the Absolute, when we view it apart from the cosmos, God in relation to the cosmos. The Absolute is the precosmic nature of God, and God is the Absolute from the cosmic point of view." Ibid., 345.

182 IVL, 343.

and experiences,[183] in a manner parallel to his experiential argument for theism. However, one must acknowledge that quite the opposite emphasis is made with equal force. "If God has no environment on which He acts, He cannot be personal. If God is personal, He cannot be the Absolute which has nothing which is not included in it in every possible sense of the word." [184] "God depends on creation even as creation depends on God." [185] "Strictly speaking, the Absolute excludes all positive and negative features . . ." [186] But for purposes of worship, the indication of Brahman by negative expressions is not satisfactory; like Bradley, Radhakrishnan affirms that: "When these negative formulas of an exact metaphysics defeat their object, we are inclined, in the interests of our religious needs, to lay a different emphasis." [187] Yet we find that God, characterized Brahman, is not a "mere self-projection of the yearning spirit:"

The criticism that Śamkara leaves us with an unbridgeable chasm at the summit of things, between the nirguṇa Brahman of which nothing can be said and the saguṇa Brahman which embraces and unifies all experience, is due to a confusion of standpoints. Thought can never overleap the distinction of subject and object, and so the highest for thought is the absolute subject with the object in it, but behind the subject and the object we have Brahman.[188]

Brahman cast through the moulds of logic is Iśvara. It is not the highest reality, since it has no meaning for the highest experience where existence and content are no longer separated. Yet it is the best image of the truth possible under our present conditions of knowledge. The saguṇa Brahman is not the mere self-projection of the yearning spirit or a floating air-bubble. The gleaming ideal is the way in which the everlasting real appears to our human mind.[189]

Thus, it seems, we have a sort of relational and perspectival intuitionism. If the "lower" forms of religious experience give "appearance," it is nevertheless appearance "of reality." "The supra-personal and the personal representations of the real are the absolute and the relative ways of expressing the one reality. When we emphasise the nature of reality in itself we get the absolute Brahman; when we emphasise its relation to us we get the personal Bhagavān." [190] The perspective may be said to include range or depth. Earlier it was said that some persons have value as their intuitive object; others have God; and others rise to awareness of

183 *Ibid.*, 342; cf. SM, esp. 280.   184 SM, 282.   185 *Ibid.*, 283.
186 Ind P, II, 541n.   187 *Ibid.*, 541.   188 *Ibid.*, 561.
189 *Ibid.*, 540.   190 HVL, 31.

identity with and in the Absolute. In a crude metaphor, some believe the program notes which say there is a play conveying certain values; some see the actors and the play upon the stage; some understand both the play and the staging. There is not exactly positive error at the earlier levels, though there is omission and incomplete understanding. Yet this is not all, apparently. The perspectival and relational consideration of the problem of God and the Absolute seemingly is not cognitive or noetic alone. It is also ontological. Discussion of this lies beyond the bounds of the present paper. To avoid a lacuna, we will simply take note of it with a few citations:

Creation marks the beginning of this world with time, though not in time.[191]

At the beginning, God is merely the knower with ideas and plans, which are realised at the end when the world becomes the express image of God. . . . When the creator and the created coincide, God lapses into the Absolute.[192]

So far as the Absolute is concerned, the creation of the world makes no difference to it.[193]

The Absolute transcends not merely its finite but also its infinite expressions taken singly or in a finite number.[194]

The question of how all this is known will be raised (but not answered) in a moment.

XI

A second difficulty that comes to our mind is not unlike one of the problems we had over Radhakrishnan's aesthetics; on this, too, we are sure that he has a view, but, to our knowledge, he gives it almost no discussion. Suppose we look at our concrete feelings—not the feeling tone of experience, which is an aspect, but the concrete current of feeling. Some of this has more pronounced cognitive aspects than other parts, but all cognition is embedded in the movement of this experience. Now let us disregard those parts or segments which approach "pure" feeling, but retain those which are "feeling that such-and-such is so," those which are qualitied as responsive to certain realities; then, among these, let

---

191 SM, 284. Several such expressions as this suggest that Radhakrishnan has gone quite a distance toward compromising with Rāmānuja's conception of the reality of creation.

192 *Ibid.*, 283. The logos tradition at times, and Whitehead's eternal objects at times, come to mind under the impact of Radhakrishnan's phrasings.

193 *Ibid.*, 285. 194 *Ibid.*, 285.

us take note especially of those which arise in reaction to the environment as a whole. Are all these alike in their deliverances? Apparently not.

It is patent that there are flagrant differences in the intuitions of different persons—even when they mean to be taking a broad view.[195] Between James Thompson and Francis Thompson, between Schopenhauer and Fichte, between Whittier and Housman, between Browning [196] and Turgeniev's bold Bazaroff who brazenly says (as so much of our practice assumes) that the world is not a temple but a workshop, not to mention between Rossetti and Swinburne, Tennyson and Arnold—between these few expressive persons who happen to come to mind, as between a host more of whom only the universe holds the inventory, there are great gulfs fixed. Within the pages of the Old Testament or of Thomas Mann or of Tennyson's *In Memoriam*, or between Browning's *Caliban* and his *Abt Vogler*, there are the familiar contrasts. Such illustrations need not, it appears, include the pathological or the willfully provincial in order to have variety; the rehearsal could contain volumes with-

[195] Of course our views of particular events are colored by their promise or threat to us; our views of "life" normally reflect our fortunes. Quite apart from glandular balances and predispositions, some persons are understandably optimistic and some pessimistic, in terms of experience. (In a sincere democracy, men are concerned to remove those inequalities that are due to arbitrary social structure; but a multitude of factors are not of this sort, and—allowing much to the promise of technical culture —there remain sources of fate beyond the most earnest attempts at human control.) But this egocentricity of perception and this subjectivity of viewpoint as functions of the individuality of destinies do not seem to us to be insuperable, at least in principle. The parent sensing danger to the child, the sentinel or the statesman alert to danger to the group, are no less real. By sympathy we can be sensitive to the needs of, and dangers to, all men—and perhaps to all sentient beings. In addition to our moral deficiencies, it is to be acknowledged, however, that usually these larger perspectives require more discursive knowledge than we have.
  Recognition that the promises and threats cited grow out of particular environments lead one to note that qualification of the universe is quite another thing. Particular prospects can be better known through science; predications concerning the universe as a whole are seldom so particularly defined, and, when they are, one is suspicious of provincial criteria on the part of him who dares to pronounce them. In principle, threats to the whole human race, for instance, are not unlike threats to the individual. Such a basis, however, substitutes anthropocentricity for egocentricity. Russell's "Free Man's Worship" is based in part upon certain astronomical forecasts. Radhakrishnan is quite ready to concur with the forecasts, but, in a manner far outstripping Russell's earlier valuational realism, he would not determine the proper vocation of man from these prospects, nor, indeed, would he assess the character of the real in terms of hedonic estimates or of futures of the subject matter of biology. (*E.g.*, cf. RR, 448.)

[196] Why, where's the need of Temple, when the walls
    O' the world are that? What use of swells and falls
    From Levites' choir, Priests' cries, and trumpet-calls?
        —In *Epilogue: To Dramatis Personae.*

out ever touching the insane or those whose reactions are routine or from authority. No wonder that some wish a dialectic to comprise all other views as lesser and partial. No wonder that the panorama inclines some to take a dramatic or esthetic view of the world, rather than an ethical one. It is not unnatural to respond with the feeling that it is the height of conceit to stand in the midst of all this, carrying one's own little view and saying, "This, I think, is the truth." Yet, in a sense, it is what we all must do. We all do have to live in this moment, and we all do have our feelings about how human life and the world runs. Normally we do not hesitate to judge the views of others, whether these be actual or presented in literature. "Thomas Hardy stacks the cards on his characters," says one. "Hardy had the courage to write what he saw," counters another. Practice and contemplation exact of every reflective person some estimate of that in which he has his present experience.

To be sure, so great a variety of mirrorings of itself as the world possesses would presumably be greatly reduced if, contrary to normal fact, we human beings had the moral property of not regarding the fortunes of ourselves and perhaps of our friends as intrinsically more revelatory as clues to the universe than the experiences of others; and, secondly, if each thinking individual possessed, at least in a general way, the knowledge possessed by all others. It would be bold, however, to assume, that even under these fantastically different conditions, the mirrorings would all become similar.[197] There is apparently less discipline of the cognizing pro-

---

[197] This is, of course, an extrapolation. Neither of the hypothetical conditions do we suppose to be exemplified in their purity, not to mention the two conjointly. But at least doubt may be based upon fragments. Admittedly, Cicero and Russell can uncover much inverse correlation among sea-faring men between their piety and the size of their ships. But some, with the smallest boats, may trust nothing but their weather eye; and some men, in the safest occupations, may have the greatest piety. Again, two men may share much astronomical or biological lore but differ greatly in their *Weltanchauungen*. One man may assess nature as a "rum 'un"; another finds it

> The anchor of my purest thoughts, the nurse,
> The guide, the guardian of my heart, and soul
> Of all my moral being.

Two men see a primrose, but Wordsworth sees something more. Everyone knows there is birth and death. One individual is more impressed with how the gourd flourishes, while Jonah's attention is focused upon its destruction by the worm; and a third, Job, rises amidst his sufferings to say "The Lord giveth and the Lord taketh away." Everyone knows that there are what are called pleasures and pains and beauties and ugliness in the world; some have a problem of evil, some a problem of good, and some a problem of neither. Everyone knows there are frustrations in life; some infer bigger ones to come; some are relieved that an end to all is in sight; others are prone to draw hopeful conclusions from the way a man's reach exceeds his grasp.

cesses on the large scale enterprize than there is in reference to the small scale objects, and—for some of the latter—sufficient [198] confirmation or disconfirmation may quickly follow.

The primary purpose here is not to stress the effect of variety upon some hesitant minds, who find an increase in their sense of doubt as to whose responses are to be trusted, but to employ these considerations as a way of asking several questions.

First, would not Radhakrishnan say that the whole formulation betrays a mistaken approach, or less than the profoundest approach, for it is founded upon the idea of characterizing an object, set over against the subject, whereas the highest wisdom transcends the attempt to know reality as an "object"?

Second, on what criteria are the total reactions of some persons rated so much more highly than those of others? This is a question of spiritual "authorities." There is no doubt that we all have recourse to value experts to some extent, nor that the race has relied upon the insights of its seers to a great extent—though, naturally, perhaps greater in the profession than in the practice. Criteria are present implicitly; greater explicitness is desired. Sometimes fruits of a moral sort are among the standards; in this case, intuitions of type (4,A) enjoy a regulative status over the validity of claims to mystic insight. (The criteria of scientific expertness are more easily formulated, though they be of more recent origin. From their standpoint, strict techniques are lacking in all such large surmising, and the various factors of the empirical self are not disciplined "down" to a hard cognitive effort.)

Third, since from a scientific viewpoint it may be urged that the babble of tongues is what results when resort is had to the "whole" man instead of to certain restricted and highly disciplined cognitive habits, are the varied cases of responding to the environment as a whole cases of knowing with the whole man, or would Radhakrishnan view all of them, except super-consciousness, as knowing with some part of man? If one does not come out with a spiritual view of reality, is he under the dominance of his passions or perhaps his mulish nature?

Fourth, the question of spiritual authority and the question of access to data frequently resolve into a question of moral qualification for certain kinds of knowing. If the highest knowing is know-

[198] Following some contemporary philosophers, we should say that even the hypothesis of the presence of a simple physical object implicitly contains an infinity of predictions, nearly all of which will remain hypotheticals contrary to fact. But this does not prevent confirmation for practical or scientific purposes.

ing with the whole man (or, perhaps, with more than the human parts), then presumably a certain internal harmony or order of the self is requisite for supreme insight. Many Hindu and Buddhist thinkers (along with Confucius, Heraclitus, Pythagoras, Plato, Aristotle, St. John, St. Paul, and others) stipulate that certain moral qualifications [199] are requisite for the successful quest after certain classes of truths. So-called "modern" conceptions have departed considerably therefrom.[200] The phrase "spiritual truth" would be taken to be meaningless by many, or else to name maxims founded on causal connections in psychical and cultural formations, accessible to anyone. Contemporary Westerners are, of course, quite familiar with the idea of getting the right conditions for an experiment to come out (despite the sporadic popular outbursts of pseudo-scientific writing), but they tend to reduce any "subjective" requirements to a minimum. Most Western thinkers would acknowledge that, besides rationality and, in the case of an empirical scientist, normal sensory equipment, or devices which improve thereon, a scientist or metaphysician must exhibit intellectual integrity specifically in his dealings with his subject-matter, but, beyond this, might practice bigamy, murder or advertising. Actually, scientists tend to be upright persons; but this is theoretically construed as a contingent fact of nature. To be sure, in certain sorts of psychological inquiry where the personal factor may enter into the technique, e.g., oral questionnaire method, there further efforts will be made to "control" the manifestations of the inquirer. But these are not particularly moral, and frequently the appearance would do just as well as the reality.

Presumably representative Indian and Western philosophers would each feel that the burden of proof lay upon the other with respect to the character of the overtures which we should make toward that in which we live and move and have our phenomenal being. Many of us Westerners will at least admit that James has a point in suggesting that commitment to certain valuations or attitudes of faith may be necessary for securing experimental evidence; if I wish to find out if my new neighbor will be friendly, I do not commence by throwing stones at him. However, perhaps only those in whom the religious tradition still breathes would find themselves disposed to apply this principle to their commerce with

199 "Moral" is used in a very broad sense, and may include not counting upon one's moral attainments to merit the reward of insight.

200 One may wonder how much this is due to, or otherwise to be correlated with, the expulsion of "ends" from nature. Values are admitted back in, as projections of those peculiar products of nature called organisms and subjective centers.

the universe as a whole. It is a fact that many Westerners assume that they "know" that the universe (whatever it may unwittingly contain collectively) is non-moral, non-beautiful, non-spiritual, and holds no spiritual meaning.

Special qualifications tend to arouse suspicion and resentment in those who are either unable or unwilling to meet them. But we certainly wish it to be clear at this point that we cannot ask our author rationally to compel people to be ready and willing to submit to a discipline. It is just a blunt fact that the conditioning of many contemporary Westerners has been such that their pride would be hurt if they were known to search for "salvation," [201] and they would feel a strong sense of "shame" if somehow they were brought to seek it through the methods of a Yōgin. To some extent this may reflect a moral judgment itself; they do not believe that there is any relevance of certain alleged bodily controls to moral or spiritual attainment. To some extent, it is a flat cultural difference in the training of feelings; though this cuts both ways, the Westerner, at least, is likely to feel that others are conditioned in odd ways, while what he does represents the simple natural truth. Thus he is very quick to urge the sharp question whether the so-called "disciplines" of alien religions are not the effective conditioners of their "results," rather than a stipulation of conditions of cognition. (A most legitimate question, provided it is reciprocally and mutually and sympathetically taken up.) And he is likely to add that "schools," and "traditions," and discipleship under "gurus," suggest just such conditioning; he is less likely to admit that there is even a mote in his own eye—that academic science and philosophy have tended to become closed corporations, and that (even against the explicit will of the members) these in fact do inculcate sets of valuations, do limit acceptable imaginings, do restrict sympathies. It may be ever so natural; it may be the price of effectiveness; but it seems to be the case.

XII

Now, with all this lengthy but still cursory attempt at classification behind us, let us turn to a few of the obvious integral questions, and thus lead into the problem of the relation of philosophy and the higher forms of intuition.

In what senses are "reason" and "intuition" to be distinguished

[201] "Adjustment" is more or less respectable, especially if it refer to competent self-management in securing sensate goods.

or "opposed"? Has our classification (in which the processes of
conducting "logical" or "rational" operations were incorporated as
one of the categories of "intuitions," namely (2) above) been a piece
of legerdemain attempting to nullify any distinctions or "oppositions" between reason and intuition, spoken of by Radhakrishnan
or other authors? What meanings of "reason" must be distinguished for the sake of the discussion?

Our incorporation of rational intuition among the types of
intuition nullifies no real distinction. Quite apart from a possible
consideration of various passages (which cannot be discussed now),
in which Radhakrishnan emphasizes complementarity and continuity of abstractly named functions, no distinction is obliterated
by subsuming the distinguished classes under some genus. A distinction is a distinction. And, it will be found, we think, that
Radhakrishnan's "oppositions" are oppositions of views which,
respectively, take some one or two or three categories as the whole
or as exhausting the ranges of all cognition.[202] There is an opposition, of course, when one protagonist claims for some part or
distinguished aspect that it is the whole and some other protagonist
does likewise for some other. We fear that Radhakrishnan does not
adhere meticulously to some one set of usages; contexts make it
reasonably clear that in different occurrences such terms as "logic,"
"reason," "intellect," have three or more quite separable meanings.
"Intuition" is likely to be viewed, correlatively, as comprising the
content or the avenues of knowledge that are omitted.

When Radhakrishnan refers to "rationalism," for instance, he
means the doctrine that the apprehension of clear and distinct
ideas and their articulation in a (supposedly unique) systematic
whole is the truth and the one kind of truth. This doctrine is in
opposition to doctrines which include species of intuition other
than (2).

In the second place, intellect and its rough synonyms are frequently used to name the consolidated capacities which achieve
scientific knowledge. Here one had better distinguish a supposed
narrower and a wider (though still not the widest) tacit meaning of
science. For, as Radhakrishnan intimates, there are views which
minimize the presence of any factors beyond sense observations and
deductions therefrom, ignoring the patent fact that the inferences

202 Cf. e.g., "Logical reflection is a special function within the concrete life of
mind and is necessarily a fraction of the larger experience. If it sets itself up as constitutive of the whole life of mind, it becomes, in Kant's words, a 'faculty of illusion.'
The different energies of the human soul are not cut off from one another by any
impassable barriers." SM, 269.

of the sciences are characteristically not so-called "immediate inferences" from particulars. Taken in its complete severity, such a view would reduce science to a chronicle of the observations made by scientists. Even in its less strict forms perhaps this should be viewed rather as a poor philosophy of science than as a narrow definition of science, though the referent of what the theory would fit would be fragments of what is ordinarily called "science." Radhakrishnan himself seems to us sometimes to employ something less than an embracing conception of science; he sometimes tacitly stipulates that scientific method must be quantitative.[203] Now we know that some logicians and theorists of probability are given to speaking of a qualitative quantification when numerical measurement is out of the question, but that does not seem to be in our author's intent. However, let it be noted that a definition or conception of science as quantitative can be perfectly hospitable to recognizing the rôle of hypotheses, of confirmed theory piled on confirmed theory; physics is an excellent example, and probably was in Radhakrishnan's mind. Still we should see no *a priori* reason why, for instance, even human history should not be the materials of a science—probably the science which would formulate its "laws" should be called "sociology"—and yet we cannot picture the whole of such science being quantitative. This, however, is to raise a mere question of definition. The point is that "intellect" may be conceived as naming the organ of science, and science may be conceived as built out of intuitions of categories (1) and (2),—or, better, out of (1), (2) and (3). In the latter case, is there anything cognitive left? There might be unused portions of (3), and all of (4) and (5) to stand under the gonfalon of intuition in opposition to reason or intellect.

Now neither "rationalism" nor "positivism"—for we can speak of the doctrine of an intellectual monopoly on cognition as generic positivism (without qualifying adjectives)—are alluded to in favorable terms by Radhakrishnan. Even were "science" free of the stipulated restriction of quantification, and were positivism to stand for the adherence (exclusively) to science in the widest sense of all knowledge attained by intellectual or discursive methods, still Radhakrishnan would disapprove. For he maintains that there is other "knowledge." It is not that he does not approve of what they do do; he would welcome them completely in what he would conceive to be their proper places; it is to the respective claims of exclusiveness that he would object.

[203] *E.g.*, IVL, 223.

A third view of "reason" in Radhakrishnan is synonymous with philosophy. This presumably is reason comprehending all intuitions, accepting data from everywhere else. Naturally it is almost always spoken of favorably—with the probable exceptions of comparisons with integral ("mystic") experience itself. We are not entirely clear as to whether it is to be conceived as (2) and (3) combined and autonomous, but differing from the intelligence of science by being universally hospitable to data, or whether in some sense it is substantially more than (2) and (3) and contains all materials in some more intimate way than as grist for its evidential mill.[204]

Our excursus shows, then, that the listing of rational intuitions among intuitions did not rob the "opposition of reason and intuition" of all meaning. There is the opposition of science to rationalism, science building upon sensory intuitions which rationalism took to be unnecessary. And *vice versa.* Secondly, there is an opposition of philosophic reason to scientism. And *vice versa.*

Again, or as a sub-point of this last, if value-intuitions (4) be conceived to have any normative cognitive rôle, there is an opposition between these claims and the account of science—no matter how extensive the latter, if the latter is confined to description and explanation, to (as Sidgwick put it) "knowledge of what is, has been and will be." [205] Owing to the limitations of space, this fascinating and abysmal subject will have to be refused any discussion in the present essay.

Lastly, there is some sort of opposition between philosophic reason and what Radhakrishnan calls "integral experience." This is more than a question of the presence of cognitive ingredients in feeling. Beside the involvement of the difficult problem of effability, some ultimate questions of authority or autonomy are implicated, and will have to receive discussion.

XIII

It may be of interest for a moment to compare Radhakrishnan's views with those of Thomism on the question of "faith and knowledge" (as it has most frequently been called in the West) or of

---

204 It has been noted earlier that philosophy is held to be dependent upon intuitions, but—as these were sketched—they seemed to function more as categories or as regulative ideals than as material postulates. We were unclear as to whether these are conceived, so to say, as constitutive of philosophy or whether they are stuff that it comes upon and works over.

205 *Lectures on the Ethics of T. H. Green, Herbert Spencer, and J. Martineau*, 2.

intuitive religious knowledge and philosophico-scientific knowledge (as we might descriptively label it for our author). For, if we count religious intuition as revelation—and Radhakrishnan does— he, like any of the more orthodox adherents of the Western religious traditions, has a problem of reason and revelation. The Thomist, whom we were singling out, and Radhakrishnan are alike in turning to revelation. Further, they are similar, we believe, in that both would say that philosophy must operate with reason, and that there is, when sound, no conflict between reason and revelation. But the differences are significant. First, the Thomist supposes himself to get further with reason "alone" than does Radhakrishnan; he believes that he can "prove" not only that God exists but that He is good and that He has revealed himself. Radhakrishnan remarks:

If 'there is no higher faculty than those involved in ordinary knowledge,' if 'the truth of religion' or the validity of religious experience is to be established, 'as reasonable inference from discursive knowledge about the world, human history, the soul with its faculties and capacities; and above all from knowledge of the inter-connections between such items of knowledge,' then it will be difficult for us to be certain about God.[206]

Purely speculative theology which cuts itself off from religious tradition and experience and works from premises which are held to be universally valid cannot serve as an adequate philosophy of religion. The proofs of God's existence from premises of a general character yield not the God of religion but a supreme first cause or being who can be construed into the object of religious experience only if we start with the latter. . . . Speculative theology can conceive of God as a possibility; it is religion that affirms God as a fact.[207]

Secondly, the Catholic philosopher has no difficulty in specifically locating where there has been Divine revelation; frequently such thinkers did not trouble themselves with considering anything beyond their own heritage of Judaeo-Christianity, and, when they did, they usually roundly condemned it as total superstition (even if, in practice, the church exhibited within her bosom extraordinary phenomena of syncretism). Indeed, the more other traditions might be found to have "insights" approximating one's

206 IVL, 133f. The internal quotations are from Tennant, *Philosophical Theology*, I: 325ff.

207 IVL, 86f.; cf. also 202, 220f., 333. He also rejects "proofs" because God is not an object, SM, 275. Cp. his comments on Śaṁkara and Kant and his repudiation of the very question of the "existence" of God, Ind P, II, 542ff.

own, in some quarters these would be regarded as the subtlest inventions of the Evil One to lure men to perdition. One would search a long time to discover a finer example of the polar opposite of all this than Radhakrishnan's view, according to which revelations of the Divine are to be found in every people and will be manifest in a consummatory way in all; the highest present attainments are confined to no one culture or religion—and least of all could they be held in the legal custody of an organized institution.

Of a third possible item of difference, it is observed that we are unclear. It relates to the conception of philosophy in the respective views. Does reason commit suicide in favor of revelation, or, in what sense does it retain its life or even retain its aegis, when accepting the data of religion? It is plausible to us that philosophy retains its autonomy in Radhakrishnan's view, and that all things are data to be considered by it, although some data do make claims and some data are found to be of much more importance than other material. On the other hand, weight could be placed on remarks which, in possibly misleading isolation, declare religious experience to be "self-certifying," *svatassiddha;* [208] or which refer to *saṁyagjñāna,* "perfect knowledge." [209] To suggest reconciliation of these by saying, as James does [210] and as Radhakrishnan may intend, that for those who have mystical experience it is the highest, while for those who don't, reason may remain supreme, does reflect the psychological realities and more, but is not as clearcut as one might desire. Perhaps Radhakrishnan further has "reason" accord the greatest revelatory power to integral experience. Unfortunately for discursive purposes, the content of such disclosures is affirmed to be ultimately ineffable at the same time as it seems to be pronounced indubitable.

XIV

In some places our author's words seem to imply that "intuition" is infallible. Verification is said to be needed in discursive knowing because of the duality between "the knowledge of a thing and its being;" this duality is allegedly overcome in intuitive knowing.[211] Speaking of pragmatic and scientific tests, he remarks, "As we do not get at the real, we await confirmation of our theories. We test

---

208 HVL, 15.   209 IVL, 147.   210 *Varieties of Religious Experience,* 422ff.
211 IVL, 138. Perhaps the need of verification obtains only of "logical knowledge" and "at the empirical level;" for it is also said that "Thought is able to reveal reality, because they are one in essence . . ."

the truth of our views by the power of prediction." [212] At other places, however, types of intuitive knowledge are spoken of as needing philosophical criticism to evaluate their validity.[213] Much of this, of course, can be taken care of by saying that he who has intuitive knowledge (a) feels no need of verification, or (b) really has no need of it because of its infallibility, whereas (c) the philosopher (who, as trusting to reason, does not have intuition) requires that it be probed. The psychological proposition (a) can be asserted without affecting one's obligations to affirm or deny (b). If (b) be right, then the practical problem is to find criteria whereby authentic intuitions can be distinguished from spurious ones. For, as Radhakrishnan observes, "Simply because the deliverances of intuition appear incontestable to the seer or happen to be shared by many, it does not follow that they are true. Subjective certitude, whose validity consists in mere inability to doubt, is different from logical certainty." [214] And possibly the discrimination of the supposed irrefragable intuitions may be as practically fruitless as it is difficult, if it is the case that "even the noblest human minds have had only glimpses of self-valid experiences." [215]

In a moment we shall consider another line which may be taken with respect to the seeming contradiction between self-validation and external validation. It may, however, have its difficulties; therefore let us explore a bit more the present possibilities. Four plausible views (and they may not be exhaustive) of the relation of intuitive or mystical insight to philosophical criticism are the following. (a) All mysticism is the highest knowledge, and is self-certifying. (b) Some mysticism, specifically pure and authentic mysticism, gives the highest knowledge and is incorrigible by any other cognitive endeavor, but this mysticism can only be discriminated on mystical grounds, by some sort of "communion of saints" which tests the spirit, or at least by some sensitivity among persons with degrees of religious intuition which points them toward the most authentic and purest. (c) Some mysticism contains the highest knowledge and most valuable experience, but it is to

---

212 *Ibid.*, 144.

213 "If we take faith in the proper sense of trust or spiritual conviction, religion is faith or intuition. We call it faith simply because spiritual perception, like other kinds of perception, is liable to error and requires the testing processes of logical thought." HVL, 16. This is one of the strongest statements indicating that the rôle of logical criticism is not simply to justify the deliverances of religious insight to those who do not have them, but also to certify them to the man who does have them. Cf. IVL, 98ff., 219, 221, 222.

214 SM, 270.   215 IVL, 94.

be discriminated—partly at least—on non-mystical grounds; "reason" may compare mystical deliverances, attempt to make them coherent; it will also draw in all other experience; but "reason" finds it reasonable to trust the claims of some of the data (in particular, mystical contents) beyond what it can certify by any other means. (d) Some mystical or intuitive experience contains knowledge, or rather what becomes knowledge, but the deliverances of intuition have to be tested one by one, and by wholly non-mystical tests.

Any scientist who realizes that hypotheses do not come automatically and mechanically will presumably be willing to entertain the fourth view, for no hypotheses are self-certifying and none need to be rejected or accepted on account of their origins or pedigree. Scientific method remains autonomous and tests the hypotheses that come to mind. Apparently this view is not enough for Radhakrishnan; in effect it is lumping all intuitions (especially of type 4C and type 5) into a species of type 3 in our classification. "Our knowledge aspires to something more than knowledge, an intuitive grasp of the fundamental unity. . . . Our knowledge is incapable of bringing us into contact with the whole. It aims at the unity, though the limitations of intellect forbid the attainment of unity." [216] Thus speaks our author.

The first theory is also rejected by Radhakrishnan. Indeed, we suppose everyone rejects it, if the popular denotation of mystical experience is accepted. Various mystics—we suppose it to be a psychological fact—do or would hold this theory *if* they may make their own normative definition of mysticism. Then it approximates to the second theory. Radhakrishnan specifically acknowledges that the "experiences of saints and mystics" has "often been confused with emotional thrills and edifying feelings." [217] Ecstasy, he remarks, "is often a perversion of mysticism rather than an illustration of it. As there is a tendency to mistake it for spiritual life, we are warned against it." [218] If there is unsound, degenerate, perverse, spurious religio-mystical experience, we want to know how it is discriminated and the source or sources of the standard by which it is discarded. "We can discriminate between the genuine and the spurious in religious experience," he writes, "not only by means of logic but also through life. By experimenting with different religious conceptions and relating them with the rest of our life, we

---

[216] RR, 434. We are assuming that "an intuitive grasp" is still essentially cognitive, although it is beyond "knowledge about" or "knowledge through symbols."
[217] SM, 276.   [218] ER, 79.

can know the sound from the unsound." [219] The authoritativeness of the authors of the Vedas is that of "experts in the field of religion." "The truths revealed in the Vedas are capable of being re-experienced on compliance with ascertained conditions." [220] He adds elsewhere: "If religion is to revive, it must be founded on verifiable truth. The centre should shift from reliance on external direction . . . to a trust in experience, intimate and personal." [221] If the "verifiable truth" in or under religion were of exactly the same sort as public science, this would associate our author with the fourth view, (d); but we take it that he is saying that it has the objectivity which is conferred by confirmation at the same time as it is private or personal in content, locus, range of jurisdiction or some other significant respect. The statements are sufficient to warrant dissociating him from the first and fourth views, and are probably enough to identify his philosophic approach as the third, (c).[222]

In these brief assertions the details are not given of just what is being tested and of just what in experience confirms or disconfirms what was entertained. There is a sense in which every verification made in science is personal or private in its locus; it occurs in someone's experience; but it is regarded as inter-subjective in its evidential function, and as public in the sense of being available to all who will meet the conditions. Now Radhakrishnan's reference to re-experiencing the truths of the Vedas under "ascertained conditions" may seem to be wholly parallel. There may be a distinction to be made, however. If the question is: Does an experience of a certain description occur under such-and-such specified conditions?—then, in principle, it is wholly amenable to public science, at least as most of our contemporaries wish to think of science.[223] But the question is: Does an experience of a certain de-

---

[219] HVL, 17.   [220] *Ibid.*   [221] ER, 61.

[222] This is definitely the impression we receive from *The Reign of Religion in Contemporary Philosophy*, as a whole. Frankly, this work impresses us—to use a vulgar phrase—as more "hardboiled" or "tough-minded" in its approach than some of his later publications. Is it not possible that our author started out to prove all things by "reason," and increasingly found that this would not yield all of which he had firm conviction, with the result that the appeal to "intuition" has been heavier and more explicit in the recent works?

[223] Some of them may, as we think, too easily leap over the problem of the apparent inaccessibility of certain data to public observation, treating this as a mere "accident" or merely the reflection of present inadequate techniques.

Further, perhaps none of those empiricists (whom we admire) have yet adequately showed how the subjective occurrence is evidential of the objective reality. We do not dispute the "reasonableness" of belief in an indemonstrable realism, but this does not settle the status of the latter. Some smuggle in a rationalistic bridge to get to

scription which includes the making of a cognitive claim occur, and does this validate the claim made?—then one has a much more complex situation. In the first case, we have a straightforward question of existence, a question of whether happenings of a certain description take place under delineated conditions. In the second case, since the hypothetical event under critical review is an event which makes a claim, the question is double-headed; it has the question of the truth of the claim superimposed upon the question of existence. We suppose that—although it is not articulated in linear inference or in a systematized itemization—Radhakrishnan holds that any and all areas of experience may play evidentially upon a part, and that it is the business of philosophic reflection to determine what actual evidential rôles are played.

At the same time as we might wish that our author were more detailed on these matters and that he had taken explicit account of the distinction that has been made, we take it that he is advocating a sort of experimentalism of the way in which a philosophy or religion is to be adopted, but that the experimentalism is not exactly scientific experimentalism. With this, we must concur. We mean this. Whatever the psychological and evidential interactions in the process, the commitment to a method is to be distinguished from the treatment of an item under that method. To validate the method by the method would be circular. There is an experimentalism of all "genuine" philosophizing on a different "level" from a doctrine of philosophical experimentalism. The reflective adherent of religion or the reflective rejector of religion is presumably "experimenting with different religious conceptions and relating them with the rest of our life." It may seem to be a matter of regret that we lack well-defined objective criteria here; it should not be surprising that the horizon is not as well defined as the objects in the foreground, that one's ultimates cannot be managed in exactly the same way as the proximates when there has already been sufficient agreement on the ultimate to determine how the proximates should be handled.

Lest these last remarks be misinterpreted as more latitudinarian than is intended, a complaint should be registered at occasional laxer usages (by our author) of the concept of "confirmation." Or, to state it objectively, his definition seems to be unconventional

---

realism. Some frankly assume the transition, whether labelled "animal faith" or otherwise. Some are trying to render the connection probable as an hypothesis; but they have not yet (it seems) adequately articulated how the schema of the object entails the subjective events which confirm it.

in instances. Evidently he is taking religious intuition as giving content of a cognitive sort (and thus tacitly making claims). He remarks that: "Discovery becomes proof when what is revealed by intuition is confirmed by the slower processes of consecutive thinking. We have now to show that the general character of the universe as known is quite consistent with this intuited certainty of God." [224] Again, "The religious intuition requires to be reconciled with the scientific account of the universe." [225] Not only does one note in this (as was observed earlier) that the religious view is to be harmonized with but not subjected to the scientific account; but one notes also that confirmation is apparently identified with reconciliation and achievement of consistency. For most of us, our definitions are such that some proposition or interpretation, being consistent with some other, is not confirmation; it may simply be showing the logical independence of the propositions, without reflecting any probability, not to mention proof, from the one to the other. Perhaps Radhakrishnan here is reflecting a Bosanquettian idealism and is accepting a rationalistic coherence theory. If, as he says, "It is not possible for thought to think what is not true," [226] then we do need some way to distinguish what is really thought and what feels so much like it.

XV

There is another line of approach for reconciling the infallibility of intuition with the need of rational criticism of the formulations derivative from intuitions—or for reconciling the "self-certifying character" of the experience of the religious seer with the dictum that "It is for philosophy of religion to find out whether the convictions of the religious seers fit in with the tested laws and principles of the universe." [227] The infallibility of intuition may be held to attach to the intuition proper but not to its interpretation or discursive rendering. Indeed, Radhakrishnan indicates as much in several places, for instance, in references to what is conveyed by

---

224 IVL, 221.   225 Ibid., 222.

226 Ibid., 157. It is to be observed that Joachim, Bosanquet himself, and other neo-Hegelians ended up by including what we would call empirical evidence in the materials to be rendered coherent.

227 And: "There is no reason why the intuitions of the human soul with regard to the ultimate reality should be studied in any other spirit or by any other method than those which are adopted with such great success in the region of positive science." Ibid., 85; cf. 86, 94, 219, 221, 222. Cf. also HVL, 16. Again: Intuition "cannot dispense with the discipline and the technique of proof." ER, 63.

religious experience and in reference to immediate knowledge of the self. A citation of the former follows:

In the utterances of the seers, we have to distinguish the given and the interpreted elements. . . . Ideas which seem to come to us with compelling force, without any mediate intellectual process of which we are aware, are generally the results of previous training in traditions imparted to us in our early years. . . . When we are told that the souls have felt in their lives the redeeming power of Kṛṣṇa or Buddha, Jesus or Mohammad, we must distinguish the immediate experience or intuition which might conceivably be infallible and the interpretation which is mixed up with it.[228]

As one would wish, he does ask "what is it that is experienced?" [229] And he answers that "The Divine reveals itself to men within the frame-work of their intimate prejudices." "To say that our ideas of God are not true is not to deny the reality of God to which our ideas refer." The personal equation "does not vitiate the claim to objectivity in sense perception and scientific inquiry," nor should it in religious experience.[230] However, we would like a still more definite answer, and we both get it and do not get it. "That the soul is in contact with a mighty spiritual power other than its normal self and yet within and that its contact means the beginning of the creation of a new self is the fact . . ." [231] Reference is made to the "fact" of a "self-existent spiritual experience." Buddha is marked out among the religious teachers of the world "as the one who admitted the reality of the spiritual experience and yet refused to interpret it as a revelation of anything beyond itself"— except under pressure, when he identified it with *dharma*, "Eternal righteousness." [232] For many Hindu thinkers, rather, is The Supreme "the very condition of knowledge. It is the eternal light which is not one of the things seen but the condition of seeing." [233] But all this—and according to our author himself—is less than satisfactory. "The unquestionable content of the experience is that about which nothing more can be said." "Conceptual substitutes for ineffable experiences" are, of course, inadequate.[234] Since, however, something has to be said, "creative imagination with its symbols and suggestions may be of assistance." [235] Thus, "Hindu

228 IVL, 98f.   229 HVL, 23.   230 *Ibid.*, 25.   231 IVL, 99.
232 *Ibid.*, 99f.   233 *Ibid.*, 101.   234 *Ibid.*, 96.
235 *Ibid.*, 97. He refers to the Platonic use of the myth; and perhaps he might well find support in the theory of "bi-representationism" (*e.g.*, diagrammatic and qualitative) of B. H. Streeter, in his work entitled *Reality*. Santayana has a rich appreciation of mythical symbols, but of course their rôle is for him much more that of projected symptoms of the wishes of men than of cognitions, more that of vehicles of values than of truths.

thinkers admit the ineffability of the experience but permit themselves a graduated scale of interpretations from the most 'impersonal' to the most 'personal.' " [236] (Our author's systematized
version of this was called a "perspectival intuitionism" earlier in
this essay.)

Now what one feels as the unsatisfactoriness of this will probably
be admitted and be attributed to the demand of the understanding
to understand what it cannot understand adequately in its own
terms. But if it will submit to the conditions of its own fulfillment,
we may be told, it will be satisfied in a larger and more integral
experience than it has dreamed of. The present writer, as is pain-
fully evident, has not enjoyed mystical experience of the more
sublime sorts, and thus, in the most important sense, does not
"know" what he is talking about. However, from his own level he
would wish to continue making a few remarks and queries.

If "the unquestionable content of the experience is a *that* about
which nothing more can be said," then it is difficult to see how its
content can be incorporated into philosophy.[237] It is not easy to see
how it can be anything cognitive at all. One does not readily apprehend how it can be affirmed that there is contact with the Divine
or "a mighty spiritual power"—although one must acknowledge
the psychological fact of the creation (to a degree) of "a new self."

---

[236] *Ibid.*, 100. Cf. HVL, 26ff.

[237] That is, into philosophy as we understand it and as it was peerlessly described
in various places in *The Reign of Religion in Contemporary Philosophy*. Philosophy
is "an intellectual attempt to deal with the nature of reality." (p. 1) "Philosophy
arises out of the logical demands and aims at theoretical satisfaction." (p. 5) While
"the method of philosophy is just the method of science," philosophy "assumes a
scientific attitude towards the whole of human experience, and not merely to the
positive facts extracted from mechanical science." (p. 4) "There are properties of the
whole as a whole, which are not considered by the partial views" of the sciences.
(p. 2) "The postulates of sciences become the problems of philosophy. Philosophy
must give a logical defence of every premise that it demands." (p. 3) (One wonders
if, in following out this program, he found that we lived by tacit premises that
could not be logically defended?—and thus recourse was needed to intuition?) "If
thought does not help us to support our beliefs, it does not follow that we should
seek for their basis somewhere else than in thought, in emotion, will or immediate
experience or intuition." (p. 2of.) "We must, as George Eliot says, try to do without
opium. We cannot discredit intellect simply because it does not give us what we
want." (p. 14) Philosophy "is an *intellectual* attempt to organize the whole of experience, intellectual, emotional and volitional." (p. 15) "When James makes out
that philosophy is a matter of passion and not logic, that the true method of
philosophy is that of direct and immediate experience, of intuition, of life, he is confusing philosophy with poetry, science with art, criticism with life. In philosophy we
do not seek for faith and vision but for a reasoned explanation." (p. 254; cf. 241, 244)
Indeed, some of these statements may seem a little too "strong;" but in the context
they are never incompatible with accepting everything as data; they are incompatible
with allowing items of data to determine their own status.

If, again, reason does test and evaluate intuitions, it is hard to understand how it performs this function except it be given propositional contents. That is, of course, unless it is evaluating an experience instrumentally; scientific intelligence could find that certain experiences are commonly followed by certain consequences; if these consequences are morally approved or disapproved, desired or shunned, etc., then an indirect appraisal would be reflected upon their manageable antecedents. We can see a sense in which an attitude in its fulness is ineffable, and yet that it gets pragmatically tested in the ongoing economy of life. If, on the other hand, an experience is the standard, then it is not judged by events. One wonders whether what is tested, according to our author, are not the formulations which must always remain inadequate.

On this view, the incorrigibility or self-certification of mystical content would seem to be essentially tied up with its ineffability. We should like to ask, if mystical experience is ineffable in any other sense than all immediacy or whether all direct experience in its ultimate concreteness is ineffable. Conceptual knowledge of existence is always partial in that it is abstract and selective. (Aristotle recognizes that primary substance is incommunicable.) Again, is the ineffability relative to those who have not shared the experience? [238]

It has frequently been said in recent days that anything is communicable because anything can be named and anything named can be talked about. This seems to us too glib. First of all, there is the qualification, tacit or explicit, that anything to be named needs to be discriminated (except perhaps the Absolute, and then the difficulty is predicating anything about it other than tautologous expressions). The act of discrimination introduces the selective factor. Second, for communication, this has to be inter-subjectively achieved. This seems to require that the similar discrimination be made by two or more people; it seems to require that they have something similar or in common in immediacy in which to make the discrimination; and it seems to require that they acknowledge that each other is engaging in the noting, denoting, discriminating. It is surely wondrous that this process ever gets going; we have no practical doubt that it obtains; presumably in our early years, by much elliptical expression with reference to the most conspicuous

---

[238] "The truths of intuition are led up to by the work of the understanding and can be translated into the language of understanding, though they are clearly intelligible only to those who already in some measure have immediate apprehension of them." SM, 269. This would suggest that effability and ineffability are relative and gives indication that communicability is a matter of shared experience.

objects standing out against their backgrounds, symbolic reference is apprehended, and then the process can "snowball," can be used to make itself cumulative. It would appear that relatively adequate communication becomes more difficult as the structure of feeling becomes more richly reticulated in its texture, and it is doubtful whether the content can ever be communicated other than in the sense that more and more of the structure may be noted and communicated literally, or may be felt out and (with luck and genius) analogically suggested or conveyed poetically, or, possibly, may have something closely similar causally produced in the communicatee by the deft choice of stimuli. Thus there is the question, whether it be listed as an independent point or not, and which can be construed as more than a matter of definition: Does "talking about" something communicate it? [239] There is no practical doubt that we do communicate about certain objects and operations in a manner that is adequate for our purposes. There is grave doubt that, if our purpose were completely to convey a feeling, this would be possible. If there be an experience of acquaintance with the Whole, we do not see how adequate communication could be possible. However, we will add that, although we can easily see how causal inquiries conducted by "reason" might invalidate as extraordinarily unlikely the claims of a particular person to have had such supernal experience (of a kind distinct from our qualitative wholistic impressions of the environing cosmos), we do not see in any practical way how reason could validate or corroborate the claim to authenticity of such a *prima facie* experience. Would reason be stretching to its maximum if it could show the possibility, rather than the actuality, of such experience?

XVI

Upon this and other matters we would be helped if we knew the relation, especially the evidential order, between philosophical absolutism and consummatory mystic experience. Have the facts of mystical experience come first, and then the theory of the Absolute has been devised as the least unsatisfactory formulation of the content of such indubitable experience? Or, sometimes at least, have philosophical reflections yielded a doctrine of the supra-rela-

---

[239] One could describe a scene for a very long time and with a great effort at accuracy and still not convey it. Is it other than sheer complexity that makes it actually incommunicable? We suspect that the "wholeness" cannot be so conveyed— but, of course, when a wholeness is recognized it can be named.

tional, supra-rational Absolute, and then, with adequate digestion of this "truth," the thinker has undergone an experience which was more than rational and that no longer felt dual?[240] Radhakrishnan impresses us as one who places much more stress upon the discipline of philosophic reason than do most mystics; on the other hand, one feels that he has a more positive theory of, and more intimate acquaintance with, actual mysticism than those objective idealists (and some analysts!) who, as we commonly say, "ended up in mysticism." His conception of the proper order of evidence would be very interesting. "Philosophy as conceptual knowing is a preparation for intuitive insight," he says, "and an exposition of it when it arises. . . . The great truths of philosophy are not proved but seen. The philosophers convey to others visions by the machinery of logical proof."[241]

If philosophical "truth" comes first or independently, considerable plausibility attaches to the possibility that integral experience is a vivid "realization" of this truth. The disciplines (intellectual and other) that are undergone suggest the gradual elimination of working assumptions contrary to it, and progressive preparation for a fullness of feeling of the metaphysical doctrine. If one believes that Brahman is Ātman, his "vivid realization" of this principle— and it would not need to be in its "fullness"—could well be a mighty and terrific experience.[242] (Thus, if the metaphysics is prior and if, as perhaps Radhakrishnan and Śaṁkara hold, it establishes Consciousness-and-Bliss to be the original unproduced and infinite Reality,[243] then presumably the rest follows well enough. But to

[240] Cf., e.g., ". . . intuition with absolutists does not mean a break with our ordinary thought or an inversion of our rational procedure, but is only an expansion or completion of the labour of intellect, a grasp or comprehension which sees things as a whole." RR, 189; cf., 194, 203, 230f.

[241] IVL, 152. Much in this and other statements would suggest that Radhakrishnan adheres to the conception, held by many Vedantists, of the self-certification of knowledge, with the function of argument being the extirpation of blinding hindrances to the perception of truth. Because of avidyā, ignorance, argument is or may be part of the discipline of getting into condition for the occurrence of "realization." Nyāya and Vaiśeṣika stances, we understand, hold that perception, inner or outer, is subject to further checking—the checking of other experience by oneself or others, and including the test of practice.

[242] We shall not consider the possibility that some ecstatic states exhibit a paralysis of the functions of cognition on confrontation with an object bewilderingly and utterly massive and complex.

[243] Cf. Ind P, II, 475ff., 497f., 502ff., 527ff., 595ff.; cf. also Chatterjee and Datta, An Introduction to Indian Philosophy, 427ff., 448ff. In another early work, Radhakrishnan urged, against Bergson, theses characteristic of objective idealism. For instance: "But that the whole reality is of the same nature as the self, Bergson cannot assume. No intuition can give rise to this view. It is due to thought. Even if we

many Westerners, as well as to many Buddhist philosophers, to
Cārvākas, of course, and, in a sense, to Vaiśeṣikas as well, "Consciousness" is a product; these will wish to be shown why it should
be taken as original. Its ubiquity in all knowing and even in sleeping is not conclusive with respect to this cosmic status.)

The problem of evidential order will not here be extended to
the hackneyed issue of the priority of epistemology over metaphysics, or *vice versa* (or of the priority rights of empirical science,
since it frequently enters the competition these days). It might be
remarked that the familiar old circularity of ethics and metaphysics
does arise, for our author apparently assigns metaphysical sources
for the moral life, but presumably the phenomena of morality are
among the data for framing a metaphysic. This does suggest the
question of how "rigid" (and "certain" or "infallible") or how
"malleable" (and "tentative" and "fallible") are moral intuitions.
But our present problem over religious mystical experience is
acute; for, at times it is held to be highly revelatory, and at other
times to be so amorphous or somehow so inapprehensible as to
resist any propositional formulation. If integral experience provides truth for metaphysics, should we not be able to say what it
means, what it says, and what it is evidence for (other than simply
evidence for its own occurrence, qualitied in whatever way it may
be)? On the other hand, if no propositional content can be found in
anubhava, then presumably it is to be described as an occurrence
and fitted into its place by theoretical structures which it does not
give—by philosophic and scientific reflection upon other things in
the context quite as much as upon it.

Perhaps a portion of the answer to the question of priority is
that the process of philosophical reflection does not exhibit the
linear order of a deductive system.

XVII

For ourselves, we can only speculate. On the one hand, it is far
from implausible to us that one should accept a notion of perception with depth. Whitehead and the Gestaltists are making it
credible to empirically minded thinkers, who long have been

---

assume for argument's sake that intuition can give us the truth of our inner life, it
is thinking that enables us to grasp the true nature of everything else than our consciousness." (One recalls Peirce's argument against immediate knowledge of the self.)
We do not know how far this expression represents Radhakrishnan's present views.
RR, 191.

dominated by a surface quality presentationism, if not outright subjectivism, which rightly or wrongly derives from the great pre-Kantian British philosophers. It seems arbitrary to assign in advance any limits to such conceivable perception in depth; although our conceptions of organic connections tend to set empirical bounds. Thus one might entertain such an hypothesis as a theory of a cognitive ingredient in mystical experience. We might add that if anyone did know all things in some such way—most hypothetical —we do not see how he could know that he was exhausting them. Indeed, we do not apprehend how any knowing can annul our ordinary plural knowing of objects selected from, we suppose, a hinterland of infinitely more potential objects.

On the other hand, we are inclined to attempt to assimilate mysticism to the realm of practice (in a very comprehensive sense) and of personal realization, where cognitive ingredients may be present but are not primary. One of the persuasive reasons is that it is not "knowledge about;" although it may have an implicit cognitive ingredient in that it is or includes the taking of a disposition "with reference to."

One may wonder, indeed, if the incorrigibility, infallibility, or self-certification are not to be construed in valuational terms rather than cognitive ones. May they not mean the "self-sufficiency" of the experience, in the literal sense that the self is satisfied, that demands for beauty, goodness, and truth are all fulfilled in the experience or all subside within it? That one trained and conditioned for the experience has complete conscious consummation in the experience of all of the self which remains after the process of discipline? Such experience, in our usage, need not be "cognitive." It might be felt by the individual to be so important as to outweigh all other possible experiences.

Less extremely, it may be suggested that the doctrine of "self-certification" is reminding us (rightly and tautologously) not only that to have knowledge by acquaintance one must be acquainted, but also of the following: that many have had an experience which they feel to be of transcendent worth; that this experience makes a great noetic impression, so great, indeed, that no detail of future experience can alter the view here had of the Whole; that thus no future experience can unverify, disconfirm, this one.

This would be an experiential analogue of the theoretic way that many theologians, "knowing" God to be good, have treated specific evils. It is hardly characteristic, on the other hand, of our aesthetic encounters that we would feel that the claims we make about their degree of beauty can never be altered. True, it will always be the case that I will have felt about this object on this occasion in just the way that I now feel about it; but this does not prove that on new occasions my appraisal will remain unchanged. If a claim, tacit or explicit, in an experience cannot be disconfirmed, what is the meaning of saying it can be confirmed? Perhaps it means that oneself or others can have other similar experiences in the future. Future experience, however, may be different. One can conceive of confirmation "failing to come" when one hungers for, or attempts to get, similar experience. Indeed, mystics have frequently registered this for us in their records of the "dark night of the soul." However, it may always be replied that the conditions are not right, as a scientist can suppose something to be wrong with his apparatus. It has long been noted that "the Spirit bloweth where it listeth."

An experience accepted as so self-certified that not even all other experiences together testifying in some opposed way could outweigh it would be functioning as an absolute. Thus this suggested doctrine eventuates in being an extreme.[244] And it is apparently contrary to Radhakrishnan's philosophy. We take it that his proper view is that philosophy may weigh the credentials of all purported messengers, and that—while perhaps it does not have messages strictly its own [245]—it performs the juridical rôle by comparing the various deliverances and attempting to make a coherent whole out of them, with no one of them wearing the mantle of authority that completely settles its own status or the final position of others that in any way bear upon it.

If this last is the view of Radhakrishnan, it would be easy to throw stones at it, remarking that it must not only start with a

[244] And to us more of an extreme than the practical-valuational interpretation of mysticism suggested above. At least, it is one thing to have a "pearl of great price" for which one will sell all one has in the valuational dimension; it is another thing to have a "pearl of great price" for which one will sell everything else that one has in the evidential dimension. Further, we can with effort see a sense in which one (e.g., a Spinoza, a pantheist) can be said to have all values comprised in his object by rising to a higher level of consciousness; although, to be sure, this does not give him the libertine's pleasure qua libertine or the partisan devotee's values qua partisan devotee. We find ourselves constitutionally unable with effort to see a correlative sense in which the abandonment of certain data gives it back to one on a higher level. Nevertheless, we take it that this is what some tell us.

[245] This, of course, is a question. We saw earlier that Radhakrishnan affirms that philosophy requires intuition; but this can be construed that it must be furnished with intuitional data from elsewhere, although admittedly our author's phrasings frequently suggest that it also contains itself general truths which can only be validated by a sort of Kantian deduction. Cf. IVL, 154ff.

motley crowd of intuitions but that it must already have been at the job of grading them for hardness of cognitive worth at the same time as it is trying to systematize them, and that thus there are too many loose ends flipping around without some one rigid linear objective procedure. However, we note that we live in a glass house, for basically we do the same thing. We believe that most philosophers do likewise—if they genuinely reflect and have not surrendered the ultimacy of philosophy to some proximate schema of the sciences. On this interpretation, if we come out differently than Radhakrishnan, it is largely because, due to our experience (including presumably its limitations), we grade our intuitions with different weightings.

Viewing mysticism from a practical perspective (which may seem irrelevant and irreverent), there is, at the lowest minimum, good sense in not precluding in advance an ultimate "at-homeness" in the cosmos. One recognizes that one is not self-existent, that one is dependent [246] on a larger nexus. There is nothing beyond the All to satisfy one, whether or not one is satisfied with It. There is a security, which Spinoza among others found, in making the Whole one's "pearl of great price." It can never be lost. All things that come will have some kind of connection (Spinoza may have mis-labelled its character, with his logical bias). A known world will be one world by being known, no matter how much differentiation or how abrupt are the changes which are found to exist within it.[247] One can be grateful for the infinite gift of being aware of It. (And also be prepared for slipping into the silence again within It.)

An analogous median position—between the extremes of assigning religion cognitive sovereignty and of excluding from it all cognitive ingredients whatever—may be taken with respect to religion at the "lower levels" of experience. The denial, or presumptive denial, of authoritative cognitive content to religion is not a denial of all cognitive content in religion. There are, historically speaking, cognitive claims made by religions in such spheres as the natural, the metaphysical, the aesthetic and the moral. Some of these, particularly in the first area, and indirectly

---

[246] Radhakrishnan does not identify religious feeling with Schleiermacher's feeling of dependence, "for then Hegel might retort that Schleiermacher's dog may be more pious than his master." IVL, 88.

[247] "We are one, and therefore the world is one." IVL, 223. There is connection (Whitehead calls it "communication") between all the worlds that can be known by one mind; but we do not see that this argument can go further as to the kinds of unity and diversity that are to be found in the content of experience.

in the last, have been shown through the developments of the sciences, to be extremely unlikely. Others have carried along in cultures—including cultures that are predominantly secular—in ways that show that the claims are, to say the least, quite plausible and viable. Some of these naturally relate in a fundamental way to man's position in the world. A minimal statement of certain of these would receive the endorsement of many naturalists who have not lost all natural piety, and, indeed, of some who simply reflect on the problem of the adjustment to the world of a being that is at once possessed of vital interests and of self-consciousness. Perhaps we should cite a point or two, admittedly elementary.

It is a plain fact of mundane experience—though sometimes obscured by the adolescent conceit of man—that the universe is vastly greater than he is. Most religions have symbolized this to him, and taught that it is appropriate of him to accommodate his will to something Greater, which is not in his control. (Some more primitive faiths may center more attention on what he can control; on our definitions, these would partake of the nature of magic; but it may be gratuitously observed that even here there are some terms and conditions to be met.)

Some religions have also taught that certain values are intrinsically good, and these merit devotion regardless of the odds. Usually such beliefs have been accompanied by physical or metaphysical assurances that the Ultimate was behind these values, supporting and sanctioning them. But it may well be (and it is in the mind of some of us) that devotion to these values is good, even though the "odds against them" may include the ultimate "Cosmic Weather." The Weather, however, has at least permitted the rise of such goods as well as of various ideal aspirations—and there is no reason why it may not do it again—although it gives no assurance that all aspirations will be fulfilled.[248]

[248] I think that Bosanquet somewhere remarks—though I cannot momentarily find the reference—that reality and value are so integral that it is impossible for London to be destroyed. I cannot believe that the world is this foolproof. London may be destroyed physically, and someday its very memory will be blotted out—save possibly in Whitehead's and Hartshorne's God. The fragmentary astronomical evidence is that the earth will be destroyed, yea, and the solar system; and, I suppose, the galaxy. At the same time, we are reminding ourselves that there is the connection of value and existence that does obtain (a description of which will not be undertaken here), and that this is presumptive evidence that the universe can "do it again"— and perhaps do it better—on other planets of suns of this or other galaxies. I take some satisfaction in this thought. (Were I moulding cosmic epochs to my heart's desire, I would stipulate that courses of evolution circumvent the emergence of carnivore and be less expensive than apparently ours has been.) Beyond these extrapolations, of course we do not know but that conditions which we pronounce

Perhaps all religions indicate that something is the matter with present conditions. Indeed, why would a faith prescribe anything, if all were well and there were not even any portents of evils? This tacit assumption surely registers a rather ubiquitous feature of life. Of course, religions usually go further, and say that there is something pretty radically wrong with man as he naturally is, whether this be classed as ignorance or as an original taint of some. sort. The salvation religions go so far as to say that only a thaumaturgical change will be sufficient to avoid catastrophic consequences. One may discount the hyperbole in the figures but none the less recognize that we are not born mature or integrated; that the achievement of maturity is relative; and that perhaps there are even socially evil forms of relatively high integration. Again, when personal structuralization starts and solidifies in certain unfortunate habit patterns, it may need a catastrophic psychical reorganization.

The "higher" religions have greatly praised a losing of oneself, a universalizing of oneself, an attaining of some higher selfhood, or a merging in the One. This teaching and its realization is patently the monopoly of no one faith, nor of all organized religions together, though assuredly lone individuals would never have attained it without standing on the achievements of the race. It can be of a sort that lives fully and, without being a "pursuit of death," is yet also a preparing for dying, as Socrates said, and as Spinoza exemplified. It can be activistic, as Radhakrishnan and Bergson teach. It seems to be the acme of maturity.

Radhakrishnan may view all such minimal suggestions as the lowest form of patronizing attitude toward the manifest spiritual elements of experience. Better an old-fashioned materialism which roundly denied the spiritual than the new-fangled naturalisms which distort it to their own petty dimensions!

Radhakrishnan, it seems, almost inveterately conceives of naturalism as reductionistic. Thus many contemporary Westerners— rightly, we think—would hardly feel that his strictures apply to them, for they proclaim themselves explicitly as empiricistic and non-reductionistic. However, our author may intend that naturalism be reductionistic by definition, and thus he may contend that the difference between the reductionist and the so-called "non-reductionist" is only a difference as to how "low" a level they are trying

---

inorganic may not be fulfillments of value; but I do not wish to argue *ad ignorantiam*. On certain of these expressions we find that Radhakrishnan has already made his comment. Cf., *e.g.,* ER, 8off.

to reduce all things, and that if you have a genuine non-reductionist, who gives full recognition to the life of mind or spirit, he is really an idealist, whatever he may call himself. Perhaps we may hazard a guess that the water-shed which will divide the views will loom up as an issue of method. If—despite any dialectical arguments from the ubiquity of the apperceptive ego and notwithstanding any intimations of "clouds of glory"—one takes the question of the status of mind in the universe to be a question of empirical fact to be settled with some degree of probability by scientific methods, then one will be called a naturalist even if he should end up (as now would surprise him very much) affirming the likelihood of a universal consciousness. On the other hand, if a dialectical devolvement from self-certainty, or considerations of valuational import, or intuitions of what one is or of a Cosmic Self, are determinative of the answer to the question, one will be called an idealist. (Such a stipulation will not be wholly arbitrary, inasmuch as it registers some of the intellectual habits and motives at work, particularly in the tie-up which so many of our contemporaries desire between naturalism and empiricism. It has to be admitted that historically many naturalists were pretty thorough rationalists, and that some idealists were quite as empirical in their day as anyone else.) [249] The suggested definition would make the use of one or more of several types of intuition which are eschewed by the naturalist into differential traits of idealism.

We trust that it will be understood that we are not saying that mysticism is self-hypnosis, or that philosophical idealism is refuted. With Savery, we should affirm that "mysticism always remains as a possibility." [250] And we cannot concur in the current Western practice of assuming antecedently that any mention of "the Absolute" is nonsense. There seems to be formal intelligibility to referring to the Context of all contexts. Granted that little can be said about the Absolute, somehow it seems philosophically appropriate

[249] Indeed, it is still an open question whether a strict empiricism does not entail a subjective idealism.

[250] The context is: "However naturalistic one may be as he follows the scientific method in philosophy, he must bear in mind that his negative conclusions can never go beyond probability and that mysticism always remains as a possibility. I do not myself accept the presumptions of the cosmic mystics, but downright honesty compels us to admit that here as elsewhere we have no certainty. It is possible that in an ideal future, when all capitalists and all dictators have perished, there will always remain a small minority of intelligent mystics." Cf. Paul A. Schilpp (ed.), *The Philosophy of John Dewey*, 513. In all consistency, Savery had better not have restricted the possibility to comprise "a small minority;" perhaps—with Radhakrishnan —we all shall awaken to mysticism.

to attempt to say it. Granted even that simple positive predications are either false or tautologously employ synonyms, there may be a leap toward a regulative idea, embodied in the repeated term. Obviously in this area one cannot resort to conventional definitions —circumscribing the limits. An effort at "definition" presumably will be more of an extrapolation than a limitation. Possibly relational statements can be made, relating the inclusive to the included. (Certain neo-Hegelians spoke of the Absolute as the subject of all predications; should they not equally have said it was the container of all predicates, though there is error as well as truth in predicating any of the predicates of It?)

We admit, however, that our mind is soon fatigued in beating on this rarified air, and we readily understand how positive specifications are to be met with "Neti, neti." Actually we suspect that there is more than one drive of the mind toward an ultimate principle,[251] and that the terminal conception is more an extrapolation of one's methodology than a securing of known content. (In this sense, there may be different absolutes.) Most notable here, in our view, might be mentioned two approaches: a very liberal empirical one and a rationalistic one.

In the rationalistic view, it is assumed or contended that some knowledge of the structure of being is had by the direct rational perception of its necessity, that not all knowledge of the world requires sensory confirmation, and that not all rational intuition is confined to the formal and empty. It may be urged that elsewhere we make "distinctions of reason" where we go from a relative whole to aspects thereof which we can infallibly separate in thought, although we cannot separate them in actuality; and it may be contended that here (in the greatest effort of metaphysics) we can make "integrations of reason" which will go from the distinguished but not ultimately separate parts or aspects of the cosmos to the Whole in which they are necessarily incorporated.

We cannot pretend to refute this view, particularly for an intelligence or reason of superlative power. As a child of our age, we are inclined not to suppose that there is knowledge without ex-

---

[251] Some are looking for an ultimate explanatory principle, and some are seeking a Being beyond our customary powers of apprehension. The latter may, in various ways, stand as the consummation of our various demands, ethical, aesthetic, religious as well as cognitive. The demand for explanation itself sometimes drives toward a Causal Source of everything; sometimes toward an integral Totality of all facts; sometimes toward a common denominator of "Being" in all entities; and perhaps sometimes in other directions.

periential material. We do not deny, rather we affirm, that integrations are attempted in contexts and at various levels of contexts which include other contexts. But the new horizons, frames, hypotheses seem to us, when non-deductive and when they are relating to a cognitively new feature of the world, to be at most probable and not certain. These intuitions were listed earlier in this essay under category (3).

The empirical view can be construed so broadly as to include intellectual enterprises which have very large theoretic edifices provided that they are evidentially tied down in experience.[252] It can accept organizing ideas and regulative ideas, provided these are not assigned prior authority as contents in knowledge. Presumably it will maintain that all ideas grow in experience, but experience will not be cut down to the sequence of sensations. Those notions which James classed as "brain-born" in their origin do emerge in experience—in "experience" in a wider sense than he used it in the last chapter of his *Principles of Psychology*. Again, concepts of "perfection" (possibly obtained by extrapolation from the comparatives of "better than") and concepts of mathematics possibly got by a "method of extensive abstraction" are not given in sensory experience. Yet such concepts may have use in organizing experience. Now conceptions of the Absolute, we suppose, will be either definitions which, apart from evidence, will be empty, or positive conceptions which may be extraordinarily speculative hypotheses. In the former case, definitions may be made with reference to some empirical data, usually of the most general sort; one may have a kind of "ontological definition," instead of an "ontological proof." Thus one may make references to the totality of existence, the whole, the all. The results of such procedure do not seem to us to be devoid of meaning, although they are devoid

252 Cf. *e.g.*, ". . . the concepts which arise in our thought and in our linguistic expressions are all—when viewed logically—the free creations of thought which can not inductively be gained from sense-experiences." "In order that thinking might not degenerate into 'metaphysics,' or into empty talk, it is only necessary that enough propositions of the conceptual system be firmly enough connected with sensory experiences and that the conceptual system, in view of its task of ordering and surveying sense-experience, should show as much unity and parsimony as possible." A. Einstein in Paul A. Schilpp (ed.), *The Philosophy of Bertrand Russell*, 287, 289. For philosophy, if not for physics, we do not see that the word "sensory" should qualify the word "experience." Whitehead would presumably note that this is a restriction of intuitions to perception in the mode of "presentational immediacy." Cf. *Symbolism, Its Meaning and Effect*, Chs. I, II; or *Process and Reality*, Part II, Ch. VIII.

of demarcations. No particular sort of unity or integration can be assumed in advance, but one specifies the general sort of unity constituted by there being nothing outside and all connections that obtain being inside the enveloping whole.

Or the empirical metaphysician may explicitly seek hypotheses or an hypothesis of widest scope. He is trying to do work essentially scientific, without confining himself to the intense specializations of the sciences as these exist. To shift vocabularies, it seems that he is trying to give a general theory of Prakṛti,[253] but he is inclined to find no "use" in the concept of Nirguṇa Brahman, for the latter affords no "positive explanation." Materialism was a rash step in the right direction, in the sense that it addressed itself to the subject, although the positive conceptions of matter were quite unequal to carrying the weight of explanation. The once popular forms of materialism, drawing heavily on a picturability borrowed from macroscopic dynamics, were found to be no good by the natural sciences themselves. Nor do materialisms constructed from contemporary concepts of matter go very far. Physics is a long way from explaining the valuations of a grasshopper or the phenomena of a social movement. Animistic materialisms and hylozoisms seem more promising, as they recognize in latent form more of the potentialities needed. Indeed, one may cling to the label "materialism" and yet quite responsibly say that the problem is to frame an adequate conception of matter. Santayana, in large measure, is an instance of one who preserves for himself much flexibility in the use of the term "matter."

We have the recurrent feeling that most of what we do in empirical metaphysics is to claim that we have "potentially" in our explanatory realities what comes out "actually" in the events of the world. Such affirmations may not seem very enlightening and may seem verbal. But if the explanatory realities are so conceived as to imply definite consequences, it is something of an achievement to frame them so that they will not entail the denial of something that exists, and it would be a very great achievement to frame them so that "there are no items incapable of such interpretation." [254]

---

253 If there are ways of determining that Prakṛti requires a catalytic agent to initiate all or certain of its processes, then of course such an agent must become a part of the cosmic hypothesis.

254 The phrase is stolen from Whitehead, Process and Reality, 4. More than the phrase is borrowed: essentially the conceptions of applicability and adequacy (common to Whitehead and many other thinkers) were here employed, and we should likewise accept the criterion of logicality. Of Whitehead's "coherence," which positively requires in the ideal that the fundamental notions "not seem capable of

Inasmuch as we take it that there is an assumed context to any statement, and that even the discrimination of denoted entities or things given proper names require some systemic connections, and that the sciences are not simply a miscellany of rules of thumb, we should hold that the attempt at formulating an empirical metaphysics [255] is a legitimate enterprise—indeed, an enterprise implicitly demanded by the sciences themselves. This is not to deny the danger of presumption and the need for caution. Thus, for the present and the foreseeable future, most of the careful work may consist of the relating of, and the eliminating of inconsistency between,

---

abstraction from each other" (p. 5) and which thus is to be distinguished from absence of contradiction, we are not quite so sure; and of "necessity" we entertain more doubt. "Necessity" (which sounds rationalistic) may name the uniqueness of the one true system of ideas at which the metaphysician aims and may be employed in the assertion that the universe as a whole, defined as all that which in any way "communicates with immediate matter of fact," is self-explanatory in the sense that no one can or need go beyond it to provide it with rationality. "This doctrine of necessity in universality means that there is an essence to the universe which forbids relationships beyond itself, as a violation of its rationality." (pp. 5-6).

We suspect that Radhakrishnan would say that Whitehead's own system does not live up to his own criterion of coherence, and that it has not exhibited its own necessity. With respect to creativity, for example, Radhakrishnan not only complains of the difficulty of conceiving it, but declares: "Unless the ultimate reality is conceived in more satisfactory terms, on the lines of the Absolute mind which has ideal being and free creativity as its features, it becomes a mere logical abstraction." IVL, 329.

255 Labels will not matter, provided that they do not inhibit the raising of ultimate questions or do not insist upon the truncation of the systematic effort at some level where smugness sets in because great satisfaction is taken in some abstracted proximate set of concepts. There is not much difference, for instance, between the following two groups, the first of which denies "metaphysics" and the second of which affirms it. *One group* says: We take science in the widest sense; philosophy is either bad poetry or a part of science; in some speculative philosophy, so-called, we find hypotheses of great scope and correlative marked tentativity. The arbitrary division of science into special sciences gives a mistaken impression of an enterprise with division of labor and (at any given time) great differences in the probability of contents, but still with a fundamental unity. Admittedly, the cross-classifications of material, and the levels of inquiry do complicate the picture. But inquiry into inquiry and into the presuppositions of inquiry is still inquiry; and whatever is inquiry we call science. The *second group* says: The special sciences are by their nature highly abstract. There is room for them; for distinctive studies which take them as subject matter; and for attempts to overcome their abstractness with a more integral and concrete view. The scientist (fortunately for us all) proceeds on assumptions; he is usually not self-conscious about them; he employs norms which he does not justify. Critique of such assumptions and norms is not science; philosophy of science is not science; such distinctive work no less belongs to philosophy than the enterprise of synthetic construction itself. Although these two views manifestly define science and philosophy differently, there need be no substantial difference between them *if* the first will really inquire into inquiry and the presuppositions of inquiry without antecedent restrictions of method and *if* the second will always keep its synthetic construction in commerce with the data of experience.

explanatory concpets in different areas of experience.[256] For there is this obvious question over metaphysical hypotheses. If these be continuous with those of the sciences though of greater generality, are they not infected with a high degree of improbability? Are they not, as it might rudely be put, hasty generalizations made by those who do not have the patience or self-discipline to wait a few millenia until the matters of lower generality have been settled sufficiently well to constitute a firm foundation for the larger generalizations? Although we admit that we have reluctantly come to accede somewhat to the attitude thus coarsely expressed, it is worth raising the question whether the assumption of an inverse order between amount of probability and level of generality holds. Is there not a tacit presupposition that the only level at which any content comes into the edifice of knowledge is that of the simple particulars, and that the hierarchy of knowledge is simply a pyramid of generalizations upon generalizations which ultimately rest on and refer to the base of particulars? Do not the enterprises of the several sciences show that this is not the case, that inquiry is carried on at various levels and that fresh and semi-independent materials are brought into the so-called edifice of knowledge at different levels? Is not the analogy of a building misleading—and even with it, cannot some rafters be shaped a bit, even though they cannot be erected before the supporting walls are up? Also is there not a failure to see that general knowledge is not completely empty, not absolutely formal, even though it does not pretend to an exhaustive knowledge of all subtended particulars? Cannot we say some things about vegetables and about plant life before we know everything about cabbages? On the level of common sense, are we not much more sure that there will be a tomorrow than we are of the specific contents of the anticipated tomorrow?

There is a strand in Radhakrishnan which suggests a dependence upon the rationalistic method in metaphysics. Reference is here made to the doctrine of Nirguṇa Brahman, of the Absolute *qua* Absolute. It seems doubtful that a consummate intuition yields the knowledge that "The Absolute transcends not merely its finite but also its infinite expressions taken singly or in a finite number," or that "the creation of the world makes no difference to it," and is "an expression of the freedom of the Absolute." [257] It is likewise

250 More or less as Broad has familiarly put it, "speculative philosophy" requires an extensive ground work in "critical philosophy." *Contemporary British Philosophy*, I, 82ff.
257 SM, 285f.

difficult to see how such propositions concerning the Absolute could be asserted with much confidence as extrapolations from the empirical materials at our disposal. It is more plausible to suppose that such theses are taken to be rational necessities or at least as coping stones in a dialectical edifice. (Of course, they might be affirmed on authority,[258] but the question would arise as to the basis of the authoritativeness of the authority.)

On the other hand, Radhakrishnan invites us on a sweeping empirical tour, after the manner of emergent theorists, encompassing matter, life, mind and personality, and leading to such statements as: "All existents are organisms, which reflect the whole, past, present and future. Even in the simplest physical entities the plan of the whole controls the character of the subordinate parts which enter into them." [259] While such results will require much further testing, they appropriately belong to an empirical metaphysics. Further, he expressly makes such stipulations as: "Philosophy does not reveal anything wholly beyond experience, but presents to us the order and being of experience itself." [260] And he recognizes that the appeal to religious experience would give evidence of an immanent aspect of Deity; "we may not know the ultimate meaning of God, though we may know something about God or what answers to God in reality through religious experience." [261]

XVIII

Let us attempt a little summing up and the recapitulation of certain tacit interrogations.

Radhakrishnan has drawn attention to very important ranges of activity, brought together under the collective term "intuition." Even for knowledge about knowledge this is a signal contribution, for there is characteristic neglect of these ranges of experiencing and of the conditions of knowledge by acquaintance and by description. Psychology has largely neglected them, partly because of a concentration, natural in a new science, upon the simpler matters, partly because of the conviction of many that a negative conclusion has already been well-established as to the existence of alleged "super-normal" phenomena, and partly, one regrets, because of motives of professional pride and unscientific dogmatism. Apart from those with specific motives in morals, aesthetics or reli-

---

258 "The truths of the ṛṣis are not evolved as the result of logical reasoning or systematic philosophy but they are the products of spiritual intuition . . ." IVL, 89.
259 *Ibid.*, 315.   260 *Ibid.*, 223.   261 *Ibid.*, 86. Cf. HVL, 29.

gion, there is among philosophers almost no concern with intuition; nor is there any shame that none can stand in the tradition of Plato's use of myth. Again, it was natural enough that, for studying knowledge, attention first went to the clearest forms of it, and this meant what was most articulated. Descartes may symbolize the ancestry of this; and it is true today, as James observed, that prestige goes to him who can "put you down with words." [262] But there are encouraging signs. In psychology there is concern with such subjects as "mental set" and "productive thinking" (and, in fringe quarters, there continues an interest in telepathy, clairvoyance, etc.). Besides the unilateral overstatement of Bergson, there are in philosophy a few strands of interest. Whitehead constructs a categorial pattern, allegedly to express immediacy; as the system comes to formulate "truths," the more general of these are found to be more difficult to lay hold upon in the complexes of prehensions, conscious and unconscious, which are constitutive of each actual occasion in an historic route exhibiting high grade personal order. Köhler, too, observes our present pre-occupation with clear and polished concepts.[263] One of the thinkers farthest removed from "trust" in intuition has not only waged continuing warfare upon formalism; he, Dewey, has noted the rôle of that which directs the processes of inquiry. Cassirer does not, to our limited knowledge, say much about that from which the great panorama of symbolic forms comes; but this matrix is presupposed, and "intuition" could conveniently be stipulated as a label for that which discriminates the relevance of the selected forms at the unfolding stages of the transactions and transformations called intellectual and human history. Mrs. Langer, seeking to give us glimpses of the process of artistic creation and to explain the language of the arts, notices the capacities of forming or selecting non-discursive symbols and the capacities of letting these do something to one in a kind of immediate insight called appreciation.

Some Western readers will thus tend to divide Radhakrishnan's thought in two: that which is suggestive to us of our neglect of pre-discursive and post-discursive apprehension, and of presentational and possibly other forms of non-discursive meaning, on the one hand; and that which seems on the surface to us to be representative of *de facto* cultural formations other than our own. To be sure, this, in a sense, exemplifies what we always do—namely, interpret or misinterpret others in terms of our own thought forms.

262 *Varieties of Religious Experience,* 73.
263 *The Place of Values in a World of Facts,* vii.

To pretend that we can wholly transcend these limitations at this time would be fanciful. On the other hand, to attempt to stabilize for the future our present sortings, acceptances and rejections, would be at once a faithless act in the face of the unity of the race and an act of folly in the face of the historical process.

It seems to us that one of the outcomes of this cursory survey is not only to be impressed with our failure to be conscious of what we are doing in our continuous uses of various sorts of intuitions but with the dearth of general theory of our cognitive apparatus and functionings. Naturalists and others who may not be convinced by Radhakrishnan's view have not gone very far in discharging their obligations to provide a general hypothesis, evolutionary and histogenetic, of emotion, feeling, sensation, efferent processes, integral intelligence, etc. Peirce suggested the need of such; the functional psychologists moved into some of the hiatus; but the mandate has not been extensively honored.

The work of Radhakrishnan on intuition is, as we see it, more one of stimulation and suggestiveness than one of linear argument or of detailed taxonomy. Thus, with the impressive ranges of material which he presents, we thought that we had the opportunity of providing some small service in proffering some scheme of classification and in setting up interrogations in its terms, among which were questions of the relationship of species as well as of the appropriateness of the outline as a whole. Admittedly, the suggested scheme may have mixed grounds of classification; its distinctions are more in terms of content intuited than of the functionings of the intuitings; probably the intended effort of unscrambling has resulted in numerous wrenchings from context and in arbitrary deployments in pigeon holes.

In the main outline, seven pigeon holes were provided.

It is arguable from some larger plausible context of thought that there must be an element of a "sheer given" in perception, even though consciously we do not find this ingredient in pure form; that there is presupposed a sort of "given in itself," although the nearest we consciously come to it is in partially interpreted givens.

Positively, we see (we believe) one kind of intuition instanced in sensory discrimination of what is sensorily discriminated.

Secondly, we think that we note by inspection—and, circularly, all rational arguments may be exhibited as presupposing—that there is another kind of intuition of the apprehension of concepts and of their relations.

In the third place, existing prior to the clear apprehension of conceptual meanings, we introspect the later steps of processes of feeling for such meanings, and of feeling for connections between somewhat removed systems of such meanings. Similarly we introspect "feeling for" facts, and for complex structures of facts; we not only "feel for" ways of re-thinking facts, but for ways of re-structuring the patterns of events. These classes of "feeling that . . ." or "feeling for . . ." can usually have their contents tested by bringing them to explicitness, seeing what these implicitly predicted or would predict, and noting whether this accords with what is known and with what does happen when certain stipulated conditions are set up. Frequently, of course, this last is "technically" impossible, as our positivist friends have willingly acknowledged for a long time.

With this third category, we arrived at the first species which Radhakrishnan calls by the name of "intuition." Some difficulty was encountered here over the question of certainty as against probability. This species includes those feelings which are the immediate source out of which, or within which, hypotheses are crystallized. They are a source, but they are not knowledge, if one means by knowledge what is proved or what is warranted with a significant degree of probability by experiment or statistical observations. This sort of pregnant feeling provides material for such probing, testing and checking. But, if one should mean by "knowledge" what is in accord with the facts, then some of these hunches and intuitions are knowledge, for some of them have been later shown to be in accord with the facts—and presumably some current newly born hypotheses will share the same happy fate. Or, if "knowledge" mean what has more probability than a random idea drawn out of the infinite blue of logical possibilities—what has some probability above zero, although assuredly one cannot quantify it—then this is knowledge. For Radhakrishnan, along with Gestalt psychologists and some earlier idealists, has shown that the picture adduced on evolutionary grounds by certain thinkers is not sound. We refer to the conception that "ideas" are to be viewed as random occurrences or purely chance variations; that all selective functions ("natural selection," in this extension of evolutionary conceptions) come into play only after the birth of the hypotheses. Some kind of pre-natal selectivity is operative,—indeed, some kind of procreative selectivity seems to be formatively present. Even the associational theory is plainly recognizing a prenatal selectivity of ideas in their causal terms, although the account appears inadequate. Rather does the contextual whole seem to have a rôle and to exercise a "gentle force of attraction," or to set up vectors to "fill the gap." There may be other accounts which may agree with the facts; this hypothesis fits as well as any with the observation that a mind familiar with the data of an area is required as the locus of the occurrence of the idea which will organize those data.

However, none of this comes near to being all that Radhakrishnan affirms. And with respect to the present range of phenomena, it may seem still too haphazard. Slight probabilities do not interest one when one believes certainty to be available. This characterizes apriorists, and it presumably is quite understandably true of those who believe there is a more direct way of attaining certain knowledge.

Recognition of the nature and context of empirical tests might provide a footing for bridging out beyond statistical probabilities and toward accepted certainties. Consideration of the processes of verification lead one to the observation of limitations of experimentation which can hardly be regarded as "technical," as functions of the state of scientific development, or even of man's location and relative size, etc. There is an ego-centric predicament and an onto-centric predicament. Roughly put, I cannot perform experiments in the absence of myself or the absence of the universe. I myself can perform no experiments without minding them, without "my" transcendental unity of apperception being involved; and nothing whatever takes place without there being being (Being, if one prefers).

However, the first of these impossibilities does not keep us from believing in "realism," and the two together do not lead us to make an identity between the transcendental unity of apperception and Being (or between Ātman and Brahman). Of course, each center of awareness must admit that concrete Being must be such as to give rise to its consciousness; the history of thought does seem to instance views which have refuted themselves by denying this.

In view of there being accepted ways of getting what is by considerable common consent "knowledge," can it not be said that it is a question of fact (to be settled by empirical test or by inspection) whether there is intuition of a certain sort or not? And, secondly, why, if we can get it, should we not have a psychological explanation of any and all intuitive powers that are found in any way?

Taking the second item first, somehow we would want all available empirical psychology before making a metaphysics of the self; but we could not propose turning over the questions of epistemol-

ogy or metaphysics to the psychologist and physiologist, who presuppose, rather than investigate, certain answers. We think all
sciences are relevant to, and should be comprised in, a metaphysic;
does Radhakrishnan regard them strictly as irrelevant? Presumably
our author would say that psychology, and the other extant empirical sciences, do, in a sense, make their explanations in terms of a
false metaphysic (although satisfactory at their own "level"). Our
next question would be whether it can be shown that, commencing
with the empirical level itself, one will be led beyond it; or whether
one must recognize that he "is" beyond it in order effectively to get
beyond it.

On the first question, similarly, the reply might possibly be
forthcoming that it illegitimately demands that the higher levels
submit to the lower for authentication; or, alternatively, Radhakrishnan may answer affirmatively and add that inspection shows
that those who are qualified find powers of pluralistic and of mystic *samādhi.* Whether telepathy and various clairvoyant powers
exist is, as we see it, an empirical question. Affirming telepathy is
asserting the presence, in certain minds under certain circumstances, of contents which can be sufficiently described conceptually to be checked by other ways of knowing. Empirical testing may
be difficult; it is hard to prove a negative, and it may not be easy
to prove the affirmative concerning something existing rarely and
in weak form. But positive cases are quite conceivable and may be
found, rendering the hypothesis practically conclusive. However,
the question of whether "we can discern every kind of reality directly" sounds like the same kind of hypothesis (except a much more
sweeping one), but one feels that it is not meant to be one that
could be confirmed by full realization. Taking it in this way, we
do not see how one could know that anything and everything can
be so known, although we could understand this as a declaration
of faith. On the other hand, perhaps the resulting kind of knowledge as well as the means are radically different from that of empirical knowing. If the contents cannot be stated to a significant
degree in conceptual terms which imply the applicably of empirical
schema, then scientific confirmation is ruled out. Possibly there
remains some kind of checking of one spirit by another spirit (if
indeed they be different); *per hypothesis,* there is no reason why
this should not be done directly; Zen masters and others, however,
evidently felt that they could check well enough by symbolic devices of expression (not of statement). If there is held to be such
other and higher knowledge of the real, tested by other and higher

ways, we are not qualified to discuss it. Although many of Radhakrishnan's phrases seemed to imply the authority of the highest experience, not checkable by any other means, we felt that his proper doctrine was the following; scientific reason, as limited in its range of data, is not autonomous; philosophic reason, as unlimited in its acceptance of data, is autonomous; but it is a fact that philosophic reason finds some of the data (data found in religion and mystical experience) to be much more significant and revelatory than other experience. If we are right in this interpretation, the next question would be that of the criteria or considerations whereby reason accords highest cognitive status to integral experience.

The next three pigeon holes were grouped as broadly in the realm of value intuitions. Here we followed Radhakrishnan's own classification into (A) Moral, (B) Aesthetic, and (C) Religious.

Intuitions of intrinsic values stand in a precarious position with respect to "verification" (which is a current but perhaps unreasonable demand). The intuition of a particular cannot be absolutely confirmed, although attempts at repetition (not strictly possible) and the checking of supposed connections may be quite sufficient for practical purposes. There is a problem of how any universal assertions are known, if they are. Full concrete particularity and defined abstract universality may stand as poles of our actual usage in the life of practice and of science. It is thus difficult to be sure that a supposed intuition of type (4) is not really of type (3); and thus that relative scientific verification is possible. If a complete judgment of a particular intrinsic value is really a prediction that acting in a specific way will result in specified results which include a specified satisfaction or to which a specified approval will be made, then it can be tested. Probable generalizations could be inductively framed by noting the repeated patterns. Confirmation of judgments of comparative intrinsic value would be still more complicated; but they might be possible to a significant degree of probability not only by finding how values get rated in *de facto* hierarchies of good, but also by indirect evidence of satisfactoriness to human nature as independently investigated. But there seems always to be a valuational assumption, whether or not concealed in a *de facto* element, in these experimental patterns. It is always possible to ask, Should we respond as we actually do, should we rest in the acceptance of our present structures? Whether these questions are answered by an absolute crystalline intuition, or whether they are answered by some process of reflectively contemplating one's clusters of more or less malleable intuitions, it seems to us that recourse must be had to intuition in ethics and aesthetics. We did not positively follow our author in the supposition that every moral decision can be made with certainty; he affirms this for saints; it is beyond our ken. Also in aesthetics we raised certain questions, for it seems doubtful whether all great art is, as Radhakrishnan seems to say, edifying.

If one knows God by acquaintance, there is nothing the outsider can say, although he may ask in what forms one is assured of the acquaintance and what analogies it bears to personal human relations. Apart from integral experience, Radhakrishnan may or may not be saying, the Absolute is only a hypothetical possibility; at any rate, apart from religious experience, God is only an hypothesis of science (or of empirical metaphysics, if we distinguish metaphysics from the special sciences). The latter seems to be correct; and many, since Laplace, have felt that it was an hypothesis with low degree of probability. Acquaintance, however, our author tells us, places it beyond practical doubt for the many who have such experience. Yet, because there may be error in spiritual perception, he prescribes "the testing processes of logical thought" not only to justify the deliverances of religious insight to those who do not have them, but to certify them logically to those who do have them. We do not suppose that religious intuitions are doubted *en toto* or justified *en toto;* it seems that our author's proper doctrine is that they, along with other intuitions of various sorts, are justified against each other, by some sort of coherence test.

In so far as religious perceptions may receive some "authentication" from other types, it is particularly interesting to ask whether it is believed that moral intuitions (4, A) support or can be in any way confirmatory of the devotional and mystical (4, C) and (5). There is little doubt that our author allows the moral a possible disconfirmatory rôle; spurious mysticism is partly judged as such through its failure to produce certain effects in spiritual character. James's voluntaristic pragmatism did allow the fruits of saintliness to enjoy a partially verificatory status with respect to the presuppositions of the saint's position. This is not strictly a scientific position. It might, however, be allowed some standing in a "coherence view." (Why resort to a coherence view here, it might be asked, since, if one resorts to it, it will also include *anubhava,* which is much more "potent"? The answer would be that no semi-independent evidence should be neglected; it would reflect some evidential favor upon mystical experience, and thus would be suggesting that these deliverances have a congruence with other deliverances which illusions lack. A coherence view is not inherently precluded from containing such categories as illusions, sports, and irrelevant mutations.) For the strictly scientific view, these intuitions carry no evidential weight; contrary to voluntaristic pragmatism, only intuitions of types 1, 2, and 3, are to be assigned any cognitive rôle, and the rôle of type 3 is one which requires its evidence from 1. To be sure, causal laws in psychology and sociology can be formulated concerning the consequences of belief in certain ideas. "Beneficial," etc., may be given stipulated definitions and these definitions together with the facts may warrant the pronouncement: "Believing in God is beneficial to individual growth and to the stability of a civilization." But the definitions are not "truths"— they are taken as conventions—and the warranted assertion says nothing to the effect that God exists.

Does the situation ultimately resolve into a matter of experience? Some few have had intense experience which produces overwhelming conviction. Many others have had mild mystical experience which leads them to sympathize with ṛṣis and to take the word of these as experts. Some do not have much experience, or at least not to a sufficient degree to be impressed by them. This may be due to an unwillingness to meet the conditions (though to some extent such experience is not under control), or to cultural and idiosyncratic inhibiting characters.

Such doctrines as "rebirth"—for which Radhakrishnan makes provocative discussion—may be grounded on the linking of two lines of consideration: first, that these doctrinal clusters are morally demanded, and, second, that the cosmos is structured in a way that is consonant with moral demands.[264] We apprehend the first point; at least our author has made it out in a way vastly more plausible than the eschatology with which we are familiar in the West. We

264 We choose to state this on the level of argument, for it is in part so stated, even though the first impression occurring in a mind from an alien culture may be that authority is the source. When one reads of rebirth, and of subtle bodies (the liṅgaśarīra which informs the physical body, and the sūkṣhma śarīra in which the physically discarnate self invests itself), one feels that Radhakrishnan's philosophy is an effort of "reconciling" the preferred siftings of a very sensitive mind working sympathetically in the great fields of religious lore with some conceptions arrived at by disciplined cognitive means, and that, not only is no monopoly granted to the latter, but sometimes the former is dominant. If this be the case, it would have been obviated if "reason" were given a larger rôle in criticism and testing. Give intuition as large a rôle as anyone may desire in originating ideas! But give reason a larger place in estimating their probability, a larger rôle than casting a negative vote only in the rather extreme cases of contradiction with fairly highly probable scientific "facts."

do not see that he has made any ordered attempt to establish the second point. Perhaps he is assured that our intuitions are so strong that no argument need be made; however, suppositions of cosmic justice have been wondrously weakened since the rise of modern "neutral" science and the widespread dismissal of final causes from its modes of explanation. (The trend may now be reversed, but it has a long way to go before it is common among scientists, or cosmic in its extent of application; and the teleology which is being exemplified is not "moral" in its character.)

Discussion was given to the relationship of (4, C) religious intuitions to (5) "integral experience"—whether this be one of continuity or discontinuity, and how reason bears upon it. Radhakrishnan's perspectival intuitionism permitted him to hold to absolutism and at the same time to affirm the relative truth of religious formulations of various levels. However, several aspects were not clear to us. We did not determine in exactly what sense our author gets his Absolute by religious experience, or precisely how he arrives at this doctrine by philosophic reason. With respect to the former, there is not only the familiar question of the knowledge one must have in order to be able to grade different levels of experience. There are also, from some points of view, the question of whether religious experience can give one data other than of an immanent divine, and, again, the question if it gave a transcendent deity, would this not be far short of the Absolute? If, indeed, "God is the Absolute from the human end," "in relation to the cosmos," or "from the cosmic point of view," [265] how do we know the extra-cosmic nature of the Absolute, the Absolute *qua* Absolute? Must not the philosophic wisdom which knows this be super-human? With the theory of the Self of Advaita Vedānta, we can understand a sense in which this may be affirmed. However, our difficulty is then the one of making the transition from the transcendental unities of apperception, which seem to be finite and plural, to Brahman.

The issue of the autonomy and supremacy of reason persistently arose, challenged by certain ascriptions of self-sufficient finality to integral experience. As has been indicated, we have inclined to interpret our author as holding to the autonomy of reason with the additional thesis that reason accords the greatest revelatory power to religious and mystical experience. However, we have not observed a step by step articulation of the processes and criteria

[265] IVL, 344f.

whereby this outcome is achieved; and there are statements indicating that the infallibility of mystical experience is tied up with its ineffability.

It is not easy to see what becomes of philosophy if one really does accept the statement, "Strictly speaking, logical knowledge is non-knowledge, valid only till intuition arises." [266] One realizes that acquaintance with an object is richer than the structures which may be abstracted therefrom for purposes of communication. (Correlatively, it is to be remarked that—to the extent that abstractions make possible—one can know many things conceptually which do not move into the realm of more intimate contact.) We can understand the value judgment that—with respect to positive goods —direct acquaintance and consumption are vastly better than "knowledge about." As James said, one real raisin is better for eating than the most elaborate printed menu. If "intuition" here be the name for some kind of valuable contact, it may be acknowledged that some little bit of "real" experience of it is more valuable than extensive symbolic references to it.

We find in ourselves the inclination to attempt to assimilate the religious and mystical to the experience of intrinsic value and in this sense to the generically practical. Much of the language of mystics could be construed as expressive of their devotion to "the pearl of great price." We can understand the sacrifice of all goods which one regards as artificial for the sake of an integral one of transcendent worth. We cannot similarly understand—if anyone proposes it —the literal sacrifice of some data or evidence for the sake of a

---

[266] *Ibid.*, 184. A familiar Advaita doctrine is that "non-cognition or non-apprehension" (we do not intend self-contradiction in the formulation) is the highest form of "cognition" or "apprehension;" this may be taken as saying that ordinary knowing partakes of a fundamental error or absence of truth. If this error is that all distinctions are supposed to be separations and especially that the knower is a self-existent reality knowing an independent self-existent object, the position is quite intelligible, although we may question whether all ordinary knowing falls into the error.

We ourselves incline, with the Vaiśeṣikas, to say that there is no objectless knowledge, though the subject may make itself an object to itself in a reflexive act of knowing; and we would hold that the differentiations involved in knowing need not contain assumptions of causal or of ontological independence. Epistemic independence does not entail metaphysical self-existence. The feeling of a unity with all things we can quite understand, and seems to us to be a most valuable experience and one which contains a profound truth. It is valuable not only for its derivative products of reducing tension and egocentricity, but for its realization of positive truth and a degree of universality of spirit. We do not think of it as annulling any distinctions that can be made; and, as long as the kind of unity asserted is not the same kind of identity as is denied in making any distinction, then there is no self-contradiction.

greater cognitive worth; one can only accept the reinterpretation of data in ways that seem legitimate.

One of the reasons, among others, why Gautama Buddha makes such a strong appeal among sophisticated Westerners is that, as Radhakrishnan says, he was very restrained in the cosmic implications which he drew from his "enlightenment;" yet, manifestly, his observations contained some of the most important psychological truths and his experience contained some of the "highest" moral values. It is to be admitted that most mystics are not as metaphysically restrained as Gautama, and that Radhakrishnan concurs with the majority in the acceptance of the inexpressible infinite ontological content of the consummatory experience.

We would be prepared to acknowledge certain uniquenesses of the Whole, of the Horizon of all horizons, the Context of all contexts. We cannot fill the concept with content—save by putting all known content into it and adding the "unknown" (with the supposition that the latter is vastly the greater part). But the Absolute, *qua* Whole, has meaning as a regulative idea, standing as a perpetual corrective of our partial formulations and as a lure beyond our ever present provincialities. In one sense, all experience is partial experience of it (though not known as It); in another sense we are having experience of It in stretching our minds to think of It as inclusive of all that is, of all possibility, of all dimensions of being as well as of actuality. In yet another sense we take up an aesthetico-practical disposition toward it in trying to "realize," to "feel," ourselves as nexūs within It; but we have not experienced this with any great vividness; probably others have. Perhaps others experience the Absolute in some other and radically deeper way of reflexive "realization," which we do not understand. We do not see how such experience invalidates the felt pluralities and distinctions of ordinary life; and to this we believe that Radhakrishnan consents, with some such added qualification as "on this level or grade of being."

We admire those souls who can rise to relatively universal points of view, and we admire some of the fruits of lives which claim the radically deeper experience of the Whole, although we cannot find it in ourselves to submit to their disciplines or fully to trust their interpretations of their own experiences. The hypothesis is always insinuating itself that these may be more the products of relatively local conditions, psychical and cultural, than of the total cosmic, or supra-cosmic, object.

If it is the case that there remains some "reign of religion" in the philosophy of radical mysticism, it is not the reign of dogmatic authoritarian religion. There are few things finer to instance than a religion so broad, so enlightened, so sympathetic as Radhakrishnan's. In him are the fruits of the spirit seen, "unshakable faith," "invincible optimism, ethical universalism, and religious toleration."

ROBERT W. BROWNING

DEPARTMENT OF PHILOSOPHY
NORTHWESTERN UNIVERSITY

4

Charles A. Moore

METAPHYSICS AND ETHICS IN RADHAKRISHNAN'S PHILOSOPHY

4

METAPHYSICS AND ETHICS IN
RADHAKRISHNAN'S PHILOSOPHY

I. INTRODUCTION

S OME years ago a book reviewer, writing about the first volume of Radhakrishnan's *Indian Philosophy*, said, "Professor
Radhakrishnan has both discovered a rock foundation and built
a house, and we think that his building will stand securely before
the blasts of criticism." [1] The house that Radhakrishnan has built
is a way of life—closely akin to the traditional Hindu orientation,
spiritualistic, and culminating in religion. The "rock foundation"
which he has built for this way of life is *absolute idealism*. The
problem of this paper, then, is the relationship between ethics
and metaphysics in the philosophy of Radhakrishnan.

Among the specific problems one must face in the process of
analyzing Radhakrishnan's handling of the problem of metaphysics
and ethics are: (1) the nature of the way of life which he advocates;
(2) the significance of ethics and of ethical values in general; (3)
the degree to which ethical conduct and ethical values are to be
transcended on the attainment of perfection or spiritual self-realization—and the implications of this transcendence for ethics; (4)
the basic tenets of his metaphysical system—insofar as they are pertinent to the specific problem of this study; (5) the special place,
meaning, and implications of the doctrine of *māyā* in this metaphysical system; and (6) the special significance of his metaphysics
and his interpretation of *māyā* for ethics and for the metaphysical
basis of ethics.

As we shall see in detail, Radhakrishnan holds that ethical conduct—in form and major content the ethics of Hinduism, properly
understood—is a profoundly significant aspect of human life, although it is to be transcended ultimately upon the attainment of
perfection; that ethics needs a metaphysical basis to provide ulti-

---

[1] Quoted by the publishers of HVL, in their announcement of Ind P, at the end
of the 1st ed. of HVL, 135.

mate support for ethical values and enthusiasm and meaning for the moral life; that ethics needs a metaphysical foundation in a reality that is basically characterized by value; and that such a sufficient metaphysical basis is provided, not by numerous Western substitutes—scientific, humanistic, and even religious—but by the absolute idealism of the classical Hindu tradition, modified and clarified in detail in the light of reason and modern knowledge and "the dialectic of history" [2] and interpreted properly so as to remove from it the exaggerated extremes which would nullify not only ethics but all significant living and the everyday world and all therein as sheer illusion.

The spirit of Radhakrishnan's philosophy consists fundamentally in the attitude of synthesis or the concept of *organic unity*.[3]

His basic approach to philosophy is the recognition of and demand for the organic unity of the universe and its many aspects, of the many sides of the nature of man, of man and the universe, of the finite and the infinite, the human and the divine. He finds such organic unity true by tradition, and also by an examination of man [4] and reality—and as the evidence even of the sciences.[5] Separatist doctrines and interpretations he rejects as false and incomplete or as exaggerated extremes.[6]

Once we realize that this is the spirit of Radhakrishnan's philosophy, we can easily comprehend and feel the force of his solution of our special problem of metaphysics and ethics, for the doctrine of organic unity or synthesis is the core of that solution. He is the Thomas Aquinas of the modern age with his remarkable ability and determination to see things in their comprehensive entirety and thus to eliminate the sharp distinctions which to the narrow and smaller mind serve as the basis for isolation and even contradiction of the several cultures and philosophical traditions. He applies this fundamental principle to all aspects of philosophy and religion—as well as to the specific problem under consideration—by virtue of his veritable genius for synthesis.

His philosophy, throughout, is one of taking the middle path between extremes, but it is not the middle path of mere eclecticism or mere moderation; it is that of keen logical analysis combined with high spiritual insight which enables him to transcend and combine contrasts in significant synthesis.

[2] RS, 118; see also HVL, 19 and Ind P II, 768.

[3] RS, 103; HVL, 31, 79, 124; IVL, 59, 72, 82, 89, 103, 114, 124, 153; ER, 82, 85, 108; BG, 13.

[4] ER, 82f, 108.   [5] IVL, 56.   [6] ER, 76.

His specific method in part consists of interpretation and clarification of concepts. He constantly rails against extremists and their interpretations and attitudes. He provides an interpretation of the perennial philosophy which does justice to both intuition and reason, philosophy and religion, and this world and the other world, in a truer exposition of that perennial philosophy than the exaggerated mysticism which is generally felt to be the basic philosophy of his native India. Thus he inevitably provides a synthesis of the old and the new and of the East and the West. He is truly the "spokesman for the East;" but his synthetic vision provides a comprehensive perspective capable of doing justice to the contrasting emphases of both East and West. In his interpretation, the East loses the extremes that the West has found objectionable; it is no longer inscrutable to the West. Nor are the values of the West ignored—but the West's materialism, humanism, and individualism are, in his synthesis, relegated to secondary importance, as, indeed, they are in all absolute idealism.

Radhakrishnan is obviously "the heir to a great tradition" [7] and "true to type" [8] in following in the footsteps of his predecessors. As a matter of fact, it is often extremely difficult to penetrate beneath his typical Indian modesty so as to discover his particular deviations from the orthodox Hindu tradition. One of the difficulties lies in the fact that, as Joad says, ". . . the reader is sometimes not as clear as he would like to be whether Radhakrishnan is speaking his own mind or revealing the mind of others, or whether, when he is quite palpably doing the latter, his tacit agreement with what he is telling us is to be assumed" [9]—although it is not really too difficult to discern when he is quoting with approval and when in opposition. Radhakrishnan is no parrot of the ancient wisdom of India, but he does seem to find there the essence of all spiritual wisdom, and, as I understand him, he makes it his task to reinterpret that great wisdom in modern terms and with a modern world perspective, showing its truth and applicability even for today.

As said above, he is a synthesizer of the old and the new and of the East and the West. He has justly been called a "philosophical bilinguist," [10] a "bridge-builder," [11] and a "liaison officer" [12] between East and West. He has the courage both to champion the "new Hinduism," [13] despite apparent conflicts with orthodox in-

---

[7] C. E. M. Joad, *Counter Attack from the East* (hereafter: Joad) 37.
[8] D. S. Sarma, *Studies in the Renaissance of Hinduism* (hereafter: Sarma), 586.
[9] Joad, 161.   [10] *Ibid.*, 53.   [11] *Ibid.*, 38.
[12] *Ibid.*, 53.   [13] *Ibid.*, 58, 170f.

terpretations of ancient Indian wisdom, and also to appreciate and to accept the wisdom of other traditions where it is pertinent and valid. In fact, one of his most effective methods of bringing East and West closer to each other is that of finding in Western writers as well as Eastern almost identical expressions of the fundamental wisdom of his own race. (He also finds that "The extravagances with which we are familiar in the East are not unknown in the West."[14]) Radhakrishnan explicitly challenges the deadening traditionalism of many thinkers in India and welcomes concepts from the West, although one does not feel that he thinks the wisdom of the West—even at its best—more than repeats the wisdom of India.[15] He does say, however, "Those who are untouched by the Western influence are for a large part intellectual and moral aristocrats, . . . They think that they have little to learn or to unlearn, and that they do their duty with their gaze fixed on the external dharma of the past."[16] "There is nothing wrong in absorbing the culture of other peoples; . . ."[17]

Radhakrishnan admits that some of his interpretations provoke opposition on the part of traditionalists, but he feels that his interpretation in the light of present-day conditions and thought[18] are thoroughly justified and that mere traditionalism can no longer satisfy the mind. As he says, "As knowledge grows, our theology develops. Only those parts of the tradition which are logically coherent are to be accepted as superior to the evidence of the senses, and not the whole tradition."[19]

Radhakrishnan's advocacy of change within the framework of the basic tradition of Hindu wisdom is a very constant theme in his writings. In most instances he accepts the basic principles of the great tradition of Hindu thought, but demands either by reinterpretation or by distinct revision important modification in the implications and applications of those fundamental ideas. "The Hindu view makes room for essential changes. There must be no violent break with social heredity, and yet the new stresses, conflicts and confusions will have to be faced and overcome. While the truths of spirit are permanent, the rules change from age to age."[20] "Though dharma is absolute, it has no absolute and timeless content. The only thing eternal about morality is man's desire for the better."[21] "The dialectic of religious advance through tradition,

[14] ER, 72. [15] Ind P, II, 773.
[16] Ibid., 775f; see also HVL, 130; RS, 138.
[17] Ind P, II, 780. [18] Ibid., 768; see also RS, 119. [19] HVL, 19.
[20] RS, 113.
[21] Ibid., 114; see also ibid., 113, 117, 118; Sarma, 627; Ind P, II, 768.

logic and life helps the conservation of Hinduism by providing scope for change." [22]

II. The Nature and Content of Ethics [23]

The ethical doctrine and the principles of ethical practice which Radhakrishnan upholds are essentially in conformity with the tradition of Hinduism—except for the several changes in detail which he recommends; but even these are not contrary to Hindu tradition for they are entailed in the essential spirit of Hinduism, which is one of growth and development within the framework of the essential spiritual outlook on life. In other words, the Hindu view of life, which Radhakrishnan describes so clearly in many of his writings, is also the essence of Radhakrishnan's view of life.

While changes in detail of moral practice are a part of Radhakrishnan's moral code, nevertheless he advocates strict obedience to the discipline,[24] which is necessary to spiritual development, and advocates the "noble and austere" [25] ethics of mysticism—consisting in large part at least of suffering and renunciation. That *dharma* is variable and progressive Radhakrishnan points out frequently and emphatically.[26] But he also insists that the principles of *dharma* are eternal.

There must be no violent break with social heredity, and yet the new stresses, conflicts and confusions will have to be faced and overcome. While the truths of spirit are permanent, the rules change from age to age . . . we cannot identify dharma with any specific set of institutions. It endures because it has its roots in human nature, . . . Though dharma is absolute, it has no absolute and timeless content. . . . The principles of dharma, the scales of value, are to be maintained in and through the stress of the new experiences.[27]

Dharma, the essence of morality, is essentially a combination of ethics and religion. The goal is the "double object" of happiness on earth and salvation.[28] On its religious side the goal is the religious one of spiritual self-realization and the attainment of some degree or form of identity with God or the Absolute. *Mokṣa* is "the aim of all human life." [29] "It [*dharma*] is the transformation of the individual into the universal outlook, the linking of our

22 HVL, 21.

23 See esp. IVL, chs. V, VII; ER, chs. II, III, IX; HVL, chs. III, IV; RS, ch. III; and HH, ch. II.

24 See HH, 14; HVL, 77.   25 ER, 295.   26 RS, 108, 113, 114, 118f; HVL, 129.

27 RS, 113-15.   28 See HH, 22f.   29 *Ibid.*, 23.

daily life with the eternal purpose that makes us truly human." [30] The purpose of the ethical life is the "discipline of human nature leading to a realisation of the spiritual." [31] There is no question that in Radhakrishnan's view of life, as in the Hindu, "The *saṁnyāsin* represents the highest type of Indian manhood." [32]

The principle of dharma rouses us to a recognition of spiritual realities not by abstention from the world, but by bringing to its life, its business (artha) and its pleasures (kāma), the controlling power of spiritual faith. Life is one, and in it there is no distinction of sacred and secular. . . . Dharma, artha and kāma go together. The ordinary avocations of daily life are in a real sense service of the Supreme. The common tasks are as effective as monastic devotion.[33]

Dharma is an extremely complex concept, including both religious aspiration and ethical and social practice. "The complex of institutions and influences which shape the moral feeling and character of the people is called the *dharma*, which is a fundamental feature of the Hindu religion." [34] "The basic principle of dharma is the realisation of the dignity of the human spirit, . . ." nevertheless, ". . . we may define dharma as the whole duty of man in relation to the fourfold purposes of life (dharma, artha, kāma and mokṣa) by members of the four groups (cāturvarṇa) [Brahmins, Kṣatriyas, Vaiśyas, and Śūdras] and the four stages (caturāśrama) [student, householder, forest-dweller, and ascetic or monk]." [35] If we add to these basic principles the concept of moral obligation, both to aspire to divinity and also to conform to the discipline of society,[36] the concept of freedom, which is indispensable to moral obligation, the law of *karma*,[37] the indispensable fact of rebirth, and the details of personal and social *dharma*, we have a clear-cut picture of Radhakrishnan's way of life.

The detailed practical code of morality is unambiguous. "The virtues incumbent on all are non-hatred to all beings in thought, word and deed, good will and charity." [38] Or, stated differently, "goodwill, pure love, and disinterestedness . . ." [39] Ideal conduct is that which "requires us to refrain from anger and covetousness, to be pure and loving in thought, word and deed, . . ." [40]

---

30 K, 43, cited in Joad, 244.   31 Ind P, I, 41, cited in Joad, 149.
32 HH, 43; see also ER, 381.   33 RS, 105f; see also *ibid.*, 108.   34 HH, 14.
35 RS, 107; see also: on the groups or castes, HVL, ch. IV, ER, 255ff; on the values of life (puruṣārthas), HVL, 80-2, ER, 352ff; on the stages of life (āśramas), HVL, 82ff.
36 See RS, 112, 131; Ind P, I, 52, 571; HH, 15, 28f, 39; HVL, 77f; ER, 37.
37 See HVL, 72ff; IVL, 274ff.   38 RS, 108.   39 ER, 83.
40 HH, 26.

"The highest virtue consists in doing to others as we would be done by." [41] "The saints love because they cannot help it. It would be strange not to love." [42] "Love is non-resistance. Conflicts are to be overcome not by force but by love." [43] (Radhakrishnan finds a justification for universal love in the Upaniṣadic doctrine *"Tat tvam asi,"* as does Deussen, who does not find such a basis in the Bible.[44]) Non-violence, of course, is emphasized throughout as the major comprehensive practical virtue.[45] Universal love, forgiveness, and non-violence, as well as renunciation and suffering are never to be considered negative, however. As Radhakrishnan says concisely, "Detachment of spirit and not renunciation of the world is what is demanded from us." [46]

Since the essence of the good life is detachment, the control of our worldly desires, and the directing of our entire life toward its spiritual destiny, the opposite attitudes constitute the major vices of the moral life. Radhakrishnan accepts Patañjali's statement of the major vices: ignorance, egoism, attachment, hatred, and self-love. "These five are different expressions of the fundamental ignorance. Only when a man rises to dispassion and acts without selfish attachment is he really free." [47]

Throughout the ethics of Radhakrishnan, as throughout the ethics of Hinduism, the supreme virtue consists in truth and life in accordance with the truth. Just as we have seen that all vices are aspects of ignorance, ignorance of the true nature of man and the universe, so the truth provides the only proper basis of the right way of life. In fact, "Truth is not so much the result of theological faith as the experience of a deeper moral life." [48]

In order to know the truth we must cease to identify ourselves with the separate ego shut up in the walls of body, life, and mind. We must renounce the narrow horizon, the selfish interest, the unreal objective. This is an ethical process. Truth can never be perceived except by those who are in love with goodness.[49]

III. The Significance of Ethics, Its Rules and Values

As we shall see in later sections of this study, the significance of ethics would seem—*to critics*—to be rather seriously undermined by three major theses of Radhakrishnan's theory: (1) the view that the real goal of human life is the attainment of per-

41 *Ibid.*, 39.   42 IVL, 117.   43 *Ibid.*, 118.
44 ER, 101f.   45 See RS, 108; HH, 35.   46 ER, 101.
47 *Ibid.*, 95.   48 HH, 25.   49 ER, 95.

fection or spiritual self-realization, which completely transcends the ethical level. (2) The view, most often expressed in the form of a criticism of Hinduism by such people as Schweitzer,[50] that, as Radhakrishnan paraphrases the criticism, "On the view of the metaphysical identity of the individual and the Absolute, *it is said*, there is no warrant for ethics. If Brahman is all, there is no need for any moral endeavour." [51] (3) The doctrine of *māyā*, which, in some interpretations, would seem to indicate that ethical action is at most only relatively important and possibly completely insignificant, since the world in which ethical actions occur is illusory. In view of these doctrines, which are interpretable as nullifying the significance of ethics, it is indispensable that we determine at the very beginning the importance and status of ethical action and its place—along with moral rules, moral values, and moral obligation in general—in Radhakrishnan's system.

Since Radhakrishnan's views are expressed both in those writings which are exclusively statements of his own point of view and also in his exposition of the views of Hinduism and of Śaṁkara, it may be wise here to call upon both sources for the clarification of his answer to this charge that ethics is insignificant. His reply takes many forms, but all of them express the view that, although ethics is eventually transcended upon the attainment of perfection and although the world in which ethical action takes place is only relatively real, nevertheless ethical action and moral obligation are vital and indispensable. His answers range from the view that life in "the historical process" and in the empirical world has *some* significance for the life of the spirit to the repeatedly expressed idea that the ethical life is the *indispensable* condition or "the essential pre-requisite" for the attainment of perfection and, in fact, for the transcendence of the entire ethical process itself.

The *general* significance of ethics as at least *one* of the ways to or stages of spiritual development and realization is expressed in the following statements: "The search of the mind for beauty, goodness and truth is the search for God." [52] "The historical process [including the ethical] is not a mere external chain of events, but offers a succession of spiritual opportunities." [53] "The Hindu thinkers combat the tendency to exalt religious devotion

---

[50] See Albert Schweitzer, *Indian Thought and its Development* (1936); and ER, 76ff.

[51] Ind P, II, 621 (*italics* mine).

[52] RS, 47; see also Sarma, 602 and IVL, 273.   [53] ER, 89.

over love of truth and practice of goodness. They know full well that emotions are not isolated functions." [54] "To reach the highest state it is not always necessary to adhere literally to the rules of *dharma.* . . . The rules of *dharmas,* however, represent the normal growth of spirit." [55] "The *dharma* helps the smouldering fire which is in every individual to burst into flame." [56]

Many times Radhakrishnan insists on the *necessity* of morality as a prerequisite to spiritual perfection: "*Jñāna,* or seeing through the veil of *māyā,* is the spiritual destiny of man. It is something more than ethical goodness, though it cannot be achieved without it." [57] "In order to know the truth we must cease to identify ourselves with the separate ego. . . . We must renounce the narrow horizon, the selfish interest, the unreal objective. This is an ethical process." [58] "While the pursuit of wealth and happiness is a legitimate human aspiration, they should be gained in ways of righteousness (dharma), if they are to lead ultimately to the spiritual freedom of man (mokṣa). Each one of these ends requires ethical discipline." [59] "The endeavour of religion is to get rid of the gulf between man and God and restore the lost sense of unity. . . . A strict ethical discipline is insisted on." [60] "The purpose of human life is to cross the line, to emerge from insufficiency and ignorance to fullness and wisdom . . . and the means to it is dharma." [61]

I think there is no clearer exposition of Radhakrishnan's view than in his defense of Śaṁkara's theory against criticism. In this explanation he says (as already quoted in part):

On the view of the metaphysical identity of the individual and the Absolute, it is said, there is no warrant for ethics. If Brahman is all, there is no need for any moral endeavour. This objection rests upon a confusion between reality and existence, the eternal and the temporal. . . . The metaphysical truth of the oneness of Brahman does not in any way prejudice the validity of the ethical distinctions on the empirical level.[62]

Further:

While it is true that the freed soul 'has no longer any object to aim at, since he has achieved all,' still he works for the welfare of the world. Besides, while Śaṁkara holds that moral *obligation* has no meaning

54 HH, 12.   55 *Ibid.,* 44.   56 *Ibid.,* 14.
57 ER, 94.   58 *Ibid.,* 95.   59 HVL, 80.
60 IVL, 111.   61 RS, 104; see also IVL, 126.
62 Ind P, II, 621; see also treatment of *māyā* in section vi below.

for the freed soul, he does not say that the moral virtues are abandoned by him. Moral perfection leads to the death, not of morality, but of moralistic individualism. Rules of conduct have their force so long as we are struggling upward, working out the beast in us. . . . As rules of murder, theft and the like do not worry the civilised man, so the spiritual man is not concerned with the conventional rules of morality.[63]

It is in this sense that ethics—in spite of all the absolutism of the idealism of Śaṁkara and Radhakrishnan—is indispensable and truly significant, though ultimately transcended.

In Radhakrishnan's view, one who has gained perfection is no longer *bound* by moral discipline and rules, but, nevertheless, is still vitally interested in the welfare of the world. As he says, ". . . the normal mystic has a burning passion for social righteousness." [64] Also, "We cannot lose ourselves in inner piety when the poor die at our doors, naked and hungry. The *Gītā* asks us [and Radhakrishnan's theory would agree] to live in the world and save it." [65]

IV. The Transcendence of Ethics in the Religious Experience

Whereas, as we have just seen, Radhakrishnan strongly defends the significance of ethics and its indispensability as the means to salvation, he is equally insistent that ethical rules and ethical values are not ultimate and must be transcended. However, the transcendence of ethics—as we have just seen briefly—does not mean the nullification of the significance of ethics, but rather its intrinsic embodiment in the self of the liberated or freed soul. Thus, here as elsewhere, a doctrine which seems open to devastating criticism from the Western point of view is found, upon clearer interpretation, not to be destructive but rather compelling in its acceptability and necessity.

Radhakrishnan feels very strongly that *mokṣa*, liberation, perfection, or spiritual self-realization, cannot be achieved by ethical action, for *mokṣa* is essentially of a different and higher order— "a new dimension altogether"—of reality and experience. He also accepts the typical Hindu doctrine that the liberated self or freed soul is beyond the distinctions of good and evil. However, in a typical illustration of his synthetic clarity, he finds in this doctrine no nullification of the significance of ethics—for reasons which

63 *Ibid.*, 620f.   64 ER, 109.   65 BG, 67.

have already been cited. In both of these aspects of the doctrine of transcendence, namely, that in which perfection belongs to another dimension than the ethical and that in which the perfected man transcends the distinctions and rules of moral conduct, it is most essential that we understand Radhakrishnan's method of synthesizing the transcendent or religious and the finite or the ethical; that method is fundamentally the method of full explanation of the doctrine so that one-sided interpretations can be avoided—for the doctrine is not one-sided.

It would be a distortion of Radhakrishnan's basic point to emphasize his middle-path perspective in this instance so excessively as to minimize his belief in the doctrine of transcendence. His doctrine of transcendence is unmistakable: "The spiritual cannot be achieved by the ethical." [66] Jñāna, or seeing through the veil of māyā, is the spiritual destiny of man. It is something more than ethical goodness, . . . The difference is that between perfection and progress, between eternal life and temporal development, . . ." [67] "To seek for liberation from the wheel of births and deaths, is nothing more than to rise to the spiritual level from the merely ethical. The spiritual is not the extension of the ethical. It is a new dimension altogether, dealing with things eternal." [68] "To realise the ideal, we must pass beyond the moral life and rise to the spiritual realisation in which the life of finite struggle and endeavour is transcended. . . . Karma cannot lead to mokṣa." [69]

"Where everything is being and nothing becomes, where everything is finally made and nothing is in the making, activity is inconceivable. When movement reaches its fulfilment, life is not a going concern." [70] "Activity is a characteristic of the historical process, and perfection is not historical. It lacks nothing and it cannot have any activity in it." [71] "Ethics presupposes the separatist view of life. When we transcend it, we get beyond ethical laws." [72] "The moralistic individualism is based on an imperfect outlook which is the root of our finiteness." [73] Radhakrishnan is fond of quoting the Upaniṣadic statement, "As the birds float in the air, as the fish swim in the sea, leaving no traces behind, even so are the paths to God traversed by the seekers of spirit." [74]

Often this theory of transcendence lies in Radhakrishnan's emphasis upon religion—such that ethics has truly been called the

[66] ER, 302.   [67] Ibid., 94; see also Ind P, II, 627.   [68] IVL, 304.
[69] Ind P, II, 626.   [70] IVL, 308.   [71] HVL, 64.
[72] ER, 103f.   [73] IVL, 305.   [74] HH, 7; see also HVL, 81.

handmaid of religion. Radhakrishnan says, for example, "Religion is not mere consciousness of value. There is in it a mystical element, an apprehension of the real and an enjoyment of it for its own sake which is absent in the moral consciousness." [75]

Religious consciousness is not reducible to either intellectual or ethical or aesthetic activity or a sum of these. If it is an autonomous form of spiritual life which, while including these elements, yet transcends them, the object of religion is not either the true or the good or the beautiful or a mere unity of them but God the universal consciousness who includes these values and yet transcends them. [76]

. . . the spiritual plane is higher than the moral plane. . . . As life emerged from matter, as mind emerged from life, and as a sense of values emerged from mind, so does God-consciousness emerge out of a sense of values. . . . It [salvation] is a rising from ethical individualism to spiritual universalism. It is an emerging from indefinite progress in time to final attainment in eternity. [77]

Passages abound in which Radhakrishnan expresses the view that the liberated man is above the distinctions of good and evil and the laws of *dharma*. For example, he quotes the *Gītā:* "The guided soul leaves behind on earth both good and evil." [78] "Hinduism has given us in the form of the *saṁnyāsin* its picture of the ideal man. . . . He is not subject to rules, for he has realized in himself the life which is the source of all rules and which is not itself subject to rules." [79] This doctrine is best expressed, I think, in the following full explanation—quoted at length because the attitude is so important:

. . . the action of the seer is of a different kind. It is creative living where external authority gives place to inward freedom. Only in this sense do the Upaniṣads declare: 'The immortal man overcomes both the thoughts "I did evil" and "I did good." Good and evil, done or not done, cause him no pain.' . . . The liberated individual is lifted beyond the ethical distinctions of good and evil. When the Upaniṣad says that 'sin does not cling to a wise man any more than water clings to a lotus leaf' it does not mean that the sage may sin and yet be free, but rather that any one who is free from worldly attachments is also free from all temptation to sin. . . . When the individual spirit realizes his divine nature and acts from it, he transcends the distinctions of good and evil. Not that he can do evil and yet be free from sin, but that it is impossible for him to do wrong. . . . Good and evil presupposes the basis of egoism. . . . While ethical life can give rise

75 IVL, 88; see also ER, 83.   76 IVL, 199; see also ER, 75.   77 Sarma, 607.
78 *Gītā* II, 50, quoted in RS, 73.   79 ER, 381; see also Ind P, II, 620f.

to a better existence, it by itself cannot effect release, which requires the shifting of the very basis of all life and activity.[80]

In another significant statement Radhakrishnan says,

These distinctions [of good and evil] belong not to reality as such but to the human world which is a part of this cosmic process, which is itself a phase in which being is alienated from itself. Not that the distinctions of good and evil are arbitrary or conventional; they are certainly reasonable and natural, and they express absolute truths of the moral order, but they are fundamentally the categories of this world. They are symbolic, not images or shadows. The symbolism is not artificial, accidental, or false. It tells us about the ultimate reality, but darkly, . . .[81]

"Perfection belongs to another dimension than the ethical, though it may express itself on the ethical plane."[82]

In an important sense, Radhakrishnan finds the doctrine of transcendence to be not a basis for the nullification of ethics but, instead, the indispensable ground of any significant ethics. "A meaningful ethical ideal must be transcendent to the immediate flow of events."[83] "As creator and saviour, God is transcendent to the true process, even as realisation is transcendent to progress. This internal transcendence of God to the true process gives meaning to the distinctions of value, and makes struggle and effort real."[84]

. . . to dwell in the realm of spirit does not mean that we should be indifferent to the realities of the world. It is a common temptation, to which Indian thinkers have fallen more than once victims, that spirit is all that counts while life is an indifferent illusion, and all efforts directed to the improvement of man's outer life and society are sheer folly. . . . To practise virtue in a vacuum is impossible. Spiritual vision normally issues in a new power for good in the world of existence.[85]

In the several aspects of this particular problem of transcendence we find almost a perfect and very distinct illustration and application—and parallel—of Radhakrishnan's metaphysics, in which the Absolute similarly transcends the finite, but in which even the doctrine of *māyā* does not nullify or relegate the empirical world to the level of illusion or insignificance, accepting it for the limited, relative, and instrumental reality which it is. Herein lies one aspect or form of his basic doctrine on the rela-

80 ER, 102f.   81 *Ibid.*, 104; see also IVL, 305.   82 IVL, 310.
83 ER, 81.   84 IVL, 345.   85 EWR, 137.

tion of metaphysics and ethics—probably the essence of his final view.

V. The Relationship Between Metaphysics and Ethics

There is no question whatsoever that for Radhakrishnan the ethical life must be rooted in ultimate reality if it is to have any significance and be more than an illusion, a product of imagination, a mere convention, or an artificial way of life void of all justification and all obligation. It is only reality itself which can provide a ground for ethics and its obligations and for its seriousness and the enthusiasm of the moral agent in seeking to do the right. It will be noted in the following two sections that Radhakrishnan argues both ways, as it were: with Kant, from ethics to metaphysics, and from the nature of reality and man to the significance of ethics. In this instance, as in all others, Radhakrishnan's interpretation is synthetic and comprehensive.

With Radhakrishnan, as with all great Indian philosophical thinkers, the fundamental problem is that of salvation, and the philosophical systems which the great thinkers construct are to provide knowledge of the truth about reality, because it is only in terms of knowledge of this truth that man can live correctly and attain his ultimate goal and destiny. Man must live in accordance with the nature of reality and himself, both as a moral obligation and as a means to salvation and infinite bliss—such is the essential doctrine of Radhakrishnan and all Hinduism. The spirit of orthodox Indian philosophy is expressed in the passage quoted by Radhakrishnan, "Out of unreality lead me to reality; out of darkness lead me to light; out of death lead me to life eternal." [86] Every Indian, including Radhakrishnan, would say, "The root cause of desire [the essence of immorality] is avidyā or ignorance of the nature of things." [87]

Not only does Radhakrishnan insist in all of his writings upon this indispensable relationship of metaphysics and ethics, but he expresses the idea in so many ways and so variously that I consider it advisable to depend almost exclusively upon his own words rather than attempt to paraphrase his fundamental thesis. The following quotations constitute clear but *varied* statements of Radhakrishnan's doctrine of the indispensable relationship between metaphysics and ethics, between the true and ultimate

[86] RS, 109.　　　　　　　　[87] BG, 52.

nature of reality and man, on the one hand, and ethical ideals and practices, on the other.

"Any ethical theory must be grounded in metaphysics, in a philosophical conception of the relation between human conduct and ultimate reality. As we think ultimate reality to be, so we behave. Vision and action go together." [88]

The question is inevitable whether the ethical ideal is a mere dream or has the backing of the universe. Is man ploughing his lonely furrow in the dark or is there a transcending purpose that is co-operating with him in his quest for ideals, securing him against the ultimate defeat of his plans? Are the values mere empirical accidents, creations at best of the human mind, or do they reveal to us an order of being which is more than merely human, a spiritual reality which is the source of the significance of what happens in the temporal process? [89]

"If the authority of the moral law is to be justified, if the ultimateness of man as a moral being is to be vindicated, then the world process which has resulted in the formation of human personalities has significance and the structure of things is spiritual." [90]

We cannot live if we do not recover our faith in life and the universe. . . . We cannot strive for . . . ideals if we are convinced that we are unimportant accidents in a universe which is indifferent, if not hostile, to them. If the nature of the world is malign, our duty is to defy.[91]

"We cannot worship what we know to be a mental fiction. . . . If we are to stick to our ideals in face of all obstacles, we need to feel certain that they are not private fancies of our own, but are somehow rooted in the universal nature of things." [92]

Moral enthusiasm is possible only if our motive includes the expectation of being able to contribute to the achievement of moral ideals. . . . We cannot help asking ourselves whether our ideals are mere private dreams of our own or bonds created by society, or even aspirations characteristic of the human species. Only a philosophy which affirms that they are rooted in the universal nature of things can give depth and fervour to moral life, . . . If ethical thought is profound, it will give a cosmic motive to morality. Moral consciousness must include a conviction of the reality of ideals.[93]

"Beliefs that foster and promote the spiritual life of the soul must be in accordance with the nature and the laws of the world of

88 ER, 80.   89 IVL, 69.   90 Ibid., 71.
91 Ibid., 55.   92 RWN, 6.   93 ER, 81f.

reality with which it is their aim to bring us into harmony." [94] "It may be argued that, although the universe may have no purpose, items in the universe such as nations and individuals may have their purposes. . . . This cannot be regarded as a satisfactory goal of ethics. . . . We long for a good which is never left behind and never superseded." [95]

"Every form of life, every group of men has its dharma, which is the law of its being." [96] " '. . . the great formula That art Thou . . . gives in three words the combined sum of metaphysics and morals.' " [97] "To know oneself and not to be untrue to it is the essence of the good life." [98] "To refuse to live up to the light within us is real sin; . . ." [99] "*Mokṣa* or spiritual freedom is the aim of all human life. . . . It assumes that the fundamental reality is the soul of man." [100] "The aim of life is the gradual revelation in our human existence of the eternal in us." [101] "Negatively, release is freedom from hampering egoism; positively, it is realization of one's spiritual destiny. The abandonment of the ego is the identification with a fuller life and consciousness. The soul is raised to a sense of its universality." [102]

"The principles which we have to observe in our daily life and social relations are constituted by what is called dharma. It is truth's embodiment in life, . . ." [103] "The rules of dharma are the mortal flesh of immortal ideas, . . ." [104] "The cosmic supplies the conditions by which personalities can be perfected." [105]

In other words—as all these passages say in *varying* ways: "*Dharma or virtue is conformity with the truth of things; . . . Moral evil is disharmony with the truth which encompasses and controls the world.*" [106]

Radhakrishnan often expresses these ideas more precisely in terms of religion—his word (along with mysticism) for absolute idealism and action in accordance therewith. "Our moral life tells us that God is not only the goal but the spring and sustainer of moral effort." [107] "There are certain vital values of religion which are met by the character of God as wisdom, love and goodness. Values acquire a cosmic importance and ethical life becomes meaningful." [108] "Simply because there is the security that God's love will succeed, the struggle does not become unreal." [109] "If

94 HVL, 17. 95 ER, 81. 96 HVL, 78; see also Ind P, I, 571.
97 ER, 101f. 98 IVL, 118. 99 EWR, 90.
100 HH, 23; see also ER, 83. 101 HH, 6. 102 ER, 97.
103 RS, 104. 104 *Ibid.*, 108. 105 RWN, 22.
106 HVL, 78 (*italics* mine). 107 IVL, 333. 108 *Ibid.*, 342; see also ER, 83.
109 IVL, 337.

the indwelling of God in man is the highest truth, conduct which translates it into practice is ideal conduct. The several virtues are forms of the truth, ..." [110] It is in accordance with religion that man seeks to realize the "ideal possibility," for religion calls for the "divinising of the life of man" [111]—because man is essentially divine.

The entire thesis of a metaphysical foundation of ethics may seem to be contradicted by Radhakrishnan's adoption of an attitude which is typical of Hinduism but which, at first impression at least, seems to nullify the correspondence between metaphysics and ethics in any significant sense. This is the doctrine that wide tolerance in the matter of belief is permitted in metaphysics, whereas a strict code of ethical practice is demanded. It seems to matter little what one believes about reality, but one must conform rigidly to the accepted code of moral practice. This seems to conflict with the theory of the metaphysical basis of ethics in any sense in which the metaphysics—the truth about reality and man—provides a basis for specific virtues and specific actions. Let us first see this point in Radhakrishnan's own words and then seek an explanation of the apparent difficulty. "For the Hindu every religion is true, if only its adherents sincerely and honestly follow it." [112]

Hinduism is more a way of life than a form of thought. While it gives absolute liberty in the world of thought it enjoins a strict code of practice. The theist and the atheist, the sceptic and the agnostic may all be Hindus if they accept the Hindu system of culture and life. . . . In a very real sense practice precedes theory.[113]

There is actually no conflict in this view, first because it is not so liberal as it appears, and secondly, because of the specific nature of the metaphysics and religion of Hinduism. For example, as Radhakrishnan says, "Hinduism insists not on religious conformity but on a spiritual and ethical outlook in life." [114] The point here is that the details of religious belief are liberally interpreted, but a Hindu is expected to have "a religious and ethical outlook in life," although I personally do not understand how this can include the sceptic and the atheist along with the theist as good Hindus. The main point, as I see it, is that the Hindu view

110 HH, 25; see also EWR, 122.   111 IVL, 123.   112 RS, 53.
113 HVL, 77; see also HH, 3; and RS, 53.
114 *Ibid.*, 77; see also HH, 21, 25. ("This does not mean that the Hindu thinkers have no right ideas of God and consider all beliefs to be equally true." HVL, 49.)

of the ultimate is such that all roads to it are acceptable since all aspects of life are aspects of reality, and therefore differences do not entail conflict or contradiction. There is also the fact that Hinduism is not a static religion or ethics but one which calls for growth and change—*provided* such change takes place within the framework and perspective of "a spiritual and ethical outlook." If these interpretations are not correct, I personally would find great difficulty in accepting Radhakrishnan's view of a metaphysical basis of ethics, because I do not understand how a metaphysics (for example, the materialism of unorthodox Cārvāka) which is significantly different from the one he presents—absolute idealism—could possibly serve as a basis for the ethical practices and ideals which his religion entails. Thus, we are forced necessarily to the next and final consideration of this study, namely, the exact nature of the metaphysical system which Radhakrishnan holds and which is supposed to provide a cosmic basis for Hinduism as a way of life. This, unless I misunderstand Radhakrishnan, is *the* metaphysics which alone can provide a sure foundation for the idealistic and spiritual ethics of Radhakrishnan and Hinduism.

VI. Radhakrishnan's Metaphysics

There is neither space nor need for an elaborate exposition of Radhakrishnan's metaphysical views here. These are being discussed in detail in other essays in this volume. It is sufficient merely to point to basic principles and to indicate how these basic principles provide the foundation for the religio-ethical life which Radhakrishnan and Hinduism consider the good life for man.

For present purposes Radhakrishnan's metaphysical doctrine may be expressed in terms of the following principles: (1) The real is spiritual—although in its ultimate character it transcends all characterization, possibly even that of "spiritual." (2) The ultimate has two aspects, *nirguṇa*, the ultimately impersonal indescribable Absolute, and *saguṇa*, the qualitatively describable and at times personal aspect.[115] (3) Reality is ultimately one—plurality is only appearance. (4) The "why" and "how" of the existence of the empirical world and individuals are a mystery, expressed in terms of the doctrine of *māyā*—a doctrine which does not entail the illusory character of the world, although it does

[115] These two are not really aspects of the Absolute, but two points of view from which man may conceive of the Absolute.

entail the non-ultimate and dependent status of the empirical. (5) The essential nature of man is spiritual, divine, but he is also human. (6) Reality is in some way characterized by value—and one gets the impression that even the indescribable Absolute or Brahman, though free of all other characteristics, and though said to be above even the category of good or value, represents (is) perfection as well as reality. (7) Although we do not know the exact "how" of the creation of the universe, we can recognize an intelligible evolutionary process by which the ultimate spiritual reality is ever more progressively expressed in advancing forms [116]—such that, in point of fact, the world we know is essentially the world of such evolution, for, as he says, ". . . the beginning and the end are merely ideal. . . ." [117] Or, as Joad expresses Radhakrishnan's view, ". . . the ultimate reality not only of man but of the universe is spirit, which as it manifests itself in and in relation to human beings is a free, a changing, a developing spirit." [118]

The Real Is Spiritual. "The ultimate principle of reality is not matter, solid, stubborn, unconscious. It is the very essence of spirit, self-active motion." [119] "Besides consciousness in the animal world (perception and action), and self-consciousness in the human (intelligence and will), we have spiritual consciousness or superconsciousness, a level of experience at which new aspects of reality reveal themselves." [120] "As we are to interpret the unknown by the known, the supreme principle is regarded as the self, not limited and particular, but infinite and universal. The supreme is the self of the universe." [121]

Radhakrishnan renounces and rejects numerous points of view which fall short of absolute idealism, most of these views, in his interpretation, being typical of the West. Most prominent among these are humanism, scientific materialism, naturalism, and mystic nationalism, as well as many specific views of individual thinkers and much of Western psychology.[122] All of these views are described as inadequate and, like materialism, "one-sided and misleading," all alike failing to do justice to the spiritual nature of reality and man.[123]

The Real Is Transcendent, Ineffable. "God is the unknown, the absolutely different, the Beyond who cannot be comprehended

---

116 See RS, 103.   117 RR, 116, cited in Sarma, 602.
118 *Ibid.,* 103; see also EWR, 138: "The world is not a snare nor its good a delusion."
119 RS, 29.   120 IVL, 301.   121 RWN, 17.
122 See ER, 75, 80-83; IVL, 24-27, 62-73, 226ff, 258-261, 269; RWN, 9.
123 RS, 40.

by our concepts or recognized by our understanding. . . . He can only be described negatively or through seemingly contradictory descriptions. . . . God is the totally other, . . ." [124] The Absolute is

the pure, alone and unmanifest, nothing and all things, that which transcends any definite form of expression and yet is the basis of all expression, the one in whom all is found and yet all is lost. . . . While God is organically bound up with the universe, the Absolute is not.[125]

The inability to describe the absolute in terms of any categories, however, does not mean the real is negative. As Radhakrishnan says, "The negative account is intended to express the soul's sense of the transcendence of God, the 'wholly other,' of whom naught may be predicated save in negations, and not to deprive God of his positive being. It is the inexhaustible positivity of God that bursts through all conceptual forms." [126]

Two Aspects of the Real. Here I think Radhakrishnan follows the wisdom of the Upaniṣads, which he describes when he says,

The Upaniṣads did not draw any hard and fast line of distinction between the simple one of intuition supported by Śaṁkara and the concrete whole of Rāmānuja. If we separate the two, it will become impossible for us to admit any distinction or value in the world of concrete existence. The Upaniṣads imply that the Īśvara is practically one with Brahman.[127]

"God, who is the creator, sustainer and judge of this world, is not totally unrelated to the Absolute. God is the Absolute from the human end." [128] "The impersonality of the Absolute is not its whole significance. The Upaniṣads support Divine activity and participation in nature and give us a God who exceeds the mere infinite and the mere finite." [129] "The supra-personal and the personal representations of the real are the absolute and the relative ways of expressing the one reality." [130] "When we look at the Absolute from the cosmic end, not as it is in itself, but as it is in relation to the world, the Absolute is envisaged as Īśvara or personal God who guides and directs the process by His providence." [131] "While the fulness of spiritual being transcends our categories, we are certain that its nature is akin to the highest kind of being we are aware of in ourselves. . . ." [132] "The Absolute is

124 ER, 298f.
125 IVL, 343.
126 *Ibid.,* 102.
127 Ind P, I, 168.
128 IVL, 344.
129 BG, 22.
130 HVL, 31.
131 ER, 92.
132 IVL, 103.

the pre-cosmic nature of God, and God is the Absolute from the cosmic point of view." [133]

The Real Is One. "When the whole universe reaches its consummation, the liberated individuals lapse into the stillness of the Absolute." [134] " 'In mystic states we become one with the Absolute and we become aware of our oneness.' " [135] "God, though immanent, is not identical with the world until the very end. Throughout the process there is an unrealised residuum in God, but it vanishes when we reach the end; . . ." [136]

If science teaches us anything, it is the organic nature of the universe. We are one with the world that has made us, one with every scene that is spread before our eyes. In a metaphor common to the Upaniṣads and Plato every unit of nature is a microcosm reflecting in itself the entire all-inclusive macrocosm.[137]

"When movement reaches its fulfilment, life is not a going concern. The historical process terminates and individuals cease to exist as historical beings." [138]

The frequent charge of an individual-annihilating unity which destroys the individual self and renders it insignificant is rejected by Radhakrishnan: "We are not, through this process [of spiritual self-realization], abolishing our individuality but transforming it into a conscious term of the universal being, an utterance of the transcendent divine." [139] ". . . we find a large number of passages in Śaṁkara which indicate that while the released soul attains at the very moment of release a universality of spirit, it yet retains its individuality as a centre of action as long as the cosmic process continues." [140] "Even Śaṁkara admits that 'This whole multiplicity of creatures existing under name and form in so far as it has the supreme Being itself for its essence is true; if regarded as self-dependent is untrue.' " [141]

The Status of the Empirical World—The Doctrine of Māyā. One of the major charges brought against Hinduism—often specifically on the ground that it undermines the entire status and significance of ethics—is to the effect that the empirical world and all that is implied in that concept, such as the individual human being, distinctions of right and wrong, etc., are unreal, both be-

---

[133] *Ibid.*, 345.   [134] HVL, 63.
[135] IVL, 105; see also HH, 135: "Throughout its long career, the oneness of the ultimate Spirit has been the governing ideal of the Hindu religion."
[136] IVL, 340.   [137] *Ibid.*, 56.   [138] *Ibid.*, 308.
[139] ER, 37.   [140] IVL, 306.   [141] ER, 31.

cause the ultimate reality is an absolute which completely transcends the empirical and also because of the specific doctrine of *māyā*, which is often translated "illusion" and thus lends support to the criticism. Since Radhakrishnan makes such repeated—and such vehement—replies to this charge, we must conclude that in his defense of Hinduism on this matter he is voicing his own strong belief. He is an absolute idealist and he holds to the doctrine of *māyā*, but he does not believe that either absolute idealism or the doctrine of *māyā*—or the two together—undermines the status of ethics or destroys its significance or that of the individual engaged in moral activities, although the individual is ultimately to be transcended along with all other empirical and finite things, qualities, and values. The solution of this problem, the answer to the charges, consists, as it does in practically every similar instance stated by Radhakrishnan, in an accurate interpretation of the doctrine as advocated by Hinduism and the consequent rejection of the extreme interpretation which, though it has gained widespread acceptance, clearly distorts the basic meaning of Hindu writers, even Śaṁkara, who alone of all great Hindu philosophers has, by his particular manner of presentation, given possible justification for the objectionable interpretation of *māyā* and of the status of the empirical world.

Radhakrishnan's theory is that which any sound absolute idealism holds, namely, that the Absolute is the only ultimate and complete reality and that the empirical world is clearly a secondary reality, relative and dependent, but that the empirical world is not for that reason unreal. The Absolute is completely independent of the empirical in the sense that changes in the finite do not affect the infinite. Radhakrishnan is expressing the essence of the great tradition of all idealism—from Plato on—when he espouses the belief that the empirical world is between being and non-being, that it is not ultimate but neither is it nothing or illusion.

The doctrine of *māyā* is, in part, expressing this concept of the *relative reality* of the empirical world, but that is only one side of the concept, and perhaps not its most important. *Māyā* is also the concept which was devised to express the *ultimate mystery* in the relationship between the Absolute and the empirical world and the reason for the existence of the empirical and its "creation" by the Absolute. Radhakrishnan insists repeatedly that we cannot answer the question "Why?" and that the concept of *māyā* expresses this ultimate mystery.

The doctrine of māyā is supposed to repudiate the reality of the world and thus make all ethical relations meaningless. The world of nature is said to be unreal and human history illusory. There is no meaning in time and no significance in life. To be delivered from this illusion which has somehow come to dominate the race of man is the end of all endeavour.[142]

In reply to this, Radhakrishnan observes that

The Vedic thinkers adopted a realistic view of the world. In the Upaniṣads we have an insistence on the relative reality of the world. . . . As Yājñavalkya puts it, everything in the world is of value as leading to the realisation of self. . . . The different theistic systems adopted by the large majority of the Hindus do not advocate the doctrine of māyā. The theory is held by Śaṁkara, who is regarded often as representing the standard type of Hindu thought.[143]

It thus becomes one of Radhakrishnan's major objectives to explain the seemingly extreme doctrine of Śaṁkara and to show that even in that doctrine māyā does not entail the illusory character of the empirical world, human history, and human endeavor.

The phenomenal character of the empirical self and the world answering to it is denoted by the word māyā, which signifies the fragility of the universe. Māyā does not mean that the empirical world with the selves in it is an illusion, for the whole effort of the cosmos is directed to and sustained by the one supreme self, which though distinct from everything is implicated in everything.[144]

"The manifold universe is not an illusion; it is being, though of a lower order, . . ." [145] "This one-sided dependence and the logical inconceivability of the relation between the Ultimate Reality and the world are brought out by the word, 'māyā.' The world is not essential being like Brahman; nor is it mere non-being. It cannot be defined as either being or non-being." [146]

Māyā also expresses the power of the absolute:

Māyā is derived from the root, mā, to form, to build, and originally meant the capacity to produce forms. . . . There is no suggestion that the forms, the events and the objects produced by māyā or the form-building power of God, the māyin, are only illusory. . . . The world is not a deception but the occasion for it.[147]

142 HVL, 61.   143 Ibid., 61f.   144 ER, 27.
145 Ibid., 30.   146 BG, 38.   147 Ibid., 40f.

". . . this universe of ours is the realization of the nature of the Absolute. . . . The infinite Being thus limits itself in order to manifest itself. This self-limiting power of the Absolute is called *māyā* by Hindu philosophers." [148]

The analogy of play (*līlā*) is employed to suggest the free overflow of the divine into the universe. It does not mean that there is nothing real or significant going on all the time. The world is the profoundest expression of the divine nature. . . . The analogy is not intended to suggest that the universe is a meaningless show made in a jest. The world is created by God out of the abundance of His joy.[149]

Māyā means *mystery:* "Māyā does not imply that the world is an illusion or is non-existent absolutely. It is a delimitation distinct from the unmeasured and the immeasurable. But why is there this delimitation? The question cannot be answered, so long as we are at the empirical level." [150] "From where we are, we can only say that it [why the divine should have permitted this particular plan of creation] is a mystery (*māyā*), or is the divine will, or the expression of his creative force." [151]

The question remains, Why does the world exist at all? To say that it is a mystery is perhaps true, but it can hardly be called an answer. . . . As to how the primal reality in which the divine light shines everlastingly can yet be the source and fount of all empirical being, we can only say that it is a mystery, *māyā*.[152]

Radhakrishnan repeatedly indicates that Śaṁkara is not an illusionist:

Śaṁkara, who is rightly credited with the systematic formulation of the doctrine of *māyā*, tells us that the highest reality is unchangeable, and therefore that changing existence such as human history has not ultimate reality (*pāramārthika sattā*). He warns us, however, against the temptation to regard what is not completely real as utterly illusory. The world has empirical being (*vyāvahārika sattā*) which is quite different from illustory existence (*prātibhāsika sattā*). Human experience is neither ultimately real nor completely illusory. . . . The world is not a phantom, though it is not [ultimately] real.[153]

". . . Śaṁkara has nothing in common with people who will not accept the visible world any more than with those who will accept nothing else." [154]

---

148 Sarma, 601.   149 ER, 92f; see also HVL, 69; IVL, 344.   150 BG, 38.
151 RS, 104.   152 ER, 90.   153 *Ibid.*, 86.
154 *Ibid.*, 100.

If we raise the question as to how the finite rises from out of the bosom of the infinite, Śaṁkara says that it is an incomprehensible mystery, māyā. We know that there is the absolute reality, we know that there is the empirical world, we know that the empirical world rests on the Absolute, but the *how* of it is beyond our knowledge.[155]

The great significance of the doctrine of *māyā*—of special relevance for ethics—is essentially the reminder that the empirical world is not the ultimate; for, to hold that it is would be the essence of ignorance, and ignorance is the cause of bondage, suffering, and false living. "When the Hindu thinkers ask us to free ourselves from *māyā*, they are asking us to shake off our bondage to the unreal values which are dominating us. They do not ask us to treat life as an illusion or be indifferent to the world's welfare." [156] "The view which regards the multiplicity as ultimate is deceptive (*māyā*), for it causes the desire to live separate and independent lives. . . . It tempts us to accept, as real, bubbles which will be broken, cobwebs which will be swept away." [157] "The negative descriptions of the Supreme and the doctrine of *māyā* which are said to be the characteristics of Hindu mysticism are employed to denote the distance between time and eternity, between appearance and reality." [158]

The Spiritual Nature of Man. Radhakrishnan's description of the essential nature of man is of great significance, of course; for upon this, as well as upon his doctrine of the nature of reality as a whole, depends the validity of his ethics and of its basis in reality. There is no question as to Radhakrishnan's doctrine of the nature of man: Man is essentially a spiritual being, ultimately identical in some way and to some degree with the Absolute; and yet man is a complex being, belonging to both orders, the infinite and the finite, the divine and the human. In this way—as in his doctrine of the relationship between the Absolute and the empirical world —Radhakrishnan metaphysically justifies both man's highest spiritual aspirations for identity with the ultimate and the significance of his ethical conduct in the empirical world.

"There is in the self of man, at the very centre of his being, something deeper than the intellect, which is akin to the Supreme. . . . The consubstantiality of the spirit in man and God is the conviction fundamental to all spiritual wisdom." [159] "The true and ultimate condition of the human being is the divine status." [160]

155 HVL, 66f.   156 ER, 47.   157 *Ibid.*, 94f.
158 *Ibid.*, 298.   159 IVL, 103.   160 ER, 102.

"For the Hindu, the spiritual is the basic element of human nature." [161] "We belong to the real and the real is mirrored in us.
The great text of the Upaniṣad affirms it—*Tat tvam asi* (That art
Thou). It is a simple statement of an experienced fact." [162] "If
there is one doctrine more than another which is characteristic of
Hindu thought, it is the belief that there is an interior depth to
the human soul, which, in its essence, is uncreated and deathless
and absolutely real. The spirit in man is different from the individual ego; . . ." [163] "The human mind is not limited to the world
of matter, and it can be raised into intimate correspondence with
the transcendental and supersensuous realm of reality." [164]

Of course, along with this doctrine goes that of the immortality
of the spiritual essence of man:

> The Hindu thinkers affirm the reality of life eternal or release from
> rebirth. It is a supreme status of being in which the individual knows ·
> himself to be superior to time, to birth and death. It is not a life
> merely future or endless but a new mode of being, . . .[165]

Nevertheless, while man is essentially spiritual, he is a creature
of this world as well, and it is important—especially in connection
with the problem we are discussing—to recognize Radhakrishnan's
doctrine that it is the whole man that is of significance. Otherwise,
the charge mentioned above in connection with the doctrine of
māyā could apply equally well here to the nullification of significant ethical conduct in the empirical world.

"The realm of spirit is not cut off from the realm of life. To
divide man into outer desire and inner quality is to violate the
integrity of human life. . . . The two orders of reality, the transcendent and the empirical, are closely related." [166]

> There cannot be any conflict between body, mind and soul. The har-
> mony of the different sides of our nature is the condition of peace and
> their mutual understanding the means of perfection. The suppression
> of any one side mars self-fulfilment. Asceticism is an excess indulged
> in by those who exaggerate the transcendent aspect of reality. . . .
> Nothing is to be rejected; everything is to be raised.[167]

"Man belongs to both orders, and his religion is here or nowhere.
Life eternal consists in another kind of life in the midst of time." [168]

161 ER, 77.   162 IVL, 103f.   163 ER, 83.
164 RS, 46; see also IVL, 72, 106, 263; HH, 43; ER, 81.
165 IVL, 303f.   166 BG, 13.   167 IVL, 115.
168 ER, 97.

"The Divine is both in us and out of us. God is neither completely transcendent nor completely immanent." [169] "Though the being of man is spirit, his nature is complex and unstable. . . . That is why he has the creaturely sense over against the transcendent majesty of God, . . ." [170] "Man is a complex multidimensional being, including within him different elements of matter, life, consciousness, intelligence and the divine spark." [171]

By way of proof of the divine nature of man, Radhakrishnan points to the evidence revealed by man in his thoughts and in his aspirations—including the ethical. "If the feeling for God were not in man, we could not implant it any more than we could squeeze blood from a stone. . . ." [172]

The relation of our life to a larger spiritual world betrays itself even in the waking consciousness through our intellectual ideals, our moral aspirations, our cravings for beauty, and our longing for perfection. . . . Man is not a plant or an animal, but a thinking and spiritual being set to shape his nature for higher purposes.[173]

The thoughts, the raptures and the deeds of the great induce in us an attitude of adoration. If the spirit were not in us, we would not have thrilled with joy when face to face with the great works of art, science or life. . . . The rhythms of the poet find correspondence in the conditions of our soul; their words an authentic echo in our speech. . . . The saint's perfection is felt as something to which we aspire and may attain. We understand an object only when there is something in us akin to it.[174]

Radhakrishnan feels that there is here a contrast between East and West and that the Western tendency is one-sided and inadequate. As he says,

There is a tendency, especially in the West, to overestimate the place of the human self. . . . It is not realised that the thought of the self which wants to explain everything, the will of the self which wants to subjugate everything, are themselves the expression of a deeper whole, which includes the self and its object. If the self is not widened into the universal spirit, the values themselves become merely subjective and the self itself will collapse into nothing.[175]

The Value-Character of Reality. It is Radhakrishnan's conviction, as expressed in many of the quotations cited earlier in this study, that the values and ideals of the ethical life must be real in

169 IVL, 106.
170 *The Cultural Heritage of India,* Calcutta (n.d.), Intro., I, xxi.
171 BG, 46; see also ER, 31f., 84.
172 ER, 83.   173 *Ibid.*, 37.   174 IVL, 207f.   175 *Ibid.*, 274.

the sense of being intrinsic to the very nature of reality itself. There seems to be no other meaning for the view that there must be a metaphysical basis for ethics. In other words, if the reality which Radhakrishnan has described for us is not characterized by value, then, the entire metaphysical system has failed to provide the basis for ethics for which we are in search, and all that has been said and quoted heretofore in this study is to no avail.

The reason for raising this question, of course, is the central doctrine that the ultimate reality is describable only negatively, and that it transcends all qualities and distinctions. Radhakrishnan firmly believes, however, that although the Absolute is completely transcendent and "totally other" than all empirical qualifications, it is, nevertheless, the very embodiment of value. I trust I am true to Radhakrishnan's conviction in making this statement; the following quotations are my justification. I find most significant of all his statements the following concise summary, as it were: "*The supreme is real, not true, perfect, not good.*"[176] A studied comprehension of that statement reveals both the value-character of the ultimate and also its transcendence of empirical designations of value in terms of value-distinctions, but does not set the two at complete variance because both perfection and good are concepts of value.

An idealist view of life [with which Radhakrishnan identifies his own theory, of course] is not expressed in any one pattern. It is many-coloured and its forms are varied; yet underneath all the variations and oppositions there are certain common fundamental assumptions that show them all to be products of the same spirit. . . . The realistic systems of Hindu thought, . . . are not in serious disagreement with the fundamental intention of the idealist tradition of the Upaniṣads, viz. *the inseparability of the highest value from the truly real.* The absolute is reality, consciousness and freedom—sat, cit, and ānanda. In the West, from Socrates and Plato to Bradley and Alexander, the idealist outlook of an ultimate connection of value and reality is maintained.[177]

An idealist view finds that the universe has meaning, has value. Ideal values are the dynamic forces, the driving power of the universe. The world is intelligible only as a system of ends. . . . Idealism in the sense indicated concerns the ultimate reality, whatever may be its relation to the knowing mind. It is an answer to the problem of the idea, the meaning or the purpose of it all. It has nothing in common with

---

176 *Ibid.*, 103 (*italics* mine). 177 *Ibid.*, 16 (*italics* mine).

the view that makes reality an irrational blind striving or an irremediably miserable blunder. It finds life significant and purposeful.[178]

"The temporal series is the scheme through which eternal values unfold themselves." [179] "Nothing in our experience can be said to be real or individual without qualification except spirit. . . . It is all that there is, all being and all value." [180] "The ethical soundness, the logical consistency and the aesthetic beauty of the universe are assumptions for science and logic, art and morality, but are not irrational assumptions." [181]

The supreme creative ground of the universe cannot be an unconscious force. . . . With the rise of organisms in the scale of existence, rudiments of mind appeared. As mental endowment improved, intellectuality, knowledge of good and evil, arose. It is difficult to imagine that this effort has no aim or significance.[182]

"Whatever may be the truth about the origin of life and the universe, the supremacy of the moral end is admitted by all. . . ." [183]

Many of Radhakrishnan's observations on this particular matter are couched in the language of religion and deal with the nature of God. It is sometimes difficult to know whether he is speaking of the ineffable ultimate or the personal deity, which is a subordinate expression or form of the Absolute. There is no question about the value-filled nature of God, and I feel there is no question, also, about the perfection of the Absolute, but the interpreter of Radhakrishnan's philosophy at this point must be extremely careful to read him aright and not to read into his view of the Absolute any doctrine which he intends to apply only at the secondary level of deity. The following are clear expressions of the value-character of reality, certainly at the level of God, if not at the supreme level of the Absolute.

. . . ethical certainty requires a highest end from which all other ends are derived, an end which flows from the very self and gives meaning and significance to the less general ethical ends. The ultimate assumption of all life is the spirit in us, the divine in man. Life is God, and the proof of it is life itself. If somewhere in ourselves we did not know with absolute certainty that God *is,* we could not live.[184]

"Humanism is concerned with value; religion relates value to reality, . . ." [185] "In mystic religion God is not a logical concept or

178 *Ibid.*, 15.   179 *Ibid.*, 319f.   180 *Ibid.*, 302.
181 *Ibid.*, 156.   182 RWN, 12.   183 HH, 29f.
184 IVL, 158.   185 *Ibid.*, 71.

the conclusion of a syllogism but a real presence, the ground and possibility of all knowledge and values." [186] "Differences in name [of the deity] become immaterial for the Hindu, since every name, at its best, connotes the same metaphysical and moral perfections." [187] Radhakrishnan quotes, apparently as his own conviction, the Upaniṣadic statement, "God is both truth and virtue." [188] Or, as Radhakrishnan's view is summarized by Joad, ". . . religion involves definite knowledge and makes a definite affirmation. The universe, it affirms, is good; it is also spiritual; it is also in some sense personal. Of these facts we have direct and immediate experience." [189]

VII. CONCLUSION

In the metaphysics just outlined it seems to me that Radhakrishnan has built a solid foundation for the ethical and religious life which he and Hinduism advocate so strongly and so effectively. As Joad correctly states,

Every word that he [Radhakrishnan] writes on ethical questions presupposes this intimate relation between ethics and religion, presupposes, indeed, as its basic assumption, the spiritual view of the universe, the spiritual nature of man and the concept of God as indwelling in man, . . . If this assumption be not granted, the ethical philosophy [of Radhakrishnan] . . . is without foundation.[190]

As just described in his own words, Radhakrishnan's metaphysics includes each of these basic principles of reality necessary to ground his particular ethical view and has thus provided a metaphysical basis for his ethics.

If reality (including man) is what he describes it to be, it is not only a basis for ethical values and morality but also the reason for ethical conduct and for the moral obligation to act in accordance with our spiritual nature. There is also justification for setting our sights upon the ultimate spiritual goal, mokṣa, in which empirical living, ethical activity, and ethical motivations are transcended. The doctrines of karma and rebirth as means of spiritual progress are justified by the value-character and orderliness of reality. There is reason to practice the comprehensive virtue of ahiṁsā or its equivalent, universal love—for we are all basically one. Morality is significant though transcended in spiritual perfection, just as the empirical world is significant though it is not the ultimate reality

186 ER, 62. 187 HVL, 46.
188 Bṛhadāraṇyaka Upaniṣad, ii, 5, 11, cited in ER, 104.
189 Joad, 63. 190 Ibid., 151.

and is transcended by the ineffable and indescribable Absolute. Complete reality and complete perfection are the goal. Ethics is an indispensable aid in the achieving of that goal by man. The reason for the obligation and for the enthusiasm of morality lies essentially in what man is and what the ultimate reality is to which he belongs and to which he aspires. Man's spiritual identity with the Absolute justifies his aspirations; his finite and worldly nature enslaves him to temporary suffering, to be sure, but it also provides opportunities for spiritual advancement and eventual perfection. The ultimate and the perfect are in all things; man's aspirations themselves and his appreciation of ultimate values provide the incentive and the means as well as the basis of his becoming divine and uniting in spirit with the Absolute—and that is the goal of both ethics and metaphysics.

VIII. Problems and Questions

I have tried to interpret Radhakrishnan's views correctly and to apply them accurately to the specific problem of this study; but there has been recurrent fear that I might have misinterpreted his doctrines or his attitude. Much of this study has been essentially descriptive; instead of being critical, I have attempted to see beyond or through the difficulties expressed by critics and to state Radhakrishnan's doctrines in his true meaning. As we have seen, the view that ethics is significant and must have and does have a basis in reality has been challenged on several counts. The doctrines of *māyā,* of tolerance in the matter of metaphysical beliefs, of transcendence of ethical values and standards, of the ultimate oneness of reality, and of *neti, neti,* serve as threats to the significance of ethics and to its having any real or significant basis in metaphysics.

The following are the major difficulties or points of doubt that have been in my mind. Perhaps some of them require clarification.

1. Will Radhakrishnan accept the interpretation of this study relative to his relationship with the classical Hindu tradition and with the theory of Śaṁkara? Does this interpretation entail any distortions of his theory? Have I underestimated his deviation from basic Hinduism on any doctrines pertinent to the problem of this study?

2. Is the view of this paper correct in its interpretation of his doctrine that morality is ultimately transcended and yet is vitally

important, not only in the empirical world as such, but also as an indispensable means to the morality-transcending experience? But, even if the interpretation offered here is correct, is it not true—as some critics contend—that morality never has more than a relative status, just as the empirical world itself is merely relatively and secondarily real? If this is true, does morality have a *metaphysical* basis; is it grounded in *reality*, as so many statements quoted above require as the indispensable ground of ethics?

3. Have I been correct in saying that Radhakrishnan believes that reality is "in some sense characterized by value"? Or, does the doctrine of *neti, neti,* to which he subscribes, remove from reality the value-connotation or value-essence without which there would seem to be no adequate metaphysical basis for ethics? Do the various value-statements in his writings—many of which have been quoted above in the section on value-metaphysics—apply to ultimate reality (Brahman) or merely to God (Īśvara), the personal deity? If to the latter, does that provide an adequate basis for ethics, the values of which must be grounded in reality itself?

4. Is there any inconsistency in holding that ethics needs a basis in metaphysics and at the same time holding that practice precedes theory, or, to put the matter differently, that there can be wide tolerance in metaphysical belief accompanied by the obligation for strict adherence to the correct ethical code? Is the attempt of this paper to explain this apparent discrepancy correct? How can an atheist, or any other disbeliever in the doctrine of idealism in some one of its forms, be considered a true Hindu and have a metaphysical basis for the spiritual ethics of Hinduism?

5. Does Radhakrishnan feel that his system provides a synthesis of East and West—whether that has been his intention or not? It seems to me that his doctrine does provide such a synthesis in the sense that great idealists of both traditions can or should accept his views. His philosophy shows that idealists in East and West are speaking the same language and seeking the same ideals. Is this an accurate interpretation, or does he feel that the idealism of the West must be transformed so as to be brought into closer conformity with the idealistic and spiritual wisdom of India? (This question extends beyond the scope of this paper, but it is suggested by the paper, and I feel that it must be clarified, if we are to understand Radhakrishnan's view adequately and in its full significance.)

CHARLES A. MOORE

DEPARTMENT OF PHILOSOPHY
UNIVERSITY OF HAWAII

5

Charles Hartshorne

RADHAKRISHNAN ON MIND, MATTER, AND GOD

5

RADHAKRISHNAN ON MIND, MATTER, AND GOD

O F the wise men and lovers of wisdom whom I have met, I think of the subject of this volume as among the chief. This essay, however, is concerned only with his metaphysics and does not aim to give anything like a complete view of his doctrines even in that field. Certain chapters (VI-VIII) in *An Idealist View of Life* render such a complete treatment unnecessary. I merely wish to indicate my general appreciation of his fine treatment of the old problems—a treatment which seems to me to combine much that is best in both Eastern and Western thought—and also to ask him to consider the difficulties that I have with a few features of his doctrine.

In saying that our author combines much that is best in metaphysics, the world over, I mean above all that he avoids one-sided extremes, such as sheer monism, or extreme pluralism, or again, such as the reduction of all causation to an absolute teleology, the sway of an all-coercing providence, or, on the other side, the sheer denial of providence. Thus he finds it possible to admit the reality of chance, disorder, and contingency, even for and in God, without giving up the divine unity of the world whereby it is a whole which contains and cherishes the values of the parts in an inclusive value. It is, I believe, such "playing fair" between contrasting poles of categorical conceptions, like unity and plurality, that East and West are coming to see as the only way to attain the whole truth, so far as it is humanly accessible.

My queries about Professor Radhakrishnan's doctrine concern, perhaps, chiefly matters of terminology, and center upon two problems. These are: (1) the relations of subject and object, or the question of "idealism;" and (2) the relations of deity and the Absolute, or the question of theism. I shall consider the two in this order.

I

Our author seems to leave the meaning of "Idealism" somewhat obscure. He does not altogether approve of Whitehead's complete translation of physical concepts into terms of "feeling," "satisfaction," "prehension," and the like.[1] He also seems to reject anything like the Berkeleyan type of subjectivism.[2] Yet I, at least, am not able to discern any third possibility for idealism. "Objective idealism" is a mere phrase. Even Berkeley's "ideas" are objective to man, for they are also in the divine mind. What further idealistic objectivity can there be, if it is denied that such things as atoms (à la Leibniz, Peirce, and Whitehead) or planets (à la Fechner and Royce) have their *own* feelings or ideas? Is it perhaps meant that matter is something different in quality from subjectivity, but dependent upon it? Then one may object that the asserted dependence is decidedly opaque. To be known is, as realists have well insisted (and our author seems to be a realist in this sense [3]), an external (better, nominal) relation of the known—unless the latter knows that it is known, and even here the internal relation is knowing-oneself-to-be-known.

It follows that matter cannot be explained by mind through the mere fact that it is known. Nothing depends upon mind merely because it is perceived. Even 'ideas' or images are not *merely* 'objects;' they are aspects of perceiving or thinking. Further, if being known means dependence upon the knowing, then the past (since it is known) depends upon the present as well as the present upon the past, and the reality of time, contingency, and freedom, upon all of which Radhakrishnan wisely insists, disappears in an absolute monism of the eternal cognitive present, in which everything implies everything else. But if matter is not dependent upon mind because it is known, what *is* the nature of the dependence?

And why, after all, does our thinker reject panpsychism? He says that, if consciousness and selectivity are taken "as defining features of human experience," it is confusing to use them in a wider sense.[4] But, on that reasoning, we should never say that beating a dog hurts the dog. Instead of 'human' in the quoted phrase, the word should at least have been 'vertebrate' or 'animal.' But are even animals the unique possessors of feelings (and in that sense, of selectivity)? Of course they are the unique possessors of *animal* feelings, just as we are of human feelings, and children are of children's

[1] IVL, 248. Unless otherwise stated, page nos. will refer to this work.
[2] *Ibid.*, 242.   [3] *Ibid.*, 246f.   [4] *Ibid.*, 248.

feelings and women are of women's feelings and woodpeckers are of woodpeckers' feelings! But there is no need to employ feeling *in general* as a distinguishing mark of adults, or of women, or of human beings, or even of animals. It is the *ways* in which these groups feel that distinguishes them. Only animals can have feelings of muscular locomotion, or of visual and auditory experiences. But a plant cell might have a feeling somewhat like the glow of pleasure we have in a warm bath; or it might have feelings we cannot distinctly imagine, as a congenitally blind man cannot distinctly imagine visual sensations. Similar remarks apply even to an atom. All that the contrary argument comes to is that just as it is hard for a blind man to know, except vaguely, what is meant by saying, "there are creatures with visual sensations," so we cannot, except vaguely or dimly, imagine the reaches of feeling beyond the human. But then no one supposes that metaphysical understanding will be as easy and obvious as trivial matters may be. Certainly Radhakrishnan does not. Also I wonder whether any way of conceiving idealism other than as panpsychism is not *more* "confusing" rather than less.

II

Let us turn now to the second topic, the nature of God. Our philosopher well says that the chief problem in the philosophy of religion has been the reconciliation of the "Absolute" with "God." That they can be simply identified is clearly not his opinion. Such identification has, indeed, been the central sophistry in our Western theistic tradition, as Hume noted;[5] but from Schelling and Fechner to James, Bergson, Montague, and Whitehead, the task of philosophical theism has been above all to find a tenable conception of some relation other than that of sheer identity between deity and absoluteness. In Fechner and Whitehead a solution has, in principle, been provided. The doctrine is not excessively complicated, and, for purposes of comparison, I wish to outline it.

"Absolute" contrasts with "relative," and thus means (roughly) non-relative, independent of relationships. Now it seems plain that to conceive something as free from relatedness we must *abstract* from all that is relative in experience, from all relations and relative terms. But what is thus conceived, by abstracting everything that is relation or relative from the concrete, can only be something extremely abstract. Why, then, try to avoid the conclusion: the

[5] *Dialogues Concerning Natural Religion.* Part IV.

absolute, as such, is a radically abstract, not a concrete, entity? More than twenty centuries have sought, nevertheless, to find a way to dodge this conclusion.

To conceive the relative there is no such need for abstraction. The concrete given whole of experience is itself relative in manifold ways; indeed, this whole must contain all the relativity (as well as all the absoluteness) that is actually given! But that which contains something relative is itself relative; that which contains the dependent or the contingent is itself dependent or contingent. For, if the least item in the whole depends on some relation, then the whole depends also on that relation, to just the extent that the item itself belongs to, contributes to, the whole; and if that extent is zero, then the item is no item. Thus to abstract from, to omit, nothing is to retain all the relativity, all the dependence, there is; whereas, to conceive the independent or absolute, we must omit from consideration all in the concrete which is due to relations. Thus the concrete is the relative; but the concrete includes the abstract, hence the relative includes the absolute, not *vice versa*.[6]

In accordance with the foregoing, the supreme concrete Reality, or deity, may be conceived as containing an absolute factor; but as concrete it must also contain relations and relative terms, and therefore, in its concrete wholeness, it must be relative rather than absolute. The absolute is a factor, an adjective, of the relative, not *vice versa*. God is the substantive, the absolute is a character of this substantive. This inverts Bradley's doctrine that the relative is a mere appearance of the absolute. On the contrary, the absolute is a mere abstract feature of what in its total reality is *more than absolute*. 'More than absolute,' superabsolute, may be seen as not really a paradox, if we recall that "absolute" is defined negatively as non-relative, and that superiority is positive and relative, as indeed is value generally (for, at least, it implies a relation of interest and object).

If we turn to Radhakrishnan, we find a doctrine which seems largely in harmony with the one above outlined, although now and then tantalizingly ambiguous in regard to it. He says that although God is organic to the universe, "essentially bound up with the life in time" (that is, relative and concrete?), the Absolute is not thus organic or subject to change and evolution (or concrete?).[7] Only the words 'abstract' and 'concrete' seem to be missing. God, we are

[6] This doctrine is explained in my book, *The Divine Relativity* (Yale University Press, 1948).
[7] IVL, 343.

told, is "but an expression of the absolute." [8] Now, disregarding the "but," which seems misplaced and misleading, the concrete may be called an expression of the abstract; thus an actual joy of joyfulness, a beautiful thing of beauty. Again, God is "the Absolute limited down to its relation with the actual possibility" (this world being but one of the possibilities that might have been actualized).[9] Just so, a concrete embodiment of an abstraction always involves a limiting down of the latter, in the sense that the possible embodiments are always infinitely more various than any actual embodiment or set of them. But the logic of concrete and abstract requires, if I am not mistaken, that we conceive the real subject of the relation between the absolute and the "actual possibility" (that is, the actualization of the chosen possibility) to be the relative actuality and not the absolute, which is only nominally thus related. The term that has the relation has also the other term. For relation-to-x includes x. Thus it is not the abstract and absolute but the concrete and relative that is more than the other. True, the abstract involves possibility of more, with respect to any concrete actuality. But possibility-of-more is not more *tout court,* it is not a greater actuality; whereas pure possibility abstracted from the actual is really and *tout court less* than the actual. For note: the possibility-of-more is itself something in the concrete, as the whiteness which another object *could* embody is the very whiteness this paper does embody; or as my capacity to be other than I am is, as capacity, part of what I actually am.

We are told that the absolute is "in a sense eternally complete." Whitehead, too, says that the Primordial Nature of God is 'complete;' but he is careful to add that it is abstract and deficient in actuality. I greatly hope that this is acceptable to the Eastern seer. The capacity to create, the matrix of pure potentials, is as capacity complete; for no possibility is missing from it; but equally all actual creation is absent from the capacity, taken merely as such (and only as so taken is it absolute). No possibility is missing *as* possibility, but all are missing as actualities.

Perhaps (I hope not) our author will object to this theory on the ground of the Thomistic contention that potentiality rests on actuality. I grant that there is no potentiality except *in* some actuality, but this actuality is to be termed complete, absolute, non-relative, immutable, only *qua* potentiality, only with regard to its fecundity for actualization. It is doubly wrong to say that there can not be complete fecundity unless there is complete actualiza-

[8] *Ibid.,* 342.   [9] *Ibid.,* 344f.

tion; first, because the meaning of fecundity implies that not every-thing is actualized (whether "already" or "eternally"); and second, because there are incompossible possibilities, so that "everything" *could not* be actualized. Paul Weiss seems right in saying that to be actual is to be incomplete; to be complete is to be non-actual.[10]

Such phrases as "the Absolute is the pre-cosmic nature of God," God is the Absolute "in relation to the cosmos," [11] can perhaps be assimilated to our theory. When, however, we read of the "free activity of the Absolute" by which the actual world is selected from the possibilities, we may wish to urge that no actual selecting can be done by the absolute factor in God; since an act of select-ing for actualization a definite possibility is as truly relative and limited as the actualization. This has been pointed out by Santa-yana.[12] It is God as relative who selected from the possibilities contained in the absolute completeness of his mere eternal potency —complete and eternal only *qua* potency, not *qua* act.

Certain remarks of Radhakrishnan suggest a view not easily reconciled with the doctrine I have sketched. He seems to hold that, as the pre-cosmic nature of God is identical with the Abso-lute, so also the post-cosmic God will return to this identity. "God . . . is not identical with the world until the very end. . . . There is an unrealized residuum in God, but it vanishes when we reach the end; when the reign is absolute the kingdom comes. God re-cedes into the background of the Absolute." [13] And Whitehead is criticized because he does not tell us what happens when the divine plan of the Primordial Nature is realized. But suppose the divine purpose is *inexhaustible!* For this supposition there is a reason, pointed out by Whitehead. No single world, however long it had lasted in time, could ever exhaust possibility, which is absolutely infinite, infinite in every dimension and respect. That is why there is time at all, because not all possibilities can be achieved together, so that whatever is actual, more remains possible, and no motive can forbid, while motives do command, that more should be actual. Radhakrishnan himself insists that there is no single eternally com-plete plan being carried out literally and irresistibly in the world: creaturely freedom and contingency, with a genuinely open or unfinished future, being real even for and in God.[14] Why then speak without qualification of the realization of the divine plan, as though it were something fully defined, exhaustible, and

10 *Reality* (Princeton University Press, 1938), 153.
11 IVL, 345.   12 *The Realm of Essence*, 162f.
13 IVL, 340.   14 *Ibid.*, 336.

destined for complete enactment? The divine plan, according to Whitehead, envisages beauty of experience, happiness, in *endlessly* increasing variety and total intensity, in the creatures and in God as embracing the creatures. So there is no "far off divine event toward which the whole creation moves;" but there is a divine purpose nonetheless. Radhakrishnan says, it is true, that "the beginning and the end are limiting conceptions." [15] But this qualification seems either not a qualification or else a retraction. It is like talking of the 'end of the number series' as a limiting conception. (I should say that the temporal series has neither beginning nor end, and that "pre-cosmic nature of God" should mean, not God before the creaturely process, but God in *abstraction* from every particular form or world-constellation which this process has actually taken. For, as all such forms are contingent, we are at liberty to conceive alternatives for every one of them, and the pre-cosmic nature is merely what all such possible forms have in common. Not before but *in* all times, actual or possible, is the meaning.)

If the temporal series were finite, of course it must have a beginning and an end. But why should it be finite? Our author seems to suggest that actuality is finite, since it is not the entire infinity of possibilities.[16] But we have the distinction between infinite and absolutely infinite, infinite in some and infinite in all respects or dimensions, to cover that point.

This is perhaps enough to show what I should like to know further about our contemporary's opinions. It might be remarked that neither my difficulty with his form of idealism nor my queries about his treatment of absoluteness represent issues between East and West. Our own (Western) traditions are mostly at least as unsatisfactory, in my judgment, as to these points, and in much the same way. If there is a difference, it is perhaps this. The West has a strong drive toward logical precision, but a drive frustrated, for many centuries, in its application to metaphysics by other strong trends in our culture, such as clerical authoritarianism, in some respects more virulent here than in India. The trend toward logic is at long last beginning to come into its own even in the philosophy of religion. The Orient never was so inhibited from applying exact logic to religious thought; but also it has had a less keen interest in logic generally. I imagine, therefore, that Radhakrishnan, for example, may care a bit less than I do about the sort of questions I have been propounding; though I should have more hope

15 *Ibid.*, 340.   16 *Ibid.*, 344.

of his being able to give an at least roughly satisfactory answer to them than I should have with reference to many a type of Western philosopher or theologian.

The thought of Radhakrishnan illustrates that convergence of traditions which some of us think one of the most hopeful signs in our world. What formerly seemed to divide, say Hinduism from Christian theology, appears more and more as due to certain arbitrary emphases found in both, emphases tending in opposite directions, but recognizable in both cases as arbitrary, and therefore as corrigible without loss of basic insights. Radhakrishnan seems to feel, for example, how slight is the gap between himself and Whitehead.[17] And it is not only these two who can easily understand each other. For Whitehead substitute Fechner, Pfleiderer, Peirce, Montague, even James and Bergson, and the distance from the Eastern thinker is still only moderate. For a really harsh and irreconcilable opposition to his views we should have to look to Roman Catholic official philosophy, on the one hand, and to positivism, dialectical materialism, or other radically anti-religious doctrines, on the other. And indeed, we shall, I believe, see more and more that the vital divisions are not between East and West, but between theism and atheism, with a cross division between intellectually reactionary and intellectually progressive versions of theism or of atheism, or perhaps better, between purely absolutistic or eternalistic and "surrelativistic" or temporalistic versions. Radhakrishnan is an illustrious representative of progressive theism, which some take to be the hope of mankind.

CHARLES HARTSHORNE

DEPARTMENT OF PHILOSOPHY
THE UNIVERSITY OF CHICAGO

17 *Ibid.*, 326ff.

6

W. R. Inge

RADHAKRISHNAN AND THE RELIGION OF THE SPIRIT

6

RADHAKRISHNAN AND THE RELIGION
OF THE SPIRIT

AUGUSTE SABATIER contrasts the Religion of the Spirit with the Religion of Authority. Authority in religion means external, divine, infallible authority. It is claimed that certain truths have been revealed which could not be known in any other way; that the custody and interpretation of these truths are in the hands of an institution, and that to doubt any part of the revelation is not intellectual error but sin. The Church of Rome is the chief example of authoritarian religion. It is very attractive to those who distrust their own private judgment, and who would rather be led blindfold than be left to find their own way. Since it makes its adherents happy, and provides well tried methods of mind cure, it may justify itself to pragmatists, who hold that, since absolute truth is unattainable, we may believe what suits us at our own risk. On the other hand, there are many who think that to submit our wills, our consciences, and our reason to the orders of others is a kind of self-mutilation. As Lucan says, it is only the shadow of freedom which we preserve when we decide to do whatever we are told. Forced belief is make-believe; we cannot make our own the dogmas which we swallow whole. The obedience of a soldier on campaign is not what is required of free and intelligent persons. We can hardly imagine a more terrible view of education than Newman's "pour truth into a child's mind, and then seal it up in perpetuity."

There are many reasons for doubting whether the institution possesses the authority which it claims. The boast *quod semper, quod ubique, quod ab omnibus* is a figment. *Quod semper* means in 1563, *quod ubique* means at Trent, *quod ab omnibus* means by a majority. Further, can there be any revelation of past and future events? Even Jesus Christ, as a man, knew no more of the future than is given to man to know. All eschatology is symbolical, imaginative, wishful thinking.

We must remember that Catholicism is not the only religion of authority. The bibliolatry of Protestants is equally groundless and even more indefensible. "Do you believe, Mr. Bryan," said the barrister at Dayton, Tennessee, "that Jonah was swallowed by the whale?" "I do, because the Bible says so." "And if the Bible told you that it was Jonah who swallowed the whale, would you believe that?" "Yes." Nor is mysticism, which means reliance on the inner light, exempt from the same danger. The inner light may itself be made too external. "Jerusalem?" an old Quaker woman is reported to have said, "it has not yet been revealed to me that there is such a place." The wisest mystical writers, like the author of the *German Theology,* are emphatic in their warnings against what they call the false light.

Are we then to infer that there has been no revelation, that God has left himself without witness, that our convictions must always be purely subjective and uncertain, the guesses of a man fumbling in the dark? Is religion like a besieged city, where the outlying defences have been captured or shattered one by one, till only the citadel is left, and that is threatened? We know that no forts are defended with more energy than castles in the air. But we have our feet on solid earth, and we ask for some assurance that our beliefs are not what nineteenth century science called mere epiphenomena, floating idly above the real world of stars and atoms. All the old outworks have been pierced. Miracles, fulfilled prophecies, an infallible Church, an infallible book, the old arguments for the existence of God, all are discredited; what is left?

Radhakrishnan does not agree that there has been no revelation. He is in substantial agreement with the great school of religious Platonism, which in Christianity has taken, not without justification, the name of *philosophia perennis,* the perennial philosophy. God has revealed himself in the life of devotion. At our best moments we are conscious that we are in communion with something or somebody above ourselves. We often say, "with a Person;" and though God is certainly not "such a one as ourselves," it seems to be true that the "I and thou" relation is never transcended. The Spirit bears witness with our spirit, as St. Paul says; we do not pray to our own best selves, nor are we ever absorbed in a super-personal absolute. This aspect of the truth is being emphasized by the new school of personalists, of whom Buber is a worthy representative. Radhakrishnan would admit that some Indian thought has gone astray by carrying the negative road too far. A journey through the unreal is an unreal journey, and leads nowhere. The "union of the knower and the known," which mysticism pictures as the ideal consummation of the soul's quest, does not mean that personality is ever extinguished. Its circumference may expand indefinitely, but the centre remains.

Besides the approach of man to God and of God to man in prayer and contemplation, God has revealed to us three attributes of his nature. We all know that the soul lives amphibiously in a world of facts and in a world of values. The values are as real as the facts, but it is their nature to be hierarchical. Some are higher, of greater worth, than others; the scale of values even includes minus signs—disvalues which are not merely defective but positively evil. Some values are instrumental, good for something or somebody in particular; others are absolute, living and active in their own right. It is in these ultimate values that God has revealed some of his attributes to us. We cannot do better than accept the traditional triplet of ultimate values—Goodness or Love, Wisdom or Truth, and Beauty. These are given to us *a priori;* they are a threefold cord not quickly broken, but they cannot be used as a means to anything beyond themselves, or even to each other. Plato would say that we have knowledge of them, opinion of everything else. The completely real, he says, is completely knowable. Not completely known, but completely knowable. This is the act of faith which is the foundation of the Platonic philosophy. It is an act of faith, but of reasonable faith. In every philosophy we come to a point where a man must trust himself. When our minds are at their highest stretch we seem to ourselves to be in contact with something supremely real and above ourselves. This is the real meaning of the ontological argument, which St. Thomas Aquinas refuses to use, and which Kant regards as an absurdity. It is a good rule not to suppose that earlier thinkers were intellectually inferior to ourselves. Kant makes the ontological argument ridiculous. Of course we may think of a hundred dollars without having them in our purse. But should we have our visions of God if there were no reality behind them? When St. Thomas says, *impossibile est naturale desiderium esse inane,* "it is impossible that our natural desires should be empty," he is conceding all that the argument, properly understood, claims. Quite strictly, it is not "impossible," but it is what Lotze calls "intolerable;" there are possibilities which we have a right to banish.

Of course this does not mean that we know intuitively what we ought to do, what we ought to believe, and what we ought to admire. We may ask, more respectfully than Pontius Pilate, "What is truth?" We may debate anxiously with ourselves as to what is our duty. We may differ in matters of aesthetics. But in so far as we know what is right, we must do it; in so far as we know what is true, we must believe it, never saying, "Where ignorance is bliss, 'tis folly to be wise;" in so far as we know what is beautiful, we must pay homage to it. The perennial philosophy, which I think is that of Radhakrishnan, will make no terms with scepticism, positivism, and pragmatism. The affirmations of religion are not merely subjective. As F. H. Bradley, no champion of orthodoxy, says:

> There is nothing more real than what comes in religion. To compare facts such as these to what is given to us in outward existence would be to trifle with the subject. The man who demands a reality more solid than that of the religious consciousness seeks he does not know what.

How does this differ from what Catholic theologians condemn as "ontologism," the theory that we all have a direct and infallible assurance of God's existence, the theory ascribed to Jacobi? It differs in this way. Our knowledge of the Good, the True, and the Beautiful is not given us to start with. It must be won by hard discipline. If we live as we ought, we shall see things as they are, and if we see things as they are, we shall live as we ought. The two grow together, and act upon each other.

Kant acknowledged the absolute nature of the moral law, but he did not put truth and beauty in the same position. We ought to recognise that the devoted pursuit of science and art is no less the service of God than the life of moral duty.

I have mentioned the three attributes of God which he has revealed to us as parts of ultimate reality. But they are far from constituting a complete revelation. There are three problems on which philosophers have exercised themselves for thousands of years, and which some of the greatest have owned themselves unable to solve. These three are Time, Personality, and Evil.

Space and Time seem to be only the warp and woof of the canvas on which we draw our pictures of things and happenings. They are nothing in themselves, unless Time is confused with our awareness of Time or with events in Time, or packed with values which do not belong to it. But the Renaissance, while dimming belief in a future life, gave rise to a secularised apocalyptism which completely captured the lay religion of the nineteenth century. Religion for Croce and Gentile is through and through historical; Bergson divinises Time, and in so doing takes *la durée* out of the Time process. A grotesque belief in a cosmic law of progress, an automatic movement towards perfection, inspired rhapsodical paeans even in real men of science. Fourier looks forward to a time when tigers and sharks will be tame and amiable creatures; Winwood Reade to a time when "population will mightily increase, and the earth will be a garden." "Man's progress towards a higher state," in Herschel's opinion, "need never fear a check, but must continue till the very last existence of history." That this is pure superstition and wishful thinking will be denied by few after the terrible events which we have witnessed in our time. We may wonder that this delirious optimism could flourish at a time when the Second Law of Thermodynamics, which the French call the principle of Carnot, was known and accepted. If the universe is running down like a clock, the ultimate doom of all earthly hopes has been pronounced. Some have seen that if the clock is running down, it must have been wound up, and have argued that whatever power wound it up once may presumably wind it up again. A process like this must have started "with a bang," as Eddington says, and this he cannot believe. A recent book on astrophysics accepts the idea of continuous "creation out of nothing," which side-tracks entropy altogether. If scientists can believe this, it is not for theologians to object. But the idea of a cosmic law of progress is, as Bradley says, "nonsense, unmeaning or blasphemous."

For the ancients Time was the enemy, not the friend; or rather they believed that history is a vast pulsation, in which they had happened on a backward period. But their philosophers spoke of an attraction which the higher everywhere exercises upon the lower. It is difficult to see signs of this except in the inner life of man. But for them all life was a return journey to its source in a higher sphere. In modern thought the idea of a *nisus*, something like Bergson's *élan vital*, has been and still is popular. Evolution is introduced into the idea of God, and God is thereby entangled in the cosmic process. William James thinks that God may draw vital strength and increase of being from our fidelity. Bergson's life-force and the emerging Deity of Alexander and Lloyd Morgan are, as Radhakrishnan says, finite and self-concatenating Gods. Indian thought has never fallen into this error, for error it is. A God entangled with the world must share its fate, and apart from miracle, for which there is no room in this philosophy, he must pass, together with his creation, into eternal death, "lost to time and use and name and fame." But our author does believe in a *nisus*, and in human perfectibility. Rejecting, as he is right in doing, the horrible doctrine of everlasting torment, he thinks that in course of time every soul must win eternal salvation. But does he not here confound eternal life with never-ending duration? Rebirth may give souls opportunities of amendment which they could not have except by living again within the time-series; but is there any evidence of moral progress in the later generations over the older? There is not the slightest evidence for human perfectibility, and, at a time of inevitable disillusion like the present, it only injures the cause of religion to associate it with a doctrine which the Catholics not unjustly call the last great Western heresy.

But the relation of Time, "the moving image of eternity," to the unchanging reality of its prototype remains and probably must remain a mystery. Medieval thinkers interpolated an intermediary which they called *acuum*, to soften the friction between the two ideas. The antinomy is not solved. Had Time a beginning? Then what was there before Time was created? Had it no beginning? How can we measure infinite duration? But of one thing I am convinced. The idea of a single unitary purpose in the cosmos is untenable. What connexion can there be between the history and fate of two worlds separated from each other by a million light years of space and a thousand million years of time? What we see is an infinite number of finite purposes, each having a beginning, middle and end. The end reached, they do not pass out of existence; "all that is at all lasts ever past recall," says Robert Browning; "nothing that really is can ever perish," says Plotinus; *non est potentia ad non esse,* says St. Thomas Aquinas. They take their place in the eternal order. An infinite purpose is eternally frustrate, and there is no evidence that anything catastrophic will happen "at the end of Time."

Physicists and astronomers give the universe a very long lease of life. But it is by no means certain that our species will rule this planet till the end. Shall we not have hydrogen bombs, and worse, to exterminate each other? A million years hence one of the next lords of creation may write about us: "Our theologians are fond of pointing to the extinction of this noxious species as a strong argument for the providencial government of the world."

The second problem, that of personality, is very difficult, but we know in what direction to look for an understanding of it. Pindar's "find out and become what you are," is a great saying. What is the real self? We speak of body, soul, and spirit. This is St. Paul's psychology; it is also the psychology of the Platonists. The Platonic *Nous* is really the same as St. Paul's *Pneuma;* the identification was made by some of the Greek patristic writers. The Indian *Ātman* is another name for what we call Spirit. Of the three, body, soul, and spirit, nobody would identify the self with body, and we are not yet spirit. Spirit is, we may say, superpersonal. "We are all made to drink into one spirit," St. Paul says. The soul has affinities both with what is above and with what is below itself. The religious life is, or should be, a spiritualisation of soul. There is an "old man," St. Paul says, which we must put off and reject; there is a "new man," which we must strive to put on. This is common ground with Christian Platonism and Indian thought; which have very much in common. It is amusing, but intelligible, that some Indians have wished to claim Pythagoras, Plato's master, as one of themselves. "Pythagoras"—why, the name is obviously *Pitta-guru*, "father-teacher." But when we ask, what is the self in which we hope to share eternal life, the answer is not easy. The lower self we do not wish to drag along with us; the higher self is not yet ours. If we could win it, is the spiritual life a Leibnizian monad, or must we think of a universal self, all members one of another? Is personal distinctness, though not separation, preserved in the spiritual world? The Platonists say yes; the Indians, as far as I know, are less in agreement.

Radhakrishnan gives importance to rebirth; the incorrect term metempsychosis is I think first used by Proclus. This doctrine has had a long history. It was held by some of the greatest thinkers, such as Plato, Origen, Plotinus, Goethe, Schopenhauer, and lately by the Cambridge philosopher McTaggart. There is much to be said for it. The germ-plasm is potentially immortal. Inherited memory, so-called instinct, is common in animals, and in man. Death may be only a recurring rhythm in the history of the individual. If eternal life is dynamic and not static, it is difficult to see how changes can take place except in the time series.

Many thinkers cannot believe in a life which has a beginning and no end. They agree with the Bhagavadgītā (E. Arnold's translation):—

Never the spirit was born; the spirit shall cease to be never;
　　Never the time it was not; end and beginning are dreams.
Birthless and deathless and changeless the spirit abideth for ever;
　　Death cannot touch it at all, dead though the house of it seems.

The Eastern doctrine of Karma was, I think, originally one of continuity, not of retribution. But the desire to find justice in the scheme of things is almost universal. Usually, in the East as in popular Platonism and Christianity, retribution is rather coarsely pictured. The whole subject of future reward and punishment is the least favourable part of historical religion. Radhakrishnan stresses continuity, not compensation. The consequence of being a bad man is to become a worse man, not to be reborn as a pig or to be roasted in an oven. But what is inherited is not only the bare form of identity, but its liabilities, and, as we have seen, Radhakrishnan believes in gradual purification by suffering.

It is not easy to believe that rebirth is literally true. There is real difference, as well as inheritance, in every new-born human being. But the doctrine symbolises a truth which should not be neglected.

No one has done more than Radhakrishnan to interpret East and West to each other. The two are drawing nearer together. One thing which we have to learn is that God does not mind whether he is called Dieu or Allah or Brahma, and that he has probably forgiven the Russians for calling him Bug.

W. R. INGE

BRIGHTWELL MANOR, WALLINGFORD
BERKSHIRE, ENGLAND

7

A. N. Marlow

SPIRITUAL RELIGION AND THE PHILOSOPHY OF RADHAKRISHNAN

7

SPIRITUAL RELIGION AND THE
PHILOSOPHY OF RADHAKRISHNAN

IN THE dreadful ordeal through which civilisation is passing men turn this way and that, searching with growing bewilderment for a sure resting-place for the spirit, a source of courage and comfort that will not fail. Some try to discover a plan in the world about them, and are met by the profoundest and most spiritual of Western philosophers with the statement that "no ethics can be won from knowledge of the universe" [1] and that we must resign ourselves to eternal ignorance; many turn to Christianity and are baffled by the contrast between the simplicity and inwardness of the words of Jesus and the pharisaism and complexity of much church organisation; many more attempt the dreary task of living divorced from all spiritual life, immersed in the outward and material, until the desert barrenness of such an existence dries up all feeling but despair and fear, for Peisistratus' words in the *Odyssey* are the simple truth, Παντες δε θεων χατεουσ' ανθρωποι,[2] "all men have need of the gods," or, as we should say, of religion.

To us in the West Radhakrishnan brings 'the refreshment that comes from another order of mind.' He offers to us in words which glow with colour and yet are suffused with a radiant gentleness a reinterpretation of the religion of spirit that seeks the deep truths of the universe within the individual soul. Deeply learned in the intricacies of the Hindu speculative systems, himself a follower of the Advaita Vedānta of Śaṁkara, much influenced in early life by Tagore, a friend and interpreter of Gandhi, and equally at home in the literature of Western thought, his outlook is catholic and his philosophy universal. Indeed it is significant that the Reverence for Life which for Schweitzer is the key to all philosophy is nearer to Hindu thought than any European system has ever been.

It is India's peculiar greatness that in her thought philosophy and religion were one and that both began at the very beginning,

[1] A. Schweitzer, *Indian Thought and its Development*, 12.
[2] *Od.*, 3, 48.

335

with the human consciousness, and prescribed continuous though not frantic discipline for the mind and even for the body. In the introduction to his monumental work on Indian Philosophy Radhakrishnan quotes with approval the conditions demanded by Śaṁkara in all who would devote themselves to philosophy. "The philosopher," he says,

is a naturalist who should follow the movement of things without exaggerating the good or belittling the evil on behalf of some prejudice of his. He must stand outside of life and look on it. . . . Only then can he stake his all on clear thinking and honest judgment and develop an impersonal cosmic outlook with devotedness to fact.

The student is enjoined to acquire tranquillity, self-restraint, renunciation, patience, peace of mind and faith. Only a trained mind which utterly controls the body can meditate and inquire endlessly so long as life remains, never for a moment losing sight of the object, never for a moment letting it be obscured by any terrestrial temptation. . . . So is he required to undergo hard discipline, spurn pleasure, suffer sorrow and contempt.[3]

Again and again in pursuing the history of Indian philosophy Radhakrishnan brings us back to these primary things. Of the Upaniṣads he writes,

The mind of a man who does not know his own self goes hither and thither like the water pouring down the crags in every direction. But when his mind is purified, he becomes one with the great ocean of life which dwells behind all mortal forms. The outward mind, if allowed free scope, gets dispersed in the desert sands. The seeker must draw it inward, hold it still to obtain the treasure within . . . only then do we become conscious of the deep peace of the eternal.[4]

The lesson of the Bhagavadgītā is the same:

What hides the truth from our vision is not merely the fault of intellect, but also the passion of selfishness. Ajñāna is not intellectual error, but spiritual blindness. To remove it we must cleanse the soul of the defilement of the body and the senses, and kindle the spiritual vision which looks at things from a new angle. The fire of passion and the tumult of desire must be suppressed. The mind, inconstant and unstable, must be steadied into an unruffled lake, that it might mirror the wisdom from above. Buddhi, or the power of understanding and discrimination, needs to be trained. The way in which this power operates depends on our past habits. We should so train it as to bring it into agreement with the spiritual view of the universe.[5]

[3] Ind P, I, 45.   [4] Ibid., I, 262.   [5] Ibid., I, 556.

This is in fact the Yogic basis of all the orthodox systems of Hindu philosophy, and Radhakrishnan adopts it in essentials as the necessary foundation for all progress in the spiritual life. Speaking of the general characteristics of the six Hindu systems, he says,

All the systems have for their ideal complete mental poise and freedom from the discords and uncertainties, sorrows and sufferings of life, "a repose that ever is the same," which no doubts disturb and no rebirths break into. . . . Our life is but a step on a road, the direction and goal of which are lost in the infinite. The development of the soul is a continuous progress though it is broken into stages by the recurring baptism of death.

Philosophy carries us to the gates of the promised land, but cannot let us in; for that, insight or realisation is necessary. We are like children stranded in the darkness of saṁsāra, with no idea of our true nature, and inclined to imagine fears and to cling to hopes in the gloom that surrounds us. Hence arises the need for light, which will free us from the dominion of passions and show us the real, which we unwittingly are, and the unreal in which we ignorantly live.[6]

This is not to say that Radhakrishnan thinks spiritual insight impossible without recourse to a whole programme of physical exercises; it is rather that he preserves for us and advocates with all his eloquence the principle behind Yoga, namely, that we should practise withdrawal of the spirit and discipline our thoughts to quietness, much in the spirit of Rabindranath Tagore, who says,

Life of my life, I shall ever try to keep my body pure, knowing that thy living touch is upon all my limbs. I shall ever try to keep all untruths out of my thoughts, knowing that thou art that truth which has kindled the light of reason in my mind. I shall ever try to drive all evils away from my heart and keep my love in flower, knowing that thou hast thy seat in the inmost shrine of my heart. And it shall be my endeavour to reveal thee in my actions, knowing it is thy strength gives me strength to act.[7]

This withdrawal of the soul is equally possible, and equally necessary, to the workman and to the scholar. When it is practised we find the immense riches of our inner consciousness. The Hindus long ago anticipated modern psychologists in their knowledge of the subliminal self.

The ālaya is sometimes the actual self, developing and ever growing. It receives impressions and develops the germs deposited in it by karma,

<hr />

6 *Ibid.*, II, 26.   7 *Gitanjali*, 4.

or experience, and is continually active. It is not merely the superficial self, but the great storehouse of consciousness which the yogins find out by meditation. Through meditation and other practices of self-examination, we realise that our waking and superficial consciousness is a fragment of a wider whole. Every individual has in him this vast whole of consciousness, this great tank, of the contents of which the conscious self is not fully aware.[8]

Radhakrishnan, along with Śaṁkara and Rāmānuja and, going back still further, with all the great thinkers of ancient India, would endorse the view of modern medical science that "no tissue is completely removed from the influence of spirit." Truth lies at a level deeper than the intellect, and can be reached only by a process of brooding. Mere thinking will not carry us far; for it is not knowledge but faith which is power, and "even untruths work when we believe in them, though they cannot work long." In a lecture on "Comparative Religion," delivered at Oxford in 1929, Radhakrishnan emphasises his belief in the efficacy of this intuitional thinking:

Brooding is thinking with one's whole mind and one's whole body. It is integral thinking. It is making one's whole organism, sense and sensibility, mind and understanding, thrill with the idea. There is no function or organ of the body which is beyond the influence of the mind or of the soul. Man is one psyche, one whole, of which body, mind and spirit are aspects. . . . We must allow the idea framed by reason to sink into the subsoil of man's life, and leaven the whole of his nature, conscious and unconscious. The word, the thought, must become flesh. Only such an alteration of the whole psychology of man, such a transformation of his whole being, such integral understanding, is creative in character. Creation is man's lonely attempt to know his own strange and secret soul and its real vocation.[9]

According to Radhakrishnan the main cause of man's unhappiness is an excess of intellectuality. To revere the intellect to the exclusion of the spirit is a form of avidyā or ignorance which to the Hindus as to Socrates was the beginning of sin.

Our anxieties are bound up with our intellectuality, whose emergence at the human level causes a fissure or cleavage in our life. The break in the normal and natural order of things in human life is directly traceable to man's intellectuality, the way in which he knows himself and distinguishes himself from others. *Firstly,* he thinks and imagines an uncertain future which rouses his hopes and fears. The rest of nature goes on in absolute tranquility. But man becomes aware of the

8 Ind P, I, 629.   9 EWR, 81f.

inevitability of death. He worries himself about ways and means by which he can overcome death and gain life eternal. His cry is, Who shall save me from the body of this death? Though he is born of the cosmic process he finds himself at enmity with it. Nature, which is his parent, is imagined to be a threat to his existence. An overmastering fear thwarts his life, distorts his reason, and strangles his impulse. *Secondly*, man's naïve at-oneness with the living universe, his essential innocence or sense of fellow-feeling is lost. He does not submit willingly to a rational organisation of society. He puts his individual preference above social welfare. He looks upon himself as something lonely, final and absolute, and every other man as his potential enemy. He becomes an acquisitive soul, adopting a defensive attitude against society. *Thirdly*, the knowledge of death and the knowledge of isolation breed inner division. Man falls into fragmentariness. He becomes a divided, riven being, tormented by doubt, fear and suffering. His identity splits, his nucleus collapses, his naïveté perishes. He is no more a free soul. He seeks for support outside to escape from freezing fear and isolation. He clings to nature, to his neighbours, to anything. Frightened of life, he huddles together with others.[10]

To recover this inner poise is the aim of religion: and it is to be sought not by blotting out all inwardness and trying to live as a member of a herd, but by delving still farther within; for all the life of eternal spirit blossoms forth in the individual soul.

Tasting nothing, comprehending nothing in particular, holding itself in emptiness, the soul finds itself as having all. A lightning flash, a sudden flame of incandescence, throws a momentary but eternal gleam on life in time. A strange quietness enters the soul; a great peace invades its being. The vision, the spark, the supreme moment of unification or realization, sets the whole being ablaze with perfect purpose. The supreme awareness, the intimately felt presence, brings with it a rapture beyond joy, a knowledge beyond reason, a sensation more intense than that of life itself, infinite in peace and harmony. When it occurs our rigidity breaks, we flow again, and are aware, as at no other time, of a continuity in ourselves and know more than the little section of it that is our life in this world. When we find the real in our own heart, we feel exalted and humbled. The memory of the eternal-illumination has enduring effects and calls for renewal.[11]

This inward rapture is the primary fact of all religious consciousness, and is expressed by mystics of all times and places. Augustine speaks of it when he stood with his mother at a window in Ostia, when all outward things were hushed to stillness and their very selves surmounted all self-consciousness in awareness of the imme-

[10] ER, 43f.   [11] ER, 50.

diacy of God.[12] Plato gives it typically Greek expression in the *Republic:*

When a man's pulse is healthy and temperate, and when before going to sleep he has awakened his rational powers, and fed them on noble thoughts and inquiries, collecting himself in meditation; after having first indulged his appetites neither too much nor too little, but just enough to lay them to sleep, and prevent them and their enjoyments and pains from interfering with the higher principle . . . when again he has allayed the passionate element, if he has a quarrel against any: when, after pacifying the two irrational principles, he rouses up the third which is reason before he takes his rest, then he attains truth most nearly, and is least likely to be the sport of fantastic and lawless visions.[13]

Thomas à Kempis reminds us, in his three stages of the mystic's ascent to God, of the stages of attainment in the Yoga system, and the words in which he describes the inward bliss of union with the spirit of Christ are very like those used by Hindu mystics in their attainment of union with the Brahman:

Venture onward, deep down into a crypt, you will find the altar, and its sacred ever-burning lamp. All His glory lies within, where Christ often comes and gives you His consoling presence—sweet the talk, the intimacy passing wonderful. Room, then, for Christ, our peace, our health, who opens the seal of the divine mysteries, having built a private chapel in the soul.[14]

The closing lines of Dante's *Paradiso* are an expression of the same bliss; and temperaments as far apart as those of George William Russell ('A.E.') and the Quaker John Woolman have the same testimony to give.

Yet there is in Radhakrishnan none of the stringency and hardness of the saints nor of the revolting self-mortification that we find in Western mystics such as Henry Suso, Ruysbroeck and St. John of the Cross. Much mediaeval devotional writing is characterized by "sweating and whining about one's condition," weighted with an intolerable sense of sin: salvation is only to be attained after extreme spiritual as well as physical agonies; the outside world is not even noticed or is regarded with hatred as when St. Bernard covered his eyes that they might not behold the beauty of Swiss lakes. Of course, both Buddhism and Hinduism provide us with mendicant ascetics whose antics are comic in their grotesque

---

[12] *Confessions*, IX, viii.   [13] *Republic*, IV, 371f.
[14] *Imitatio Christi*, II, i (tr. Canon Liddon).

pathos: who walked about on all fours or barked like dogs (had the cynic Diogenes come into contact with them?) or drank urine or never sat down; but in their case the bodily mortification is regarded as a piece of preparatory ritual, efficacious in itself and compelling the hoped-for spiritual bliss to come in its train. In the West the mortification of the body is an outward sign of an inward spiritual writhing, an agony of self-abasement wholly unnatural in its excess; as though the soul were torturing itself as well as the body. The utmost that Radhakrishnan, to judge from his writings, would admit is what Tauler called "an inward disconnection and distance of the soul from all things." [15]

The religion of spirit which Radhakrishnan believes to be the ultimate faith of mankind is hard to define; but it has its roots far in the past, in the ecstasy of union with the Brahman experienced by the Brahmin priests in the beginnings of Indian history. This ecstasy, induced as it was sometimes by the drinking of *soma* and sometimes by self-hypnotism, was at first essentially a physical experience, a feeling of being exalted above the universe, and has never lost the characteristics of such a trance-like state. It has given rise to the sense of inner power, the feeling that the Absolute Spirit is in each individual consciousness, and conversely that it is possible to overleap the bounds of the ego and achieve a larger, more wondrous experience of union with the Absolute, a sense of being greater than this mortal body. "I am large," said Walt Whitman, "I contain multitudes." Sometimes this experience of union is felt as a submergence of the self and at others as an enlargement and enhancement of the self, and it is even seen to be both together. Thus it has eluded logical statement; it lies behind the austere brooding of Śaṁkara with his doctrine of *māyā;* it finds expression in many a passage of the Upaniṣads concerning the World Spirit: "That verily from which these beings originate, by which they live, to which departing they return again—endeavour to understand that—that is the Brahman." [16] "The Soul of created beings is a unity, only divided between creature and creature; unity and plurality at the same time, like the moon mirrored in many waters." [17] "The Brahman serves as a dwelling for all living things and dwells in all living things." [18] "This is the truth; as from a bright fire come thousands of sparks like itself, so from the Unchanging come all kinds of living beings and return to it again." [19]

---

[15] *Sermon XXV for St. Stephen's Day*, tr. C. Winkworth.
[16] Taittirīya Upaniṣad, iii, 1.   [17] Brahmabind Upaniṣad, xii.   [18] *Ibid.*, xxii.
[19] Mundaka Upaniṣad, ii, 1.

"Who sees himself in all beings and all beings in himself, enters into the highest Brahman without any other reason." [20] "The highest Brahman, the soul of all, the great mainstay of the universe, more subtle than the subtle, the eternal Being, that art thou, that thou art (*Tat tvam asi*)." [21]

This is the uncompromising monism of the early Brahmanic religion, standing above and apart from ethics; and it is too deeply rooted in Indian thinking for Radhakrishnan's interpretation of the religion of spirit to have escaped its influence. Yet from the earliest times popular Hinduism had filled the void in Brahmanic ethics by a doctrine of *bhakti* or devotion to the infinite Being, who became a person and was identified variously as Indra, Mitra, Varuna, Agni or another god of the Hindu pantheon. In the Bhagvadgītā this devotion to God expresses itself in activity and is praised equally with the older ideal of withdrawal from the world. From Rāmānuja to Tagore, Indian thinkers have given to the devotion of activity an increasingly predominant place, and even Śaṁkara is constrained to admit that pious worship of the Brahman imagined as God has a place subordinate to the ideal of union with the Brahman through perfect knowledge. With Rabindranath Tagore this activity of *bhakti* has almost completely ousted the more ancient ideal of union through withdrawal, though, true to the universal Hindu tradition, he attempts to find it in the Upaniṣads.

Leave this chanting and singing and telling of beads! Whom dost thou worship in this lonely dark corner of a temple with doors all shut? Open thine eyes and see thy God is not before thee!

He is there where the tiller is tilling the hard ground and where the pathmaker is breaking stones. He is with them in sun and shower, and his garment is covered with dust. Put off thy holy mantle and even like him come down on the dusty soil!

Deliverance? Where is this deliverance to be found? Our master himself has joyfully taken upon him the bonds of creation; he is bound with us all for ever.

Come out of thy meditations and leave aside thy flowers and incense! What harm is there if thy clothes become tattered and stained? Meet him and stand by him in toil and sweat of thy brow.[22]

For Tagore the whole world is a manifestation of benevolent spirit, where evil is considered as error and is destined to be swallowed up in good. For Tagore every action in which man steps

---

[20] Kaivalya Upaniṣad.   [21] Kaivalya Upaniṣad, vi.   [22] *Gitanjali,* 11.

out of the narrow bounds of the *ego* helps to realise the supreme purpose of the world. This is the recurring theme of *Sādhanā,* his most considerable attempt to expound his personal philosophy. We should aim at so immersing ourselves in the life of the world around us that we experience a feeling of breadth, of expansion and at-oneness. First, of course, we must so withdraw into ourselves that we experience the truth of this Brahmanic mysticism, and then we must live our lives in the knowledge that a universal spirit is working through us and attempting to fulfil its purpose in every individual striving for an ampler scope and environment.

Radhakrishnan was strongly influenced by Tagore, and, in his first major work, *The Philosophy of Rabindranath Tagore,* published in 1918, we find many an expression of this religion of spirit, in language glowing with colour, because the writer was carried away by the beauty and charm of the poetry and prose with which he is dealing. Like the old commentators, Radhakrishnan is led to express his own views merely by way of expounding the writings with which he deals. Like Tagore he traces the religion of spirit to the life in the forest led by primitive Indians, which gave them a sense of oneness with nature, so that they never felt, as did Western philosophers, the opposition between self and not-self. On this view the raptures of Thoreau are but continuing what the ancient Indians began. "If we adopt the right attitude to nature, we feel the pulse of spirit throbbing through it. A true seer sees in natural facts spiritual significance. The poetic temper hears the voice of spirit crying aloud in nature." [23]

God has called the world of māyā into being through pure creative joy, in order to find himself by creating. Joy has created separation in order to realise union through obstacles. "This self-sundering of the whole in which the world is contained is but the expression of his joy and the law of the universe." [24] This sense of union with the universal spirit can only be attained by intuition, and not by intellect—this is a theme to which Radhakrishnan will return again and again: like Tagore he has the deepest distrust of the intellectual systems of the West, though he can claim to know much more about them, being a professor of philosophy. Again, the body is not a sign and symbol of division from God. "For him man is bound up with nature; the human spirit is wedded to the material organism. Contact with the body, instead of being a tainting of the purity of the soul, is just the condition necessary for fulfilling its nature." [25] And the fulfilling of the soul's nature is to be

[23] PRT, 18f.   [24] *Ibid.,* 30.   [25] *Ibid.,* 68.

found in renunciation of the self for the more-than-self, in losing the isolation of selfhood. It is here that Radhakrishnan, like Tagore and indeed like Rāmānuja and the authors of the Bhagavadgītā, finds an ethical content for the religion of union with the Brahman. It has been pointed out more than once—by Albert Schweitzer for example, in *Indian Thought and its Development*—that it is difficult to conceive how far human activity can be in union with the spirit of the universe. Monistic mysticism must for ever be content to leave the spirit of the universe an unfathomable secret, or import more or less arbitrary ethical schemes into its world-view. The doctrine of renunciation for the sake of larger experience does, however, arise out of this monistic mysticism; renunciation can be interpreted ethically and can extend to the ordinary intercourse of life. "Loyalty to God the highest universal is meaningless if it does not embody itself in work for man the finite particular. The one is not beyond the many but is in the many." [26]

In the third chapter of his book on Tagore, Radhakrishnan writes of the poet and the painter as engaged in the task of revealing the world spirit. "The function of the artist or the poet is to exalt the natural towards its destined spiritual perfection. The poet releases the spirit imprisoned in matter." [27] Tagore's whole message is summed up by Radhakrishnan thus:

His supreme spirit is not an abstract entity residing at a safe distance from the world, but is the concrete dynamic life at the centre of things, giving rise to the roar of the wind and the surge of the sea. It is the final truth of the cosmic dance of life and death. Rabindranath's is a wholeness of vision, which cannot tolerate absolute divisions between body and mind, matter and life, individual and society, community and nation, and empire and the world. Mystic experience the whole world over has this philosophy underlying it. Rabindranath's religious message is simple: Stick to religion, let religions go. Happiness is for those who realise this oneness and wholeness of spirit. . . . To realise this goal, it is not necessary that the traditional paths should be followed; for the path of devotion is trackless.[28]

For Radhakrishnan, from the earliest to the latest of his writings, this is the message of Hinduism. He is ready in his early works to discard the caste system, though in *Religion and Society,* published in 1942, he seems to be defending a modified form of it; for he elaborately explains its working and essential basis in human nature from a point of view resembling that of Socrates in Plato's

[26] *Ibid.,* 77.　　　　[27] *Ibid.,* 143.　　　　[28] *Ibid.,* 177.

Republic. He also follows Tagore in his aversion to the mechanics of Western civilisation.

Yet there were other strong influences upon him, probably fostered by his years of study at the Madras Christian College. Here he absorbed the spirit of the West as few Indian writers have ever done. This is most noticeable in his writings, which have a lucidity and a range wholly Western; he can write of religion and philosophy with the felicity and sanity of Gilbert Murray and drive home his points with exactly the right quotation from Bergson or Alexander or Bradley. From his earliest student days, he tells us,[29] he was interested in the practical bearing of philosophy on life. Here too he showed the influence of the West, and that is why the West listens to him as it listens to few Eastern philosophers.

Radhakrishnan's next work, *The Reign of Religion in Contemporary Philosophy,* published in 1920, was an attempt to evaluate the systems of Leibnitz, Ward, Bergson, Bertrand Russell, William James, Eucken, the Pragmatist school, and the new Idealists. These schools of thought have in common a more or less developed pluralism which at times bears a striking resemblance to the pluralistic systems of the Sāṁkhya and other Hindu schools. Radhakrishnan's aim is to show that all pluralistic systems, if thought out far enough, end in absolutism of the kind which the Upaniṣads sketch as being the ultimate truth of things and of which in the last chapter he gives us an admirable exposition.

The work proceeds dialectically, analysing and criticising the various systems before expounding that in which he himself believes. Scattered throughout are isolated judgments which foreshadow the faith, for such it can be called, professed in the last chapter, a faith in spirit as the source of all things. Here one may be pardoned for remarking a tendency to diffuseness and repetition in all Radhakrishnan's works. He writes of the religion of spirit with such an epigrammatic charm that one is beguiled into overlooking the fact that all has been said many times before. This tendency is no doubt due to the indefiniteness of the subject. As he himself says, "Religious souls have after all to employ the current philosophical jargon;"[30] and, although he repeats himself, his sentences glow with so luminous an insight that we accept them as meditations on a theme. Another point to beware in his criticisms of other philosophers is that, after a lucid exposition of a point of view, he passes on, in the same paragraph and without a break in the shape of a 'but,' to put down his own comments and criticisms,

[29] *Contemporary Indian Philosophy,* 257 (various authors).   [30] RR, 283.

so that the utmost care is always necessary to discern where the break comes. In the second volume of his work on *Indian Philosophy*, particularly in his criticisms of the Nyāya school, this characteristic is very marked. In *The Reign of Religion in Contemporary Philosophy* the expressions of personal faith throughout the work remind us rather of the author of the Fourth Gospel who makes Jesus develop his doctrine by repetitive discourses.

Of the pluralistic philosophers we feel that Bergson has the greatest appeal for Radhakrishnan, and it is in the chapter dealing with him that the religion of spirit is first set forth.

For in the historical evolution of the world first comes inert matter, then life, and so, whether Bergson calls matter the relaxation of spirit or the negative effect thereof, matter presupposes spirit. Only in matter, spirit has not come to itself. . . . Reality is one, though we can describe it as a struggle of two tendencies. . . . It is a current which we call upward when the creative spiritual tendency is conquering and downward when the non-creative tendency is conquering. . . . The relative grades of the objects are determined by the more or less of the creative or the spiritual tendency. The hierarchy of values is determined by the more or less of the spiritual nature. The universe from its beginnings in crude matter to its heights in human persons is struggling towards the attainment of the whole. The life tendency moves on, creating endless forms which advance in the direction of, and beyond, man. When man gives up his subordination to matter, then spirit comes back into its own. But in the universe this goal is never reached.[31]

Radhakrishnan, like Tagore, is an optimist. "As a matter of fact, belief in a cosmic spirit which is friendly to us is the verdict of the religious consciousness."[32] And belief in this, philosophically stated, leads to absolute monism. "We are led to it, whether we take our stand on the life and faith of the mystics or the certainties of the understanding."[33] It alone can aid us in life; for to Radhakrishnan as to Royce the Absolute is "the most pervasive and omnipresent and practical, as it is also the most inclusive of beings."[34] The purpose of philosophy is to bring out the innate reason of this view, not to abstract a two-dimensional system from reality and impose it on the intellect. "Philosophy has an essential function in the life of spirit, if it only rests on experience and develops on its basis."[35] "Spiritual life expresses itself in art, philosophy and religion, beauty, knowledge and perfection. None of these exhausts the fulness of it."[36] Religion if it be no more than

31 RR, 167f. 32 *Ibid.*, 283. 33 *Ibid.*, 283.
34 *Ibid.*, 289. 35 *Ibid.*, 300. 36 *Ibid.*, 303.

pious conduct or activism is no higher manifestation of it than knowledge, which to be true must be an act of the whole self. "He does not truly know who is not stirred to his very depths by the consciousness of the infinite in him." [37] Spiritual salvation is the end of man, but those are wrong who seek it in a break between nature and spirit, in a mortification or crushing of ordinary normal desires and the acquisition of spiritual grace from outside.

It is because we already possess the ideal of spiritual perfection we agree to those laws which serve its ends and repel all those hostile to it. If man possesses a sense of higher values, how can Eucken say that the higher spiritual life of man is newborn? It is there because human life is part of the universal life of spirit. . . . It is meaningless to argue that man is weak and finite by nature and cannot therefore by the unaided exercise of his natural capacity develop spiritual perfection. If he is really so completely lost, if he is essentially and unalterably sinful or "natural" in Eucken's sense, he cannot and would not think of God at all. No life of spirit would commend itself to such a being. . . . The pathway to salvation is not through sudden conversion but gradual growth. What is required is not a letting in of divine energy from outside, but only a development of the spiritual note he already possesses. This view of man as potential spirit and of salvation as the development of his spiritual side is satisfactory, but it is the view of absolutism; the view of man as merely natural and of perfection as involving a second birth is Eucken's, but it is unsatisfactory.[38]

In the final chapter of the book Radhakrishnan bases his own view of life on the passage in the Upaniṣads where Bhrigu asks his father Varuṇa the nature of reality, and rejects in turn the views of the Absolute as matter, life, consciousness, and intellect, finally resting in the view of it as Ānanda or the bliss of union with the infinite Spirit. For the Hindu reality includes all these things and each is striving to attain the level above it.

According to the Vedānta philosophy it is not correct to speak of a sudden revelation of spirit when we come to life, for even matter is spirit, though in its lowest mode of manifestation. When matter reaches a certain climax of development then life breaks out. Life is a later development or stage of the Real. The Real gradually progresses from one stage to another. . . . Life is not an extension of matter. It is something different in kind from matter. The evolution of the world is not a mere development, but is a development of the whole or the Real. Both matter and life fall within an all-developing spirit whose very nature is to push forward from one to another and thus reach full real-

37 *Ibid.*, 305f.   38 *Ibid.*, 310f.

isation through the very impulse of its own movement. The Vedantic
view does not involve the sundering of matter from life.[39]

The world-spirit gathers up all stages from the lowest to the highest, so that all arbitrary divisions which stop short of the mystic
experience and all attempts to sunder matter and spirit do wrong
to man's inner nature. Intuitional truth is higher than that of the
intellect, and in the state of Ānanda man becomes conscious that
there is but one Absolute within him and without. The Vedānta
becomes the Advaita Vedānta. This is the view of life expressed by
Radhakrishnan in 1920 and it is substantially his view today.

This infinite spirit, which though it transcends the self is yet
revealed at its fullest in the self, in that deep well of being that
remains in dreamless sleep when all distinction of subject and object vanishes and the immortal principle and substratum of Being
alone remains, is to Radhakrishnan the object of all faith and
worship, the source of all joy and the ground of all morality. At
times it is in danger of being conceived as very like the *nirvāna* of
Buddhism, and at others it resembles the *anima mundi* of the
Stoic, who conceived of God as the universal Reason pervading all
that is, the world-soul of which a divine spark is in gods and men
alike, the divine principle of subject limited by contexts of object;
for Radhakrishnan as for all the Stoics every soul is part of the
deity and must therefore be kept inviolate, not dishonoured by
unnatural passions and abnormal desires. For both there is a moving purpose, Φύσις, in the world, which shapes the acorn into the
oak, the child into the man. In the two volumes of his *Indian
Philosophy*, published in 1923 and 1926 respectively, all the great
schools of Hindu thought and the six Brahmanical systems are
examined with an undertone of criticism from the point of view of
their attitude to the problem of an Absolute Spirit. So great is
Radhakrishnan's imaginative sympathy with the various systems
that he almost reminds us of Vācaspati Misra, who "commented
on almost all the systems of Hindu thought, wrote on each, as if
he believed in its doctrines." But it is the Advaita Vedānta of
Śaṁkara which attracts him most, with its austere thinking and
its resolution of all reality into the one and undivided Brahman.
It is here that he finds the philosophical expression of the Absolute
which his intellect requires, and in his exposition of the other systems we find ourselves moving towards the system of Śaṁkara in
many an anticipatory comment. "To separate individuals from

[39] *Ibid.,* 416.

universals," he says for instance at the conclusion of a note on a small point of Nyāya logic, "is to miss the unity of the two in things," [40] or again, he quotes the Nyāya theory of comparison with a certain amount of sympathy: "If the theory of medicine propounded by the sages of old is tested and found true, then the science of individual freedom as expounded by them must also be true." [41] Or again: "The distinctness of souls is due to the earthly life in which they partake. The finite beings, though rooted in matter, strive to flower in spirit. The perfected souls live within the spirit's fire when the smoke of their bodies passes away." [42]

There is inevitable confusion here in the discussion of the Absolute God, a confusion inherent in all Hindu thinking and succinctly expressed by Surendranath Dasgupta:

No attempt is made anywhere in the Upaniṣads to show how from this one reality of a pure perceiving consciousness the diverse experiences which make up our psychological being can be explained; we are however sometimes told that this universe is only Brahman, or that this universe has sprung out of Brahman and would return back to it, or that this universe is a transformation or manifestation of the nature of Brahman, or that this universe has for its inner controller the Brahman who is of the nature of our inmost self; no attempt is made to explain by what operation the inmost self of man can be regarded as the source or cause of this manifold world. In understanding the nature of the self we are gradually pushed to a mystical conception of it, which is so subtle as to transcend the realms of thought; it cannot be grasped by the senses or by the cognitional modes of our experiences, it can only be realised through self-control, the cessation of all desires, and the meditation of the spiritual reality. . . . How the "many" of the world can arise out of one, the self, and in what sense the reality of the world can be regarded as spiritually grounded, remains a question which has never been explained in the Upaniṣads. [43]

This is precisely Radhakrishnan's difficulty. He posits of course a qualityless Absolute as a ground of all spiritual life, yet the life of the spirit can in practice never attain to union with it:

A "Personal God" has meaning only for the practical religious consciousness and not for the highest insight. To the finite individual blinded by the veils, the Absolute seems to be determinate and exclusive of himself. Bondage and redemption possess a meaning for the finite individual, whose consciousness is fettered and repressed by his lower nature. If a personal God exclusive of the individual were the

40 Ind P, II, 64, note 2.   41 Ind P, II, 104.   42 Ind P, II, 160.
43 S. Dasgupta, *Indian Idealism*, 49f.

highest, then mystic experiences would become unintelligible, and we should have to remain content with a finite God. God is no God if he is not the All; if he be the All, then religious experience is not the highest. If God's nature is perfect, it cannot be so, so long as man's imperfect nature stands over against it; if it is not perfect, then it is not the nature of God. There is thus a fundamental contradiction in religious experience, clearly indicating that it belongs to the province of avidyā.[44]

This Absolute is the object of the highest religious experience in which all sense of personal identity is lost; here Radhakrishnan would appreciate Gaudapada's statement in the Kārikās that he adored the man who by knowledge as wide as the sky realised that all appearances were like the vacuous sky; that he has known the mystic trance which is ineffable to Plotinus and Eckhart, who can only describe it by saying that he seemed to exchange his identity with that of God:—"*Got der ist dor um worden ein ander ich, uf daz ich würd ein ander er.*" [45]

Yet this ineffable mystery is for the few. In his Hibbert Lectures for 1929, printed as *An Idealist View of Life,* the most elaborate and reasoned statement of his personal faith, Radhakrishnan speaks of feeling for the Absolute God as the highest spiritual experience.

While the character of God as personal love meets certain religious needs, there are others which are not fulfilled by it. In the highest spiritual experience we have the sense of rest and fulfilment, of eternity and completeness. These needs provoked from the beginning of human reflection conceptions of the Absolute as pure and passionless being which transcends the restless turmoil of the cosmic life. If God is bound up with the world, subject to the category of time, if his work is limited by the freedom of man and the conditions of existence, however infinite he may be in the quality of his life, in power, knowledge and righteousness, he is but an expression of the Absolute. But man wants to know the truth of things in itself, in the beginning—nay, before time and before plurality, the one "breathing breathless" as the Ṛg Veda has it, the pure, alone and unmanifest, nothing and all things, that transcends any definite form of expression, and yet is the basis of all expression, the one in whom all is found and yet all is lost. The great problem of the philosophy of religion has been the reconciliation of the character of the Absolute as in a sense eternally complete with the character of God as a self-determining principle manifested in a temporal development which includes nature and man.[46]

Do we not then worship a personal God? And is this blankness of spiritual absorption into the infinite, a darkness of blinding

44 Ind P, II, 650f.
45 Jostes, *Meister Eckhart und seine Jünger,* No. 82, 97.   46 IVL, 342f.

light, the message of the Upaniṣads, or the natural culmination of the religion which consists in giving due recognition to everything in us, the religion which Radhakrishnan portrays so winsomely in the last chapter of *The Reign of Religion in Contemporary Philosophy*? The answer would seem to be that for him religion is the latter, with a striving in a few rare souls towards the attainment of the second; but he would be quite justified in answering that it is impossible to pigeon-hole an experience; when you have it you know it. Hinduism has always been notoriously tolerant of creeds, in fact has prided itself on this tolerance, and the moving way in which Radhakrishnan expounds Śaṁkara's twofold truth shows that he is in sympathy with it:

We cannot worship the Absolute whom no one hath seen or can see, who dwelleth in the light that no man can approach unto. The form-less (nirākāram) Absolute is conceived as formed (akaravat) for the purposes of worship. Worship of God is not a deliberate alliance with falsehood, since God is the form in which alone the Absolute can be pictured by the finite mind. The highest reality appears to the indi-vidual, who has not felt its oneness with his own nature, as possessing a number of perfections. The conception of a personal God is the fusion of the highest logical truth with the deepest religious conviction. This personal God is an object of genuine worship and reverence, and not a non-ethical deity indifferent to man's needs and fears. He is regarded as creator, governor and judge of the universe, possessing the qualities of power and justice, righteousness and mercy, omnipresence, omnipo-tence and omniscience. Holiness of character and moral beauty are prominent aspects of Śaṁkara's God. He is set over against the human soul, who stands to him in the relation of a beloved to a lover, a servant to a master, a son to a father, and a friend to a friend. . . . Religion for Śaṁkara is not doctrine or ceremony, but life and experience.[47]

In this tolerance of the worship of a personal God for those in their spiritual infancy Radhakrishnan is thoroughly and typically Hindu, and indeed in this respect Hinduism typifies much that is best in the ancient world. This defence of the conception of a personal God is in the spirit of Maximus of Tyre: "If a Greek is stirred to the remembrance of God by the art of Pheidias, an Egyptian by paying worship to animals, another man by a river, another by fire—I have no anger for their divergences; only let them know, let them love, let them remember." [48]

Radhakrishnan discusses the notorious tolerance of Hinduism

47 Ind P, II, 649.
48 Quoted by Gilbert Murray, *Five Stages of Greek Religion,* 77 note.

for all shades of belief, and the Upton lectures at Oxford in 1926, reprinted as *The Hindu View of Life,* are in the main an eloquent defence of Hinduism for this reason.

. . . Hinduism developed an attitude of comprehensive charity instead of a fanatic faith in an inflexible creed. It accepted the multiplicity of aboriginal gods and others which originated, most of them outside the Aryan tradition, and justified them all. It brought together into one whole all believers in God. Many sects professing many different beliefs live within the Hindu fold. . . .

Hinduism is wholly free from the strange obsession of the Semitic faiths that the acceptance of a particular religious metaphysic is necessary for salvation, and non-acceptance thereof is a heinous sin meriting eternal punishment in hell. Here and there outbursts of sectarian fanaticism are found recorded in the literature of the Hindus, which indicate the first effects of the conflicts of the different groups brought together into the one fold; but the main note of Hinduism is one of respect and goodwill for other creeds.[49]

A whole chapter of *Eastern Religions and Western Thought,* published in 1939 as Radhakrishnan's statement of his ideals and aspirations from the chair of Eastern Religions and Ethics at Oxford, traces the history of Hindu religious tolerance from the Harappa and Mohenjodaro civilizations to the present day. "Toleration," he says, "is the homage which the finite mind pays to the inexhaustibility of the infinite." [50] The Vedic and Upaniṣadic religions, Buddhism as represented by Aśoka, the popular religion of the great epics, even the Vedānta of Śaṁkara were conspicuous examples of tolerance in forms and ceremonies, and impressive examples are given of hospitality to Christians and Moslems which was not returned. Even Buddhism was killed in India by a fraternal embrace.

As a result of this tolerant attitude, Hinduism itself has become a mosaic of almost all the types and stages of religious aspiration and endeavour. It has adapted itself with infinite grace to every human need and it has not shrunk from the acceptance of every aspect of God conceived by man, and yet preserved its unity by interpreting the different historical forms as modes, emanations or aspects of the Supreme.[51]

This is not to say that Radhakrishnan is blind to the faults and failings of Hinduism. Indeed he tells us that it was these very faults and failings which urged him first to study its philosophy intensively. "I remember," he says,

[49] HVL, 37. [50] ER, 317. [51] *Ibid.,* 313.

the cold sense of reality, the depressing feeling of defeat that crept over me, as a causal relation between the anaemic Hindu religion and our political failure forced itself on my mind during those years. What is wrong with Hindu religion? How can we make it somewhat more relevant to the intellectual climate and social environment of our time? [52]

And he goes on to catalogue its shortcomings, the "tragic divergence between the exalted idea and the actual life," the timidity in following the ethics of *ahiṁsā* to their logical conclusion, the empty ceremony, the superstition, the degeneracy of the priesthood, the weakening of moral fibre. Elsewhere he writes, "After these many centuries, Hinduism, like the curate's egg, is good only in parts. It is admirable and abhorrent, saintly and savage, beautifully wise and dangerously silly, generous beyond measure and mean beyond all example." [53] Yet he is convinced that the heart of Hinduism, with its crude appanages discarded, is what the world needs. "While there is a good deal in Hindu religion and practice which merits just criticism, dark aspects of brutality, cruelty, violence, ignorance of nature, superstition and fear, in its essence the religion seemed to me to be quite sound." [54] The shell of error must be retained for the sake of the kernel of precious truth; it is vandalism, not to say folly, to lay hands on what has been patiently built up through so many centuries.

Hinduism requires every man to think steadily on the life's mystery until he reaches the highest revelation. While the lesser forms are tolerated in the interests of those who cannot suddenly transcend them, there is all through an insistence on the larger idea and the purer worship. . . . So while Hinduism hates the compulsory conscription of men into the house of truth, it insists on the development of one's intellectual conscience and sensibility to truth.[55]

And in the middle of the recent war, speaking from Calcutta in 1942, he has become more convinced than ever of India's mission.

Indian culture is not racially exclusive, but has affected men of all races. It is international in feeling and intention. As the typical religion of India, Hinduism represents this spirit, the spirit that has such extraordinary vitality as to survive political and social changes. From the beginning of recorded history, Hinduism has borne witness to the sacred flame of spirit which must remain for ever, even while dynasties crash and empires tumble into ruins. It alone can give our civilisation a soul, and men and women a principle to live by.[56]

[52] *Contemporary Indian Philosophy*, 258. [53] ER, 338.
[54] *Contemporary Indian Philosophy*, 258. [55] HVL, 49. [56] RS, 43.

It follows that all religions of authority are mere stages of error on the road to truth, halfway houses for those not equipped by nature or training to worship in spirit. In the early pages of *An Idealist View of Life* authoritarianism is severely censured, as is natural in an exponent of that religion which according to Oldenberg afforded "the most absolute liberty of conscience that has ever existed."

Every religion has its popes and crusades, idolatry and heresy-hunting. The cards and the game are the same, only the names are different. Men are attacked for affirming what men are attacked for denying. Religious piety seems to destroy all moral sanity and sensitive humanism. It is out to destroy other religions, not for the sake of social betterment or world peace, but because such an act is acceptable to one's own jealous god. The more fervent the worship the greater seems to be the tyranny of names. . . . The view that God has entrusted his exclusive revelation to any one prophet, Buddha, Christ, or Mohammad, expecting all others to borrow from him or else to suffer spiritual destitution, is by no means old-fashioned. Nothing is so hostile to religion as other religions. . . . The world would be a much more religious place if all the religions were removed from it.[57]

In *Eastern Religions and Western Thought* the same fact is stressed:

Even if life be aimless, man must pursue some dream. To deny him hope is to take away his interest in life. Religions exploit this need, this fundamental insufficiency of an all-pervading positivism, this primitive hunger for fellowship. The fugitive character of life makes man fondly hope that his life is not at an end with the death of the body, that it cannot be true that the suffering of the innocent meets with no reward and the triumph of the wicked with no requital. It must be that man does count. Religions attempt to satisfy this fundamental need of man by giving him a faith and a way of life, a creed and a community, and thus restore the broken relationship between him and the spiritual world above and the human world around. While the prophet founders of religions declare that the community is world-wide and make no distinctions between the Jew and the Gentile, the Greek and the barbarian, the traders in religion declare that the greatness of one's own creed and group is the end and coercion and violence are the ways to it. They develop group loyalties at the expense of world loyalty. Such a bellicose condition is the only one in which life becomes worth while for a larger number of people. There is not much to choose between these religions, which exalt belief, bigotry, and preservation of group loyalties and vested interests, and the older, cruder, primitive cults. The

57 IVL, 44f.

later, which are the more sophisticated, are the more dangerous, for they are constructions of intellect interfering with the natural relations of man.[58]

Here one notes the recurrent stress on the danger of intellectualism and the necessity for intuitive thinking which are the kernel of Radhakrishnan's message. The mellowness of expression reminds us constantly of Gilbert Murray, to whom it may not be fanciful to suppose Radhakrishnan to owe a considerable debt.

It is a sign of the times that authoritarianism is on the increase, both in religion and in those secular creeds which attract their followers with all the intolerance of a religion.

The spiritual genius who can think out a religion for himself is one in a million. The large majority are anxious to find a shrine safe and warm where they can kneel and be comforted. For them it is a question of either accepting some authority or going without religion altogether. It is catholicism or complete disillusion. The leaders enlarge on the beauty and richness of the worship, the antiquity and order of the tradition, the opportunity for influence and service which the historic church offers. If we are not to languish as spiritual nomads, we require a shelter, and the church which is majestically one in creed, ritual, discipline and language, a corporation in which racial and national barriers are obliterated, a kingdom without frontiers, attracts the large majority.[59]

Christianity is criticised strongly by Radhakrishnan, who writes of its shortcomings in a manner reminiscent of Lecky's *History of Rationalism*. He is inclined to agree with those Hellenists who regard it as an "unhappy interruption of human progress," [60] and reminds those who defend its superiority to race and creed that mediaeval universities were hotbeds of nationalism. The faults of historical Christianity are that it is too definite—"We cannot say that definiteness in conception makes for depth in religion"—and that it makes excessive demands on credulity.

For example, in Christendom theology is busy with such questions as, Are the Scriptures inspired? How shall we explain the divergences in the accounts of the life of Christ? How shall we reconcile the Biblical account of creation with modern science? Were the Old Testament prophecies fulfilled? Shall we believe in the New Testament miracles? Acute thinkers spend their time and energies in finding modern ideas in ancient texts or reading meanings into them which are not there. So long as the life of Jesus is regarded as a mere event in history which

58 ER, 39.   59 IVL, 78.   60 ER, 7f.

occurred nineteen hundred years ago there can be no understanding
of what that life should mean to us. A study of comparative religion
has broken down the barriers by which dogmatists seek to entrench
themselves and show that their own religion is unique.[61]

(The influence of Tylor, Frazer and Marett is patently discernible
in *East and West in Religion* and *Eastern Religions and Western
Thought,* in the attempt there made to find a common basis for all
religions by examining existing ones.) Again, Christo-centrism
turns many away. "For the orthodox Christian, the coming of the
Kingdom is catastrophic and not the peaceful outcome of an ever-
widening process of evolution, an intervention of God cutting
right *into* history and not springing *from* it."[62]

In the light of our present knowledge of man's history and the vastness
of the cosmos it seems anomalous, if not absurd, to imagine that the
earth or the human species or any historical individuals in it form the
centre of things. Our earth is parochial and our citizenship on it a triviality. Geocentrism in cosmology and anthropocentrism in philosophy
and Buddhocentrism or christocentrism in religion are on a par.[63]

Radhakrishnan also draws attention to the untrustworthy documents and to the destructive effect of Higher Criticism on certain
cherished beliefs, though he cannot mean to push this argument
far, as it recoils with tenfold effect on Hindu scriptures.

Christ's followers have used their dogmas and fixed institutions
in a manner destructive of spiritual life. Radhakrishnan would
echo with conviction A. E. Housman's remark that religion was
prized by mankind chiefly as an excuse for making other people
unhappy. "Religious men seem to have developed unduly the instinct for being unhappy. They seem to have a perverted ingenuity
for finding out new contents for sin." "Is it an accident," he asks
in a footnote, "that Hitler and Mussolini have been brought up in
Roman Catholic societies, where it is blasphemous to criticize infallible authority?"[64] And elsewhere he pours scorn on those who
"invoke the religion of Jesus for the programme of Moscow."[65]

The personality of Jesus himself is treated with scrupulous reverence in *Eastern Religions and Western Thought;*[66] but Radhakrishnan seems unable to make up his mind whether or not
Jesus' teaching was influenced by Buddhism. On the whole he is of
the opinion that there must have been some influence; he approves
the statement by the Bishop of Oxford in 1931 that the teaching

61 *Ibid.,* 59.   62 *Ibid.,* 74.   63 IVL, 27.
64 ER, 60 note.   65 IVL, 72.   66 ER, 163-187.

of Jesus was "an erratic block whose provenance—other than in his direct intuition of supernatural truth—must remain for ever unknown." He recounts the impressive list of resemblances in the stories told of Jesus and Buddha—the supernatural birth, the temptations, the miracles, the transfiguration, the sending forth of disciples, the condemnation of ceremonial and sacrifice, the triumphal entry into a great city, the parables, the exhortation to do good to one's enemies. He even hints, in a footnote, that Jesus may have travelled in the East in the hidden years before his baptism, but hastens to add that there is no trustworthy evidence of this.[67] It is undeniable that the conclusions of Pfleiderer and Winternitz, that the parallels between Buddhism and Christianity are too striking to be ignored, have much in their favour; but, as if realising that scholarship is by no means unanimous in this matter, he cautiously adds: "As for the resemblances, other causes than borrowing may be assigned. If religion is the natural outcome of the human mind, it would be strange if we did not find coincidences." [68] What Radhakrishnan is seeking, without being provocatively downright, to establish throughout these lectures is the probability of a continuing influence of the East upon the West in religion and particularly in Christianity, and the certainty that the core of the spiritual and ethical teaching of Christ is reproduced and even anticipated by Buddha and the Upaniṣads.

Authoritarianism, rampant in politics as well as in religion, is to Radhakrishnan the chief evil in the world today. The first chapter of *Religion and Society* is an examination of Marxism from this viewpoint, which often finds trenchant expression in other books also. In the Hibbert lectures of 1929 he had written of Communism as if it were really religious in a spiritual sense; but the later book is full of disillusion. Though it contains nothing strikingly new, yet it says with the author's characteristic insight what others have said with less compelling quietness, and repeats once more the plea for spirituality between man and man arising out of each man's possession of his own soul. The fact that Radhakrishnan is now Indian Ambassador in Moscow, that he has found favour there and that he has the courage of his convictions, is one of the greatest single influences for peace in the world today.

How are we to live out in the world this religion of spirit? Now that we are converted from nature to grace by our inward experience, how are we to be converted again from grace to nature? Schweitzer poses this question in his *Indian Thought and Its De-*

[67] ER, 165 note. [68] *Ibid.,* 184.

velopment, and Radhakrishnan thinks it necessary to devote a chapter of *Eastern Religions and Western Thought* to answering him. Schweitzer's whole aim in his book is to show that Indian thought has what Western thought lacks—a perfected monistic mysticism which has the courage to stand apart from ethics and to realise that ethics cannot be won from knowledge of the universe.

Every world-and-life view which is to satisfy thought is mysticism. It must seek to give to the existence of man such a meaning as will prevent him from being satisfied with being a part of the infinite existence in merely natural fashion, but will make him determine to belong to it in soul and spirit also, through an act of his consciousness.[69]

Yet union with the Absolute is not ethical but spiritual. "Of this deep distinction Indian thought has become conscious. With the most varied phrasing it repeats the proposition: 'Spirituality is not ethics.' . . . 'Mysticism is not a friend of ethics but a foe. It devours ethics.' " [70] The old Brahmin priests attained a state of intoxication by drinking soma, and by it felt themselves raised above the whole universe; thenceforth their whole aim was to experience in themselves the sovereignty of spirit over matter. Their philosophy strides majestically on, putting aside good and evil. The rapture which they felt is akin to the rapture men feel on beholding a lovely landscape or listening to music.

Spring sunshine, trees in flower, passing clouds, fields of waving corn provoke it. A will-to-live which announces itself in many forms in magnificent phenomena all around them, carries their own will-to-live along with it. Full of delight, they want to take part in the mighty symphony which they hear. They find the world beautiful. . . . But the transport passes. Horrid discords allow them once more to hear only noise, where they thought they perceived music. The beauty of nature is darkened by the suffering they discover everywhere within it.[71]

Moreover—and this is the most searching criticism to which the religion of spirit could be subjected—there is a danger that communion with Absolute Being may become meaningless, or degenerate into self-hypnotism.

But reality knows nothing about the individual being able to enter into connection with the totality of Being. As it knows of no Being except that which manifests itself in the existence of individual beings, so also it knows of no relations except those of one individual being to another. If mysticism, then, intends to be honest, there is nothing for

69 *Civilization and Ethics*, 234.   70 *Ibid.*, 235.   71 *Ibid.*, 212.

it to do but cast from it the usual abstractions, and to admit that it can do nothing rational with this imaginary essence of Being. The Absolute may be as meaningless to it as his fetish is to a converted negro.[72]

Radhakrishnan's answer is firstly that the experience authenticates itself—it is beyond logical definition and in spite of the gulf in logic between mysticism and ethics a course of conduct issues inevitably from the experience. One is so happy that one wishes for the happiness of all mankind and does one's utmost to promote it. Perhaps the commonest error of Western philosophers has been precisely this insistent attempt to find a logical ground for kindness to one's fellows and Schweitzer himself gives it up.

To be rapt is not to pass beyond oneself but to be intensely one's self, not to lose self-consciousness but to be greatly conscious. Man is not torn out of the setting of his ordinary earthly life. He still has a body and mind, though he knows them to be the instruments of his higher life. He does not exult in his own intelligence or seek for his own soul, for he has it no more. If he has gained a transcendent personality and an independence which nothing in this world can touch, it is because not he but the Super-spirit lives in him, making him illimitable.[73]

Mysticism is defended in one of those noble passages which occur so often in Radhakrishnan, which convey conviction by their lofty dignity and insight and in a way contain the whole of his doctrine, which cannot be expounded without repetition, since it is a statement of the same elusive truth in many ways:

Religion begins for us with an awareness that our life is not of ourselves alone. Religion as man's search for this greater self will not accept any creeds as final or any laws as perfect. It will be evolutionary, moving ever onward. The witness to this spiritual view is borne, not only by the great religious teachers and leaders of mankind, but by the ordinary man in the street, in whose inmost being the well of the spirit is set deep. In our normal experience events happen which imply the existence of a spiritual world. The fact of prayer or meditation, the impulse to seek and appeal to a power beyond our normal self, the moving sense of revelation which the sudden impact of beauty brings, the way in which decisive contacts with certain individuals bring meaning and coherence into our scattered lives, suggest that we are essentially spiritual. To know oneself is to know all we can know and all we need to know.[74]

The ethics to which this spiritual knowledge leads us are quite positive. They are the active counterpart of the negative *ahiṁsā*,

---

72 Schweitzer, *op. cit.*, 237f.   73 ER, 78.   74 *Ibid.*, 61.

not merely the avoidance of all injury but the doing of good. As Schweitzer says, "all ethics are pity," and the illumined soul must go out and enter imaginatively into the lives of others; so the ethic of renunciation for the sake of deeper life is predominant.

The individual strives to make God-control entire by throwing off all that is impure and selfish. All this means effort. Wisdom is not cheaply won. It is achieved through hard sacrifice and discipline, through the endurance of conflict and pain. It is the perfection of human living, the ceaseless straining of the human soul to pierce through the crushing body, the distracting intellect, the selfish will, and to apprehend the unsheathed spirit. It is intent living, the most fruitful act of man by which he tries to reach reality behind the restless stream of nature and his own feelings and desires.[75]

These spiritual communings are not only productive of active ethics but they are themselves the crown of the most strenuous moral effort.

Spiritual realization is not a miraculous solution of life's problems but a slow deposit of life's fulness, a fruit which grows on the tree of life when it is mature. The soul, in the state of ecstasy, enters the stream of life, is borne along in the flowing current of it, and finds its reality in the larger enveloping life. This life of spirit, where freedom from the sense of bodily or even mental limitations and emergence into a space of unlimited and infinite life are felt, is not the same as magical mysticism.[76]

"But intuition, though it includes the testimony of will and feeling, is never attained without strenuous intellectual effort." [77]

So too the religion of spirit is creative in the world of art. There is not the deplorable enmity between taste and goodness that has marred so much of Western evangelical religion. Radhakrishnan here draws much upon the philosophy of Tagore, and puts forward his own views largely as a commentary on those of the poet.[78] Since spirit has for them this inclusive psychological meaning of a consummate vital principle, all art as its product is spiritual in essence, and to the fully developed spiritual mind there is no such thing as bad taste—that is due to an admixture of the earthy element according to the traditional Hindu view of the elements in life.

In making spirit a creative principle Radhakrishnan once again shows how deeply he has been influenced by Tagore on the one hand and by the West on the other. To his contemporary Mahen-

---

[75] *Ibid.*, 96.   [76] *Ibid.*, 77.   [77] *Ibid.*, 63.   [78] PRT, ch. III.

dranath Sircar nothing is more plain than that spiritual life transcends all action, all qualities, all feelings even of mystic bliss. It is the transcendent silence beyond joy. This according to Sircar is the essence of the mysticism of the Upaniṣads.[79]

Radhakrishnan shows the influence of the West especially here. Though he regards Śaṁkara as the greatest Indian thinker, yet in this respect he is following Rāmānuja, whereas it is Sircar who is apparently nearer to the spirit of Śaṁkara. "What a man takes in by contemplation he must pour out in love," said Eckhart, and Radhakrishnan would welcome this as the most succinct statement possible of his religion. And yet, while his insistence is on action and though his own career has splendidly exemplified his beliefs, he remains I am sure a true Oriental at heart. His *Idealist View of Life* is noble and inspiring as a statement of Hindu views; but his treatment of Western philosophers and the problems of Western society is artificial, and, when he tells us that he owes his inspiration to Plato and Śaṁkara, we suspect that Plato's name is brought in with the aim of appealing to the West. Again, he is acutely alive to suffering, as his *Religion and Society* shows, but I fear his solution—the appeal to the spiritual in each man—is too simple. He told me that when he visited Manchester in 1929 to deliver the Hibbert Lectures he was approached at the station by a student— he was apparently alone and a little confused as well as burdened with luggage—who insisted on helping him. That trivial incident has remained vivid in his memory for more than twenty years, and as he recalled it he said to me, "One does not have to seek far to find beauty." This is the lofty, noble side of spiritual religion; but many will ask, "What of the darkness of the terrible streets?"

Here one steps out from books into life. This is a major criticism of such a religion as Radhakrishnan brings to us. Does it not tend to make light of sin and evil? In *Religion and Society* he seems to be defending the caste system, or at least showing how much good the system contained; but bearing in mind the amount of suffering in India as a result of this system, is this not going too far? Does it not imply a belief in *karma* and the inexorability of justice for one's deeds? Is there nothing in the Christian doctrine of personal salvation, and have the downtrodden millions in the world only their *karma* to blame that they have been born to such a lot? I know that Radhakrishnan has been outspoken and untiring in his championship of the poor and suffering; but I feel that this is an expression of his sensitive and lofty sympathies rather than a

[79] Sircar, *Hindu Mysticism*, passim.

necessary outcome of his beliefs. To him reincarnation on the human level only is an accepted doctrine; does this not show a tendency to compromise, to take what is good in a religion and leave what is bad? Can eclecticism ever be a driving force that will save the world? Is it not remarkable that the beginning, over a century ago, of active work for the poor in India coincided with the first full impact of Christianity?

Criticism could also be levelled at this form of religion on the ground of its lack of outline, of firm belief. A good deal of this criticism is unjustified, and with the unthinking Westerner a religion of spirit with its roots in Indian thought would be ignorantly classed with Theosophy or stigmatized as another Eastern fad—"the eternal quest of the indefinite in man," as Sircar says,[80] or "the idle flapping of our wings in the vacuum of the Absolute," [81] to use a phrase of Radhakrishnan's own. Yet, though this sort of criticism is unjust, it cannot be denied that the view of life which he expounds as being that of the Upaniṣads is almost pure pantheism.[82]

I could quote many a passage from Radhakrishnan that answers individual objections, but I persist in my view that on the whole such questions as I have raised are bound to occur to one trying to live by the religion of spirit.

A chapter of *Religion and Society* is devoted to war and nonviolence. Here again it is not easy to be certain of Radhakrishnan's final view. In this imperfect world we must be prepared to use force when justice demands it. Sayings from Buddha, the *Bhagavadgītā,* the laws of Manu and many other sources are adduced as evidence that the wrongdoer must be punished.

Non-violence as a mental state is different from non-resistance. It is absence of malice and hatred. Sometimes the spirit of love actually demands resistance to evil. We fight, but filled with inward peace. We must extirpate evil without becoming evil. If human welfare is the supreme good, peace and war are good only in so far as they minister to it. We cannot say that violence is evil in itself. The violence of the police aims at social peace. Its aim is restraint of lawlessness. . . . When its aim is human welfare, when it respects personality, then war is permissible.[83]

If Radhakrishnan is doing no more here than expound the Hindu view one may again remind him of Vācaspati and of "writing of

80 *Ibid.,* 25.   81 Ind P, I, 467.
82 RR, ch. XIII.   83 RS, 202f.

each system of thought as if one believed in it." But when he goes on to say,

We live in a society governed by certain laws, codes and customs which are not ideal, but have made compromises, which use armies, police and prisons. Even in such a society, we can live a life inspired by love to all men. While keeping the ideal before us and always striving towards it, the Hindu view recognises the relative justification of laws and institutions because of the hardness of men's hearts,[84]

one may be excused for thinking that this is his own view, too.

The Christian attitude to war, Radhakrishnan says in effect, is hampered by the contradiction in the words and actions of Jesus. Although the Sermon on the Mount is resolutely in favour of non-violence, yet he denounced the scribes and Pharisees, drove the money-changers from the temple, insisted that salvation was of the Jews, snubbed the Syro-Phoenician woman, and knew that he "came to bring not peace, but a sword." Christians, consequently, can point to sayings and deeds of their Master which seem to condone violent action, and they have not failed to take full advantage of this.

When Radhakrishnan comes to deal with the attitude of Gandhi he decides that whole-hearted non-violence is after all the only way to save even this imperfect world. He quotes long statements by Gandhi and an extract from Bertrand Russell's *War and Non-resistance* to attest the practicability of passive resistance (a method long dear to the Hindu spirit and precisely legislated for in the Laws of Manu); but even then he is not sure. "As a policy for a nation, non-violent non-co-operation is justifiable only if we are fairly certain that the nation is really prepared to act on such a policy."[85] *Ahiṁsā* remains a way of life for the individual who is willing to face martyrdom.

The attempt to fuse all religions into one has been made intermittently in India since the time of Akbar. It was the dream of Ram Mohan Roy, who wished to establish an institution where men of every creed could assemble for common prayer; it affected the work of Keshab Chandra Sen and Pratap Chandra Mazoomdar; it was the main theme of Tagore's *Sādhanā,* it inspired Aurobindo Ghose's *The Life Divine* and it is, as we have seen, the chief aim and motive of nearly all Radhakrishnan's published work, to proclaim that spirit is one and indivisible and that names, forms, and observances are local, and all effective merely as means to an end.

---

[84] *Ibid.,* 206. [85] *Ibid.,* 235.

On the whole these famous Hindus are more convincing in writing of things from a Hindu point of view and when describing with sincere warmth and richness their own spiritual *ascesis*. It is this warmth, richness, and sweetness of the inward experience which they describe more appealingly than any others; and it is their *ascesis* that remains their richest gift to the life of spirit. This discipline leads to a religious experience quite different from that of a devout believer in a credal religion or in a personal saviour; it is the quintessence of the wholeness of self, in which by a paradox the fulness of selfhood leads to a feeling of self-transcendence. It cannot be described or analysed; it can only be felt; but with milleniums of attempts at description of states of consciousness in their spiritual make-up the Hindus are more adept at it than we. One can sense the stiffness and artificiality with which Western analogies are brought in—although Eckhart and the pseudo-Dionysius and William Law use the same language at times as that of Indian mystics, there is a subtle difference resulting from the wholly different physical and intellectual and even economic background. In *Eastern Religions and Western Thought,* for example, the most eloquent and moving passages are those describing what is best in Hindu religion; the chapters expounding the history of gnosis in Greek and mediaeval Christianity are good, but they are part of a framework seemingly imposed on the book from without. It is to some extent the same with Radhakrishnan's other works, particularly with those delivered in the form of lectures to Western audiences. For this reason I think the two volumes on *Indian Philosophy* to be by far his greatest work. Here he shows himself an absolute master of the subtlest intricacies of logic and dialectic, while never losing a quiet glow of enthusiasm that suffuses the most arid speculations of the six systems with insight and feeling. There is often in a single footnote enough of both these qualities to sustain a whole chapter. I know of no single modern book so full of maturity of spiritual experience.

It seems that a religion of the kind that Radhakrishnan advocates is appearing increasingly the only possible life of the spirit for those to whom belief in a personal saviour is no longer tenable. It cannot escape notice how near this 'Nameless Faith' comes to Schweitzer's 'Reverence for Life,' which also recognises that no ethics are perceptible in the outward world as we perceive it and yet that the need for ethics is grounded in man's inmost being, whither alone the philosopher can turn and need turn for the basis of all his speculations. The reality of the inward experience leads by a paradox to the observance of the highest outward moral life; the gulf between monism and ethics is bridged in the soul. This view of spirit does, in the words of Gilbert Murray, describing the Stoic school,

build up a system of thought on which, both in good days and evil, a life can be lived which is not only saintly, but practically wise and human and beneficent. It does for practical purposes solve the problem of living, without despair and without grave, or at least without gross, illusion.[86]

But to be consistent and effective it must retain the inwardness and *ascesis* of Hinduism and resolutely discard the jumble of beliefs and customs that have grown out of it.

A. N. Marlow

Department of Classics
University of Manchester
England

[86] *Five Stages of Greek Religion*, pp. 100-1.

8

Lawrence Hyde

RADHAKRISHNAN'S CONTRIBUTION TO UNIVERSAL RELIGION

RADHAKRISHNAN'S CONTRIBUTION TO UNIVERSAL RELIGION

I

SIR SARVEPALLI RADHAKRISHNAN is widely acknowledged as the greatest living Indian philosopher. At the same time he has contributed more powerfully than perhaps any other Asiatic to the immensely important undertaking of creating a synthesis between Eastern and Western thought. It is entirely appropriate that he should have been appointed the first Professor of Eastern Religions and Ethics in the University of Oxford.

Before proceeding to consider his conception of universal religion I must say a word regarding the meaning to be attached to the term. Universality in this field has two aspects. It can mean a tolerant recognition of every form of religious belief and practice which brings man nearer to the Divine, together with the rejection of the claim that any one type of faith has an absolute and final value. But it can mean also the impulse to enrich one's own form of religion by incorporating within it as wide a range of creative elements as possible. Broadly speaking, we find that most apologists for universalism in the religious realm concern themselves almost exclusively with the first, and the more negative, of these two liberalizing tendencies. This is certainly true of Radhakrishnan, as it was also of that other eminent exponent of the *Philosophia Perennis,* the late Ananda K. Coomaraswamy.

The importance of the second aspect of catholicity must not, however, be neglected. It is possible to have a generous sympathy with those of other communions and yet lack true universality through leaving out important elements in the building of one's own spiritual edifice. It is questionable, for instance, whether any cult can provide really adequate nourishment for the soul if it pays little or no attention to the possibilities of spiritual communion with those in the Unseen (not, of course, on the level of vulgar spiritism, but in the sense implied in the Christian Communion of Saints), or of esotericism (again not as popularly understood, but as an element in a high spiritual tradition). But I shall not follow up this line of enquiry here, but concern myself only with religious universalism in the first sense indicated above.

With respect to the work of Radhakrishnan, one must begin by noting that he has not arrived at his conclusions exclusively by the path of philosophical investigation. Firstly, he is fully sensitive to the fact that the development of contemporary events is presenting us with a choice between catastrophe and the creation of 'One World.' The crisis may have transcendental implications, but it can be detected plainly enough by those who restrict their view to the material scene.

For the first time in the history of our planet its inhabitants have become one whole, each and every part of which is affected by the fortunes of every other. Science and technology, without aiming at this result, have achieved the unity. Economic and political phenomena are increasingly imposing on us the obligation to treat the world as a unit.[1]

This is, of course, a principle which is accepted by every serious student of world affairs today.

But account must also be taken of the fact that Radhakrishnan's universalism has its deepest roots in his belief in the primary function of love. Besides being an acute dialectician, he is a profound mystic who consciously takes his stand upon the insight that we associate ourselves with Reality most surely when we go out in sympathy to others. His plea for tolerance and inclusiveness is not therefore confined to an appeal for intellectual comprehensiveness. Fundamentally he stakes everything upon the realisation of unity between selves, or souls. No one can doubt this who has read with sympathy the moving final pages of his autobiographical sketch, "My Search for Truth," published in *Religion in Transition.*[2]

Our concern here, however, is with his attitude to the problem of universality as a philosopher. And here we must begin by recognising that as an Eastern thinker he has behind him an ancient and powerful spiritual tradition, in which emphasis is constantly laid upon the variety of ways in which man can approach the Divine. "Him who is the one Real sages name variously." We must look, not to the externals of a particular cult, but to the metaphysical insight which it embodies. At the core of every form of true

[1] ER, 2.   [2] London, 1937.

religion there is to be found a mysticism which is universal in character. It is therefore quite unproductive to become involved in doctrinal disputes or concern oneself unduly about creeds or definitions. On the importance of this principle Radhakrishnan is emphatic:

We need not adopt the official attitude of the Churches to the mystic developments. They may fight furiously about the dogmas of the divinity schools, but the common notions of spiritual religion remain, the plain easy truths, the pure morals, the inward worship, and the world loyalty. . . . They are of the very stuff of truth, however hostile they may seem to the orthodoxies.[3]

Moreover, it is the mark of Hinduism, of which Radhakrishnan is such a distinguished exponent, that it displays an extreme sensitiveness to the claims of different aspects of spiritual truth. To begin with, the Hindu religion is an elaborate and flexible synthesis of a wide range of cults and beliefs. And its basic scriptures may fairly be said to be universal in their significance. "The Gītā," writes Radhakrishnan,

represents not any sect of Hinduism, but Hinduism as a whole, not merely Hinduism but religion as such, in its universality, without limit of time or space, embracing within its synthesis the whole gamut of the human spirit, from the crude fetishism of the savage to the creative affirmations of the saint.[4]

And of the Vedānta he remarks that it "is not a religion, but religion itself in its most universal and deepest significance." [5] Further, Hindu philosophers have always taken it for granted that the claims of non-Hindu religions must be treated with the greatest respect:

The Hindu thinker readily admits other points of view than his own and considers them to be just as worthy of attention. . . . Hinduism developed an attitude of comprehensive charity instead of a fanatic faith in an inflexible creed. . . . Heresy-hunting, the favourite game of many religions, is singularly absent from Hinduism.[6]

II

It should now be sufficiently clear that the form of religion on which Radhakrishnan takes his stand is completely universal in character. He finds himself in sympathy with all creative forms of

[3] ER, 296.   [4] BG, 12   [5] HVL, 23.   [6] *Ibid.*, 19, 37.

religious life, wherever they may be found. But the problem of discovering the principles in accordance with which they could be
reconciled reduces itself, as he himself recognises, to that of bringing about a synthesis between Eastern and Western thought. For
they clearly represent the two complementary poles of spiritual
experience. If Oriental inwardness and Occidental activism could
be truly co-ordinated, the problem of world religion would substantially be solved. In this essay I shall, therefore, deal with Radhakrishnan's religious philosophy from the point of view of this
relationship alone.

We have first to consider the more negative aspect of his contribution: his analysis of the attitude adopted to religious and philosophical problems by the typical Western thinker. It is marked, he
contends, by an exceptional degree of intolerance. He is particularly disapproving of the spirit pervading missionary religions, of
whatever type:

Each claims with absolute sincerity that it alone is the true light while
others are will-o'-the-wisps that blind us to the truth and lure us away
from it. When it attempts to be a little more understanding, it affirms
that the light of its religion is to that of others as the sun is to the stars,
and the minor lights may be tolerated so long as they accept their position of subordination.[7]

The roots of this attitude go very deep. The typical Occidental
thinker delights in disputation and controversy, and derives great
satisfaction from the 'clash' of personalities and viewpoints. If he
is a philosopher he places great faith in dialectic. If he is a scientist
he is likely to become fanatically attached to any theory with which
he has identified himself. If he is a theologian he devotes himself
to the search for 'finality' in religion, places his trust in a 'special
revelation,' and exercises his powers in repudiating the claims of
'rival' creeds. If he is only a 'plain man' he instinctively stands up
for his 'rights,' and thinks of democracy more from the point of
view of the scope it offers for the expression of 'personality' than
from that of the possibilities it provides in the direction of unity
and inclusiveness.

From the standpoint of the Oriental all this is the expression of
a distressing immaturity. The root of the matter, as he sees it, is
that the basis of our Western culture is less spiritual than intellectual. Although our way of thinking owes a great deal to our Christian heritage, the decisive factor is still the rationalism which is

[7] ER, 345.

our legacy from Greece. The situation can be radically overcome only by the cultivation of a widely different form of discipline directed to the attainment of inward realisation.

Our trouble lies in our individualism. And we have at last begun to realise the dangers to which it exposes us. It is now nearly half a century since, under the impulse first provided by Freud, we awakened to the fact that the root of our troubles lay in unacknowledged emotional drives which distort to a serious degree the operations of our conscious minds. And we have by now developed an elaborate psychological technique for correcting these disturbances. We make a great deal of integrating the personality, of achieving a proper adjustment to 'reality.' For one who has been brought up in the Eastern tradition, however, such re-education is not radical in character, and this for the following reason: The ideal of the Western psychologist is to liberate the individual from 'irrational' impulses. His proper condition is one in which the forces at work in his so-called 'unconscious' are enriching, but not disturbing, the processes of his conscious mind.

So far the Oriental philosopher would approve. But he would go on to point out that we cannot safely afford to stop at that point. For, according to the teachings of Eastern metaphysics, that self whose free functioning has thus been secured is itself a very conditioned manifestation in relation to a still higher state of being. Viewed from a more transcendental standpoint, this rational, self-conscious ego, acutely, and even morbidly, conscious of its separation from other centres of consciousness, and filled with an unwarranted confidence regarding its capacity to arrive at truth by a process of clear and consistent reasoning, is not the basic element in the personality of man. On the contrary, it represents only the most interior and refined aspect (the *ahankara* principle) of a transient, biological organism which is essentially relative in character, and consists of nothing more substantial than an impermanent aggregate of psychic forces. It is the *ātman* alone—the universal Brahman within the soul—which is truly real. In other words, the conscious mind, which for the Western philosopher is a *subject,* is for the Oriental metaphysician of the nature only of an *object.* A full realisation of this fact constitutes, according to the traditional schools, 'emancipation.'

For Radhakrishnan this principle is basic. "There is a tendency," he writes,

especially in the West, to overestimate the place of the human self. Descartes attempts to derive everything from the certainty of his own isolated selfhood. It is not realised that the thought of the self which wants to explain everything, the will of the self which wants to subjugate everything, are themselves the expression of a deeper whole, which includes the self and its object. If the self is not widened into the universal spirit, the values themselves become merely subjective and the self itself will collapse into nothing. . . . If the deeper spirit in us sees the truth unveiled and enjoys freely the delight of being, then it and not self-conscious mind is the original and fundamental intention of nature which must emerge eventually.[8]

Our misleading sense of separatism is the outcome of succumbing to the subtle influence of Māyā, which

is a term employed to indicate the tendency to identify ourselves with our apparent selves and become exiled from our spiritual consciousness with its maximum of clarity and certainty. This tendency *is the expression of the working of self-conscious reason.* Intellectual activities are a derivation, a selection, and, so long as they are cut off from the truth which is their secret source, a deformation of true knowledge (avidyā) which has its natural result in selfishness.[9]

This statement can be exactly paralleled by two observations made by the late Ananda K. Coomaraswamy in his *Hinduism and Buddhism:* "In the doctrine of the un-self-ish-ness (*anātyma*) of all physical and mental operations he [the Buddha] dismisses the popular *Cogito ergo sum* as a crude delusion and the root of all evil." And again: "You will observe that amongst these childish mentalities who identify themselves with their accidents, the Buddha would have included Descartes, with his *Cogito ergo sum.*" [10]

In this principle we are provided with a valuable key to the psychology of the Western thinker. Although, if he is instructed, he recognises the difference between the transcendental and the empirical ego, he falls into the error of identifying the higher phases of the latter's activity with the true metaphysical self. He philosophizes over-confidently from out of a limited, relative consciousness, under the misguided impression that he possesses in his conscious, rational self a really reliable organ for judgment and interpretation. He cannot get beyond the conception that *ratio est capabilis.*

8 IVL, 274, 305.   9 ER, 28 (my *italics*).
10 Ananda K. Coomaraswamy, *Hinduism and Buddhism,* 55 and 59. Compare the Jewish philosopher Erich Gutkind: "Philosophy, which takes consciousness of the ego or thought, *i.e.,* psychological or logical data, as its starting point, must inevitably come to grief, as we can see from the plight of German idealism." (*The Absolute Collective,* 26.)

One of the most tell-tale expressions of this identification of the lesser with the greater is the tenacity with which the Occidental religionist clings to the notion of the immortality of the soul. He hopes and believes that his 'self' as at present known to and ex-perienced by him will—with due provision for perfection—endure throughout eternity. It has been taught for millenia, however, in the Orient that, at whatever point in its history we consider it, a self is but a phase in the history of an ever-changing complex of forces. When analysis is carried to its conclusion it is found that the only abiding principle in man is the supreme I AM, which remains the same within all its diverse manifestations. The self as a unit of consciousness cannot go out of existence. But the collec-tion of ideas, sentiments and impulses, of which it is the centre, will be constantly modified in character as the individual continues in his pilgrimage towards liberation. We can safely identify our selves with the *ātman,* but not with any one of its transient mani-festations.

III

An inescapable consequence of this wrongful conception of the self is dogmatism and intolerance in the realm of theology and philosophy. Insofar as the individual lays the accent upon the fac-tors of rationality and self-awareness he is intensifying his con-sciousness in a dangerous mode. For he thereby becomes unduly closely identified with the opinions and conclusions which are most satisfying to his mind at that particular point in his history. If I am acutely aware of myself on this level I am acutely aware also of those aspects of the outer world in which my distinctive charac-ter is reflected. Through not having gone sufficiently far inwards I am excessively sensitive to what comes within the limited range of my cherished empirical ego. My views reflect to a perilous extent the historical and cultural setting in which my mind has devel-oped. And they appear to me to be final, unquestionable, and im-mutable just because they are correlative with my intense sense of myself as a separate personality. This may explain both the classic *odium theologicum* and the compulsive nature of all deeply pon-dered philosophical convictions: the nature of my inner self is mirrored most completely in general ideas—an indirect testimony, incidentally, to its basic universality. But when the more profound levels of consciousness have not yet been touched then, instead of a true vision of the universal, we meet with attempts to univer-salize limited conceptions, with all the intolerance and unimaginativeness which this entails. The individual is still unable to make the passage from 'I think' to *'es denkt in mir.'*

We are here brought face to face with the crucial issue as between the Western and the Eastern mind. The Occidental religious thinker is firmly convinced that his philosophical and theological arguments are sound, and is prepared to develop them *ad infinitum*. But he fails to enquire sufficiently closely into the nature of the personality by which they are advanced. Preoccupied with logical considerations, he is correspondingly indifferent to the principle within himself which has impelled him to select at the beginning of his enquiry certain data at the expense of others. So his picture becomes out of focus, he fails to see the significance of alternative possibilities, and only too easily succumbs to that tendency which Aldous Huxley has aptly characterized as 'theological imperialism.'

What it comes to is that we in the West have not yet fully awakened to the dangers of what may be described as 'dialectical sinning.' We convert what the Hindu thinks of as a *darśana*—a point of view—into a dogma or a credal definition. As I have suggested earlier, the discipline on which we rely in this field is intellectual rather than spiritual. But the East knows better; for its sages have always taught that the key to discerning thinking is purity of being. To emancipate ourselves from partisanship and exclusiveness we must devote less attention to criticism and analysis and come interiorly into union with that Universal Self which is the principle behind all possible formulations. But this calls for the relaxation of the mind and will; and it would seem that the significance of this essentially mystical adaptation is realised at present only by relatively few minds in our restless and over-individualized West.

The doctrine that liberation comes primarily through interior realisation is essentially Oriental, and Radhakrishnan takes his stand firmly upon it: While "faith in conceptual reason is the logical counterpart of the egoism which makes the selfish ego the deadliest foe of the soul," [11] "we are saved not by creeds but by gnosis, *jñāna,* or spiritual wisdom." [12] He writes also:

The Upaniṣads protest against the exclusive sway of the dialectical spirit, against the rigid limitation of experience to the data of sense and reason. They believe in the possibility of a direct intercourse with the central reality, intercourse not through any external media such as historical revelations, oracles, answers to prayers, and the like, but by a

[11] ER, 25.   [12] *Ibid.,* 24.

species of intuitive identification in which the individual becomes in very truth the partaker of the divine nature.[13]

We are saved not by creeds, but by wisdom. The key to emancipation lies in a knowledge of our true nature. When the obstructions have been removed, the truth is spontaneously disclosed and the mind perceives things in a correct perspective. We then, he insists, see things from the standpoint of the universal. And one of the most important consequences is that we can no longer assign a unique importance to one particular type of revelation.

This impulse towards universalizing the sympathies is not, for the Eastern philosopher, a matter of sentiment alone. It is an inescapable consequence of accepting a particular system of metaphysics. The significance of the great equation, "That Thou Art" (*Tat Tvam Asi*), lies in the fact that it is *each* 'thou' which is 'That.' To the degree that I come into union with the One Self within all I necessarily develop a sympathetic understanding of the religious practices, symbolizations, and formulations of my fellow-pilgrims on the Way. To be attuned to the all-inclusive Brahman is to become endowed with the power of seeing *from the inside* what is being accomplished within the souls of others. It is transcendence of egotism alone which can ensure true imagination. But it is the complaint of all Oriental philosophers that the Western mind is capable for the most part only of observation from the outside—the contemplation of one region of the phenomenal from within the confines of another. Hence unremitting division, contention and misrepresentation. But few in Europe or America are fully awake to the significance of this principle. For the average Occidental intellectual it is just another thesis on the same level as all the others—which means that he is considering it on the very plane to which he has descended as the result of denying it!

IV

So far we have been concerned with Radhakrishnan's contribution to an East-West *rapprochement* from the Oriental end. We have seen that he is intensely aware of the limitations of our rationalism and of the need to balance it by an Asiatic understanding of inwardness. Now we have to consider how far he shows a true sympathy with the creative elements in our Occidental way of thinking. We shall find, I suggest, that, thanks to his exceptional

13 *Ibid.*, 129.

acquaintance with Western culture, he shows a full recognition of our distinctively Western genius.

This is first of all decisively revealed by his attitude towards our Occidental activism. Although like all civilized persons he deplores the abuse of scientific thinking and the extravagances of a 'sensate' culture, he is completely with us in accepting the fundamental principle that the visible world has true worth and meaning and provides the appropriate field for the development of our powers. His views regarding the characteristically Eastern doctrine of *māyā* will doubtless be closely examined by experts elsewhere in this volume. My own non-professional view is that his standpoint is much nearer our own than that of Śaṁkara—at least, as his ideas are usually interpreted. The world is not illusion, but appearance. This preserves the conception of God as a true creator, and at the same time does not rob action of its spiritual significance. "*Māyā* does not imply that the world is an illusion or is non-existent absolutely. It is a delimitation distinct from the unmeasured and the immeasurable." [14] And again: "The different theistic systems adopted by the large majority of the Hindus do not advocate the doctrine of *māyā*." [15]

As to the Supreme, Radhakrishnan's attitude would seem to be nearest of all to that of the great sage Rāmānuja, and closely allied with that which has been so suggestively developed in recent years by Śrī Aurobindo. For the illuminated the purely transcendental Divine can be a true object of experience. But—the great message of the Gītā—it manifests as the Lord, and these two are in essence one. The conditioned, provided that it is seen in relation to the Unconditioned, is not to be regarded as the lesser.

It is not true to contend that the experience of the pure realm of being, timeless and perfect, breeds in us contempt for the more familiar world of existence, which is unhappily full of imperfection. Reality and existence are not to be set against each other as metaphysical contraries. . . . For one who has the vision of the supreme, life, personality, and history become important. The life of God is the fullness of our life.[16]

In making these statements Radhakrishnan is taking his stand upon traditional Hindu philosophy: "The Supreme in its absolute self-existence is Brahman, the Absolute and as the Lord and Creator containing and controlling all, is Īśvara, the God." [17]

This means that action has essential meaning and worth. It is not merely a discipline which prepares the soul for realisations and

14 BG, 38.   15 HVL, 62.   16 ER, 31.   17 BG, 24.

experiences which cannot be gained within the space-time world. In acting rightly we associate ourselves truly with the Real. On this point Radhakrishnan lays great weight. He compares ascetics to cut flowers in metal vases, beautiful to contemplate for a while, but which soon wither through being without nourishment from the soil. He believes in "the full active life of man in the world with the inner life anchored in the Eternal Spirit." [18]

It will be plain that through attaching true creative value to action Radhakrishnan links himself in a very definite manner with the West. For as a result of the cultural influences which have worked upon us for so many centuries we are committed to the principle that, provided that in so doing we truly express the life of the Spirit, we gain rather than lose by converting our thoughts into deeds. Activism, if it does not involve seduction by the phenomenal, is a natural and inescapable expression of the spirit of man.

We have to ask, however, how far Radhakrishnan is prepared to accept the gospel of action as we interpret it in the Occident. In his firm rejection of that feverish and fatal preoccupation with externals at the expense of inwardness which has brought our civilization to the edge of the abyss he is, of course, taking the same line as all enlightened thinkers in Europe and America. But, as is to be expected, he still reveals in his pages an Oriental preference for quietism. For the Eastern thinker the surest road to reality is through contemplation. Even though he may have accepted the positive teachings of the Bhagavadgītā, or has become imbued with the realistic spirit of Mahāyāna Buddhism, the fact remains that his philosophy is non-naturalistic. Although he believes in unflinching adaptation to the demands of life as it has immemorially existed, he is greatly averse to making any extensive changes in the world around him. He is concerned to ensure such things as good husbandry, wise government and appropriate social organisation, but only in order that suitable conditions may thereby be provided for the realisation of higher purposes in the field of contemplation and art. And the more cultivated he is, the smaller his demands on life will tend to be.

In the West, on the contrary, we have for centuries past been working on the assumption that Nature is to be regarded, not simply as an external reality to which we must accommodate ourselves, but as a realm of being which is to be explored and 'mastered'— the scientific attitude. Although this has led to an appalling abuse

[18] BG, 66.

of knowledge, to the point of threatening today our very physical existence, it is also true that it has opened up vast vistas of cosmic knowledge and released almost limitless possibilities of creative power. Further, this is not merely a scientific but also a religious issue. The world as it was known to the ancients—Nature infinitesimally modified by eotechnics—was clearly sufficient to enable the spiritually-minded to learn from it the lessons which their souls needed. The important meanings have been, and always will be, communicated by the simplest means.

But is it not part of our spiritual adventure also that we should regard the realm of matter as an obstacle, a resistant medium, which we are called upon to penetrate for the glory of God? It is not simply that in the mode of philosophical contemplation we can come to know it as a mirror or projection of our deeper being, so that through the senses we are being shown in a reflected form realities which are less accessible to us through a process of spiritual introversion. Do we not rather have to conclude that it is part of our human destiny, not only to gain a vastly more extensive picture of the universe in which we live, but to break through the superficial levels of physical matter by scientific research and thus drastically alter the relations of things as we originally found them, release thereby natural energies of extreme potency, and become the masters of the forces to which our ancestors were subject, so that we are free to pass on to greater achievements? Today what we are principally witnessing is, of course, the terrible effects of a scientific knowledge which is not co-ordinated with wisdom. But there is undoubtedly a future path indicated for humanity on which science, like art, will be the handmaiden of theology, and will both lighten our burdens and extend our vision without corrupting us in the process.

This advance has, however, been effected almost exclusively by the West, in which science as we know it came to birth and developed. But it is undoubtedly regarded by almost all Eastern philosophers with very great suspicion. And, although Radhakrishnan is in this respect wider in his outlook than most, one feels that he has a certain Oriental unresponsiveness to the possibilities of action when it threatens to transform externals, even constructively, beyond a certain point. Apart from this minor limitation, however, we can safely regard him as being sympathetic to our Western concern with the more dynamic aspects of experience.

V

A word must be said regarding Radhakrishnan's attitude towards Personalism. It is sometimes claimed that true appreciation of the dignity and worth of the individual is a distinctively Christian contribution to culture. But this view is rendered plausible only by contrasting the teachings of Jesus with the debased attitude towards human beings which was characteristic of ancient civilizations in their decline. To the disinterested student of these questions it is sufficiently plain that respect for the individual and veneration of the divine life expressed through his being has been a basic element in the ethical teachings of all the great sages, whether we consider Zarathustra, the Buddha, Confucius, Lao-Tzu or Socrates. And of course Radhakrishnan as a Hindu thinker takes his stand on the same principles. But this spiritual humanism permeates his thought so completely that he feels no necessity to advance a special plea for personalistic values. For they are implicit in the whole philosophy of the Upaniṣads and the Bhagavadgītā.

It may be suggested that the reason why Oriental personalism is misinterpreted in the West is that in Eastern thought the *empirical* self is not considered as being of any metaphysical significance. The true source of all goodness, illumination and spiritual power is the great Unconditioned, and realisation of this fact is regarded as the key to emancipation. Preoccupation with the mere vehicle of the divine life is strongly discouraged; for there is only one ultimate Agent. This essentially ascetic attitude towards the human instrument is, however, easily misunderstood. It is certainly inimical to that insatiable interest in 'personalities' which has had such a baleful influence in the West. But at the same time it does not in any way diminish the Oriental's interest in human individuals and their characteristics. In fact, we meet in the East with the highest manifestations of what we think of as 'Humanism.' The difference lies only in the fact that the Eastern thinker is sufficiently well instructed to refer the spiritual element in the activities of a human being to something more ultimate—the Universal Spirit. His veneration is addressed, not to individuals as such, but to the Divine which manifests through them. And this process of transcendentalization is the sovereign corrective of that ego-centric mode of thinking by which the West has been so deeply corrupted. True Christian humility makes, of course, for the same result; but it has to compete in the West with powerful rationalistic influences which are less markedly fostered by the Eastern tradition.

Finally, Radhakrishnan has made a very important contribution towards a synthesis between the cultures of the two hemispheres by his elaborate and carefully documented work, *Eastern Religions and Western Thought*. With immense erudition he traces the different channels along which Eastern mystical and metaphysical ideas have penetrated into our Western world, making always for an emphasis upon inwardness, charity and tolerance rather than upon conflict and bondage to externals. He has a very real understanding of what we value, and of the direction in which our genius lies. But he remains true to his vision of metaphysical realities. He is convinced that human beings can only develop by expressing their freedom in thought and action in a world which is in an important sense real. But as an Asiatic he has a deep realisation that in order to think and act effectively men must attain to insight into a Reality which lies beyond the realm in which mind and will are exercised. To change things effectively we must establish ourselves inwardly in a sphere of being which no changes can affect. It is this mystical secret which the Eastern thinker is peculiarly qualified to impart to seekers after wisdom in the West. And Radhakrishnan has perhaps more to teach us in this field than any other living Oriental philosopher.

LAWRENCE HYDE

REIGATE, SURREY
ENGLAND

9

Clement C. J. Webb

THEISM AND ABSOLUTISM IN
RADHAKRISHNAN'S PHILOSOPHY

THEISM AND ABSOLUTISM IN
RADHAKRISHNAN'S PHILOSOPHY

I HAVE been invited to contribute a discussion of Radhakrishnan's views on 'theism and absolutism' to a projected volume
on *The Philosophy of Sarvepalli Radhakrishnan*. The antithesis
requires some explanation. It is obvious that it belongs to the
philosophy of religion, and would find no place in a metaphysic
which would take no account of religious experience as a genuine
apprehension of ultimate reality.

Thirty years ago Professor Radhakrishnan published a work—it
is the second in chronological order of those credited to him in
Who's Who—entitled, *The Reign of Religion in Contemporary
Philosophy*. It fell to me to review this book—the first by its author
to come my way—in *The Times Literary Supplement*. At that time
I criticized it as diminishing the force of a powerful polemic against
certain tendencies, which were prevalent in the philosophical
literature of that period, by the vagueness with which the word
'religion' was used in it. As employed in the title of the book, this
would seem to refer not to the religion of Radhakrishnan's own
people, the people of India (which was also his own religion), but
to that of Western Europe and America,—that is to say (if I may
quote my own words in the review in question), "Christianity, with
the emphasis laid upon those aspects of the Christian tradition
which are least akin to the religion of India;" a type of religion
which might be classed as 'theism' in contrast with the 'absolutism'
exemplified in the "approach to Reality based upon the *Upaniṣads*," which was outlined in the last chapter of *The Reign of Religion in Contemporary Philosophy*, a chapter added, as the author
tells us, "to rescue the book from the charge of being wholly polem-
ical and negative in its results." Moreover, "if in this way" (to
quote myself again) Radhakrishnan "is inclined to take 'religion'
in too narrow a sense, he sometimes seems to give to the word too
wide an extension of meaning," and "goes near to identifying 'reli-

gion' with 'democracy' and with the 'philosophy of change' in which democracy" had "lately tended to seek an intellectual justification for its faith," and "even with any 'extra-philosophical demands' which 'enter into philosophy and spoil it.' " By 'absolutism,' on the other hand, Radhakrishnan understands the 'monistic idealism' which is, in his opinion, the natural outcome of such philosophical systems as "play the game of philosophy squarely and fairly, with freedom from presuppositions and religious neutrality." In contrast with this, 'theism' is 'pluralistic.'

Now, when *The Reign of Religion in Contemporary Philosophy* appeared, the philosophic scene was very different from that of today. 'Pragmatism' was fashionable, and 'Logical Positivism,' with its denial that philosophy should aim at propounding a satisfactory *Weltanschauung*, had not yet become so. A reaction against Hegelian and kindred systems of 'absolute idealism' had brought several forms of pluralism into favour, and some of these were no doubt inspired by the suspicion that the confession by such a thinker as Bradley, that the distinction of God from his worshipper was in the end 'appearance' and not 'reality,' would be found to contradict an essential claim of religion. But, as was sufficiently evidenced by Radhakrishnan's inclusion, in his survey of contemporary philosophies which failed to play the game out to the end, of the 'new realism' of Bertrand Russell, not all pluralism need be 'theistic' in any possible sense of that comprehensive term.

I cannot but think that the same failure that I noted, at the time of its publication, in the title of *The Reign of Religion in Contemporary Philosophy*, to observe consistency in the use of words which, not forming part of the terminology of exact science, are especially liable to vagueness and ambiguity, is responsible for much that is unsatisfactory in Radhakrishnan's treatment, there and elsewhere, of the contrast expressed in the antithesis of 'theism' and 'absolutism,' and leads to a misunderstanding of the real difference which underlies it. This must be my excuse for prefixing to a criticism of his teaching on the subject an attempt to state it in a form less open to objection, even though we may thus find ourselves concerned with questions which may seem to belong to the sphere of historical theology rather than to that of general philosophy.

The word 'theism,' used in this connexion, indicates that we have here to do, as I have already pointed out, with a philosophy which takes account of the witness borne by religious experience to the nature of reality; for it is without meaning except in relation to

the object of religious experience, which we call God. The word
'absolutism' does not, indeed, in itself involve such a reference;
but, when thus opposed to 'theism,' 'absolutism' implies that quest
for complete union with ultimate reality which is no less characteristic of religion than is the reverence and love for a Being
conceived as capable of reciprocal 'personal' intercourse with a
human 'person,' which the term 'theism' suggests.

To use a phraseology which I have found convenient, a combination of *ultimacy* with *intimacy* will be found on reflexion to be the
distinctive note of all that we should call 'religious.' A Being, real
or imaginary, is not 'God,' with which or whom a conscious emotional relation is impossible ("Speak to Him, for He heareth, and
Spirit with Spirit can meet"); nor one, on the other hand, a relation to whom or which does not involve access to whatever is at the
back, or at the heart (we may vary the metaphor) of all existence.
But in some types of religious experience, the desire of the worshipper may be rather to *speak with,* in others rather to *be united
with* his God: the latter type of religion being that which is often
designated by the word *mystical.* Among historical religious systems, some emphasize the one, others the other type. In Hinduism,
the religion of Radhakrishnan's people, emphasis on union with
the Divine, as the goal of spiritual endeavour, is more marked than
in the religion of most Christians. Yet there are Christian mystics,
and, on the other hand, *bhakti,* viz., passionate devotion to a divine
being conceived as personal, is a well known form of Hindu piety.
We find Radhakrishnan himself calling attention to these facts.
"The personal category," he observes, "is transcended in the highest experience of the Christian mystics: Hinduism affirms that some
of the highest and richest manifestations which religion has produced, require a personal God." [1]

In an essay which Radhakrishnan has done me the honour of
quoting, contributed by me to a book, published in 1925 with the
title, *Science Religion and Reality,* I suggested that, of the principal religious systems which still at this date enjoy the allegiance
of great numbers of men and women, Christianity and Hinduism
may be considered especially capable of developing into a religion
for all mankind. It is not surprising that of these two Radhakrishnan should regard Hinduism as the better suited for this purpose;
his reasons for doing so are set forth in the Upton Lectures for
1926 on *The Hindu View of Life,* where he obviously has Christianity in mind as the religion with which he is comparing and con-

[1] HVL, 30.

trasting his own. Incidentally he remarks that, in the essay I have mentioned, I had not been quite fair to Hinduism in suggesting (I quote his words) "that for Hinduism there is nothing to choose between one revelation and another. Hinduism does not," he continues, "mistake toleration for indifference. It affirms that, while all revelations refer to reality, they are not equally true to it." [2] It is indeed likely enough that I was not quite fair. It is perhaps almost impossible not to take a more external view of a religion which one only knows from books and a few occasional contacts with its professors than of one in which one has been brought up and which has been one's principal guide in the conduct of one's life. I might plead that Radhakrishnan has sometimes criticized his own ancestral faith as inadequately sensitive to *ethical* defects in cults and practices which it tolerates; and I am well aware that his own valuation of such cults and practices is in the main determined by ethical considerations and coincides with that of Christians, for the generality of whom such considerations are apt to appear so obviously the most relevant that Matthew Arnold's definition of religion as "morality touched by emotion," open, as it is, to grave objection on more grounds than one, is yet only an exaggeration of a view congenial to their traditional way of regarding it. Nevertheless, it is to be noted that, when Radhakrishnan gives us a classification of religious attitudes, the main principle upon which he determines the relative position of these is clearly not the ethical, but rather the metaphysical. He tells us that

the worshippers of the Absolute are the highest in rank; second to them are the worshippers of the personal God; then come the worshippers of incarnations like Rāma, Kṛṣṇa, Buddha; below them are those who worship ancestors, deities and sages; and lowest of all are the worshippers of the petty forces and spirits.[3]

Radhakrishnan frequently declares that Hinduism—unlike some other religions, Christianity among them—is not a form of thought, a doctrine or a creed, but "a way of life." [4] Here, I confess, I find myself in a difficulty. What is this 'way of Life'? "Hinduism," we read in one place,[5] "insists on a moral life" and is "a fellowship of all who accept the law of right and earnestly seek for the truth." I cannot help feeling that this conception of Hinduism is not easily reconciled with the admission which our author often is ready to make, that its tolerance of practices which he would not deny to be rightly described as 'immoral' is excessive. I should

2 HVL, 48.   3 HVL, 32.   4 HVL, 77.   5 *Ibid.*

willingly grant that Christianity, though it seems to me more obviously characterized as a 'way of life,' in that for many of its
professed followers its ethical code appears to them to be what is
most distinctive of it, so that its doctrines are accepted chiefly because they are held to sanction this code and encourage its observance, may yet be criticized as having permitted and even approved
cruel persecution of the unorthodox; and this plainly in consequence of the importance which (as compared with Hinduism) it
has attached to the holding of certain beliefs as to the nature of
God and as to the historical circumstances of his revelation of
himself to man. But, although we may thus be led to question the
goodness of the 'way of life' which Christianity prescribes and to
doubt the truth of the doctrines with which it associates that 'way
of life,' it still seems to me to be more justly described as in its
nature a 'way of life' than Hinduism, which latter confessedly
allows a number of very different 'ways of life' and rules of conduct
to be, not indeed *equally,* but all in their own degree genuine
modes of serving God. For my own part, I should not find the
main contrast between Christianity and Hinduism in that one is,
and the other is not, a 'way of life' rather than a creed; although I
could wish that Radhakrishnan had made it clearer than he seems
to me to make it, what is, in his view, the distinctive character of
the 'way of life' which is Hinduism. What he appears to me inadequately to recognize is that the fundamental contrast between the
religion which he generally has in mind as representative of
'theism' and that which, although not *excluding* 'theism,' attributes
an intrinsic superiority to 'absolutism' lies in the Christian view
of *history* as belonging to ultimate reality in a sense in which it
does not for an 'absolutist' (such as Bosanquet, for example, for
whom it is, at the best, a 'hybrid form of experience').

The upshot of this discussion is that, in my judgment, Radhakrishnan's use of language in his contrast of 'theism' and 'absolutism' is less clear and consistent than could be wished; but that
he unquestionably holds the superiority of 'absolutism,' in the
sense of a view for which personality is a transient phenomenon,
to a 'theism' which ascribes to personality an abiding significance
in the ultimate reality. It is also plain that, as a consequence of
this estimate, he looks upon Hinduism as a religion which, though
finding room for devotion to a God conceived under the form of
a personal object of worship, decidedly regards the quest for absorption in the Absolute as a higher form of piety and as, on this
account, better suited to be the germ of a universal religion than

Christianity, which latter attaches to personality, and therefore to history, a significance which does not permit of it being ultimately transcended.

CLEMENT C. J. WEBB

OLD RECTORY
PITCHCOTT, AYLESBURY
ENGLAND

10

Edgar Sheffield Brightman

RADHAKRISHNAN AND MYSTICISM

RADHAKRISHNAN AND MYSTICISM

N O ONE who has even the slightest acquaintance with Sir
Sarvepalli Radhakrishnan can fail to be impressed by his
really extraordinary combination of versatility and integrity. His
interests and abilities are varied and complex, yet all of them seem
to come to an integral expression in his every act and thought.
For this reason, it is no simple matter to disentangle any one aspect
from the living whole and treat it by itself. Particularly is this
true of Radhakrishnan's attitude to mysticism. On the surface it
is plain that he lives in a milieu thoroughly impregnated with
mystical experiences. The noblest souls of India for centuries have
regarded mystical "realization" of God as the goal of their existence—not merely as the highest good, but as the only real good, in
comparison with which all other goods vanish into "Māyā and
illusion." On the surface it is also plain that Radhakrishnan is,
among other things, a great historian of Indian philosophy, and,
as such, has occupied himself intensively with the objective understanding of intellectual theories about mysticism.

But what goes on under the surface, in Radhakrishnan's mind
and soul? Is he a mystic? If so, of what type? This question is not
easy to answer. Radhakrishnan is self-contained and reticent, in
this respect like the great Jewish mystics.[1] Some mystics are
voluble and expressive confessants. Although declaring that the
heart of their experience is ineffable (is it more ineffable than *any*
qualitative experience?), they have much to say about it, pouring
out their story in journals, letters, poems, essays, sermons, and
confessions—telling all. Other mystics find the inner light within in
the silence of their own souls, and then let their light shine without
accompanying clamor of words. They do not say, "Lo, thus and so
I felt when I found the light; thus and so did my heart throb, my
body shake, my spirit melt." These two kinds of mystics may be

---

[1] G. G. Scholem, in *Major Trends in Jewish Mysticism* (1946), 16, speaks of the
"personal reticence" and "sense of shame" of Jewish mystics.

called the autobiographical, those who describe the light that they have seen; and the radiant, those who let the light shine without telling how it came to shed its rays on them. These two kinds are not mutually exclusive. An autobiographical mystic may often be radiant; and a radiant mystic may sometimes be autobiographical. The distinction is, however, useful in application to Radhakrishnan. If he is a mystic, he is not autobiographical. We search in vain for introspective confessions. His mysticism, if it exists, is radiant.

The investigation before us, then, is not simply an inquiry into Radhakrishnan's theory of mysticism, important as that is. Rather, it is an inquiry into the resources of his inner life. Does his power as an effective personality lie primarily in his will-power, in his intellect, or in his direct experience of the divine? Is he primarily a moralist, a philosopher, or a mystic?

At the Sixth International Congress of Philosophy, held at Harvard University in 1926, India was represented by two great men, Surendrenath Dasgupta and Sarvepalli Radhakrishnan. Everyone recognized both men as scholarly philosophers. In Dasgupta the intellect predominated. Objective reason was his ideal, his keynote. But many commented on Radhakrishnan to the effect that he sounded more like a prophet or a preacher than a pure philosopher. Dasgupta had reasons. Radhakrishnan had a message. Such at least was the impression gained by more than one member of the Congress. Is this a clue to the solution of the problem which we are facing? At any rate, one cannot infer hastily from the fact that Radhakrishnan is a Hindu that therefore he holds one specific theory or indulges in specific spiritual practices. For, as he writes himself, "Hinduism . . . allowed room within its pale for all the different types of thought and temperament." [2]

I

In order to understand Radhakrishnan's relation to mysticism, it is desirable first to underline the versatility of his mind. He is in no sense a fanatic. He suffers from no monomania. Versatility is his most obvious trait, and every aspect of his thought must be seen in relation to a rich complexity of other aspects.

Radhakrishnan was the son of Hindu parents of conventional outlook, but his own outlook transcends the conventional. He was

[2] Ind P, II, 653. See also H. Glasenapp, "Pragmatische Tendenzen in der Religion und Philosophie der Inder," in E. S. Brightman (ed.), *Proceedings of the Sixth International Congress of Philosophy*, 1926 (New York: Longmans, Green and Co., 1927), 102-107, where the variety of views in Hinduism is given an original turn.

educated in Madras Christian College, and is familiar with Christianity without being a Christian. It is reported that no Indian philosophy was taught in that college, a circumstance which would not lead a young Hindu to admire Christian intelligence. Although he was thoroughly Hindu in feeling, Radhakrishnan's first book was a conventional elementary text in Occidental psychology.[3] His greatest scholarly contribution is as an historian of Indian philosophy. Yet he is thoroughly acquainted with European thought, especially with modern British absolute idealism.

He is a vigorous critic of materialism and his interest in that criticism is almost equally metaphysical, ethical, and religious. He is a competent interpreter of great figures like the Buddha, Rabindranath Tagore, and Mahatma Gandhi. He is a close student and interpreter of the Upaniṣads and the Bhagavadgītā. He is also a philosopher of history in a world-wide sense, and is intensely concerned about the political present and future of his own country and other countries. Although a patriot, he is no provincial. He is a university teacher, who has recently been dividing his time between the Hindu University of Benares and Oxford University in England, and still more recently has resigned as vice-chancellor of the University in Benares. He has travelled and lectured extensively in the United States. At present he is India's ambassador to the U.S.S.R. in Moscow. Like many Orientals, he is critical of the West, but never without assigning rational and ethical grounds for his criticisms.

If such a man is a mystic, he is also a scholar, a man of affairs, an active and many-sided personality. This versatility must be continually borne in mind as our investigation advances. If a mystic, he is no hermit, no solitary, no professional mystic.

II

No man can be fully understood in terms of his environment. Every man is more than his environment. Yet no man can be understood without regard to his environment.

The Hindu environment of Radhakrishnan is very complex and one may find in it as many different philosophical ideas as one finds in the West—a fact which Professor F. C. S. Northrop has considered insufficiently in his brilliant work, *The Meeting of East and West*. Nevertheless, it would hardly be too much of an oversimplification to say that, in the main, there are but two varieties

[3] *Essentials of Psychology* (1911).

of Hindu mysticism. It is difficult to find names for these two varieties which are not misnomers. One might call them the passive and the active: yet the so-called passive certainly engenders activity, and the so-called active has its moments of passive bliss. One might name them for their chief exponents, Śaṁkara and Rāmānuja, but this would be awkward. They may be distinguished in terms of their goal. The chief goal of one is identity with Brahman; the chief goal of the other is love of the divine. Both aim at the mystical experience of "realization" of God. Both (with some differences) inspire their devotees to activity in the world, in the spirit of the Bhagavadgītā. But the one is essentially contemplation in which (as in the Buddhistic Nirvāṇa) "the dewdrop slips into the shining sea" and the devotee realizes his essential identity with God; whereas the other is love, in which the devotee enjoys an essentially social, emotional, and ethical relation to God and to man. Contemplation-mysticism eventuates in "nondualism," or, in Western terms, absolute idealism or pantheism; whereas love-mysticism is always "dualistic," in the Hindu sense, or, in Western terms, inclines to a personalistic and pluralistic idealism.

This does not mean that all Hindu thought is idealism of one type or another, but only that the majority of mystics, in so far as they are philosophical, tend in one of these two directions. It must be added that there is a remarkable trend in each view toward the empirical justification of the other, and therefore toward some sort of synthesis. The extremes of contemplation-mysticism and its accompanying philosophy are the spiritual property of a relatively small élite group. The love-mysticism of bhakti is practised by Vaishnavas and others, and hence by the majority of truly religious Hindus. We shall find reason to regard Radhakrishnan as inclined philosophically toward "nondualism" and its impersonal absolutism, but practically toward bhakti, with its "dualism" and its emphasis on the personal and the social. Those who think of him as a prophet, in the Hebrew sense, are not far wrong. In any event, his nature is profoundly ethical, and in his exposition of the most nondualistic thought his central interest is in ethics. In describing nondualism, he says: "If we are called upon to love our neighbor, it is because all are one in reality." [4] This doctrine, familiar to Occidental philosophers through Schopenhauer's view of all as One Will, combines the practical with the theoretical reason, yet with a definite coloring of the primacy of the practical reason.

4 Ind P, I, 209.

III

Let us now turn to a closer examination of Radhakrishnan's thought. There is much evidence to support the suggestion already made that his basic theoretical preference is for nondualism and the related contemplation-mysticism. He finds thought driven to "a system of absolute idealism," which, however, "cannot be grasped by the intellect." When we think "in the acquired dialect of the intellect" we are, it is true, led to theism, and have a (deplorable!) finite God. But when we take the full range of reality into account we become absolutists.[5] His line of argument and his conclusions are indicated by the frequency with which he quotes approvingly from F. H. Bradley and Dean Inge.[6] The ultimate is the One of Plotinus—experienced in "the flight of the alone to the alone"—or the absolute feeling of Bradley, which somehow includes, yet somehow transcends all thought. Radhakrishnan interprets Śaṁkara with special warmth and sympathy; his view is that "a spiritual perception of the infinite as the real leads to peace and joy." [7] In a quotation from the *Ṛg Veda,* he sets forth the essence of Hinduism, the nondualism of which he seems to endorse: "Priests and poets, with words, make into many the hidden reality which is but one." [8] Evidences of Radhakrishnan's essentially monistic idealism could be multiplied, but no new light would be gained.

More instructive is it to make clear with what qualifications Radhakrishnan guards the interpretation of his view. First of all, he seems to assert it unqualifiedly by his rejection of theism. The point of his book, *The Reign of Religion in Contemporary Philosophy,* is not, as one might expect from him, that religion reigns over philosophy and should reign, because it alone reveals the ultimate nature of reality. On the contrary, his point is that the reign of religion has been deleterious, because the religion which has reigned has been theistic, and theism leads (as we have seen) to a finite God and thence to pessimism and despair.[9] This seems to commit him to nondualistic absolutism.

---

[5] RR, 432, 434.　　　　[6] RR, 439f. *et passim.*　　　　[7] Ind P, II, 614.

[8] Art. "Indian Philosophy," *Encyclopaedia Britannica* (1937), XII, 247-253.

[9] See the Preface to RR. Later Radhakrishnan says: "The mystic vision is accepted by Russell as constituting the true essence of religion. The fact of mysticism itself is a refutation of the dualism which is the fountain-spring of all pessimistic thoughts" (RR, 362). It is true that the use of the word "dualism" in this context may be tinged with Western usage; but for Radhakrishnan it always means any view that does not include all things in God—and hence theism is meant. On his opposition to theism, see E. L. Hinman's review of RR in *Philosophical Review,* 29 (1920), 582-586.

In the second place, however, we find him, in common with so convinced an absolutist as Hegel, dissatisfied with the description of his thought as pantheism. If theism be false, if the mystical realization of Brahman reveals man's identity with God, why not avow pantheism? It is Radhakrishnan's view that pantheism tends to identify God with the world, i.e., with physical nature. He wants it to be clear that the divine reality is richer, deeper, more spiritual than anything that can be found by the methods of science in the world of nature. "God is more than nature." [10]

It should be noted, in the third place, that Radhakrishnan shares the widespread Hindu view that all types of genuine religious mysticism are justified. He quotes from a Upaniṣad, without documentation, this statement: "The worshippers of the Absolute are the highest in rank; second to them are the worshippers of the personal God; then come the worshippers of the incarnations." [11] For an Occidental this view is very difficult, for it seems to assert that, as the different experiences are justifiable, so the pantheistic and theistic philosophies which interpret them are both, in a sense, true. The Occidental asks: In what sense? The best that Radhakrishnan can say in answer is to refer to Bradley's doctrine of degrees of truth and reality.[12] In this mood, although all genuine mysticism is accepted, contemplation-mysticism is essentially the highest. Radhakrishnan quotes the Taittiriya Upaniṣad that "the highest is ānanda," "the delight of life and mind, the fullness of peace and eternity." [13] He points out explicitly in this context that in the Upaniṣads ethics is "subsidiary to this goal."

There is, in the fourth place, a point which Radhakrishnan never surrenders and which brings him nearer to theism than some of his other statements. He never doubts or denies that the mystical experience and the God realized in that experience are of the nature of the highest possible consciousness. The language of super-consciousness may be used, but this is not meant to convey the idea of a stage that is absolutely unconscious. On the contrary, it always refers to sat-chit-ānanda, a combination of being, knowledge and bliss, which utterly transcends ordinary consciousness, yet is itself consciousness on the highest possible level. This, of course, is what Western personalists and theists mean by divine personality; so that the contrast in the Upaniṣads between the Absolute and the personal God is far from being as sharp as Radhakrishnan feels it to be. He can say that "we may not know God,

10 See especially, RR, 445f.   11 Cited in HVL, 32.
12 See RR, passim.   13 Ind P, I, 208.

but God certainly knows us." [14] What more could a "dualistic" theist—be he Berkeley, Barth, or Bowne—ask than this clear distinction between the divine and the human, and this clear assertion of knowledge as a divine attribute?

But, most important, in the fifth place, Radhakrishnan avows a typically Hindu view which frees him, in principle, from absolute commitment to any philosophy or theology. It is a doctrine so empirical and so undogmatic that one might for a moment wonder whether one is hearing the voice of John Dewey,[15] or even John Wesley, with his emphasis on religious experience, and his freedom in "non-essentials." Radhakrishnan dwells on the basic religious importance of the actual mystical awareness of the divine, in contrast to any and all theoretical assertions about it. "Hinduism," he writes, "is wholly free from the strange obsession of the Semitic faiths that the acceptance of a particular religious metaphysic is necessary for salvation." [16] Although this may be a polemic sharpened by its attack on Jewish and Christian—especially Roman Catholic—orthodoxy, it is striking for its tacit repudiation of the religious importance of his own criticisms of both theism and pantheism and of his defense of absolutism. If he means what he says, a demand to accept Śaṁkara's metaphysics would itself be a "strange obsession." Repeated statements make clear that this religious empiricism combined with intellectual agnosticism is no casual or careless aside. "The intellectual representations of the religious mystery are relative and symbolic." [17] "One metaphor," he says, "succeeds another in the history of theology until God is felt as the central reality in the life of man and the world." [18] The experience is the vital fact here: "God is felt;" and Radhakrishnan comes close to Schleiermacher's "feeling of dependence." It is "the half-religious and the irreligious [who] fight about dogmas, and not the truly religious." [19] Here we find the actual experience of God made supreme, and the road is cleared for the full appreciation of contemplation-mysticism and love-mysticism, without regard to the contradictions that might be entailed by adherence to the absolutism of Śaṁkara and the theism of Rāmānuja.

In the sixth place, there is the qualification that arises from a consideration of Radhakrishnan's practical interests. He is not

---

[14] HVL, 50.

[15] See S. C. Ackley, *John Dewey's Conception of Shared Experience as Religious* (Boston University Dissertation, 1948), especially the treatment of Dewey's critique of dogma as opposed to scientific method.

[16] HVL, 37. [17] HVL, 36. [18] HVL, 129. [19] HVL, 60.

exclusively devoted to philosophy and education. He gives the impression of primary concern with an ethical criticism of civilization. Wherever there is social injustice, human suffering, man's inhumanity to man—whether arising from selfishness or from materialistic ideals—there Radhakrishnan is aflame with the zeal of a prophet and a reformer. He attacks abuses in family life, in the economic order, in politics, in diplomacy, in man's tendency to war. One of his recent works is *Religion and Society* (1947), in which the reader might be inclined to see in him merely a secular social reformer, were it not for one striking passage, which we quote, and which is almost the only explicit reference to mysticism in the entire volume:

> When we dispute over dogmas, we are divided. But when we take to the religious life of prayer and contemplation, we are brought together. The deeper the prayer, the more is the individual lost in the apprehension of the Supreme. The hardness of the ego melts; the tentativeness of the creed is revealed; and the intense focussing of all souls in one utter Being is grasped.[20]

Here the mystical and the social so interpenetrate as to be inseparable. The spirit of Radhakrishnan here is one with the spirit of the martyred Mahatma Gandhi. Its kinship with love-mysticism and with personalistic theism is further revealed in another brief passage: "The mystic religion of India . . . affirms that things spiritual are personal"[21]—a statement in apparent conflict with the view that worship of the Absolute is superior to the worship of the personal God.

These six qualifications, taken together, make it clear that Radhakrishnan is not absolutely committed to absolutism, and that his personal faith is rooted in immediate mystical experience of the divine rather than in any metaphysical system.

IV

So far, our approach to Radhakrishnan has been through his attitude toward philosophy, as modified by his religious experience. Let us now reverse the process, and consider his view of mysticism and its effects on his philosophy.

In considering Radhakrishnan's account of mysticism it is well to divest our minds of all that we have learned from William James and other Western writers. Valuable as their insights are, they have

---

[20] RS, 53.   [21] *Ibid.*, 49. Cf. 68.

schematized the mystical and standardized it to such an extent that their theories have become normative for many in the West who know nothing about the mystical experience beyond what they have read in psychology books. In Radhakrishnan we have a writer who stands closer to the sources and to the living reality of mysticism than does any Western scientific analyst.

If we look at the mystical states through Radhakrishnan's eyes, the first item that strikes us is the fact that mysticism is experience independent of dogma—independent in the sense of not requiring any dogma as a prerequisite to the experience. It is true that every good Hindu of every sect regards the Vedic scriptures in the light of a divine revelation. But the mystic is not required first to accept the revelation and then to seek an experience within the revealed framework. On the contrary, the experience is the test of the revelation. This empirical and experimental basis of mysticism is made especially emphatic in *The Hindu View of Life* (1927). There Radhakrishnan says, for example, "the truths revealed in the Vedas are capable of being re-experienced on compliance with ascertained conditions." Even more explicitly, he declares that "the Hindu philosophy of religion starts from and returns to an experimental basis." [22]

This experience, moreover, is both immediate and objective—in terms of theory of knowledge, it asserts an idealistic epistemological monism. All other authority, therefore, is secondary to the primary authority of the direct experience itself. "The mystics," Radhakrishnan says, "are the specialists in religion who attempt to see God face to face and not merely through the eyes of tradition and history." [23] This appeal to immediate experience is one of the factors that have led some critics to regard mysticism as merely private and subjective delusion. But Radhakrishnan comes near to losing his patience in the face of such criticism. When it was raised in discussion at a Congress of Philosophy, his very restatement of the criticism implied his rejection of it. He said that "mystics, we were told this morning, are highly suggestible folk, given to externalizing their private fancies." [24] Over against this solipsistic view, he expounds most sympathetically Śaṁkara's objective description of mokṣa, the highest mystical state, as a "direct realisation of something which is existent from all eternity," and as an apprehension of "the heaven which is all the time here, could

[22] HVL, 17, 19.   [23] RR, 262.

[24] Brightman (ed.), *Proceedings of the Sixth International Congress of Philosophy* (1926), 546.

we but see it." [25] The claim to objectivity, then, is one of the most fundamental traits of mystical experience, as direct and as certain as is its very immediacy.

Closely connected with the foregoing is the certainty of the experience. It always contains or arouses a "feeling of certitude." It has an "unquestionable content." [26] Like many others, it is true he also refers to the ineffability of the experience.[27] But, if a criticism is here in order, it does not appear that ineffability is a very important trait of mystical experience, for two reasons. First, most mystics have been able to talk about their experience in language that is perfectly intelligible to other mystics and even conveys some meaning to a nonmystical secularist. Autobiographical mystics have made a business of expressing the inexpressible; and even radiant mystics somehow convey the meaning of their source of light. Second, there is a sense in which all direct experience is ineffable. The color yellow which you experience cannot be conveyed in words to your blind friend. Effability is simply the possibility of appealing to a like experience in another. Nothing is strictly ineffable save an experience or content totally unique and of a kind totally inaccessible to anyone save the experient. The denial of any ineffability based on such totally inaccessible experience is a first principle of most mysticism of both East and West. Mystics in general cry with one voice, "Taste and see that the Lord is good." The mystic experience is ineffable only in the sense that the taste of good food is ineffable. It shows sound instinct and good judgment in Radhakrishnan that he makes very little of the asserted ineffability of mystical states. He might, however, have analyzed the concept of ineffability with greater care.

Radhakrishnan also mentions the transiency of the mystical experience. "The moments of vision," he tells us, "are transitory and intermittent." [28] But this is so obvious, so unimportant, and so uninstructive regarding the importance or validity of mysticism that Radhakrishnan rightly makes little of it. It is doubtless true that the full import of the theory of relativity is present in the mind of Einstein himself only in transitory and intermittent moments of insight. No one, however, would think of taking this fact as shedding any significant light on the truth or falsity of relativity; it is merely a statement about the nature of the human mind.

For Radhakrishnan there is another and more important attribute of the mystical, namely, its organic relation to the ethical. It is true, he grants, that in the Gītā "the freed soul is beyond all good

25 Ind P, II, 636.   26 IVL, 95, 96.   27 IVL, 95.   28 IVL, 94.

and evil." [29] This may, we infer, mean that the divine realization is beyond anything that human striving can produce; as St. Paul says, "It is the gift of God." So, in the hands of Nietzsche, the highest good of man is beyond and above all conventional standards of the common mores. But whatever it means, Radhakrishnan utterly repudiates the idea that it implies any indifference to or relaxation of the highest moral standards. Stating the case mildly, he declares that there is "no inconsistency between mysticism and the most exalted ethics." [30] More emphatically, he points out that mysticism is a critique of immoral attitudes, such as a narrow nationalism, and he declares with visible pride that "we did not make our country a national goddess." [31] In expounding the teachings of the Upaniṣads, he finds in them "a direct challenge to the spiritual activity of man," and he ascribes to them the "undermining of class hatreds and antipathies." [32] In formulating the essence of Śaṁkara's thought, he makes the ethical very prominent. The fulfilled experience is "life in the spirit full of meekness and peace, holiness and joy, and not sinking into a state of contemplative inertia." [33] In short, whatever the gift of God may be, however receptive and passive the soul may be in mystical experience, it is not Radhakrishnan's view that the experience is wholly or even characteristically passive. Its function is to stimulate moral activity and to expel moral impurities.

Radhakrishnan's view of mysticism prevents him from indiscriminate acceptance of everything that claims to be mystical. In the light of the highest experience, some mystical claims must be regarded as unworthy deviations. Obviously, whatever is unethical, he condemns as perversion, and he, like many other Hindus, takes umbrage at Schweitzer's unappreciative interpretation of the place of ethics in Indian mysticism.[34] He also frankly faces and condemns the immoral life of Kṛṣṇa as related in the Puranas.[35] Just as he rebukes immoralism, so does he reject mystical fanaticism. The extreme other-worldliness and asceticism which many regard as almost the essence of mysticism, he would abjure as mere excrescences. Ecstasy itself is "often a perversion of mysticism." [36] "Fanatical asceticism is not," he declares, "indicative of a true

---

29 Ind P, I, 579.   30 ER, 108.   31 ER, 54.
32 Ind P, I, 219, 223.   33 Op. cit., II, 619.   34 See ER, Chap. III.
35 Ind P, I, 496.
36 ER, 79. However, the use of the word "ecstasy" is confusing. The term may denote fanatical emotionalism, or it may refer to the heights of disciplined mystical experience. Radhakrishnan might have been more exact in definition.

renunciation, but is only another form of selfishness." [37] Perhaps Radhakrishnan is too severe in calling all such excesses selfish, however poor the judgment of the devotee may be.

At this point we may summarize Radhakrishnan s conception of mystical experience. It is immediate, certain, objective, spiritually active, morally purifying experience of the divine (transient, of course, in its givenness, though not in its effects, and ineffable in a sense), repudiating both immoralism and fanaticism. This obviously differs at several points, not necessary to belabor, from current Western clichés. It illustrates his practical dualism.

In the second place, Radhakrishnan's conception of the mystical experience may be further illuminated by inquiring more specifically into his view of its goal. Here we shall find evidences of his theoretical nondualism, which contrasts with the practical dualism and bhakti devotion which have just been alluded to, and which will emerge again later. Yet even in statements of the goal, the evidence is not all on one side. For example, perhaps in a largely historical mood, he speaks of the mystic's goal as "a return from the plurality into the One" as being "the ideal goal, the most ultimate value." [38] Yet more recently he has written that "the end of man is to let the spirit in him permeate his whole being, his soul, flesh, and affections." [39] The former statement is more monistic and metaphysical. The latter is more personalistic, pluralistic, and ethical. But the monistic, "nondualistic," descriptions predominate. "The freedom of spirit, the delight of harmony, and the joy of the absolute" are traits of the goal, as are peace, perfect fruition, and being one with the infinite. "Only when the God in him realises itself, only when the ideal reaches its fruition, is the destiny of man fulfilled." [40] This nondualism is explicit in the definition of ānanda which is supreme joy or bliss. "Ānanda or delight is the highest fruition, where the knower, the known, and the knowledge become one." Reality itself is ānanda, and therefore is not indefinable—in contrast with Rāmānuja's belief and with Radhakrishnan's own assertion of ineffability. [41] Ātman, the self or soul which is Brahman, is "positive bliss," and "the completest consciousness." [42] But such assertions are never meant to be taken as pure theory. The goal of union with Brahman is something to be verified empirically. In short, "the possibility of becoming one with God can be established only by the actuality of

37 Ind P, I, 216.
39 MST, 39 (1946 offprint, 30).
41 Op. cit., I, 165-167.

38 Ind P, I, 208.
40 Ind P, I, 206.
42 Op. cit., I, 162. See also RR, 424.

it." [43] This means substantially what Occidental Unitarians mean who declare that all can become what Jesus was. When that occurs, "the absolute is felt as a boundless spirit, pervading the whole universe and flooding the soul of man. . . . [Thus] ideal religion overcomes the duality with which it starts." [44] In the highest phase of experience—nirguna bhakti—"the individual and his God become suffused into one spiritual ecstasy and reveal themselves as aspects of one life. Absolute monism is therefore the completion of the dualism with which the devotional consciousness starts." [45]

The goal of mysticism may be seen clearly in Radhakrishnan's account of the stages of yoga, or union with God, which are the *via purgativa* (the way of purification), the *via contemplativa* (the way of concentration in which to be completely "one-pointed" is the aim), and finally the *via intuitiva* (which is actual identification with God in the experience of samādhi).[46] This ultimate samādhi he describes more fully as "ecstatic consciousness, . . . a sense of immediate contact with ultimate reality, of the unification of the different sides of one nature." [47]

Another name for the mystical goal is mokṣa, which is spiritual realization or liberation. "This is what gives ultimate satisfaction, and all other activities are directed to a realisation of this end." [48] Even for Śaṁkara, Radhakrishnan holds, in mokṣa individuals "retain their individualities as long as the world process continues. The released souls at the moment of release do not pass into the stillness of the Absolute, but secure a steady vision of the oneness of it all." [49] Here dualism and nondualism seem to be successive stages of realization of the mystic goal, nondualism lying in the indeterminate future. On the other hand, in the very same context it appears that the nondualistic goal is immediately available, for Radhakrishnan declares that "Mokṣa is freedom from historicity or temporal process or birth, which are the forms of time. Historicity ceases with realization." [50]

Yet even in the most extreme statements of the goal, the basis in experience and the empirically verifiable content remain. Of

---

43 *Op. cit.,* I, 230.   44 *Op. cit.,* I, 234.

45 *Op. cit.,* I, 565. It seems strange for Radhakrishnan to interpret any type of bhakti as absolute monism, since bhakti is so fundamentally dualistic. It is also to be remembered that Radhakrishnan has warned against the extreme of ecstasy.

46 ER, 48.   47 ER, 51.   48 HVL, 81.

49 In Brightman (ed.), *Proceedings of the Sixth International Congress of Philosophy* (1926), 685f. Some would question Radhakrishnan's interpretation of Śaṁkara. They would hold that Śaṁkara envisages the possibility that certain individuals may be released from individuality here and now.

50 *Ibid.*

samādhi, for example, he declares that it is "not a simple experience," rather, "it is a succession of mental states which grow more and more simple until they end in unconsciousness." [51] This might appear to be a cutting of all relation to any empirical base of supplies. But careful consideration of related passages reveals that "unconsciousness" is a relative, not an absolute term, which would be expressed better by "superconsciousness." In samādhi, the subject is, to be sure, unconscious of the physical world and of sensation; he is unconscious of the presence of other human beings. But he is supremely conscious in the dimension of the divine, to such a degree that his consciousness is incomparably intensified beyond all ordinary human experience, so that it is almost equally true to call it unconsciousness (of the ordinary human) and superconsciousness (of the extraordinary superhuman).

In view of his repeated and emphatic statements of the sublime goal of mysticism, it is noteworthy that Radhakrishnan can discuss religion at considerable length in some contexts with relatively little stress on the nondualistic goal. In his striking book, *The Religion We Need,* almost his only direct reference to the mystical is in a description of "the true religious life" that might as well have been written by a devout Catholic or Protestant Christian or a Jew or a Moslem as by a Hindu. He says:

> It is spiritual certainty offering us strength and solace in the hour of need and sorrow. It is the conviction that love and justice are at the heart of the universe, that the spirit which gave rise to man will further his perfection. It is the faith which grips us even when we suffer defeat, the assurance that though the waves on the shores may be broken, the ocean conquers nevertheless.[52]

Such true religion, he goes on to say, is "an utter self-surrender, a pure self-giving."

Brief, but very decisive and unambiguous, in the third place, are the statements which identify the mystical experience with love, and thus emphasize the dualistic aspect of Radhakrishnan's mysticism and his kinship with bhakti devotion. In expounding Rudolf Eucken's thought, he summarizes his view of mysticism in the words: "The religious souls commune alone with the Alone, and find it to be Infinite Love." [53] This is evidently also Radhakrishnan's own view. When speaking of the "unconditioned value" of God, he declares that "human love is a shadow of the divine

---

[51] Ind P, II, 360.   [52] RWN, 27.   [53] RR, 325.

love." [54] More emphatically, he states that "developing disinterested love is the essence of all true religion." [55] In another connection, Radhakrishnan declares that "to have one's heart and mind absorbed in love seems to invert the mystery of the universe." [56] Evidently for him, mysticism without love is false mysticism, and love without mysticism is false love.

In the fourth place, we turn to a problem that is perplexing for other thinkers and no less so for Radhakrishnan, namely, the relation of reason and intuition in the mystical experience. The task of unraveling these factors and assigning each its proper place is troublesome, to say the least. In education and in temperament Radhakrishnan is a combination of the East and the West. He rightly reflects his twofold training and experience when he says that the dominant feature of Eastern thought is "creative intuition," whereas the dominant feature of Western thought is "critical intelligence." [57] But this should not and does not mean that the Oriental trusts every intuition uncritically or that the Occidental criticizes every intuition away. Immanuel Kant's thought has been paraphrased in the formula, "Form without content is empty, and content without form is blind." Yet few would hold that even Kant's synthesis of the intuitional and the rational is perfectly satisfactory.

Radhakrishnan is a philosopher, not an ecstatic, and he demands a rational basis for belief. "We cannot believe a thing," he declares, "simply because we wish to. We cannot worship what we know to be a mental fiction." [58] No external authority can compel his assent. In fact, he points out that "both Buddhism and the Upaniṣads repudiate the authority of the Vedas." [59] He criticizes the Upaniṣads themselves for "the vagueness of [their] doctrines." [60] He points out the rational difficulties in the Bhagavadgītā. "The critical intellect has to work on it with care before it can deduce a consistent system from it." [61] He asserts with great frankness that "religion must establish itself as a rational way of living." [62] Very earnestly does he protest against religious irrationalism. Mysticism for him "is not a flight to unreason or a glorification of ignorance and obscurity." [63] At the same time, he is aware of a certain danger in the use of analytic intelligence in religion. He finds that the Buddha, although influenced by the Upaniṣads, sought so predominantly

54 Ind P, I, 217.   55 Op. cit., I, 216.   56 IVL, 93.
57 ER, 48.   58 RWN, 9.   59 Ind P, I, 470.
60 Op. cit., I, 241.   61 Op. cit., I, 532.   62 MST, 20 (1946 offprint, 10).
63 ER, 63.

for "clear and definite thought" that "he became deficient in depth and lacking in organic character." [64] Yet it can hardly be said that this statement manifests any hostility to reason. In fact, it is irrational to concentrate exclusively on areas of thought where clarity is easily attained to the neglect of areas where vaguenesses abound; but the need of clarification is therefore all the greater. Radhakrishnan finds reason a necessary tool for the mystic.

But when we turn to Radhakrishnan's account of intuition, the picture becomes less clear. First of all, exactly what does he mean by intuition? It is characterized, he tells us, by "integral oneness," and he quotes the Upaniṣads, St. Paul, and Ruysbroek in support of this conception.[65] He speaks of "the intuition of the all-pervading unity of the self and the universe." [66] Thus intuition is in some sense a synoptic grasp of totality—a sort of *Gestalt* experience. There are statements which identify it with the "peace, power, and joy" of mystical realization, and that claim for it self-sufficiency and completeness.[67] If taken literally, this last assertion would place it above all rational criticism, unless the "completeness" is intended to include all possible experience and all possible thought, thus being identical with the Hegelian Absolute for which the true is the whole, or with the Spinozistic *scientia intuitiva*. But if this be meant, then all ultimate difference between intuition and reason vanishes, and complete intuition is simply a name for complete reason. Some utterances of Radhakrishnan incline one to this interpretation. Intuition, he tells us, "stands to intellect as a whole to a part, as the creative source of thought to the created categories which work more or less automatically." [68] Intellect is the step by step, piece by piece movement of the mind toward the total truth, whereas intuition is the perception of the whole in one grasp—a point of view which reminds one of W. E. Hocking's interpretations in *The Meaning of God in Human Experience*.

On the other hand, there are hints of a somewhat humbler place for intuition. "Intuitive realisation," we are told, "is the means to salvation." [69] But if it is means only, it is not the end, and so is not the all-inclusive whole. If, as he tells us, "integrated lives are the

64 Ind P, I, 469, 470. Some would regard this as too sweeping a criticism of the Buddha.

65 *Op. cit.*, I, 196f.

66 IVL, 125.

67 See IVL, 92f.

68 S. Radhakrishnan and J. H. Muirhead (eds.), *Contemporary Indian Philosophy* (1936), 269.

69 IVL, 128, cf. 138-143.

saved ones," [70] then intuition is really the experience of the unity of the human self.

Besides being an experience either of ultimate wholeness or of human integration, intuition testifies to objective reality in a special way. It "tells us that the idea [of God] is not merely an idea, but a fact," [71] although it is not quite clear how intuition, apart from the claim to immediate knowledge, accomplishes this objectification. The relation is clearer when stated in terms of hypothesis and verification. "To say that God exists means that spiritual experience is attainable. The possibility of this experience constitutes the most conclusive proof of the reality of God." [72] Here we have the ordinary logic of rational induction and experiment. So is it also when Radhakrishnan declares that "the chief sacred scriptures of the Hindus, the Vedas, register the intuitions of the most perfected souls." [73] On the other hand, there are dark limits of mystery, which may be regarded either as humble statements of human ignorance or as adumbrations of something essentially irrational in the universe.

Such, for example, is the flat assertion that mysticism "is the admission of mystery in the universe." [74] This would be well and good if it meant only that "now we see in part" or that no deductive system could ever find concrete reality entailed by premises which did not contain it. Yet, when he says that

Rāmānuja's view is the highest expression of the truth, though Śaṁkara would add that the real is something larger and better than our thinking has room for,[75]

he seems to hint that reality contains something accessible to mystical intuition, but forever hidden from reason. This is confirmed by his statement of Śaṁkara's view (and his own) that "the relation between the Absolute Spirit and the changing multiplicity is an incomprehensible one." [76] If it be utterly incomprehensible and ineffable, how can one believe it to be real, or have any idea what one is believing? Yet it may be, as he goes on to say, that this is merely a "wise agnosticism," and not an ultimate irrationalism. One must, however, frankly admit that the relations between reason and intuition are not fully cleared up.

[70] MST, 39 (1946 offprint, 30).   [71] MST, 39 (1946 offprint, 30).
[72] *The World's Unborn Soul* (1936), 21. Hereafter referred to as *WUS*.
[73] HVL, 17.   [74] ER, 61f.   [75] Ind P, II, 712.
[76] Brightman (ed.), *Proceedings of the Sixth International Congress of Philosophy*, (1926), 688.

As in every mystical absolutism, so in Radhakrishnan's, a fifth problem arises, namely, that of "the value and destiny of the individual." Here again, one confronts the question of ultimate "dualism" or "nondualism"—that is, in Occidental terms, of an idealistic (or personalistic) pluralism or an idealistic singularism. There are many statements by Radhakrishnan which evaluate the individual so highly as to imply almost a commitment to "dualism" or personalistic pluralism. "The Supreme has an individual interest in and a delicate care for human beings." [77] No Christian theist, not Whitehead himself, could state the ultimate nature of individuality more strongly than this. Again, there are many statements of self-realization as the ethical ideal, in which the self by no means melts away in the face of the statement that "to realise oneself is to identify oneself with a good that is not his alone." [78] In expounding the bhakti marga of the Gītā, he states (with obvious sympathy) that "devotion to the Supreme is possible only with a personal God, a concrete individual full of bliss and beauty." [79] If you deny bliss and beauty, you deny the whole sum of mystical meaning. But if you affirm bliss and beauty, according to this passage, you affirm a personal God, and the principle of concrete individuality as the basic principle of mysticism.

Here one comes upon the most puzzling feature of Radhakrishnan's thought, and of Hinduism in general. Is God personal or is he not? We have just seen the assertion that if mysticism is valid, God is personal. Then we read that in the Upaniṣads "the Absolute becomes a personal God. Though it is not the final truth, ordinary religious consciousness requires it." [80] This means to an Occidental that God is truly not personal, but that, for purposes of accommodation, he may fruitfully, but falsely, be treated as personal by the ignorant. But the Hindu repudiates both of the bold statements just made, and concludes that "the Absolute is both personal and impersonal." [81] Here the Occidental mind reaches an impasse. The Occidental feels much more at home with the thought of Rāmānuja, as Radhakrishnan reports it:

> Mystics try to "melt their souls in God." But there is no evidence that any mystic achieved such a goal. . . . He who has become God cannot return to tell us of his experience. . . . [He] who narrates his story has not become God.[82]

---

[77] MST, 13 (1946 offprint, 3).　　[78] Ind P, I, 210, 212. See IVL, 111, and RWN, 30.
[79] Op. cit., I, 559.　　[80] Op. cit., I, 233.　　[81] Op. cit., I, 234.　　[82] Op. cit., II, 712.

For Rāmānuja, "mokṣa" always implies an "other" and in the highest state the released soul "attains the nature of God, though not identity with him." [83] If Radhakrishnan could persuade himself to adopt the view of Rāmānuja, he would be more consistent with his own religious and ethical experience and far more intelligible to the Occidental mind.

Whatever his conclusion, Radhakrishnan dwells often on the individual, human and divine. "The soul in solitude is the birthplace of religion" [84]—words which suggest both Plotinus and Whitehead. Radhakrishnan recognizes the "endowment, personal, racial, and historical" of each religious genius.[85] He sees that religious experience is not the pure unvarnished presentment of the real in itself, but is the presentment of the real already influenced by "the ideas and prepossessions of the perceiving mind." [86] The individual is, then, an important factor. Religion as "the inward life of the spirit" is "the personal sense of the divine." [87] He dubs those mystics "fanatics" for whom "the will to live is not the highest good." [88] There is, then, in Radhakrishnan a large body of interpretation of mystical experience which is clearly a personalistic pluralism, nearer to Rāmānuja than to Śaṁkara, and therefore "dualistic" in the Hindu sense.

But there are other, nondualistic utterances. The individual's divinity is "a part of God aspiring to be the whole." [89] Radhakrishnan declares real the experience which Rāmānuja deemed impossible, when he said that "the privacy of the individual self is broken into and invaded by a universal self which the individual feels as his own." [90] Again: "it is impossible for man, a child of eternity, to distinguish himself from God in the long run." [91] To use his more poetic expression, "heaven and earth are felt to flow together." [92] In expounding the Gītā, Radhakrishnan remarks that "the distinctness of particular persons . . . [is] only accidental." [93] Although there are times when the ethical is primary for Radhakrishnan, there are other times when nondualism triumphs and the ethical is only a means to the all-inclusive mystical. In the highest mystical state "the individual being is absorbed in the Supreme. This alone has transcendental worth, but the moral struggle as preparing the way for it is not useless." [94] Or, the mystical may be more essential to the moral, even on the nondualistic levels, for:

83 Op. cit., II, 710.   84 ER, 53.   85 HVL, 25.
86 HVL, 24.   87 IVL, 89, 91. See also WUS, 19.
88 ER, 99f.   89 Ind P, I, 209.   90 IVL, 92.
91 RR, 424.   92 Ind P, I, 237.   93 Op. cit., I, 552.   94 Op. cit., I, 230.

It is when we destroy the exclusiveness of our individuality and therewith the sense of separateness that we enter the joy of religion and realise the full freedom of the spirit. The possibility of this religious realisation is the presupposition of all morality.[95]

The ultimate nondualistic mood appears in the sublime words: "Apart from eternity there is nothing that can, strictly speaking, be called human." [96] It can hardly be said that Radhakrishnan's thought about the individual achieves clear and coherent unity. Different aspects of the mystical experience lead him to irreconcilable theories and assertions of ultimate mystery.

The sixth aspect of mystical experience which Radhakrishnan considers is the mystic's evaluation of the world of nature. Inherent in all mysticism is the claim to supreme value—a value transcending all material values, if indeed the material has any value at all in comparison with the mystic intuition. Radhakrishnan would agree that the world has, indeed, no intrinsic value, and no independent "material" reality, of the kind that materialists or naturalists would assert. But he strongly insists that it is false to the meaning of Indian mysticism to hold that it implies that the world is unreal. He holds Deussen responsible for the spread of the erroneous view which ascribes to Hindu mystics the belief that the world is mere shadow and illusion. On the contrary, Radhakrishnan holds, the mystical experience is a vision of the world as rooted in Brahman. "The world," he says, "is God's revelation of Himself." [97] He sees clearly, of course, that the mystic's insight is perception of a reality that transcends the world. But he holds that illusionism and pantheism are equally false to the mystic experience. Illusionism asserts that God alone is real and the world nothing. Pantheism asserts that the world, being identical with God, is everything. In Radhakrishnan's eyes, the mystical experience, far from denying the world, glorifies it; and, equally far from identifying God with the world, reveals God's transcendence of it.

Such is the import of statements like this: "The Upaniṣads declare that the universe is in God. But they never hold that the universe is God. God is greater than the universe, which is His work." [98] This combined assertion of immanence and transcendence brings the mystic meaning very close to personalistic theism—nearer to Rāmānuja than to Śaṁkara. Radhakrishnan's condemna-

95 Op. cit., I, 226.   96 ER, 81.
97 Ind P, I, 186, 190f.   98 Op. cit., I, 203.

tion of "false asceticism," to which reference has already been made, rests on the belief that such asceticism "regards life as a dream and the world as an illusion," a view "which has obsessed some thinkers in India." [99] This view, he declares, is foreign to the Upaniṣads, however much it may fascinate some Hindus and some Occidentals. The mystic view, then, is not an acosmism, but an idealism which sees the world to be "one with consciousness." [100] Even for Śaṁkara, Radhakrishnan insists, mokṣa is "not the dissolution of the world, but only the disappearance of a false outlook." [101] Schweitzer, then, is wrong in distinguishing between Hinduism and Christianity on the ground that one is world-denying and the other world-affirming. Both Hinduism and Christianity, Radhakrishnan declares, are "both world-affirming and world-denying." [102]

We may summarize Radhakrishnan's interpretation in this area by saying that, for him, the mystic experience illuminates the world as a revelation of God, rather than denying the world as an enemy of God. Mysticism gives the key to the divine meaning of the world rather than condemning the world as meaningless. Thus his view of mysticism is more friendly, as we have seen, to ethical activity in the world, and, we may add, to physical sciences, than is the traditional *contemptus mundi*.

V

He who undertakes a general appraisal of Radhakrishnan as an interpreter of mysticism is indeed rash. Yet to that rashness we are committed by any attempt to understand his thought.

1. It must be said that Radhakrishnan stands out as an authority for the whole world of scholarship in the objective and appreciative interpretation of Hindu mysticism in all of its standard historical forms, although one misses a treatment of so great a philosophical mystic as Swami Vivekananda. Perhaps Radhakrishnan regards Vivekananda as too near to our own time for appraisal in perspective. Radhakrishnan's treatment is distinguished for its high evaluation of the ethical and social implications of mysticism.

[99] *Op. cit.,* I, 219.
[100] In IVL, 44, he cites Eddington, *The Nature of the Physical World*, 321, in support of such idealism.
[101] Ind P, II, 637.   [102] ER, 65-76.

In this, perhaps, he has been affected by the noble example of the late Mahatma Gandhi.

2. Despite the soundness and breadth of his scholarship, it is noteworthy that Radhakrishnan, although in many ways a mediator between East and West, pays relatively little attention to the kinships and contrasts between Hindu mysticism and Christian mysticism, either Biblical or post-Biblical. One might almost speak of a blind spot for much non-Hindu mysticism, whether Jewish, Christian or Moslem. In view of Radhakrishnan's generous and universal mind this is difficult to understand, unless it be ascribed to the accident of scholarly specialization.

3. Although Radhakrishnan sheds much light on the nature of the mystical experience—his understanding of it being far richer, more discriminating and more sympathetic than that of William James—yet his chief interest is not psychological, but philosophical. He is one of the greatest philosophers of mysticism in modern times.

4. Nevertheless, it cannot be said that his philosophy of mysticism is wholly consistent at all points. To the present writer, Radhakrishnan seems not to arrive at a coherent decision about the problem of singularism and pluralism—in Hindu terms, "nondualism" and "dualism;" not to be fully clear about the nature of God as personal or impersonal; not to assign a clear place to the individual, although his view of physical nature is clarifying and harmonious with mystical experience.

5. It is evident that Radhakrishnan is deeply moved by all types of mysticism, and is remarkably gifted in his powers of insight and analysis. Yet he shows greatest kinship with bhakti, the mysticism of love and devotion. As he grows more and more mature, and the needs of the world more acute, his stress on the moral and social implications of mystical faith becomes more dominant.

6. There remains the question: Is Radhakrishnan himself a mystic? To what extent are the experiences of "realization" and "liberation" his own experiences? As was said at the start, he is surely not an autobiographical mystic. He is reticent. He is one of the radiant, not one of the self-descriptive personalities. But what is the inner nature of the experience which is for him the source of radiance? He has not chosen to reveal this side of his nature and it would be presumptuous to judge it. Yet Radhakrishnan himself might describe it in the terms in which he describes Hinduism itself: "Hinduism is therefore not a definite dogmatic creed, but

a vast, complex, but subtly unified mass of spiritual thought and realisation." [103] Be that as it may, to know the thought of Radhakrishnan is more than the acquisition of further philosophical knowledge. It is a spiritual experience.

EDGAR SHEFFIELD BRIGHTMAN

DEPARTMENT OF PHILOSOPHY
THE GRADUATE SCHOOL
BOSTON UNIVERSITY

[103] HVL, 21.

11

K. J. Spalding

MYSTICAL RELIGION AND THE
MYSTICISM OF RADHAKRISHNAN

MYSTICAL RELIGION AND THE
MYSTICISM OF RADHAKRISHNAN

I AM so far in agreement with Professor Radhakrishnan's views on religion that I shall attempt, in this essay, not so much to criticise them as to throw what light I can on their mystical aspects. I shall speak, in the first place, of the gradual attainment by man of that experience which forms the basis of the mystic's religion; secondly, of the arrest of that progress in men of smaller attainment; and, thirdly, of the work of the mystic in discovering to his fellowmen something of the truth of his own religion and philosophy.

I. Man's Rise to Mystical Religion

I

"Religion," says Radhakrishnan, "is native to the human mind, integral to human nature itself. Everything else may dissolve; but belief in God, which is the ultimate confession of all the faiths of the world, remains." [1] Native as religion is to the human mind, men are as little born with a religious experience as they are with an artistic or scientific experience. The greatest of men are as subject to this fate as the least of them. A child may become an Einstein, a Shakespeare, a Śaṁkara. But in the cradle the experience which is to distinguish these men is still implicit in them: it is an experience of which they are no more aware than are the mothers who bore them. The unusual experience of such men is not on that account unnatural to them. It belongs to them to develop their particular powers as naturally—as natively—as it belongs to their bodies to become the developed bodies of men. The wisest men appear in the world like seeds destined to continue growing till they have developed the flower and fruit natural to them.

It is not without difficulty that such men grow to their full stature. Their bodies' environment forms for them their first experi-

[1] EWR, 18.

ence of the universe. Like other youthful animals, they touch, and look, and listen in the interest rather of their animal desires and aversions than of the things their senses present to them. The sun may become for them a thing of glory; but they may first have loved it for its warmth, and hated it as much for its heat.

Conscious of a natural environment, the youthful genius is not less conscious than his fellows of a human environment. Instinctively measuring men by his animal desires and aversions, he may rate men as he rates the things of nature, as they please or pain his body rather than for anything they may be in themselves. He may presently come to consider his father a perfect Hyperion; but he may first have loved him for his sweetmeats, and hated him as much for his blows.

A child is rarely born into a society that has no word for God. Be the child who he may, his God may be at first as much the subject of his body as the sun or his father. His God may become for him a Being in whose consuming Presence he dies to every thought of himself. But in his childhood he may be as prone as another to worship Him for His toys and to loathe Him as much for His pains.

II

Things may, however, sometimes call to man with a voice of their own; and in boyish moments men may discover that what things are in themselves is of more importance to them than what they are for their bodies. Still aware, like the animal, of "the use of the useful," they may, with the Chinese philosopher Chuang-tse, also become aware of "the use of the useless." [2] The future man of science may discover in the motion of a marble something to set his mind wondering; the future dramatist, in the tale of a fairy may find something mysteriously reminiscent of his mother's butcher; the future prophet, in a myth of his people, may divine something in God of more wonder than his works.

What things are in themselves becomes a question more attractive to minds of this kind than what things may be for their bodies. They begin to find their life in the objects that have arrested their attention: for one, it may be in the motion of a star; for another, in some hero of his imagination; for a third, in a God of his own thinking. The animal identifies himself with his body and separates himself from the world. But these are thinkers who would rather identify themselves with the world and separate themselves

[2] Chuang-tse, chap. IV.

from their bodies. A creature wholly careful of his body is an 'egoist.' Whereas a mind which has found 'itself' in another is a lover. The objects of its love grow dearer to it than its hands and feet; and in a star, in a man, in a God, it comes to, it knows "itself;" a creature no longer immature like the Prodigal Son; but one, rather, who has found "himself in" returning from the far country of his body to his native home in the universe.

III

In the mind of the 'lover' lies an implicit philosophy unrecognised by men of a·more animal experience. The mind of the animal is properly directed to those objects of its environment which maintain its life or threaten its death. For the consciousness of the animal these objects are-presented to its senses without thought or understanding of its own. Their stimuli impress the animal mind as accidentally as print a blank surface of paper; and, thus supplied with the daily news of the world, the animal develops a mind capable of dealing with its various environments. A nature-based philosophy like that of Locke develops naturally out of such premises: only as man has a body can he have a mind. Attractive as a philosophy of a mind-engendering body may be, it is yet not without its difficulties; and philosophers like Berkeley, Hume, and the modern Logical Positivists are enough to frighten an animal about its very existence. True or false as this philosophy may be, it is not the philosophy implicit in the mind of the 'lover.' In unity as he feels himself to be with the world, he is conscious of an intimacy of his mind with its objects rather than of its accidental and unpurposed relation to them. A partner of the world rather than a puzzled stranger in it, he feels himself moved to take hold of its objects and to discover himself and his universe like Helena and Hermia in the play, "both in one key," things "seeming parted, but yet an union in partition." [3] Desire is the energy that moves the mind, and it is therefore through an "intellectual desire" that the mind of the lover finds itself constrained to seek its ends. The Object of its search must be a thing that is: a thing, therefore, for its perfect thought, not limited but limitless: a thing, accordingly, not now existent and then non-existent; nor here existent and there non-existent: but rather a thing 'eternal' and 'infinite.'

The eternal and infinite expanses of nature welcome a mind which, in virtue of the world's affinity with itself, must find what

[3] Shakespeare, *A Midsummer Night's Dream*, 3, 2, 206; *As You Like It*, 1, 3, 99.

its reason must think. For nature, in the words of Parmenides, is a Being "complete, immoveable, and without end: nor was it ever, nor will it be; but now it *is;* all at once; a continuous one." [4] In the "profoundest rest" of nature the mind for a moment wins its own. Nature, however, is a kind of being which presently vexes the mind that rests in it. Not knowing *what* it is, or *that* it is: for the mind an "All," but in itself nothing: Nature plays the lover false; and, a truant from his thought, becomes for him a thing in want of the true Being that can alone satisfy his reason.

Reason which sought to find its end in a nature Eternal and Infinite can now only wonder at a being discovered to be thus anomalous; and, ceasing to require, must lose its power to control it. Left a prey to chance and uncertainty, Nature is discovered to be a being multiple rather than One. It falls into a strange disruption, and, in a void deprived of the 'being' expected of it appear galaxies in motion: the roving sun; man's earth—a scurrying speck; bodies formed alike of turbulently moving particles that mock the eyes of men. Reason might appear to be outwitted by a seething chaos so offensive to its thinking. But, estranged as it is from the world, the world is still no stranger to reason. Rather, reason renews its claim upon nature, and, present to accuse, is present also to remedy what it accuses. In the multiplicity of nature a Newton —an Einstein—in time discover a rational Unity: a Unity which, reminiscent of "The One," makes for their ears a new "music of the spheres." Modified though it may be, reason's control of the world is not destroyed by Nature's lapses; its seeming chance gives way to the 'necessity' of a mind which must find what its reason must think. The inductive sciences of nature form only a limb on the infinite tree of man's knowledge. But, still imperfectly explored as nature's secrets may be, the genius of science continues to play its part in revealing to man's thought something of the rational truth of the universe.

In controlling the physical world science, however, cannot remove the defect inherent in its enigmatic mode of 'being;' and, in creatures that know *what* they are and *that* they are, reason meets, beyond the physical world, with beings more real than the things the senses perceive. "If the universe," says Pascal, "were to crush him, man would still be more noble than that which kills him, because he *knows* that he dies . . . the universe knows nothing of this." [5] A self-knowing creature like himself is what the lover is looking for; and, having found him, he becomes as much one thing

4 Fragment 8 (tr. by J. Burnet).   5 Pascal, *Pensées,* 347 (Temple Edition).

with him as he became with nature. Man, however, is a being destined presently to vex the mind no less than nature had done. Though for its thought men may appear as "glittering and sparkling Angels," and as "strange seraphic pieces of life and beauty," [6] yet none possesses that perfect mode of Being which can alone fulfill man's perfect thought. A Being which, altogether un-becoming, altogether *is;* a Being, like nature's Ideal, Eternal and Infinite; which is not the being conceived in the spirit of man; and, finding joy in it, the lover looks still for the true Being that can alone satisfy his reason.

Reason that sought its end in the life of Spirit must wonder again at a Being which, superior as it is to the whole world of nature, is yet discovered to be thus strangely defective; and, ceasing to require a thing estranged from its own thought, must once more lose its power to control it. Left a prey to chance and uncertainty, human beings appear in the world as wanting to their proper truth as are the strange phenomena of nature. In place of a "seraphic piece of life and beauty," may appear a Salome; instead of a "glittering and sparkling Angel," a Judas. A society of lovers disappears into a riot of egoists. Creatures "behaving unseemly;" "easily puffed up;" "seeking their own"—these are the tragic beings the lover discovers he must measure against beings who can say of one another "Thou and I am One." "What a piece of work," the disillusioned lover may now mutter,

is a man! How noble in reason! How infinite in faculty! In form and movement how express and admirable! In action how like an angel! In apprehension how like a god! The beauty of the world! The paragon of animals! And yet what, to me, is this quintessence of dust? Man does not delight me; no, nor woman neither . . .[7]

Present to accuse reason, however, is also present to redeem what it accuses. To its thought man is not a stock or stone, doomed by its nature to remain for ever unaware of what it is. Prodigal Son though man may be, he may become aware of his error; and, coming "to himself," he may bring to birth in him that reason which, as "native" in himself as in the saint, shall leave him at the last a "glittering Angel," a "seraphic piece of life and beauty."

In such a redeemed world of the Spirit reason must, however, still meet with a Being which, for ever 'becoming,' never wholly *is;* with a nature which, wanting an Eternal and Infinite Being, must still leave the lover longing. A Being as Self-knowing as Spirit,

6 Traherne, *Centuries of Meditations*, III, 3.
7 Shakespeare, *Hamlet*, 2, 2, 315-322.

yet as Infinite as nature, is the Being the lover must now expect. In One who in His single essence unites the perfection of all that reason has hitherto been able to think of, the lover divines at last the end of his pursuit. That "whose nature demands everything that perfectly expresses Being" [8] is to be seized at last by the thought of the lover of 'Being.' For, "the Good which is the object of the will is therein wholly gathered, and outside It that same thing is defective which therein is perfect." [9]

The lover finds his reason holding him all the more closely to the Being which now appears to him because of the trouble it has taken to attain It. He seizes It the more eagerly for having been kept for a while from It by inferior objects which now, beside Its sole Reality, look like unreal wraiths of things. The Being which in boyish moments may have captivated his emotion now holds his reason more completely than the best of beings that had formerly attracted it. His reason knows now that, entire in God, no one "who looks upon that Light can turn to other object, willingly, his view." [10]

That which perfectly fulfils the truth of reason cannot fail to *be*. Absolved by thought of all defect of Being, It cannot assume, like nature and Spirit, forms which, uncontrollable by reason, must leave the mind in doubt of what It is or is not. The defective forms of nature and Spirit leave the mind continually straying. A sun may be imagined to exist where no sun is; a Spirit may be fancied which is of no more reality than a mythical elfin of fairyland. But, unable itself to assume an empirical form undetermined by reason, the Being of God is one immune from the doubts that shadow lesser forms of being.

The End of man's being is therefore not such as to find a way into his fancy. By no effort of his mind can man conceive the Thing that fulfils him to be a mere object of fairyland. Without that Being through whose sole attainment he can be 'himself,' man can not be; but assured as he must be that 'It is,' he must be as sure that he himself is. Uncertain as he may remain of the fortuitous manifestations of nature and Spirit, he remains more certain of his unassailable fulfilment in the Being of God than of his sight of the sun. Just as once a world of Living Things more real than nature broke in on his mind, so now a One more real than either breaks in on it. The unchallengeable Whole of Being, in which it

8 Spinoza, Letter 36.   9 Dante, *Paradiso*, xxxiii, 103-105 (Temple Classics).
10 *Ibid.*, xxxiii, 95-97.

is his reason's lot to rest, stands plain at last before him. In the presence of the Eternal and Infinite he feels, his breathing stilled, Its Peace, and his. Men under the constraint of their senses may fail to feel the Presence of a Thing inaudible, invisible, intangible. But to lovers of 'Being,' to the "pure in heart," [11] there comes at times a sense-less sight of It, and to them it grows as plain as to the astronomer does the still abyss of the skies.

In the Light of this Being the seer at first discerns that which his own human nature must discover in It. In its living Spirit something of man's proper being must appear to him. The love that holds himself to the world he now perceives to be an image of the love which holds God to it. In God the lover first sees the love which is the truth of himself; and, reaching beyond the 'righteousness' of men, he perceives in Him the Universal Father of the world. In a philosophical Vision he encounters Very Being living into being, and every part of It in love. But, presently withdrawing from It everything of human origin, he turns at last to contemplate It in Itself. Come wonderingly to That before whose Infinite Existence "all nations are as nothing," [12] he looks into Its "naked Being:" [13] all that is concerned with man forgotten, he feels himself "as one who is placed in a profound and vast Solitude whither no creature can come:" [14] and, having therein found a Being who has done all for him that can be done for him, he finds out all it means to be a man.

Such seers have found themselves in time to be more than they thought they could be. They come so near the flame that "like unto hard iron which so assumeth . . . the form of the fire that it almost turneth into fire," so, "united with God," they "almost become Divine and transformed in God." [15] Though man cannot "touch bottom," [16] yet he is not without attaining at last some sorrowless feeling of what it is to be God. "On a par" [17] with God rather than with man, he feels that "Thou and I am One;" and, knowing with Spinoza, that "Love directed towards the Eternal and Infinite feeds the mind with pure joy, and is free from all sadness," [18] he enters at last "the dark Silence where all lovers lose themselves." [19]

[11] *St. Matthew*, V, 8.   [12] Isaiah, XL, 17.   [13] *The Cloud of Unknowing*, V.
[14] St. John of the Cross, *The Dark Night of the Soul*, II, xvii.
[15] B. Angela of Foligno, *The Book of Divine Consolation*, Tr, iii, c. 6 (tr. by M. G. Steegmann).
[16] Meister Eckhart, *Tractate*, 11.   [17] Eckhart, *Sermon* LXXVI, 4.
[18] Spinoza, *De Intellectus Emendatione*.
[19] Ruysbroeck, *De Ornatu Spiritualium Nuptiarum*, III, 4.

IV

"Native" to the human mind as this divine experience must be; alive as it may therefore be in the heart of a child: yet, like other rare experiences, it lies undeveloped in the common thought of mankind, and blossoms wholly in the life of only a few. Wonderful even to these as such an experience may seem, yet presently it appears to them as only the promise of a further wonder, to be the prologue only to a new experience in which the Self which still remains in them is to be transmuted wholly into God; when their intellectual 'reason' is to become a super-intellectual 'intuition.' As Radhakrishnan puts it:

This religious or intuitional experience is the summit of the whole evolution. It is the crowning round of human life. It is the completion and the consecration of the whole struggle. It is "the light that never was on sea or land, the consummation, and the poet's dream." Here terminates the philosopher's quest for reality in which thought can rest.

If self-consciousness is the distinctive mark of the intellectual experience, self-forgetfulness characterises the *Ananda* (bliss) condition. . . . The release from this world of trouble, risk and adventure can be had only by losing the separate self. Absolute surrender of self to God, a perfect identification with the divine will, will "let us pent-up creatures through into eternity, our due." The *Swetswatara Upaniṣad* says: "In this wheel of Brahman, which is the support as well as the end of all beings, which is infinite, roams about the pilgrim soul when it fancies itself and the supreme ruler as different. It obtains immortality when it is upheld by him," i.e., when the soul thinks itself to be one with him (v, 61).[20]

The place 'reason' has given to the Self in its universe might seem to be one of which reason could not also deprive it. The ground of the truths of its reason, the Self is not, it seems, of a nature capable of being humbled by its reason. Yet, reason must conclude that, in filling the Self wholly, the Self's Final Object empties the Self wholly.

"Self-identical; always, endlessly, Complete,"[21] this Final Object of the Self is a "One-without-a-Second,"[22] which sums, Alone, all Being in Itself. There can be in the universe, so long as It is in the universe, no room for anything but Itself. As much an outcast from Being as a physical body lying outside the wholeness of In-

20 RR, 437, 449; *cp.* also IVL, 138.
21 Plotinus, *EN.,* III, vii, 11 (tr. by S. Mackenna).
22 Śaṁkara on *Chāndogya Upaniṣad,* vi, 16.

finite Space, every being outside God must be as "less than noth-ing" beside Him. That Being which the Self most wholly owns it learns as well to be a Being which must cause it to disown itself. For the Self to add itself to the All must be for the Self at once to withdraw itself from the All. The All has made a prey of that whose life lives only through the All; and He who wholly makes the Self is now perceived to be a Whole who wholly unmakes the Self.

In the presence of the One-without-a-Second the Self, obedient to its Aloneness, would resign its other being. It would become the nothing it must be in order that it may leave The One the All The One must be. But, eager to do away with itself, it discov-ers that it cannot do away with itself. Leaving itself, it is keep-ing itself still; and in saying, "I am not," it is still saying "I am." As sure at first of itself as of any of the truths of its reason, now the Self, perplexed and baffled, is only sure of its unsureness. Com-pelled alike to be and not to be, it lets go its hold of itself; it knows that it can be itself only as it is another than itself. In a truer nature than its own it craves to be that which its own nature must be. At the summons of its reason the Self now looks beyond its Self, and betrays its Self in order to be loyal to its Self. Having "grasped all of the divine that lies within its scope," the Self dreams boldly of a new seeing, and, not yet seeing, now knows that "Until the seeing comes, it will still be craving something which only the Vision can give." [23]

The animal identifies itself with its body; the lover rather with the world. "Thou and I are two," is the thought of the animal; "Thou and I am one," that of the lover. Yet, an union only "in partition," love, the yearning lover learns to feel, severs while it marries, and parts while it unites. "When I am from him I am dead till I be with him; when I am with him I am not satisfied, and would still be nearer him." [24] If in man the lover seeks a "love with-out partition," in the presence of the One-without-a-second, he must needs boldly assert it. Having become aware that, while the All exists apart from the Self, the Self, in conflict with its Second-lessness, cannot co-exist with It, he is aware that till "The parting be parted; the Severance at last be all severed," [25] he cannot reach "the crowning round of human life." The lover dreams to be a One with God rather than to remain a second beside Him. He

---

[23] Plotinus, VI, ix, 11.
[24] Sir Thomas Browne, *Religio Medici,* Part II, sect. 6.
[25] From the *Divan* of Jelaleddin Rumi (in W. Hastie's *The Festival of Spring,* No. VIII).

aspires to put away the knowledge of his 'reason' which makes him an other than God and to acquire a super-rational 'intuition' which shall make him the same with God. With a knowing that is an "un-knowing knowing"[26] he would surprise the super-rational truth of his own being: by "a transcending of all creatures, a perfect going forth from oneself; by standing in an ecstasy of mind,"[27] he would find the nothing that he is the All that he must be.

Looking to find its Self atoned with God, the Self runs in front of its reason and foretells a Being whose Secondlessness is not Its Aloneness. To its longing the "One-Alone" for its completed knowledge of It is to be a "One-Together;" and the God whose Being has naughted its own, to be a God whose Being consummates it.

Consider, I beseech you; grasp the unheard of! "God" and "God-head" are as distinct as Heaven and Earth. Heaven stands a thousand miles above the Earth, and so the Godhead is above God. God becomes and disbecomes. . . .[28] For when thought passes then God also passes. Man should not have a God merely intellectually conceived. Rather, man must have an essential God, who is high above the thoughts of men.[29]

In wholly knowing God the Self must cancel His Aloneness; but in wholly knowing itself it must cancel itself. "Where two grow one, one loses its nature."[30] To be completely quit of a Self, un-able to bear the Being of God, the Self must dare to die to its "first life and nature."[31] Foreseeing the Thing it is to be, the Self revokes the thing it is. "To be inwardly convinced of one's own non-being, and of one's Being solely in God and through God,"[32] is the end the Self now craves for itself. It stills the will that showed it the universe, and, no longer "knowing," presses no longer to be One with a God not One with itself. Now with an "unloving love" it looks to love God, as with an "unknowing knowing" it looks to know God. "It is as lover and beloved here, in a copy of this union, long to blend."[33] Now the Self "will give herself no foreign name, not man, not living being."[33] Quickened "to behold God purely, and looking to gather all its being and its life and whatever it is from the depths of God," in a fathomless self-simplification the Self

[26] Eckhart (e.g. I, pp. 7, 9, 12, 13, 55 of C. de B. Evans' transl.)
[27] Thomas à Kempis, De Imitatione Christi, III, xxxi.
[28] Eckhart (tr. by Rudolf Otto in his Mysticism, East and West, 14).
[29] Ibid., 134.   [30] Eckhart, Sermon V.   [31] Ibid.
[32] Fichte, The Way Towards the Blessed Life, Lecture IV.
[33] Plotinus, VI, vii, 34.

now looks to know "no knowing, no loving, nor anything else what-soever." [34]

Not by its own will can the Self appropriate the Being of an other than itself; not by a becoming of itself can it become an other than itself. Only by God's own bliss-bringing Substitution for itself: Only by His gift to it of His sole knowledge, "Thou and I am One:" can the Self at last identify itself with That whose Being must redeem its own outcast state. "The wind bloweth where it listeth, and thou hearest the sound thereof, but can'st not tell whence it cometh or whither it goeth: so is every one that is born of the Spirit." [35] The waiting lover knows not how that doom comes on him which is his salvation. But, as if riven by lightning, he who can endure his end knows suddenly that "That Art Thou" [36]—that, super-rationally One with God, he "hath eternal life, and is passed from death into life." [37]

No movement now, no passion, no outlooking desire: reason is in abeyance, and all reasoning, and even, to dare the word, the very Self: caught away, filled with God, man has in perfect stillness attained to aloneness. All the being calmed, he turns neither to this side nor to that, not even inwards towards himself. But, wholly at rest, he is as though he had become Immutability itself.[38]

V

The Self that has thus "won to the term of all her journeyings" [39] now perceives anew those lesser Objects of its universe which had seemed to dissolve with itself in the all-extinguishing Presence of God. "Immoveable in Itself, yet from this Immobility all things are moved, and all receive life." [40] "Without assent, or will or motion of any kind" [41] the super-rational One, outside the sight of reason, begets in peace to Itself all that whose being had seemed discreated by Its Secondless Existence.

The worlds He thus creates God knows with a Knowledge that keeps them nearer to Himself than any knowledge of man may keep his own remote mind-exiled Objects. "Flowing forth from Him

34 Eckhart, The Book of Benedictus, Part II. 35 St. John, III, 8.
36 Chāndogya Upaniṣad, vi, 8-16. 37 St. John, V, 24.
38 Plotinus, VI, ix, 11 (tr. by S. Mackenna. The translation of the final sentence is by B. A. G. Fuller).
39 Plotinus, VI, vii, 34.
40 Eckhart (tr. by R. Otto, in Mysticism, East and West, 174).
41 Plotinus, V, i, 6.

while remaining within Him," [42] they lie transformed from what they were in the inescapable Embrace of God. It is in "another glory" that the worlds the lover lost are found by him again. With a Love that holds them as near to Himself as the Knowledge emparts, He is a Father closer to his worlds than a man is to his children. Though He makes the nations "less than nothing," yet there is in God "nothing to be afraid of; everything in God is altogether loveable." [43] The human love that strains to be the thing it loves is the glimmer of the unjourneying Love with which God loves the universe. His nearer Knowledge keeps Him nearer to the worlds of His creatures than any lonelier love of man can ever keep the things his reason severs from him.

He who through his reason saw the world of nature in part only, knows her now wholly as she lies secure in God. "The Infinite Dwelling of the Infinite Being is everywhere: in earth, water, sky and air." [44] No longer baffled by a lifeless world unaware of itself, he sees her being now, "a many-splendoured thing," in the super-rational Presence of God. Comprehending the whole world, "both here and beyond the sea, and the abyss and ocean and all things," the creature given to perceive the World sustained in God "beholds naught save the Power divine alone, in a manner that beggars description; so that through excess of marvelling the soul cries with a loud voice, saying, 'this whole world is full of God.' " [45]

As near to Him as nature, spiritual creatures flow in turn from Him "while remaining within Him." Perceiving their presence there, the soul who once knew man, as she knew nature, in part only, sees him now, with everything that lives, complete in God; and, aware of her own consummation with them in this world, perceives, at peace, her self-owned, alien life extinguished in the only Life of God.

But when the soul is naughted, then of herself she neither works, nor speaks, nor wills. And in all things it is God who rules and guides her; and she is so full of peace that, though she press her flesh, her nerves, her bones, no other thing comes forth from them than peace.[46]

Winning the Worth his reason misses in him the "naughted" creature leaves the phantom-life of things away from That in which

---

[42] Eckhart, *Sermon* LXXXVIII.
[43] Eckhart, *In Collationibus*, 23.
[44] Kabir (tr. by Tagore, No. LVI).
[45] B. Angela of Foligno, *The Book of Divine Consolation*, Treatise III, Third Vision.
[46] St. Catherine of Genoa, *Life and Doctrine* (condensed).

RADHAKRISHNAN'S MYSTICISM 431

alone they have their being; and, aware of being an exalted Energy of God, in a secondless union with Him enjoys a bliss unyielded to his human nature. "Before the Unconditioned, the Conditioned dances: 'Thou and I are One,' this trumpet proclaims. The Guru comes, and bows down before the disciple: this is the greatest of wonders."[47]

At peace in the world of God, the creature thus naughted finds a peace still deeper silently awaiting it. A last transformation is to give it all that may be given it till, through God's total Substitution for itself, it finds itself unfalteringly the One it is eternally with Him. In the peace of its temporal life in God, there dawns at times on it the peace of a creature beyond time. In God it learns to live in repose a life where "all remains the same within itself, knowing nothing of change, for ever in a Now, since nothing for it has passed away or will come into being, but what it is now, that it is ever."[48] In "flowing forth from God while remaining within Him," this Life derives from Him a nature ignorant of any Self of its own existing "in and through itself."[49] Of the self of man that seeks and strives for itself it knows nothing. It has no sense of a self of its own to be "naughted." It knows itself for ever the unchangeable Rest of God which it for ever is; and in the Peace of God enjoys eternally the life He has appointed to it.

With new eyes these beings, unknown to temporal man, perceive in repose a new World of their own. The super-rational tie which keeps their being One with God's keeps them also one with one another and with all things. Themselves atoned with all things, they now know in turn all things atoned with all: the things which, even as creatures "self-naughted in God," they had still seen as many, they see now as One. "Within Its depths ingathered," each, like Dante—as he momentarily joined their company—, in joy perceives "together bound by love in one volume the scattered leaves of all the universe; . . . as though together fused, after such fashion that what I tell of is one simple flame."[50]

The nature these beings behold in God is free from the conflicting plurality which in the distant world of human sense startled man's toiling reason. Its quilt of many patches there, lies Here a web without a seam.

Here all blades of grass, and wood, and stone, all things are one. This is the deepest depth and thereby I am completely captivated. . . . Black

[47] Kabir, No. XXVIII.   [48] Plotinus, III, vii, 3.
[49] Eckhart, *Sermon* XL.   [50] Dante, *Paradiso,* xxxiii, 85-90.

does not cease to be black, nor white white—the opposites coincide without ceasing to be what they are in themselves. . . . In the Kingdom of Heaven all is in all, all is one, and all is ours.[51]

One with a Nature that is itself a One, the eternal Selves are here in turn harmoniously One with every other: and with a love-without-partition make together an eternal company-without-partition. With the penetration of a black that is white and a white that is black, all alike atone with all "without ceasing to be what they are in themselves." "Each has all, and is all, and is with all" in a world in which "no individual is severed from the whole."[52] Loving one in all things and all things in one, none can find themselves excluded from the universal meeting. "Those drunken with this wine, filled with the nectar, all their soul penetrated by this beauty, cannot remain mere gazers; no longer is there a spectator outside gazing on an outside spectacle: the clear-eyed hold the vision within themselves."[53]

In the peace of the eternal world the clear-eyed gaze beyond its beauty to the Peace whose Love impartibly unites them. "Tranquil in the fulness of glory;" "lapped in pure light;" "all good and beauty, and everlasting;"[54] the World the eternal creature folds in Peace is, with its Self, for ever "centred in the One, and pointed towards It . . . never straying from It."[55]

II. THE ARREST OF RELIGION

"Religious experience" thus implies, for the mystical thinker,

an integral, undivided consciousness in which not merely this or that side of man's nature but his whole being seems to find itself. It is a condition of consciousness in which feelings are fused, ideas melt into one another, boundaries broken and ordinary distinctions transcended. Past and present fade away in a sense of timeless being. Consciousness and being are not there different from each other. All being is consciousness and all consciousness being. Thought and reality coalesce and a creative merging of subject and object results. Life grows conscious of its incredible depths. In this fulness of felt life and freedom, the distinction of the knower and the known disappears. The privacy of the individual self is broken into and invaded by a universal self which the individual feels as his own. . . . He affirms that the soul has dealings, direct, intimate and luminous, with a plane of being different from that with

---

51 Eckhart (tr. by R. Otto, in *Mysticism, East and West*, 61).

52 Plotinus, I, viii, 2; III, ii, 1.   53 Plotinus, V, viii, 10.

54 Plotinus, III, viii, 10.   55 Plotinus, III, vii, 6.

which the senses deal, a world more resplendent but not less real than the conventional one. The experience is felt as of the nature of a discovery or a revelation, not a mere conjecture or a creation. . . . He claims for his knowledge of reality an immediate and intuitive certainty, transcending any which mere reason can reach. No further experience or rational criticism can disturb his sense of certainty. Doubt and disbelief are no more possible. He speaks without hesitation and with the calm accents of finality. Such strange simplicity and authoritativeness do we find in the utterances of the seers of the Upaniṣads, of Buddha, of Plato, of Christ, of Dante, of Eckhart, of Spinoza, of Blake. They speak of the real, not as the scribes, but as those who were in the immediate presence of "that which was, is and ever shall be." [56]

Few as those may be who attain to this Vision, it still remains, for all its rarity, "native" to men; it still remains a blossom to flower presently in them. Reared in the cold climate of this world, man's religious experience is commonly arrested in him; and the nature of this arrest constitutes a further subject for Radhakrishnan's discussion of religion. Man's experience is one which rises, like Jacob's ladder, from earth to Heaven; and on any of its rungs men may be unwittingly arrested. Some climbers may attain a mystic height without attaining the supreme Height, where, no longer men, they know that "Thou art Thou."

Others, rising to a 'rational' knowledge of God, may fail to attain to the lowest 'intuition' of God; and, on a giddy height though they may be, to the few above them they will appear as arrested in their ascent to the Divine: "While there abideth in thee any image or *like* thou art never the *same* as God." [57]

On a lower rung than these, other rational men may find themselves lovers of man rather than of God, and, without attaining to the felicity of the saint, may yet discover a felicity of their own in a creature "how noble in reason!, how infinite in faculty!" All that lives may become the prize of these lovers; and they may find 'themselves' in every beast and flower. In the "poetic experience," Radhakrishnan observes, "the mind grasps the object in its wholeness, clasps it to its bosom, suffuses it with its own spirit, and becomes one with it. 'If a sparrow came before my window,' Keats wrote, 'I take part in its existence and pick about the gravel.'" [58] "The endless variety of the sensible world" may become for the mystical climber a "symbol" only of "an invisible world which is behind and within it;" (*ibid.*) yet in the world's own living beauty

[56] IVL, 91f, 95.   [57] Eckhart, *Sermon* VII.   [58] IVL, 184.

the human poet or musician may revel in glories not guessed by lesser men and not despised by the greatest.

Still other men may find themselves lovers rather of nature than of man or of God. "Matter" is "at the highest an imperfect repre-sentation or translation of the truth into a lower plane." [59] Yet those who have reached this plane may discover themselves one with a world of strange wonders; in its "boundless spaces, and superhuman silences and profoundest rest," like the poet Leopardi, they may feel a peace peculiar to themselves. The multiplicity of nature's objects may be seized by these lovers; and, finding 'them-selves' in every beauty in it, with Traherne they may feel that "You never enjoy the world aright, till the Sea itself floweth in your veins, till you are clothed with the heavens and crowned with the stars." [60]

The scientist who finds 'himself' in this world is not less near to it than the poet or the artist. "The interpretability of nature is proof positive of the kinship of object with subject, nature with mind." [61] In his world of stars and atoms the scientist surprises a rational Unity as captivating to his mind as the rhythmical form of a rose is to the eye of a painter; and in his meeting with this beauty he feels himself to grow incorporate with it.

It is not man's study of physical science which sometimes alarms the 'metaphysician.' There is nothing in that study to prevent the scientist's continued progress up the ladder of knowledge. A physi-cist like Newton may find in the 'spiritual' doctrines of a Boehme mysteries as alluring to his mind as those of the heavens. Engaged in probing the dark secrets of nature other men of science may want the leisure to transcend the task which nature has allotted to them. The disciples of such men may, however, be less aware than their leaders of the position of physical science among other rational studies. Not yet conscious of the station which reason assigns to the physical world in the universe, they set foot on it as if it were the topmost rung of the long ladder of knowledge; and, with no incentive to move to anything beyond it, like the behav-iourist they may deny the existence of mind, and, like the atheist, the existence of God. One may agree with these ardent thinkers that "philosophy should be empirical in the sense that it must arise out of and be built upon experience. The difference," however,

between true empiricism and false is that, while the false wants to con-fine experience to the world of sense or the world at its surface, the true

---

[59] ER, 88.   [60] Traherne, *Centuries of Meditations*, I, 29.   [61] RR, 431.

takes for its field the whole of experience. . . . True empiricism is radical in that surface phenomena and highest religious intuitions both form its data.[62]

We often hear the complaint [a saint might parley with some doubting Thomas of a modern laboratory] that the Brahma of the Upaniṣads is described to us mostly as a bundle of negations. Are we not driven to take the same course ourselves when a blind man asks for a description of light? Have we not to say in such a case that light has neither sound, nor taste, nor form . . . ? Of course it can be seen; but what is the use of saying this to one who has no eyes? He may take that statement on trust without understanding in the least what it means, or may altogether disbelieve it, even suspecting in us some abnormality. [And the saint might continue his parley:] Does the truth of the fact that a blind man has missed the perfect development of what should be normal about his eyesight depend for its proof upon the fact that a larger number of men are not blind? The very first creature which suddenly groped into the possession of its eyesight had the right to assert that light was a reality. In the human world there may be very few who have their spiritual eyes open, but, in spite of the numerical preponderance of those who cannot see, their want of vision must not be cited as an evidence of the negation of light.[63]

If "there is a tendency to otherworldliness in Eastern religions" and to "this-worldliness" in "Western types," [64] yet in all countries of the world are to be found many who have still scarcely started to climb the ladder of knowledge. The egoism which belongs to all men in their cradles is, in these lingerers, rather nurtured than suppressed or annihilated. What things are for their bodies is of more concern to them than what things are in themselves; and, increasingly aware of "the use of the useful," they grow increasingly suspicious of "the use of the useless." One may grant, with these seekers, that the body—as a mind-borne thing of life and beauty— must have its part to play in the world. But, whereas animals (the lover may remind them) naturally live "by bread alone," the man who lives thus rather starves his life than feeds or entertains it.

For the genius of the animal man nature becomes a being to be artfully exploited—to be used like an engine rather than to be enjoyed like a friend. Man, accordingly, fills his world with devices of his own contriving; and endless objects of 'utility' take the place of nature's less luxurious articles.

---

62 *Ibid.,* 17.
63 R. Tagore, in his "Foreword" to Radhakrishnan's *Philosophy of the Upaniṣads,* xif.
64 EWR, 56.

[65] Men no less than nature are instinctively designed by the animal man to become his domestics. Aware from the very beginning of the use to him of his parents, he grows up in a society which, training him, like them, to serve them, offers him their services in return. His right to the care of men he thus learns to associate with a duty of his own towards them. Having become conscious that, on the performance of their duty rests, together with their own, the life of their society, a few men rise above the unthinking morality of the multitude; and, acknowledging the sanctity of 'moral imperatives,' these men acquire a 'self-mastery' obedient to the customs of their people. Moving downwards, other men may only so far follow custom as to reason themselves into a belief in their own innocence when they run counter to custom. The duties customarily required of men are, however, less generally acceptable to them than the pleasures derived from other men's duties towards themselves. "Wherefore should I," asks Edmund in *King Lear* (I, 2.2), "stand in the plague of custom?" Men of this persuasion learn in time to condemn the duties thrust by men upon them. They begin to assert their right to have no duties. To pay the wages they were forced to pay in return for other men's services they now conceive to be a sin against 'nature;' and, like Thrasymachus in Plato's *Republic* (I, 336-347), they proclaim the 'justice' of men to consist in an unconditional obedience to the 'strong' man's imperatives. To win, through the acquisition of absolute power over men, such unconditional dominion over them is thus as much a natural propensity of men as to win dominion over a plough or a locomotive.

If the lover's understanding of nature and man thus delays its appearance in the mind of 'animal' man, the lover's religious experience is no less delayed in it. The things his senses perceive in the world suggest even to primitive man the presence in the world of a mysterious Power as wide as the seas and as immeasurable as the heavens. 'Something,' it seems, omnipotently controls those objects on which his body's welfare wholly depends. At Its bidding the sun lightens the world; rains fall at Its summons; harvests ripen at Its commands. Less explicably this Power at times withholds Its expected services. In place of light comes darkness; in place of rain, drought; in place of plenty, withered harvests. A God conceived as 'righteous' is perceived in time by a few to be of more worth than divinities with egotistical tendencies; and, of greater discernment than

---

[65] The following passages contain quotations from an address by the present writer on "Mystical Experience," published in the journal, *Faith and Freedom* (1950).

other men, an Eliphaz or Zophar may attribute men's bodily disasters to an infringement of the social duties imposed on them by the laws of the Almighty.[66] Others, grown sceptical of the utility of their Deity, may presently lose all faith in His merits; and, discovering in the scientist's control of natural law an alternative for the Almighty's, may prudently dismiss Him from the universe. To make this capricious Power his servant must, nevertheless, remain a desire of the natural man more imperative in him than to make servants of men and of things. By bountiful services to men he wins their service to himself: by more bountiful services to this Power man naturally conceives a likely means of winning his way also with It. Prayers, sacrifices, incantations become the wages to be given expectantly to the Omnipotent in payment for Its attentions. Thus to win dominion over the mysterious Controller of the universe becomes as much the desire of the natural man as to win dominion over the wills of men and over the forces of nature.

Men, thus desiring, may, at times, actually experience the delights they look to win from their use of the world. But, with their world's sudden changes, come sudden disappointments and sorrows. "Joy and sorrow," the mystic Chuang-tse tells them, "come and go, and over them I have no control." [67] Now, rejoicing in a world of objects of use to the body, man is cast down by one which seems rather to misuse his body than to support and delight it. Nature's fertile harvests fail. Man falls out with man; and society with society. Identifying themselves with their bodies and severing themselves from the world, men are apt to dissolve the ties of custom which maintain the health of their societies. And, failing to form such ties with 'foreign' powers, societies are apt to whet their swords rather than their wits. Not yet understanding that "true love regards the whole world as one's country and all mankind as one's countrymen," [68] they inflict on themselves abundant pains unknown to the lover. Religion itself may be the food of man's grief-engendering egoism: fostering the pride he enjoys in being more favoured with the knowledge of God's will than ignorant neighbours or strangers, the unwary Puritan or Patriot may bring a strife upon men which may be as inimical to their bodies' interests as nature's plagues and famines. If animal men are thus apt to torture themselves, they may seem to be no less tortured by God. Even a righteous Job may find his Deity an undutiful servant—

66 The Book of *Job*.
67 *Chuang-tse*, chap. XXII (transl. by H. A. Giles).
68 EWR, 83.

unjustly repaying His wages with a service of disaster. Appearing no better than an uncontrollable Power, the God of animal man may show Himself at times an irresistible and unpetitionable Master: a Cause of the world not to be argued with; a Cause as able and as likely to destroy the body of man as to maintain and perpetuate it. "Vanity of vanities!" says the Preacher, "all is vanity." Expecting evil rather than good, man now becomes the prophet rather of the woes than of the joys of men. Willing his delights in vain, man's will itself becomes a thing of woe to him: like Schopenhauer he can only decry the vanity of its fierce energies; like the modern Existentialist he can discern nothing better in it than a *"passion inutile."* The Conqueror who has mastered the world lies as insecure in it as his scavenger. He must remain uncertain of his treatment by his servants. Nature respects a palace as little as a hovel; men betray the greatest; and, though he may conceive the Omnipotent to be his, he remains, for all his fancies, at the mercy of It. And there remains for him at last—as there remains for all men—"the inevitable graveyard:" non-existence; darkness; death.

III. The Progress of Religion

Arrested as religion may be in the mind of the 'animal' man, yet it remains as "native" to the least as to the greatest of men to climb the ladder of knowledge which leads to it.

The ideals we cherish may be still remote and unaccomplished, but the fact is we possess the ideals, and love them so much as to condemn the world because it does not conform to them. "We grant that human life is mean," wrote Emerson, "but how did we find out that it is mean? What is the ground of this uneasiness, of this old discontent? What is the universal sense of want and ignorance, but the fine innuendo by which the soul makes its enormous claim?" [69]

Finding that his world "is not a pleasure garden, but is full of pain and suffering," [70] man looks upward for some other; and, out of temper with the world of the egoist, moves at moments towards the world of the lover. An indolent animal may "wish to pick up religion as easily as a shell from the sand." [71] But more suffering souls become aware of an adventure, of a daring ascent, that shall in time transform them from the lowly beings they are into immortal creatures of "life and beauty." The risen lover is not called to relinquish the life of mankind. "The saints do not refuse to sit

[69] IVL, 56.   [70] *Ibid.*, 57.   [71] EWR, 86.

at the rich man's table; nor do they object to the scent of precious ointment." [72] The rich man's table, notwithstanding, may need to be left for a while by men who have not yet perceived the universe to be their table; and precious ointment abjured by such as have not yet found more precious perfume in a wild-flower. "Stepping over corpses," Hegel teaches us, "is the way in which the objective spirit walks in order to reach fulfilment;" [73] and men must die to live that they may later live to laugh.

To be unable to endure is moral weakness. We need not ask for pain, but it is a proof of strength to be able to face it. It is not for nothing that religions impose ardours and endurances. If religion asks us to renounce the good things of life . . . , it is because it believes that wrong can be righted and truth established by means of sacrifice deliberately undertaken.[74]

The code of ethics adopted by mysticism is noble and austere. It insists that suffering and renunciation are the life-blood of religion. In the splendid phrase of Wilamowitz, we must give our blood to the ghosts of our ideals that they may drink and live.[75]

To gain the higher, we must give up the lower. Unless our little self is sacrificed, progress is not possible. Every step on the upward path of realisation means sacrifice of something else. This sacrifice, which means friction, opposition and pain, is the penalty we have to undergo in rising to ourselves on account of our finiteness. Throughout we have these incidents in the growth of a soul. Pain and suffering are phases of all progress. The process of the life of self is also a process of death.[76]

To climbers thus prepared to suffer, the saint speaks of his own knowledge; and, coming down to them in the form of a Buddha, a Christ, a Mohammad, he gives them news of the Things known to him above. The saint rebukes the world in order to comfort it. "He dwells in God; and yet his heart goes out towards all creatures." [77] To men pregnant already with his truth, the saint urges self-examination, meditation, self-knowledge. "There is the need," he tells them,

for the single eye within, the closest correspondence between the secret thoughts and the overt desires. We cannot find out easily our secret impulses or deep desires. We cannot find ourselves, unless we use our leisure and solitude in contemplation. However difficult it may be, it is still the appointed way. Religion does not consist so much in prayers and rites as in those silent hours of self-communion which will help us

72 *Ibid.,* 139. 73 *Ibid.,* 104. 74 *Ibid.,* 121f.
75 ER, 295. 76 RR, 447.
77 Ruysbroeck, *De Ornatu Spiritualium Nuptiarum,* ii, 65.

to control our character, . . . purify our emotions and let the seed of spirit grow. The art of letting things grow in quietness, action in non-action, as the *Bhagavadgītā* has it, is Yoga.[78]

The sage pursues the path of the Socratic philosopher when he points men to that principle of "dharma" which "rouses us to a recognition of spiritual realities not by abstention from the world, but by bringing to its life, its business and its pleasures, the controlling power of spiritual faith." [79] "The basic principle of dharma is the realisation of the dignity of the human spirit, which is the dwelling-place of the Supreme." [80] Know and practise this, and you will "refrain from doing unto others what you will not have done unto yourself." [81] For men still drooping in the world of animal desire, the lover of man has a remedy of his own. Distinguishing between a "remote ideal" and a "practical programme," [82] he recommends to the Statesman that Principle of Adaptation advised of old by the Taoist philosophy,[83] and thus he leads men step by step towards the spiritual knowledge of themselves. The dharma of the true reformer

is an elastic tissue which clothes the growing body. If it is too tight it will give way, and we shall have lawlessness, anarchy and revolution. If it is too loose it will trip us and impede our movements. It should not be too far behind, or too far ahead of, intelligent public opinion.[84]

To men not born, like the saint, to become familiar with the wonder of God, the comforter offers the consoling knowledge of faith.

Thou wilt say, "How can that be? I have no knowledge of it!" I answer: What does it matter? The less thou knowest and the more firmly thou believest, the more laudable is thy faith . . . for perfect faith means, in mankind, a great deal more than make-believe. Therein we have actual knowledge. True faith is the one thing needful.[85]

Men are not without faith in a knowledge still to be born in them. If Fate, as Matthew Arnold felt, foresaw

> How frivolous a baby man would be—
> By what distractions he would be possessed,
> How he would pour himself in every strife,
> And well nigh change his own identity, . . .

---

[78] EWR, 96f. [79] RS, 105. [80] *Ibid.*, 107.
[81] *Ibid.*, 108. [82] *Ibid.*, 201. [83] *Chuang-tse*, chap. XXV.
[84] RS, 119. [85] Eckhart, *In Collationibus*, No. 20.

the poet might add:

> But often in the world's most crowded streets,
> But often in the din of strife,
> There rises an unspeakable desire
> After the knowledge of our buried life;
> A thirst to spend our fire and restless force
>
> In tracing out our true, original course;
> A longing to inquire
> Into the mystery of this heart which beats
> So wild, so deep in us—to know
> Whence our lives come and where they go.

In the least of men this faith in things not seen may pass at moments into sudden sight:

Occasionally perhaps each of us has had a few moments of impersonal joy, when we seem to tread not on solid earth but on uplifting air, when our whole being is transfused with a presence that is unutterable, yet apprehensible, when we are bathed in an unearthly atmosphere, when we touch the very limits of beatitude, where seeking interests and yearnings unfulfilled yield to attainment and serenity. Such moments of insight and moods of joy are a heightening and expansion, a deepening and enrichment of oneself, and yet of identity with the universe. In these experiences of shattering profundity, of intense exhilaration, when we are raised on wings into contact with reality, when we are filled with light and environed with the presence of spirit, we acquire a wonderful clarity of mind and feel ourselves to be parts of a friendly universe.[86]

K. J. SPALDING

BRASENOSE COLLEGE
OXFORD UNIVERSITY
ENGLAND

[86] RS, 44.

12

Joachim Wach

RADHAKRISHNAN AND THE COMPARATIVE
STUDY OF RELIGION

RADHAKRISHNAN AND THE COMPARATIVE
STUDY OF RELIGION

THE comparative study of religions has never been merely an academic concern for the great Hindu scholar to whose philosophy this volume is dedicated. He has been existentially interested in such studies since the days of his youth. In "My Search for Truth," the moving autobiographical sketch which he contributed to a volume entitled *Religion in Transition* (1937), he reports how the challenge by Christian critics of Hinduism, his own faith, impelled him at the time of his student-days at Madras to "make a study of Hinduism and find out what is living and what is dead in it."[1] Again and again in writings, he has traced historically phases of development in Western (Greek and Christian) and Indian (Brahmanic, Hindu and Buddhist) religious thought, and has analyzed in systematic fashion basic notions in Hinduism and Christianity.[2] Moreover, he has devoted at least one part of one of his books[3] to "Comparative Religion." Here he recapitulates briefly the growth of this science, discusses some of the current objections, shows its value, characterizes the spirit in which such study must be undertaken, and finally points up some problems which it must face. Here are some of the convictions to which the comparative study of religions has led the distinguished Hindu thinker: "It increases our confidence in the universality of God and our respect for the human race. It induces in us not an attitude of mere tolerance which implies conscious superiority, not patronizing pity, nor condescending charity, but genuine respect and appreciation."[4]

"The different religions have now come together, and if they are not to continue in a state of conflict or competition, they must develop a spirit of comprehension which will break down prejudice and misunderstanding and bind them together as varied expressions of a single truth."[5] Finally, by investigating parallels and

[1] MST, 19.   [2] E.g., ER (1939).   [3] EWR, Lecture I.
[4] *Ibid.*, 32.   [5] ER, 306.

analogies, such study "broadens our vision." [6] In addition to psychological and historical inquiries it poses the philosophical problem of value and validity. "How far can the facts gathered by Comparative Religion be accepted as expressing the reality of an unseen ground?" [7]

This sketch of the nature and the task of a comparative study of religions proves that Professor Radhakrishnan (a) is familiar with the expressions of the age-old quest for a definition of the relation of the different great religions of the world with each other and with the development of the sciences (history) of religion, such as was conceived in the 19th century by Max Mueller and his successors; (b) that he has contributed to our increase of knowledge of several of the great world faiths and their relations with each other; (c) that his studies have convinced him that all religions have developed in a peculiar ethnic, sociological, cultural, and intellectual environment; (d) that he is aware of resemblances and differences in their expressions; (e) that he regards them as "tentative adjustments, more or less satisfactory, to the same spiritual reality, after which the human spirit feels and by which, in some manner, it is acted upon;" [8] (f) that none of them ought to be regarded as "absolute," a conviction which Professor Radhakrishnan shares with E. Troeltsch; [9] (g) that understanding any form of religion requires sympathy and empathy.

The work of the Indian philosopher shows a preoccupation with two of the world religions: Brahmanism and Christianity. Buddhism comes next in his attention and appreciation. There are fewer references to Islam; which is surprising in view of the importance of this religion for the history of India.[10] He rarely refers to what is known as the tribal national religion and the "primitive" cults. The reasons for this preference are partly to be sought in his own personal development (Hindu home, Christian instruction), partly in his primary interest in the intellectual expression of religious experience or, in other words, the philosophical bent of his nature, and, last but not least, in his often voiced conviction that we have to "get behind and beneath all outward churches and religions, and worship the nameless who is above every name." [11] Though he finds this attitude in all parts of the world, especially in the mystics, we are led to believe that Brahmanism, in addition to

---

6 EWR, 36.   7 Ibid., 36.   8 Ibid., 19.
9 Die Absolutheit des Christentums.
10 But cf. the chapter on "Islam and Indian Thought" in HH, 65ff.
11 RWN, 24.

being the thinker's physical and intellectual home, represents to him very possibly the highest form of the eternal religious quest of man.

The student of the history of religions will have to ask: Does he do full or adequate justice to both, Brahmanism and Christianity? This question cannot be answered here, inasmuch as it would have to be discussed at length and with considerable documentation. There can be no doubt of the profound insight into the nature and history of Brahmanism and the intimate acquaintance with the religious, literary and political manifestations of the spirit of India to which Radhakrishnan's *oeuvre* testifies. It is significant, however, that it is the earlier, the Brahmanic phase of Hindu religion, that it is the classical Vedānta, on which he concentrates his attention and which commands his affection and loyalty. It is Śaṁkara's rather than Rāmānuja's version of the Vedānta to which he adheres, and it is the Brahmanic phase rather than the medieval form of Hinduism which represents for him "the" religion of India. It is actually a double option which determines Professor Radhakrishnan's explicit and implicit evaluation of religion: his preference for the apprehension of ultimate reality as proclaimed by the seers and sages of India and, within this tradition, his preference for the teachings of the Upaniṣads in the peculiar interpretation of the Advaita-school. The philosopher, Western or Eastern, may well agree with this second emphasis; but the scholar interested in the comparative study of religions may well ask if certain other manifestations of Hinduism should not be more fully included when we attempt to discuss the essence of the religion of India. Especially Occidentals seem all too prone to identify the latter with the metaphysics of the Vedānta without doing justice to the characteristic spirit of devotion to which the earlier and later mediaeval documents of Hinduism testify. The work of such scholars as Pope, Grierson, R. Otto, Schomerus and others is not widely enough known. The result is the one-sidedness in the presentation and appraisal of the religion of India which we find in so many publications of Western scholars and amateurs. Few of them betray any familiarity with the work of Bhandarkar, the great pathfinder in the exploration of Viṣṇuism, Shivaism and the minor cults, or of his modern successors.

Let us return once more to the autobiographical sketch in which Radhakrishnan outlines the growth of his interest in the two great religious traditions with which he has been confronted all his life, the Indian and the Christian. It is regrettable that until recently this meant the Indian and the Western. If we recall the identification of Christianity and the West in the minds of Occidentals and —hence—in the minds of the peoples of the East throughout the Victorian age and into the 20th century, we shall better understand the critical attitude towards Christianity which Professor Radhakrishnan's writings betray. Or rather, we shall appreciate even more highly the untiring efforts on the part of this great Hindu scholar to do justice to Christianity. From the days of his youth he had met with a form of Christian apologetic which could be nothing if not ineffective and which could only have adverse effects upon him, because it was uninformed and proceeded from unexamined presuppositions. Not that the conviction on the part of Christians that Christ, rightly understood, is "the light of the world" would have had to be offensive; but the claim that Hinduism, whatever its form, was all darkness and that Christianity, whatever its expression, is all light. The advocates of this latter doctrine all too frequently were prone to forget how woefully deficient, how necessarily limited by their own background, their understanding and interpretation of the *kerygma* of Christ was, how compromised by colonialism, provincialism, and conventionalism. Not that the truly Christian spirit and the splendid achievements of many selfless workers for the cause of Christ in India and elsewhere could be denied by anyone; but many Westerners conceived of the meeting between Christian and Hindu as entirely a one way traffic, which consisted in condescendingly presenting for total acceptance a parcel in which the gospel was wrapped in sheets often not as clean as could be desired. All this one has to bear in mind if the reaction which many highly educated Indians have been exhibiting to efforts of this kind is to be understood and properly assessed. There is a notable trace of bitterness in a great number of references to Christianity in Radhakrishnan's writings. Here he speaks as the apologist of Hinduism, that is, of Hinduism as he interprets it, of a reconstructed Hinduism, or better, of the ideal of Hinduism.

I am not sure that he always applies the same procedure—carefully distinguishing between the empirical and the ideal—when he discusses what is to him the great religion of the West. Granted that there are valid reasons for the criticism which he voices in the section on Christian Missions and Indian faiths. However, I find little evidence that he considers the Christian faith seriously as a live option for India. To reject unwarranted attempts at "Westernization" or, for that matter, any imposition of "foreign" notions is one thing; however, the only alternative to such attempts is not necessarily the somewhat relativistic idea of *sharing.* "The different religious men of the East and the West are to share their visions and insights, hopes and fears, plans and purposes." True, this is desirable; but in which spirit, and why not in the Spirit of Christ? The West does not possess a monopoly on Him. Before Him there is neither Jew, nor Greek, nor Indian. The God of justice and love of whom he testified is either truly our—and that is for *all* of us "our"—creator and redeemer or not the true God at all. There is a profounder difference than Radhakrishnan seems to be willing to admit between tribally or nationally bound Brahmanic Hinduism and the constitutionally universal message of Christ. But this is not the difference of the faith of one part of the world as over against that of another.[12] There is no reason why Indian Christians should not teach any number of Western Christians a deeper insight into the *kerygma* of the Christ who judges all.

Or is Radhakrishnan merely objecting to the *methods* by which Christianity so often has sought converts? It could seem so; because he does not level as harsh a criticism against Buddhism, another universal faith, as he does against Christianity. After all, to find the truth in Christ and in his teachings need not prevent anyone from studying with profit and admiring the thought of the great Indian sages. In fact, whoever expects important contributions from Indian Christianity to Christian theology and philosophy will have every reason to familiarize himself with those sages' search for truth.

However, it is not necessarily in the realm of intellectual endeavor—monumental though Hindu contributions in this field may be—certainly not *merely* in this realm, that one would seek and find unexpected treasures. Religion is above all *devotion,* and the intensity and fervor of the devotional life of India's Saints must put many lukewarm Western Christians to shame. Here we feel that much that is admirable can be found in Medieval Hinduism alongside of other things which are gross and perhaps even repellent.

The sincere and relentless effort to understand the religion of peoples different from our own is certainly highly desirable. Radhakrishnan himself is an eminent example of such endeavor. Yet we do not feel that it is all said with the simple formula: let us share. The problem of *validity* and of *truth* has to be faced, as the author of *East and West in Religion* himself reminds us. We agree with him: "revelation is a universal gift, not a parochial posses-

[12] Christianity is, after all, an "Eastern" religion. Cf. EWR, 46.

sion." [13] But we cannot follow him when he continues: "with regard to religions, the question is not of truth or falsehood but life or death." [14] It is right to say that "every living religion has its part in the spiritual education of the race;" [15] but these parts are not necessarily equal. We feel that William Temple, who was a believer in universal revelation, made an admirable distinction in saying, "all therefore is alike revelation; but not all is equally revelatory of the divine character." [16] In great fairness Radhakrishnan distinguishes between the early forms and later developments of both, Christianity and the religions of India. He contrasts the "pure and simple teachings of Jesus" with the developments which Christianity has undergone in the West.[17] In his analysis of the rôle of intellectualism, scholasticism, social solidarity, and activism, and of their historic causes, there is much truth. Yet some of the more recent investigations in the field of New Testament exegesis and theology do not quite confirm the picture he draws of the "religion of Jesus." It is doubtful if we have a right to say that "he founded no organization, but enjoined only private prayer." [18] There is no reference here to the passion and crucifixion, the central events in the life of Jesus, the supreme tests of his teaching. Of these, which for the Christian are of paramount importance as the incomparable instances of divine love and suffering, it can not be said that they, as "the characteristics of intuitive realization, non-dogmatic toleration, insistence on non-aggressive virtues and universalist ethics, mark Jesus out as a typical Eastern seer." [19] The Christian is convinced that Jesus was something else and something more than that. For the Christian the cardinal question remains: *What do you think of Christ?* [20] Hence this Christian will not be satisfied with the prospect of a time when "faith in God and love of man will be the only requisites for mutual fellowship and service." For the Christian who deserves the name, belief in Christ and in his spirit is not something which is added to other basic beliefs and which can, therefore, be omitted; rather, it is the one central affirmation by which alone all others receive their meaning. It should be said in all fairness that a majority of Christians themselves do not see this vital point too clearly. In this chapter, "The Meeting of Religions," in *Eastern Religions and Western Thought,* Radhakrish-

13 EWR, 38.   14 *Idem.*   15 *Idem.*
16 *Nature, Man and God*, 315.   17 EWR, 47, 57ff.   18 *Ibid.*, 58.
19 *Idem.*
20 Cf. the chapter "Christendom I" in ER, esp. 163ff, 176, for Dr. Radhakrishnan's answer.

nan remarks that "the man of faith, whether he is Hindu or Buddhist, Muslim or Christian, has certainty;" but he adds: "yet there is a difference between the pairs." [21] Faith, he says, for the Hindu does not mean dogmatism, implying that for the Christian it does.[22] But a Christian would have no difficulty in subscribing to the statement that "it is not historically true that in the knowledge of truth there is of necessity great intolerance." [23] He would agree with the Indian thinker that "religion is a matter of personal realisation;" although Radhakrishnan seems to consider this as a typically Hindu attitude,[24] and would most certainly hold that "one's religiousness is to be measured not by one's theological affirmations but by the degree to which one brings forth the fruit of the spirit." [25] However, it is difficult to follow the author of *Eastern Religions and Western Thought* in his protest against the "view of Christ as 'the only begotten son of God' " who "could not brook any rival near the throne." [26] Should Christ too, then, be regarded—by Christians—as merely one "symbol" among others? It does by no means follow that to accept Christ for what he claimed to be must lead to intolerance and to the persecution of others. Certainly, "no doctrine becomes sounder, no truth truer, because it takes the aid of force." [27]

It is in the concluding paragraphs of his chapter on "The Meeting of Religions" that Radhakrishnan invites Christians to cease propagating their faith. He rightly objects to Karl Barth's denial of universal revelation. It is not in defense of Barthian theology, therefore, or because we believe that "only one religion provides divine revelation and others have nothing of it," [28] or because we regard the Christian religion as unique,[29] that we hold that ours cannot be the way which this Indian scholar suggests. He cites with approval the example of the Syrian Christians in India—as well as the Hindus—who are "opposed to proselytism." [30] However, to surrender all attempts of inviting and winning others to the cause of Christ, would actually be to deny him. This is not to advocate "religious imperialism." Responsible religious leadership —such as the recent meetings of the International Missionary Council, to which Radhakrishnan himself refers,[31] represent—is well aware that there are pressing tasks which require the wholehearted co-operation of the faithful of all religions. Surely,

21 ER, 314. 22 *Ibid.*, cf. 316f, 324. 23 *Ibid.*, 314.
24 *Ibid.*, 316f, but cf. 319. 25 *Ibid.*, 320. 26 *Ibid.*, 324.
27 *Ibid.*, 326. 28 *Ibid.*, 343. 29 *Ibid.*, 344.
30 *Ibid.*, 345ff. 31 *Ibid.*, 345.

if we do not bring together in love those who sincerely believe in God and seek to do his will, if we persist in killing each other theologically, we shall only weaken men's faith in God. If the great religions continue to waste their energies in a fratricidal war instead of looking upon themselves as friendly partners in the supreme task of nourishing the spiritual life of mankind, the swift advance of secular humanism and moral materialism is assured.[32]

There is much more mutual contact, exploration, exchange, and understanding necessary among the sincere followers of all faiths than is now in evidence. We must, indeed, all recognize the insufficiency of our interpretation of the meaning of faith within our own religious community. This has already been pointed out above. But a Christian would not be contributing his best, if he would not make manifest, in word and in deed, upon what spiritual food he feeds, where he has found the springs of hope, of joy, and of strength. Surely he should expect the Hindu, the Buddhist, and the Moslem to do likewise. In this area grave errors and many sad mistakes of the past will have to be undone. It is when each believer opens himself completely that he witnesses most honestly. There is no more reason why an Easterner should not accept Christ as readily and as naturally as a Westerner. Christ, the Buddha, Muhammad—we are beginning to understand this better today than did the 19th century—are *universal options*. It is wrong for a Hindu to say that these names stand for provincialism. The interpretation of their teaching or the failure to act in conformity with that teaching may often be provincial. It is wrong for a Westerner to say: because my forbears were Christians, I had better be one also. No less a theologian than Søren Kierkegaard has pointed out how difficult it is for a Christian, that is to say, for one brought up in and hence "accustomed" to Christianity, to become a Christian. Modern determinism assumes many subtle forms: one is cultural determinism. Many anthropologists, sociologists, and psychologists —even philosophers—regard religion merely as an expression or a function of civilization. That means that I confess a religion because it happens to be the prevailing one in the culture or society to which I happen to belong. Should we not respect a Westerner who, out of conviction, turns Buddhist or Moslem higher than a *soi-disant* "Christian"? And is not, therefore, the mutual understanding and hence communion of Arab, Hindu, Chinese, and Western Christians profounder than that based merely on mutual "toleration"? It would be difficult to prove to a Ceylonese or to an

[32] *Ibid.*, 347.

African Christian that he is wrong if he hopes, prays, and works for the acceptance of Christ by all men.

Radhakrishnan has devoted a chapter to Hindu thought and Christian doctrine in his book on *The Heart of Hindusthan* (1932). There he points out that he finds the same fundamentals emphasized in all religions, namely "that God is; that man stands in some relation to God; and that intercourse of some kind is possible between God and man who has in him the desire to be in harmony with God." [33] It is not difficult to agree with this statement, even if one considers it possible to go beyond the three points in the enumeration of "universals" in religion.[34] But for the reasons stated above, objections must be raised to the explanation—or at least to the phrasing of it—Dr. Radhakrishnan gives for the differences among "the living progressive religions of the world." They relate, according to him, to "accents and emphases, which are traceable to social environment and historic circumstances." This formulation sounds highly relativistic and evades altogether the problem of truth. More specifically, however, it has to be said that the Hindu philosopher does not quite do justice to the difference which exists between the Indian concept of Avatars and the Christian notion of 'the Son of God.' The view that "Jesus is an avatar," [35] which has recently been elaborated by Radhakrishnan's fellow countryman, Swami Akhilananda, in his book, *The Hindu View of Christ*, implies the denial that "He had a special relation to God, which it is not possible for others to acquire," and cannot, therefore, be accepted by those who see in Christ the supreme manifestation of the Divine love; which does not exclude other manifestations but supersedes them. If the life and passion of Jesus Christ reveals as much of the nature and purpose of God as Christians believe it does, it is inadmissible to grant that as much of that nature and purpose is made known in any of the various "incarnations" of Viṣṇu, Rama, Krishna, *et al.* Even the most pronouncedly Johannine understanding of the life and work of Christ and of the destiny of man, for whom he died, would not permit us to say that "the resources of God which were available to him are open to us, and if we struggle and strive even as he did, we will develop the God in us." [36] Radhakrishnan thinks that it is "a pious delusion" to think that "none else than Jesus attained this consciousness of spiritual oneness with God." I wonder why anyone should call himself a "Christian," if he does not hold this 'uniqueness' to be

33 HH, 88.   34 Wach, J., *Types of Religious Experience*, Chap. II.
35 HH, 101.   36 *Ibid.*, 102.

true. It does not follow that, if the light of God blazed forth in such unique splendor in Jesus—as Radhakrishnan puts it very beautifully—we should not object if the followers "say, of Confucius and of Buddha, set up similar claims for their heroes." Actually, the followers of Confucius have never made such a claim. And, as concerns the founder of Buddhism, we feel that at this point a real *decision* between Christ and the Buddha is demanded, not just a simple addition. The issues which make such a decision necessary, implying quite fundamental differences as they do, cannot be discussed here.[37]

Our distinguished Hindu philosopher rightly states that "God has never said his last word on any subject; he has always more things to tell than we now can hear (John 16, 12)." But this does not mean that we are not called upon to respond to God's precious invitation which he extended to *all* men when He became incarnate in Christ or that we should not see everything that came before, has come since, and will come, in the light of this His, until now—we cannot say more, but also certainly not anything less— supreme revelation. This view, it might be reaffirmed again, does not exclude the recognition of deep spiritual insight won by and of revelatory grace granted to Christian and non-Christian seers, prophets, and saints. Rather, it demands such an interpretation. We whole-heartedly agree with William Temple: "Only if God is revealed in the rising of the sun in the sky, can He be revealed in the rising of a son of man from the dead; only if He is revealed in the history of Syrians and Philistines"—and we add: in the history of the Indians—"can He be revealed in the history of Israel." [38] But that is by no means the same as Radhakrishnan's assertion: "Hinduism believes that every guru is a Saviour, in as much as he quickens in his disciples the life of God and develops the seed of the spirit capable of fructifying in them. Any one who helps us to a complete harmonisation of the finite will of man with the perfect will of God has the power to save us." [39] The present writer has found great inspiration, much truth, wisdom, and beauty, fervent witness to the *numinous* character of ultimate reality in the great Hindu writings through the ages, and hopes to learn still more from them; but he cannot agree with Radhakrishnan's conclusion that "Jesus' own testimony, philosophical truth and religious ex-

---

37 In his book, *Types of Religious Experience, Christian and Non-Christian* (1951), the author of this paper has attempted an analysis of the differences between the Christian and the Mahāyāna-Buddhist faith. *Cf.* chap. VI.

38 *Nature, Man and God*, 97.   39 HH, 103f.

perience alike demand that He should be brought in line with the other great saints of God, who has not left himself without a witness in any clime or age." [40] True enough; but "neither is there salvation in any other name: for there is none other name under heaven given among men whereby we must be saved." (Acts 4, 12) It may be the case, as this great Hindu thinker intimates, that for some time now a "more critical attitude towards the divinity of Jesus" has been developing among Christian theologians of the West, "who are tending to emphasize more and more his [Jesus'] humanity." [41] However, tendencies in modern Western theology stand in need of evaluation. The mentioned trend has not remained unopposed and, if we are not mistaken, is of late being reversed quite decidedly. Theologians are only a part, and very possibly not the major part, of the Church—and by that we do not mean the ecclesiastical, denominational, and sectarian institutions, but the Great Church of which it was said by its master that the gates of Hell shall not prevail against it. This Christian Church, which started with the confession: Jesus Christ is Lord, will abide by this confession, lest it betray its true foundation. It does not have to subscribe to any of the "classical" theories of the Atonement; but Radhakrishnan's suggestion that it should forget about the notion that "God was in Christ reconciling the world unto himself" [42] it cannot possibly heed. Nor will it be ready to admit that "the sacrifice of Christ has no significance for man as a propitiation for sin." [43]

Some will protest that statements such as these are "dogmatic." However, such characterization would be correct only if these formalizations had no experiential roots. Here they are introduced as the expression of a living experience. "A man's religion," Radhakrishnan rightly observes, "must be his own and not simply accepted on trust or imposed by authority." [44] It is readily granted that otherwise, if they were merely the results of mechanical indoctrination, they would possess little or no validity. What kind of validity *do* they possess except that of being a witness to some subjective experience which might be contradicted and, as some would say, invalidated by expressions of different or even contrary "convictions?" The criterion cannot be the strength or power of the belief. It rather appears to be the degree to which, in and through the experiences to which these statements point, there is effected an actual deepening and widening of spiritual insight into the nature of

40 *Ibid.*, 165. 41 *Ibid.*, 104. 42 *Ibid.*, 109.
43 *Ibid.*, 109, 121. 44 RR, 287.

ultimate reality, of human existence and of the destiny of man. The possibilities which such experiences entail are potentially open to *everyone*. There is nothing esoteric or exclusive about them. Those who believe in a genuine democracy of the spirit will not be afraid of or adverse to contests from which no "competition" will be excluded and where the *true* will prevail.

We come to the crux of the matter when we confront the Hindu scholar's statement with regard to the Indian branch of this Church in which he expects to "*combine* the best elements of Hinduism with the good points of Christianity." [45] An evaluation of the implications of this statement will lead both to an affirmative and a negative conclusion. Neither Hinduism nor Christianity, as we have intimated before, will or ought to remain as it is. We are one with the Indian thinker in stressing the necessity of theological and philosophical "re-thinking" (to use W. E. Hocking's term) in the universal search for truth. But a combination in the sense of mere addition, even in the sense of a synthesis of the Hindu and Christian religions, seems unfeasable. We have elsewhere [46] indicated why, from our point of view, the concept of a "world faith" on a syncretistic basis is not a live option. The crux of the matter, in a very real sense of the word, is indicated by the question: What do you think of Christ? Ever since Jesus' life and work has revealed to man the great two alternative possibilities, it has been impossible to *bypass* this question. But there are no monopolies for West or East, Jew or Greek, for high or low, for rich or poor, as far as the interpretation of the implications of the supreme act of God's redeeming love are concerned. At this point all, wherever found and whoever they may be, are called upon to respond and to contribute their deepest feeling, their profoundest thought, and their most concentrated efforts in action to testify that they are truly redeemed.

We have indicated in an earlier part of this paper that we thoroughly agree with Radhakrishnan in the unqualified rejection of any use of compulsion in spiritual matters. It indicates a lack of confidence in the power of truth, if directly or indirectly force is applied in the service of a religious cause. If we speak of the "great invitation" to accept Christ as one's master, we are not advocating any "*coge intrare.*" The only means open to us are an effective example and the winsome word. It is understandable that, in view

---

45 *Ibid.*, 122.
46 "The Place of the History of Religions in the Study of Theology," *Journal of Religion*, XXVII (1947), 157ff.; *cf.* also *Types of Religious Experience*, chap. I.

of vast and grievous mistakes in the past, considerable apprehension exists in the souls and minds of non-Christians—in the West and in the East—lest they be subjected to reprisals, discriminations, and persecutions for not "conforming." Christians must feel a deep sense of shame that many of the peoples of the East have begun to feel secure only after they have won their political independence. But it might also mean that to accept Christ has again become a test or a risk rather than an insurance or a matter of material and social advantage. Moreover, the difference of the situation in the East and in the West is now not much more than one of degree, inasmuch as it takes courage in the Occident too to want really to be a Christian. To guard against any possible misunderstanding I want to reiterate my insistence that our considerations pertain to the realm of the spiritual quest for truth. They are in no way meant to endorse any form of coercion.

The author does not wish to conclude this brief discussion of some points in the writings of Radhakrishnan which seem to him of a controversial nature without adding some remarks of a different character. It may seem picayune to pick out sentences, formulations, or passages in books of a scholar or thinker whose total work is of such imposing character and which testifies to so noble and profound a spirit in its author as that of Sir Sarvepalli Radhakrishnan. The present writer owes much to the beautifully written studies, in philosophy and religion, of the most outstanding living Indian thinker, one whose guiding star throughout has been the quest for truth. By virtue of these commitments he is entitled to expect a similar approach on the part of anyone who becomes his attentive reader. How lengthy would this essay have become, if it would have listed the theses, negative and positive, with which the writer is in profound agreement, such, for example, as the rôle which Radhakrishnan assigns to religious experience, and his criticism of scepticism, radical materialism, environmentalism, and behaviourism! He is also in full accord with the definition: "Religion is, in essence, experience of or living contact with ultimate reality." [47] This author is aware of the mighty advance which Radhakrishnan's studies in the history of thought represent over the provincial outlook of so many Western and Eastern presentations of the development and the various types of philosophy and religion. He is conscious of the magnificent way in which Radhakrishnan upholds the ideals of justice, of order, and of freedom. There could be no more impressive attempt to combine love for one's

[47] RR, 275.

country with the desire sympathetically to understand the genuine aspirations and achievements of other nations and civilizations. What remarkable insight and appreciation are revealed in some of his portraits of outstanding leaders in the intellectual and spiritual world of men! No aspect of civilization is overlooked in his studies in Eastern and Western life, past and present.

It would be a rewarding task, though one for which this essay has no place, to attempt to trace and assess the influences which various movements and trends in the Western intellectual world have had upon Radhakrishnan's thinking through the years. Some such influences are detectable in the ideas with which this paper has been concerned: his notion of the nature, the task, and the significance of the comparative study of religions. The frequency with which the distinguished thinker himself refers to this subject seems to indicate that it is one to which he attaches considerable importance. There is, moreover, a great and lively interest in these problems today. That may justify our choice of topic and the insistence upon some considerations with regard to which a weighty question remained in the mind of at least one reader of Radhakrishnan's books.

JOACHIM WACH

FEDERATED THEOLOGICAL FACULTY
UNIVERSITY OF CHICAGO

13

Swāmi Agehānanda Bhārati

RADHAKRISHNAN AND THE OTHER VEDĀNTA

RADHAKRISHNAN AND THE OTHER VEDĀNTA

F ROM pious platforms all over India we have been hearing for quite a few decades now that India and India alone can save the world from disaster. There is also a fairly large audience abroad that agrees and that tries to supplement its faith by some kind of organized action. We are not talking about the many sects formed during the last century which claim to have their doctrinal and ritualistic bases in India, sects building eerily esoteric systems around a nucleus which is Indian by name, but very un-Indian in thought. The Indian way of philosophizing presupposes more inspiration than information. It has been claimed by many a well-meaning lover of Indian Philosophy, monastic and lay, that inspiration is all and information nothing, with the result that Vedāntic and Buddhist societies have sprung up wherever there has been dissatisfaction with indigenous ways of thinking and where the heart's cry has favored pristine and serene primitivity. Vedānta, as absorbed through popular literature, through the words and writings of very colorful saints, certainly quenches the thirst for the primitive, but we wonder whether this is quite what the Āchāryas sought to teach or wanted to perpetuate. Probably it would be wrong to assume that Śaṁkara was not inspired; but certainly he was informed; perhaps not so much about the original teachings of his ancient doctrinal opponents, as about those of his contemporaries. In reading his delicate refutations of the Buddhists, it is difficult to eliminate the feeling that Śaṁkara was refuting a Buddhism of which we no longer know anything. We find a very striking parallel, in this regard, with the Western Schoolmen, particularly with their doyen, the Aquinate. A compendious portion of the third book of the Summa (where one would least expect it) refutes the theories of the old, the "false" gnostics, and establishes his own, viz., the "true" gnosticism; but no trace of what Thomas refutes is found either in Basilides or in Valentinus.

461

Europe finished its scholastic period some 500 years ago; since then many other choices of philosophic method and attitude have been tried. Scholasticism might have returned into the philosophic arena for a new trial, but, for reasons mainly historical and psychological, it did not. Most Western philosophers are fed up with dogmatism; the present-day philosopher in the West tries to be as undogmatic as possible, or at least he introduces his own dogma in a form that does not smack conspicuously of the didactic. Yet his readers, the enlightened public, that is to say, are experiencing once more the urge for the learned childlikeness and philosophic naïveté of scholastic surety. Fear of Roman and other Church dogma leads the security-seeker to look for something that is new in content yet old in method. Naturally, his hopeful gaze has long fallen on India and China, where there are so many well-elaborated systems apparently ready for quick digestion; they are attractive, moreover, because they are pagan—they are often chosen out of philosophic spite.

In the Indian sector there have, in the main, been two sources upon which the intent reader of the West could draw: Vivekānanda and Radhakrishnan. There have been many other sources, no doubt; but here I am picking the most up-to-date and the most typical two—the one standing for inspiration alone, the other for information also. There are many who know Vivekānanda and praise Radhakrishnan; there are few who retain their full enthusiasm for the former after having studied the latter; but studying Radhakrishnan means working through his two volumes of *Indian Philosophy,* and not reading merely his two *Views of Life.*

We find that reading Vivekānanda opens the door, but no more; he is a kind of appetizer, an aperitif, as it were. He who stops here —and there are many who do, believing that Indian philosophy is exhausted in Rāmakrishna and Vivekānanda and perhaps Ramana Maharishi—he who stops here will not be informed about Indian philosophy, though he may be inspired by it. Many frustrated people are deeply in love with Vedānta and Buddhism; but, of course, their structured ideas about the systems are vague and very faint. This sense of a vague security may be quite sufficient for the individual who wishes to feel both sure about himself and convinced of having made a right decision; such a position is, however, quite insufficient for the serious student. The latter need not necessarily be inspired, but he must be informed—that is why he can well do without Vivekānanda, but not without Radhakrishnan.

It is said that the time has come for a rapprochement between

Indian and Western philosophy. In the form in which this statement has been advanced, it is probably nothing more than a trite pleasantry. We often talk of political and social rapprochements in order to bridge a gap in our conversations or business dealings, as an expletive, at parties or between nations. Personally I cannot but feel that, by such remarks, popular philosophers are doing not much more than uttering a truism. Two lines of thought cannot be reconciled without compromise on either side, if they are radically and technically different. If such a compromise is possible, it is a matter of indifference as to whether the two lines of thought have been hatched in one and the same place or continents apart. We have some misgivings about school-philosophers, therefore, who advocate this joining of issues. The stress is on *school*-philosophers, whom I distinguish from comparative philosophers. I would call him a "school-philosopher" who has surrendered his mind to one particular tradition of philosophic thinking, and submit that all his further research must be biassed. The "school-philosopher" certainly explores other systems of philosophy, but with the sole object of finding grounds to refute these philosophies, or to deny whatever in them stands against his chosen philosophy. Scholasticism, Indian and Western alike, is the way of biassed philosophizing. It is an interesting coincidence that scholasticism's teachers were called "Schoolmen" long before the opposite approach, the comparative, had been seriously considered.

Let us propose, then, that the said rapprochement is not possible, for the problems are, on the one hand, purely technical, and are neutral in terms of value, on the other; they do not lend themselves at all to an emotional analysis. If emotion is to be brought in at all—let us call it "aesthetic judgment" in order to sound more philosophical and less psychological—we may just as well plan an eternal segregation of the two ways of philosophizing, each right for itself because its advocates like it; tastes are, after all, no further analyzable. It is difficult to understand why to unification should be assigned the highest general value, as if desire for synthesis were a psychic *a priori*. This is, however, only an enthusiastic postulation. Quite a lot can be done: Pension off the school-philosopher; the man of philosophic goodwill—the *bona philosophi voluntas* of Mendelssohn—then can become accustomed to the comparative method, which, of course, requires the gathering of more and wider information. Moreover, in the process of mastering other schools, each will have to sacrifice his agreeable conviction of being right. Scholasticism breaks down along with self-complacence. Satisfaction with the philosophic status quo and a determination to preserve it are the hallmarks of scholasticism and of most types of gnostic thought. The schoolman feels absolutely sure of his position; he considers doubt a kind of disease or a symptom of immaturity; but this is not necessarily a philosophic approach. The comparative philosopher does not mind keeping conclusions pending, for he belongs, as Bowne put it, to the happier breed of thinkers who can live without a system. Doubt is his method. (We shall return to this point at a later stage.) The comparativist returns the charge of being without a system by saying that surety is for the theologian; doubt is for the philosopher. The latter clause is Cartesian in diction, but ancient in content. The schoolman *in extremo*, therefore, is a theologian, and little of a philosopher.

In India there has always been the tendency to make the two one, philosopher and theologian. This is a bit tragic, for it has hampered free philosophic enquiry in this country. We definitely claim that India has not left its scholastic era nor does it desire to do so; on the other hand India is steeped in schoolmanship, in utter theology. The fact that, of the six classical systems of Indian philosophy (which Radhakrishnan calls the Brahmanical systems), virtually only one is extant, so far as followers are concerned, seems to be fair evidence concerning the validity of this statement. It is Vedānta which counts today; and Vedānta is theology far more than the other five systems. The Hindu philosopher nowadays is a Vedāntin by implication; and, what is worse, he is a branch-Vedāntin, a monist, a dualist, or holds a modified position in varying degrees. There is far more mutual strife among the votaries of the various Vedāntic exigeses than between them taken together and the propounders of extra-Vedic systems. The main reason for this is the small number following non-Vedāntic, i.e., non-scholastic, systems. I have met few philosophers who professed to be Naiyāikas or Sāṃkhyans, although all claimed to know the subject matter of these systems. But I have met hosts of Vedāntins, lay and monastic, of all shades. Vedānta, however, is theology. Without hesitation I would call any philosophy a theology which puts its entire emphasis on ontology and metaphysics (apart from its stress on revelation in cruder cases) at the cost of the other philosophic disciplines, viz., logic, ethics, and perhaps aesthetics, if the last be claimed as an essential discipline. All the schools of Vedānta do this.

This much had to be prefaced to establish our main contention:

we hold that Professor Radhakrishnan is a theologian, and that *he is the theologian of Hinduism.* This is the highest tribute a monk can pay to a layman.

The problem of oneness or distinctness of philosophy and theology has been a puzzle ever since philosophy usurped a place confoundingly near to theology. The fact that at the outset philosophy was everywhere ancillary to theology is a chronological statement and only of historical relevance, and one which does not concern us here. Nor are we concerned with the fact that philosophy was often a reaction against the ordained faith. To the earlier Schoolmen of the West, the proof of their oneness or at least their mutual inextricability was the main task, and Scholasticism (at least the Dominican form) ended when their separateness had been established. In India, the possibility of a separation between philosophy and theology has not even yet been conceived. Merely mentioning such a possibility is indignantly silenced on a soil which apparently is too sacred for profane philosophizing. That India has not emerged from its scholastic era seems only too clear to the modern observer, quite apart from the data supplied by the history of Indian philosophy. In addition, the Indian philosopher must be an ascetic or give himself an ascetic appearance; he must call his house an Āśrama (a cloister), and is expected to contribute funds to pious people for their pious purposes. If he happens to be married, he can never quite hope to be considered a full-fledged philosopher by the average Hindu. Such a man may be a reformer, a preacher, and a good man; but at best his holy laymanship is incomplete. The Hindu wants to see this man go the whole hog; moreover, theology being one with philosophy, this attitude is intelligible. It is, lastly, the monk alone who commands Platonic and Kantian respect, a fact which is deplored by the monk who may, incidentally, also be a philosopher. I fear that this is the reason why even Radhakrishnan is not known to *the Hindu,* who knows and refers to the output of the Dayānandas, Rāmatīrthas, and Vivekānandas (to that of genuine monks, that is), rather than to the genuine knower—to the man who actually masters all the issues of Hindu thought. It is generally agreed that there is more toleration in Hinduism than anywhere else. One may propound virtually any doctrine from crass nihilism to the most elaborate ritualism, implying a crude monotheism in a polytheistic shape; one may teach and preach realism and idealism, nominalism, love, hatred, and all opposites, *provided* one does not deny the formal authority of the Scripture. One may explain as one likes, but one must not overtly impugn Scriptural validity. One can "torture the text," to quote Vivekānanda, if one must make a bluntly dualist dictum monistic; but don't deny the authority of the Book. Those who ever dared to do so—Buddhists, Jains, Chārvākas—were branded *Vedabāhya* and *Vedanindaka* (outsiders and abusers of the Scripture). Anathema, despite all toleration! Society suffers the disloyal, indeed; but orthodox literature, which is standard for the same society, condemns them as being in darkness; it is delightful to read Rāmānuja's preamble on the Śaṁkarites, which reminds one strongly of zealous missionary literature on the poor heathens.

All those who wished to remain in the fold of the Vedas in spite of their urge to liberate philosophy, to emancipate thought, merely had to assuage their conscience and that of the public by paying sporadic homage and occasionally stressing their loyalty to the Veda. It cannot be denied that this often involved compromise. The change from *Nirīśvara* to *Seśvara Yoga* is remarkable —God is inserted quite surreptitiously in the course of time. Sāṃkhya with Kapila—whoever he was—was certainly atheistic. If the mythical founder of the Sāṃkhyan dualism was indeed identical with the great seer whom the Gītā, the catechism of theism, styles the greatest among Munis—the Lord Himself having been especially manifested in him—, then it certainly speaks for the Lord's impartiality to have chosen to manifest Himself as an atheist from among all other possibilities. Gauḍapāda, the spiritual grandsire of Śaṁkara, in all probability was a Buddhist, using, as he did, even the Buddhist terminology, e.g., *samvṛti* for *vyavahāra*. A cogent comparison can be made with certain Western philosophers who had to be Christians for far more acute and serious reasons. The great Descartes launched his philosophy with an admirably well-effected compromise: most of his contemporaries thought he was a good Christian; so perhaps did he himself. The lesser Gassendi did without the compromise; yet it took another three centuries before the philosopher could do, on the whole, without pious pretexts.

We love to take words as literally as possible and to avoid their later connotations as far as is feasible. Philosophy means the "love of wisdom," *sapientiae amicitia* in Seneca's definition, and that covers enough—it is a method and an attitude. Now, if we as Indian philosophers claim this word for our work, and yet at the same time emphasize that *this is also religion,* we bring in a new and unnecessary connotation—it is a mistake of terminological parsimony. The West virtually has overcome this particular connotative complex by disposing of theology as a separate faculty in life as well as in the *Alma Mater*. We in India have not yet taken the initial step and most of us do not want to, thinking we are quite right in our present view; and, if the very best among us perpetuates this state, we have little hope of complementing the emancipated thinking of our Western colleagues. No Indian philosopher in this century has suggested anything new—we find nothing but the old stuff dressed in impressive, up-to-date language. If one wants to read some standard philosophy of the West, a confident librarian may suggest the Kantian *Critiques*. There, God is postulated. If one wants Vedānta, because, by many, it is held to be the essence of Indian philosophy, one must sooner or later take to the *Brahma Sūtras* with their commentaries. There, God is posited. The approach is thus fundamentally opposite; and our rapprochement of the best with the best has once again fallen into abysmal depths. If we take a foreign term—philosophy—to denote our method, we are not really entitled to attach a new meaning to it; and, in the West, this particular term has been clearly differentiated from theology by a successful and complete separation which seems to be final. It is a mistake to mix up matters afresh at this end. It is now only some eighty years since we attempted to express our thoughts and systems in Western terminology, and the chances for a hopeless medley are given. The only Indian, viz., Sanskrit, term usable and used for philosophy is *Darśana,* and indices of philosophic literature in Indian languages use this term throughout.

Darśana is derived from the root "*dṛś*" (Greek—*deix-*, *deiknymi*), "to see," and the idea of some kind of supra-intellectual realization or intuition is therewith deeply ingrained, a notion invariably present in our minds. We thus know quite a lot about Darśana, but little about philosophy; yet, we have no better word for interpretation. That the Rāmakrishnas and Vivekānandas, and almost all of our anchorites and coenobites, scoff at systematic, discursive philosophy is not only due to their own lack in method and information, as may often be the case, but it also reflects a general Hindu attitude. That the Hindu view is so popular with wide circles in the discursive West is because the West has had a surfeit of discursive thinking and because many are to be found there who long for the primitive. Non-discursiveness is related to primitivity (again in the literal sense of the term), in which latter we are said to be, and believe ourselves to be, the masters. There is also much agreeable emotion and melodrama in sitting at the feet of masters belonging to very exotic regions; and the mention of lotuses and seers, of sacred groves and mountains easily thrills the primitivity-starved Westerner.

The antagonism towards discursive perfection is strangely taken over by many who would otherwise go in for philosophy rather than for Darśana. When the question comes to points of logical exclusion, for instance, the Indian philosopher recedes into the region of metaphysics and dogma, becoming essentially apologetic. But apologetic philosophy is a contradiction in terms, and what really results is theology. Philosophy, as love of wisdom, is not apologetic, for it avoids a mediator between wisdom and itself; whereas for theology the scripture is the only source of—and mediation to—wisdom. Theology claims, in India at least, superiority for direct, mystic experience; but that is not what the Darśanist (to avoid the now equivocal term "philosopher") actually cares for. He is ever bent on refuting the Buddha who has had such experience (even though at the cost of the Scripture), and he goes to the extreme of denying the validity of the Buddha's or any other opponent's intuition; the Vedānta-Āchāryas, ancient as modern, are specialists in that. On the other hand, if the irrefutability of one's own intuition is claimed apriorically, then volumes of commentary—in fact all literature—become redundant, as, indeed, it was and is with the full-fledged mystics and laconic Ṛṣis of yore like Raikva, or the deceased Ramana of late, whose gospel covers some ten small pages. To doubt the validity of a second person's individual intuitive experiences on the ground of their not tallying with Scripture is just as absurd as to deny them because they contradict one's own—the former being the attitude of the dogmatic, the latter that of the fanatic.

If we use philosophy in its original and fairly-well defined academic sense, we cannot flout any of its various disciplines. The very core of Vedānta is illogical, as are its *Mahāvākyas* or great dicta, when compared with one another; the Absolute is bereft of all qualities in one place and bestowed with all qualities in another. Now, if we are to believe that the Upaniṣads mean one and the same philosophy throughout, then this clearly ignores the law of the excluded middle, as the newly matriculated student can see after his very first classes in philosophical propaedeutics. It is not a-logical, as some would have it, for this is only a verbalism; what is not logical can only be illogical in this discipline; else, by upsetting the principle of the excluded middle in its very own sphere, we arrive at a tricky sort of *petitio principii;* nor will another name, such as a-logical, help, nor the usual shifting of the topic out of its discipline, i.e., from logic into metaphysics. If I am a philosopher and want my non-Vedāntic colleagues to take me for one, I must agree on some common axioms: the three laws of deductive logic and at least the main one of the scientific method must hold. If I want my Brahman to be vaster than the vast and smaller than the smallest, I must skip logic and eventually change over to the theological chair, or else renounce the claim to the philosophical unimpeachability of my system. In saying that my teaching surpasses human understanding, I precisely effect this change-over to the other faculty; and by stating that logic cannot grasp the matter, I automatically forfeit my claim to the philosophic chair, which has logic as one of its legs. Philosophy may believe that there are problems beyond understanding, and that their number is legion indeed; but it carefully avoids dealing with any of them once they are chalked out to be beyond its ken. Thanks to Kant, philosophy rather works at safely determining what cannot be understood, and about this field it then loses no further word. Here the theologian commences—a very elevating thought no doubt; he builds up his premises on the things that have been earmarked as not comprehensible and laid aside by the philosopher. The philosopher wants to know what he can know and keeps a proper respect towards the unknowable; the theologian wants to describe what he cannot know by any discursive means, for he becomes discursive only after his premises have been established. He must invoke intuition and revelation as his final authority, hence he must be apologetic. The Brahma Sūtras take the Unknown for granted—*"athāto Brahmajijñāsa"* ("here therefore begins the quest into Brahman"). The conclusions are built on a premise which might be called a theological *a priori*. In failing to work out this point, Radhakrishnan again makes philosophy one with theology, something which has to be avoided if we agree on the axioms given above. *"Janmādyasya yathāh"*—("from which (Brahman) birth, etc., viz., our universe of function and form, originates"). Vedānta is apologetic, it is theology. Radhakrishnan actually hints at that in one place; yet his endeavor is to expose such texts as philosophy, though they are theology and irreparably so. The various commentaries contain much philosophic matter, no doubt; so does all scholasticism. The conclusions are masterfully drawn and their logic is more often than not faultless. But not so their premises; authority, which does not bother about logic, is consistently substituted for the *ratio*. This makes the fundamental difference between philosophy and Darśana. Darśana is the philosophy of the theologian, it is scholasticism, plus a margin of mysticism.

There are naturally very many and quite different ideas concerning the ingredients of a philosopher. My distinction between Darśana and philosophy will not be acceptable to the majority of Indian philosophers, least of all, I am afraid, to Radhakrishnan. We have been admiring him for his austere ethicism, for his genuine knowledge of Eastern and Western thought, and for his orthodoxy. Radhakrishnan is not only a fine theologian, but he also is a good Hindu. As a matter of fact, quite a number of intellectual Hindus take him to be a modern Ṛṣi or even the modern Śaṁkara, and, as a monk of the order whose founder has found his most eminent modern disciple and propounder in Radhakrishnan, I can subscribe to this epithet. He has very many opponents in this country, as all great men have had in all countries. It is clear that a non-Śaṁkarite will fight Radhakrishnan with all his means. There are circles in Hindu society where Śaṁkarism or Rāmānujism or Madhavism are a matter of honor to generations; and the Western reader may wonder at the heat with which the adherent of one school inveighs against that of the other. Here emotions play their major part, and these need, of course, not be taken seriously from a philosophic viewpoint. Even terminology plays a great emotional rôle here; and it is odd to notice that authors of all systems wax eloquent over verbalisms, the content of which they know and admit to be identical in both schools. But a "feeling" cannot provide a basis for the work of the philosopher. We hold that philosophy and philosophic discussion can never be harnessed by emotions at all. A most complex method is involved in eliminating all non-philosophic issues, which can be said to have sprung from emotion and which cause emotion, from philosophic discussion. We must beware of "liking" or "disliking" a philosophy; even if we hold that assent or dissent in intellectual enquiry involves an affective tone, we shall have to pay attention to this warning. We shall have to see that our assents and dissents are as methodical as possible, that is as unemotive as we can honestly conceive. This statement, therefore, is to be understood as one of subjective method. We doubt whether philosophy should inspire—we believe that it should inform. Here is the danger in Radhakrishnan: his philosophy inspires as it informs;

and we have had an unwholesome surfeit of inspiration, from Yājñavalkya to Vivekānanda.

Are these charges damaging to Radhakrishnan and his works? We hope not; nor do we think they are. But we certainly miss information we would like to have, and this has hitherto been withheld by Radhakrishnan. We must presuppose that the pioneer in modern exegesis masters all that is available and important in the branch he chooses to explore; the amazingly short treatises on the non-Śaṁkarite readings of the Vedānta seem to be points at issue. We do not possess an adequate treatment of the other monistic expositions of the Vedānta, of the Tāntrik systems for example, or of the non-monistic and qualified systems. Mādhava, Nimbarka, Vallabha, and Bhāskara are mentioned only briefly, and even Rāmānuja and his school do not receive the elaboration in analysis such a school would be entitled to in a book which devotes so much space to Śaṁkara. It is impossible to contend that one Vedānta in its final form has more gaps or dialectical defects than any of the others. We do not have to pay heed to enthusiasts who make unreasonable claims for the excellence of their exposition. Professor Malkarni once pointed out quite correctly that India would be intellectually poor if Vedānta were the only philosophic system developed. We should add that she would be poorly off if Vedānta were the finest achievement. It is enough to say that Vedānta is among the most searching thought patterns created in this country. When Vivekānanda declares apodictically that Advaita must arise at the end of all thinking, as its consummation, we must understand and value this saying rhetorically. We know that he, as a true enthusiast, never found time to investigate or discuss schools he did not like. Vivekānanda disposes of the Madhavite Vedānta, the extreme dualist Vedāntic system, as crude and primitive; he was not aware of the fact that the Madhavite school has had the keenest dialecticians in all Vedāntic thought— Jayatīrtha and Vyāsatīrtha. It must be surmised that Vivekānanda had never heard their names, else he could not have been so rash in his verdict. He gives Rāmānuja's teachings a higher place no doubt, but certainly not for Rāmānuja's own or Veṅkaṭa's magnificent dialectic, but simply because modified monism, *Visiṣṭaadvaita,* is generally believed to be in closer proximity to Advaita of the Śaṁkarite type. Vivekānanda likes Advaita best and consequently comprehends it best though not necessarily well. We understand that "most of the time he [Vivekānanda] spent in feeling deeply for the downtrodden masses," as a renowned modern Indologist has put it.[1] For all that, it is inaccurate to call Vivekānanda a philosopher, although a nation and many outsiders believe he was. It now appears that a similar value-gradation can be traced in the case of Radhakrishnan. That would be awkward, if it were a result of his earlier susceptibility to the teachings of Vivekānanda, the man to whom Radhakrishnan has often referred as one of those who inspired and assured him. In any case, Radhakrishnan with his vast reading knowledge is even more entitled to such valuation than was "the Hindoo monk of India," Vivekānanda.

Radhakrishnan does not despise the non-Śaṁkarite Vedānta, but neither does he care very much for it. So much is this true that, when we want to be informed about the whole of Vedānta, we can consult Radhakrishnan only on Śaṁkarite Advaita and, to an extent, perhaps on Rāmānuja. In bulk that does not total even one third of Vedāntic philosophy. For the rest we must turn to other, more elaborate studies or to the originals, which latter are always the best source of information.

The predilection for Advaita on the part of modern scholars can be explained on several grounds. For this topic we should like to refer our readers to a relevant monograph by Professor T. M. P. Mahādevan.[2] The point which seems the most significant—one which has been held by us, incidentally, for several years—is the complete novelty of the system of Advaita in its appeal to the West. There have been many monistic and absolutist philosophies, but Advaita, ideologically and methodologically, is quite unparalleled; its similarities with Berkeley are probably not close enough to make the Western student of Advaita feel that there are striking parallels with English idealism or with several other similar lines of Western thought, a parallelism carefully analyzed by Radhakrishnan.

It has been repeatedly pointed out that Advaita leaves the least number of problems unsolved and that that is why we should accept it as the best philosophy. The lay Smārtas and the monastic Sannyāsins claim this with loud tones and it is emotionally quite justifiable. Who would not elevate the teachings of his spiritual ancestors? On sober study of the non-monistic Vedānta and of the other classical systems of Indian thought, we have, however, come to the conclusion that the claim for the eventual superiority of

[1] See Professor Hiriyanna's article in *Philosophical Quarterly*, 1949.
[2] *Vedanta Kesari*, Madras: 1950.

Advaita has no rational foundation at all. The eternal parallels of God, Soul, and Matter contain crude philosophic difficulties no doubt, and so does *Sankocha-Vikocha* doctrine of the qualified monists. Yet the main counter-issue against the Śaṁkarite *Māyā-vāda* is clear: if the sullied Māyā be one with the Pure Brahman, then Brahman is no longer pure; and if the impure Māyā is separate from Brahman, then monism is gone (*a*-dvaita negates a second entity after Brahman, "*a-*" being the Aryan privative prefix). In comes the explanation of the two levels of truth—higher and lower, absolute and relative, *pāramārthika* and *vyāvahārika;* and out goes all logic that grasps one degree of existence only.

We shall now try to substantiate what has been stated up to this point. The effort can only be incomplete within the scope of this contribution. What Prabhākara called a *sūtravana,* a "forest of quotations," cannot be adduced here. A few pieces of evidence must suffice for our commentary, but we have attempted to select such as seem most typical and closest to the point.

It is essentially a philosophical solution, since Śaṁkara lifts us, through the power of thought which alone can reconcile and ennoble the different sides of life, into the ideal of joy and peace.[3]

This statement by Radhakrishnan typifies the theologian. We have defined philosophy formally as a method and an attitude and deduce, therefore, that "joy and peace" can be no criteria for a philosophic solution. We cannot deviate completely from the classical subdivision of academic philosophy into its basic disciplines. Logic treats the validity and the form of thought; ethics describes the goods and the highest good in terms of speculative value; and metaphysics is concerned with the content of philosophic thought. "Joy and Peace" are not admitted as subject-matter in any of the three disciplines; their occurrence, whether as a sequel of philosophic thinking or as the stimulus to philosophic discourse, is—philosophically speaking—totally accidental. Neo-Platonism, as well as romantic philosophy, insisted on aesthetics being introduced on an equal footing as a fourth and indispensable discipline in philosophy. Many modern philosophers, perhaps including some existentialists, may feel inclined to support this view. But even then "joy and peace" cannot gain admission as philosophic criteria, since it is the beautiful which is the subject-matter of aesthetics. Such experiences may be objects of observation, but only on a line with other aesthetic objects, as

[3] Ind P, II, 656.

form, setting, or environment. "Joy and peace" are certainly on the list for investigation by the psychologist—as emotional phenomena; but this psychological approach is not what Radhakrishnan seems to be after.

The sentiment that Śaṁkara's philosophy lifts us up toward the "ideal of joy and peace" intimates that Śaṁkara's solution is essentially unphilosophical. As an anchorite or monk in Śaṁkara's line, I may experience in meditation an insight which yields joy and peace; meditation, however, completely excluding, as it does, discursive thought, is contrapolary to philosophy, which is the very culmination of discursiveness. The equating of contemplation with philosophy—which then is styled "the true philosophy" by its propounders—is at best enthusiastic thought which appeals to the pious. This medley has been perpetrated not only by Vivekānanda, but, as is well known, by real philosophers too, such as Pythagoras and Plato.

Śaṁkara is not unmatched for his logical powers, as Radhakrishnan holds. The very rudimentary fact that the main tenet of Śaṁkara's philosophy is illogical (as indicated above) shows that the Ādiguru Śaṁkara himself did not care as much for logic as his successors did and found it necessary to do. (Madhusūdana Sārasvati can be said to have been the pastmaster in that trade.) Śaṁkara did not have to care too much for a faultless dialectic at his time; for the great anti-monistic dialecticians had not yet been born. The impact of his unique metaphysics and, most of all, of his grand personality must have played a distinct rôle in establishing his usually unquestioned *Digvijaya*, i.e., the doctrinaire conquest of the contemporaneous philosophers. It takes about a century or two for the philosophic world to recover from the charm the extra-ordinary individual philosopher has cast; only then do the opponents' voices gain clarity and rigour.

That the Śaṁkarite Advaita completes and crowns the edifice of Indian philosophy is a very enthusiastic—and almost Vivekānandian—statement, and is certainly that of a schoolman. But the comparative philosopher cannot commit himself that far. A very thorough study of the Vedānta classics, including the less known and therefore less appreciated, such as Nimbarka and Vallabha, readily proves to the unprejudiced student that their respective dialectics are equally strong; the final choice of a particular school is emotionally conditioned—and then *de gustibus non est disputandum*. Radhakrishnan has been called a panegyrist, and he surely is that so far as the Śaṁkarite Vedānta is concerned.

But a string of abstractions cannot do justice to the wealth of reality unless we assume that the ultimate reality is thought as such. It is this absolute judgment that is implied in our mind from the first, that thought and being are one.[4]

This contention of Radhakrishnan's makes a strong appeal to Śaṁkara's notions and gives them value in opposition to Rāmānuja; but there are some fallacies involved in the process. This "judgment" is *not* "implied in our minds" *unless* we believe ourselves to be born as absolutists; but we do not necessarily have to believe that. Surely such was not implied until the rationalists and the absolutists told us. The empiricist, on the other hand, teaches that the conception of this oneness is not only not essential for philosophic method, but proffers the directly opposite approach. The empiricist schoolman could possibly claim that the distinction between thought and being is implied in our minds from the first, and do so with just as much right. Radhakrishnan's dictum *sounds* Hegelian; it *is not* Śaṁkarite. There is an insuperable difference in the respective elements of the two systems (if the Śaṁkarite philosophy can be termed a system at all, which is doubted by several scholars). The Hegelian "thought" has little to do with the Śaṁkarite concept; it is not the contentless *cit* of the Vedānta which has no locus and which defies all connection or correlation with a personal, thinking subject, and which is rather pure *cit* because it does not have any object either. The *grāhaka* ("grasper," cognizer) and the *grāhya* ("grasped," the cognized objective world of the Śaṁkara Bhāṣya) is a strange mongrel indeed; the former being equated with the objectless noumenon on the one hand, and explained in terms of the empirical *jīva,* on the other. But for this equation, the Śaṁkarite *grāhaka* might be the Hegelian "thought," which the consistent absolutist metaphysician must needs equate with "being." The empiricist—whether he be a Nāgārjuna or a Locke—will admit the equation only for empirical thought and empirical being, though this would not bother the absolutist schoolman. It remains yet to be worked out whether any Western philosophy in the Critical tradition has ever conceived of thought and being as so totally abstracted an entity. If the negative can be proved—and we are inclined to think it can—then any correlation of the Advaitist with Western absolutism and monism will have to be abandoned, and even the approximation of Śaṁkara to Berkeley will become questionable.

[4] Ind P, II, 713.

The absolute of Western philosophy, its thought-being, is thus not so readily equable with the *sat-cit* of the Upaniṣad, where it is spoken of as inseparable from and coterminous with the equally impersonal subject-objectless bliss-*ānanda*—which finds no place whatever in Western absolutist systems, even as a nominal entity. The Aupaniṣadic trinity, *sat-cit-ānanda*, is a true *"Dreieinigkeit,"* a tri-unity and, like the Christian trinity, is an entirely theological notion; yet, up-to-date comparative religion with vested interests on either side will have to work hard to establish the popular equation of *sat-cit-ānanda* with the Christian trinity—the necessary identity of *ānanda* with the "Holy Spirit," Paraclite, seems far-fetched and somewhat difficult to swallow.

It is also unwholesome to impose a more recent method on a previous or ancient dogmatic proposition. The Hegelian "trinity" of thesis, antithesis, and synthesis is a highly developed philosophic method and the summit of a long speculative tradition. The theological trinities of the Upaniṣad and the less certain Comma Joanneum are not accessible to any discursive enquiry; we may take them as statements of intuition or revelation or dogma. Their superficial analogy seems adventitious, unless history proves some mutual influence. We suggest that there is a proclivity to the figure "three" rooted in the magical setting of primitive societies— this is a problem for the ethno-psychologist. But as modern philosophers we must disclaim a discursive, methodical explanation of theological dicta; to supply the Hegelian method as an ontological basis for the revealed "trinities" is an impermissible superimposition, what our *Bhāmati* calls a *mūḍhādhyāsa*.

According to Radhakrishnan, the "dualist realism of the Saṃkhya is the result of a false metaphysics;" [5] here again the absolutist speaks. We cannot admit that the pluralist's arguments or the empiricist's metaphysics are false, or at least that they are any more false than the rationalist's and the absolutist's. The history of philosophy shows that the real strife is between the empiricist and the absolutist, between the Heraclitean and the Eleatic. But we are philosophizing in the post-Kantian era, and we have learned that school-philosophy is a strenuous and fatiguing affair, and a thankless one besides; our best energies are spent in refuting others or trying to do so. Not only the radical empiricist, who is the schoolman of the antagonist camp, but even the mildest syncretist must take objection to this assertion. Metaphysics deals with the contents implied in the ontological formula. It speculates and

[5] Ind P, II, 320.

hypothesizes on that mysterious *"Ding an sich,"* the noumenon. Hence there can be no false metaphysics, unless a false dialectic precedes it. The Sāṃkhyan dualist dialectic of the *Kārikas* of Īshvarakrishna is quite workable and the often mentioned [6] flaw in the Sāṃkhyan *exemplum magnum* [7] is really the only hitch in their dialectical make-up. The eternally parallel existence of the two principles can well be postulated and conceived, and the non-interference of the *Puruṣa* with the *Prākṛti* could be compared with the catalytic effect in the relevant chemical reactions; the scientist here does nothing but state the self-evident fact; nor is he particularly disturbed in his doings before he can spot the cause.

Metaphysics, then, cannot be false in the sense logic can be. The Advaitist dicta attributing qualities to the noumenon in one place and denying them in the next are false logic, if we reject the validity of a graded existence—of the absolute and the relative planes. But this rejection is incumbent on the pure logician; by analogy, Advaita metaphysics could be held to be falser than Sāṃkhyan, which is certainly dualistic and realist. It is only logic, and probably only of the deductive variety, that can be directly charged when fallacious. Logicians of all schools have at least more common ground than do metaphysicians of opposing schools; for there are the three simple laws of deductive logic and there is the more elusive scientific method available for the logicians as common tools; there are no such common tools for the metaphysician. Given an equal mastery of the basic logic, it is finally left to the taste of the individual metaphysician to decide in favor of monism or of pluralism.

The contention that Advaita metaphysics must be acceptable at the end of all studies is very dogmatic; but it is in vogue among most of the monks of the order of its first propounder. They, however, can be connived at for their loyalty until they can be given to understand that loyalty to one's preceptor means agreement in life and deed, not necessarily in thought as well; but it seems there must be different readings of loyalty; we feel, consequently, that for the time being, we should argue the point with the scholarly

[6] Cf. Ind P, II, 327.

[7] The *Puruṣa* and *Prākṛti* are likened to a seeing, lame man and a blind man with normal legs, respectively. The lame man sitting on the blind man's shoulders can direct his gait, and so they carry on by mutual aid. The argument against this classical Sāṃkhyan simile is that both of the men are sentient beings and that their communication is perfectly possible; whereas the mute, insentient Prākṛti cannot be susceptible to conscious coercion or influence.

layman only. Even the scholarly layman becomes difficult, however, when he takes to the attitude of the apodictic monk.

The Puruṣa, "who is over and above the continuum of mental states, cannot be experienced in empirical metaphysic." [8] Now, if Radhakrishnan means the sādhana-complex by "empirical metaphysic," viz., what is called the "spiritual life" in the vulgarly hackneyed jargon of edifying literature, we fail to see how anyone, including the Advaitin, is to experience his Brahman which cannot be any more positively qualified than the Sāṃkhyan Puruṣa. Its main characteristics are also negative—neti, neti, "not this, not this." It is qualified as eternal, indivisible; and this dangerously resembles the Puruṣa of the Sāṃkhya in whatever is predicated about the Brahman. The Brahman of Śaṃkara figures just as little among the dramatis personae of the witnessed play as does the Puruṣa.

"Man cannot live on doubt," [9] writes Radhakrishnan;—but the philosopher can, though the theologian may not be aware of it. The dogmatist of all times and climes condemns doubt as a crime —it is the sin against the Holy Spirit, which is the only sin that cannot be forgiven. This is understandable, doubt and dogma being mutually exclusive. De omnibus dubitare has been postulated as a criterion of the philosopher's attitude. Doubt is a method of philosophy; dogma is the method of the theologian; which fact again justifies the separation of the two faculties on the academic level. Whether the hopes and aspirations of the sincere Ṛṣis, the seers and sages, are to be doomed or fulfilled when philosophic method checks the validity of their works, this does not concern the philosopher.

It is indeed very easy to find fault with minute details; any student of philosophy can find statements that can be refuted or at least contravened by some other thesis. The admissibility of a graded reality; the impossibility of a pluralist system yielding a consistent metaphysic, etc.—all these claims can be critically dealt with at great length. It was the basic outlook with which we were mainly concerned in this paper; and what we were driving at was the establishment of a criterion of philosophizing in general, and of comparative philosophizing in particular. In this procedure, the philosophy of Radhakrishnan served as the antithesis.

In summing up we offer an apology. It is not only insolent, but also unwise to try to pull down what a universally acknowledged specialist has built up in a lifetime. Wide learning, prodigious

[8] Ind P, II, 320.   [9] Ind P, II, 19.

reading, prolific writing, and the mastery of a fine language are praiseworthy in themselves; where they are found the critic can only attack a very small sector—he must find a very narrow and limited topic, a subtle aspect for his point of attack. Kant has been challenged and even "refuted" by many lesser contemporaries; but it was not really Kant who was challenged, but at best a few sentences he wrote or taught. But a man and even a philosopher is more than all his sentences put together. Radhakrishnan is so much more than the two volumes of his *magnum opus* and his important monographs. There may be many pundits in India who know Sanskrit better and show more specific erudition than does Sir Sarvepalli. Yet on the scale of world-wide cultural contacts, which may yet give some hope in a mire of hopelessness, their weight must be less than that of the man who in our days holds out to the world the light of an ancient, serene, and sometimes mysteriously profound way of thinking and living.

Swāmi Agehānanda Bhārati

University of Delhi
Delhi, India

14

Suniti Kumar Chatterji

DYNAMIC HINDUISM AND RADHAKRISHNAN

DYNAMIC HINDUISM AND RADHAKRISHNAN

APART from his rôle as interpreter of Hindu philosophy, in which by his clear and lucid exposition through the medium of the English language he has created quite an epoch, Sarvepalli Radhakrishnan stands unrivalled today as the most convincing exponent of a Dynamic Hinduism which, true to its original character as a synthesis of diverse faiths and philosophies of life, is now offered as a Universal Doctrine capable of embracing the whole of humanity—as a *Sanātana Dharma* or "Perennial Philosophy"—on which the wisdom and experience of the nations in the domain of the spiritual converge. Like all great poets and thinkers adding to the extent and content of the emotional and mental experiences which they set forth,—and like all great artists and sculptors exalting by their plastic creations the mythological and other conceptions which they seek to visualise—a master mind like Radhakrishnan's has enriched by his exposition the thought content and the spiritual experience as well as the social implications of the Hindu religion, not only as a thing of the past but also in its dynamic, ever-moving aspect as an indication of the present, and as an aspiration for the future as well.

The views advanced by the present writer are not those of a professed student of philosophy, a subject in which he cannot claim any training or special competence. They are offered with great diffidence and with a profound sense of inadequacy before the concourse of experts in philosophy to whom these essays are primarily addressed. The present writer is a student of philology—of linguistics and literature, and of a few ancillary human sciences like anthropology and history of culture. The living interest which he feels in the religion and culture of India, past and present, as one of the most significant human achievements in the last 3,000 years, and in the writings and work of Professor Radhakrishnan as the most convincing among the living exponents of this religion and culture in both their personal and universal aspects, causes him to accede, with a full sense of his deficiencies, to the request to write on the topic of "Dynamic Hinduism and Radhakrishnan." As a layman who appreciates with his objective historical sense the dynamics of a cultural and spiritual force, which Hinduism most assuredly is, he is seeking to present it in its character and its working; and, at the same time, to trace the part Radhakrishnan has been playing in making it understood and in consciously helping to direct its line of progress and action. He offers these pages as a tribute of respect to one of the greatest sons of Mother India in the present age, and one of the accredited thought-leaders of the world, with whom he has had the honour and privilege to be associated as a colleague in the same seat of learning for a considerable number of years.

Panta rhei—all things are in a state of flux, including things of the mind and spirit. Life is movement. Whether we feel it or not, or see it as such or not, the environment in which we find ourselves is never static. A non-stop, unending, and never-repeating moving picture show is this so-called Being in the universe. Being is nothing static—it is Becoming, it is dynamic, ever changing into something new, into something which shows some difference, however small or great. This is true also of the way of life and the domain of thought which we call Hinduism. The life and thought of the Indian people, at any definite stage of development, present nothing immobile or fixed, static or unchanging. The process of life is more nearly comparable to the continuous flow of a stream than to a chain consisting of detached links. Dynamic Hinduism thus is Hinduism as a living process—Hinduism in its historical venue of growth which is still going on.

If we believe in determinism, then man is a helpless automaton. There is, of course, as all believers agree, the Supreme Will which directs things—the *Demiurge*. The Supreme Will works through its manifestations on earth, the wills of men, the wills of saints and sages. The affairs of men are the playground of a divine polo-player; but man, when he rises to the full height of his being, is not merely the ball which moves to and fro when hit, but is also a fellow-player. The saints and sages are co-actors in the scene with God. Or, as the *Gītā* has put it, "whatsoever being there is, endowed with glory and grace and vigour, know that to have sprung from a fragment of My Splendour."

If the participation of the wise man in directing the affairs and shaping the mentality of his fellow-beings has something of the

mystic in it, then still more mystic is the dispensation of circumstances by which a particular people builds up its initial mental
attitude which seems to give its special tone to all subsequent developments. As Radhakrishnan himself has put it, "the only revolutions that endure are those that are rooted in the past." The
seen and the unseen, the historic and the mystic, are but the two
faces of the same *événement*. What happened or is happening is
always capable of a two-fold explanation or interpretation, the
outer and the inner. The outer refers to the background of the
area, the time, and the people (*déśa, kāla, pātra*) which requires an
objective and historical investigation; the inner refers to the wider
human and super-human implications which it is the province of
philosophy to establish. As regards the former, Hinduism, the
Hindu attitude and the Hindu way of life, can, from the standpoint of its origin and historical development, be an object of
anthropological and sociological study. Such studies have been undertaken, and, they are, with the advance of these social sciences,
becoming more and more intensified and detailed. It used to be
the habit to think of Hinduism (as, indeed, in the case of most
other religions) as scriptural in origin, emanating in all its entirety
and full growth from the mind of the Divinity or its interpreters,
the sages and saints of a hoary antiquity, which, in orthodox opinion, was too hoary to be computed in mundane centuries or even
millennia. In its pristine form it was supposed to transcend time and
race and country, just as the Jew would claim for Judaism and the
Muslim for Islam. However, the scientific study of history with all
its ramifications is scoring a slow but certain victory at this point.
The age, the country, and the people are coming to receive their
proper recognition in the evolution of a national religion or ideology, just as the man and the moment are being given their due
regard in considering the right emphasis to be put upon certain
aspects of this religion or ideology.

Thanks to some six generations of students and investigators,
scholars and thinkers, and persons who have lived this religion in
one or more of its manifestations, the basic ideas of Hinduism as
a system are gradually becoming enunciated. From pulpit and platform, from the retreat of monks and mendicants, from books and
journals by scholars and investigators, we are gradually becoming
accustomed to certain lines of thought as representing the most
characteristic expression of Hinduism. Some of the greatest minds
in India, who regard themselves as expositors of Hinduism as a
path for the attainment of the highest good, have, in recent years,

even formulated some of Hinduism's basic ideas in pithy epigrammatic sentences in the form of the *Sūtra*, a style characteristic of ancient Indian philosophic and scientific statements. We are reminded of statements like Ramakrishna Paramahansa's "as many doctrines, so many ways," and "it is not pity for all creatures—it should be service to creatures knowing them to be the Supreme," or Swami Vivekananda's "Vedānta recognises no sin, it only recognises error," and "he is the atheist who does not believe in himself," and similar sayings from most of the Indian saints and sages of the present age, conveying many significant ideas. Radhakrishnan has great facility for stating profound truths, for which Hinduism is his inspiration, in terse and piquant statements as good as the best epigrams of any age. This ability has been one of the great strengths of his style: his epigrams, which often are more convincing than any sermon or discourse, are forged out of the depth of his convictions. It would be easy to make a good-sized selection of these from his writings. I shall cite just a few, taken from only one of his books, his *Hindu View of Life: viz.,*

"The Divine reveals itself to men within the framework of their intimate prejudices." (p. 25)

"It is a sound agnosticism which bids us hold our peace regarding the nature of the unknown spirit." (p. 25)

"Truth wears vestures of many colours, and speaks in strange tongues." (p. 36)

"No type can come into existence in which God does not live." (p. 42)

"Error is a sign of immaturity. It is not a grievous sin." (p. 43)

"Hinduism hates the compulsory conscription of men into the house of truth." (p. 49)

"Religion is not correct belief but righteous living." (p. 51)

"The unity of religion [is] not in a common creed but in a common quest." (p. 58)

"Gorgeous flowers justify the muddy roots from which they spring." (p. 60)

"The law of karma encourages the sinner that it is never too late to mend." (p. 76)

"Disguised feeling is masquerading as advanced thought." (p. 88)

"The last part of life's road is to be worked in single file." (p. 90)

"Every state is necessary, and in so far as it is necessary it is good." (p. 91)

"When the wick is ablaze at its tip, the whole lamp is said to be burning." (p. 92)

"Service of one's fellows is a religious obligation. To repudiate it is impiety." (p. 116)

"We cannot put our souls in uniform." (p. 116)

We shall now consider Hinduism or the Hindu way of life in its basic aspects as it developed in ancient India as the result of the forces of the age, or rather, of various ages, with the diverse races and the various economic *milieus* interacting among each other. National cultures grow out of international contacts and conflicts. Similarly great nations never develop from small tribes; rather, they arise out of the fusion of great races, meeting in war and peace. The Indo-European Hellenes mingled with the Mediterranean Aegean people, and, with a sprinkling of Semitic people in its composition, we have the Indo-European-speaking Greeks of history from the 10th century B.C. onwards. In the formation of the Roman people we have not only the various Italian tribes commingling with the basic Latin tribes of the same Italian group, but also Celts and other Indo-Europeans, and, what is more important, the Asianic Etruscans. The basic Iberian type of man was overlaid by the Indo-European Celtic, and then there was the strong Germanic infusion to give rise to the English speaking people. America today shows the greatest wide-scale miscegenation of peoples in history, but here we have a fusion of people mainly belonging to one group of humanity only, the white or so-called Caucasian race. In India, racial fusion has been going on for the last four-thousand years and more, and the basic or component races show much greater diversity in the fundamental physical types and their mental and spiritual attitudes and aspirations than anything we see in Europe or America. According to the most recent authoritative scientific opinion on the matter, as many as six distinct races in their nine sub-types or variations have entered into the composition of the present-day Indian people. Members of these races came into India at different times, and, beginning from a prehistoric period of unknown antiquity, right down to a thousand years before Christ, this commingling of peoples, or racial fusion appears to have been in full swing, giving rise in North India at about that time to a definite Hindu type of man with a special physical character and a peculiar mental attitude of his own. The process did not cease with that date—it continued with unabated vigour all over India, and has continued to our day, and is still in active operation in certain parts of India where the so-called aboriginals or backward tribes are becoming slowly but inevitably converted to membership in the common Hindu or Indian body-politic—e.g., in

Central India, in Orissa, in Chota Nagpur, in Himalayan India, in North Bengal, and in Assam.

It is not necessary here to go into anthropological details about the various races which contributed to the formation of Indian humanity. There were great and apparently unbridgeable differences in physical appearance at the outset—in colour (white, or yellow, brown, or black), in head-formation, in stature; there also was great diversity of speech and of the culture-type which is linked with a particular mentality as expressed by the speech. For our purposes, we can speak of the various "language-culture" groups which were fused into one common "Hindu" culture—the racial miscegenation has never been uniform to the same extent that cultural fusion has been. In some areas, racial fusion has been very marked indeed; in other parts, original races have remained largely unaffected physically, but the common culture in which, although evolved elsewhere, these original races had a share, came to be adopted and assimilated. We cannot think of three groups more distant in their outward physical type, their language and their original ways of life than the Austric-Dravidian people of Malabar, the fair "Aryan" Brahmans of Kashmir, and the Mongoloid people of Nepal. Yet all of them have accepted the common Hindu ways of life, and have no other mentality or attitude than the Hindu one. Variations are merely regional or in dialect; but they are all of the same archetype.

No kind of primitive man seems to have evolved on the soil of India proper; all her human inhabitants are descended from outsiders who came to the country at various epochs. The first people who came to India were short-statured Negroids, properly Negritos who were not exactly pygmies, who came into India from Africa, one does not know how many thousands of years ago. They trekked along the coastlands of Arabia and Iran, and settled in Western and Southern India, and pushed into Eastern India as far as Assam, whence they passed on to Burma, Malaya, and beyond—and to New Guinea, for example, and from the tip of South Burma they crossed over to the Andaman Islands, where a few hundred of them still live in a very primitive condition. On the soil of India itself they have been either killed off or absorbed by subsequent peoples—only in South India they survive as members of a number of wild tribes, speaking dialects of Dravidian, which they acquired from Dravidian-speaking peoples who influenced them culturally; traces of these Negroids are also found among the Mongoloid Nagas of Assam. These Negroids, who started the drama which humanity has played on the soil of India, had no very high type of culture. They were a food-gathering community, living in forest lands. Apart from some tree cults (e.g., the cult of the fig tree) and some notions of life after death (e.g., an avenging demon who meets the individual after his death), anthropologists think that they did not contribute anything to the thought-world of man in India. Ideologically they do not appear to have given anything to humanity, and even on the material plane these primitive food-gatherers apparently had no contribution to make.

The Negroids were followed by four other peoples who represent the basic elements of the Hindu population. Speaking in a loose way, with greater emphasis on language and culture rather than on race, they were the Austrics, the Dravidians, the Indian Mongoloids and the Aryans or Indo-Europeans. They were known in India, respectively, as *Nishādas, Drāviḍas, Kirātas* and *Āryas.* The diversity in skin-pigmentation noted among these peoples— dark or black, brown, yellow, and white, forms one of the bases of the caste system as a characteristic organization of Hindu Society— the Sanskrit word for caste, *varṇa,* meaning just "colour." Three of these four groups, like the Negroids, came from the West; only the Kiratas or Mongoloids came from the East.

The Austrics formed a very old off-shoot of the Mediterranean race who came to India in pre-historic times in the wake of the Negroids, with whom they doubtless intermingled. In their primitive state, before they had lived here for centuries, modified their type and found the bases of their culture within an Indian *milieu,* they are described as *Proto-Australoids.* In this *Proto-Australoid* stage they passed out of India through Burma and Malaya into Indonesia, and thence into Australia, where today's Australian aborigines are their modern representatives. But on the soil of India they developed a higher type of culture, including primitive agriculture with the digging stick, the culture of rice and of some vegetables, the domestication of the elephant and of the fowl, and the spinning and weaving of cotton into thread and cloth. They dispersed all over India, particularly in the Ganges valley; and the bases of the village culture of India were supplied by these Indian Austrics. At the present time, medium-sized, dark-skinned, long-headed and snub-nosed, they form an important element in the lower castes of the whole of India. From India, these Austrics with the culture they developed in India, both material and spiritual (some notions about the beginning of things and of creation, of life after death, and some cults and rituals), passed on to Farther India

(Burma, and Indo-China, including Siam, Cambodia, Vietnam, and Cochin China) and Malaya, and thence to the islands beyond— to Indonesia, Melanesia, Micronesia, and Polynesia. It can be said, therefore, that, from Western Panjab and Northern Kashmir to distant Hawaii, Easter Island and New Zealand, there is an Austric basis in the population. The present-day peoples speaking languages derived ultimately from the primitive Austric speech as it developed in India (this Austric speech has largely been ousted on the soil of India, particularly in the plains, by the Aryan speech, by virtue of the fact that the Austric-speaking masses accepted the Aryan language along with Hinduism) are divided into two main groups—(1) Austro-Asiatic, and (2) Austronesian. There is evidence of considerable intermingling of original Austric peoples with other races in this vast area of mainland and islands—with Negroids and Mongoloids, for instance. The Austro-Asiatic group includes the Kol or Munda aborigines of India, speaking Austric languages like Santali, Mundari, Ho, Korku, Savara, Gadaba, etc.; the Khasis of Assam; the Nicobarese of the Nicobar Islands; the Mon or Talaings of South Burma and South-Siam; the Paloung and the Wa of North Burma; and the Khmers of Cambodia; besides some other peoples of French Indo-China. The Austronesian group comprises the Indonesians (Malays, Javanese, Sundanese, Madurese, Balinese, Bugis, and other peoples of Indonesia, the Filipinos, and the Malagasis of Madagascar), the Melanesians, Micronesians, and the Polynesians. An underlying linguistic unity between these two groups suggests the existence of at least a basic common culture throughout this area, with a certain amount of racial affinity, say, between a Santal and a Malay, a Cambodian and a Maori.

This basic element, the Austric, in the people of India was overlaid by the Dravidian and the Aryan elements, and by the Indo-Mongoloid at its northern and north-eastern fringes. It is believed that the original Dravidian-speaking group of India came from the Mediterranean area, and racially and culturally they were an East Mediterranean people. The question of linguistic affinity between Dravidians of India and the Aegeans and Asianics and other East Mediterranean peoples has not yet been solved, as we have no connected specimens of the ancient East Mediterranean languages of sufficient length and certainty in meaning to enable us to compare with Dravidian: individual words have been, however, plausibly compared. The Dravidians of Mediterranean origin were great city-builders, and the remains of a wonderful city culture in South Panjab and Sindh, which were discovered some three decades ago, evoke our wonder and admiration. This civilisation goes back to at least 3500 years before Christ; so that the advent of the Dravidian people can be placed a few centuries before this date. The Dravidian-speaking people gradually spread over the whole of India—as far east as the Brahmaputra Valley and as far south as the Tamil land and Malabar; moreover, in the south they founded solid blocs of people where their language became strongly established. Culturally they were more advanced than the Austrics, who lived with them side by side over a great part of the country, particularly in North India. They brought with them elements of their religion from the Mediterranean area which included the worship of a great Mother Goddess as the most active force in nature and life, with a passive male counter-part in the form of a God who seemed to be overshadowed by her. In Hinduism, certain profound notions about the nature of the godhead, and certain mystic cults, rituals, and ideologies are the gift of the Dravidians. The Aryans and the Dravidians, with the Austrics contributing their own quota, really built up the Hindu world of ideas and the Hindu way of life by 1000 B.C.

The third non-Aryan element (equally pre-Aryan, too, though perhaps not so old in India as the Austrics and the Dravidians) is presented by the Indo-Mongoloids, the Kiratas. They spoke languages and dialects of the Sino-Tibetan family, to which Chinese and Siamese, Burmese and Tibetan, and the non-Chinese aboriginal languages of China like Man and Miao-tsze, and Karen of Burma, equally belong. They arrived in India sometime before 1000 B.C., from the East and North-east, either along the valley of the Brahmaputra or through the passes in the Himalayas leading from Tibet into India. We find them already known to the Vedic Aryans as a people living in the caves and hills of the North. These Kirata Mongoloids of India were settled all over Assam, East and North Bengal and North Bihar as well as along the tracts to the south of the Himalayas as far west as East Panjab. Culturally backward, they appear not to have made much of a contribution to the formation of the Hindu world of ideas, except in North Bihar, Bengal, Assam, and Nepal. They just touched the fringe of Hindudom, and their participation consisted largely in the nature of an acceptance of the Hindu religion and culture which was developed in the Ganges plain, with certain modifications brought in by their peculiar racial character.

The Aryans formed one of the great Indo-European speaking group of peoples which has now taken the leadership in civilisation from the Hamito-Semites of antiquity and the Mongoloids in the East. Like their linguistic brothers, the Iranians and their cousins the ancient Greeks, the Romans, the Celts, the Germans and the Slavs, they were not creators of any great material civilisation, but they were great as organisers. They came into India from their original homeland in the South Ural steppes by way of Northern Mesopotamia and Iran, where they are found between B.C. 2500-1500 and later; and their advent into India appears to have been after 1500 B.C. A group of semi-nomad and only partly agricultural tribes, they arrived with their flocks and herds, and found the city-dwelling Dravidian people in Eastern Iran and North-western India, and the Austrics living mostly in their forest hamlets. The Dravidians they appear to have known at first as *Dāsas* and *Dasyus* (in Iranian pronunciation these words later became *Daha* and *Dahyu*) and the Austrics as *Nishādas*. The Aryans established their *nidus* in the North-west of India, in the land of the seven rivers (Punjab and the Northwest Frontier Province and Western U. P. or *Uttara Pradēśa*), and from the very beginning they found the earlier inhabitants disputing their advance. Gradually, however, Aryan discipline and solidarity, plus their physical vigour and certain moral qualities they possessed (imagination, adaptability, and a sane attitude towards women), combined with the want of solidarity among the pre-Aryan peoples (who had no linguistic or cultural cohesion among themselves, speaking as they did languages of three totally distinct groups, the Dravidian, the Austric, and the Sino-Tibetan), caused the Aryans easily to acquire the place of a *Herrenvolk*, of a group of puissant *Conquistadores*, who could impose their will, while accepting whatever they had to accept in the land they had come to live in and to rule—at least for some time. The longer the Aryan stayed on in India, and the further he pushed into the non-Aryan domains of the East in the Ganges Valley and of the South in the Deccan, the more he leavened the local cultures and brought about their unification, which was effected largely by his language supplying the need for a common medium to bind together a new people being brought into existence by racial mixture. By 1000 B.C., judging from the evidence of Hindu tradition as preserved in the Hindu scriptures—the *Vēdas* with the *Brāhmanas* and the *Grihya-sūtras,* the great national epic of the *Mahābhārata,* and the repositories of the traditions of the various peoples, Aryan and non-Aryan, which are the *Purānas*—this mixture was far advanced, and a people of Aryan-non-Aryan (*Ārya-Drāvida-Nishāda-Kirāta*) origin had come into being, with the

Aryan speech as their common language. The wise men of these various groups, and their men of action too, came to collaborate in the formulation of a common culture. No racial exclusiveness was tolerated, although the Aryan had a certain prestige by virtue of his being the conqueror and of his language being the vehicle of this culture. But his claim to racial superiority or pre-eminence was soon modified or restricted by the development of the Hindu ideas of caste, in which race and colour became subordinated to function and social value of the work done by a group. The pantheons of the Aryans and the various non-Aryans were synchronised and they were combined to give rise to a common pantheon, no longer purely Aryan, or Dravidian, or Austric, or Mongoloid, but Brahmanical or Hindu; and the mystic and philosophical notions of these various groups were brought to bear upon each other. Ultimately they were formulated into Brahmanical beliefs and doctrines, philosophy and rituals, in which each group could honestly feel at home, since there was an acknowledgment of the value of his particular point of view.

It has been a very good fortune for India that, instead of racialism, there developed a tacit acceptance of universalism. The philosophy of the Vedānta helped it: "he who sees all creatures in his own soul, and his soul in all creatures, he cannot hide himself away (or hate) any one," so says the *Īśā Upaniṣad*. We may not be conscious of it scientifically here in India, but we have a vague idea of kinship with the whole world through the complexity of our racial make-up. An Indian who knows the racial bases of his people and of his culture cannot but feel himself the most cosmopolitan person in the world. Thus our Aryan languages, although profoundly modified by the non-Aryan languages (Dravidian languages had as much to do with the formation of Sanskrit in India as did Aryan languages), form a great mental and spiritual link with the Eur-American world—the Indo-European world of the West, where Sanskrit also occupies a place of honour. We are linked up with the peoples of South-eastern Asia and of Austronesia (Indonesia, Melanesia, and Polynesia) through our Austric heritage, racial, cultural, and linguistic. Similarly the Kirata or Indo-Mongoloid elements in our culture make us feel a kinship with the worlds of China and Japan, Siam and Vietnam, Burma and Tibet, Mongolia and Korea. The Dravidian languages may show some deep affinities with the Ural-Altaic world. Then, our long contact with Islam, through Arabs, Turks, and Iranians, bringing its ideology and its great culture to us, has made us familiar with the Muhammadan world also; and we can, therefore, accept the Semitic, Arab and other Islamic worlds with more than a mere nod of acquaintance; for the mystic side of Islam especially has found a congenial nest in the Hindu soul also. We have, furthermore, expanded our Hindu soul by our contact with Christianity also. The diversity of race, which Destiny brought to us, with an attendant attitude of not emphasizing this diversity on the basis of any petty jingoism, has been responsible for this initial note of internationalism in our national character, particularly in the domain of ideas.

Racialism and the idea of being "the chosen people" of God could, fortunately, find no place here, where the climatic and economic situation brought about a great levelling of the people. The "Mestizos," i.e., the mixed descendants of non-Aryans and Aryans, were the most natural bridge-builders over this initial gulf among the various elements. Hindudom has, therefore, been giving divine honour to two of the greatest among those Mestizos in history, who, in all truth, may be said to have given its special orientation to the Hindu way of life and its attitude to religious culture in general; who, in fact, set Hindu culture on the path on which it has progressed for the past thirty centuries. These were Kṛṣṇa Dvaipāyana Vyāsa, "Kṛṣṇa the Island-born, the Arranger," and Kṛṣṇa Vāsudeva Vārshṇeya, "Kṛṣṇa the son of Vāsudeva, of the Vṛishṇi clan."

They were among the most important heroes of the *Mahābhārata* epic, the historical basis of which, according to three competent authorities who arrived at the same conclusion by totally different lines of enquiry (viz., F. E. Pargiter, H. C. Ray Chau· dhuri, and L. D. Barnett), goes back to the 10th century B.C. Kṛṣṇa Dvaipāyana Vyāsa is looked upon as the author of the Sanskrit epic itself. He was the grandfather of the Kaurava and Pāṇḍava heroes, cousins belonging to a royal house who fought in the great 18-days' battle of Kurukshetra; Vyāsa is a veritable Nestor in the Indian epic, who was also like an Ossian celebrating the deeds of his own grandchildren who passed away before him. Vyāsa stands at the head of the Hindu religion, in a way: it was he who gave it its basic scriptures, the *Vēdas*. According to tradition, Vyāsa is so known (the word means "the Arranger") because he collected the mass of religious hymns and ritualistic texts which were current orally among the Aryan-speaking people of mixed origin, like himself; and he divided them into the four *Vēda* books, the *Ṛg-Vēda*, the *Yajur-Vēda*, the *Sāma-Vēda*, and the *Atharva-Vēda*—the first three of which were in use in Brahman ritual, whereas the last showed a phase of popular religion and poetry in its charms and incantations. The historical bases of Vyāsa's career are not known. But he was a quadroon, three-fourths non-Aryan in blood; his mother Satyavatī (Matsya-gandhā) was the daughter of possibly an Austric-speaking chief of fisher folk living by the river, and his grandmother was a woman of the Caṇḍāla tribe, supposedly non-Aryan. Possibly it was his non-Aryan affinities or connexions which enabled him to employ for his Aryan speech an alphabet based on pre-Aryan Dravidian writing, which was a sort of Proto-Brāhmī— the ancestor of the finished Sanskrit alphabet, the Brāhmī, of the 4th century B.C. Vyāsa also gave an impetus to the collection of the legendary, historical, and other traditions of the mixed people, which began to be gathered together in a series of works known as the *Purāṇas,* which in later times formed 18 voluminous works, with subsidiary treatises, all of which were fathered upon Vyāsa. The spirit which actuated these collections was that nothing was thrown away as unhistorical, improbable, or un-Aryan; it was an all-inclusive affair. On more questionable authority, Vyāsa is also credited with the formulation of the Brahmanical philosophy of the Vedānta, such as we find in the *Upaniṣads,* in a work of aphorisms on philosophy known as the *Vedānta-sūtras,* which are of the highest authority, along with the *Upaniṣads* and the *Gītā* (a section of the *Mahābhārata*), for the study of the Vedānta. This all-inclusiveness of Vyāsa, who gave Brahmanism its scriptures, marked the Hindu attitude from the beginning.

Now let us take the case of Kṛṣṇa. He was at least a half-caste— his mother Devakī, according to the tradition, was the sister of a non-Aryan king, king Kansa of Mathurā. He stood up against the exclusive Aryan position in its pantheon and ritual—he supported on one occasion a pre-Aryan cult of the Govardhana hill against the Vedic worship of Indra, and sought to give a moral interpretation to the Brahmanical fire-rites; and, in the *Gītā* (Chap. IX) he gave the charter of equality to all types of religious ceremonial, those of non-Aryan origin like the *pūjā,* along with the orthodox Aryan ritual of the *hōma* or fire-sacrifice.

The unknown philosophers of the later Vedic and Upaniṣadic age, working in the same spirit as Vyāsa and Kṛṣṇa, created the distinctive philosophy of Brahmanism with items from the religious experience and perception of the *Nishāda,* the *Drāviḍa,* the *Ārya* and possibly also the *Kirāta.* Among the Aryans—as we notice among their kinsmen in Iran, in Greece, in Italy, and in the Germanic world—man after his death was gathered unto his fathers, in a *pitṛi-lōka* or "Abode of the Manes," an Elysium or a Valhalla.

There was no further speculation. The Dravidian believed in a continuance of personality after death, as a ghost which had to be nurtured and kept alive by periodical offerings of food, in order that the "ghost" might use its beneficient influence for the well-being of the living. The Austric believed in a plurality of the human spirit which passed on into or manifested itself as various beasts or plants. All these were evidently discussed, and finally the Brahmanical philosophy of *Karma* and *Saṁsāra* came into being, with the moral background added by a more advanced mental and spiritual outlook; although notions of an abode of the fathers and the necessity to feed the spirits of the ancestors by means of a *śrāddha* ritual were allowed to remain. The non-Aryan, very probably the Dravidian ritual of the *pūjā* (with possible influences from the Austric world as well), is one in which the Supreme Spirit or Brahma (like *Mana*) is forced by means of a rite to be present in an image or symbol, for the special benefit of the worshipper, and is then treated like an honoured guest. This rite has been completely accepted by Brahmanism, the original Aryan rite of the *hōma* still retaining its place no doubt, but losing much of its appeal or force. Śiva and Umā, Vishṇu and Śrī, divinities of stupendously cosmic and moral significance, together with the ideology of *Yōga* and its practice, derive from the non-Aryan (possibly Dravidian) world, before whose greatness the Vedic anthropomorphisations of nature powers like Varūṇa, Indra, Sōma, Sūrya, Ushas, and others have paled into insignificance. It was later, by a frank recognition of the Vedic or Aryan tradition in religion as *Nigama* (= "that which has come into it, i.e., society at large") and the distinct non-Vedic or non-Aryan tradition as *Āgama* (= "that which has come down through it"), and by giving these equal value as paths to spiritual progress, that the Hindu mind came to feel at ease. Further, Buddha sought to bring about a total denial of Brahmanical pretensions and claims to privilege and prestige, in so far as these claims were Aryan. Buddha, for aught we know, might have been an Indo-Mongoloid, and not a pure Aryan. Earlier, the Jinas like Ariṣṭanemi and Pārśvanātha, historical predecessors of Mahāvīra who was contemporaneous with Buddha, took up the promulgation of other ideologies than the purely Aryan, some of which, like physical austerity, chastity and the doctrine of non-injury, were to form essential parts of the Hindu way of life.

In all these and some other though similar ways, we may say

that, at the turn of the 1st millennium B.C., the Hindu world-view, as taught by Vyāsa and Kṛṣṇa, took definite shape. Certain things marked this world-view from the beginning, and we may try to formulate the most important of them. The ancients, it must be remembered, had no need for a formal statement or formulation of the Hindu or Brahmanical attitude or ideology, since they lived and breathed and had their being in its atmosphere. It was a thing both *in esse* and *in posse* for them, always enlarging its scope, as fresher and newer elements, with contributions in the line of religious experience not envisaged before, were coming within their ken. With this explanation, we may state the following salient points about the Hindu view of the universe and the Hindu way of life, as giving to these their proper *cachet*.

To begin with, Hinduism is a religion without any formal or official creed. Its dynamic character is brought out by this fact more than by anything else. A creed is likely to be a static thing, particularly if a literal interpretation is made to stick to it. Hinduism is a federation of different kinds of religious experience rather than a single type excluding or denying all other types of religious experience. Nevertheless, some of its major characteristics may be noted as follows.

1) It believes in, or seeks to establish by reason, an Ultimate Reality, which man (who, in his essential being, which continues after death, is a part of this Reality) can attain through self-culture, knowledge and intuitive experience, or through Its own grace (the grace of God); a Reality which both transcends life as we see it and is immanent in it.

2) It recognizes and seeks to remove the various kinds of sorrow and suffering that are in life.

3) It embraces Life and the Universe (which are unending throughout the *kalpas* or aeons) in all aspects, and does not look upon man as something detached from the world of nature to which he belongs. Man and the Universe are the expressions of the same Divine Spirit (*Paramātman*) or Energy (*Śakti*) or Order (*Ṛita*) working through them.

4) It does not pin itself down to the experiences and opinions of any single individual—incarnation or prophet—although it reverences all. It recognises that the Ultimate Reality manifests itself in various forms, and that Truth is approachable by diverse paths; therefore, it does not insist upon or inculcate a particular creed which must be accepted by all and sundry. It believes that man can

attain to the *niḥśreyas* or the *summum bonum* in life through the best that is available in his environment, if that best is followed in a spirit of sincerity and charity.

Like all other religions, Hinduism developed its two wings; and on these two wings it has been floating through the centuries, never remaining static at any given point, but covering wider and wider circles of experience. These two wings are those of (i) thought, philosophy, or theory, and (ii) life or practice. The second is based on the first, but it also colours the first. The practical aspect of Hinduism is known as *Dharma, i.e.,* "that which holds" —in other words, "the way or rule of life." Dharma or religion in practice is two-fold—(a) *Nitya-dharma* or the universal and eternal laws of morality and fellowship with others, which must be followed by all, and (b) *Laukika-dharma* or the secondary rules of life which may differ with different lands, ages, and peoples. The theoretical side is *Darśana, i.e.,* "sight," or "view-point," or "insight," where we have ratiocination and perception, intellectual approach and emotional experience.

Approached from another angle, we may say that the following three things constitute the outstanding characteristics of Hinduism.

(1) Tolerance of all other points of view. This is not merely an expression of a superior condescending attitude that there is truth in every religion, although there is only one wholly true religion which is that of the respective believer. Rather, Hinduism admits the essential truth of any particular religious experience for particular individuals as much as one's own religion is held to be true by the one who professes it. This leads to the great principle (or the principle is naturally deduced from it) that Truth has many facets; and different religions are different paths, as Ramakrishna Paramahansa said, or are just like different languages, as Swami Vivekananda explained it, and that God is in all religions and fulfils Himself in many ways. Name and form do not change the nature of the Ultimate Reality: "That which is, is One; sages describe it in manifold ways," as the *Ṛg-Vēda* has put it.

(2) The second great thing noticeable in Hinduism is its uncompromising Adherence to Truth when one is using reason for arriving at a conception of the Ultimate Reality. Even if a logical line of argument were to lead one to atheism, one is not to fight shy of it. The highest prayer of Brahmanism, the Vedic *Gāyatrī* verse, asks only inspiration or guidance from the Supreme Spirit in matters intellectual ("may He direct our thoughts"). What has been condemned in unequivocal terms, is *pramāda,* or "mental

intoxication," and *ajñāna,* "absence of knowledge." Hence the variety of philosophical schools within Hinduism, all seeking to reach the same truth. As Radhakrishnan has quoted from Mahatma Gandhi: "Hinduism is a relentless pursuit after truth. It is 'the religion of truth.' Truth is God. Denial of God we have known. Denial of truth we have not known." [1]

(3) The third notable thing in Hinduism is the Principle of *Ahiṁsā* or Non-injury to any life. This principle is conceived in a spirit of highest altruism and of a most enlightened and cultured negation of self. *Ahiṁsā* is not incompatible with a necessary modicum of cruelty which is inevitable in life; just as one might use a thorn to extract another thorn embedded in the flesh. On the negative side, our attitude towards our fellow-creatures (not merely fellow human beings) is characterised by this abstention from injury; but on its positive side it is *Karuṇā* or "Pity" and *Maitrī* or "Active Good-doing."

Renunciation (*Tyāga*) and Chastity (*Brahmacarya*), when some great ideal is burning within one, these are the other two characteristic aspects of Hinduism in practice.

It would be easy to give quite an extensive positive and negative characterisation of Hinduism, both in its theory and in the practices it enjoins. There is the whole range of Indian literature for the last three-thousand years to draw from; and there are the lives of the saints and prophets as practical demonstrations of it. Over a period of thirty centuries we are able to see how dynamic and ever-extending in its scope Hinduism has been. There have, of course, also been some narrow-minded sects within Hinduism (human failings and limitations are to be found everywhere), which sought to pin their faith upon this or that historical manifestation or special emphasis in the history of Hindu experience, and to deny the value of others. Witness, for example, the exaggerated zeal for the pure monotheistic Vedic faith as some conceived it to be, belittling the rich experience of faith in Puranic divinities like Śiva or Vishṇu, which latter were in their essential conceptions no less monistic. All this richness of experience—not easily found elsewhere—opens up before us the kaleidoscopic and permanent diversity of the forms of the spiritual life: a gamut of many notes from which harmonies may be extracted according to the taste and capacity of the respective individual.

To name only the most representative works and authors—saints and sages, philosophers and devotees—would be to give an ample

[1] ER (2nd ed.), 313.

indication of the variety and the quality of this spiritual feast: Vedic poetry and mysticism; the Upaniṣadic vision of truth; the wisdom and orderliness of the *Hindu Dharma* as in the *Mahābhārata* and the *Purāṇas*, combined with the romance and mysticism of Hindu myth and legend; family ideals, as in the *Rāmāyaṇa;* the theory of the four castes and the four stages of Hindu life; the *abandon* of faith in early Tamil religious and devotional poetry as of the Sivite *Sittars* and the Vishnuite *Azhvārs*, "Adepts" and "God-mad" people; the calm philosophical attitude of the various philosophical writers and commentators; the cold reasoned morality and active good-doing of the Hīnayāna Buddhists; the warm faith and transcendent love of the Mahāyānists; the high pedestal of self-culture through love and non-injury and through an objective desire (with its great predilection for symmetry) to see the innate truth of existence and the nature of salvation which characterises the Jainas; the various Tantric schools—Buddhist and Brahmanical, with their desire to make the lower life a stepping stone for the higher; the pure light of a revived Vedānta; and of Vedānta coloured by *Bhakti* or devotion, and coloured again by Muslim *Taṣawwuf* or Sūfī mysticism, of the medieval mystics and saints of North India; the eclectic schools, with elements from Tantra and Yōga, Vedānta, *Bhakti* and Sūfīism, characterising North Indian saints like Kabir; the *Śākta* devotees of Bengal, with their childlike devotion to God the Mother; and the singers of the Rāma and Kṛṣṇa cults with their special lines of approach to the Divinity in medieval North India and Bengal; the self-realization of Ramakrishna Paramahansa, accepting all forms of experience; the mysticism of Rabindranath Tagore with its over-powering aesthetic beauty, with the conception of God as the Great Sweetheart of Man—the *Ewig-Weibliche* or "Eternal Feminine" of Goethe which "draws us upwards" (*zieht uns hinan*) and which, in the figure of his *Jīvan-dēvatā* or "Life's Godhead" (*Divinité de la Vie*) has been Rabindranath Tagore's own exquisite and poignant contribution to mystic poetry; the spiritual perception of Ramana Maharshi, and of a whole host of others, for the last three thousand years of Hindu history, not to consider the precursors, Dravidian, Austric, Indo-Mongoloid, and Aryan, before the formation of the Hindu tradition. All this is the rich Hindu heritage, and a heritage, moreover, which the Hindus have not neglected.

In fact, the Hindus have sought to enlarge the scope of this heritage from age to age, following the Hindu notion that a good thing should not only be preserved in its goodness, but its effectiveness and value should be extended: *Kshēma* and *Yōga,* "Flourish-ing" and "Addition or Expansion," both are needed. When the Hindu view and way of life became established in North India, it became an irresistible force for good, and began in a few centuries, after annexing the whole of India to its empire, to expand and overflow into other lands. India thus became a *Kalyāṇa-mitra,* a Friend in the Quest of the Good, for the greater part of Asia. A feeling for the deeper things of life, while making fullest use of the environment available, came to actuate neighbouring peoples, when, in the wake of peaceful commerce through Indian merchants and adventurers, this overflow of intellectual enquiry and spiritual fervour reached them from India. For the merchants were followed by Buddhist monks, Brahman priests, and teachers visiting and settling in Indo-China and Indonesia, in Iran, Central Asia, and China; and from China the influence travelled to Korea and Japan. In this way, a *Greater India* developed during the first 500 years after Christ, extending from Central Asia to the Far East and Indonesia.

The great land of China, although maintaining her own spe-cial culture and her soul, was able to participate in a fellow-ship of spirit with India through her own Taoism on the one hand and the Mahāyāna Buddhism from India on the other. In this great age, India was, in a vague way at least, conscious of this spiritual dynamism of hers. Her best minds were eager to assimilate new ideas, and did assimilate new ideas in spirituality and in science; although they were reticent about their curiosity. The Indians took a great deal from the Greeks in astronomy and in the fine arts, possibly also in the drama. In literature, certain ideas appear to have been inspired by China (e.g., the note of apprecia-tion of Nature and the motif of forcible separation from one's loved one). And at least one enlightened person, Bhāskara-varman, the king of Prāgjyotisha or Assam, in the first half of the seventh century A.D., expressed his desire to have a Sanskrit translation of the *Tao-teh-King* of Lao-tzŭ. "Make the universe Aryan"—this in-junction of the *Ṛg-Vēda,* and "Exalt again the fallen"—this prayer from the *Atharva-Vēda* doubtless actuated the spirit of those who were moved by the working of a Dynamic Hinduism at its best.

The conquest of Sindh and North India by the Arabs and the Turks in the 8th and the 11th to 13th centuries was a sudden dis-ruption of the line of progress in Hindu Dynamism. For a few cen-turies there was the vital need for defence—from violent onslaughts from the outside—and for conservation from within. But, the spirit of dynamism soon again triumphed. India had sent abroad her

Vedānta to help Islamic mysticism with some of its most fundamental concepts—concepts which took some time to be assimilated
into Islamic mentality, but not before causing the martyrdom of
a fine soul like Manṣūr al-Hallāj (921 A.D.). Her *Yōga* ideas and
practices were also partly assimilated by the Sūfī mysticism of Iran
and Central Asia. These came to India in the wake of the Turkish
conqueror's Islam, and they supplied a *pou stō* for dynamic Hinduism to form a spiritual understanding with Islam. In this way,
Hindu dynamism also influenced Indian Islam; just as we have the
acceptance of certain Sūfī practices (methods of *sādhanā* or spiritual discipline) in some medieval schools of Vaishnavism in India.

Active response came from the other side also. To name only two
of the most illustrious spirits who were actuated by the great universalism of the Hindu mind, we may mention the Mogul Emperor
Akbar (1554-1605), who founded a religion on an eclectic basis, the
Dīn-i-Ilāhī or "Divine Religion," and instituted what may be
called the first series of Conferences on Religion in which the various forms of Hinduism (Buddhism and Jainism included), Islam,
Zoroastrianism, and Christianity were represented; and Akbar's
great-grandson, the highly-gifted and chivalrous, but ill-fated
Prince Dārā Shikōh, who got the *Upaniṣads* translated into Persian
(as Akbar earlier had the *Mahābhārata* and some of the *Purāṇas*
rendered into Persian) and compiled a work like the *Majmaʿu-l-
Bahrain* (in Sanskrit, *Sāgara-Saṅgama*) or "the Union of the Two
Oceans," in both Persian and Sanskrit, showing points of agreement
between Hinduism and Sūfīistic Islam.

Just before the advent of the English, the old line of progress in
Hinduism went on on its own inertia. Political and other reasons
were producing an inevitable stagnation in Hindu life and thought.
Nevertheless the old type of scholars and philosophers was quite
active in the 18th century also, when men like Madhusūdana
Sarasvatī composed their works on the Vedānta and Baladeva
Vidyābhūṣaṇa their formulations of certain aspects of late
Vaishnava philosophy and ideology. The foundation of two centuries of British rule was laid at Plassey in 1757, when the East
India Company came in virtual possession of the huge province of
combined Bengal, Bihar, and Orissa. At the turn of the century, we
note a quickening of the Hindu intellect by its contact with the
mind of Europe through England. When confronted by the compelling material civilisation and intellectual pre-eminence of England and Europe, the Hindu spirit realised that it must either fight
for its very existence and try to hold its own, or else absolutely sur-

render and perish. In this situation great minds arose, some actuated by the spirit of compromise, others by that of unyielding
resistance (both the attitude of compromise and that of resistance
were, unfortunately, based on an imperfect understanding of
Hinduism as a dynamic process). Raja Ram Mohan Roy (1770-
1832) represented this progressive, but compromising spirit; while
Raja Radhakanta Deva, contemporary of Raja Ram Mohan, and
compiler of the great Sanskrit lexicon, the *Śabda-kalpa-druma,* was
the leader of the orthodox group in this initial period of a conscious cultural contact and conflict in Calcutta, early in the 19th
century. Ram Mohan Roy was a curious amalgam of Tantric mysticism and Islamic monotheism, who found support in the *Upaniṣads* for his rather narrow monotheism which he derived from
Islam through his Persian and Arabic studies; this was later
strengthened by his contact with Christian Unitarianism. From
this limited point of view, he conceived of Hinduism more as
something fallen from the high standard of the monotheism of the
Upaniṣads than as a dynamic force expanding its scope. Nevertheless, his services to the Hindu people were inestimable, for he put
heart into them and impelled them to study the bases of their religion; and he put confidence in them by making them realize that,
even if they were deficient in material civilisation, they had
treasures of spiritual experience, as in the *Upaniṣads,* which gave
them their unique position in the community of peoples.

It must be said that in a way it was the curiosity of Europe
which rediscovered our past for us. European Orientalism, in spite
of the superior European (Greek, Roman, Christian and English)
bias manifested by a few of its exponents, was on the whole a
splendid thing which was interested in studying the culture of the
East as a common human inheritance (even with the development
of liberal culture among educated persons, this view-point took, of
course, some time to establish itself as such). The culture of India
slowly came into its own, together with its auxiliary or derivative
forms in other parts of Asia; and it became possible to appraise
Hinduism in its world context. While all this was slowly going on
during the 19th century, a deeply religious saint, Ramakrishna
Paramahansa, in his own way realised the vital aspects of Hinduism. And he, in turn, was able to inspire two of the most remarkable intellects of his time—well-trained in the philosophies both of
India and of Europe—viz., Kesava Chandra Sen and Narendranath
Datta. The former founded "The Church of the New Dispensation," (*Nava Vidhāna Mandira*) as a branch of the *Brāhma Samāj*

or "Community of the Supreme;" this latter was a sort of Protestant Hindu organisation established in Bengal and inspired by Ram Mohan Roy. Narendranath Datta, who assumed the name of Swami Vivekananda, when he took the vows of a Saṁnyāsin or Hindu monk, became, during the short span of his 38 years (he died in 1902), the greatest revivalist of Hindu thought, culture, and dynamism.

Vivekananda's active and revolutionary personality infused new life into the Hindu body-politic. While relying on and retaining his firm hold upon the sheet-anchor of Hindu acceptance of all religions, he preached with the deepest conviction (born out of his studies and discipline on the one hand and his spiritual fellowship with his master, the Saint Ramakrishna, on the other) the Universal Aspect of Hinduism as an all-embracing doctrine, which did not and could not exclude any religion on earth which mankind anywhere found useful as a path to the attainment of the Ultimate Reality. Swami Vivekananda was the first one in our age to realise the dynamic character of the Hindu religion, and this realisation made him irresistible. A Republic of World Faiths, with the universal character presented by Hinduism as the background—that was his message proclaimed before the whole world in the World Conference of Religions in Chicago in 1893. This shocked the protagonists of Imperialism or Totalitarianism in the domain of religion in their respective spheres. But slowly the world has been coming around and listening to the voice of Vivekananda and to the message of Dynamic Hinduism. In fact, with the exception of those who are unable to free themselves from the confusion of ideas of an exclusive and intolerant faith, civilised man is gradually coming to an attitude of acceptance and appreciation of all alien faith and cultures, of humility and of harmony. Swami Vivekananda himself was fully conscious of the dynamic aspects of Hinduism and hence his views gained general acceptance. He stated his position in straightforward and unmistakable terms.

Confronted, on the one hand, by an aggressive Islam using the methods of the proselytising Muhammadan *mullah* and having no scruples even to use force in religious matters if necessary, and, on the other, by a scarcely less aggressive Christianity with its conversion-preaching *padres* (both Catholic and Protestant), Hinduism, being much more tolerant and universalistic in outlook, almost shrank back into itself, and was "inclined to leave the field to the aggressors, in patient, deep disdain." The Hindu spirit was not in favour of "tooting its own horn," claiming to be the only pure brand—hence it was indifferent to foreign proselytising work among its own people; many foreigners were far more worldly wise in this matter. The result of all this can be easily seen in the phenomenal increase in the number of adherents to Islam and to Christianity in some parts of India in recent years. The whole Hindu attitude is most clearly revealed in the reply I got from a Brahman priest in Bali Island, the far-flung easternmost outpost of Hinduism in Indonesia (during my visit to the Island in 1927 in the company of Rabindranath Tagore), when, upon my calling his attention to the fact of an occasional Balinese conversion to Islam, he said in the calmest manner possible: "What harm? The Muslims, too, pray to God." This Hindu indifference and acquiescence were opening the door to the undermining of Hindu society by depletion of its ranks, and to a loss of nerve by always having to be on the defensive and even ready to beat an orderly retreat.

Swami Vivekananda, with his robust personality, first saw the social and moral danger in this sort of thing and stood up, taking the offensive. He preached a strong and virile Hinduism which, so far from being perpetually on the defensive and apologetic, was to make a bold stand and take up an aggressive position, proclaiming Hindu dynamism and universalism as a challenge to all religion and to the whole of humanity. This attitude of his was the greatest miracle in Hindudom in our age.

That large-hearted Irish lady, truest disciple of Vivekananda, Sister Nivedita, understood her beloved master's point of view, since, having been born abroad, she was able to see the battle more clearly. She published a little book of 40 pages, containing three short essays, which she called *Aggressive Hinduism.* "The land of the *Vedas* and of *Jñāna Yōga* has no right to sink into the rôle of mere critic or imitator of European letters." She preached to the Indians: "Instead of passivity, activity; for the standard of weakness, the standard of strength; in the place of a steadily yielding defence, the ringing cheer of the invading host." Hinduism was not to remain merely the preserver of Hindu customs, but was to be the creator of Hindu character:

No other religion in the world is so capable of this dynamic transformation as Hinduism. To Nāgārjuna and Buddha-ghosa, the Many was real, and the Ego unreal. To Śankarāchārya, the One was real and the Many unreal. To Rāmakrishna and Vivekananda, the Many and the One were the same Reality, perceived differently and at different times by the human consciousness. Do we realise what this means? It means that CHARACTER IS SPIRITUALITY. It means that laziness and defeat are not renunciation. It means that to protect another is infinitely greater than to attain salvation. It means that *Mukti* (salvation) lies in overcoming the thirst for *Mukti*. It means that conquest may be the highest form of *Saṁnyāsa* (Renunciation). It means, in short, that Hinduism is to be aggressive.

Her aggressive Hinduism was to absorb all the good things of the modern spirit. But "only the fully national can possibly contribute to the cosmo-national." The national idea "must be realised everywhere in the world-idea." A Hinduism which knows itself, realises its strength, and takes up its duty to serve mankind—that is the ideal which Nivedita saw Vivekananda place before India.

Both on the intellectual and on the emotional plane Rabindranath Tagore laid the greatest stress on the dynamic ever-expanding character of Hinduism. For him Hinduism was not its theology or ritual, but the sum total of the thought and being of India which were ever receptive to great things, ever hospitable to new ideas which might help to evoke the latent powers of man. He founded the Viśva-bhāratī University as a centre of World Culture in its Indian setting, and his motto for the University was applicable to the Hindu spirit also—"where the world has its one nest." By his poems and other writings, his lectures and discourses, and his wanderings all over the world as the most eloquent preacher of internationalism and of Indian universalism, Rabindranath, like Swami Vivekananda, was a great exponent of dynamic Hinduism. Vivekananda, the prophet, and Rabindranath, the poet, were both mystics and lovers of man; they had realised the spirit of a dynamic Hinduism or Indian universalism by a sort of intuitive conviction. Like poets and prophets, they took their part in adding to its lustre and in speeding it on its progress with a wider message for mankind as well as for the Hindu world. They were among the most creative forces in the modern evolution of Hinduism—and by their own contributions they furthered its dynamic and universal aspects.

And now we have the sage, following the prophet and poet and taking up the same task—the philosopher Radhakrishnan, after Vivekananda and Rabindranath. I can only repeat what I said at the beginning—Radhakrishnan also has enriched what he sought to explain; he has not kept it static. Thinker that he is, his convictions about the character of Hinduism and its value for humanity are due in the first place, to a study of its background and of comparative religion and culture; and also to a perception of its values in actual Hindu life around him and to the witness of his own spirit. Radhakrishnan is a man of science in the realms both of thought and of emotion—of philosophy and of mystic insight. It is the function of a man of science to divide a composite thing into its component parts, to analyse; it is also his function to build up the original total entity from scattered fragments, i.e., to synthesise. Moreover, the man of science also registers the process, the historical sequence, which is always operative in things endowed with life or movement. In his study of Hinduism, Radhakrishnan analyses and at the same time seeks to give a comprehensive and synthetic picture. But inasmuch as Radhakrishnan is more than a mere man of science (who moves only within an objective viewpoint), most of his readers feel (and many of his competent critics have also noted it) that he is also a man of religion, who is moved to passionate eloquence by his conviction and faith in the Ultimate Reality. Moreover, it is this aspect of his personality, his possession of true spiritual insight and not mere theoretical book-knowledge or dry intellectual interest, which fit him to speak on such profound matters as religion and religious experience.

Radhakrishnan's works deal with Hindu religion, and no aspect of it has remained untouched or unexplained in them. His great two volume work on *Indian Philosophy* will remain the classic work on the subject, a work which, because of its expository value, will be a *sine qua non* of modern scholarship, both in India and abroad. Radhakrishnan's lucidity of thought is amply sustained by the felicity of his expression, and a combination of the two has enabled him to make difficult and abstruse subjects appear simple and easily understandable. To make the difficult easy is to add lustre to it, to shed light upon obscurity. His work on the *Upaniṣads,* which has been separately reprinted, gives a systematisation of the opinions and intuitive experiences of the seers of the age when Hindu thought was taking definite shape. Inasmuch, moreover, as it indicates a plan and a structure in the midst of apparent planlessness and disjointedness, it significantly adds to the comprehensability of it. He had accomplished the same end in his *Philosophy of Rabindranath Tagore,* where he successfully sought to indicate the sequential coherence of the poet's utterances, apparently independent and disjointed, whether in prose or in verse, which were the expressions of his spiritual perceptions and convictions.

It would be difficult to name a person of such comprehensive acquaintance with the philosophical literature of the world today as Radhakrishnan. Of him it can be said most truly: "knowing all, he has entered into all." When I consider the all-inclusive range of Radhakrishnan's philosophical vision as indicated by his published writings, I am reminded of the Iranian scholar of 900 years ago—Al-Bīrūnī. In the entire civilised world of his day there probably was no other individual who could command such a wide sweep of the science and thought of his age. Al-Bīrūnī was an Iranian from Turkish Central Asia, who had access to everything available in Persian and Turkish, as well as some indirect knowledge of the Chinese world. An excellent Arabic scholar, Al-Bīrūnī was completely versed in the Islamic sciences and was familiar with whatever was procurable of Greek letters, philosophy, and science by way of Arabic translations. In addition he seems to have had proper historical sense, such as was in vogue among the intellectual *élite*. He had also acquired a very extensive knowledge of Hindu civilisation and history and of Hindu thought and science, by studying many original Sanskrit works. All this had endowed him with a broad humanism unique in his time and unique in any age. No other scholar of his period anywhere in the world, whether in Western Europe, in Byzantine Greece, or in Hindu India, or in China, could claim precedence over this true inheritor of the civilisations of the ages—in either the vastness of his erudition or in the liberality of his spirit. Today, of course, there are many polymaths whose range of studies in different branches of letters and science in the various languages of the world would be considered phenomenal. Yet even today there can be only a few persons who could rival Radhakrishnan in his assimilation of the various schools of thought in the Western world, old and new, as well as those of India; nor has he neglected the philosophies of Islam and of the Chinese world. When he speaks about India and the West, therefore, he is always listened to with respect. The Hindu world, more particularly, will remain for ever grateful to him for his vindication of practical Hinduism—Hindu Dharma—in its human aspect, more specifically in his two works, the *Hindu View of Life*, and *Religion and Society*.

Nor does Radhakrishnan ever forget the rest of the world whenever he speaks about Hinduism and India. For the solutions to the problems of life which Hinduism offers relate not merely to the Indian, but to the whole of mankind. The exposition of Hinduism in its world context is, therefore, of special value. And herein lies Radhakrishnan's greatest contribution to dynamic Hinduism: by bringing it into relief before "the eyes and ears of the world."

One is tempted to compare Radhakrishnan with Mahatma Gandhi; but the philosopher and politician-saint are on quite dif-

ferent planes of thought and spheres of action. It would be just as
futile as to compare Rabindranath with Gandhi. To say the least,
Gandhi was not metaphysical, and he had little interest in matters
of the intellect. He also lacked imagination and poetry. And he was
moved by the immediate problems confronting him. On the other
hand, he had a most tenacious faith in himself and in his mission,
as well as in the position at which he arrived as being an indication
of God's will. This mystic quality, combined with the fervency of
his faith and his readiness to suffer physical pain, won for him the
almost blind homage of his followers; and the moral fervour which
he manifested obtained the loving homage and admiration of very
excellent personalities who often did not see eye-to-eye with him in
many matters. Radhakrishnan also appreciated the greatness of
Gandhi and came under the spell of his personality; this becomes
quite clear in a series of papers on the Mahatma's life and work. I
am not competent to give an opinion on Radhakrishnan's reaction
to Gandhi's ideology or personality. But I feel inclined to agree
with the view expressed by the reviewer of Radhakrishnan's book
on Gandhi in the London *Times Literary Supplement:* "One of
Gandhi's successes has been securing the devotion of a man like
Radhakrishnan, who, if he has less experience in the rough and
tumble of political life, has higher intellectual attainments and a
finer quality of soul than Gandhi himself."

There has been a tradition in India, some 1500 years old, that
all who wish to expound certain philosophical ideas of Hinduism
do so in the form of commentaries to three of the fundamental
texts of Hindu philosophy, viz., the *Upaniṣads,* the *Vedānta-Sūtras*
of Vyāsa, and the *Bhagavad-gītā.* In this way the dynamic character
of Hinduism has been maintained throughout. New expositions,
new experiences leading to new doctrines, have thus been put into
commentaries which, supposedly, merely explain ancient texts; nor
did the new wine do any damage to the old bottles, admitting their
all-embracing and elastic nature. Even in modern times, the writing of such commentaries had not been disdained by modern
teachers. Rabindranath Tagore's little sermons in Bengali forming
the *Śāntiniketan Series* of his religious discourses are commentaries
and expansions, in his inimitable poetic style, of passages from
the *Upaniṣads.* Bankim Chandra Chatterji, the great Bengali novel-
ist and thought-leader of India of the second half of the 19th
century, wrote a Bengali translation and commentary on the
Bhagavad-gītā. Aurobindo Ghosh, Mahatma Gandhi, and B. G.
Tilak, Indian political and religious leaders, each has written his

own commentary on the *Gītā,* respectively in English, in Gujarati and Hindi, and in Marathi. Radhakrishnan also was unable to escape this tradition; he, too, has published an English version of the *Gītā* with a commentary or exposition in English, preceded by a rather complete Introductory Essay on the *Gītā.* Here Radhakrishnan does not follow any of the old schools of Vedānta exposition, whether Śaṁkara's, or Rāmānuja's, Madhva's, or that of any other great commentator. The exposition is his own, and the work can truly be declared to be among Radhakrishnan's most distinctive contributions to the thought content of a dynamic Hinduism. He has similarly translated and commented upon the principal *Upaniṣads*—and these are expected to be published soon.

Just as it requires a poet to appreciate a poet, so a philosopher must wait for a philosopher, or at least for one who has mastered the discipline of philosophy, before he can get a correct resumé of his views. Some day a competent person will come forward and formulate an account of Radhakrishnan's exposition of Hinduism from his books, scattered writings, and discourses. This will be no simple task. But when it is done, the world will be enriched by the formulation of a Dynamic Hinduism as a current which has not stopped, but which is continuing on its life-bringing course, quenching the spiritual thirst of men as the decades and centuries pass.

Men without philosophy, men without a fine quality of soul, men without a proper perception of the thought-worlds which have swayed their people for generations, men without imagination and distant vision, thinking only of the immediate—such men can be but indifferent guides of their fellows in the path of progress, and unreliable leaders to their followers. Plato was perfectly right in suggesting that philosophers should be rulers. Like Rabindranath Tagore, Radhakrishnan has been working as the great cultural ambassador of India: on pulpit and platform and on the teachers' rostrum, through his books and papers, he has, for one whole generation, successfully been bearing and furthering the message of a dynamic and ever advancing Hinduism. There has not been the least taint of chauvinism or of national patriotism in his mission of illumination. He carries the whole of humanity with him; he makes it clear that the desire of the nations for the good life and for the realisation of Ultimate Reality has been India's desire also, and that India's élite have attained to that desire in a way which is worthy of the consideration of men everywhere, without any transfer of allegiance. His country has appreciated Radhakrishnan's achievement. He has been selected to exert his influence in a sphere where it might be possible for him to create a bridge between today's conflicting ideologies (ideologies, which, unfortunately, concern themselves only with matters relating to this ephemeral existence, without any reference to or much interest in things of abiding value). In this position Radhakrishnan's unending "Search for Truth" is an echo of the query put to Socrates 2400 years ago by another wandering teacher like himself from his own country: "How can we inquire into human phenomena, when we are ignorant of divine ones?"

It may be that the political bosses of his own land, arbiters of power and pelf, will not tolerate a philosopher's trespass into the administrative affairs of his own country, affairs which they consider their own preserves. But of this we can be certain: Radhakrishnan's name as a bearer of the eternal message of India regarding a universal, all-embracing, and perpetual philosophy, helping man everywhere in whatever environment he may be to discover himself and to find the Ultimate Reality, will shine for ever, and most worthily, beside those of two other of his great contemporaries and compatriots, Vivekananda and Rabindranath, persons with that rare quality of soul which alone gives us hints of the Supernatural.

SUNITI KUMAR CHATTERJI

DEPARTMENT OF
INDIAN LINGUISTICS AND PHONETICS
CALCUTTA UNIVERSITY
CALCUTTA, INDIA

15

P. T. Raju

RADHAKRISHNAN'S INFLUENCE ON
INDIAN THOUGHT

15

RADHAKRISHNAN'S INFLUENCE ON INDIAN THOUGHT

I

EVERY philosopher is both a creature and a creator of his age. An adequate estimate of his influence can therefore be made by the future, when his work shall have produced tangible and substantial results. Yet in the case of outstanding personalities, the effects begin to be felt even in their own life-time, though the task of their estimation is not easy. And it becomes more difficult when the philosopher is the product of the two main philosophical traditions of the world, the Western and the Indian, enters into the spirit of each, looks at each as the expression of the same spirit in man in different conditions of existence, and, with a steady gaze on the essentials, treats the details and technicalities of interpretation as of secondary importance.

Radhakrishnan has been bred and brought up in both the Western and the Indian philosophical traditions. He is known throughout the world as the liaison officer between East and West. He is not only an interpreter of the culture and civilization of the East to the West and of the West to the East, but also a formulator of a new synthesis. His influence both on Western and Indian men of thought is therefore more subtle, pervasive and profound than that of only interpreters or system-builders. He has given a new bent to the current of the world's philosophy, and opened up a new line of work for many of the young generation of philosophers who have come to realise that the East has as good a philosophy as the West and that a true philosophy of life should incorporate the best elements of both in each tradition. Radhakrishnan is the protagonist of a new school of cultural synthesis, which is contributing to the formation and growth of the idea of world-philosophy. He writes: "The modes and customs of all men are now a part of the consciousness of all men. Man has become the

515

spectator of man. A new humanism is on the horizon. But this time
it embraces the whole of mankind." [1] Again,

the supreme task of our generation is to give a soul to the world-consciousness, to develop ideals and institutions necessary for the creative
expression of the world-soul, to transmit these loyalties and impulses to
future generations and train them into world citizens. To this great
work of creating a new pattern of living, some of the fundamental insights of Eastern religions, especially Hinduism and Buddhism, seem
to be particularly relevant. . . . No culture, no country lives or has a
right to live for itself. If it has any contribution to make towards the
enrichment of the human spirit, it owes that contribution to the widest
circle it can reach. The contributions of ancient Greece, of the Roman
Empire, of Renaissance Italy to the progress of humanity do not concern only the inhabitants of modern Greece or modern Italy. . . . In
the life of mind and spirit we cannot afford to display a mood of provincialism. At any rate, a mobilisation of the wisdom of the world may
have some justification at a time when so many other forms of mobilisation are threatening it.[2]

It may be said that the idea of a world philosophy, of a philosophy that would meet the spiritual and intellectual questionings
of men in all parts of the globe and make available to each the
cultural and intellectual achievements of different countries at
different times, is not entirely new; but it has a new significance
for us now. Philosophy started its work as the love of wisdom, and
the philosopher was the spectator of all existence. Such were the
Greek conceptions of philosophy and of the philosopher. It was
only of late, in the eighteenth and the nineteenth centuries, that
philosophy began to be national and came to be regarded as the
expression of a national outlook. Thereby it lost its universality
of appeal, and philosophical truth tended to be relative to the
culture of the nation in question. It is true that scientific truth
is relative to the stage of our intellectual progress; but universality
is its aim and presupposition and thus acts as a proper check on
the extravagances of speculation. But, if such universality is not
recognised in philosophy, there would be little to prevent the
rationalisation of racial, national and even individual idiosyncrasies and prejudices. There has been some justification for treating philosophy as national. Inasmuch as it deals with problems of
experience, and since experience is often coloured by conditions
of national and racial existence, and, further, because different
aspects of existence seem to be basic to different peoples at differ-

1 ER, Preface, vii.   2 *Op cit.*, viii.

ent times, the patterns which philosophy took in the main centres
of culture and civilization in the past were different. In addition,
human knowledge, in philosophy as in science, is never complete,
but growing. When the various countries of the world were comparatively isolated, their philosophers worked with ideas that were
peculiar to themselves; if for no other reason than the lack of proper
opportunities to compare their ideas with those of others. Hence
arose different philosophies of different culture groups. But now
conditions have changed. Even the main difference between the
two cultural traditions, East and West, are likely soon to be
obliterated,[3] and will have to be cancelled, not only politically but
also culturally. Radhakrishnan writes: "Those who separate themselves from the rest of the world in the name of religion or race,
nation or polity, are not assisting human evolution but retarding
it." [4] Here lies much of the significance of Radhakrishnan's life
work. His influence on Indian thought has to be adjudicated in
the light of this momentous cultural transformation which has set
in. He is the philosopher of a new East-West synthesis. With him
starts a new line of philosophical activity.

II

Radhakrishnan is a product of the Indian Renaissance. During
his youth the nationalist politicians were rousing Indians from
their lethargic acceptance of cultural and political dependency
and holding before them the achievements and glories of ancient
India. Social and religious reform movements like the Brah-
mosamaj and the Aryasamaj showed to the critics of Hinduism that
Hinduism did not and does not mean mere caste-system or idol-
worship. It was far deeper and more fluid than they had imagined.
The Theosophists were declaring that the religion of the *Upaniṣads*
and the Buddha were among the most spiritual and profound and
could not be replaced by anything supposedly better. Christian
critics were being told that the religion of India was more spiritual
and philosophical than they understood it to be. India became the
battle-ground of East and West, both politically and culturally;
Radhakrishnan himself is a philosophical product of that conflict.
    The Indian Renaissance has its own peculiarity. It was itself the

---

3 It is interesting to note that the East-West problem has now changed its forms
and significance. It is now a problem of the conflict between the Communist and
non-Communist groups in the West itself.
    4 RS, 18.

result of a clash between East and West. Some may think that it
was a revival of the bygone past; but it was very much more. It
was the scholars, educated in Western universities, who were bringing the past back to the present in India. The past was therefore
re-interpreted and made meaningful to the present by men with
Western education. The past therefore did not sweep the present
before it as an irreconcilable opposite or even in order to dominate
and suppress it. This reconciliation of the past and the present—
which in India were practically identical with East and West—was
philosophically accomplished by Radhakrishnan. For this reason,
his work is significant not only for India but also for the West: it
is a reconciliation not only of past and present for India, but also
of East and West for the world. It lies in discovering, through serious research, the essentials of the human spirit as it expresses itself
under varying conditions; the similarities and differences of that
expression, and, after due evaluation, the attempt of building them
into a new comprehensive pattern. Neither East nor West, neither
the past nor the present, should be ignored. We cannot break away
from the past; nor can we march back to it. The West has come to
stay in the East; and the East has supplied a spiritual leaven to the
West; neither can disentangle itself from the other. The future of
mankind lies in their conscious reconciliation and synthesis.

III

The genius of Radhakrishnan lies in seeing through details and
finding the spirit behind them. He could see through the minutiae
not only of any single system but also through those of several systems of any tradition, and discover their spiritual affinity. That is
one of the reasons why, in spite of the profundity of his thought,
his writings appear easy to read and do not present the usual technicalities of detailed exposition and argument. The details need
to be worked out now by his disciples and followers. When review-
ing Radhakrishnan's *Idealist View of Life,* Professor Muirhead
wrote:

He modestly disclaims any originality for the view his book expounds.
But if originality in philosophy as in poetry consists, not in the novelty
of the tale, nor even in the distribution of light and shade in the telling
of it, but in the depth with which its significance is grasped and made
to dominate over the details, this book certainly does not fail in this
quality.[5]

[5] *Hibbert Journal,* October 1932.

Radhakrishnan is not only the philosopher of Indian Renaissance but also of a new renaissance in the West. He writes:

The West is passing through a new Renaissance due to the sudden entry into its consciousness of a whole new world of ideas, shapes and fancies. Even as its consciousness was enlarged in the period of the Renaissance by the revelation of the classical culture of Greece and Rome, there is a sudden growth of the spirit to-day effected by the new inheritance of Asia with which India is linked up. For the first time in the history of mankind, the consciousness of the history of mankind has dawned on us. Whether we like it or not, East and West have come together and can no more part.[6]

He himself played no small part in helping to bring about the dawning of the new Renaissance in the West.

Though Radhakrishnan is a philosopher of both Renaissances in the contemporary world and appears to be showing the importance of the East to the West and *vice versa,* and though he is avowedly a follower of Śaṁkara and, even to his critics, a modern follower of Śaṁkara, he has something new to suggest, a new viewpoint and insight into some specific problems. His study of many philosophies and his observation of the cultural movements and ideologies of the world have enabled him to see a new humanism arising, although it has not yet taken definite form. He says, in his *Eastern Religions and Western Thought,* that "a new humanism is on the horizon." He is impressed by the great emphasis which the West lays on science, logic, and humanism; as well as by the emphasis which the Eastern philosophies placed on spiritual and creative intuition. The East and the West can, therefore, give to each what the other did not care, or did not have the occasion, to develop. Yet the dignity of man, either in the East or the West, cannot be doubted; the fact that, in an important sense, he is "the measure of all things," cannot be rejected. The thought which thinks is human thought. Though democracy and Communism are now great enemies, each criticises the other for not being humanistic enough; thereby showing that both of them are offshoots of the same humanistic upsurge. In India the Gandhian movement is ancient religion turned humanistic in practice. Even in philosophy, both absolute idealism and materialism could still be humanistic. Although a follower of Śaṁkara, Radhakrishnan points·out that the conception of a personal God is unavoidable, because God is the Absolute humanised, pressed into the moulds of thought,

[6] ER, 115.

which cannot be otherwise than human. Man cannot but think as man; humanism, therefore, is in the core of Radhakrishnan's philosophy. This is how humanism is more and more consciously being recognised and entering the life and thought of India; it is, so to speak, in the air. It has influenced leaders of both thought and action in India: Radhakrishnan, Tagore, Gandhi, each in a different way and in different fields; and each has voiced and expressed it in his own way.

The modern criticism of established religions and the consequent sceptical attitude towards them do not disconcert Radhakrishnan, who is able to appreciate the humanistic motive behind much of the criticism and is convinced that it cannot conflict with the essential spiritual nature of man. He therefore writes: "The indifference to organised religion is the product not so much of growing secularism as of deepening spirituality." [7] He feels that "the dogmas which were once paths to divine life, should not be allowed to interpose a barrier between man and God and spoil the essential simplicity of spiritual life." [8]

A spiritual as distinct from a dogmatic view of life remains unaffected by the advance of science and criticism of history. Religion generally refers to something external, a system of sanctions and consolations, while spiritual life points to the need for knowing and living in the highest self and raising life in all its parts.[9]

The revolt against religion is the revolt of spirit even though masquerading as matter. A true appreciation would enable us to give the revolt its true spiritual form. It is humanistic, but not necessarily materialistic.

What is the nature of the humanism that Radhakrishnan had in mind when he asserted that a "new humanism is on the horizon"? There have, after all, been various types and sub-types of humanism, cultural, religious, philosophical and political. There is the humanism of Dewey, which may be called cultural humanism, but which has its roots in naturalism. The humanism of Schiller takes man as he appears—a very vague idea, indeed,—as the centre and standpoint of philosophy. There is the new idea of a scientific and evolutionary humanism, given impetus by Professor Julian Huxley as the philosophy of UNESCO. But the word, *scientific*, is again vague when applied to humanism and may be made to yield a materialistic conception *a priori*. If man is to be made the centre of philosophy, he has to be critically understood, and the presupposi-

7 *Ibid.*, 59.   8 RS, 42.   9 ER, 61.

tions of his being should be uncovered. He should not be treated as a merely material, biological or psychological being, at least not *a priori*.[10] A critical analysis of man's nature, which may uncover great spiritual depths, such as have been revealed by all major religions, is now of utmost importance. Moreover, the recognition of man's spiritual nature is as necessary as is that of the material, biological, mental and social. The new form which humanism should and will take in the near future should be that of *critical humanism*.

In the history of thought, whenever it was felt that conflicting lines and traditions of thought had each its own truth which could not be ignored, reconciliation and synthesis were effected through criticism. Kant started his Critical philosophy, when he confronted the truths of both rationalism and empiricism. The critical realists made their appearance under similar circumstances. It is really time for critical humanism to make its appearance and play its rôle. The new humanism which Radhakrishnan sees on the horizon and which is to do justice to the dignity of man and to the truths of human reason, and yet not ignore the spiritual depths discovered in man by the great religions of the world, would necessarily be critical, not naive; it would, therefore, prevent an undue appeal by philosophers, to "man as such," when reason and experience fail to support them.

Radhakrishnan is in no small way responsible for the new humanistic bent in many of India's contemporary academic philosophers. This humanistic direction is expressed either in a complete denial of any negativistic attitude in ancient philosophies or at least in dissatisfaction with it, if it is thought that they were negativistic. And the new spiritual bent in many of the Western writers and thinkers is also due, to an appreciable extent, to the influence Radhakrishnan's writings have had on them. There is a strong desire that Indian philosophy should be made more humanistic and applicable to the constantly changing complexities of life in this world. But a consistent philosophy which expresses and works out this attitude has still to be written; moreover, while being humanistic, it will still be spiritual: for true humanism is spiritual and cannot be opposed to spirituality. And it will be *critical* humanism: for it is only the critical method and approach which can give due recognition to all important truths, however apparently conflicting they may be.

One difficulty in appreciating the human, if not the humanistic,

10 *Ibid.*, 21.

approach of Radhakrishnan to cultural and philosophical problems is due to his repeated criticism of materialistic and unspiritual
cultures, showing where and how they need the spiritual factor;
whereas he does not as generally criticise those cultures, in which
spirituality is unbalanced and over-emphasized. He writes: "A
spiritual view is sustained not only by insight but by a rational
philosophy and sound social institutions." [11] This statement should
not only mean that social institutions, if they are to be sound,
should be oriented towards the realisation of spiritual values, but
also that spiritual values, in order to be actualised, need sound
social institutions. Indeed, Radhakrishnan criticises on more than
one occasion the wrong negativistic approach to *Upaniṣadic*
thought made by some Indian thinkers of the past. It was a common theme of several philosophic songs to exhort man not to do
anything since he was already the Brahman; for, when everything
is the Brahman, what is there to achieve and what is there to give
up? Even the Kaśmīr school of Śaivism, for which the world is real
and positive, sometimes adopts this attitude. Abhinavagupta, the
greatest exponent of this school, writes in his *Annutarāṣṭikā* that
inasmuch as the world is not ultimate reality, there can be no bondage and therefore no salvation. In that case, what point would there
be in trying to get rid of bondage and in attaining salvation? But
Radhakrishnan had the courage to insist that this trend of thought
does not correctly represent the *Upaniṣadic* and therefore the Indian attitude to life and the world. There was a time, particularly
while writing *The Philosophy of Rabindranath Tagore,* when
Radhakrishnan felt dissatisfied with Śaṁkara or at least with one
line of thought running through Śaṁkara's works, for over-empha-
sizing the negative element in the Absolute and for ignoring the
positive. But later, and more particularly in his *Eastern Religions
and Western Thought,* he seems to justify Śaṁkara, because intellect cannot grasp the positive relation between eternity and time.
He takes greater pains to show that spiritual values are involved
in the ethical and that the ethical are not self-sufficient than to
show in detail or in any systematic form how ethical values gradually lead to the spiritual and transform themselves into the spiritual. The latter is what is needed if the strands in Radhakrishnan's
philosophy are to be united.

In Radhakrishnan's philosophy two lines of thought are discernible: one assuming the self-sufficiency and self-completeness of
Indian thought, and the other assuming its incompleteness and

11 ER, 76.

exhibiting a desire to incorporate elements from Western thought. The latter is easy to find in his pre-nineteen-hundred-and-thirty writings. One may clinch the point thus: Either Radhakrishnan should say with the traditionalists that India's past philosophy is sufficient in itself or that it is incomplete and needs transformation, application and expansion in those directions and to those fields of experience, not covered by our ancient systematic philosophers. If the former view is taken, then Indian culture, it will have to be said, has developed sound social institutions; in which case we shall have to explain why its systematic philosophers did not care to make even a defensive critical study of social ethics, why Indian philosophy was called *mokṣaśāstra* or the science of salvation, and why Śaṁkara, in his commentaries, and some of his followers in other books also, say that cosmologies are only conventions, not to be taken too seriously; for it is only in cosmologies that we develop a categorial scheme for the world of plurality, including the social.

I believe that Radhakrishnan would still accept the second alternative. He has been writing and preaching in defence of the important spiritual truths contained in ancient Indian philosophy and religion, as against the attacks of Christian writers, who overlook the spiritual truths of Hinduism and their real implications for all religions. One important point brought out by him is that the real contrast is not between Hinduism and Christianity or between any two spiritual religions, but between spirituality and self-sufficient humanism. The third chapter in his *Eastern Religions and Western Thought* clearly makes this point. Yes, the historical is true; but by itself it has no significance. He says that "the historical process is not a mere external chain of events, but offers a succession of spiritual opportunities. Man has to attain a mastery over it and reveal the higher world operating in it. This world is not therefore an empty dream or an external delirium." [12] The human world of history and its values are therefore true; but they should be so transformed as to reflect the spiritual world and its values. The gulf between the merely humanistic and the spiritual values has to be bridged.

If the human world and its values are true, it is necessary for us to understand their real nature. It may be conceded that Western thought has given more attention to the human world and its values than has the Indian; though, on the whole, the conclusions reached may be one-sided. However, any truths it contains will have to be incorporated by Indian thought in its development; re-

[12] ER, 90.

moving, of course, the undue emphases put on certain values by a self-sufficient kind of humanism.

That human values are not unimportant for Radhakrishnan is supported further by his view that the liberated individual has to work for the welfare of the world.

It is improper for man to remain without sharing in the work of the world when even God consents to work for the universe. Besides, so long as man lives, he cannot remain even for an instant without activity. Love to God expresses itself in love to creation. The sage is not ego-centric in the sense of caring for his own soul, or altruistic in the sense of caring for others, or theocentric in the sense of wishing to enjoy God in the solitude of his soul. He is at the heart of the universe in which he himself and others live, move and have their being. He is conscious of the wider destiny of the universe. The question is not, what shall I do to be saved? but, in what spirit shall I do? Detachment of spirit and not renunciation of the world is what is demanded from us.[13]

In Radhakrishnan's philosophy, the problems of the relation between eternity and time, the Absolute and the historical process, and intuition and intellect are being solved along a similar line of approach. The terms of each pair are not really opposed to each other. In each case, the first is the completion of the second. Human values, which belong to the temporal and historical process and so to the world of discursive intellect, find their completion in the spiritual. Our attitude to the human values, therefore, should be positive; but they need transformation into spiritual values, which guide our pursuit of the human. Radhakrishnan has succeeded in showing this need; but he has not yet given a detailed or systematic exposition of the positive movement from the human to the spiritual. Certainly this would be the direction in which Indian thought would have to move, if, on the one hand, it does not wish to break with its past and yet recognises, on the other hand, the need for inclusion of worldly, i.e., human, values. What Radhakrishnan, with his mature experience and first hand acquaintance with most of the important philosophies and cultures of the world, could contribute along these lines would be of immense value to those of us who wish to work out the implications of such a positive movement.

After having discerned the birth of a new type of humanism in the world and saying that the revolt against religion is not a danger to spirituality but only to sacerdotalism and institutionalised re-

13 ER, 101.

ligion, Radhakrishnan would now have to say that the next important step for Indian philosophy is the development of a humanism
which will be true to man by recognising the value of every factor
of man's being, including the spiritual. As a matter of fact, the acceptance of the Kantian approach by many Indian academic philosophers, following on the trail of Radhakrishnan, has already
caused the starting-point to shift from Brahman to the *human* individual. The alleged dialogue between Socrates and the Indian
philosopher suggests that Western philosophy begins its argument
with man, whereas the Indian begins with God. But Radhakrishnan writes: "The proof of the validity of the intuitive principles
is somewhat similar to Kant's proof of *a priori* elements. . . . They
belong to the very structure of our mind." [14] Again, he says our
knowledge of the unconditioned is *a priori*.[15] This is an important
shift towards humanism. Radhakrishnan refers appreciatively to
Socrates' assertion that the noblest of all investigations is the study
of man and of what man should be and pursue.[16]

IV

As a re-interpreter of the past, Radhakrishnan is not merely himself a product of the Indian Renaissance, nor merely a contributor
to the solution of the problems involved, but also a creator of the
Renaissance on the philosophical side. He has given new life to
ancient concepts; moreover, by the felicity of his expressions, his
happily chosen and pregnant phrases, he has lighted up new meanings in unexpected corners. The vision of his readers has broadened and new perspectives have been opened up to them.

As a religion, Hinduism is said to be all-absorbing: its assimilative power is stupendous. Radhakrishnan is fully conscious of it.
He writes: "There is hardly any height of spiritual insight or rational philosophy attained in the world that has not its parallel in
the vast stretch that lies between the early Vedic seers and the modern Naiyāyikas." [17] The assimilative power of Indian religions is
reflected in Indian philosophy, and Radhakrishnan was not slow
in seeing this and giving expression to it in his interpretations. The
philosophical systems which had their roots in the same religion
represent several varieties of realism, idealism, pluralism and monism, all claiming to uphold, more or less, the same spiritual tradition of the *Upaniṣads*. Philosophers even in the past attempted

14 IVL, 156.   15 *Ibid.*, 165.   16 ER, 1.   17 Ind P, I, 8.

to reconcile the rival systems as philosophies of the same life understood at different levels of intellectual maturity. No new system of philosophy was obnoxious to the Indian, provided it was not anti-spiritual. Just as Indian religion was all-assimilating and all-absorbing, so Indian philosophy could make room for a great variety and therefore could also contain parallels to several philosophical doctrines of the West. In the exposition and interpretation of Indian philosophy, Radhakrishnan set the practice of drawing parallels between Indian and Western philosophers, wherever possible. Such comparisons became an important part of research after him. In the writings of some less careful men, of course, comparisons might sometimes have been overdrawn, basic differences ignored, and undue claims might have been made that ancient Indian philosophy contained all the latest doctrines. Yet the whole idea of comparative philosophy took concrete form under Radhakrishnan's influence. And the Renaissance idea that ancient Indian culture was rich, varied, and comprehensive, and still possessed potentialities of progress waiting to be worked out, was given clear expression by him. In India, comparative philosophy is an outcome of the Renaissance which followed the advent of the West; and in the West it is the result of the inroads of Eastern ideas.

Though much literature appeared on comparative *religion,* the idea of comparative *philosophy* was only vaguely in the air when Radhakrishnan started his career. Very little work had actually been done on the subject. There were even misgivings about its usefulness. Yet Radhakrishnan continued his work in this field in spite of criticisms. For the basic experiences of men are after all the same everywhere. In the traditional spirit of India, Radhakrishnan kept his eyes more on essentials which were common and basic than on the differences which were incidental. As George V Professor of Philosophy in the University of Calcutta, he trained several scholars and research students, working under him, in this spirit. Slowly but surely, the idea of comparative philosophy has taken shape.

It should be added, however, that the idea is still somewhat vague and amorphous. There is first the idea of comparative philosophy as a phenomonological study, propounded in Masson-Oursel's *Comparative Philosophy.* Different philosophers are studied in relation to their environment and interpreted and estimated in terms of their functions. In the second place, comparison is made of different schools, systems or philosophers, not necessarily of different traditions, but even within the same tradition. Every philosophy is a philosophy of supposedly the same universe and in its own way aims to be a rounded-out system. Any concept in a philosophical system gets its significance from the place it occupies in that system and is, therefore, practically a function of that system. Thus, though a concept is apparently the same in two systems, it might have a very differing import in each. Comparative philosophy thus assumes the form of the study of the comparative significance of concepts with reference to the various philosophical systems.

The relation between the two kinds of comparative study can easily be seen. Whereas the first is interested in treating a system, school, or tradition as a function of its environment, the second treats a concept as the function of a system. The two types of study are mutually interdependent and useful, but not opposed.

In the third place, comparative philosophy started as the study and evaluation of similarities and dissimilarities between the philosophies of the two main philosophical currents of the world, the Western and the Indian, with the main purpose of co-ordinating and synthesising the basic values of life which those two great traditions are taken to represent. The former two types of comparative philosophy apparently constitute a disinterested inductive study; but this third type has a specific purpose. It is more directly interested in life and its values than the others. The first two also can be made to serve the purpose of a philosophy of life. But their direct aim is a disinterested study like mathematics; yet the necessity for such studies and their utility for the third type are easily discernible. The third started as a result of the conflict of cultures and of the philosophies of the East and the West. Cultural reconciliation involves reconciliation at the philosophical level as well. Further, some Western thinkers have begun to feel that the West is making a rather one-sided progress, resulting in the disturbance of life's equilibrium and that the Western outlook needs the values of the Eastern as a check to restore the lost balance. There is a corresponding feeling in the East as well. Consequently some philosophers of both East and West undertook a deeper study of philosophies other than their own. The same kind of effort is required by the coming together of distant peoples of the world, both politically and economically, particularly after World War II. The world is becoming more consciously one now; it is impossible for any culture to continue to exist in isolation. Moreover, if the world is bound to become more and more one, every culture should profit from the best elements and values of each. Hence the need for a comparative and critical study and evaluation of every culture and philosophy. Radhakrishnan's work belongs to this third category of comparative philosophy.

With such an aim in view, Radhakrishnan brought the need for a critical study of our ancient systems to the attention of Indian scholars. He writes: "The authors of the systems are worshipped as divine. A study of Indian philosophy will conduce to the clearing up of the situation, the adopting of a new balanced outlook and the freeing of the mind from the oppressing sense of the perfection of everything that is ancient." [18] Ancient philosophies were born and grew in a spiritual atmosphere: they were philosophies of life with special reference to the reality of the spirit within. The discoverers of spiritual truths were indeed great seers and saints. But they were not opposed to a critical, let alone a rational, understanding of the nature of spirit. Even to prove that spirit is above reason involves the use of reason. Nor did any of them ever claim that the discovery was the monopoly or prerogative of anybody. As discoverers they are to be respected by us. But our duty does not end there. We have to understand their discoveries and transmit them to others. Only then can we realise that their discoveries have life and meaning, and appreciate the significance they have for our contemporary life.

A rational and unbiased study of philosophy, Eastern and Western, is bound to result in comparison, in the discovery of some common denominators and in co-ordination and synthesis. The corresponding effect on life should be balance and comprehensiveness. Yet workers in the field may appear to the worshippers of tradition to be misguided. It would not be surprising, therefore, if Radhakrishnan should appear to some as reading too much of Western thought into Indian and too much of Indian thought into Western. There are, for example, some Indian scholars who think that Radhakrishnan gives a more positive estimate of Śaṁkara's concept of Māyā than it deserves. There are some who think that he followed some of the latest followers of the Śaṁkarite tradition rather than Śaṁkara himself. Some Western critics regard him as a mystic and say that the Western philosophical tradition, which is essentially logical and rational, is different from the Indian, which latter is mainly intuitive and mystical, and that therefore there cannot be any significant similarities between the two. But when a given concept is first re-interpreted and seen in a new light, it is likely to disclose a new meaning unseen by us before. Sometimes not only the concept but also the system to which it belongs

[18] Ind P, I, 55.

is thrown into a new perspective with the result that new inter-relations between the same concepts and therefore new meanings might be discovered in them. This was done not only by Radha-krishnan but also by the later followers of the ancient tradition itself, who felt bound to define their concepts in the light of criti-cisms of the other schools.[19] This much is admitted tacitly by the second type of criticism referred to above. In answer to it, it may also be said that, so far as Indian philosophy is concerned, every system began with inchoate and unclarified concepts, and devel-oped by clarifying them as it came into more and more conflict with rival systems. The logical significance of a concept can be found more clearly in the writings of the later followers of a school than in those of the earlier.

Regarding the third type of criticism, it is often forgotten that the history of Western philosophy itself contains several names of admittedly great philosophers who pointed up the shortcomings of mere reason and intellect. Bradley is one of the latest examples. The Neo-Hegelian tradition comes closest to the *Upaniṣadic,* by insisting that reality can best be understood as self, the highest real-ity of which we know. And this tradition in the West culminated in the Bradleyan denunciation of intellect and logic as finally in-capable of grasping reality. To compare Bradley to Śaṁkara, there-fore, does not amount to a mistaken reading of Indian into West-ern thought. Even Plato was aware of the inability of reason to answer ultimate questions or to grasp ultimate reality; and he therefore resorted to myths. Further, we should not forget Plotinus or the other Neo-Platonists as also the Augustinian trend of Chris-tian philosophy. Schopenhauer openly made use of the concept of Māyā as the inexplicable principle of individuality; and it is diffi-cult to imagine that his contemporaries, Schelling and Hegel, were uninfluenced by the conception of the *Upaniṣadic* Absolute. For Schelling in particular, the Absolute was an object of intuition. Then again, on the Indian side, the pluralistic schools of Nyāya and Vaiśeṣika, the dualistic schools of Sāṅkhya and Yoga, and the Jaina and the early Buddhist schools are undoubtedly realistic. And none of these schools, whether realistic or idealistic, based its con-clusions on intuition. Neither did Western philosophy glorify rea-son consistently and continuously throughout its history; nor, on the other hand, did Indian philosophy neglect its use.

[19] One may compare the definitions of Māyā as given by Madhusudana in his *Advaitaniddhi* and *Siddhantabindu* with that given by Śaṁkara himself in his commentary on the first of the *Brahmasutras*.

One important point not to be forgotten is that Indian philosophy has its academic side, which is logical, dialectical, and metaphysical. This is often ignored by Western critics. Consider, for instance, the Western criticism that Buddhism, in its later developments, ceased to be ethical and religious and turned into dry metaphysics. This criticism assumes further that religion and metaphysics are mutually exclusive alternatives. This complaint disproves the view that Indian thought, including Buddhism, is merely intuitive and not logical or intellectual. The assumption it makes is not true of Indian philosophy in the past: metaphysics and religion were never opposed. To declare intellect to be defective is not equivalent to saying that it is by nature opposed to intuition. That the two are not opposed by nature is demonstrated by the long development of logical and metaphysical thinking in India. Even the traditional logicians, metaphysicians and dialecticians never referred to their intuitions in support of their arguments. Many of them, moreover, were not regarded as saints or seers primarily, but as scholars and academicians. The great scholars Vācaspati in the North and Appaya in the South, the great logicians Raghunātha and Udayana and the great dialectician Sri Harṣa were first and foremost academicians.

With more than two thousand years tradition of logical and metaphysical development, it is easy to find parallels between Indian and Western thought. It was not too difficult, therefore, for Radhakrishnan to discover several factors common to both of them, some of which are due to cultural contacts in ancient times and others to independent but parallel developments. Moreover, both the common factors as well as even the differences, whenever found to be important, can be utilised for a new comprehensive synthesis. A rational and unbiassed study of both Eastern and Western systems is a great desideratum, therefore; nor need such study lead to any misunderstandings or to a wrong reading of Western into the Indian or of Indian into the Western concepts.

V

Radhakrishnan's plea for a logical and rational approach to the study of ancient philosophers did not prevent him from being a follower of the Śaṁkarite tradition. It is a part of the Indian philosophical tradition itself to be loyal to tradition and yet be devoted to truth. Thus conservatism and progress have been peculiarly reconciled in India's philosophical development. In spite of the great divergence of their doctrines from each other, almost all Indian philosophical systems claim the authority of the *Upaniṣads* in their support. This loyalty made it possible for them to belong to the *Upaniṣadic* tradition, although developing quite distinct views of their own.

Though a great admirer of Śaṁkara and in general a follower of his way of thinking, Radhakrishnan holds that some of Śaṁkara's later followers gave his philosophy an unduly negativistic interpretation. The view that Māyā should not be taken as a value judgment but only as a logical concept of inexplicability is a position upon which Radhakrishnan is insisting. That the world is not unreal, that Māyā does not mean unreality, is ever and again emphasized by the dialecticians of the later Advaita, while clarifying and defining their concepts. But some of the followers of the tradition continued to equate it with unreality and to use it as a value-judgment as well, which is not consistent with the logic of the Advaita. Further, Śaṁkara's Advaita is only one of nearly a dozen schools of Vedānta, and by none of the others is the world or Māyā treated as unreal. For them, Māyā is a positive and inexplicable creative power of the Absolute and/or God. Hence the negativistic interpretation of Indian thought is consonant neither with the Vedānta in general nor even with the logic of the Advaita. Radhakrishnan maintains that it is not correct to say that Indian philosophy preaches a negative attitude to the world; it contains only so much of negativism as does every religion which believes in a reality beyond and behind the mundane world. Moreover, Radhakrishnan's interpretation of this point is accepted by almost all liberal minded philosophers of India. This new re-emphasis on the positive attitude, which Radhakrishnan has given both in his writings and lectures, was so suitable to the changing and renovated India that it has practically been accepted as the norm.

VI

The main emphasis of Radhakrishnan's philosophy is on the primacy of the spiritual in the nature of man. Man is more than matter, life, or mind, or all these put together. Radhakrishnan believes that the pessimism of modern existentialists like Sartre [20] is due to a wrong analysis and understanding of human existence, which excludes from it the higher spirit within. Such philosophies completely leave out of account the truths preached by the great

[20] BG, 254.

religions of the world for thousands of years. Due very largely to
the influence of Radhakrishnan, the academic philosophers of India still maintain the primacy of the spiritual, in spite of the inroads of several materialist philosophies from the West. Radhakrishnan believes that the new outlook which is needed to solve
the world's problems and conflicts must essentially be spiritual,
and the new philosophy must give primacy to spiritual values.[21]
The conflict between the political ideologies of the present day is
due to viewing man as only a social unit, society being *a priori*
identified with either the democratic or the Communist type of
society. But the nature of man reaches to the Universal Spirit beyond society. As Radhakrishnan puts it:

> There is a fundamental difference in regard to the nature of the in-
> dividual between historical religions and totalitarian faiths. Religions
> teach that God is in man, that man is possessed of the power to choose
> between good and evil; and this power to make a choice makes him
> a man and distinguishes him from the animal and lends sacredness to
> human life. The real unit of life is the individual with the beating
> human heart, the baffled human will, the sense of vast dignities and
> strange sorrows. Democracy is our expression of the faith in man and
> his right and duty to perfect himself and to build a society in which
> self-expression is possible. The human being is treated by living reli-
> gions as a sacred entity. Whereas for Marx it is only an 'ensemble of
> social relations.' [22]

Not all democracies follow this philosophy. However, the teaching
of Gandhi was based on the conviction that man is essentially
spiritual.

Like Gandhi, Radhakrishnan interprets the *Bhagavadgītā* (usually called *Gītā*) as preaching non-violence. He writes:

> The ideal which the *Gītā* sets before us is ahiṁsā or non-violence
> and this is evident from the description of the perfect state of mind,
> speech and body in Chapter XII. Kṛṣṇa advises Arjuna to fight without
> passion or ill-will, without anger or attachment, and if we develop such
> a frame of mind, violence becomes impossible.[23]

The *Gītā* occupies a unique place in Indian philosophical literature. It is one of the philosophical triad, the *Upaniṣads*, the
Brahmasūtras, and the *Gītā,* which constitute together and individ-

21 "To gain the ends which Marx and his adherents have in view, to achieve the
extinction of unhappy hates, we need a spiritual revival. The new world order must
have a deep spiritual impulse to give it unity and drive. It alone can give a rational
basis to the social programme." RS, 42.

22 RS, 55.   23 BG, 68.

ually the main scriptural authority for all the orthodox schools of Indian thought. But, whereas the *Upaniṣads*, as part of the Veda, were forbidden by traditional orthodoxy to be read by the lower castes, which constitute the majority of the inhabitants of India, the *Bhagavadgītā*, as part of the epic *Mahābhārata*, could be read by all alike.[24] Consequently the *Gītā* has naturally been more popular. Not only did the protagonist of almost every school of Indian thought write a commentary on the *Gītā* from his own point of view and even made it yield his own views, but also every leader in India today finds it useful and even necessary to furnish a commentary on it in order to make his views reach as many people as possible. Tilak wrote a commentary on it in order to preach his philosophy of action, and Gandhi his of non-violence. Radhakrishnan followed their example and has written a translation with notes and comments, not only to preach a life of action and non-violence but also a universal world-outlook, which could really be the outlook of UNESCO. In Radhakrishnan's opinion, "inertia or non-action is not the ideal (of the *Gītā*). Action without any selfish desire or expectation of gain, performed in the spirit that 'I am not the doer, I am surrendering myself to the Universal Self' is the ideal set before us." [25] In view of the fact that, according to Radhakrishnan, every religion contains elements which are universal truths, the *Gītā*, which was able to yield such divergent interpretations as realism, idealism, monism and pluralism, should contain such universal truths to an even greater degree, and its doctrines should be interpreted as of universal applicability. "The *Gītā* cannot be used to support the existing social order with its rigidity and confusion." [26] This statement is of a piece with his general spirit of approach to philosophical problems and interpretation. Philosophy is and ought to be universal and therefore rational. Our interpretations and solutions of problems should get at truths of universal validity and appeal. He say that the *Gītā*

represents not any sect of Hinduism but Hinduism as a whole, not merely Hinduism but religion as such, in its universality without limit of time and space, embracing within its synthesis the whole gamut of the human spirit, from the crude fetishism of the savage to the creative affirmation of the saint. The suggestion set forth in the *Gītā* about the meaning and value of existence, the sense of eternal values and the way in which the ultimate values are illumined by the light of reason and

[24] This condition no longer obtains in the contemporary academic circles of India.

[25] BG, 352.   [26] *Ibid.*, 364.

moral intuition provide the basis for agreement in mind and spirit so very essential for keeping together the world which has become materially one by the acceptance of the externals of civilisation.[27]

The universal world outlook which Radhakrishnan has been endeavouring to preach has now, in fact, become the fashion of the day in contemporary philosophical circles of India.

VII

The great contribution which Radhakrishnan has made to Indian epistemology and which has influenced many Indian writers is the idea that intuition is not opposed to intellect but is its completion. The two are often treated as opposed to each other in both the East and the West. The ancient philosophers of India, particularly Śaṁkara and some of the later Buddhists, denounced intellect, though they made elaborate use of it in order not only to prove the shortcomings of intellect but also to criticise each other. The Vedāntins as a whole placed scripture above reason as a source of valid knowledge, and the Mahāyāna Buddhists gave *prajñā* (intuition) the highest place. As a result, this wrong practice of opposing intellect to intuition became a fashion among many Indian thinkers: to appeal to the shortcomings of intellect became an easy way of escape from a difficult logical situation in philosophical controversies. On the other hand, some intellectualist philosophers, who dub others as mystics, consider any reference to intuition as derogatory.

In contrast to both such extreme positions, Radhakrishnan maintains that intellect is not opposed to intuition, and that intuition is not irrational knowledge but supra-rational. Intuition is the completion of the intellect: intuitive knowledge is the perfection of rational knowledge. He recognises different ways of knowing: sensation, imagination, instinct, perception, reason, and intuition. Pure sensation does not reveal "what" an object is; perception does so. In imagination the object is non-existent; it has only psychical existence. Rational knowledge needs verification, because, although thought is able to reveal reality, thought and reality are different in existence at the empirical level. "What intuition reveals is not so much a doctrine as a consciousness; it is a state of mind and not a definition of an object. Logic and language are a lower form, a diminution of this kind of knowledge." [28] And there are aspects of reality where intuition is efficient. The highest of them is found in

27 *Bhagavadgītā*, Introduction.   28 IVL, 138.

religion. We generally tend to deny the reality of the spiritual, because it cannot adequately be grasped and understood by intellect. But we forget that there is a higher type of knowledge than intellect, although some deny even such a possibility. Radhakrishnan emphasized this truth and thereby is able to save the reality of the spiritual. Intuition is a presupposition of the intellect and is its completion; similarly, the spiritual is a presupposition of the empirical reality and is its completion. A philosophy which deals only with empirical reality deals only with a part of reality and cannot, therefore, be adequate as a philosophy of life.

Although pointing out the place and importance of intuition and of the spiritual in philosophy in general, Radhakrishnan exhorts Indian thinkers to adopt a new attitude toward scripture and its authority. Too much dependence on the verbal statements of scripture is detrimental to philosophy. Otherwise, philosophy reduces itself to mere grammar and etymology, and the philosopher would be at the mercy of the grammarian and the etymologist. Indeed, our ancients pointed out the inherent logical defects of intellect in order to prove the superiority of scripture. However, from the so-called inherent defectiveness of intellect, it does not at all follow that everything that every scripture says must be true. We have already realised, moreover, both in the East and in the West, that all statements of scriptures can not be equally true. The most reasonable attitude, therefore, we can adopt toward the scriptures is to treat them as a body of the intuitive utterances of our ancient sages. Thereby we remove the stigma that our scriptures and Indian philosophy are anti-rational. Scriptural truths are religious and spiritual truths; they can be grasped by intuition, which is above intellect. This new teaching of the relation between intellect and intuition has strengthened the spiritual tradition of philosophy in India, in spite of all intellectualist attacks.

In fact, even in ancient India some sensationalist and materialist conclusions for a philosophy of life were drawn by means of a demonstration of the so-called inherent defectiveness of reason and perception. It has often strongly and rightly been emphasised that philosophy in India has been, from the very beginning, a philosophy of life, intimately connected with religion, which latter has never been weighted down by any dogmas about God. Whenever, therefore, a philosophy turned out to be materialistic, conclusions of a materialistic philosophy of life were drawn at once. God is invisible like spirit. The reality of both has to be inferred. But the materialist tried to show, with the same logical acumen as that displayed by many modern logicians, that inference was inherently incapable of giving truth and so could not prove the reality of spirit or God. Thus, while Indian materialists deduced the unreality of spirit and God from the inherent defectiveness of reason and inference, the Vedāntins, following Śaṁkara, deduced from the same premises the conclusion that spirit (ātman) and the Brahman (Absolute) were beyond intellect and could only be directly experienced through intuition. But they did not take the trouble to show clearly that this direct experience is a form of knowledge involved in and presupposed by the discursive knowledge of the intellect, and that intellect is not necessarily opposed to this higher experience but is absorbed in and completed by it. By Radhakrishnan, this experience is called "integral experience" and, as a form of knowledge, intuition. He writes: "The proof and validity of the intuitive principle is somewhat similar to Kant's proof of a priori elements. We cannot think them away. We cannot disbelieve them and remain intellectual. They belong to the very structure of our mind." [29] In proving this thesis he makes use of Kant's philosophy and method. He says: "We have not only an a priori consciousness of good and evil, but also that of the unconditioned." [30] Further,

the self-evidencing and underivative character of intuition is the lesson of Kant's philosophy, though he was himself not conscious of it. Kant thinks that intuitive understanding is a prerogative of God and not a possession of the human spirit. Such a misconception is traceable to the arbitrary limits he imposed on human knowledge.[31]

Both intellectual and intuitive kinds of knowledge are justified and have their own rights. Each is useful and has its own specific purposes. Logical knowledge enables us to know the conditions of the world in which we live and to control them for our ends. We cannot act successfully without knowing properly. But if we want to know things in their uniqueness, in their indefeasible reality, we must transcend discursive thinking. Direct perception or simple and steady looking upon an object is intuition. It is not a mystic process but the most direct and penetrating examination possible to the human mind. Intuition stands to intellect in somewhat the same relation as intellect stands to sense. Though intuition lies beyond intellect, it is not contrary to it. It is called saṁyagjñāna, or perfect knowledge. Reflective knowledge is a preparation for this integral experience.[32]

This clarification of the relation between intellect and intuition has made a deep impression on the minds of contemporary thinkers, particularly in India.

[29] IVL, 156.   [30] Ibid., 165.   [31] Ibid., 166.   [32] Ibid., 146f.

VIII

Though Radhakrishnan is anxious to continue the ancient Vedāntic tradition, he often pleads for creative work. But ancient Indian philosophy is too profound and rich in variety; it will not be easy, therefore, to start something new which will be true, useful, and significant at the same time. That is one of the reasons why there is not much novelty in the work of most contemporary Indian thinkers. So long as the importance for life of our ancient philosophy is not lost sight of, creative work will take the form of a development and widening of the scope of our ancient systems rather than of starting something new. Radhakrishnan's influence is strongly in favour of this attitude. So far as the articulation of a spiritual outlook is concerned, ancient philosophy had much to say, and there will not be much that can be absolutely new. But this overwhelming interest in matters spiritual has, in the past, limited the scope of philosophical activity. What is needed, therefore, is the breaking of limits and an expanding of scope in order to include matters that are as intensely human as matters spiritual.

The present is a sociological age. We are more concerned with social problems than with the purely scientific. In the West, the latest developments of science and industry have given rise to new problems for man and society. In India, religion and communal antagonisms have been the occasion for similar difficulties. Man, instead of being master of science and industry, has become their slave. Both ancient institutionalised religions in the East and the new social ideologies in the West have made the individual completely subservient to communalism and to party leaders. Ancient Indian philosophy solved the problem of religious communalism to a degree at least by turning religion into a philosophical and spiritual quest, instead of treating it as a set of dogmas to be obeyed without question and exploited by political leaders. Radhakrishnan repeatedly brings this peculiar nature of Indian religion to the attention of his readers, and insists that the essence of the spiritual life is the pursuit and realisation of spiritual·perfection, not adherence to any dogmas. This extrication of the spiritual, for our understanding, from social and other incidental entanglements by ancient Indian philosophy has strengthened it and made it so far healthy. But, unfortunately, a similar approach has not yet been made to the study of social forms, in which the spiritual life tends to be embedded. In the West, at the time of the Renaissance, science and reason were liberated from the dogmas of religion, but not so social thought and practice. The twentieth century is the century of the liberation of the sociological from religious studies, the need for which was foreseen by Dewey. When this liberation is accomplished, we shall have facilitated an intensive rational study not only of the sciences of matter and mind, but also of man, society, and spirit in the near future, for a final and harmonious integration again. In order to achieve this end Radhakrishnan's insistence that religion must be treated as a pursuit of spiritual values and not as adherence and subservience to some official dogmas would, if consistently followed, be of immense help. What Indian philosophy and religion tried to do more or less unknowingly, may be done consciously and deliberately. The influence of Radhakrishnan's teaching on young Indian thinkers is, moreover, very great. Indians are prepared to follow him, provided the leaders of institutionalised religions will not treat them, for so doing, as the followers of another sectarian religion. For it is far easier as well as more convenient and comfortable for the majority of human beings to observe a few externals, to wear a particular type of clothes and have their hair dressed in a particular way than to analyse their inner being in order to discover the Universal Spirit within. The adherents of traditional religions may, therefore, treat the new approach as a new institution, not their own.

Radhakrishnan has influenced not only the academic philosophers but also the educated people of India in general. He is not only a clear and charming writer but an impressive personality and a fluent speaker. He has the gift of presenting the most technical ideas in easy, simple language. In his lectures, the old and the new, in other words, East and West, are made to meet without conflict. Both are presented as complementary to each other. Men of ancient outlook come out of his lectures with the satisfaction that their views and opinions are not absolutely useless; and men of progressive views find an equal supporter in him. Radhakrishnan says that it is neither desirable nor necessary to break away from the past; yet he maintains that the past cannot be made to live again, that progress is necessary.

The peculiar conditions in which the Renaissance in India took place have made Radhakrishnan not only the philosopher of the Indian Renaissance but also the philosopher of East-West philosophical co-operation and synthesis. Schlegel, the great Austrian philosopher of history, said that the introduction of Sanskrit into Europe was next in importance to the Renaissance. But philosophically the effects of that introduction have hardly been appreciable till now. Only now has the Western attempt to understand Indian thought seriously been begun. And this beginning is not a little due to the work of Radhakrishnan.

Similarly, the attempt of Indian philosophers and scholars to bring ancient Indian thought into line with Western thinking and to make it possible for the former to progress by incorporating the best and the most useful of the latter is equally largely due to the influence of Radhakrishnan's work. Radhakrishnan is the philosopher not only of the Renaissance in India but also of a second Renaissance in the West, which is becoming effective four centuries after the first. Besides, he is a philosopher of the modern and young Indian nation, recognised to be the best fitted to shape her educational policies in conformity with her great spiritual traditions in the past and with high ideals of continuous progress for the future. The important recommendations which he made to the Government of India as the Chairman of the Universities Commission will further strengthen the influence of his ideas on the educated men of this country.

P. T. RAJU

DEPARTMENT OF PHILOSOPHY
JASWANT COLLEGE
UNIVERSITY OF RAJPUTANA
JODHPUR (RAJASTHAN), INDIA

16

M. N. Roy

RADHAKRISHNAN IN THE PERSPECTIVE OF INDIAN PHILOSOPHY

RADHAKRISHNAN IN THE PERSPECTIVE OF
INDIAN PHILOSOPHY

THE various currents of philosophical, as distinct from religious, thought of ancient India eventually contributed to the rise of Buddhism. Because it grew out of a background in which faith in the supernatural was subordinated to human reason, Buddhism, though counted as one of the Great Religions of the world, was not a religion in the strictest sense. Therefore, it could not fill up the spiritual vacuum created by the disintegration of the early Vedic natural religion. On the one hand, it flourished as an intellectual movement (the Hīnayāna school) with a limited scope; and, on the other, it compromised with the vulgarities of the decayed natural religion. In this latter form, it could not hold its own against the rationalised religious revival buttressed upon Śaṁkaracharya's scholasticism.

The downfall of Buddhism buried its philosophical foundation in the ruins of time. The triumphant Brahmanical reaction not only falsified ancient philosophical thought, which had dared deny the authority of the Vedas and even the existence of God, so as to combat it conveniently; but the blasphemous works of atheists, materialists, and nihilists were mostly destroyed. India entered her Middle Ages, during which theology, scholastic as well as anthropomorphic, dominated thought. What has come down as orthodox Hindu philosophy was elaborated in that period of intellectual reaction. Being primarily concerned with the nature of God, which conception was taken for granted, of the soul, and how the latter could return to its transcendental home, it was not philosophy but theology.

By her own effort, India never emerged from the intellectual twilight of her Middle Ages. In the 16th and 17th centuries, individual religious reformers preached devotionalism which would dispense with the priestly intermediary between God and his devotees. But their influence was local and transitory. India experienced neither a Renaissance nor a Reformation. The intellectual stagnation lasted until the middle of the 19th century, when a faint echo of the modern rationalist and liberal thought reached India to disturb it partially. During the latter half of the century, the intellectual life of the country was influenced by a number of men who preached revolt against religious orthodoxy, intellectual parochialism, and social injustice. There was no great philosopher amongst them. They were social reformers. None of them thought of going behind the twilight of the Middle Ages in search of India's philosophical heritage. The attitude of the more advanced amongst those forerunners of an Indian Renaissance toward her past was negative. They drew inspiration from the West and held that India as a whole must do the same in order to emerge from mediaevalism.

Unfortunately, the impact of modern Western thought came in the wake of the British conquest. It made some headway until discontent and then hatred against the foreign political rule became the predominating passion of the educated classes. Then all Western influence was decried as de-nationalising materialism to be opposed and rejected in favour of the spiritual genius of Indian culture. Speculative thought of any kind had been for centuries eclipsed by priestly bigotry, superstitious ritualism and practice of social injustice, such as the caste system, untouchability, etc., which passed as religion. In that atmosphere, the democratic simplicity of Christianity had a strong appeal not only for the victims of social injustice, but also for many liberal intellectuals.

A movement of religious reform and of revival of the spiritualist philosophy of India were the reaction to that process of the disintegration of an intellectually stagnant society. Return to the pristine purity of Vedic ritualism was the religious reform advocated. The orthodoxy of the reformers was more bigoted than the current variety. Such a reactionary movement being incapable of meeting the situation, it was reinforced by the modern prophets of India's spiritual mission, who sought to provide a philosophical sanction to religious revivalism. It was discovered in the post-Buddhist scholastic theology, which had expounded Vedānta as the quintessence of the philosophical thought of ancient India.

The credit for raising the politically motivated religious and cultural revivalism to the level of academic philosophy belongs to Radhakrishnan. Before him, the rejection of Western philosophical thought as materialistic was dogmatic, and the exposition of Indian philosophy, on the other hand, fell short of academic erudition. He was the first exponent of the post-Buddhist Indian philosophy to back up his criticism of Western philosophical thought with an adequate knowledge of it; though knowledge does not always make for appreciation. His exposition of the Hindu view of life was a "counter-attack from the East," as C. E. M. Joad characterised it. The *Hindu View of Life* expounded in the Upton Lectures was much too apologetic to be a positive statement of principles; it was a criticism as well as a defence. The full-blast counter-attack was the Hibbert Lectures on *An Idealist View of Life*. On that occasion, Radhakrishnan took a negative attitude to all the schools of contemporary Western philosophy—naturalism, atheism, agnosticism, scepticism, humanism, pragmatism, so on and so forth, which rejected the traditional religious view of life and spiritual conception of the universe. In the same lectures, he took up a position which has been described as Absolute Idealism. But the central theme of Radhakrishnan's philosophy is God, and the conception is very different from the Hegelian World Spirit. Radhakrishnan's God is almost anthropomorphic; in any case, an *ad hoc* postulate, an article of faith—a very unstable foundation for a system of rationalist thought. Spinoza also was "God-inebriated;" but he did not allow God any place in the geometrical structure of his philosophy of nature. Therefore, Spinoza's pantheism was hardly distinguishable from materialistic metaphysics. In Radhakrishnan's philosophy, God pervades the universe, which is a spiritual reality. The knowledge of reality, therefore, is identical with the knowledge of God; philosophy is theology. That is the tradition of the Vedāntic pantheism which Radhakrishnan expounds as the Hindu philosophy.

Radhakrishnan's idealism is not subjective; therefore, he is not confronted with the problem of solipsism. But the fallacy of Absolute Idealism is more formidable: the Absolute Being is Absolute Nothing. How could the phenomenal world of experience come out of nothing? Radhakrishnan evades the question by postulating an anthropomorphic God, and falling back upon Śaṁkaracharya's subterfuge of the *Māyāvāda*—the world is an illusion, and as such a reality!

God as the universal mind working with a conscious design, who is at once the beginning of the world, the author of its order, the principle of its progress and the goal of its evolution, is not the God of religion unless we take into account the facts of religious consciousness.[1]

[1] IVL, 333.

How do we discover this fundamental fact of metaphysics?, this conclusive notion about the unfoldment of the Absolute into the actual? "Our moral life tells us that God is not only the goal but the spring and sustainer of moral effort." [2] So, the absolute reality is known, and its nature comprehended, intuitively; in other words, mystic or religious experience "declare[s] the presence of the one Supreme. The universe seems to be alive with spirit, aglow with fire, burning with light." [3]

Nowhere except in the Hibbert Lectures has Radhakrishnan expounded a philosophy of his own. Even therein he is mainly preoccupied with finding fault with the modern naturalist and rationalist trends of thought. When offering his alternative, he talks always about God. In his conception, philosophy therefore is not differentiated from religion. As a matter of fact, if he expounds any philosophy, it is admittedly the philosophy of religion; that is to say, theology, which tries to rationalise the belief in God. "The great problem of the philosophy of religion has been the reconciliation of the character of the Absolute as in a sense eternally complete with the character of God as a self-determining principle manifested in a temporal development which includes nature and man." [4]

In the Upton Lectures, Radhakrishnan makes his conception of philosophy still clearer.

The history of philosophy in India as well as Europe has been one long illustration of the inability of the human mind to solve the mystery of the relation of God to the world. The greatest thinkers are those who admit the mystery and comfort themselves by the idea that the human mind is not omniscient.[5]

One need not be a great thinker to admit that man's capacity to know is not perfect. At the same time, it is undeniable that there is no absolute limit to it. Human mind is not omniscient, but it knows so much more today than in the past; therefore, it can be reasonably assumed that it will know more and more as time passes; and there will be no end to that process. Any doubt or dogma about the endlessness of the cognitive faculty of the human mind results only from the blind faith that reality, being spiritual, is inaccessible to it. One may ask the philosopher who preaches this esoteric doctrine, how does he know that there is such a reality. If it is unknowable to the human mind, the philosopher, being also a human being, cannot have any idea about it. Therefore, the spiritual real-

---

[2] *Ibid.*   [3] *Ibid.,* 109.   [4] *Ibid.,* 343.   [5] HVL, 67f.

ity is only a figment of his imagination. Such imaginary reality is "the wide and stormy ocean, the true home of mirage," as Kant aptly described it.

Any judgment of Radhakrishnan's philosophy, therefore, must be backed up by a statement of the critic's criterion. What is philosophy? Pythagoras defined it as "contemplation, study and knowledge of nature." This definition generally holds good even today. Speculation about the supernatural is not philosophy; and anything beyond the reach of the human mind is supernatural. Because, human mind being a part of nature, it is capable of penetrating all the secrets of nature. If philosophy is defined as the love of knowledge, then speculation about the *unknowable* evidently is *not* philosophy.

Speculation about the causes of natural phenomena begins as soon as man reaches an intellectual level where his spiritual needs are no longer satisfied by the superstitions and fantasies of natural religion. Intellectual growth impels and emboldens him to seek in nature itself the causes of all natural phenomena; to seek in nature a unity behind its diversity. Science and philosophy, therefore, in the last analysis, are identical. As a matter of fact, the priority goes to science, which lays down the foundation of philosophy, if it is to be defined as the logical co-ordination of the progressively expanding totality of human knowledge. If it starts with the assumption, which is really a preconceived belief, that the causes of phenomena are transcendental, then philosophy cannot perform its function—to explain nature. But the necessarily limited knowledge of the time compelled early philosophy to fall back on speculation about the ultimate reality. Speculative philosophy is the attempt to explain the concrete realities of existence by referring them to a hypothetical absolute. It is the way not to truth, but to dream; not to knowledge but to delusion. Instead of trying to understand the so-called phenomenal world, the only reality given to man, speculative philosophy ends in denying the existence of the only reality and in declaring it to be a figment of man's imagination. An enquiry which denies the very existence of its object, is bound to get bogged down in idle dreams and hopeless confusion.

With the postulation of a creator or the Final Cause, human thought is caught in the vicious circle of a teleological metaphysics. Starting from the assumption that the phenomena of nature are caused and governed by some supernatural agency, call it God or Universal Spirit or First Principle, or anything you like, philosophy makes room for faith, and merges into religion. The supernatural must necessarily be beyond the reach of the mind of man, himself a part of nature. As soon as the ultimate reality is placed beyond the reach of human knowledge, the world itself becomes incomprehensible. That marks the end of philosophy. Man must not aspire to solve the problems of the universe, which is a spiritual unity. He should simply believe that the world is so because God wills it to be so. One must not ask why God wills it to be so, and who made God. Because, these questions cannot be answered. "We can only say that it is much too difficult for us in the pit to know what is happening behind the screens. It is *māyā* (hallucination), or a mystery which we have to accept reverentially." [6]

That is Radhakrishnan's philosophy. There is nothing peculiarly Hindu in it. Western philosophy was equally rooted in religion until the rise of modern science. Even today, it can claim many adherents. But, like ancient Greece, India also had known naturalist, secular, and rationalist currents of philosophical thought. Jacques Maritain may still believe that theology is the queen of the sciences; but more than two thousand years before Radhakrishnan, the founder of the Sāṁkhya system of philosophy, Kapila, denied the existence of God because there was no evidence. And Kapila's agnostic naturalism was preceded by the materialist (atomist) rationalism of the Nyāya-Vaiśeṣika system expounded by Kaṇāda and Gautama. As an historian of Indian philosophy, Radhakrishnan does not ignore those ancient currents of thought.[7] But he expounds the post-Buddhist Vedānta system as the Hindu view of life.

His Absolute Idealism is the pantheistic monism of the scholastic theology of Śaṁkaracharya, expounded in the language of modern academic philosophy. As against the ancient systems of truly philosophical thought, which had resulted from the metaphysical speculations fragmentarily recorded in the *Upaniṣads,* Śaṁkaracharya picked up the pantheistic theology of the Vedānta to oppose Buddhism, which had inherited the rationalist and atheistic traditions of ancient Indian thought. As the name suggests (Vedānta literally means end of the Vedas), the Vedānta system is conventionally believed to be the quintessence of the Vedas, and therefore, since Śaṁkaracharya's time, has been regarded as *the* Hindu philosophy. But criticism must doubt the philosophical validity of a system which draws authority from the scriptures. Although traditionally Vedānta is counted among the six systems of the philosophy of ancient India, there is ground for doubt about its

6 IVL   7 Cf. Ind P, 2 vols.

authenticity as such. The alternative theory that it was formulated on the basis of older religious beliefs to combat Buddhism, and that Śaṁkaracharya himself was the author, appears to be quite plausible. The Vedānta *Sūtras* (aphorismic texts) are very enigmatic, open to any kind of interpretation. They provided the authority for qualified monist and out-and-out dualist theologies. The *Gītā* is believed to contain the most authoritative (because it was preached by God incarnate) elucidation of the Vedānta philosophy. It is a part of the epic *Mahābhārata*, which evidently is a compilation of often contradictory pieces written in different times. The *Gītā* must have been a very late, most probably post-Buddhist, interpolation.

In any case, the six systems of philosophy, whether they belonged to the same period or not, fall into two distinct categories, both resulting from the metaphysical and theological speculations quickened by the decay of the Vedic natural religion. The earlier three —Vaiśeṣika, Nyāya and Sāṁkhya—record the development of naturalist and rationalist thought, which disputed the divine authority of the Vedas, rejected the belief in creation and therefore the idea of God, and preached rebellion against the priesthood. The other three—Yōga, Uttar Mīmāṅsa and Purva Mīmāṅsa—did not break away from the Vedic tradition, relied on scriptural authority and constructed a partly anthropomorphic, partly impersonal, monotheistic religion superimposed upon the earlier polytheism. The last three systems, one of which deals with Vedic ritualism, collectively came to be subsequently called the Vedānta. The suggestion was that the earlier three did not flow from the Vedas, and therefore were not recognised as part of India's intellectual heritage. Yet, they constitute India's contribution to philosophical thought, as distinct from religious doctrines and theological speculations.

Dissatisfaction with the Vedic natural religion gave rise to the speculation about the origin of things. Those speculations are recorded rather enigmatically in the *Upaniṣads*. But the speculation about the origin of nature did not start from the repudiation of the prejudices of the primitive natural religion, because it was done mostly by the Brahmins, whose very existence as the leaders of society was dependent upon the maintenance of the rituals and ceremonies of natural religion. Therefore, the evolution of thought in ancient India was a headlong plunge into theological speculation.

Evidence of dissatisfaction with the Vedic natural religion can be traced in a sufficiently early period—when the *Upaniṣads* were composed. They contain fragmentary records of that primitive spirit of enquiry into the origin of things. But the enquiry was not the result of the rise of a non-priestly class which was opulent and therefore intellectually advanced enough for the purpose. It was mostly confined to the priestly class itself, although some Kṣatriyas appear also to have participated in it. In any case, little record of the non-priestly contribution to that early enquiry has come down to us. Whatever tended towards the origin of a true philosophy, that is, to the discovery of the causes of natural phenomena in nature itself, must have been suppressed by the Brahmins who retained the spiritual monopoly for a long time to come. In the hand of the Brahmins, the primitive inquisitiveness did not prove disruptive to old traditions. It did not undermine the position of the priesthood. On the contrary, it constructed a speculative system which stabilised the decayed structure of the Vedic natural religion. Instead of challenging the authority of the Vedic gods, and consequently of their ministers, the all-powerful Brahmins, the orthodox Hindu speculation of the *Upaniṣads* sought to establish its doctrines, and refute other, more philosophical systems, on the authority of the Vedas themselves. Therefore, the metaphysical speculations of the *Upaniṣads* could not even lead to a clear monotheism. It could set up only a very precarious form of monotheistic religion. The conception of Brahman was precarious because it did not necessarily do away with the pantheon of the anthropomorphic natural gods.

The Brahman of the *Upaniṣads* is a purely *a priori* assumption —an unverifiable hypothesis. That assumption regarding the origin of things categorically put an end to all enquiry in that direction; therefore, it rendered positive knowledge impossible; philosophy was out of court, and priestly monopoly of the intellectual life was perpetuated. The basic defect of ancient Indian philosophy was that the origin of nature was not sought in nature itself. The *a priori* assumption of a super-natural factor inevitably blocked the way to empiricism—the gate to positive science and true philosophy. Later on, there appeared bolder thinkers, such as Kaṇāda, Kapila, Gautama, Chārvaka, and others who came more or less near to a mechanistic conception of nature. But even most of them could not completely liberate themselves from the prejudice of some sort of unknown force giving the first impulse from outside. Owing to that basic weakness, ancient Indian materialism was eventually overcome by spiritualism, and philosophy degenerated into dogmatic theology. There developed the elaborate form of logic which so successfully fettered the human spirit to the prejudice of the ideal of releasing individual souls from the bondage of physical existence. Brahmanical domination, completely re-established after the Epic Era, checked the "heretical," that is to say, philosophical tendencies of the primitive enquiry recorded in the *Upaniṣads*.

Hindu philosophy is, strictly speaking, theology. With the exception of the Nyāya, Vaiśeṣika, and Sāṁkhya, no other speculative system tried to explain the origin, evolution, and phenomena of nature independent of an assumed supernatural agency. With such an assumption, speculative thought becomes theology—a fruitless enquiry or dogmatic assertion about the nature of the supernatural spiritual being which, by its very nature, is beyond all enquiry or description. Orthodox Hindu philosophy offers the most classical example of the contradictions and confusion of speculative metaphysical thought. As most authoritatively expounded in the *Gītā* by God himself, the basic doctrine of orthodox Hindu philosophy is that there is no difference between the material and the immaterial: the formless, invisible, and uncreated immaterial becomes materialised in the same way as water is crystallised into ice. Though false as the gleam of a polished shell, or as a mirage caused by the sun's rays, yet no one at any time, past, present, or future, can rid himself of the delusion (of the world).

The most obvious contradiction is the admission of the reality of that which is declared in the same breath to be a delusion. A thing that existed in the past, exists in the present, and will exist in the future, is eternal. The eternity of the "delusion" of the world thus granted, Brahman necessarily ceased to be what it is assumed to be, namely, "only one without a second."

If the immaterial is really immaterial, the material can never grow out of it. Two things having nothing in common can not stand in the relation of cause and effect. If the material comes out of the immaterial, then, the latter can not be what it is supposed to be: it must also be material. Thus there is but one substance in existence. The dualism is only a sophistry, a verbal contrivance to defend a useless hypothesis. Should immateriality be conceded to the origin of things, the very existence of immateriality itself would be denied. For, existence, which means, extension in space, is not compatible with the conception of immateriality. Water exists

materially; therefore, it can change itself into ice, another material
existence. The material phenomenon of ice could never happen
unless water existed as a material substance. Therefore, the material is the only reality, and it exists eternally. That admission is
the logical inference to be drawn from the above passages. But
such an admission would be highly damaging for the entire system
of Hindu metaphysical thought. It does not leave any room for a
creator. The conception of an eternal existence dispenses even with
the more elusive hypothesis of a First Principle. Therefore, the
start is made from the other end, which eludes verification.

The hypothetical absolute Supreme Being, possessed of flagrantly
contradictory attributes, which violate its supposed absoluteness,
is assumed to be the only reality; and the undeniable reality of
the material world is declared to be a "delusion." Further, "there
is no difference between the material and the immaterial." Yet,
according to orthodox Hindu philosophy, true wisdom consists in
the ability to distinguish between the material and the immaterial.
Endless confusion, naturally, results from such arbitrary splitting
of the unity of being.

The sum and substance of Indian metaphysical speculation can
be stated as follows (to make its absurdity evident): Proposition:—
the finite is not the infinite; problem:—how, then, can the finite
know the infinite? Solution:—the finite must become the infinite!

The Vedānta Sūtras, as interpreted by Śaṁkaracharya, represent
the acme of orthodox Hindu philosophy. It is an admirable work
of scholastic argumentativeness and speculative extravagance, full
of self-contradictions. For instance, Śaṁkaracharya admits: "If
(there) is a second entity, co-existing with Brahman from eternity,
it follows that Brahman has a second." [8] He saw the fallacy of this
inextricable dualism which invalidates the basic theorem: "When
Brahman is known, everything is known;" therefore, he tries to
explain it by declaring the parallel existence identical with Brahman. But that hardly improves the situation. Śaṁkara is generally
believed to have expounded a system of monotheism almost as
perfect as Hegel's absolute idealism. A study of the Śaṁkara-Bhāṣya,
however, shows that this belief is baseless. The work begins with
the following passage: "It is a matter not requiring any proof
that the object and the subject, whose respective spheres are the
notions of the 'Thou' (non-ego) and the 'Ego,' and which are
opposed to each other as much as darkness and the light are, cannot
be identical." [9]

---

[8] *Brahma-Sūtrabhāṣya*, Book II.   [9] *Brahma-Sūtrabhāṣya*, Book I.

No less than two major fallacies are involved in this point of departure. In the first place, the basic principle of the system is simply taken for granted; it is not proved. And, secondly, an absolutist dualist conception is made the premise of a monistic philosophy. Consequently, Śaṁkara had to invent the absurdity of the Māyāvāda (which cannot be traced in the Sūtras themselves) to establish the purely spiritual unity of being.

The doctrine of Māyā is expounded as follows:

Brahman is associated with a certain power called Māyā or *Avidyā*, to which the appearance of this entire world is due. This power cannot be called 'being,' for being is only Brahman. Nor can it be called 'non-being' in the strict sense, for it at any rate produces the appearance of this world. It is in fact a principle of illusion: the undeniable cause, owing to which there seems to exist a material world. Māyā thus constitutes the *Upādāna*, the material cause of the world. Māyā belongs to Brahman as a Śakti. We may say that the material cause of the world is Brahman in so far as it is associated with Māyā.[10]

This doctrine obviously contradicts the conception of Brahman as the unitary and absolute existence. Brahman is devoid of all qualities. Yet, Māyā is assumed to be its Śakti. Moreover, Māyā is conceived as an existence parallel to Brahman. The idea of "association" presupposes two entities; similarly does the idea of "belonging."

The object of the Vedānta Sūtras was to systematise the Aupaniṣadic speculations into a homogeneous whole, and to prove that the heretical doctrines of Kaṇāda, Kapila, Gautama, and others were not borne out by those speculations.[11] The *Upaniṣads* contain speculations which cannot be reconciled in one coherent philosophical system. For example, in the Chāndogya, Bṛhadāranya and Taittirīya, ether or space (*ākāśa*), fire and air are visualised as existences without origin. This view cuts across the basic dogma also set forth in all the *Upaniṣads*, that in the beginning there existed the Brahman, "only one without a second;" and this dogma constitutes the premise of the cardinal doctrine of Hindu religious philosophy, namely, "when the Brahman is known, everything is known," also propounded in the *Upaniṣads*.

In the face of this flagrant contradiction, the entire body of the Aupaniṣadic speculation could not logically be the basis of a single system of philosophy. Unorthodox thinkers, daring to challenge the authority of the scriptures, pointed out this contradiction.

10 Cf. *Brahma-Sūtrabhāṣya*, Book II.
11 *Vide* the *Brahma-Sūtrabhāṣya*, Book II.

They argued: If none but Brahman exists in the beginning, then ether, air, fire, etc., have an origin; that is to say, they are created; but the hypothesis of creation renders the absolute conception of Brahman untenable. On the other hand, if the elements are without origin, then the Brahman ceases to be what it is assumed to be —"only one without a second." If one of these views is correct, then the other is not. Thus the infallibility of the scriptures is shaken. Their claim to absolute authority can no longer be maintained. The monism of the Vedānta, as interpreted by Śaṁkaracharya, is, however, based on precisely this contradiction. In order to obviate any disturbance of the absoluteness of Brahman, the elements must be without origin. The difficulty (of dualism or pluralism) is overcome by declaring them to be identical with Brahman.

Śaṁkara's commentary on this Sūtra is highly interesting. It gives a graphic picture of Hindu speculative thought and shows a curious logic.

These premissory statements (regarding the unity and exclusiveness of Brahman) are not abandoned, that is, not stultified, only if the entire aggregate of things is non-different from Brahman, the object of knowledge; for, if there were any difference, the affirmation that by the knowledge of one thing everything is known, would be contradicted thereby. Non-difference again of the two is possible only if the whole aggregate of things originates from the one Brahman. And we understand from the words of the Veda that that affirmation can be established only through the theory of the non-difference of the material cause and its effect. . . . If the ether, etc., were not effects of the Brahman, it could not be known by Brahman being known, and that would involve an abandonment of a (previous) affirmation; an alternative which, as invalidation of the authoritativeness of the Vedas, is of course altogether unacceptable.[12]

The logic here is remarkable. If the Vedas contradict themselves, that should not be allowed; since that would affect their authoritativeness! The incontestible authority of the scriptures is the absolute standard. Should the evidence against the infallibility of the scriptures be found in the scriptures themselves, that should not be admitted, because that would shake the authority of the scriptures. The basic principle of this remarkable logic is to submit everything to the test of an unverifiable hypothesis, and to reject all evidence against that hypothesis, simply because such evidence would expose the absurdity of the hypothesis and render it, therefore, untenable.

To have found unity in diversity is claimed to be the greatest

12 *Brahma-Sūtrabhāṣya*, Book I.

merit of orthodox Hindu philosophy. But, as a matter of fact, the unity was not found. It was simply assumed or imagined. It is an ideal conception which brushes aside all the problems to be solved. Inasmuch as the rise of the material world out of the assumed immaterial root-cause is not logically possible, dualism persists, defying all metaphysical verbal jugglery. From the Aupaniṣadic Rishis down to Śaṁkaracharya, no orthodox Hindu speculative thinker has been able to prove how the diversities of nature could arise from a common cause. The sheer impossibility of this task ultimately drove Indian speculation to the monumental absurdity of the *Māyāvāda*. Vitiated by the baffling and obstinate problem of dualism, the speculation concerning the origin of the world must necessarily come back again and again to the good old conception of an anthropomorphic god, whose venerable appearance keeps casting a sinister shadow on the sublime light of philosophy. Śaṁkaracharya's laboriously constructed *Advaitavāda* solved the problem of the world by the simple contrivance of declaring it to be a dream. Nevertheless, it still was unable to get rid of a personal god. And a personal god is utterly incompatible with the philosophical conception of unity in diversity.

All existing records, dealing with the various schools of philosophic thought in ancient India, bear testimony to the fact that dissatisfaction with the Vedic natural religion gave rise to speculations about the origin of the world, which inevitably developed tendencies to explain the world in physical terms. In India, too, physics preceded metaphysics! Much of the really philosophical thought of ancient India has, unfortunately, been lost. But, from the fragmentary evidence remaining, that forgotten chapter of the spiritual history of India can be reconstructed. As everywhere else, so in India also, philosophy was, originally, materialistic. The materialistic outcome of the speculations of the rebels against the Vedic natural religion, contained in the three systems of philosophy proper, namely, Vaiśeṣika, Sāṁkhya, and Nyāya, provided the inspiration for the greatest event in the history of ancient India— the Buddhist revolution. The spiritual development of India during nearly a thousand years, beginning from the seventh century B.C., was very largely dominated by materialistic and rationalistic tendencies. It is highly doubtful whether the Vedānta system was formulated before the end of that Golden Age of Indian history. Internal evidence clearly would indicate the opposite. The main purpose for which Vedāntist pantheism was developed was to combat the materialistic systems of Kaṇāda and Kapila as well as the revolutionary doctrines of Buddhism and the unsettling logic of the Jains. Even as late as the fourth century A.D., in the period of the triumphant Hindu restoration under the Gupta dynasty, the Chinese traveller, Fa Hien, found in India no less than "ninety-six heretical sects, all of which admitted the reality of worldly phenomena."

Śaṁkaracharya constructed his rigidly logical, but philosophically ambiguous system of monism in order to combat Buddhist idealism. But the real enemy he had to contend with were the materialistic traditions of pre-Buddhist philosophy. His works are full of long polemics against materialistic and naturalistic doctrines; so much so that the fragments profusely quoted by him can serve as a reliable foundation for reconstructing the latter.

From fragmentary evidences contained in his own works, therefore, the following can be reconstructed as a summary of the "atheism and materialism" which Śaṁkaracharya combatted.

Religious doctrines are all meaningless words. Their foundation is the idea of God, whose very existence can not be proved. God is the creator, but he himself has no origin. If it is admitted that there must be a creator and ruler of the world, then there arises the question: Who created the creator? Whence did he come? The creator is said to be without beginning and without end; without any limits. But, after all, he is said to be a creator, which implies a personality on his part. God is, indeed, considered to be the creator. But a person can not be without beginning or end nor without other limits. If God is limited, then, is it not possible that there may exist a power over and above him? God is believed to be all-powerful and all-pervading. But these attributes of God cease to be what they are believed to be as soon as they are imagined by man. Thus, the essence of God, the creator, disappears. Moreover, it is taught that desire is the cause of creation. From this it follows that God himself is not free from desire. Further, if the universe is created by the will of God, then God himself must have the feeling of want; for wish grows out of want. The feeling of want destroys omnipotence, omniscience, completeness and all other superhuman attributes ascribed to God.[13]

What has come down to us as the most authoritative as well as most representative Hindu philosophy was the creation of Śaṁkaracharya. He was the ideologist of the Brahmanical reaction and patriarchal society which were re-established on the ruins of the

[13] *Vide* the *Brahma-Sūtrabhāṣya*.

Buddhist revolution. But Śaṁkaracharya's effort for liquidating the traditions of the really philosophical thought of ancient India was a failure. This very important fact in the spiritual history of India is not realised. Yet it is obvious from a critical study of Śaṁkaracharya's own works. He failed to meet the materialists on their own ground. But neither could he refute their arguments. He, therefore, had to fall back on the authority of the scriptures, the repudiation of which had been the starting-point of all philosophical thought in ancient India. Of all the great ancient rationalists, Kapila alone had admitted scriptural testimony as evidence. But that was only a formal concession. For, in declaring that the existence of God could not be proved, inasmuch as there was no evidence, Kapila does not take scriptural testimony into account. Even the Vedānta Sūtras themselves do not accept the scriptures as answering all questions raised by those dissatisfied with the dogmas of natural religion.

So highly developed and powerful were the materialist and naturalist schools combatted by Śaṁkaracharya that, whenever he tried to refute their arguments logically, he was driven to take up an essentially materialistic position himself. His pantheistic monism is really an inverted materialism. The *Māyāvāda* is a shame-faced recognition of the reality of the external world. It is only by degenerating into a dogmatic system of theology, which tries to reconcile even the gods of the Vedic natural religion with the metaphysical conception of Brahman, that Śaṁkaracharya's system apparently escapes the fate common to all systems of consistent pantheism. The fate is to corroborate the materialistic view from the opposite direction.

The unreality of the phenomenal world is the fundamental dogma of the Vedānta system. But, in order to refute the idealistic school of Buddhism, Śaṁkaracharya himself rejected this very dogma. The Buddhist idealists held that cognition was exclusively an internal process; not that it had no connection with the external object, but that it was self-contained; the external objects existed only in their relation to the mind. The substantial residue of objects is atoms, the rest being form; but the atom cannot be conceived by mind.

In combatting this doctrine, Śaṁkaracharya writes: "The non-existence of external things cannot be maintained, because we are conscious of external things. Why should we pay attention to a man who affirms that no such thing exists?" Why, then, should we ourselves, in turn, take Śaṁkaracharya seriously when he talks of Māyā? He proceeds:

That the outward thing exists apart from consciousness, has necessarily to be accepted on the ground of the nature of consciousness itself. Nobody, when perceiving a post or a wall, is conscious of his perception only; but all men are conscious of posts and walls as objects of their perceptions. Even those who contest the existence of external things, bear witness to their existence when they say that what is an internal object of cognition appears like something external. No one says that Viṣṇumitra appears like the son of a barren mother. If we accept the truth as it is given to our consciousness, we must admit that the objects of perception appear to us as something external. Because the distinction of thing and idea is given in consciousness, the invariable concomitance of idea and thing has to be considered as proving only that the thing constitutes the means of ideas, not that the two are identical. It cannot be asserted in any way that the idea, apart from the thing, is the object of our consciousness; for, it is absurd to speak of a thing as the object of its own activity. The variety of mental impressions is caused altogether by the variety of external things perceived. This apparent world, whose existence is guaranteed by all the means of knowledge, cannot be denied.[14]

Here Śaṁkaracharya is combatting his own whole philosophy. Once the issues are joined on philosophical ground, the triumph inevitably goes to materialism. When Śaṁkaracharya himself had to expound the above purely materialistic theory of cognition, it is evident how powerful was the current of materialistic thought which influenced the spiritual life of ancient India for nearly a thousand years, until the downfall of Buddhism.

Although the fundamental principles of ancient Indian materialism were originally stated in the Vaiśeṣika system, the dominating position in the intellectual life of that period came to be occupied by the Sāṁkhya system of Kapila. The latter deviated largely from the strictly materialistic ground, and developed instead a rational-naturalistic system of metaphysics. Nevertheless, the physical principles of materialism were elaborated philosophically by Kapila. He is known as an atheist who maintained that the existence of God could not be proved by logical evidence. But the real merit of his philosophy is the recognition of the objective reality of the physical world. The Sāṁkhya system decidedly rejects the doctrine that the external world has no objective existence or that nothing exists except thought. Arguing against some earlier

14 *Brahma-Sūtrabhāṣya*, Book II.

philosophers, who are characterised by the commentators as "heretics" or "nihilists," [15] Kapila says: "Not thought alone exists; because there is the intuition of the external world. . . . Then, since, if the one does not exist, the other does not exist, there is a void." [16]

The most authoritative commentator, Vijnana Bhikshu, interprets the Sūtras as follows:

> The reality is not thought alone; because external objects also are proved to exist, just as thought is, by intuition. If external things do not exist, then a mere void offers itself. Because, if the external world does not exist, then thought does not exist; for it is intuition that proves the objective; and, if the intuition of the external world did not establish the objective, then the intuition of thought also would not establish the existence of thought.[17]

The theory of cognition is definitely materialistic. The underlying principle of the Sāṁkhya theory of knowledge is identical with the modern materialist principle that consciousness is determined by being. The defenders of the religious doctrine of creation tried to silence the enquiry about the origin of things by denying the reality of the world itself. They argued that a thing of dream —an unreality—did not need any substantial origin. Kapila retorted: "The world is not unreal; because there is no fact contradictory (to its reality), and because it is not the (false) result of depraved senses (leading to a belief in what ought not to be believed)." [18] This is clear enough. But Kapila goes farther—to the extent of stating the fundamental principle of the rationalist-materialist view of the world: "A thing is not made out of nothing." With this the bottom is knocked out from under the doctrine of creation. The origin of the physical world is traced to an endless process of causality, and that process is inherent in nature. Existing eternally by itself, the world does not need any creator or creation. Nor is there any beginning. Because, in that case also, something would have to be coming out of nothing. Thus, the Sāṁkhya system rejects even an "immanent teleology."

Kapila visualised existence as a hierarchy, so to say, composed of twenty-five elements. In addition to the soul, nature, mind, and self-consciousness, there are "subtle" elements, sense organs, and "gross elements." The pyramid stands on the apex. Reverse the order, and you have a process of evolution. Although the process

---

[15] Cf. *Brhadaranyakhopaniṣad*, Book II.
[16] *Sāṁkhya-Sūtra*, Book I, Sūtras 42 and 48.
[17] *Vijnana-Bhikshubhāṣya*, Book I.   [18] *Sāṁkhya-Sūtra*, Book I.

of evolution is set on its head, the "realities" are derived inductively from the immediately perceptible gross elements. The existence of the "subtle elements" (sound, colour, touch, taste and smell)
is inferred from the "gross elements," which are directly perceptible. The logic is obvious: everything which is gross is formed
of something which is less gross. The process is traced to the primal
state of nature, in which everything lies in a state of inaction. But
nature is not only eternal, but self-operative. "Since the root has
no root, the root is rootless." [19] Thus nature is herself the final
cause. Since mind and self-consciousness are placed within the
scheme of nature, they are included in the materialistic system.
Only the soul stands outside; but, like Newton's *deus ex machina*,
it is completely unnecessary for explaining the being and becoming of the world. The existence of nature is inferred from its perceptible phenomena. These are real; they must, therefore, have a
real cause. That is to say, the constituents of the world exist
eternally. Those ultimate elements, in the Vaiśeṣika and Nyāya systems, are called atoms. Kapila reduces them to an all-pervasive
existence, and calls it nature in a state of inaction.

Nature in its primal state, in the Sāṁkhya system, is like
Spinoza's *"beseelte Materie."* Three qualities (goodness, passion,
and darkness), inherent in nature, are the lever of all natural operations. Atomism is rejected, because pain and pleasure are not
properties of the atom. Everything in existence is an aggregate of
pain, pleasure, delusion, etc., which are clearly perceptible. But
here arises a very pertinent question: What is the cause of these
categories or qualities? Kapila himself asserts that something cannot come out of nothing. Obviously, therefore, in order to avoid
this dilemma, he makes nature an all-pervading primal substance,
having the three qualities in a state of equilibrium. The atomists
would contend that the atom could just as well represent the
equilibrium of qualities.

The most important contribution made to the development of
philosophic thought by the Sāṁkhya system, however, is its sensationalist theory of knowledge. Kapila was an out and out empiricist. He holds, with an admirable logical rigour, that sense
perception is the only reliable source of knowledge. "Determination (right apprehension) of something not previously known is
right notion (knowledge). What is in the highest degree productive thereof is evidence." [20]

19 *Sāṁkhya-Sūtra*, Book I, Sūtras 114 and 115.
20 *Sāṁkhya-Sūtra*, Book I, Sūtra 87.

Evidence is defined as perception, inference, and testimony (scriptural). By admitting inference among the categories of evidence, Kapila anticipated the rise of inductive logic. His contribution to the scientific mode of thought is, therefore, very considerable. The above Sūtra is interpreted by one of the commentators as follows: "The proof or evidence, or whatever we may choose to call that from which right notion results, is just the conjunction of an organ (with the appropriate object)." [21]

The Sūtras themselves are very categorical about the rôle of perception in the process of acquiring knowledge. A decisive answer to the questions raised even by modern epistemological nihilists was given by Kapila. "Perception is that discernment which, being in conjunction (with the things perceived), portrays the forms thereof." [22]

It is held that the organs (external, that is, of perception, and internal, that is, of inference) are products of nature. They are not "depraved;" that is, they do not portray as real what is not real. Therefore, whatever is established on their evidence is real. Since the organs bear testimony to the existence of the external world, the reality of the external world is established.

The Upaniṣads themselves record not merely strands of rationalist, naturalist, and agnostic thought, but also out and out atheism and materialism. At least one of the eighteen main books [23] is entirely devoted to an exposition of rationalist and naturalist thinking and to the most outspoken heretical views. It denies the existence of God as well as of soul; it holds that nothing but matter exists, and that there is no other world beyond this world. Its thesis can be summarised as follows:

There is no incarnation, no God, no heaven, no hell; all traditional religious literature is the work of conceited fools; nature, the originator, and time, the destroyer, are the rulers of things and take no account of virtue or vice in awarding happiness or misery to men; people deluded by flowery speeches cling to God's temples and priests when, in reality, there is no difference between Visnu and a god.[24]

The origin of the naturalist and sceptic thought, developed in some of the major Upaniṣads, can, indeed, even be traced in the Ṛg Veda; for instance, the Creation Hymn which concludes the dialogue between the parents of mankind—the twin brother and sister, Yama and Yami.

---

[21] *Bhikshuvaṣya*, Book I.
[22] *Sāṁkhya-Sūtra*, Book I.
[23] Viz., the *Swasanved Upaniṣad*.
[24] *Vide* the *Swasanved Upaniṣad*, Sūtra II.

There are Vedic hymns which refer to heretics and unbelievers. They evidently were the pioneers of the revolt against natural religion and as such were the forefathers of Indian philosophy. In other words, in India as elsewhere, the first attempts of the human intellect to explain nature in natural terms gave birth to philosophy.

The Vedas and the early *Upaniṣads* refer to the *Swahāvabadins* (naturalists) and their doctrines. They disputed the reality of the gods of natural religion and scoffed at the pretensions of the priests. From the scant references made only to refute them it can be inferred that those early pioneers of Indian philosophy were empiricists; they held that perception was the only source of knowledge as well as the only reliable evidence. They were, therefore, called *darśaniks,* and the term subsequently came to mean philosopher. The Sanskrit word *darśana* means perception (insight).

The authorship of the *lokāyata darśana,* the earliest Indian philosophy, is traditionally ascribed to Bṛhaspati, the legendary preceptor of the gods. The legend indicates that in the olden days the naturalist rebels against blind faith and orthodoxy were held in high esteem. The fact that Bṛhaspati has gone down in history as the founder of the Chārvaka system developed in a later period proves that, until the fall of Buddhism—that is, for more than a thousand years—, materialism was a continuous current of thought in ancient India. The fundamental principles of the *lokāyata darśana* (Indian materialism), as it developed over this long period, were recorded as follows by Kṛṣṇa Misra, who was a younger contemporary of Buddha:

"In it only perceptual evidence is authority. The elements are earth, water, fire, and air. Wealth and enjoyment are the objects of human existence. Matter can think. There is no other world. Death is the end of all." [25]

The long process of the development of naturalist, rationalist, sceptic, agnostic, and materialist thought in ancient India found its culmination in the Chārvaka system of philosophy, which can be compared with Greek Epicureanism, and as such is to be appreciated as the positive outcome of the intellectual culture of ancient India. The greatest of the *Paribrajaks* mentioned in the earliest Buddhist literature, those Sophists and Stoics of ancient India, was Bṛhaspati. His name occurs in ancient Indian literature frequently

[25] Quoted by Dr. D. R. Shastri in his *Indian Materialism.*

in various connections over a period of many hundred years, during which naturalist, rationalist, and materialist thought developed
and wielded considerable influence. Bṛhaspati is mentioned as the
founder of *Swabhāvabad* and *Lokāyata*, and he was also the founder
of the Chārvaka system—Indian Epicureanism. The Bṛhaspati
Sūtras are referred to frequently in contemporary Buddhist and
Brahmanical texts. But only some remnants of the Sūtras survived
the downfall of Buddhism. From them we learn that Bṛhaspati
condemned Brahmins as "men devoid of intellect and manliness,
who uphold the authority of the Vedas because they yield them
the means of a comfortable livelihood." [26]

The Chārvaks laughed at the notion that the Vedas were divinely
revealed truth; they held that truth can never be known except
through the senses. Therefore, the idea of a soul is a delusion. The
Chārvaks thus anticipated the modern philosophical trend of ultra-
empiricism. They held that even reason was not to be trusted,
because every inference depended for its validity not merely on
accurate observation and correct reasoning, but also upon the
assumption that the future would behave like the past; and of
this there was no certainty. That was anticipating modern agnosticism more than two thousand years before Hume. But the Chārvaks
were not mere nihilists, agnostics, or sceptics. They developed an
elaborate system of positive philosophical thought.

All phenomena are natural. Neither in experience nor in history do
we find any interposition of supernatural forces. Matter is the only
reality: the mind is matter thinking. The hypothesis of a creator is useless for explaining or understanding the world. Men think religion
necessary only because, being accustomed to it, they feel a sense of loss
and an uncomfortable void when the growth of knowledge destroys
faith. Morality is natural; it is a social convention and convenience, not
a divine command. There is no need to control instincts and emotions;
they are commands of nature. The purpose of life is to live; and the
only wisdom is happiness.[27]

The rationalist, materialist, and naturalistic teachings of
Kaṇāda, Kapila, Gautama, Mahabir, Chārvak, and others were
ultimately buried under the ruins of the Buddhist revolution.
Brahmanical reaction, reasserting itself in the scholasticism of
Śaṁkaracharya, choked all spiritual progress so successfully that a
renaissance of the liberating thought of antiquity was delayed until
it was too late. General prostration and stagnation precluded the

[26] *Bṛhaspati Sūtras.*
[27] Quoted by Dr. D. R. Shastri in his *Indian Materialism.*

rise of new social forces corresponding to those which rescued Europe from the darkness of the pious and spiritual Middle Ages. India remained spiritual because, owing to historical reasons, she was deprived of the blessings of modern science. Her spiritualism is the badge of social backwardness, which brought her people slavery, degradation, and degeneration.

What is preached by Radhakrishnan as the orthodox Hindu philosophy represents the intellectual reaction which followed the fall of Buddhism and was galvanised by a social stagnation lasting for the centuries of the Indian Middle Ages.

M. N. ROY

INDIAN RENAISSANCE INSTITUTE
DEHRA DUN, INDIA

17

T. R. V. Murti

RADHAKRISHNAN AND BUDDHISM

17

RADHAKRISHNAN AND BUDDHISM

I. Radhakrishnan's Approach to Buddhism

OF ALL the significant services rendered by Radhakrishnan to our understanding of Indian philosophy his interpretation of Buddhist thought is by no means the least. His appreciation of the importance of the subject is evinced by his devoting approximately half of the first volume of his *Indian Philosophy* to Buddhism. First published in 1923 and revised subsequently in 1929, this is Radhakrishnan's basic work on the subject. He returns to the topic whenever he has an opportunity to do so.[1] When invited to deliver the British Academy Lecture, under the Henriette Hertz Trust, on a Master Mind, he chose—not Śaṁkara or Rāmānuja, but Gautama the Buddha. For,

In Gautama the Buddha we have a master mind from the East second to none so far as the influence on the thought and life of the human race is concerned, and sacred to all as the founder of a religious tradition whose hold is hardly less wide and deep than any other.[2]

He approaches the subject in the best traditions of Hinduism:

Though a Hindu by religion, I have the highest respect for the great Gautama and the attractiveness of his message. This attitude of reverence for the majesty and winsomeness of Buddha's personality is the normal one for the intellectuals of India. . . . His influence on India's thought and religion has been profound and latterly very much on the increase.[3]

Buddhist studies are still far from complete or adequate. The fact that no large additions or drastic modifications are called for

---

[1] In 1933 Radhakrishnan inaugurated the Don Alphina Ratnayaka Trust Lectureship, in Colombo, Ceylon, with his discourse on "The Teaching of Buddha." (Reference to this work will hereafter be abbreviated: TB.) And, on the invitation of the Chinese Government in 1944, Radhakrishnan delivered a series of lectures on Buddhism and Hinduism in various university centres in China.

[2] GB, 1. [3] TB, 2.

in Radhakrishnan's exposition and appraisal of Buddhism is
sufficient proof of the abiding value of his work in this field. He
has created, in Indian universities, a lively interest in Buddhist
studies and has guided research work on comparative and critical
studies of Buddhist systems. The writer of this essay owes a great
debt to Professor Radhakrishnan for his inestimable help and
advice in his study of the Mādhyamika philosophy.[4]

There are admitted difficulties in Buddhistic studies. For one
thing, their vastness is frightening. An extensive literature, canon-
ical, exegetical, and systematic, covering a period of more than
fifteen centuries, is scattered in a score of languages, Pali, Sanskrit,
Chinese, Tibetan, and several Mongolian languages. Its complexity is equally formidable; the schools and sub-schools are bewildering in their number and in the twists and turns of their
thought. The greatest difficulty, however, is caused by the absence
of a continued tradition which might set aright many an incorrect
interpretation. For a considerable time to come, therefore, our
knowledge of Buddhism is bound to be tentative and patchy. In
spite of these discouraging factors, it is the duty of the historian
of philosophy to reconstruct and relive the past. Radhakrishnan's
basic approach to Buddhism, as to any other philosophy, is that of
a constructive philosopher. He enunciates this in his *Indian
Philosophy:* "The historian of philosophy must approach his task,
not as a mere philologist or even as a scholar, but as a philosopher
who uses his scholarship as an instrument to wrest from words the
thoughts that underlie them." [5] I find myself in complete agreement with this mode of approach.

It is not possible, nor even desirable, to go over the ground covered by Radhakrishnan in such masterly fashion. I propose confining myself to indicating Radhakrishnan's standpoint on some
important problems connected with Buddhism and to showing how
far one might accept his lead.

The first question to claim our attention is the relation (not
merely historical) of orthodox Hindu (Brāhmanical) thought to
Buddha and Buddhism. Secondly, we may consider the development of the several Schools belonging to Hīnayāna and Mahāyāna
Buddhism. An allied question is their relation and logical affinity
to the corresponding Brāhmanical systems. The peculiar feature
of Buddhism as a religion requires consideration in order to bring

---

[4] This will shortly be published under the title, *The Central Philosophy of
Buddhism*, by George Allen & Unwin, London.
[5] Ind P, I, 671.

out its distinction from Brāhmanism. Lastly, the spread and disappearance of Buddhism from the land of its birth is to be
accounted for. In the absence of an adequate explanation this
might remain a puzzling phenomenon.
These problems do not exhaust the questions which call for
interpretation or information. Purely literary and linguistic questions have, of course, no place here. It would also be fascinating to
trace the spread of Buddhism outside India, in Ceylon, Burma,
China, Tibet, etc. But this topic properly belongs to the history
of religions. Biographical and chronological details are not considered here. Our knowledge in these matters is still largely
conjectural, and for a philosophical understanding of Buddhism
they are not essential.
The main feature of Radhakrishnan's treatment lies in the fact
that he fully demonstrates the unity and affinity of Buddhism with
Brāhmanism. This is indeed the case; for, Buddhism has to be
understood as a growth or modification of Hinduism. Both belong
to the same genus. It is also, however, necessary to establish their
specific differences. Radhakrishnan does not, it appears to me,
sufficiently emphasize their differences; in fact, he even tends to
minimise them. This is evident especially in his treatment of the
relation between the *Upaniṣads* and Buddha and to a certain extent
also between the absolutisms of Mādhyamika, Yogācāra, and
Advaita Vedānta. The view suggested here is that, although their
generic identity is undeniable, the specific differences are equally
undeniable. This seems to me essential for a balanced appraisal of
Indian philosophical systems.

II. Buddha and Upaniṣads

What is the distinctive nature of Buddha's teaching? Is it the
same as that of the *Upaniṣads*? [6]
All our accounts agree that Buddha taught the Four Holy
Truths: the Truth of suffering, its Cause, its Cessation, and the
Path leading to its Cessation. For him all empirical existence is
pain, and no being is exempt from the Law of Karma. "Birth is
sorrow. Decay is sorrow. Sickness is sorrow. Death is sorrow. . . .
To be conjoined to things which we dislike, to be separated from
things which we like—that also is sorrow." [7] Sorrow is not un-

[6] Radhakrishnan deals with this topic in his Ind P, I, 360ff, 676ff; GB, 28ff;
and TB.
[7] GB, 16.

caused or self-caused; for in either case it could not be removed. Buddha rejected all philosophies that were inconsistent with the possibility of Freedom from Suffering and with the endeavour towards such freedom. He was therefore not only opposed to materialism or nihilism, which advocated the fortuitous origin of things and denied the existence of the Soul apart from the body, but also to those conceptions which took the Soul as a permanent substantial existence impervious to change. Discarding these as the two principal extreme and false views, Buddha taught the Dharma (Law) from the—so-called—Middle position. An unchanging eternal soul is a stumbling block to our spiritual life; in that case we would be neither the worse nor the better for our efforts. This would lead to inaction and stagnation. Nay more; the ātman is the root-cause of all attachment, desire, aversion, and pain. When we take anything as a self, as a substantial and permanent entity, we become attached to it and dislike other things which are opposed to it. Substance-view is ignorance *par excellence,* and from it proceed all passions. Denial of ātman or Substance is the very pivot of Buddhist metaphysics, as it is of its doctrine of salvation. The oft-recurring strain in the Pali Canons is that things are transitory: "How transient are all component things; growth is their nature and decay. They are produced; they are dissolved again; to bring them all into subjection that is bliss." [8]

Buddha formulated the Holy Eightfold Path for purifying the mind of passions, anger, lust, craving, and aversion, and to enable it to perceive the Truth. Buddhist spiritual discipline has always been of the three-tier type—Virtues, Concentration of Mind, and Wisdom. It repudiated the mechanical performance of ritual and sacrifice as meaningless. There is no appeal to extraneous inducements, reward or punishment; there is no invocation to God. The entire discipline is a severe form of self-culture, directed towards the elimination of all craving, of all clinging to the 'I' and the 'Mine.' Insight into the nature of the Real as anātman (substanceless) is the final stage of the path of purity. On the attainment of this enlightenment (bodhi) one becomes an Arhat (Saint); this itself is Nirvāṇa. Final Release (Parinirvāṇa) follows on the cessation of the aggregates of mind and body-functions which constitute the stream of individual life.

Though real, the state of Nirvāṇa is inexpressible. "There is the not-born, the not-become, the not-created, the not-compounded . . . If there were not this not-born, . . . there could be no escape

---

[8] *Mahāparinibbāna Sutta,* vi, 10.

from this world of compounded things." [9] It is even spoken of in more positive terms as "a reality beyond all suffering and change, as unfading, still, undecaying, taintless, as peace and blissful. It is an island, the shelter, refuge and the goal." [10] We are expressly forbidden to consider Nirvāṇa—the state of the Tathāgata (The Perfect One) after death—as annihilation. It is one of the four sets of questions declared inexpressible by the Lord. The earlier schools, however, tended to conceive Nirvāṇa negatively as a state of extinction comparable to the blowing out of a lamp. In the Mahāyāna Schools (Mādhyamika and Yogācāra) it was taken as the underlying ground identical with the phenomenal world in essence. This latter conception is probably in greater accord with Buddha's real teaching.

It is also on record that Buddha affected silence when questions of a metaphysical nature were asked; he declared them inexpressible. They are invariably enumerated as fourteen and always practically in the same order. Actually, there are four sets of questions, three of which have four alternatives each, whereas the last one concerning the soul has only two. The questions are: whether the world is eternal, or not, or both, or neither; whether the world is finite (in space), or not, or both or neither; whether the Tathāgata exists after death, or does not, or both, or neither; whether the soul is identical with the body, or different from it. For a correct understanding of Buddha and Buddhism it is essential to have a proper appraisal of this 'silence.'

Such in brief outline is the teaching of Buddha as it can be gathered from the earliest works, the Pali and Sanskrit Canons. It is difficult to decide how much of it could be attributed to Buddha himself and how much to later accretion. This topic has proved a fruitful field for scholars on which to exercise their ingenuity. Did Buddha accept the *Upaniṣadic* (ātma) tradition?; and, if so, to what extent?

Some Orientalists, like Mrs. Rhys Davids, try to discover a simple 'soul-affirming' primitive teaching of the Master as distinguished from the 'soul-denying' later scholasticism and monkish elaboration. Others, like Poussin, Beck, etc., aver that Yōga and practice of virtue, without any metaphysic, formed the original teaching of Buddha. Many consider him even as an agnostic and take the 'silence' as decisive in this regard.

It is no doubt true that Buddha and Buddhist schools paid great attention to the practice of virtue and concentration of mind. They

[9] *Udāna*, viii, 3.   [10] *Saṁyutta Nikāya*, IV, 368ff.

brought to light deeper and subtler distinctions, and gave us a minute map of the entire terrain of our inner life. However, there is nothing peculiarly Buddhistic about this. We have all the ingredients, if not the detailed prescriptions as well, of a moral code in the Śikṣāvallī of the *Taittirīya Upaniṣad* and similar texts. Yoga-practice was much older than Buddhism. Buddha himself was taught Yoga, all our accounts agree, by two Sāmkhya teachers, Āḷāra Kālāma and Uddaka Rāmaputta. It is an accepted tenet of Indian Philosophical systems that an impure and distracted mind is incapable of perceiving the truth. To reduce Buddhism to a technique of mind-concentration or a code of morals amounts to a failure to appreciate the individuality of Buddha's genius and his metaphysical insight. It is the failure to discern that even a way of life implies a view of reality.

Radhakrishnan interprets Buddha as accepting the *Upaniṣadic* tradition. He bases this interpretation on the following grounds. Buddha cannot be understood except in the historical setting of his age. "Great men are as much the creatures as the creators of their era." [11]

Those who tell us that for the Buddha there is religious experience but there is no religious object are violating the texts and needlessly convicting him of self-contradiction. He implies the reality of what the *Upaniṣads* call Brahman, though he takes the liberty of giving it another name, *dharma,* to indicate its essentially ethical value for us on the empirical plane. The way of the Dharma is the way of the Brahman.[12]

And when the Buddha asks whether anything which is changeable and perishable can be called the self he implies that there is somewhere such a self. . . . When the Buddha asks us to have the self as our light (attadīpa), the self as our refuge (attasaraṇa), surely he is referring not to the transitory constituents but the universal spirit in us.[13]

As a matter of fact, nowhere did Buddha repudiate the *Upaniṣad* conception of Brahman, the absolute. In the *Kathāvatthu,* where different controversial points are discussed, there is no reference to the question of the reality of an immutable being. All this indicates, if anything, Buddha's acceptance of the *Upaniṣad* position.[14]

The 'silence' of Buddha unmistakably implies a Transcendent Reality as the foundation of all phenomena. Radhakrishnan rightly rejects the agnostic and the nihilistic interpretations of the silence. Moreover, it is not true that Buddha's attitude was merely suspen-

---

[11] TB, 4.   [12] *Saṁyutta Nikāya*, i, 141; GB, 49.
[13] *Ibid.,* 51.   [14] Ind P, I, 682.

sion of judgment and that he was awaiting a more favourable opportunity to publish the truth. He tells us expressly that he has taught the truth without reservation and without any distinction of the exotic and the esoteric; unlike a tight-fisted teacher, he had kept back nothing. Nor is Buddha's silence ignorance of metaphysics. He was not only conversant with the philosophical speculations of the time, but was himself a metaphysician of no mean order. By his penetrative analysis he had reached a position which transcended and annulled the dogmatic procedure of Reason. His rejection of speculative metaphysics was deliberate and sustained. Criticism itself is philosophy for him. Radhakrishnan unerringly indicates the nature of Buddha's silence: "If the Buddha declined to define the nature of the Absolute or if he contented himself with negative definitions, it is only to indicate that absolute being is above all determination." [15]

Why, then, did Buddha not admit in express terms the reality of the absolute? Buddha refused to describe the absolute, for that would be to take a step out of the world of relativity, the legitimacy of which he was the first to question in others. The absolute is not a matter of empirical observation. The world of experience does not reveal the absolute anywhere within its limits.[16]

This correctly represents the Mādhyamika standpoint, which is the real heart of Buddhism. All that I would like to add to this analysis is that Buddha's implicit acceptance of a Transcendent Reality does not mean that he accepted the *Upaniṣadic* tradition, for nowhere does he identify it with the ātman. For, ātman must mean a permanent substance.

On the other hand, we have to state that Buddha and Buddhism can be understood only as a revolt not merely against the cant and hollowness of ritualism—the *Upaniṣads* themselves voice this unmistakably—but against the ātman-ideology, the metaphysics of the Substance-view. Buddha nowhere acknowledges his indebtedness to the *Upaniṣads* or to any other teacher for his characteristic philosophical standpoint. Though reference is made several times to Brahmā, the deity, Brahman is never referred to. On the contrary, Buddha always speaks as one initiating a new tradition, as opening up a path never trod before. In the *Brahmajāla*, the *Sāmaññaphala Suttas* and elsewhere, current philosophical speculations are reviewed, and all of them are rejected as dogmatic and as inconsistent with the spiritual life. This is not the way of one

---

[15] GB, 59. [16] Ind P, I, 682f.

who continues an older tradition. If the ātman had been a cardinal doctrine with Buddhism, why was it hidden under a bushel so that even the immediate followers of the Master had no inkling of it? The *Upaniṣads,* on the other hand, blazen forth the reality of the ātman in almost every line.

Passages must not be counted, but weighed.[17] We must consider the entire body of texts together and evolve a synthesis, weighing all considerations. We require a synoptic interpretation of the Buddhist scriptures. It is necessary to make a doctrinal analysis of the contents and to assess their value philosophically.

Nothing is gained by the theory of a soul-affirming primitive Buddhism followed by a soul-denying scholastic Buddhism. Even if,—what is impossible—it could be proved that the historical person—Gautama the Buddha—did teach a soul doctrine, fundamentally at variance with the doctrines we associate with classical Buddhism, we should still have to explain Buddhism and to relate it to the *Upaniṣadic* tradition. Excluding Buddha from the charge of preaching the denial of the ātman might save *him* from any 'guilt.' But the question is not a personal one. We should merely have added one more problem: in the act of bridging the difference between the *Upaniṣads* and Buddha, we would have increased the distance between Buddha and Buddhism immeasurably. We can-

---

[17] Radhakrishnan quotes the *Mahāparinibbāna* passage "attadīpa attasaraṇa" and translates it: "Be ye as those who have the self as their light. Be ye as those who have the self as their refuge. Betake yourselves to no external refuge. Hold fast to the truth as to a refuge." (GB, 11). This interpretation is not borne out by the context. There was no doctrinal discussion of the soul or the self. Buddha was telling Ānanda that he had become old, eighty years of age, and that he had taught all that he knew without reservation and that he did not hold anything up his sleeve like a "tight-fisted teacher." Therefore, the Order should do well without him. "Ānanda, be a lamp unto yourself, be a refuge unto yourself; seek not any outside help (anañña-saraṇa) in this matter." To treat this passage as inculcating a metaphysical tenet about the self is not warranted by the context. Radhakrishnan himself translates it elsewhere (Ind P, I, 428) in the usual way as: "Be ye lamps unto yourselves; be ye a refuge to yourselves." The *Dhammapada* text: "attāhi attano nātha" and similar ones admit of the interpretation that the empirical reality of the self as a doer and enjoyer of the consequences is accepted. The Mādhyamika teachers have made commendable efforts to reconcile these texts. According to Nāgārjuna, Buddha has affirmed the existence of the ātman against the materialist; for there is the continuity of Karma and its result, act and its responsibility; he has denied it as against the eternalist who takes it as an immutable identical essence; he has also said, from the ultimate (paramārtha) standpoint, that there is neither the self nor the not-self. Buddha, like a skilful physician, always graduated his teaching according to the need and the capacity of the taught. Radhakrishnan himself makes pointed reference to this interpretation in his Ind P, I, 389. Much cannot be built on the use of such terms as 'brahmacariya,' 'brahmapada' and 'brahmavihāra,' for they connote purity, blessed state and serenity; they have lost all implications of a Brahman (ātman) metaphysics.

not find any sufficient or compelling motives for the alleged distortion of the original teaching. Either the monks were too stupid to grasp the master's basic teaching, or they were too clever and fabricated and foisted on him an opposite doctrine. Neither of these alternatives can seriously be entertained. Why and when precisely the falsification is supposed to have occurred is not specified. *Prima facie,* those systems and schools of thought which owe allegiance to the founder of this religion have a prior and greater claim to represent and understand Buddhism than the moderns who are removed from him by centuries of time as well as by distance of culture and outlook.

The entire development of Buddhist philosophy and religion is proof of the correctness of the anātman-interpretation of Buddhism. There is no Buddhist school of thought that did not deny the ātman; and it is equally true that there is no Brāhmanical or Jaina system which did not accept the ātman in some form or other. It may be objected that the ātman which the Buddhists deny is the material self identified with the body or with the particular mental states, and that such denial does not touch the position of the Vedānta or the Sāṁkhya. But Buddhism never did accept the reality of the ātman, of a permanent substantial entity impervious to change. The Real for Buddhism is Becoming. And any species of the ātman-view must take it as a changeless identical substance. The Buddhist schools differed among themselves to a great degree; but at least one thing they have in common—the denial of any permanent substance (ātman). It is a mistake to think that the Mahāyāna schools reversed the denial of the ātman and re-affirmed its reality. If anything, they are more thorough in carrying out the anātman-doctrine. They deny not only substance (pudgala-nairātmya), but extend the denial to the Elements too (dharma-nairātmya), which the Hīnayāna schools had uncritically accepted as real.

The Buddhists are not the only ones to take their philosophy as a 'no-soul doctrine.' Jaina and Brāhmanical systems too invariably characterise Buddhism as denying the ātman (substance or soul). The modern exponent may not feel committed to the estimate of Buddhism by Buddhists and others. But he is required to pause and explain the unanimity with which Buddhism has been taken as a 'no-soul doctrine.' He is also required to consider the teachings of Buddha in relation to Buddhist schools of thought, which *prima facie* have the right to be considered as embodying the founder's tenets. This problem is at least as important as relating Buddha to the *Upaniṣads*.

A possible objection to the view that Buddha denied the soul might be that it may seem contradictory to his other doctrines accepted as basic, such as the efficacy of Karma, of the adoption of spiritual life and the attainment of Nirvāṇa, and of the doctrine of rebirth. Karma without a permanent agent who wills and reaps the fruit of his action seems inconceivable. And, what is the value of spiritual life if there is none at the end of it? Buddha's doctrine would be the acceptance of pain without *any one who* feels it, a spiritual discipline without any person who undertakes it, and a final release (nirvāṇa) without any being to enjoy it. Such an absurdity, it might be said, could not have been seriously meant by Buddha.

But, Buddha himself was fully aware of these alleged absurdities. He *replaced* the soul by the theory of a mind-continuum, with the psychical states rigorously conditioned as to their nature by the causal law governing them. According to him this alone provides for progress (change, efficacy) and continuity (responsibility), in as much as each succeeding state (good or bad) is the result of the previous state. Thus it avoids, on the one hand, the futility of Karma, which is an inescapable predicament of the acceptance of a permanent soul, and nihilism which follows from the non-acceptance of continuity, on the other. Rebirth does not mean the bodily transportation of an individual essence from one place to another. It only means that a new series of states arises, conditioned by the previous states. Memory and recognition are also similarly explained. If there are difficulties on the Buddhist hypothesis, the difficulties on the other hypotheses are equally formidable.

In every aspect of things we find two opposing standpoints. In causation, we may emphasise the emergence of the effect as something new and different, or we may emphasise its necessary connection and continuity with the cause. In any presented object, we may attend to the particular and the changing, or to the universal and the abiding feature. The latter may be termed the static or space-view of things and the former the dynamic or the time-pattern. On the first view, change and difference may be taken as appearance; on the second, the permanent and the universal will be appearance. One emphasises unity, the other difference. What is real for one is appearance for the other and *vice versa*. The Buddhist and the Brāhmanical schools each evolved a coherent metaphysic and epistemology in consonance with their respective standpoints. It is not contended that Buddha himself formulated the anātman-doctrine in systematic form, with all its implications fully worked out. It is, however, suggested that he gave the inspiration and the impetus to the anātman-view, which came to be formulated in such sharp contrast to the ātman-view. That there are insuperable difficulties on either conception of the real, on any conceptual pattern, no one realised perhaps more strongly than did Buddha. He was thus led to discredit all attempts at *conceiving* reality, and in consequence to reject all speculative metaphysics. This is the real meaning of his 'silence.' To this conclusion he would have been led because two or more opposed points of view were tried and found unsatisfactory. If the ātman-tradition alone had held the field, Buddha could not have arrived at his characteristic 'no-metaphysics' position. The systematic form of this 'silence' is the Mādhyamika system. This system could arise only after the two traditions had developed sufficiently to make it possible for the conflict between them to be appreciated in all its intensity and universality. That alone could engender the dialectical consciousness.

Indian philosophy must be interpreted as the flow of these two vital streams of thought—one having its source in the ātman-doctrine of the *Upaniṣads* and the other in the anātman-doctrine of Buddha. Each branched off into several sub-streams with a right and a left wing and several intermediary positions. There were lively sallies and skirmishes between them, but no commingling or synthesis of the two traditions. One took Being as real, the other Becoming; for the former substance typified the real, for the latter the modes. In their extreme form, the former denied the reality of Becoming, the latter that of Being.

The relation of Buddha to the *Upaniṣads* may be stated thus. For both, phenomenal existence is imperfection and pain; they are also one in placing before us the ideal of state which is beyond the possibility of pain and bondage. The *Upaniṣads* speak of it more positively as a state of consciousness and bliss; Buddha emphasises the negative aspect of it: nirvāṇa is the annihilation of sorrow. Both have to speak of the ultimate as devoid of empirical determinations, as incomparable to anything we know: silence is their most proper language. They also agree that no empirical means,—organisational device, sacrifice or penance,—can be of any avail: Only insight into the nature of the real can take us to the goal. For the *Upaniṣads,* the ātman is real; its identification with the body, with the mental states, or with any other empirical object is accidental. Only by negating the wrong identification, its unreal limitations, can we know its real nature; ātman is brahman; it is all that is. No fear, aversion, or attachment could afflict it. Buddha reaches this very goal of desirelessness, not by the universalisation of the 'I' (ātman), but by denying it altogether. For, only as we consider anything as permanent and pleasant, i.e., take it as a self, do we get attached to it and are averse to things that are opposed to it. The ātman is the root-cause of all passions; and this notion has to be rooted out completely to attain Nirvāṇa. For Buddha, then, the self is a primary wrong notion. Buddha does not speak of the knowledge of any specific entity as the saving knowledge. For him the awareness of the nature of pain and its cause is itself the knowledge which sets man free. Times without number we are told that the Tathāgata knows what is pain, how it arises and how it ceases. This can mean that for him the saving knowledge is the self-conscious awareness of the world-process; to realise the inexorability of the Causal Law is to stand aside from it. "Freedom is the knowledge of Necessity." Again, the *Upaniṣads* appear to start with an intuitive or extra-philosophical knowledge of Brahman and then lead the disciple to that knowledge by arguments and analogies. They are not aware, except in a vague form, of the conflict in Reason; theirs is not a dialectical approach. Buddha, on the other hand, is more rational in his procedure. Buddha ascends from the Conflict of Reason to the inexpressibility of the absolute. Both reach the same goal of final release, but by different means. The spiritual genius of Buddha carved out a new path, the negative path.

I am happy to find that there are observations in Radhakrishnan's writings which indicate the difference between Buddha and the *Upaniṣads:* "If there is a difference between the teaching of the *Upaniṣads* and the Buddha, it is not in their views of the world of experience (saṁsāra) but in regard to their conception of reality (nirvāṇa)." [18]

The fundamental difference between Buddhism and the *Upaniṣads* seems to be about the metaphysical reality of an immutable substance, which is the true self of man as well. . . . It is true that Buddha finds no centre of reality or principle of permanence in the flux of life and the whirl of the world, but it does not follow that there is nothing real in the world at all except the agitation of forces.[19]

[18] GB, 33.   [19] Ind P, I, 375.

Is not a *fundamental metaphysical difference* the source of all other differences? If Buddhism is "only a restatement of the thought of the *Upaniṣads* with a new emphasis,"[20] it is desirable to emphasise this 'emphasis,' especially because it is of a fundamentally metaphysical nature. The *Upaniṣads* and Buddhism belong to the same spiritual genus; they differ as species; and the differentia are the acceptance or rejection of the ātman (permanent substance).

III. DEVELOPMENT OF THE SCHOOLS

Nowhere is our knowledge of Buddhism more deficient than in the emergence and growth of the schools. Of most of the early ones we know next to nothing, and the little that we know is not very intelligible. Early Buddhist historians like Vasumitra, Vinītadeva and Bhavya speak of 18 different Schools, all rightly claiming to embody the true teaching of the Master. Of these, only four main schools deserve consideration: Sthaviravāda (Theravāda), Sarvāstivāda, Mahāsamghika, and Sāmmitīya; others are off-shoots of these. The differences began to manifest themselves soon after the death of Buddha, and the first recorded division of the Buddhist Order occurred at the Council of Vaiśāli. The rise of the schools is proof that the teaching of Buddha was sufficiently rich and pregnant with metaphysical possibilities, but was not sufficiently definite. The basic teaching, its anātmavāda (denial of substance), is differently interpreted by the different schools. As Radhakrishnan says:

Philosophy is a natural necessity of the human mind and even the Buddha did not succeed in compelling his hearers to adopt an attitude of suspended judgment on the ultimate questions. In the absence of definite guidance from the teacher, different metaphysical systems were fastened on him early in the career of Buddhism.[21]

I venture to think that the correct approach is to consider Buddhism as a *matrix of systems,* rather than as one unitary system. It does not exclude legitimate different formulations. The attempt to treat Buddhism as one unitary system is a species of over-simplification and engenders a partisan spirit in writers; they begin taking sides with one or the other school of Hīnayāna and Mahāyāna, and consider *that* as *the* teaching of the Buddha. Such procedure prevents a correct understanding of the development of Buddhist philosophy. It would be less fallacious to consider Bud-

[20] *Ibid.,* 676.   [21] GB, 64.

dhism as a critical tendency or direction rather than as a finished system.

Each of the systems of Hindu thought (Sāṁkhya, Yoga, Nyāya, Vaiśeṣika, Vedānta and Mīmāṁsā) is treated by Radhakrishnan with sufficient thoroughness and definiteness in separate chapters of his *Indian Philosophy*. We should naturally expect the same thoroughness with regard to at least the four classical schools of Buddhism: Vaibhāṣika (Sarvāstivāda), Sautrāntika, Mādhyamika and Yogācāra (Vijñānavāda). This is, however, not the case. The reason for this is two-fold. Paucity of material is still a great handicap: many of the basic works of some of the systems are not available either in the original language or in translation; although important works are being published from time to time. It would, therefore, be necessary to revise one's exposition and evaluation of the systems with the constantly increasing addition to our knowledge.[22] It is also incumbent upon one to make a determined and consistent effort to understand the Buddhist systems from their own inherent and internal standpoint, instead of looking at them through the eyes of the Nyāya-Vaiśeṣika or the Vedānta. They should not be considered as halting approximations to the Advaita Vedānta. I may, possibly, be wrong, but one gets the impression that Radhakrishnan evaluates every system of philosophy, including schools of Buddhism, in terms of the Advaita Vedānta of Śaṁkara. This is understandable since the Advaitism of Śaṁkara represents a very consistent and complete form of Absolutism; and absolutism, some (among them Radhakrishnan) would maintain, is the end of all philosophy. I should like to state that the Mādhyamika, and the Vijñānavāda too, are equally commendable attempts, though from a different approach. A necessary implication of this is that philosophical differences are ultimate and are, therefore, perhaps incommensurable. Refutation and criticism, indulged in by systems of philosophy, ostensibly in order to annul differences and to unify the systems, only serve to distinguish and differentiate them.

There were three principal turning-points in the history of Bud-

[22] Since the publication of *Indian Philosophy* (vol. i) in 1923 and its revision in 1929 the following are some of the important original works that have been made available: *Tattva-Saṁgraha*, (2 vols.), *Adhidharmakośavyākhyā* of Yaśomitra (complete Tokyo Edn.), *Catuḥśataka* of Āryadeva, *Madhyamakāvatāra Candrakīrti* (in part), *Abhisamayālaṁkārāloka* of Haribhadra, *Madhyāntavibhāgaṭīkā* of Sthiramati (Nagoya Edn.) *PramāṇaVārttika, Hetubinduṭīkā* and *Vādanyāya* of Dharmakīrti. Some other works like Nāgārjuna's *Mahāprajñāpāramitā Śāstra* and Asaṅga's *Mahāyānasaṁgraha* etc., are available in French translation.

dhism. The earlier realistic and pluralistic phase, comprising the Hīnayāna Schools: Theravāda and the Vaibhāṣika (Sarvāstivāda). This can be called the Ābhidharmika Philosophy. The Sautrāntika, as a critical realism, is a partial modification of this earlier dogmatic realism. The middle phase is the dialectical absolutism of the Mādhyamika system founded by Nāgārjuna and Ārya Deva (2nd cent. A.D.). The third is the idealism of the Yogācāra, systematised by Asanga and Vasubandhu (4th cent. A.D.) and continued by Dignāga and Dharmakīrti.

The *Śālistamba Sūtra* says: "Whosoever sees the Pratītyasamutpāda (Law of Dependent Origination) sees the Buddha and whosoever sees the Buddha sees the Dharma (Truth or Reality)." [23] Nāgārjuna expresses himself similarly: "One who perceives truly the Pratītyasamutpāda realises the Four Sacred Truths, Pain, its Cause, Cessation and the Path." [24] Buddhism has always been a Dharma-theory based on the Pratītyasamutpāda, and every Buddhist system has claimed to be the Middle Path. Pratītyasamutpāda has, however, received different interpretations at different times. The earlier Buddhism of the Ābhidharmika systems took it as denying the permanent ātman and at once establishing the reality of the separate elements. Pratītyasamutpāda is the causal law regulating the rise and subsidence of the several elements. The Middle Path is the steering clear of both, Eternalism (substance or soul) and Nihilism (denial of continuity). The Mādhyamika contends that this is not the correct interpretation of the doctrine. Pratītyasamutpāda is not the principle of temporal sequence, but of the essential dependence of things on each other, i.e., the unreality of separate elements. The entire Mādhyamika system is a re-interpretation of Pratītyasamutpāda. This is now equated with Śūnyatā— the empirical validity of entities and their ultimate unreality.[25] The Middle Path is the non-acceptance of the two extremes—the affirmative and the negative views—of all views. In the Vijñānavāda, Śūnyatā is accepted, but with a modification. The formula now is: That which appears (the substratum, i.e., consciousness) is real; the form of its appearance (the duality of subject and object) is unreal. The Middle Path is the avoidance of both, the dogmatism of Realism (acceptance of the reality of objects) and the Scepticism of Nihilism (the rejection of object and consciousness both as unreal).

23 *Śālistamba Sūtra*, opening passage.
24 *Mādhyamika Kārikās*, XXIV, 40.
25 *Mādhyamika Kārikās*, XXIV, 18.

The Sarvāstivāda is a radical pluralism erected on the denial of substance and the acceptance of discrete momentary dharmas. 'Dharma' is the ultimate factor or element of existence—a sense which the term has only in Buddhism. Dharmas are ultimate, as they are simple and not compounded of simpler entities. A thing (e.g., chair, tree, man) is an aggregate of these elements; the aggregate or the whole is not a reality, one more reality as in the Vaiśeṣika. The elements are impermanent: they are momentary and durationless. There is no inherence of one element in another, hence no substance apart from qualities; no matter beyond the separate sense-data, and no soul beyond the separate mental data (Dharma = Anātaman). . . . The Dharmas are classified and defined in the Abhidharma treatises, notably in the *Abhidharmakośa* of Vasubandhu. The Sarvāstivāda lists 75 dharmas in all, 72 conditioned phenomena and 3 unconditioned noumena.

According to the Abhidharma conception there is a real transformation of the unconditioned into the unconditioned noumenal state through the force of insight. Nirvāṇa is conceived almost as a state of negation or extinction of the phenomenal forces. This implies that Nirvāṇa and phenomena (Saṁsāra) are totally different. The Mādhyamika controverts these points.

The dogmatism of the Ābhidharmika, its tendency to hypostatise subjective notions and words into objective realities and especially its doctrine of the existence of the elements at all times, evoked criticism from other schools. The Sautrāntika, which discards the Ābhidharma works and bases itself on the direct discourses (Sūtras) of Buddha, represents the systematic form of this criticism.

The Sautrāntikas cut down the inflated list of dharmas drawn by the Vaibhāṣika. Not only did they reject the past and the future phases, but also Space, Nirvāṇa, and the non-mental forces. In the final analysis, a list of 43 elements was drawn up.

The real contribution of the Sautrāntika to the development of Indian thought is the discovery of the subjective—the transcendental function of the mind in constructing the empirical world. Dignāga (5th cent.) and Dharmakīrti (7th cent.) have formulated a rigorous and revolutionary logic and epistemology along Kantian lines. There are two modes of knowledge, immediate and mediate; they are mutually exclusive and exhaustive taken together. The function of the one is to *receive* or acquaint us with the given, and that of the other is to *think* it through concepts. Their respective objects are the particular and the universal; the particular alone is real; the universal is a thought-construction having merely conventional reality. Experience is the synthesis or identification of these two heterogeneous factors. Hindu writers invariably characterise the Sautrāntika as advocating that the external object is inferred, not directly perceived. This is not exactly correct. The essence of representationism is that we do not directly perceive objects, but are aware of our ideas only (the copies of things). The Sautrāntika emphatically asserts, however, that we are in direct contact with the real in perception. His doctrine only means that the subjective factor in knowledge is mistaken for the objective, the thing-in-itself. This mistake is not, however, empirical in origin. The Hindu misconception might have arisen from the fact that the Sautrāntika considers determinate perception as mental construction.

One would like a fuller treatment of the Sautrāntika logic and epistemology in a work of the dimensions of Radhakrishnan's *Indian Philosophy*. This is all the more desirable because the corresponding Nyāya epistemology has been treated with such thoroughness and because the Sautrāntika logic has played such a great part in deepening Indian Philosophy. Fortunately, Dharmakīrti's basic treatise, *Pramāṇavārttika,*—long thought lost in the original —has lately been discovered and published; we also have his shorter *Nyāyabindu* and *Hetubindu;* Stcherbatsky has made a notable contribution to the subject by his *Buddhist Logic*.

In the second phase of development there was a revolutionary change in Buddhism: from the earlier radical pluralism it became as radical an absolutism. The part played by some of the philosophical schools, notably the Sāmmitīyas and the Sautrāntikas, which proved to be a sort of transitional link, must be mentioned. Universally condemned as heretical by all other Buddhist schools, the Sāmmitīyas held tenaciously to their doctrine of the Individual (pudgalātman) as a quasi-permanent entity, neither completely identical with the mental states nor different from them. However halting this conception may have been, it is evidence of the inadequacy of a stream of elements to account for the basic facts of experience—memory, moral responsibility, spiritual life, etc. The theory of elements is discredited: the mental states cannot completely substitute the ātman: a permanent synthetic unity must be accepted. Of course, the Sāmmitīyas could not attain to the fully critical position of the Mādhyamikas, viz., that there are no states without the self, nor is there a self without states, and therefore both are unreal since they are relative. The Sautrāntika by his insistence on the creative work of thought directly led to the dialectic of the Mādhyamika and to the idealism of the Yogācāra. To the former it became clear that the subjective was much deeper and wider in scope. Not merely the categories of substance, but causality, change, being and non-being were equally subjective. The Yogācāra takes the constructivity of thought to prove that the object itself is a construction of thought. We have the Western parallel of the Fichtean and Hegelian idealistic criticism of the Kantian dualism of the thing-in-itself and the categories of thought. The other in thought (object) is itself a creation of consciousness; the dualism of subject and object presupposes a non-dual consciousness which alone is ultimately real.

Radhakrishnan gives a full and very sympathetic account of the Mādhyamika and Yogācāra absolutisms, especially of the former. His interpretation and evaluation of these two great systems shows his unerring understanding and insight. I shall undertake to point out some differences between these systems and the Advaita Vedānta.

The absolutism of the Mādhyamika is established by the dialectic. Dialectic is the consciousness of the interminable and total (antinomical) conflict in reason and resolution of the conflict by rising to a higher level of consciousness. In Hegel, the conflict is resolved by synthesising the opposites in a higher, more comprehensive, unity which is their identity. The Mādhyamika dialectic tries to remove the conflict by rejecting both the opposites, whether taken singly or in combination. The Mādhyamika is convinced that a conjunctive or a disjunctive synthesis of views (as in the Jaina theory of the Anekānta) is merely another view; it labours, therefore, under the same difficulties. Rejection of all views is the rejection of the competence of reason to comprehend reality. The Real is transcendent to thought. Views are not rejected on any positive grounds nor because another view is accepted. The rejection is based solely on the inner contradiction implicit in each view. Four alternatives are possible on any subject. The basic alternatives are two: Being and Non-Being, Affirmation and Negation. From these, two others are derived by affirming or denying both at once. It may be thought that while avoiding the two extremes, the Mādhyamika accepts a middle position between the two. No; he does not hold any third position; the middle position is really no position, since it is beyond concept or language. How does the Mādhyamika reject any and all views? He uses only one weapon. By drawing out the implications of any view he shows its inherent self-contradictory character. The dialectic is a series of *reductio ad absurdum* arguments. Every thesis is thus turned against itself; it is self-convicted, not counter-balanced. The Mādhyamika disproves the opponent's thesis, but he does not prove any *thesis* of his own. The principle of the dialectic is that the relative is unreal; mutual dependence is a mark of the unreal. Reason which understands things by way of distinction and relation is a principle of falsity, for it distorts and thereby hides the real. In causation, for instance, we must differentiate between the cause and the effect and at once identify them; the relation between them cannot be conceived as either identity or difference or both nor can we give it up. Nāgārjuna says: "Neither of those things is established (as real) which cannot be conceived as either identical with or different from each other." [26] The substance-view believes that it could have substance without attributes or modes (as in the Advaita Vedānta); the modal or anātman-view entertains the opposite belief, that it could dispense with substance altogether (as in the Ābhidharmika and Sautrāntika systems). There is, however, no attribute without substance nor any substance without attributes. They are not intelligible even together; for, we could not then distinguish them. There is no whole apart from the parts and *vice versa*. Things that derive their nature and being by mutual dependence are nothing in themselves, they are not real.

Philosophical consciousness attains its fruition through the working of its inner dynamism, through the three moments of the dialectic: dogmatism, criticism, and intuition. In its natural speculative employment, philosophy is dogmatic; this finds expression in the various systems of thought. As this invariably leads to conflict, philosophy becomes critical, self-consciously aware of the assumptions and inadequacies of reason. This is the consciousness of the relativity of phenomena, their unreality. Phenomena are Śūnya, because they are dependent and are thus devoid of the essence of reality. The completion of criticism effectively does away with the speculative or conceptual function of reason. Philosophy then culminates in intellectual intuition. Here knowledge (reason) and its object (the real) coincide; there is non-duality. This too is Śūnyatā, since Prajñā or the Absolute is devoid of duality (free from 'is' and 'is not').

The great contribution Radhakrishnan has made to our understanding of Buddhism is his unequivocal interpretation of Śūnyatā. This is the fundamental concept of Buddhism. The whole of Buddhist Philosophy turned on this concept. The earlier realistic phase

26 *Mādhyamika Kārikās*, II, 21; XIX, 6.

of Buddhism, with its rejection of substance and uncritical erection of a theory of elements, was clearly a preparation for the fully critical and self-conscious dialectic of Nāgārjuna. Not only is the Yogācāra Idealism based on the explicit acceptance of Śūnyatā, but the critical and advaitic trend in the ātman-tradition is also traceable to this. Thanks to Radhakrishnan's lead, the nihilistic interpretation of Śūnyatā has come to be rightly discredited. It is now generally accepted that Śūnyatā stands for the Transcendent Ground, inexpressible by thought-categories. It is thus devoid of empiricality, not void or nothing. As Radhakrishnan says:

About the ultimate reality we cannot say anything. To attain truth we must cast aside the conditions which are incompatible with truth. The absolute is neither existent nor non-existent, nor both existent and non-existent, nor different from both non-existence and existence. To the Mādhyamikas reason and language apply only to the finite world. To transfer the finite categories to the infinite would be like attempting to measure the heat of the sun by the ordinary thermometer. From our point of view the absolute is nothing. We call it śūnyam, since no category used in relation to the conditions of the world is adequate to it. To call it being is wrong, because only concrete things are. To call it non-being is equally wrong. It is best to avoid all descriptions of it. Thought is dualistic in its functions, and what is, is non-dual or advaita.[27]

The Absolute is not one reality set against another, such as the empirical. The Absolute looked at through thought-forms is phenomenon. The latter, freed of the superimposed thought-forms, is the Absolute. The difference is epistemic (subjective), not ontological. Nāgārjuna declares, therefore, that there is not the least difference between the absolute and the world. Transcendent to thought, the absolute is, however, thoroughly immanent in experience. A distinction has to be made between what is by itself and what appears to the finite intellect. Nāgārjuna declares that those, who do not distinguish between the unconditioned truth and the conventional, do not understand the heart of Buddha's teaching.

The Mādhyamika dialectic, which culminates in intuition, is, however, the fruition not only of the theoretic consciousness, but it is the fruition of the practical and the religious consciousness as well. The dialectic as non-conceptual knowledge takes us beyond the possibility of phenomenal existence; it is freedom itself (Nirvāṇa). The dialectic as Prajñāpāramitā is identified with the Tathāgata, the *Ens perfectissimum*, which all beings are in essence

27 Ind P, I, 663f.

and which they attain by spiritual discipline. Religion is the mystic pull of the Transcendent (the Ideal) on the actual. The dialectic consummates the union of all beings with the Perfect Being. In Vijñānavāda, Śūnyatā is accepted, but with a significant modification; it rejected as unreal the duality of subject and object with which consciousness is apparently infected. For the Mādhyamika, phenomena are unreal because they are mutually dependent; he considers the *logical* constitution of a thing and finds it lacking in essence. The Vijñānavādin views it *psychologically:* the object cannot stand by itself; it is nothing without the consciousness on which it is superimposed; but consciousness can exist without the object. It is Vijñāna that can undergo modifications, and it can purify itself by getting rid of the superimposed duality. With his bias in favour Vijñāna as the sole reality, the Yogācāra criticises the Mādhyamika for denying the reality of Vijñāna. His most effective argument against the Mādhyamika is that everything may be dialectically analysed away as illusory; but the illusion would imply the ground on which the illusory construction itself would have to take place. Accepting the Śūnyatā of the *Prajñāpāramitās* and even protesting that they interpret it more correctly, they give substance to the Śūnya by identifying it with Pure Consciousness that is devoid of duality. They consider themselves the true Mādhyamika—adopting the middle course between the extremes of Nihilism and Realism. The Yogācāra-school is the third and last comprehensive synthesis of Buddhist doctrines. It could certainly incorporate the Vaibhāṣika 'dharmas,' taking them as mind and mental states; the Yogācāra even increased the number of 'dharmas' to a hundred.

Vijñāna then, is *real,* not apparent; but Vijñāna *alone* is real, not the object. It is however infected, without beginning, by the primordial ignorance of duality (the subject-object relation). Owing to this ignorance, which is aided by subsidiary passions, Vijñāna is defiled and undergoes modifications. The modifications are three-fold: Ālaya, Manovijñāna and Viṣayavijñāna. They are the different stratifications of consciousness. Ālaya can be compared, as Radhakrishnan so happily does, to the Unconscious, deep and potential. The Manovijñāna is the transcendental process of intellection or categorisation, the activity of the mind, by which the potential is actualised, and experience is synthesised. The third mode of consciousness comprises the six kinds of sensa, including introspection. The external object is a projection of consciousness; there arise from it the apprehension of such things as houses, trees, mountains, etc., as existing independent of consciousness; but they do not so exist. Dream-objects are concrete examples of this false projectivity. The object is unreal by its very nature. Although the tree may have no external existence, it might at least be thought that the "tree-idea" exists as a subjective fact. Unlike Berkeley and other subjective Idealists, however, the Vijñānavādin rightly holds that, with the unreality of the object, the idea too loses its distinctive character as this or that idea. The modifications of consciousness, including the Ālaya, are called Paratantra, the Dependent. They are unreal in so far as they depend on the object for their determinate character. They are, however, not unreal in themselves. For, they are unreal only in the form in which they appear to us, being infected, as they are, with a false duality. Shorn of this duality, by the force of insight and intuition, they are the Ultimate. Hence the subjective world of ideas is said to be neither identical with nor different from the Absolute; not identical, because it is infected with the duality of subject and object; and not different because the Absolute is none other than this, being free from the false duality. The Pariniṣpanna (Absolute) is also called Dharmatā or Tathatā, the *Thatness* of things. It is of one undifferentiated nature like space and is identical with the essence of things, the Dharmakāya of the Buddha.

IV. Influence of Buddhist Philosophy

Influence does not necessarily mean acceptance or borrowing of doctrines. That too is influence which stimulates the systems of thought to modify, revise, or even re-affirm their original standpoint. Influence may be expressed as much by opposition as by acceptance. In this sense alone the Vedānta, the Nyāya, and other systems of the Brāhmanical tradition have been influenced by Buddhism, and *vice versa*.

The subject of the relationship between Brāhmanical and Buddhist systems in itself is a vast and interesting field of study. Material of importance is to be found in the polemic scattered in the Śāstra literature of the systems. Encouraging work has been and is being done to trace the influence of the Sautrāntika on the Nyāya-Vaiśeṣika and of the Mādhyamika and the Yogācāra on the Advaita Vedānta.[28]

It is generally admitted that the Sāṃkhya was the first system of

[28] Reference may be made to Stcherbatsky's *Buddhist Logic* (2 vols.), and to Professor Vidhushekara Bhattacharya's *Āgama Śāstra* of Gauḍapāda as cases in point.

philosophy to arise in India; and in its earliest formulations this is pre-Buddhistic. The Sāṁkhya grew as the first synthesis, on a rationalistic basis, of the chief tenets of the *Upaniṣads*. The Sāṁkhya shows no Buddhistic influence. On the other hand, the Sāṁkhya itself exerted considerable influence on Buddhism. The teachers of Buddha, Ālāra Kālāma and Uddaka Rāmaputta, were Sāṁkhya philosophers. Change or becoming is the central problem in Buddhism, as in the Sāṁkhya; but with this difference: in Buddhism this and every other problem was approached from the predominantly ethical point of view. There is no doubt that the Ābhidharmikas had before them the developed Sāṁkhya and that they moulded their own system closely on the Sāṁkhya model. "Viewed as a step in the evolution of Indian philosophical thought," says Stcherbatsky,

Buddhism was probably preceded by a fully developed form of the Sāṁkhya system in the elaborate thoroughly consistent shape of an Indian science. . . . Both doctrines are sometimes called radical systems, because the one adheres to the doctrine of eternal existence only, while the other maintains universal impermanence. It is out of place here to go into a more detailed comparison of both systems. Their close affinity has not escaped the attention of scholars. What I should like to insist upon is the fact that a close connection may be expressed not only by points of similarity, but also by opposition, nay by protest.[29]

We may consider the Ābhidharmika conception of 'Dharma' as the Buddhist version of the Sāṁkhya conception of Prakṛti. The Dharma, like Prakṛti, is a space-time entity; though, unlike Prakṛti, it is a momentary durationless point-instant. The Sarvāsti-vāda explanation of the mode of existence of an entity in all the three times (past, present and the future) is inspired by the Sāṁkhya. The great contribution Buddhist thought made to Indian philosophy was the discovery of the subjective, the theory of mental construction and appearance. Whereas the Sāṁkhya took only the relation between Puruṣa (spirit) and Prakṛti (matter) as appearance, the Buddhists with their anātman-bias relegated substance, the permanent, the whole, and the universal to the realm of the subjective. They maintained that these were merely thought-constructions lacking reality. Not empirical in origin, these are *a priori* forms which the uncritical mind superimposes on what really are momentary particular elements of existence. Thus is created the illusion of the soul, the permanent, the whole, and the

29 Stcherbatsky, *Soul Theory of the Buddhists*, 824.

universal. The Sautrāntika elaborated a very consistent and rigorous epistemology on these lines. The Mādhyamika, as we have seen,
extended and deepened the emphasis on the subjective.

This revolution in Buddhist thought exerted a decisive influence
on subsequent philosophy. Each system began re-modelling, re-
forming and re-adjusting its tenets in the light of this disturbing
and devastating discovery of the subjective. Systems with a monistic bias, such as the Vedānta and the Vijñānavāda, accepted the
subjective, the *a priori* function of thought, and profited by the
result. But they restricted the subjective to certain limits. They
seem, therefore, to condemn the extremism of the Mādhyamika—
his so-called nihilism. The Advaita Vedānta with its insistence
upon the reality of Pure Being, its identity and universality, defined avidyā as that which makes Being appear as Becoming, the
Universal as particulars, the identical as different. For the Vijñānavāda, avidyā consists in the transcendental activity of the mind
whereby the non-dual consciousness projects a false duality of
subject and object. Both absolutisms employ dialectic to safeguard
their absolutism, though not for establishing it in the first instance.
Their absolutes partake of the form of the Mādhyamika Śūnyatā
in being transcendent to thought and being accessible only to non-
empirical intuition. They also have recourse to the device of two
kinds of truth and two texts by which to explain apparent inconsistencies in experience and in the scriptures.

The reaction of the realistic and pluralistic systems was to reject
the subjective and to re-affirm their realism all the more vehe-
mently. The Nyāya and the Mīmāṁsā on the one hand and Jainism
on the other take thought-forms as forms of the objectively real
also. Thought, for them, *discovers* or *represents* things in a different medium; it does not distort or construct. For the absolutist
systems, thought distorts reality and makes it appear as something
other than what it really is. They had thus to make the distinction
between what is *in itself* and what merely *appears;* they had thus
to accept the notion of two types of truth and the distinction between phenomena and noumena. The realist systems required no
such distinction; their reals are merely systematised or crystallised
forms of empirical thought; they are very close to empirical moulds
of experience.

The initial phase of the Nyāya-Vaiśeṣika shows no Buddhist influence. From its inception it has been a realistic pluralism, advocating atomism and the mechanical combination and separation of
things. The influence of Buddhism made it still more realistic; it

tended to make the Nyāya-Vaiśeṣika a very consistent and self-conscious realism. The Nyāya-Vaiśeṣika, which emerged at the end of its centuries-long duel with Buddhist systems, rigorously establishes the objectivity of relations, of the whole, of the universal, and even of negation. It minimised and even denied the work of thought. It objectified and externalised all thought-forms and put them up as categories of the object. One has to look into the polemic found in the works of Vātsyāyana, Udyotakara, Vācaspati-miśra, Jayanta, Udayana, Śrīdhara and a host of others in order to realise the truth of this remark. The Nyāya thus brought its ontology and epistemology into full accord with its basic principle. The Nyāya resisted the critical and subjectivistic attitude of Buddhistic schools all along the line.

In the rise of the Mahāyāna, with a religion and a philosophy radically different from the Hīnayāna and even opposed to it, the influence of the Upaniṣadic tradition has been surmised, and with some justification. Kern sees distinct parallels between the *Bhaga-vadgītā* and the *Saddharma Puṇḍarīka*. Stcherbatsky says: "That the Mahāyāna is indebted to some Aupaniṣada influence is probable." [30] Radhakrishnan suggests this at several places: "Bhūta-tathatā is the absolute which persists throughout all space and time as the basis of all. This universal eternal substratum answers to the Brahman of the Upaniṣads." [31]

The Dharmakāya answers to the impersonal absolute, the Brahman of the Upaniṣads. It is not so much the body of the law as the fathomless being or the norm of all existence. When the absolute principle assumes name and form we have the transformation of the Dharmakāya into the Sambhogakāya. The substance which persists becomes the subject which enjoys. The Brahman is now the Īśvara. He is the God in heaven, determined by the name and form, omniscient, omnipresent, omnipotent, the Ādi Buddha, supreme over all the Buddhas. When we pass to the Nirmāṇakāya, we get the several manifestations of this one activity into avatārs, or incarnations. . . . So far as the Mahāyāna is concerned, there is practically nothing to distinguish it from the religion of the *Bhagavadgītā*. The metaphysical conception of Dharma-kāya, or the ultimate foundation of existence, corresponds to the Brahman of the Gītā. As Kṛṣṇa calls himself the Supreme One, even so Buddha is made into a Supreme God.[32]

This defines the nature of the possible influence. The earlier atheistic and positivistic phase of Buddhism is transformed into a

---

[30] Stcherbatsky, *The Buddhist Conception of Nirvāṇa*, 51.
[31] Ind P, I, 593f.   [32] Ind P, I, 599.

pantheism with a host of deities; a radical pluralism becomes an absolutism. The influence might have been with regard to the absolute as the transcendent ground of phenomena, an idea which is well-defined in the Upaniṣadic conception of Brahman; the conception of Godhead and the doctrine of *bhakti* (personal devotion) may be traceable to the theism of the *Bhagavadgītā*. If there was borrowing, it was, in any case, only indirect and circumstantial. It is more probable that Buddhism, impelled by its own inner dynamism, was heading towards absolutism in metaphysics and pantheism in religion.

To appreciate the possible influence of the Mādhyamika and the Yogācāra on the Advaita Vedānta, we have to understand the nature of the revolution in Upaniṣada thought ushered in by Gauḍapāda and Śaṁkara. Pre-Śaṁkara Vedānta is best described as a monism; it is not an absolutism or non-dualism. For, it did not find any incompatibility in ascribing a real modification of Brahman to the world of phenomena; Brahman has real parts or aspects and possesses attributes; he has both form and no-form. Mokṣa (Freedom) is not through knowledge alone; karma (performance of enjoined duties) is a co-ordinate means. In Gauḍapāda and Śaṁkara, all this is repudiated. Brahman does not change; there is only an appearance of that. Brahman is transcendent to thought and no predicates can apply to it; there can be no real parts or aspects of Brahman, for it is an Infinite Whole and not made up of parts. The cause of bondage is our wrong identification with the body or mental states, owing to which there arises the false distinction of 'I' and 'Thou.' This wrong notion of difference is to be annulled and this can be attained only by enlightenment or knowledge. The advaitism of Śaṁkara is a conscious and sustained rejection of duality and difference. Brahman is established not positively, but by the denial of duality. In essence all these ideas are present in Gauḍapāda's *Māṇḍūkya Kārikās*. In the first three chapters of the book, he shows, by appeal to texts and arguments, that non-duality (advaita) is the real import of the *Upaniṣads* and that duality is an appearance, etc. The question is: If pre-Gauḍapāda Vedānta is monistic, not advaitic, then how could it suddenly take an absolutist turn? Two hypotheses are possible: one that of borrowing, or at least copying, from the absolutism and dialectic already well-established in the Mādhyamika and the Vijñānavāda; and second, that, owing to its inherent dynamism, the Upaniṣadic tradition also was heading towards absolutism. There is nothing incongruent about either hypothesis, nor are they mutually exclusive.

Radhakrishnan clearly defines the nature and extent of the influence:

We need not say that the Advaita Vedānta philosophy has been very much influenced by the Mādhyamika doctrine. The *Alātaśānti* of Gauḍapāda's Kārikās is full of Mādhyamika tenets. The Advaitic distinction of vyavahāra, or experience, and paramārtha, or reality, correspond to the saṁvṛti and paramārtha of the Mādhyamikas. The Nirguṇa Brahman of Śaṅkara and Nāgārjuna's Śūnya have much in common. The force of avidyā introducing the phenomenal universe is admitted by both. The keen logic which breaks up the world into a play of abstractions, categories and relations appears in both. If we take an Advaita Vedāntin like Śrī Harṣa, we find that he does little more than develop the Mādhyamika theory, expose the self-contradictions of the categories we work with, such as cause and effect, substance and attribute, and deny the reality of things on account of the impossibility of explaining them.[33]

One cannot fail to be struck by points of close similarity between the *Kārikās*, especially the IV Chapter of it and Mahāyāna works. These fall under three heads: use of technical terms which have significant meaning only in Buddhist philosophical literature; verses which are almost verbatim quotations or adaptations from well-known Mādhyamika and Yogācāra works; and third, such doctrines as non-origination, the non-predicability of the four kinds of alternatives of the real, the object as the creation of the mind, etc. The conclusion is irresistible that in the *Māṇḍūkya Kārikās*, Gauḍapāda, a Vedānta philosopher, is attempting an advaitic interpretation of Vedānta in the light of Mādhyamika and Yogācāra doctrines. He even freely quotes from and appeals to them. This conclusion is, however, subject to two important reservations, one textual and the other doctrinal. To take the first. We have proceeded on the assumption that all the four chapters of the *Māṇḍūkya Kārikās* are by a single author. The different parts of it, however, are loosely connected; they may have been the work of different authors. Moreover, only the IVth Chapter shows indisputable Buddhist influence. This might well have been the work of a Buddhist, since it begins with a salutation to Buddha and ends with another; there is no reference to the ātman or the Upaniṣadic texts here, such as we have in the previous chapters.

It is also difficult to conceive how philosophers belonging to the ātman-tradition could borrow doctrines from those of the opposed anātman-tradition. The Vedāntins stake everything on the reality

[33] Ind P, I, 668.

of the ātman and accept the authority of the *Upaniṣads;* the Buddhists denied the reality of the ātman (soul, substance, the permanent, the universal) in any form. The barrier, therefore, was always there. Besides, it is readily assumed that there is no difference between the absolutisms of Nāgārjuna, Śaṁkara and the Yogācāra. A closer analysis should bring out their differences as much as their generic affinity. Consistent with the above contention, we could only expect the Vedāntin to have profited by the technique or method of the Mādhyamika. He had before him the Mādhyamika distinction of Paramārtha and Saṁvṛti, of texts into Nītāratha (primary) and Neyārtha (secondary) and of the Mādhyamika method of reaching the real by negating the real. The Mādhyamika and Yogācāra also had a theory of illusion to account for the emergence of appearance. Knowledge of this turn in Buddhism must have sent the Vedāntin back to his own texts and enabled him to perceive the truer meaning of the *Upaniṣads* in Advaitism. The upshot of all this, therefore, would seem to be that there has been borrowing of technique rather than of tenets.

This leads us to the intrinsic problem about the correct interpretation of the three absolutisms, the Śūnyatā of Nāgārjuna, the Vijñaptimātratā of the Yogācāra, and the Nirguṇa Brahman of Śaṁkara. Do they differ merely in name? I should like to suggest that, although agreeing with regard to the *form* of the absolute, these absolutisms differ considerably in the mode of their approach and in the nature of the entity with which they identify the absolute. This may also explain why these systems criticise each other and distinguish their respective positions so sharply. In all these systems, the absolute is transcendent, i.e., totally devoid of empirical determinations. The absolute is immanent too, because, it is the reality of appearance; the absolute is but the phenomena in their essential form. They all speak of the absolute as realisable in a non-empirical mode of intuition called variously, Prajñāpāramitā, lokottarajñāna and aparokṣānubhūi. They further agree with regard to the nature and status of phenomena as appearance. Every absolutism is really an advaita or advayavāda, i.e., non-dualism; they do not establish the absolute; they merely reject duality as being illusion.

The differences among the absolutisms, at least in the manner of their approach, should, however, not be overlooked. The Vedānta starts with an extra-logical or theological revelation of the Vedānta texts (*Upaniṣads*) about the sole reality of the ātman; and this is attempted to be realised by means of rational thought and contemplation. The Mādhyamika takes hold of the dialectical consciousness which emerges logically in the conflict of viewpoints. The Yogācāra is convinced of the sole reality of consciousness on the basis of the experience of trance-states, where consciousness continues to exist even though the object may be absent. The Vedānta and the Vijñānavāda begin with an analysis of an empirical illusion,—such as misperceiving a piece of shell for silver,—and then apply that analysis to phenomena as a whole. For the Vedānta, the real is the given, answering to the 'this' in the illusion-context: 'This is silver.' The 'silver,' as subsisting within consciousness only, is appearance. The Vedānta analyses illusion from the standpoint of knowledge wherein the object is or should be independent of the knowing act; knowledge merely discovers or reveals the given being and does not create it. The Vijñānavādin approaches this problem from an opposite angle; the given ('this') is an unreal or free projection of consciousness, which latter alone is real. Vijñāna (consciousness) is understood not as Pure Being (static), but as creating and constructing the object out of itself by a free act. Vijñāna can be construed as Cosmic Will, much like the Absolute Ego of Fichte. Differing from both the Vedānta and Vijñānavāda, the Mādhyamkika addresses itself directly to the transcendental illusion created by the opposition of standpoints; it reaches the absolute through this dialectical consciousness. If Brahman is Pure Being (static and permanent), Vijñāna is Creative Force or Will. Śūnyatā of the Mādhyamika is identified with nothing that we empirically experience; it is the Critical or Reflective Awareness itself.

V. Buddhism as a Religion

Many might be tempted to consider Buddhism, at least its Hīnayāna phase, as a positivism in religion. It denied revelation, did not accept God, and, repudiating grace and personal devotion, relied entirely on knowledge and works. If religion means the consciousness of a Supreme Personal Reality and our intimate relation to that Reality, then Hīnayāna is not a religion. This position is radically modified in the Mahāyāna, which accepted the divinity of Buddha. Even Hīnayāna can be considered as a religion in so far as it canalises every aspect of man into the non-worldly ideal of salvation (Nirvāṇa). As Radhakrishnan puts it:

The essential quality of religion is to deal with the invisible environment of absolute worth. If this unseen environment or absolute reality does not exist, religion has no basis and no meaning. This reality is for the Upaniṣads absolute wisdom, and for Buddha it is the moral order. Whether we call it the order of truth or the order of righteousness, it is absolute in its claim. Religion is nothing more than the recognition of this claim. . . . Schleiermacher says: The only way for a truly individual religion to arise is to select some one of the great relations of mankind in the world to the Highest Being and then, in a definite way, make it the centre and refer to it all the others. The absolute can be apprehended by man in numberless ways. Each religion emphasises a special way and is in a sense a special intuition of the infinite, though the whole is always present in each. The Buddha emphasised the ethical aspect of the infinite and the ethical striving of man. Round these are organised the metaphysical and mystical truths of Buddhism.[34]

Both Brāhmanism and Buddhism are types of Spiritual Religion. They try to realise a state of utter negation of the ego, the abolition of selfishness. Positively, it is the attainment of the Universal where all differences and conflicts cease and where there is perfect concord and harmony. Again in both, the highest state is attained by mystic intuition, a kind of non-discursive intellectual absorption. A strenuous spiritual discipline is enjoined as the indispensable means to it. All this is brought out with fullness and clarity in Radhakrishnan's account of Buddhism as a religion. I should now like to define the differences between Brāhmanism and Buddhism as religions.

The source of religious inspiration in Brāhmanism is revelation as given to us in the Vedas; in Buddhism it is reason. Not that Brāhmanism is antagonistic to reason or is unmindful of the value of reason; but it is only revelation which can give us intuitions of the transcendent; the function of reason is to analyse and clarify the revealed truth. Innovations are only interpretations of the given truth, and the entire mode of development is authoritarian and traditional. Buddha asks us not to receive anything on trust nor to accept any authority, but to test it by reason and experience. He himself did not owe allegiance to any authority, Vedic or non-Vedic.[35]

A curious paradox arose soon after Buddha's death. His discourses, edited, codified and preserved, attained the sanctity of Canons or Scriptures like the Vedas. Buddhists began to be as much exercised over exegetical considerations as were their Brāhmanical compatriots. Owing to the diversity of languages in which the Discourses of Buddha were preserved and the want of an ac-

[34] TB, 22f.   [35] *Majj. Nik. Sutta* 26; *Saṁyutta Nik.*, II, 105.

curate system of oral transmission, their dictional purity, obviously, could not attain the standard of the Vedas. This was remedied in the course of time; and disputes came to be settled, in the orthodox Hindu fashion, by appeal to texts. The *Kathāvatthu* (3rd cent. B.C.) adopts this method in deciding issues. The situation continued to be fluid for a long time, however. New canons of the Mahāyāna began to make their appearance not very long after the death of Buddha, and soon their number became a veritable flood. Both Hīnayānists and Mahāyānists appealed to the Word of Buddha; the former were literalists and conservative, the latter were liberal and progressive. Even the Word of Buddha is defined by the Mahāyāna as what is not incompatible with the Norm and whatever is well-said.

Orthodox Hinduism does not rest on any historical fact nor on the advent of any person; its incarnations are mythological and legendary, and the non-appearance of any or all of them would not affect it. It is not an historical religion. Buddhism, on the other hand, is an historical religion. The advent of the human Buddha (Gautama) is vital to it. Buddha is but an exalted human teacher. The advantage of having a human teacher as the founder of a religion is obvious; it makes for concrete and intimate personal relationship. There are, on the other hand, also distinct disadvantages: with the lapse of time the personal intimacy ceases to be felt, and doubt arises about the founder's historicity; legends and exaggerations complete the process. By dynamic necessity, therefore, Buddha came, in the course of time, to be deified like any other founder of a new religion. The divinity of Buddha came to be the chief ground of difference between the Mahāsamghikas and the Sthaviravādins.

If we look at the *Nikāyabheda-Dharma-Mati Cakara Śāstra* of Vasumitra, we come across the following passages. The fundamental and common doctrines of the Mahāsaṁghikas, the Ekavyavahārka, the Lokottaravāda and the Kaukkuṭika schools are:—The four schools unanimously maintained that the Blessed Buddhas are all supermundane, the Tathāgatas have no worldly attributes, the words of the Tathāgatas are all about the Turning of the Wheel of Law, Buddha preaches all doctrines with one utterance, in the teaching of the Bhagavān (Buddha) there is nothing that is not in accordance with the Truth, the physical body of Tathāgata is limitless, the majestic powers of Tathāgata also are limitless, lives of Buddhas are limitless and Buddha is never tired of enlightening living beings and awakening pure faith in them, etc.[36]

---

[36] Kimura, *Hīnayāna and Mahāyāna*, 86f.

We can see in these rather undeveloped notions the incipient stages of the Mahāyāna Buddhology, Śūnyatā and the Bodhisattva ideal which came to be developed with such thoroughness in the *Prajñāpāramitā, Sadharmapuṇḍarīka,* and other treatises. The conception of Buddha as God is as foundational in religion as is that of Śūnyatā in metaphysics. It represents the de-historiza-tion of Buddha; Mahāyāna just escapes being an historical reli-gion. In one sense Buddha loses some of his concrete personal character in as much as he is now identified with the Dharmakāya (the Absolute) or Śūnyatā; he is one of the numerous free phenom-enalisations of the Absolute. In another sense, Buddha becomes more human: he is the inner essence of all beings and Buddha-hood is latent in all; every being is a *bodhisattva* destined, in the fullness of time and effort, to attain complete Buddhahood. By a logical necessity, therefore, "the Buddhas were subjected to a six-fold process of evolution: they were multiplied, immortalised, deified, spiritualised, universalised, and unified." [37]

The dual nature of Buddha as one with the Absolute (Śūnya) and at the same time actively pursuing the welfare of beings sup-plies the philosophical basis for the theological conception of the Trikāya of Buddha. The three bodies or aspects of Buddha are: the Dharma- Kāya or Cosmical body, which is his essential nature as one with the Absolute; the Samhogakāya is the body of Bliss, by which he contemplates and enjoys himself as a Divine, Glorious Person; and the Nirmāṇa Kāya is the body which he assumes as an act of grace in order to teach the Law and save beings. Gautama the Śākyamuni is merely one of the countless manifestations of the Buddha.

The need for a mediator is felt in all absolutism; Vedānta has recourse to Īśvara, distinct from Brahman, to account for the rev-elation of truth; in the Mādhyamika and Yogācāra that function is performed by the Tathāgata. It is not a necessary part of Truth that it should be known and declared as truth: it is not constituted by our knowing or not knowing it. The Absolute (Brahman or Śūnya) does not reveal itself, being the Truth itself; and finite beings confined to the phenomenal sphere do not know the truth. Only a being who enjoys a sort of amphibious existence, having one foot in phenomena and the other in the Absolute, can possibly know the Absolute and reveal it to others. But Īśvara or the Tathāgata is a lower principle than the Absolute, which is the impersonal reality of all beings. Though this position is common

37 Har Dayal, *The Bodhisattva Doctrine,* 28.

to both the Vedānta and the Mahāyāna, there are, however, some differences. To Īśvara is assigned not merely the function of revealing the Truth; creation, sustenance, destruction, and other cosmic functions are also performed by him. In Buddhism, the Law of Karma takes the place of Īśvara in this regard. Īśvara reveals the Truth to phenomenal beings through some extra-ordinary mechanism of communication, probably in the beginning of creation; he does not incarnate himself as man for this purpose. The Tathāgata, on the other hand, descends from his divine plane and takes birth among men, conforms to their modes of life, gains their sympathy, and reveals the truth through ordinary modes of communication. The Tathāgata is, to all intents, Man perfected by the destruction of ignorance and passions. The most characteristic feature of God in Mahāyāna Buddhism is the Mahākaruṇā (Great Compassion) that is prepared for any sacrifice for any being and for all time. This active and unceasing effort for the welfare and final release of all beings makes the Tathāgata a very loving and lovable God. It is easily one of the purest and most exalted conceptions of Godhead. Not that Īśvara is not conceived as benign and loving, but that the ideal of Mahākaruṇā and Sarvamukti (Salvation for all) is not so intimately and intensely expressed there as in Buddhism.

It is not to be supposed that Buddhology was a complete innovation of the Mahāyānists. It is present in implicit form in the Pali Canons too. In the *Mahāpadāna* and the *Mahāparinibbāna Suttas*, we have an account of the spiritual lineage of the Buddhas. The Mahāyāna is the unequivocal expression of these anticipations. In its philosophy, Mahāyāna is an absolutism; in religion it is a Pantheism, a diversity of divine beings with a background of Unity of Godhead. There is greater affinity between Mahāyāna and Brāhmanism than between the former and Hīnayāna.

Though Hīnayāna cannot, on philosophical grounds, find any place for God, Buddha serves the same purpose which God performs in other religions. There are temples, in all the Southern countries professing Hīnayāna, where the image of Buddha is worshipped more or less in the Hindu fashion. Every form of ritual and worship in the Brāhmanical religion is symbolic and mystical; they stand for the transcendent. In Hīnayāna it is mostly relic-worship, the veneration of the physical remains of the historical Gautama or his Saints; Stūpas have been erected on these relics (teeth or bones). The need felt by the common man for a personal god was too strong to be resisted. However, scholars and monks in

these countries would still in theory profess atheism, strict govern-
ance of the law, etc., although in practice it is otherwise.

Buddhism is a religion of the elect, despite the fact that it was
thrown open to all without distinction of caste or status. It is
expressly meant for the few who choose the life of the monk and
conform to the rules of the Order. The layman was not expressly
provided for in this scheme. His function seems to have been to
provide food and raiment to the Order and to listen to the discourses of the monks. The benefit of Buddhism to the layman is,
therefore, indirect and circumstantial. The content of the Buddhist religion is principally, if not wholly, spiritual. There was
no ceremonial, social or juridical side to it. In other religions,
ceremonies are enjoined on the birth of a child, at the time of
marriage, funeral, etc. The *Gṛhya Sūtras* of Brāhmanism are devoted to this aspect of life. Festivals and services also form an
integral part of other religions. The religious society is also usually
governed by a code of law, governing inheritance, adoption, etc.;
the *Dharma Śāstras* perform this juridical function in Hindu
society. It is not owing to an oversight or to disinclination that
such rules were not framed for the lay society in Buddhism.
Buddha himself formulated minute rules regulating every aspect
of the life of the monks comprising the Order. The *Vinaya Piṭaka*
is a massive code which even to-day regulates the life of Buddhist
monks. The conclusion is forced on us, therefore, that the content
of Buddhism is chiefly spiritual. It was not committed to any
specific social or racial milieu, as is the case in Brāhmanism.

This freedom from the social setting enjoyed by Buddhism is
at once an asset and a drawback. It could address itself exclusively
to a compact and well-disciplined order. It could also be easily
transported to other environmental conditions, since it was not
tied to any rigid social cast like orthodox Hinduism. Buddhism
is Hinduism meant for export. Only the spiritual message needed
to be propagated in other countries. Buddhism could thus take
on the colour and hue of the societies and racial groups to which
it spread. This accounts for the wide diversity of its forms. It
could synthesise and fuse with varied racial and social structures,
as in China with Confucianism and Taoism, in Japan with Shinto-
ism, in Tibet with Lamaism, not to speak of its divergent forms
in the Southern countries of Asia. In this sense, Buddhism is
more universal in its appeal than orthodox Hinduism. But this
should not blind us to the fact that it was an exclusive religion.
It did not accept alternative paths or modify its teachings accord-

ing to tastes and temperaments. The Councils and Synods held from time to time were meant to define the Orthodox Norm and persecute heresy by the application of sanctions. The Mahāyāna differed greatly from Hīnayāna in this regard. It was not only more liberal and prolific, but it also could genuinely provide for different approaches. As the Ultimate is Śūnya, devoid of empirical determinations, it could be reached by not merely one official path but by several. The gradation of teaching according to the spiritual bias and capacity of the individual is a great tenet of Mahāyāna. This is the celebrated doctrine of Buddha's "excellence in the choice of means." Buddha does not blindly, mechanically, prescribe one remedy to all and sundry; he varies and graduates it according to the need and the occasion. The indeterminacy of the absolute allows freedom of approach.

VI. THE SPREAD AND DISAPPEARANCE OF BUDDHISM

Orthodox Hinduism was content to leave the propagation of religion to unofficial agencies. In consequence, all its institutions were decentralised. But Buddhism, from its very inception, believed in organised and directed effort. Buddha founded the First Church in history. It is not that the order of monks was his innovation. There were literally countless groups of recluses and homeless wanderers in India before and during the time of Buddha. Moreover, many of the rules adopted by Buddha for his Order were admittedly borrowed from current practice, e.g., the institution of observing the Fortnightly Convention. But such a great and closely knit organisation, actuated by a single purpose, shows Buddha as a unique organiser and administrator. The *Vinaya Piṭaka* may well be compared to the *Laws* of Plato, although Buddha is concerned here to lay down detailed rules not for any imaginary city-state on earth but for the monks bent on achieving freedom from earthly existence.

The speed with which the message of Buddha spread and the succession of high-souled men of incessant energy whom the Order could attract to its ranks are attributable to the unique personality of Buddha, to his universal spiritual message, and to the efficiency of the Order. "The causes of the success of Buddhism as a religion are the three jewels or triratna, of (1) Buddha; (2) the dharma or the Law; and (3) the saṁgha, or the brotherhood." [38] The Saṁgha, as a devoted body of selfless men drawn from all ranks, especially

[38] Ind P, I, 473.

from the highest classes, not only carried the message far and wide in India, but spread it in distant countries. They were the first missionaries in history.

The missionary spirit contributed considerably to the spread of the gospel. Buddha bade his disciples: "Go into all lands and preach this gospel." Tell them that the poor and the lowly, the rich and the high, are all one, and all castes unite in this religion as do the rivers in the sea.[39]

Buddhism had a universal appeal; it did not require, as was pointed out above, any specific social or caste background. And there was the Order charged with the task of spreading and preserving the teaching of the Master. But the factors which made for its rapid spread were themselves also the cause of its decline in and disappearance from India.

We must discount all accounts of persecution of Buddhism by orthodox Hinduism. As Radhakrishnan says: "Buddhism died a natural death in India. It is an invention of the interested to say that fanatic priests fought Buddhism out of existence. . . . The violent extermination of Buddhism in India is legendary." [40] Persecution of different religious groups and sects is totally contrary to the Indian spirit. Buddha preached for over forty years after his enlightenment; and, during all that time, he freely moved about the country. We do not hear of any molestation or persecution. He was received everywhere with reverence and honour, even by those who disagreed with him. In fact, he received injury from a faction in his own Order instigated by his cousin Devadatta. The Jaina Order too offered him some opposition. But no mention is made of any civic or other disability imposed on the Saṁgha at any time during its existence. Stray cases of persecution on either side cannot be ruled out; but it is more likely that the Buddhist Order was militant and intolerant. Any organised and deliberate persecution does not appear to have occurred.

Moreover, external persecution has never resulted in extinction. A religion with such vitality and dynamism could not be stamped out by unfavourable circumstances; for, it could not only rise above the circumstances, but also could effectively mould conditions to its own norm. The causes for the disappearance of Buddhism must, therefore, be inherent and internal. Two principal causes might have contributed to the decline and disappearance of Buddhism from India; one, the secularity of the Order, and the other that

39 Ind P, I, 475.   40 Ind P, I, 607f.

Buddhism was never rooted in the soil, since it had only a spiritual content. When this spiritual content became indistinguishable from a resurgent Hinduism, there was no *raison d'être* for Buddhism's separate continuance.

The Monastic Order was certainly a potent source of strength. But it was inherently secular, unspiritual; all organisation is so of necessity. Individual monks could not have belongings or own houses; but the Order could and had to acquire property. So long as the monks were few, they could subsist on alms by begging from house to house. But to feed by means of alms several hundred monks gathered in some of the *vihāras* was a difficult problem. They had also to set up establishments near flourishing towns and cities instead of residing in solitary places, as the first monks had done. The Order also needed quite a number of men to perform necessary secular duties in order to maintain a few monks who could then attend to their spiritual affairs. It is recorded that Buddha had to make the following appointments: "I sanction a Bhikkhu endowed with five qualities . . . as Food-controller. . . . I sanction a Superior of Lodgings who will know what is assigned and what is not assigned. . . . I sanction a storehouse keeper and a receiver of robes." [41] As some of the Vihāras were fair-sized towns, they must have presented problems in sanitation, transport, and other civic amenities. Thus the world, which the monks had ostensibly renounced, comes in through the back door.

Moreover, a different psychology motivates the Order. What one would not do for his individual gain, one would do in the interests of the Order. He would be importunate and callous when it concerned the Order. The impersonality of the Order could, therefore, easily deaden the monks' moral susceptibilities. The interests of the Order would also preclude exposing the failings of its members. Thus the Order becomes a vested interest. Rivalry and competition for position are inseparable from an Order. It becomes a power, and "power corrupts." We also know from history that many of the Heads of the Vihāras wielded considerable power and interfered in the politics of the states; and, in view of their international affiliations, they even conspired at times with foreign invaders.

An Order is secular and unspiritual by its constitution. A spiritual Order is a standing contradiction. It could exist only by an unceasing compromise between two opposing forces, selfishness and altruism. As long as there was a preponderance of the unselfish ele-

41 *Cullavagga*, VI, xxi.

ment in the Order, it could forge ahead as a real spiritual force. But when the rot set in, as the egoistic trends soon asserted themselves, the Order became a potent source of evil. The Lord (Buddha) must have perceived the inevitable decay of the Order, when he is reported to have said, on the occasion of the admission of women to the Order, that his Dharma would have lasted a thousand years, but now its life would be shortened to five hundred, because of the admission of women. Actually, Buddhism has lasted much longer than the predicted period. But there was a limit to its usefulness determined solely by its own inherent reasons.

The other reason for the disappearance of Buddhism from India is to be found in its special form. We should not forget that Buddhism was never a rival religion competing with or contending against Hinduism, as Islam and Christianity are and have been doing. Its difference from Brāhmanism was solely on the spiritual plane. It had no rival social and legal institutions. It is wrong to think that Buddha or Buddhism was opposed to caste as a *social* institution. It is true that in the Order of Monks there was no distinction of caste, and caste-values had no meaning. But this does not mean that Buddha ever preached a crusade against caste. According to the Canons, Buddhas could be born in the Brāhman or Kṣatriya caste, and not in any other. The popular notion that there was a period called Buddhist India, when the majority of people were converted to Buddhism and that on the revival of Hinduism they were reconverted to Hinduism has no basis in fact. As has been pointed out already, Buddhism had a spiritual side only, and the layman was never converted to Buddhism, as one can speak of conversion to Christianity or Mohammedanism. Indeed the Upāsaka expressed his spiritual or moral sympathy; but he was never required to renounce in theory or practice the religion he had been following; there is no mention of any formula or ritual of conversion, and there was nothing to distinguish him from his Hindu brethren. Initiation into the Order of Buddhist Monks is a different matter altogether; there were elaborate ceremonies for that. Only the Monastic Orders could be called specifically Buddhist at any time, and they must have formed a microscopic community. The moral and spiritual influence of the Order on the layman was, however, enormous and continuous.

Since Buddhism confined itself to the spiritual side, it had no separate roots in the general society. With the emergence and spread of the Mahāyāna philosophy and religion and the resurgence of the Vedānta religion and the Advaita philosophy, the difference between them must have become almost indistinguishable. "Buddhism and Brāhmanism approached each other so much that for a time they were confused and ultimately became one. Slow absorption and silent indifference, and not priestly fanaticism and methodical destruction, are the causes of the fall of Buddhism." [42] This analysis of Radhakrishnan is eminently reasonable and true.

The disappearance of Buddhism, as a separate entity, from India is no measure of the disappearance of its influence, however. It has profoundly influenced the philosophy and religion of India. It has deepened our spiritual life and has given us a purer ethics. The absolutist and critical trend in Indian philosophy is largely owing to Buddhism. The Dialectic as a weapon of refutation and as a spiritual mode of approaching the Absolute is distinctly a contribution of the Mādhyamika. In the field of epistemology, the debt that the Nyāya, the Vedānta and the other systems of thought owe to the Sautrāntika is immense. To crown all, we have with us the ideal of the *Bodhisattva,* unceasingly active in the well-being of all creatures, high and low; he is a shining example of egoless personality.

Professor Radhakrishnan's own philosophy stems as much from the absolutism of Śaṁkara as from that of Nāgārjuna. His ethical ideal of the philosopher realising his unity with all beings, not in retirement from the world into a private enjoyment of his own freedom, but in bringing spiritual freedom to others, is as much the ideal of Sarvamukti of the Advaita Vedānta as it is of the Mahāyāna.

T. R. V. Murti

Department of Philosophy
University of Ceylon
Colombo, Ceylon

[42] Ind. Phil. I, 608.

18

Edgar L. Hinman

RADHAKRISHNAN AND THE SUNG CONFUCIANISM

18

RADHAKRISHNAN AND THE SUNG CONFUCIANISM

IN MARCH of 1944 an invitation was extended by the Chinese Government to Sir S. Radhakrishnan to visit China, and lecture before various Chinese universities. Disturbed conditions had prevented an earlier visit, in connection with a portrait of Rabindranath Tagore presented to China. But the Chinese Ministry of Education would not allow the project to drop. The lectures were given in the various institutions about Chungking in May of 1944, and the charming little book, *India and China*, gives to the world a deposit from them. Its treatment of Confucius and of the later maturing of Confucian thought may serve to introduce the theme of the present paper.

The exposition of Confucius is normal. From the critical evaluation I wish to quote a few passages:

His religious views and his ethical and social views are not integrated into a system. . . . The strict observance of the ethical rules which Confucius lays down is possible only with the regeneration brought about by religion. . . . To exercise control over the natural man, we must seek support in something higher, in the power of Heaven. This power operates in man, as the power of control. . . . There are humanists at the present day who believe in the force of moral ideals, the value of tradition, in international good behaviour, which are all a part of the Confucian faith. They are, however, an outward expression of inward piety. The dharma is the true nature of man. It is based on Heaven, and shows its action on earth through social duties (li) which make for mutual confidence and harmony. . . . There is a deeper consistency in his thought and a spiritual background to it, but as he did not develop it, he left it to his followers to provide the spiritual background and give his social code stability and direction. In so doing they were only following out the implications of Confucius' thought.[1]

These comments I support. But as we read farther, and particularly as we approach the great thinkers of the Sung dynasty, who

[1] IC, 64f.

gave with power the systematic development which our author has here desiderated, we begin to feel that something is the matter. First we note the extreme brevity of the treatment—two pages for two centuries of formulation, and seven centuries of regnancy. Buddhism and Taoism rate a chapter each, although neither was ever so influential over the minds of thinking Chinese men as the Sung Confucianism has been. Possibly this brevity is in part due to the fact that the author's message from India could be more adequately conveyed by the discussion of Buddhism and Taoism. But I think that the difficulty goes farther, and indicates a genuine lack of sympathy. True, he generously comes to the support of the later Confucianism by indicating the influence of Buddhism and Taoism in the construction of the Sung School. But even that commendation might have lost much of its point, if he had indicated that these factors had operated negatively, as furnishing something that the Confucianists were striving to surpass. But he thinks of it otherwise:

The satisfaction of the metaphysical need and the spiritual aspirations of men are secured by the acceptance of the religious postulates of Taoism and Buddhism. These were not altogether alien to the Confucian doctrine.[2]

Radhakrishnan means, I take it, that a Chinese gentleman of worthy culture would feel the humanistic need for Buddhist and Taoist ideals, and that he would be right in doing so, because man is more than Confucian analysis brings out; but that Confucianism in its own development is too intellectualistic and political in its mentality to be able to attain to the higher and more mystical appreciations that are at home in India. And to this many a Christian thinker might also yield a rather ready agreement.

But there is need of a closer analysis of the genuine relation which "the religious postulates of Taoism and Buddhism" may rightly bear to matured Confucianism. Such an analysis may show, I suppose, that for the student who has rightly apprehended the essential logic and purpose of philosophical Confucianism, much of the religious and mystical quality of these other faiths will prove to have been developed also from the intrinsic life of Confucian teaching; whereas, whatever is not to be so developed must be regarded as a baneful heritage, which should not be permitted to attach itself by an external syncretism.

The problem, I think, is that of evaluating properly the nega-

[2] Ibid., 71.

tive movement, which enters so powerfully into all competent philosophy, but which is particularly evident in the dominant philosophies of both India and China. In China this negative movement ran wild in the philosophy of Taoism. In Buddhism also it was excessive, although rather less so in developed Chinese Buddhism than in the original Hīnayāna Buddhism of India. But still we have to say, what Radhakrishnan so justly says of Buddhism in India, that it "emphasizes overmuch the negative side." [3] The Sung Confucianism, from its first formulation and throughout the centuries, has also made a forceful use of negation. But it has so defined the negative function, within the concrete system of Chinese life and experience, that the negative movement did indeed cut out that which was untenable, but moved steadily towards a wholesome reconstruction of life. Not only was it required to test all things and hold fast that which is good, but it was also required to recognize that the actualities of Chinese society, as Confucius found them, were not in accordance with his high teachings. It must therefore reconstruct according to the vision. But the Sung Confucianism never toyed with the conception of the Empty Absolute (which is the normal goal of ill-defined negation, as negation abstracts from the phenomena of sense). Its essential commitments were to a type of monism, idealistic indeed, but concrete, rich with differences, and able to provide a differential foundation for the factors within a manifold system.

The appropriate use of negation and affirmation in logic has been compared to that of differentiation and integration in biology. An organism, through differentiation, establishes manifoldness of organs and functions. Normally, however, this does but enhance the integration of the organism, its maturity and viability. Likewise the normal use of logical negation, operating within an affirmative scene, is to serve, foster, and help to bring out the positive content of discourse. In this use it may be pervasive and dynamic, as in the competent and constructive use of modern criticism. At lower levels of discourse, however, this affirmative implication of the negative is allowed to remain unnoticed. In that case serious results may ensue. Among people of untrained minds, argument then tends to become eristics; among people of somewhat more advancement, criticism becomes dominantly destructive; among people of still more advancement, strange and paradoxical philosophies emerge.

The negative movement has taken a very prominent place in

[3] Ind P, I, 527.

the philosophical thinking of India. There, however, it has sometimes assumed forms which attempt to deviate from the theory of
negative predication just sketched—unless, perhaps, to illustrate the
last clause.

The Vedas implied a rich religion; and when its development
culminated in the noble literature of the *Upaniṣads*, the literature
itself easily became sacrosanct and authoritative. But now, within
that literature, and seeming to be its "finest hour," there are scores
of passages which enforce the doctrine of the unity of all Being
by a method of disregarding all differences. Of course, there are
also manifold passages which do otherwise. And so it had to be that,
when the commentators came into being, to give to the Vedāntic
philosophy its most adequate statement, the issue concerning the
sound interpretation of these passages became fundamental. Since
so much of Vedāntic interpretation turned upon this logical issue,
it really became the main ground of the differentiation of the
schools of thought.

In the eighth century of the Christian era abstract idealistic
monism received its classical formulation at the hands of the great
commentator on the Vedānta Sūtras, Śaṁkara. This thinker's life
indeed was short, but his work and influence were tremendous.
Like Aristotle, he was almost too efficient. Śaṁkara seized upon the
key passages in the *Upaniṣads* which exhibit a universal principle
by throwing away the differences—the "nothing but" passages—
and constructed the entire philosophy of Vedāntic thought in the
light of these.

"Just as by a lump of clay everything that consists of clay is
known; transformation depending upon words, a mere name—in
truth it is nothing but clay." [4]

And so we get the doctrine of a Brahman that is devoid of all
differences whatever, being indeed the only true reality; and of
a world of manifold differences, which is utterly fictitious, unreal,
not even founded in deeper differentiations within the Brahman.
This last would be Māyā, in the meaning given to that ancient
term by Śaṁkara's monism.

Māyā is the realm of appearances, but with the peculiar over-
tone that these appearances are neither real themselves, nor are
they authentic expressions of anything that is real. Here we may
not apply Herbart's maxim, *So viel Schein, so viel Hindeutung auf
Sein.* It is as if all affirmations had been funded into one Everlasting Yea, the Brahman; and all negations into one Everlasting Nay,

[4] *Chāndogya Upaniṣad*, 6, 1, 4.

the Māyā. It is as if a biological writer having an organism under study should prepare one set of charts exhibiting all the integrations, but no differentiations; and then another set of charts, exhibiting all the differentiations, but no integrations. And yet, if the form of logic that it uses is indeed logic, then I suppose that Śaṁkara has given us the most logical formulation in history of abstract monism—Advaita Vedāntism.

But there remained many factors in Vedāntic thought that were not at ease in the formulations of the Advaita monism. These factors gained an effective treatment, some three centuries later, in the commentaries of Rāmānuja. The outcome was a monism which attempted to provide for differences and to interpret them. The resulting doctrine was a monism still, but with a unity defined as carrying within its life modifications—Visistadvaita. This teaching aspires to provide an affirmative basis for finite individuality, although not going to the extreme of making such individuality to be absolute. For Rāmānuja, then,

The word 'Brahman' denotes the highest Person, who is essentially free from all imperfections, and possesses numberless classes of auspicious qualities of unsurpassable excellence.[5]

These two schools of Vedāntic interpretation are thoroughly expounded, with discerning criticism, in the *Indian Philosophy* of Radhakrishnan, and indeed widely throughout his writing. It is important here to gain some statement of his general assessment of truth and error in the two.

We may first note that Western thought has maintained a sustained criticism against abstract monism. From the time that Aristotle opened his invective against the "friends of Ideas," the argument has been that though we may operate, logically, with abstractions, we must not, metaphysically, hypostatize them. In the Middle Ages the shift from Plato to Aristotle turned largely upon that issue. The victorious moderate realism held that universals exist only as embedded in individuals. The Tree of Porphyry, then, is "the tree that never grew." The Leibnizian teaching has fortified that view, and has been taken over into much of post-Kantian philosophy. Idealism has presented itself as the doctrine of "the concrete universal;" and critics of idealism who suspect that its universal is still an abstraction tend to become pragmatists—vigorously to pursue the concrete, even at the cost of surrendering the universal.

[5] *Sacred Books of the East*, v. XLVIII, 4.

I understand Radhakṛishnan to accept, essentially, the force of Western criticism against abstract universals; but to judge that this criticism does not rightly touch the things most significant in the philosophy of Śaṁkara. In particular, the quietistic mysticism which the Advaita sustains is quite beyond the critic's reach. Meanwhile Rāmānuja's thought is judged to have much to commend it; but still, his attempt to maintain both immanence and transcendence seems to get him entangled in "the problems of theism," and his position becomes difficult to hold.

This attitude may be shown by a few quotations from Radhakrishnan:

Śaṁkara would not agree with Bergson's view that the intellect breaks up the flow of life. . . . Intellect not only dissects reality, but attempts to reconstruct it. It is both analytic and synthetic in its functions. Thought displaces contingency by law. It does not sunder reality into parts, but holds these in the bonds of unity by means of space, time, and causality. To the concrete life of experience our intellects are quite adequate. . . . If Śaṁkara regards intellect as not the highest mode of man's consciousness, it is because the completed world of logic still leaves us with a riddle. The completed world of logic is not the completed world of life and experience. . . . The triumph of thought is the triumph of the concrete, but the most concrete thought is abstract in the sense that it is incapable of apprehending reality as it is. In pressing forward and upward in the quest of reality, with the aid of intelligence, we reach a reality seemingly full, rich, and profound, that of Īśvara, the only way in which Brahman can be envisaged at the level of finite thought. But Īśvara is not the highest Brahman, and the unity of God is not an intelligible one. . . . The inconsistencies and incompletenesses in which Śaṁkara's theory of knowledge is content to remain are not due to any defects of his reasoning, but are the inevitable imperfections of a philosophy which tries to go to the depths of things.[6]

So then our author seems to agree with Western criticism concerning the inadequacy of abstractions, and may even accord with the ideal of the "concrete universal" when that is interpreted as the goal of science. But since this is then understood to refer only to our intellectual recasting of the realm of phenomena, he may still hold that "for substance of doctrine" Śaṁkara was correct regarding the fundamental meaning of it all.

We should notice, however, that the teaching of our author at this point will differ rather sharply from Western idealism. For

6 Ind P, II, 523-524, 526.

the Western thinker all formulations—even the best and most critical science—are couched in terms of conceptions that are more or less mutilated, incomplete, and abstract. So then the goal of systematic concreteness is an immanent ideal, approached indeed in varying degrees, but never actualized. It is militant indeed, but not largely triumphant. "We touch it in life's throng and press, and we are whole again." Yet it is the compelling faith of science, and according as the integrating wholeness gives congruence to our experience and judgment, we are getting at the real meaning of our world. Partial meaning is reaching out for integrating wholeness, and so is grounding itself in reality. The integration, however, may well go far beyond the purely intellectual side of life.

But in Radhakrishnan's thought as here expressed, our knowledge may be wholly concrete. It is flatly opposed, however, to a reality which it can never seize, even to the slightest degree. The two realms fall apart. And thus our author re-enacts, after all, the theory of affirmation and negation as representing two distinct packets. And the result is complete agnosticism—relieved, however, by the mystical intuition, defined according to the negative way. Truth in its best estate is asked to correspond to a reality that is outside it; and it can never show any evidence that it has been able to do that. But Western idealism has turned the flank of that difficulty, and vindicated in principle the possibility of knowledge, by maintaining the congruence conception of truth; and that is what I meant to imply in the modified passage from Whittier just quoted.

We may take a few sentences more:

Since Śaṁkara repudiates the conception of a concrete universal as the ultimate category, it is thought that he dismisses the world as meaningless. Śaṁkara's Brahman, which has no other, nothing independent of it, seems to be an abstract unity, a sort of lion's den, where all that enters is lost. Śaṁkara holds that we cannot construe the relation between Brahman and the world in any logical way, but he is as insistent as any advocate of the theory of the concrete universal that nothing is real apart from the ultimate reality. Though the world and Brahman are not regarded as complementary elements in a whole, they are not set in absolute antagonism. And yet great scholars [Deussen, Max Müller] have rushed to this conclusion. Śaṁkara's view that the problem of the relation of reality and appearance remains for us finite souls a riddle is the result of a greater maturity of thought.[7]

7 Ind P, II, 586.

However, the difficulty found by such thinkers as Rāmānuja, Deussen, Max Müller, Thibaut, and even Śaṁkara himself, is not exactly that there is nothing independent of Brahman. It is rather that there is no negativity within this abstract affirmation, therefore no difference or "parts," and that therefore it could not ground or engender anything whatever. And yet there exists the entire universe of fact, although its manifold of existence has just been denied. Our author goes on to explain that such universe exists by reason of Cosmic Ignorance (Avidya), and is in fact a system of Cosmic Illusion (Māyā). And this may avoid subjectivism, since the illusion is cosmic. But in place of the critic's problem that in such a system there could not be any grounds for truth in science, duty in ethics, rights in politics, our author substitutes the consideration that we have difficulty in defining to ourselves, in a logically powerful manner, the metaphysical foundations of such values. But that is not what these great scholars understood Śaṁkara to be saying.

The large value found by mystics in Śaṁkara is that he has been very zealous for the "Brahmahood of the soul of man," and that he has given an exposition of the negative way by which release may be secured, it is believed, from the trivialities and frustrations and sorrows of ordinary living. And of these considerations much of Indian thinking is keenly aware. Neo-Confucianism, however, as we shall see, finds that by such logic the movement to the higher values of a philosophy of civilization seems confused. Although I have understood our author to be more sympathetic with the former, he really has points of attachment with both. Broken selections from the booklet on *The Religion We Need* may bring this out:

The supreme reality is difficult to grasp and impossible to define. We can be sure of what God is not, but not of what God is. He is not an emergent deity . . . not an exceedingly able mechanical engineer . . . not a supernatural proprietor of the universe interfering with it at all odd moments. He is not a God to whom we are bound by a covenant . . . or who takes sides and has preferences . . . He is not the remote ground of the structure of the universe, but an immanent spirit working in and through all . . . He is the ceaseless creative activity which has actualized us, which is working in us, through us, and beyond us . . . When we rise to the human level, conscious purpose takes the place of unconscious variation. Man knows that the power which has produced personalities with spiritual, rational, and moral endowments is alive at the centre of the universe claiming adventurous co-operation.

The creative process is still going on and is unfinished in several respects and waits for man's willing and heroic service. The future evolution of man on earth is not likely to be on the organic side; it will be in the ideal direction.[8]

These passages move from a beginning essentially assuming the teaching of the Vedānta to a close which is highly congruous with the philosophy of the Confucian "masters" of the Sung dynasty. If the emphasis were changed from the earlier part of the citation to an adequate development of the concluding portions, a different treatment of affirmation and negation would become regnant, and a different system of values and perspectives would be fostered. I would favor reading the citation with such an emphasis.

For the passages do not represent a logical development—probably were not intended to do so, in these high matters.

From Śaṁkara's teaching that the Brahman really has no attributes, our author had previously ridden over to the statement that we do not know the attributes which it really has. And this yields the form in which the negative way has been current in both agnosticism and mysticism. But critics have long since pointed out that a consistent agnosticism is impossible. So then, from "We do not know the real as a mechanical engineer," one slips over to "We know that God is not a mechanical engineer." And then the thrust of affirmation, implied in all significant negation, begins to install other traits which we must believe to be real. He is the immanent spirit working in and through it all. And ultimately affirmation becomes vigorous indeed. "Man knows that the power which has produced personalities . . . is alive at the centre of the universe claiming adventurous co-operation [possibly free will]." "Unfinished in several respects [not only immanence but transcendence]."

We may now turn to the Chinese side of the story.

The Sung philosophers conceived that the Neo-Confucianism which they were defining remained essentially true to the teachings of the sages Confucius and Mencius; that they were but giving to those teachings a closer logical integration and a more adequate philosophical basis. From their extensive writings we may bring into view only a few, and especially such as bear upon our problem of affirmation and negation, of abstraction and concreteness in the quest of unity.

Incorporated in the writings of Chu Hsi is a student's question, which he, the master, commends. The setting for the question I quote for comments:

[8] Radhakrishnan, RWN, 22, 26.

There is only one Law of Heaven and Man [monism]. The root and fruit are identical [concrete] . . . The realization of the fruit does not mean separation from the root [like Aristotle, opposes *chorismos*]. Even those whom we regard as saints spoke only of perfecting the relationships of human Life. The [Chinese] Buddhists [abstract monists] discard man and discourse on Heaven, and thus separate the fruit from the root. . . . The indispensable relations between father and son, sovereign and minister, husband and wife, senior and junior [and thus all natural rights], they regard as accidental. . . . Now there are no two laws in the universe; how then can they take Heaven and man, the root and the fruit, summarily asserting one and denying the other, and yet call this Tao? . . . Those who follow the sacred Confucian school, on the other hand, "from the study of the lowly understand high things [Analects]." . . . For the Moral Law which the noble man follows after is far reaching and yet mystical. Far reaching, it embraces the whole of his daily life; mystical, it is Divine Law. With this Divine Law, then, in daily life—in the relation between sovereign and minister, father and son, senior and junior, or when engaged in the toasting and pledging of social intercourse, or when eating, resting, seeing, and hearing—there is not one sphere of activity that is not under the guidance of Law, and not one that can be confused—for wherever there is confusion, Divine Law has perished. What is there in Buddhism adequate to express this? The reality and unchangeableness of Divine Law and man's mind they have not apprehended. What they call "culture," also, is nothing more than the control of the mind and sitting in silence. Discarding human relationships, destroying the Divine Law, they reap no good that can be perceived.[9]

I have quoted this statement in order to get before us the emphasis of the Sung School upon the concreteness of the real as a unity involving differences, and their attack upon the abstractionism of Buddhism. Such abstractionism results, they hold, from the fact that Buddhism separates too sharply the affirmative factor, Heaven, from the negative factor, the self-defeating quality of human life. The Confucian does not deny that in the study of "the lowly" we test, criticize, use analysis and negation; but it sees negation as aiming at the objective of bringing out more adequately the staunchness of "high things"—of clarifying the affirmative movement in the entire process.

Some time during the reign of Richard I of England a Chinese college student, Ch'en An Ch'ing, living near Changsha in south central China, tendered to his professor, Chu Hsi, a philosophical essay on the Mind. Ratified and given publicity by the professor,

---

9 Bruce, J. P., *Philosophy of Human Nature*, 280-282.

it assembles in a manner available for us important Neo-Confucian conceptions. In particular, he may be understood as attempting to formulate the conception of the concrete universal, so far as it had been made available to him by his teachers of the Sung School:

> 'The Decree of Heaven, how profound it is and undying' [Odes]. That by means of which it rules over the production of things is the Mind of Heaven. Man receives the Decree of Heaven and so is born; and because this by which Heaven gives me birth is received by me in its entirety to reside in me, spiritual and intelligent, continuously illuminating and unclouded, living and imperishable—this we call the Mind of Man. . . . Therefore, though the substance [actuality] resides in a very minute spot, that which constitutes it the substance is really as great as Heaven and Earth; the countless laws of the universe are present in their completeness, and there is not a single thing outside their scope.[10]

Here, five hundred years before Leibniz, we are getting the conception of the genuine individual as a *microcosmus*, truly at home in a world of universal law, when that law is of a type which founds and fosters individuality. But our student goes forward, to introduce the problem of knowledge:

> Although its operation proceeds from a very minute spot, that which constitutes its operation is really in union with the pervading activity of Heaven and Earth; the countless phenomena of the universe are united in it, and there is not a single law which does not operate in them. Herein lies the mystery of the mind; it unifies activity and repose, the manifest and the hidden, the external and the internal, the source and the issue, to the exclusion of all barriers. But man is fettered by the limitations which fall to his lot, to which is added the entanglement in the desires of the senses; and thus the Mind is cramped by material form.[11]

Thus far he has taught what a recent writer calls the "privileged position of the self in knowledge," but without surrendering to the subjectivism which is latent in Descartes, explicit in Berkeley, and perhaps not entirely overcome by Kant. As Bosanquet has formulated this teaching, "Reality is the norm of the Mind."

> Thus, before being affected by the external world, the Mind is pure and brilliant. . . . After being affected by the external world, the response depends upon this particular phenomenon. For this Law is all comprehensive, and resides in every single thing as the law of its individual existence. . . . In repose the substance of Heaven and

---

[10] *Ibid.*, 217f.   [11] *Ibid.*, 218.

Earth remains—one source with an infinite plurality of phenomena. In activity the operations of Heaven and Earth go forth—an infinite plurality of phenomena, but united in one unity. The substance constantly enfolds its operation within itself, and the operation is never separated from the one substance.[12]

He is saying, I suppose, that in developed logical theory the ultimate ground of knowledge would have to be identical with the world ground. At this point, however, a fellow student passes criticism upon the somewhat soaring character of the paper of Ch'en An Ch'ing; and the young Confucian reverts to type in a manner which I must quote:

On thinking over the matter further it seems to me that speaking in an ontological sense it is still correct to say 'The mind-substance is as great as Heaven and Earth, and its operation is in union with the all pervading activity of Heaven and Earth;' but to express it only in this way would be to fall into the opposite error of speaking on too lofty a plane, and of not bringing the subject into touch with our own faults. It seems best to speak from our own point of view, and say, 'That which is all comprehensive within is the substance; that which is affected by the external world and responds thereto is the operation' as the most pertinent statement of the matter. I recall that the saints and sages spoke in common speech.[13]

There may then be plenty of "fault," frustration, and negativity within our execution of the logical process; but the affirmative meaning of it all is still lodged in the nature of supreme reality—such, at any rate, is the faith of human intelligence, for Neo-Confucian analysis, even if it be denied by the Vedānta; lodged, indeed, in the real. But, as we shall see, this does not necessarily mean that the intellect, even in its best consummation, completes the measurement of the real.

Our mode of approach must be inductive—the study of particular phenomena, and the attempt to define first the laws which pervade their individualities, and the immediate and proximate connections of individual facts. But it must still remain true, as the philosopher Chang Tze has said, that "The egoistic mind cannot be in union with the Mind of Heaven." The quest of the universal is what activates intelligence, even when the universal is defined at a higher level than generalized law.

But our young collegian's Essay on Mind has also a section expounding the Neo-Confucian teaching regarding the foundation

12 *Ibid.*, 218f.   13 *Ibid.*, 220.

of ethics, and especially aiming to put into clear light its interpretation of the selfhood of man as truly universal. This will contrast
with modern positivism, which may admit the social self, indeed,
but can give no meaning to a universal self; and contrast also with
the Vedāntism of Śaṁkara, which recognizes indeed the universal
self, but is unable to connect it with human ethics. I quote:

> Permeating the whole universe there is but one Law as the ultimate
> reality, the pivot of creation and transformation received alike by men
> and all other creatures. Yet among all creatures it is man who is spirit.
> So true is this that I embody and receive congregated in my Mind all
> those principles which are comprehended in that one Law. . . . But
> although these principles are thus congregated in my mind, they are
> never severed from the Divine. What in my Mind is called Love is the
> Divine principle of Origin [and so Reverence, Righteousness, Wisdom].
> . . . They are really identical, and are not simply used as illustration.
> . . . But when I call it the substance of my Mind, then, from the point
> of view of law as it is inherent in me, there is an arch-controller, and
> its operations are traceable [resisting the theory of the empty Absolute].
> . . . This Law I receive into my Mind in its entirety; and being in my
> Mind there is not a moment when it is not productive and in union
> with the all-pervading activity of Heaven and Earth. . . . Take, for
> example, the feeling of solicitude. In the case of those who are near, it
> is manifest in family affection. When we are affectionate towards those
> to whom we ought to be affectionate it is the pervading activity of the
> Decree of Heaven. I simply unite with it in its pervading activity, and
> then I do not defraud the objects of my affection. . . . Or in a wider
> circle, in the sphere of love to men, such as the obligation to comfort
> the aged, to treat the young tenderly, and to be apprehensive for one
> falling into a well, this, too, is the pervading activity of the Decree of
> Heaven. . . . In a still wider circle, in the sphere of kindness to in-
> ferior creatures, such as sparing the young sapling, saving the life of
> pregnant animals, and avoiding the destruction of young creatures,
> this, too, is the all-pervading activity of the Decree of Heaven. . . . If
> in only one thing there is not the appropriate response, it is because in
> that one thing Divine Law is impeded.[14]

In this teaching of Neo-Confucianism there is as sharp an assertion of the essential identity of the human self with the universal
self as we find in the Vedānta; but it is an identity which involves
difference, an assertion which involves negation subordinated
within it. In Indian debate, opponents of the Advaita had attacked
such assertions on the ground that they violate the law of the excluded middle. They are indeed of the order of paradox involved

14 *Ibid.*, 222f.

in the poet's assertion that "Unless above himself he can erect himself, how poor a thing is man!" But the Confucianist judges that this overriding of our smug distinctions is of the very essence of sane thinking and sane acting, and can be rejected only by a type of logical theory which does not understand situations that are sufficiently intelligible. The allowables of competent logical theory are indeed overstrained, however, when we fund all assertion of reality into an undifferenced Brahman, all negation into nonentity, and then insert, between these two, the realm of systematic illusion, Māyā, which is neither real nor unreal. Such a "middle" should indeed be "excluded," and the members more properly integrated.

Now the teaching of our Neo-Confucian student is indeed mysticism. That is, it holds that the human self is in vital unity with the oversoul. It holds that the intellectual activity is a relatively low and secondary stage of "production" from that unity. It holds that the feelings of man are powerfully charged with the life of the Absolute—indeed, it may go as far in this direction as Schleiermacher did. It sees the entire system of individual and social ethics as based upon this fact. And it sees the climax and meaning of it all in Love in the individual responsive to Love in the Whole. One might almost judge that it went forth deliberately to prepare the metaphysic which should enable the Quaker poet, some seven centuries later, to express his mysticism in the prayer, "Let our ordered lives confess the beauty of Thy peace."

Before we move too far away from our student's paper, we may comment upon his relation to Kant. He recognizes, as clearly as does the German master, a transcendental synthesis in the Mind; a "mystery" by which it "unifies the manifest and the hidden, the external and the internal, the source and the issue." But for him this also unifies activity and repose. The Nature and the Decree are one. So then he does not, like Kant, establish an absolute duality of method between the indicative mood and the imperative mood, between the facts of human nature and the imperatives of humanism. And he thereby avoids the ethical formalism which is so troublesome in Kant's philosophy. He has entered upon the pathway of Fichte to the primacy of will, and could interest himself in much of the message of Professors James and Dewey. But if and when the pragmatists should deny the reality of universals even in the concrete sense, he would need to break away.

Confucianism bases its entire interpretation of human life and the interests thereof upon the study of human nature; and that is the objective of psychological, biological, and other natural sciences. It may be taken, then, as an example of *Naturalism*, in one of the meanings of that highly ambiguous word. But it groups with what some have called the Higher Naturalism—the philosophy of "both-and" rather than "nothing but."

Mencius had taught that human nature, in the essential law of its being, is fundamentally good. Taoists replied that human nature has no such law that is intrinsic to it. Rather, it is like the waters of a stream, which whirl entirely under the control of bank and rock. The Confucianists recognized here the philosophy of "nothing but," or, in more technical phrasing, the reductive form of naturalism. Mencius vigorously opposed, then, the Whirling Waters Heresy; and the Sung School carried forward the war. Man is both an organism struggling to survive, and also to some degree aware of the farther possibilities of the situation. In rejecting the whirling waters fallacy, then, Neo-Confucianism is committing itself to the metaphysics of Elizabeth Barrett:

> The little more, and how much it is!
> And the little less, and what worlds away!

The Sung philosophers' treatment of this situation fails indeed in point of literary skill, but not of logical discernment. Chu Hsi puts it thus:

> It is necessary to recognize the differences in the unity and the unity in the differences. In the beginning there is no difference so far as Law is concerned, but when the Law is deposited in the Ether there is likeness only in the coarser features, such as the capacity for hunger and thirst, and seeking what is advantageous and avoiding the injurious, which birds and beasts have in common with men; so that, apart from moral principles, man would not differ from them. . . . The Philosopher has said, 'The people hold within themselves a normal principle of good.' This represents the difference. The saying, 'The mass of the people cast it away, while the noble man preserves it,' means that we must preserve this difference. Only thus are we distinguished from the brute.[15]

We may note that this asserts immanence and continuity, so dear to the Western heart. The struggle for life may be, even for bird and beast, a 'struggle for the lives of others.' For man it may be a struggle for sovereign and country, for parents, for brothers, for friends. But such factors are intrinsic and essential, and are not to

---

[15] *Ibid.*, 96f.

be sacrificed to the "nothing but" abstractionism of the whirling waters fallacy.

This line of thought grounds also one of Chu Hsi's main criticisms against abstract idealistic monism:

We must not say that the wriggling movement of the worm holds the spiritual within it; that all things have the Buddha nature like ourselves.[16]

Now, of course, for Chu Hsi "The Mind of Heaven and Earth" is as truly present, in the plenitude of its power, in the nervous organization of the wriggling worm as it is in the brain of a Confucius. "As full, as perfect, in the hair as heart." But the levels of expression into fact and history are enormously different. They differ, therefore, in their competence to display reality. These differences must be conserved by our theory of life, and must not be handed over to the leveling type of egalitarianism.

The Mind of Heaven and Earth carries within itself, as of its very essence, the constructive ends of wholesome humanism; so therefore the possibilities of life at its very best lie open to the human spirit, according to the measure to which any given personality may overcome his frustrations. Lower life has indeed its interest, but it remains lower life.

Chinese Buddhism speaks indeed of the Heart of Compassion as supreme. But since it regards all the objectives of human aspiration as vain, futile, and self-defeating, it has thrown away all the differences which Confucianism has so carefully established between animalism, cheap human life, and noble humanism. Buddhism may indeed, as Sir Edwin Arnold thought, have "made our Asia mild;" but Confucianism was aspiring to give to Asia a rich and stable civilization, with citizens minded to maintain schools, enlightened laws, and affectionate families.

I wish to allude briefly to certain characteristics of the history of the Sung School.

The first thinker of this movement, Chou Tun I, was a contemporary of Edward the Confessor in England, and of Rāmānuja in India. He wrote many books, of which the two most important are fully preserved. Of these the first gave a brief interpretation of the Chinese theory of the universe in terms of monism; and the second, more extensively, traced the dominant ethical categories of Confucius and Mencius back to their metaphysical grounding. There now ensued a very remarkable movement, at the hands of

16 *Ibid.*, 97.

several gifted thinkers who were also men of outstanding personality. With the death of Chu Hsi, A.D. 1200, the movement may be regarded as having made a competent presentation of its case. Chou Tze's first book opens with five Chinese words, which have become the slogan of the school. Professor Bruce translates them, "Infinite! And also the Supreme Ultimate!" [17] And this shall stand as a declaration of a concrete monism.

But certain Chinese critics pointed out that the two ideographs here translated Infinite simply mean the denial of the finality of the factual world; that abstract monism in the Vedānta and in Buddhism had already done that, with the Empty Absolute as the result. But in extensive debates, summed up effectively by Chu Hsi, the Confucianists repulse this abstractionist rendering, and defend the concreteness of the Supreme Ultimate. In the light of this discussion, I venture to tender as a translation, "Searching for the integrating basis of the world of finite hard-and-fastness; and finding the supreme pivot of all that is real!" The negative movement is there, indeed, and in power, but it is not made all-destroying.

The second representative of the school, the elder brother Ch'eng (Ming Tao), adding also a dash of paradox, sought to give enhanced emphasis to both the negative and the affirmative factors in the slogan. "Void like the boundless desert, but filled with innumerable forms like a dense forest." Chu Hsi renders it obvious that the second member of this famous formula represents the controlling interest. No finite thing shall stand up in its own right; but in and through the power of the Concrete Universal, vast constructive results shall be established.

Want of space forbids us to follow the detail of the analysis by which the older Confucian ethical views were overhauled in the light of this metaphysic; but certain passages relevant to the general problem that faces a matured philosophical ethics become important. We have first the account given by Chu Hsi of the method of conventional morality, particularly when, as in the Chinese case, the conventional tradition had already been edited by revered men who were competent sages, indeed, but not metaphysicians:

> The infinite greatness of the substance of the Moral Law, and at the same time the necessity that the student in his study of it should be 'accomplished, distinctive, contemplative, and all-searching, and not allow error even to the extent of a hair's breadth: this is what the saints

17 Bruce, J. P., *Chu Hsi and His Masters*, 128.

and sages exhibited in discoursing upon the Moral Law. . . . It embraces the three hundred rules of ceremony and the three thousand rules of demeanor. . . . And in their instruction to the scholar in the task of 'actualizing the Moral Law by the cultivation of virtue' . . . they of necessity go on to show that 'none of its exquisite and minute points may be omitted.' [18]

But twelfth century Chu Hsi did not need to wait for the nineteenth century, in order to learn what may happen when "The Great God lets loose a Thinker on this planet." The age of criticism was then already at work, his own school was helping it on, but in too many cases it had reached only the "acids of modernity" stage.

Modern teachers in expounding the meaning of the Moral Law are very different. In discussing its vastness, they rejoice in its comprehensive completeness, but dislike research into its ramifications. They rejoice in its transcendental mystery, but gloss over its infinitesimal minuteness. So far as concerns its 'broadness and greatness,' they do not differ materially from the sages, but they do not examine into its 'exquisite minuteness.' So that they are not in position to discuss the true account of its entire substance.[19]

Such students, he thinks, are suffering from an education that is underdone. For them, criticism has indeed "made ancient good uncouth." And this is a necessary negative stage. Shall they therefore stand mute in modern debate? Not so, in the opinion of Chu Hsi, if they have used negation wisely, and have advanced to the affirmative stage of Neo-Confucian teaching:

Is it maintained that Tao is lofty and distant, inscrutable and mysterious, and beyond the possibility of human study? I answer that Tao derives its name from the fact that it is the principle of right conduct in everyday life for all men. . . . I say that Tao, present as it is in all the world in the relation between sovereign and minister and between father and son, in down-sitting and uprising and in activity and rest, has everywhere its unchangeable clear law, which cannot fail for a single instant. The student of the sages must not be satisfied with examining the letter only. . . . He must discuss their teachings intelligently, and examine them . . . in order to . . . manifest them in the business of life. Only thus can he fulfil his mission, and take his place in the universe. He must not examine the letter only, for the mere purpose of tracing out and compiling.[20]

[18] Bruce, J. P., *Philosophy of Human Nature*, 277.
[19] *Ibid.*, 277f.   [20] *Ibid.*, 278f.

If Chu Hsi had consciously applied to this problem the maxim of Ming Tao, which he so cordially approved, and which I suppose he was implicitly using here, it would probably have read something like this: "Void, of the precepts of dogmatic and traditional ethical maxims, as a boundless desert; but filled, with innumerable forms which issue from the ground of an enlightened humanism, as a dense forest is filled with trees." In a similar spirit I would like to amplify for ethics the translation which I offered of the slogan originally given by Chou Tze:

Searching for the integrating ground of our Confucian ethics, which cannot be acceptable in the form of dogma and tradition; and finding its root in the mystic union of the finite self with the Mind of Heaven and Earth conceived as the Concrete Universal, and as productive Love operating in the establishment of individualities; finding its fruitage also in a vast system of humane morals, law, and culture, which can be seen as adapted to the expression of the true nature of man in his relation to the nature of the world.

The sages of China, by their systematic study of the literary monuments of ancient Chinese civilization, may now be seen as correctly perceiving extensive areas of this law and culture; but they may also be seen, the Sung philosophers judged, to be subject to critical revision in detail and indeed often in principle. We would thus gain a new conservatism, which in point of definition is difficult to distinguish from the new liberalism, after liberalism shall have passed beyond its negative stage. In the social medium of China, however, Neo-Confucianism could not be permitted to develop its liberalistic logic.

Early in its career the Sung School found itself in need of a brief formula which should express with some success the spirit of the laws—something to correspond to the Golden Rule of Jesus, or the formulations of Kant. Confucius himself had suggested the idea of Reciprocity. "Whatever you do not wish others to do to you, do not do that to them." But this remains in the negative stage characteristic of conventional ethics, and besides, it has not moved through the development we have been noticing. About A.D. 1060 the youthful Ming Tao wrote a paper on *The Steadfast Nature*— a two page paper which became a Neo-Confucian classic. His historic statement reads:

The highest attainment is with broadness of mind to be actuated by a high altruism, and to respond naturally and fittingly to each phenomenon as it presents itself.[21]

21 *Ibid.*, 245.

Probably no statement of this type can be fully successful; but any such statement is at least entitled to be correctly understood. In the case of Ming Tao, we must remember that the high altruism is interpreted by the thought of the great constitutive relations of society. So also breadth of mind does not mean, as for some liberals, a want of fidelity to the essential ends of life at its best. Rather, it is more like the breadth of mind of a highly competent judge, "a man learned in the law." A natural response, also, is not one dictated by one's immature and perhaps animalistic organization, but rather one in accordance with our "high calling" as human beings. That which is fitting, again, is not simply adapted to the conveniences of our parlor intercourse, but to our dealings with a person who, like ourselves, participates in the Mind of Heaven and Earth. Further, the last clause does not represent pragmatism or cheap opportunism. The element of Law which is there is as inexorable as Stoic or Puritan ever supposed; but it is the Law of human life at its most adequate consummation. And then too, we should note that the Steadfast Nature means what Ming Tao meant it to mean, "neither more nor less," and it does not mean stubbornness or stolidity. It should be closely compared, however, with a statement by a writer of quite different antecedents, speaking also in his own way:

We have repeatedly endeavored to explain that all sorts of Heroes are intrinsically of the same material; that given a great soul, open to the divine significance of life, then there is given a man fit to speak of this, to sing of this, to fight and work for this, in a great, victorious, enduring manner; there is given a Hero,—the outward shape of whom will depend on the time and the environment he finds himself in.[22]

My present interest is to loiter neither with the "common speech" of the Confucian, nor with the "high things" of the Scotsman. I am interested in the deliberate attempt to avoid in ethics the formulation of generalizing universals, whether set up in terms of German Koenigsberg or American Middletown; to avoid these, however, not by giving up the moral universal, but rather by recasting it in concrete form; and to maintain clearly and vigorously that this recasting carries an affirmative meaning which is intelligible and of vital import to society. The generalizing statements may then still be retained, as facets within the synthesis, but they lose their absoluteness and their power to domineer. They declare "It is not in me," and on occasion become amenable to critical revision.

[22] Carlyle, Thomas, *On Heroes and Hero-Worship*, Lectures IV and VI.

We now move on to consider the evaluation which the Sung philosophers came to place upon Buddhism—the most appealing form of abstract idealistic monism which had come within their ken. This evaluation was a matter of prolonged and searching study—a study that was critical indeed, but, until after the verdict had been rendered, not hostile in spirit. When rendered, however, the verdict was indeed decisive, and has remained so to this day, as I suppose, for those who have clearly understood Neo-Confucianism and the issues involved. Only those who have failed to understand, or who have yielded to a weak spirit of lackadaisical syncretism, can rest at ease in the curious three-fold medley of Taoism, Buddhism, and Confucianism—however common that medley may have been for many centuries in China.

And the verdict is that Confucianism under its own motivation is ticketed to develop all that is humanistically valuable in Buddhism; whereas Buddhism contains inevitably baneful elements which prevent it from being a worthy and adequate philosophy, religion, or scheme of life for a society of civilized men.

The second writer of the Sung School, the elder brother Ch'eng, a cultured personality (already noticed as Ming Tao), not only read widely in the writings of the philosophers of all schools, but devoted ten years to the study of the teachings of Taoism and Buddhism. Ultimately, however, he remained staunchly Confucian, and indeed, in association with his gifted younger brother, added much to the development of the School.

But it was more than half a century after the death of the younger Ch'eng, namely in A.D. 1160, that the issue now under study reached its decision. This came as a consequence of a series of historic debates between two scholars of splendid power and training. A third man, also known to literary history, but of secondary rating on this issue, also participated. We may give brief space to these historic figures and the historic event.

Chu Hsi ultimately threw the decision by surrendering his protracted defense of the merits of Buddhism. At this time he was thirty years of age. A prodigy in childhood, he had in youth studied the Confucian masters with an industry even surpassing that so famous among Chinese students. For three years, early in his 'teens, he had enjoyed the tuition of his father, Chu Sung. The father had been one of the very best students under Lo Ts'ung Yen, the latest of the Sung masters; and in active life he had been an important minister in the government of the Emperor. When he was about to die, he placed his son under the best Confucian teachers.

Chu Hsi took his doctorate at the age of nineteen. Early distinguishing himself as a writer, he received his first appointment as a magistrate at the age of twenty-two. By the time he was twenty-eight, however, he was appointed to a sinecure position as guardian of a temple near Changsha, where he might have the opportunity to teach and write. In the meantime, from boyhood forward, he had taken great interest in Buddhist thought, and had read its literature with deep sympathy.

Li Yen Ping, older by one generation, had been accounted the very best of the students under Lo Ts'ung Yen. In his school days he had also formed a life friendship with Chu Sung, and was a frequent visitor in his home. Thus he became also the friend, and ultimately the teacher, of Chu Hsi. Some nine years after his father's death, when enroute to his first magistracy, Chu Hsi visited Li Yen Ping at the home of the latter. Their conversations ranged widely over their field of scholarly interests, but soon came to touch upon the literature and teaching of Buddhism, then viewed very favorably by Chu Hsi. Li Yen Ping issued a sharp logical challenge, which set the younger man back on his heels, but did not cause him to give ground. He did, however, enter upon a very close study of the issues involved, a study lasting for several years.

Some seven years later, A.D. 1158, Chu Hsi again visited Li Yen Ping, for a stay of several months. They retired to a summer cottage in the mountains, and in company with Hu Chang, the third, they worked systematically upon their problem of the evaluation of Buddhism. "They spent each day in reading, and in the evening and early morning compared notes, correcting and criticizing the results of each other's labors." [23] Li Yen Ping brought to bear a splendid appreciation of the history and logic of Neo-Confucianism; Chu Hsi brought "incomparable ability and power of concentration which his teacher characterized as 'terrific.' " [24] The younger man could not readily yield the advantages which Buddhism had to offer. It had already in being, for instance, a vast literature, much of which was of high nobility and fitted to appeal to the public; it had a priesthood able to interpret that literature to the people; it had an ecclesiastical organization able to advance and disseminate its influence. Confucianism, by comparison, was simply the books of the sages and the influence of the student class. Further, one may believe that the idealistic monism of Buddhism may have made upon Chu Hsi at that time an impression similar to that which an idealistic rendering of Spinoza made upon Lessing,

[23] Bruce, *Chu Hsi and His Masters*, 68.   [24] *Ibid.*

Goethe, and many another figure in European literature. So then, during the 1158 session at least, the issue was not solved.

The two came together again for several months in 1160, this time in the "Western Park" as guests of another friend. At this session the verdict was cast. Buddhism lost all part and share in Confucianism, except as the latter produced similar values from its own substance—there should be no external syncretism with the "religious postulates of Buddhism." And when Chu Hsi surrendered, he surrendered "all over." His manifold later references to Buddhism are regularly in terms of adverse criticism. And he had remaining forty years of active literary work in which to maintain that criticism.

There is of course no adequate literary history of this significant debate. But the form which the issue ultimately took in the mind of Chu Hsi is abundantly evident in Chinese books, although these are not available for Western readers. The distinguished Sinologist, Professor J. P. Bruce, who has studied these books, and whose work is most available here, gives the following summary statement:

These, then, are the essential features of the two systems. Buddhism says: There is one mind in the universe, the Buddha mind. We receive it, and it is ours. Our mind, therefore, is part of the universal mind. But our individuality consists in our entanglement in the mesh of connections with external things, and what we call our mind, that is our individual mind, is not our real mind. So, then, our real mind is outside what we call our mind, and the Law of the Universe is to be found outside our hearts. Our business, then, is not to develop, but to sink our individuality, to lose our individual mind that we may find our true mind, the universal mind of Buddha. The result is the destruction of the social relations and the cardinal virtues. Chu Hsi, on the other hand, says: There is one mind of the universe, the manifestation of Divine Law. We receive it, and it is ours. And because the mind of the universe is ours, the Law of the universe is also ours, inherent in our hearts. Our business is to develop our mind to the utmost and bring it into harmony with its source. To do this means that our individuality will be not obliterated, but intensified, and the cardinal virtues perfected.[25]

I suppose that this is a sound statement of the issue; and on this statement, I do not see that syncretism with Buddhism would ever be possible to the clear-minded Confucian philosopher.

It is beyond doubt that the Sung philosophy, like every other

[25] *Ibid.*, 253f.

human scheme of thought, requires growth and completion. It appears to have been trying to say what Tennyson said,

Thou seemest human and divine,
The highest, holiest manhood Thou!

I am not tendering Western metaphysics to help it out. India indeed could offer much, especially from thinkers not dominated by orthodox Vedāntism, Buddhism, or the Negative Way. Our own author, Radhakrishnan, in scores of discussions, has borne a worthy part. Let me adduce a key passage from an important book:

Only a philosophy which affirms that our ideals are rooted in the universal nature of things can give depth and fervor to moral life, courage and confidence in moral difficulties. We need to be fortified by the conviction that the service of ideals is what the cosmic scheme demands of us, that our loyalty or disloyalty to them is a matter of the deepest moment not only to ourselves or to society, or even to the human species, but to the nature of things. If ethical thought is profound, it will give a cosmic motive to morality. Moral consciousness must include a conviction of the reality of ideals. If the latter is religion, then ethical humanism is acted religion. When man realizes his essential unity with the whole of being, he expresses this unity in his life. . . . In the higher religions of mankind, belief in the transcendent and work in the natural have grown together in close intimacy and interaction.[26]

The manifold passages of this type, which I would prefer to stress, associate themselves with the later portions of our citation from *The Religion We Need*. But there remain many others— dozens, scores—which join better with the earlier portions. Our author then normally suggests interpretations from the Vedānta or kindred thinkers, which may serve to make the contrast less oppressive. But the Vedāntic interpretations sometimes seem open to challenge by competent scholars; and when using Bradley, for instance, he quotes indeed the well known negative passages, but remains silent concerning the affirmative passages which throw a different light on the situation. On this particular matter, however, I venture to suggest that Bradley be rated as less significant than Chu Hsi; and, more broadly, that the entire Sung movement be brought into focus, for the valuable contrast it affords with the overdriven quietistic tendencies which issue from certain Indian philosophies.

EDGAR L. HINMAN

DEPARTMENT OF PHILOSOPHY
UNIVERSITY OF NEBRASKA

26 ER, 82.

19

F. S. C. Northrop

RADHAKRISHNAN'S CONCEPTION OF THE RELATION
BETWEEN EASTERN AND WESTERN
CULTURAL VALUES

RADHAKRISHNAN'S CONCEPTION OF THE RELATION BETWEEN EASTERN AND WESTERN CULTURAL VALUES *

O NE of the unique facts of our time is the shift of the political focus of the world from Western Europe toward Asia. In Japan, following Perry's visit, in China with the revolution of Sun Yat Sen, and in Indonesia and India more recently, Oriental peoples have thrown off the control of their fortunes by Western powers and insisted upon directing their affairs in terms of their own traditional indigenous values. At the same time the two major economic, political and military powers in the world are the United States and Soviet Russia. Both of these powers ground their social institutions and values in the economic, political and religious, or anti-religious, principles of modern Western civilization.

Under such circumstances, with Oriental peoples taking over command of their own affairs while Westernized nations are also dominant internationally, one major contemporary problem becomes obvious. It is that of understanding, and then in the light of this understanding properly relating, the differing values of the East and the West. Few men, if any, bring to such a task a more fortunate background of education and experience than Professor Radhakrishnan. Even the statesmen of his country testify to his practical as well as theoretical competence, as is witnessed by his present appointment as the Ambassador of India to Moscow.

It happens also that Professor Radhakrishnan has directed his attention explicitly to this question of the relation between Oriental and Occidental values. This occurs in his two books, *East and West in Religion* [1] and *Eastern Religions and Western Thought.* [2] It is important, therefore, that a serious examination be made of the conclusions at which he arrives and the validity of the reasons which he gives for them.

* The author is gratefully indebted to the Viking Fund for a grant which makes this and other research possible.

[1] George Allen and Unwin, Ltd., London, 1933. Hereafter referred to as EWR.

[2] Oxford University Press, 1940, 2nd ed. Hereafter referred to as ER.

It will be well to begin with his final constructive suggestions. We can then work back to the conclusions of his analysis and his reasons for them. This approach has the advantage also of enabling us to see his conception as a whole before we turn to his appraisal of Western values, part of which is critical.

As their titles·indicate, these two major works treat of religion. It must be remembered, however, that, for any citizen of India, religion and philosophy are identical. Thus Radhakrishnan's approach to the values of the West must not be thought of as neglecting philosophy or science or the technological values which follow from Western science. Even in the West, religion, philosophy, science and technology are essentially connected, even if the departmentalization of Western education tends to obscure this fact. Radhakrishnan is referring to values, Oriental and Western, in the widest and most all-inclusive sense.

Even so, his emphasis upon religion is very much to the point. For religion perhaps more than explicitly articulated philosophy takes one to the more unconscious values and emotionally sustained responses which define the truly living laws and practices of any culture.

Sensitive to the aforementioned events of our time, he puts his positive suggestion as follows:

To-day the whole world is in fusion and all is in motion. East and West are fertilizing each other, not for the first time. May we not strive for a philosophy which will combine the best of European humanism and Asiatic religion, a philosophy profounder and more living than either, endowed with greater spiritual and ethical force, which will conquer the hearts of men and compel peoples to acknowledge its sway? [3]

Needless to say, he answers this question in the affirmative.

Radhakrishnan is not so naive, however, as to suppose that this can come about without some very important changes in present attitudes, particularly in the West. This new attitude he puts as follows: "We must recognize humbly the partial and defective character of our isolated traditions and seek their source in the generic tradition from which they all have sprung." [4] Forthwith he refers to Professor Hocking's statement, "We have to recognise that a *world religion exists.*" [5] Radhakrishnan then ·concludes as follows:

Owing to a cross-fertilization of ideas and insights, behind which lie centuries of racial and cultural tradition and earnest endeavour, a great

[3] ER, 259.   [4] *Ibid.*, 347.   [5] *Ibid.*, 347.

unification is taking place in the deeper fabric of men's thoughts. Un-consciously perhaps, respect for other points of view, appreciation of the treasures of other cultures, confidence in one another's unselfish motives are growing. We are slowly realizing that believers with different opinions and convictions are necessary to each other to work out the larger synthesis which alone can give the spiritual basis to a world brought together into intimate oneness by man's mechanical ingenuity.[6]

In his earlier book he puts this constructive development and proposal in the form of "the doctrine of love" which he notes is common to all the major religions of the world. He is careful, however, to define the doctrine in a way which may not be quite so universal: "To love one's neighbour is not to compel him to share our opinions, but to renounce one's own standards and see with the other man's eyes, feel with his heart and understand with his mind." [7] Radhakrishnan is explicit in saying that this involves not supplanting another's religion with one's own, but in respecting other religions precisely as one respects one's own.

It is at this point that Radhakrishnan's final positive conclusion and suggestion passes over into and in part derives from his findings concerning the differences between Oriental and Occidental religious values. One of the differences he affirms between (a) the three theistic Semitic religions of the West and Middle East and (b) the Far Eastern religions is that the latter, as part of their own religious beliefs and values, have this respect for religious and cultural values other than one's own, whereas traditionally and for the most part the three Semitic religions—Judaism, Christianity and Mohammedanism—do not.

He does note that there are exceptions to the latter rule. As we shall see, however, he makes out a good case for the thesis that they are exceptions rather than the historical rule.

Let us begin with his account of the basic values of Far Eastern Oriental tradition and religion. The manner in which Chinese families embrace Buddhism, Taoism and Confucianism and welcome insight into Western religions is well known. Certainly Chinese values at this point equal those of India. We shall, therefore, follow Radhakrishnan in taking the Far Eastern culture and religion with which he is most intimately acquainted as the basis for his conclusions concerning Far Eastern religious values generally. We shall follow him also in taking Hinduism, which he knows best, as typical of India generally, apart from the Semitic

6 *Ibid.*, 348.   7 EWR, 112f.

Mohammedanism which is there also. Certainly, if anything, the case within Buddhism for Radhakrishnan's appraisal of Oriental values is even stronger than the case which he rests primarily upon Hinduism.

"Hinduism," he writes,

recognizes that each religion is inextricably bound up with its culture and can grow organically. While it is aware that all religions have not attained to the same level of truth and goodness, it insists that they all have a right to express themselves. Religions reform themselves by interpretation and adjustment to one another. . . . The permeation of the Indian religious spirit from the Pacific Ocean almost to the Mediterranean is not based on a conviction of the finality of its particular faith and the futility of the rest.[8]

He supports this conclusion by the following quotations among others. "Gandhi says: 'If I were asked to define the Hindu creed, I should simply say: Search after truth through non-violent means. A man may not believe in God and still call himself a Hindu. Hinduism is a relentless pursuit after truth.' " [9] Professor Radhakrishnan agrees, for he writes, "The Hindu welcomes even the atheist into his fold, for if the latter is earnest in his search for truth and gains a true inwardness, he will discover the inadequacy of his faith." [10]

One is reminded of Junjiro Takakusu's statement that Buddhism not merely welcomes atheists but in itself is positively atheistic.[11] Professor D. T. Suzuki, to be sure, denies this characterization of Buddhism as atheistic. There are reasons for believing, however, that the differences between Takakusu and Suzuki upon this point are more verbal than real. The heart of the matter centers in the Nirvāṇa factor in Buddhism. This factor is religious. In effect it comprises, according to all Buddhist teaching, the religious element in man and nature. Thus in this sense Suzuki is correct. Buddhism is not atheistic in the sense of being irreligious. It is atheistic, however, in the sense of not being religious in the Western theist's sense. In other words, it is atheistic in the sense of being non-theistic. Thus in this sense Takakusu is right.

That such is the case is shown by the character of Nirvāṇa. As Suzuki would agree and, as Takakusu writes, "The true state [i.e.

---

[8] ER, 335f.   [9] As quoted by Radhakrishnan, ER, 312f.   [10] Ibid., 320.
[11] See my chapter VIII, Philosophy East—West, edited by Charles A. Moore (Princeton University Press, 1944); also J. J. Takakusu, The Essentials of Buddhist Philosophy (University of Hawaii, Honolulu, 1947).

Nirvāṇa] is the state without any specific condition." [12] It is, in other words, an ultimate religious factor in human nature which is not determinate in character after the manner of the theistic divinity and the underlying determinate immortal soul of all Western theistic religions, and hence it is not designated by any determinate thesis. As Takakusu adds, "It is simply the negation of an independent reality or the negation of specific character." [13] The important point, therefore, to note is that the attitude of both Buddhism and Hinduism, not merely to other religions, but even to atheists, is not a mere generous afterthought to their basic beliefs concerning the divine, but flows out of the very nature of that basic belief. Radhakrishnan puts the matter thus: "The Hindu view is not motived by any considerations of political expediency. It is bound up with its religion and not its policy." [14] It should be added that Brahman has the same indeterminateness, and hence non-theistic character, as Nirvāṇa or Void in Buddhism.

Radhakrishnan brings forth other quotations in support of the encouragement of other religious and cultural values than its own as an essential part, if not the very heart, of the Far Eastern Oriental outlook. He quotes a statement made by perhaps the greatest of all the Emperors of India, Aśoka: " 'He who does reverence to his own sect while disparaging the sects of others wholly from attachment to his own, with intent to enhance the splendour of his own sect, in reality, by such conduct inflicts the severest injury on his own sect.' " [15] At this point Radhakrishnan quotes our own late Professor J. B. Pratt as follows:

The attitude of the great majority of Buddhists towards Christians and toward Christianity is one of genuine friendliness. If there is to be a fierce and long continued war between the two religions, it will be all the work of Christianity. For its part Buddhism would be only too glad to ratify a treaty of enduring peace, alliance and friendship with its great rival.[16]

Radhakrishnan notes that Śaṁkara ". . . did not believe in a god who denied the existence of his rivals." He adds that "this non-dogmatic attitude has persisted in Hindu religious history." [17]

The *Bhagavadgītā* not merely reaffirms this attitude as the essence of its own religion, but also lays down explicit practical

---

12 Takakusu, *op. cit.*, 45, n. 11.   13 *Ibid.*, 106.   14 ER, 316.
15 *Ibid.*, 309.
16 As quoted by Radhakrishnan from Professor Pratt's *The Pilgrimage of Buddhism*, 735f. ER, 309, n.
17 ER, 311.

injunctions in order to put the attitude into effect. Thus Radha-krishnan continues, "The *Bhagavadgītā*, with a clear grasp of the historical, warns us against taking away the psychological comfort of people by unsettling their faiths. We are required to confirm the faith of others even though we may not have any share in it." [18]

The reasons for these injunctions are also made evident: "Tradition is society's memory of its own past. If we tear up the individual from his traditional roots he becomes abstract and aberrant." [19] Certainly at this point the *Bhagavadgītā* came long ago to the conclusion at which contemporary cultural anthropology and the philosophy of culture in the West have but recently arrived. [20] Robert Louis Stevenson's letter to a lady missionary is very much to the point: "Remember that you cannot change ancestral feelings of right and wrong without what is practically murder. . . . see that you always develop them: remember that all you can do is to civilise the man in the line of his own civilisation, such as it is." [21] Also most relevant is George Santayana's more concrete statement:

If the Englishman likes to call himself a Catholic, it is a fad like a thousand others, to which his inner man, so seriously playful, is prone to lend itself. He may go over to Rome on a spiritual tour: but if he is converted really and becomes a Catholic at heart, he is no longer the man he was. Words cannot measure the chasm which must henceforth separate him from everything at home. For a modern Englishman with freedom and experiment and reserve in his blood, to go over to Rome is essentially suicide: the inner man must succumb first. Such an Englishman might become a saint but only by becoming a foreigner. [22]

Radhakrishnan correctly concludes: "Religion is like the string of a violin: if removed from its resonant body, it will give the wrong tone, if any." [23]

Let us turn now to Radhakrishnan's appraisal of the attitude of the three Western or Middle Eastern Semitic religions. The position of Mohammedanism is clear. Of it Radhakrishnan writes:

18 *Ibid.*, 328.   19 *Ibid.*, 328.
20 See Pitirim A. Sorokin's *Society, Culture and Personality* (Harper and Brothers, New York and London, 1947); Harold D. Lasswell, *The Analysis of Political Behaviour* (Routledge and Kegan Paul, London, 1948), ch. II; Clyde Kluckhohn, "The Philosophy of the Navaho Indians" in *Ideological Differences and World Order*, ed. F. S. C. Northrop (Yale University Press, 1949); F. S. C. Northrop, *The Meeting of East and West* (Macmillan, New York, 1946), hereafter referred to as MEW.
21 As quoted by Radhakrishnan, ER, 328 n.
22 As quoted by Radhakrishnan, *ibid.*, 327f.
23 *Ibid.*, 328.

Islam is the creation of a single mind and is expressed in a single sentence. 'There is one God and Mohammad is his prophet.' Mohammad claims to be the final link of the great chain from Adam through Noah, Moses, and Jesus. His simple faith, with its real brotherhood and hatred of idolatry, hurled itself on the world, bidding it choose between conversion and subjection.[24]

In other words, it recognizes a partial validity in the other two Semitic religions—namely Judaism and Christianity—but regards itself as realizing perfectly what they realize only in part and imperfectly. Radhakrishnan points out that Mohammedanism "borrowed its idea of Messiah from Judaism, its dogmatism and asceticism from Christianity, its philosophy from Greece, and its mysticism from India and Alexandria." [25] "The dogmatism of Islam," which derives from Christianity was, as Radhakrishnan notes, "toned down in India." [26]

The other two Semitic religions, Judaism and Christianity, are treated together by Radhakrishnan. This is justified because of the derivation in considerable part of the latter from the former. "The Jews," he writes,

first invented the myth that only one religion could be true. As they, however, conceived themselves to be the 'Chosen People,' [Deuteronomy xiv.2.] they did not feel a mission to convert the whole world. The Jews gave to Christianity an ethical passion and a sense of superiority; the Greeks gave the vague aspirations and mysteries of the spirit a logical form, a dogmatic setting; the Romans with their practical bent and love of organization helped to institutionalize the religion. Their desire for world dominion transformed the simple faith of Jesus into a fiercely proselytizing creed. After the time of Constantine, authorities, clerical and secular, displayed systematic intolerance towards other forms of religious belief, taking shelter under the words 'He that is not with me is against me, and he that gathereth not with me, scattereth.' [27]

Radhakrishnan continues:

Unfortunately Christian religion inherited the Semitic creed of the 'jealous God' in the view of Christ as 'the only begotten son of God,' and so could not brook any rival near the throne. When Europe accepted the Christian religion, in spite of its own broad humanism, it accepted the fierce intolerance which is the natural result of belief in 'the truth once for all delivered to the saints.' [28]

Max Radin has attempted to repudiate such an appraisal of the Hebrew religion in a recent review of the English translation of

24 *Ibid.*, 339.   25 *Ibid.*, 339.   26 *Ibid.*, 340.
27 *Ibid.*, 10.   28 *Ibid.*, 324.

The Code of Maimonides. To this end he quotes as follows from the work of "the physician of Saladin prepared for the general use of his co-religionists" nearly eight centuries ago:

The Sages and Prophets did not long for the days of the Messiah that Israel might exercise dominion over the world, or rule over the heathens, or be exalted by the nations, or that it might eat and drink and rejoice. Their aspiration was that Israel be free to devote itself to the Law and its wisdom, with no one to oppress or disturb it, and thus be worthy of life in the world to come.[29]

It seems clear, however, that Radhakrishnan comes nearer to putting facts such as this one in their proper proportions with respect to the whole, when he quotes Bishop Barnes concerning

the thousand instances in which it [the intolerant attitude of the Jewish and Christian tradition with respect to other religions] can be justified from the Old Testament, notwithstanding that it seems the natural product of the deepest piety, true though it may be that since the time of Constantine it has been practiced by every great branch of the Christian Church. . . .[30]

It may be said that contemporary liberal Jews and Christians have departed from this traditional predominant attitude. Radhakrishnan points out with respect to contemporary Christians that there are three groups which he terms right, center and left. The contemporary right wing position is represented by Karl Barth "of 'Dialectical Theology' fame. He," writes Radhakrishnan, "brands non-Christian religions as foes to Christendom, which must in no circumstances 'howl with [those] wolves.' A true Christian's response to other faiths must be an intolerant No! . . . The other religions are [according to Barth], in fact, untouchable." [31]

The middle contemporary Christian attitude is expressed by the Report of the Commission on Christian Higher Education in India which was presided over by Dr. A. D. Lindsay (now Lord Lindsay of Birker). Radhakrishnan quotes from this report as follows:

The Christians are convinced that they have a message which alone is a solution for the problems of humanity and therefore of India. They believe themselves to be bearers of good news which they wish to share with others. Their hope and desire is that India may become Christian. They can never acquiesce in the position that different religions are good for different communities, that all religions are fundamentally

---

29 *The Review of Metaphysics,* Vol. III, 4, June 1950, 521f.
30 ER, 326.
31 *Ibid.,* 341f.

the same and that it is for each religious community to seek to make the best of the possibilities of its own religion.[32]

Radhakrishnan summarizes the difference between the right and center group attitudes thus:

The second view recognizes the divine element in the other religions of the world, but contends that Christianity is the peak of the development of religion. It is the crown and completion of the religion of humanity, the standard by which all others are judged. While on the first view no recognition is given to the workings of the spirit in other religions, here it is conceded that others also sought to know God and do His will, but they are merely preparations for the Christian religion, which is unique. . . . The difference betweeen Christianity and any other religion is that of the best and the good, and the good is the enemy of the best.[33]

The center group of contemporary Christians is therefore like the Mohammedans.

Radhakrishnan's left group of contemporary Christians "is definitely against proselytism." [34] This attitude is represented in the report of the International Missionary Council which met at Jerusalem in 1928. This Council wrote, "We would repudiate any symptoms of a religious imperialism that would desire to impose beliefs and practices on others in order to manage their souls in their supposed interests. We obey a God who respects our wills and we desire to respect those of others." [35]

Radhakrishnan concludes his survey of the three contemporary Chistian attitudes in the following words:

the hopes of the future are under the left wing of liberals and not with the reactionaries or conservatives . . . if we persist in killing one another theologically, we shall only weaken men's faith in God. If the great religions continue to waste their energies in a fratricidal war instead of looking upon themselves as friendly partners in the supreme task of nourishing the spiritual life of mankind, the swift advance of secular humanism and moral materialism is assured.[36]

Radhakrishnan emphasizes that many statements in the accepted texts of the sayings of Jesus do not support the majority opinion. There are other sayings of Jesus, however, such as "I am the way, and the truth and the life; no one cometh unto the Father but by me," [37] which most certainly do.

[32] *Ibid.*, 342.   [33] *Ibid.*, 344.   [34] *Ibid.*, 345.
[35] *Ibid.*, 345.   [36] *Ibid.*, 347.
[37] The Gospel according to *St. John*, XIV, 6.

Having thus determined Radhakrishnan's conception of this difference in attitude of the Far Eastern religions and the three Western and Middle Eastern Semitic religions, it is now necessary to examine the reasons which he gives for believing in the correctness of the Eastern rather than the majority opinion Western attitude.

One of these reasons has already been noted. People often become artificial, superficial, and spiritually empty if an attempt is made to replace rather than develop and build upon their traditional religious and cultural values. Judged by its fruits, therefore, the majority opinion attitude of the three Western theistic religions is unproductive and hence erroneous.

There is, however, a deeper reason also hinted at in the foregoing analysis. This reason has its roots in the basic naturalistic and philosophical conception of Far Eastern Oriental culture, philosophy and religion. Their basic object of religious devotion, naturalistic empirical scientific knowledge and moral and legal value is variously designated by the words Brahman, Ātman, Nirvāṇa, Tao and the source of *jen*. This ultimate object of empirical intuitive knowledge and religious devotion has two characteristics. First, it is not inferred by logical methods; instead it is a factor within the totality of immediacy of experience which can be known only immediately by direct apprehension. Second, it is to be distinguished from other immediately apprehended factors in the totality of immediacy by the fact that it is indeterminate and undifferentiated.

The first of these two distinguishing traits insures that the ultimate factor in Far Eastern culture and philosophy and knowledge generally is given in the strictest sense of the word inductively and positivistically. As Swami Nikhilananda has written of Hindu culture, "Direct experience reveals the final reality . . . , reality is immediately apprehended." [38] This purely inductive and positivistic character of the ultimate factor in Oriental culture and values is none the less present notwithstanding that the totality of immediacy exhibits this ultimate factor as differentiated by the sensuous data and the introspected sensing of the data. Writing on the spiritual emphasis of the Orient as exhibited in Tagore, Radhakrishnan says: "In the struggle between the sceptics and agnostics who doubt whether there is anything behind the universe, and the spiritual positivists who affirm that the most vital reality is behind the universe [i.e., the sensed differentiations within

38 "Foundations of Hindu Culture," *Calcutta Review*, Feb. 1950, 91.

the all-embracing otherwise indeterminate immediacy], Rabindranath is with the latter." [39] Note the designation of Oriental thinkers as "spiritual positivists." [40]

This purely inductive positivistic character of the Oriental ultimate object of knowledge and religious value has very important implications with respect to toleration of opinions other than one's own. That which is given purely inductively and with positivistic immediacy is pure fact. Pure fact is neither true nor false; it merely is. Any differences of opinion, therefore, with respect to such knowledge must necessarily center in differences in the propositions used to designate the object of knowledge and value rather than in the object itself. It follows, therefore, directly from the nature of an Oriental culture rooted in such knowledge and in the values which such knowledge gives, that differences in the propositionalized formulation of what one believes must be largely verbal rather than real. The differences center in the symbolism chosen to denote the immediacy of experience rather than in the immediately experienceable object of knowledge which is symbolized. It is natural, therefore, for a culture grounded in such purely inductively given, positivistically immediate knowledge to regard differences in belief as a mere quibble over words.

Strictly speaking, for any culture or philosophy which bases itself upon purely inductively given positivistic immediacy, the real and true object of knowledge cannot be expressed in symbols. Strictly speaking everything can be shown, nothing can be said. This is what the Oriental sage means when he says that, if you have not already experienced, and hence if you do not already know, what he is talking about, nothing that he can say can convey it to you. It is to be emphasized that this is just as true of the data given with immediacy through the senses, such as green, as it is of the all-embracing immediacy which is Brahman, Ātman, Nirvāṇa and *jen*, of which the sensed data are the differentiations. I happen, in fact, to be color-blind with respect to green. No amount of discourse is able to convey this particular color to me.

If positivistically immediate knowledge must be known apart from the symbols which are by convention assigned to denote that which has to be known apart from the symbol, then semantically exact, scientific, philosophical, aesthetic and religious wisdom consists in moving behind the different conventional symbolic

[39] EWR, 132.
[40] See also MEW, chs. IX, X, XI, especially pp. 378, 384ff. and 447.

formulations of immediacy to immediacy itself. This is what Radhakrishnan means when he says that "life consists in breaking free from conventions and penetrating into true being." [41] Such is the importance of the exceedingly intuitive positivistic method of obtaining knowledge upon which the cultural values and ethical, legal and religious norms of the Far Eastern peoples rest.

The most important factor in the totality of immediacy is not its *esse est percipi* relativistically sensed and introspected differentiations, but the otherwise undifferentiated immediacy termed Brahman, Nirvāṇa and Tao, of which the sensed and introspected data are the transitory differentiations. This factor has important implications with respect to the Oriental attitude toward legal norms, ideological doctrines and religious conceptions other than its own. Only the all-embracing undifferentiated immediacy is knowledge universally valid for all men. This immediacy embraces the distinction between subject and object. Moreover, since both subject and object are relative to one another, all knowledge referring to the differentiated factors and experiences will be relative from culture to culture, standpoint to standpoint, object to object, and person to person. Hence it follows from the intuitive nature of the basic knowledge underlying Oriental culture and religion that there not only will be but must be, if men are empirically and scientifically honest, different formulations of the relativistic *esse est percipi* differentiated factors in experience. There is, therefore, no question of one formulation of determinate, differentiated knowledge contradicting another formulation, so that the acceptance of one would entail the rejection of the other. Each is valid for its own standpoint.

This failure of any formulation of differentiated, determinate knowledge to contradict any other formulation follows also from the purely inductive, positivistic character of the Oriental method of knowing. If differences center only in the way of symbolizing and in the immediacy of unsymbolized fact, which is the object of knowledge, then clearly there can be no contradiction in real knowledge, since true knowledge must always possess the immediately apprehended fact with immediacy before it can assign the symbol. Clearly, facts cannot contradict one another—only propositions—that is, certain concatenations of symbols can be mutually contradictory.

Thus the Oriental assumption that any two differing formulations of knowledge refer to purely inductively given factors which

41 ER, 317.

must be known with positivistic immediacy apart from the formulation and which, strictly speaking, cannot be said but can only be shown, as well as its doctrine that all differentiated factors in knowledge are relative to perceivers—leads straight to the conclusion that a battle between religious groups, scientific or philosophical thinkers or nations is a stupid and misguided quibble over words, or a failure to take the *esse est percipi* character of what is knowable with immediacy into account. For a culture reared on such methodological, positivistic and relativistic foundations, different doctrines and beliefs are but different conventions concerning the same object of immediacy or else true descriptions of different relativistic differentiations of immediacy.

Notwithstanding this extreme relativism of all determinate differentiated knowledge, there is the all-embracing otherwise undifferentiated immediacy which is the same for all objects and all subjects. It is this which is for the Oriental the true self, the only true *non esse est percipi* object, the only timeless factor in knowledge or in the realm of values. It is this which Radhakrishnan has in mind when he speaks of "The formless blaze of spiritual life . . ."[42]

Both knowers and objects are relative to one another and are differentiations, in polar opposition, of the all-embracing otherwise undifferentiated immediacy which is Brahman, Nirvāṇa, Tao and the source of *jen*. By what the Hindu terms "māyā masking," the undifferentiated infinite all-embracing immediacy, perpetually differentiates itself into the transitory, relativistic polarized finite subject-object differentiations. This is why Radhakrishnan is able to write: "Toleration is the homage which the finite mind pays to the inexhaustibility of the Infinite."[43]

It now appears that Radhakrishnan's tolerant attitude toward cultures, doctrines, and religions other than his own does not have quite the world-centered, rather than Hindu Oriental culture-centered, basis that he assumes. It is instead a consequence of applying to the rest of the world the standards defined by the epistemology and specific philosophy of Oriental culture. This will become more evident when we turn now to a similar analysis of the basic method of knowing and the specific content of the scientific and philosophical doctrines of the West.

One essential characteristic of Western doctrines should have already suggested itself to us. In Western science and philosophy there are doctrines which are real contradictaries. To accept Ein-

[42] *Ibid.*, 317.   [43] *Ibid.*, 317.

stein's physics entails a rejection of certain assumptions in Newton's physics. Similarly, to accept Newton's physics entails a
rejection of certain doctrines of Aristotelian physics.

The same is true of the basic doctrines of Western philosophy.
Aristotle tells us that, to accept the philosophical systems of either
Democritus or Plato, is to cause the most important truths of
mathematics to totter. The impossibility of being both a Platonist
and a Democritean atomic materialist at one and the same time is
equally obvious.

Western religious doctrines illustrate the same logical incompatibility. Witness the debates between Abelard and William of
Champeaux, which shook Catholic Christendom at the time to its
very foundations, a debate which turned around the difference between Platonic and Aristotelian universals. The logical incompatibility of certain modern Protestant religious values, with their
Kantian rejection of ontology, and Thomistic Roman Catholic
theological doctrine, which roots religion in the ontology of nature, is equally obvious.

This logical incompatibility so characteristic of different Western scientific, philosophical, and religious beliefs and values, points
to a type of knowledge and a theory of value fundamentally different from that of the Orient. The significance of this should not
be passed over lightly. It means that there is a different concept of
the spiritual in the West from the concept of the spiritual in the
Orient.

The crucial question immediately arises. What is the source of
this different concept of the spiritual in the West? Why is it that
contradictions are impossible within the Oriental mode of knowing and its concept of the spiritual, whereas contradictions between
diverse doctrines are of the very essence of the Western type of
knowledge and its attendantly different concept of the spiritual?

It frequently happens that Oriental thinkers affirm the difference between Oriental and Occidental culture to be that merely
between a civilization based on spiritual values and one concerned
primarily with efficient technological instruments. This would
mean that the Orient has a perfect and complete comprehension
of the spiritual ends of human existence and that the sole contribution to be made by the West is greater technological efficiency
in the achievement of the Oriental ends and values. Radhakrishnan
suggests this when he says that "Efficiency is the quality in which
the West is supreme." [44] The fact, however, that the West has a

44 *Ibid.*, 322.

different concept of the spiritual from the Orient shows this notion to be erroneous.

At times Radhakrishnan also writes as follows:

On the whole, the Eastern civilizations are interested not so much in improving the actual conditions as in making the best of this imperfect world, in developing the qualities of cheerfulness and contentment, patience and endurance. They are not happy in the prospect of combat. To desire little, to quench the eternal fires, has been their aim. . . . While the Western races crave for freedom even at the price of conflict, the Easterns stoop to peace even at the price of subjection. . . . The qualities associated with the Eastern cultures make for life and stability; those characteristic of the West for progress and adventure.[45]

Such statements entail that Occidental civilization differs from Oriental not as efficient means to spiritual ends but with respect to a difference in the ends themselves or in other words because of a difference in the concept of the spiritual goal of human existence.

We must now seek out the grounds for this difference. Radhakrishnan touches upon them in the following statements:

The Greeks laid the foundations of natural science for the European world. To analyse and explore, to test and prove all things in the light of reason, was the ambition of the Greek mind. . . . Plato tells us that the universal or the general idea determines the nature of a particular individual and has greater reality than the latter.[46]

The last sentence is the heart of the entire matter. Because of a failure to go behind Plato's more popular writings to the technical science of his Academy, apart from which the popular writings cannot be understood, the significance of Plato's doctrine upon this point has not been appreciated even by most Western scholars. What he was saying here is nothing more than a commonplace of Western scientific knowledge and the philosophical theory of ideas and of the moral individual to which this scientific knowledge leads.

Western scientific knowledge does not stop with purely inductive methods and with positivistic immediacy. With the ancient Greeks for the first time an additional, new scientific method and an attendantly different way of knowing was discovered. As Morris Cohen and I. E. Drabkin have written: "all the evidence indicates that the ideal of rigorously deductive proof, the method of developing a subject by a chain of theorems based on definitions, axioms, and postulates, and the constant striving for complete generality and abstraction are the specific contributions of the Greeks. . . ." [47] It is this novel, distinctly Western scientific method and its equally novel way of knowing which lies at the basis of the unique spiritual values of the West, just as the exceedingly intuitive, excessively positivistic method of the Orient with its emphasis upon pure immediacy leads to the unique concept of the spiritual of the Far East.

This new scientific method is that of indirectly verified, deductively formulated theory, where the postulates of the deductively formulated theory refer not to the entities and relations given inductively with immediacy but to theoretically designated, directly unobservable entities and relations. The remarkable discovery was made that there are factors in human knowledge which are not directly experienced. Nonetheless we can know these factors to exist, because by deducing consequences from the assumptions of their existence and then testing these consequences against the inductively given data of immediacy we can verify the existence or nonexistence of the theoretically designated factors indirectly. Einstein, among others, has made it abundantly clear that this has been the method of Western science since the time of the Greeks.[48]

Note the radically different character of beliefs grounded in knowledge of this kind as compared with beliefs of the Oriental type grounded in immediacy: Only the proposition conveys the object of knowledge. This follows necessarily from the fact that what the proposition designates is not given with immediacy. Were the factors, which the postulates of Western scientific knowledge designate, given with immediacy, then the indirect method of verification of Western scientific method upon which John Dewey and Albert Einstein, among others, have placed so much emphasis would not be required.

But when the proposition alone gives the object of knowledge, then beliefs expressed in terms of such propositions no longer possess merely a verbal significance. To throw the symbolism of the propositions away would be to throw all means of knowing the object of knowledge away. For knowledge of this type, without the proposition there is nothing known. Consequently, in any culture whose concept of the spiritual derives from such knowl-

47 *A Source Book in Greek Science* (McGraw-Hill Book Company, Inc., New York, 1948), 1.
48 See my "Einstein's Conception of Science" in *Albert Einstein: Philosopher-Scientist*, Vol. VII, Library of Living Philosophers, ed. Paul A. Schilpp (Evanston, Ill., 1949); also my *Logic of the Sciences and the Humanities* (Macmillan, New York, 1947), chs. III-VII. (Hereafter referred to as LSH.)

edge, the symbol is of the essence, and it is literally true that one is saved not by intuition but only by the word.

Also, since this Western deductively designated object of knowledge has to be arrived at by trial and error through the scientific method of hypothesis, it happens automatically that different hypotheses concerning its nature not only can be but are often mutually contradictory. When beliefs are logically contradictory, the acceptance of the one renders toleration of the other impossible. Instead, acceptance of one logically entails the rejection of the other. Thus the criterion of truth and of spiritual value grounded in such truth must be different for this Western type of knowledge from what it is for the Oriental type. Also, the ethical attitude to doctrines other than one's own must be different. Consequently, to apply, as Radhakrishnan does, the doctrine of toleration, which is appropriate to Oriental beliefs grounded in its mode of knowing, to Western beliefs and spiritual values grounded in their different mode of knowing, is to impose a theory of value of one culture upon the domain of another culture where its application is inappropriate.

Respect for beliefs other than one's own is permissible, providing the beliefs are not related to one another by the logical relation of contradiction. This is the case with the beliefs of the Orient precisely because of the purely inductive or intuitive mode of knowing upon which they rest. Respect for a belief other than one's own is, however, not only impossible but also immoral if the relation between the two beliefs is that of logical contradiction. To hold one's own belief, in this latter case, with spiritual seriousness is of necessity to deny the contradictory belief, since with respect to logical contradictions both cannot be true.

This does not mean that a basis for toleration cannot exist in the West. What it does mean is that the tolerant attitude does not apply between different Western religious, political, ethical and legal norms in the unqualified sense in which it is appropriate between diverse Oriental religions; also, in the West its basis has to be centered in the method of free inquiry and free discussion used to arrive at the content of the diverse doctrines rather than in the essential identity of the content itself.

This point is not of mere academic interest. Unless it is grasped, the exceptionally dangerous character of contemporary world Communism will not be realized. Not only do the contemporary Communists, because of the logical incompatability of the assumptions of their doctrine with the doctrine of any other culture and religion, believe and act upon the principle that any culture or religion not based on Marxist principles as applied by Lenin and Stalin, is evil and immoral and hence justifiably attacked wherever it is expedient, without any regard for the indigenous moral values or legal procedures of the other culture, but the Communist elimination of any free inquiry into or free discussion of ideological differences and of the ends of human existence, excludes the tolerant attitude even from the *method* of arriving at the determination of cultural and spiritual ends.

The failure of India to realize that Westerners governed by theistic beliefs, such as the Mohammedans, the Portuguese, the Dutch and the British, cannot be handled after the manner in which Oriental beliefs are handled by the Oriental attitude of toleration is probably the major explanation of the historical fact that India, through almost the entirety of her history, has been under the domination of Western or Middle Eastern theistic peoples and powers. Supposing that theistic values are identical with those of the Far Eastern religions, India has welcomed theistic invaders under the assumption that the invaders would respect the intuitively grounded Indian values after the manner in which an Oriental respects values other than his own. Having done this, India has continuously suffered the disillusionment of finding that theists, whether they be Mohammedans, Portuguese Roman Catholic Christians or Dutch or British Protestant Christians, automatically believe and insist upon the uniqueness and priority of their own values. Unless India recognizes that an attitude of toleration which is appropriate for Oriental differences of belief is not in the same sense appropriate for Western ones, she will have rid herself from the recent domination of the Western British only to welcome and find herself again under the yoke of the even more doctrinaire and dangerously intolerant Western Marxist Communists. What must be realized is that the relation between different beliefs of the Western type is not that of the relation between different Oriental beliefs, and that an ethics which is appropriate for handling the one is not appropriate for handling the other.

So much for the difference between the Oriental and Occidental concepts of the spiritual insofar as this difference depends on differences in scientific method and in modes of knowing. There is also, however, the difference arising out of diversities in the content of knowledge to which the two modes of knowing lead.

In deductively formulated, indirectly verified Western scientific knowledge, determinate relations and entities are verified to be valid knowledge for all perceivers in all frames of reference. Hence, propositions referring to determinate differentiated factors in natural man and nature describe knowledge which is not *esse est percipi*. For example, the basic law in Einstein's general theory of relativity is that any body at any time moves in a path which is geodesic in a four-dimensional space-time which has the determinate metrical properties of a Riemannian chrono-geometry. This is determinate knowledge of nature. It is knowledge designating a determinate structure of nature and a determinate property of all physical objects in nature which is true for any observer in any frame of reference anywhere and always. This means that the ultimate factor in Western knowledge which holds for all knowers is not the indeterminate, undifferentiated formlessness which is the source of value in Oriental religion. In terms of content, this is the real difference between the concept of the spiritual in the Orient and in the West. In the new scientific method discovered by the ancient Greeks the West came upon the remarkable discovery that there are *determinate* factors in nature and man which hold for all men.

This Western type of scientific and philosophical knowledge with its radically different concept of the spiritual has one other unique characteristic: Every individual particular thing is an instance of a universal law. For example, in Newton's physics every physical object in the universe is an instance of the laws of Newton's mechanics. Similarly in Einstein's general theory of relativity every physical object in the universe is an instance of its determinate geodetic law. It is this and not the transcendental nonsense usually attributed to him which Plato had in mind when he said, as paraphrased by Radhakrishnan, that "the universal or the general idea determines the nature of a particular individual." [49]

The implications of this concept of the nature of an individual are tremendous. When different scientific or philosophical postulate sets concerning such an individual appear, then the concept of the moral and spiritual individual becomes a fundamentally different thing in a culture based on the one set of postulates from what it is in a culture based on another set. Hence Western doctrinal or ideological differences are not merely verbal, but raise the basic question of the moral nature of a person.

According to Thomistic doctrine the concept of the moral and

49 ER, 3.

spiritual is one thing. According to Cartesian and Lockean doctrine it is a second thing. According to Hegelian doctrine it is a third thing, and according to Marxist Communist doctrine it is a fourth. Since such a moral person is not given with positivistic immediacy, but is known only by means of a doctrine indirectly verified, it follows that without the doctrine, there is no knowledge of what morality and spirituality mean. This is the reason why in the Western concept of the spiritual, issues of doctrine are issues of moral and spiritual life and death.

In the traditional Western concept of the spiritual, the true self of a moral person is not the indeterminate, indescribable Brahman, Nirvāṇa and Tao, knowable with immediacy when all the directly inspected differentiations of immediacy are neglected, but is instead a determinate being knowable only by means of postulated propositions indirectly verified. This is why faith in formulated doctrines plays a much greater part in Western religions than in Oriental ones. In other words, moral man is not merely determinate man but also propositionalized man. This is what the West means when it asserts that a moral man is a man of principle. In contrast to this the true moral man of the Orient cannot be known by propositionalized, determinate theses or principles, but is instead a man of intuition.

It follows that when, as has been the case throughout Western history, the scientists and philosophers have been led to new propositionalized conceptions of the nature of man and of things, different conceptions of moral and religious man and of the good society result. When also, as is the case often, these propositionalized conceptions turn out to be self-contradictory, then ideological conflict is the result. Not only is the Western concept of the spiritual generically different from the Oriental concept, but even within the Western concept there are literally different and often mutually incompatible concepts of moral and spiritual man and of the good society.

This is why ideological conflict is of the essence of the spiritual and cultural life of the West. Witness the present logical and practical incompatibility of Marxist Communism and traditional French and Anglo-American democracy, both of which are different answers to the basic theoretical and spiritual problems of modern Western thought and culture. Note also how the doctrinal debate between Abelard and William of Champeaux concerning the validity of the Platonic or the Aristotelian theory of universals shook Medieval Christendom to its very foundations.

This means that an end cannot be put to the present Cold War in the world after the manner suggested by Radhakrishnan and the Quakers, by appealing from the Foreign Secretaries and the militarists to ethics and to religion, nor by acting toward Communists as if they were Quakers or non-dualistic Vendānta pacifists. For, as soon as the Western concept of the moral, religious, and spiritual is comprehended, it becomes evident that the Cold War is the result of the essential nature of Western morality and religion and hence cannot be cured by it. If it be said, then, that one should appeal to the Oriental concept of the spiritual, the answer is that the world's culture is as genuinely and inescapably Occidental in part as it is inevitably Oriental in part, and to the Occidental cultural and spiritual values the application of the Oriental concept of the spiritual is inappropriate.

The problem of peace in our world and the problem which Radhakrishnan has attacked of relating Eastern religions and Western thought and values must, therefore, be approached in a different way. To respect a religion or culture other than one's own requires first that one understand its basic assumptions and the method of knowing by which those assumptions are validated. To do this for the West is to discover, as we have noted above, that differences of Western doctrine do not have the relation of compatibility which characterizes differences of doctrine in the Orient, and hence to learn that the attitude of toleration appropriate to the latter is not *in the same sense* appropriate to the former.

How then are we to proceed? What is the correct method for bringing Oriental and Western values together and for preventing mutually contradictory Western concepts of moral and social man, such as Marxist Communism and the French and Anglo-American more traditional democracy, from driving mankind into a suicidal atomic war?

Clearly two things are required. First, the relation between the two different components of things and their respective different ways of knowing, from which the Oriental and the Western concepts of the spiritual derive, must be determined. To put Oriental culture and Western culture together is to formulate and apply the vision of a truly world society in which the differing spiritual values of Far East and West are related after the manner in which scholarly investigation reveals the two modes of knowledge, from which they derive, to be related. Second, the method within the concept of the spiritual of the West for resolving conflicts between logically incompatible Western propositionalized conceptions of moral and social man must be specified and applied.

These two tasks are too difficult to be treated in detail upon this occasion. The nature of the solution in both instances has, however, been indicated elsewhere.[50]

Curiously enough, it is within the analysis of the methods and content of contemporary Western mathematical physics that the solution of the first problem has been found. Actually, however, this is not surprising. For Western mathematical physics begins with inductively given positivistic immediacy, notwithstanding the fact that it passes on to postulationally designated entities and relations which are not directly apprehended. Furthermore, Western indirectly verified, deductively formulated, scientific and philosophical knowledge can be verified only by deducing consequences from its propositionalized postulates and checking these consequences against the data of the all-embracing immediacy. It follows, therefore, that, within the method of Western scientific knowledge, the relation between its immediately apprehended component, upon which the Oriental concept of the spiritual rests and the propositionalized theoretically known, non-immediately apprehended component, from which the Western concept of the spiritual derives, must be contained. It is not a miracle, therefore, that the analysis by the contemporary logicians and philosophers of the method of mathematical physics should have revealed this relation. It suffices to state that the relation is a two-termed relation; not the relation of appearance to reality which has been traditionally assumed in the West since the time of Democritus and Plato.

The important consequence is that this makes the immediately known aesthetic component of things upon which the Oriental concept of the spiritual rests, as ultimate, irreducible, and real as the propositionalized theoretic component of things in which the Western concept of the spiritual has its roots. In short, a new vision for our world is philosophically formulated, according to which both the Orient and the Occident enlarges its concept of the nature of things and of spiritual, moral, and social man to include that of the other.

How is the second aforementioned task of our time to be resolved? What is the method for resolving issues between logically

50 MEW, ch. XII; LSH, chs. VIII, XVI, XVII, XVIII, XXI-XXIV; and Henry Margenau, *The Nature of Physical Reality* (McGraw-Hill Book Co., New York, 1950), chs. III-V.

incompatible Western concepts of the spiritual? The answer to this question is the same as the answer to the first. One must go to the method by which this Western type of knowledge is validated. This method will necessarily give us the criterion for determining the particular Western doctrine to choose.

The character of this method has been roughly sketched already. It is that of deductively formulated, indirectly verified theory. This method is unequivocal for the criterion to be used to decide between incompatible doctrines to which its usage through time leads one. If, given any two such doctrines, one of the two, through its deductive consequences, accounts for all of the facts accounted for by the other and for additional directly inspected facts as well, then it is the one to be chosen and the doctrine which is incompatible with it must be rejected.

In point of fact, however, the issues between the Western propositionalized doctrines of moral, social, and spiritual man which are now competing internationally for the loyalty of mankind wherever Western values are in part at least wanted, is not as simple as this. These conflicting Western moral, social, and spiritual doctrines have the power they exhibit because there are certain considerations arising out of the basic theoretical problems of modern Western civilization which justify each one of them. We are not, therefore, in the more simple situation in which one doctrine takes care of every consideration for which the others account and additional considerations as well. It cannot be said, therefore, that one of these Western ideologies is the correct one and that the others must be rejected.

Nevertheless, the method of obtaining Western knowledge specifies how in such a situation we are to proceed. In contemporary mathematical physics there is a similar situation. There are at present at least two theories—the one termed relativity theory, the other quantum mechanics, which are mutually contradictory. There are certain directly inspectible facts for which only the relativity theory accounts. There are other immediate data explained only by quantum mechanics. Neither theory, therefore, is capable of taking care of all the facts. Competent mathematical physicists such as Einstein and Dirac know that in such a situation the only solution is the construction of a new theory which takes care of both sets of facts without contradiction. This may be done in one of two ways: Either by generalizing one of the theories so that it takes care of the facts accounted for only by the other. This is what Einstein is attempting to do at the present moment in his latest unified field theory. The other method is to drop the basic assumptions of both of the present theories and introduce thoroughly novel assumptions which, without logical contradiction, account for all the facts explained by the present mutually contradictory theories. In the last two chapters of my *Meeting of East and West,* I have suggested the manner in which this procedure can be applied to the incompatible ideologies of the contemporary Western world.

The Western method of knowing provides a novel basis for toleration. This becomes evident when one examines its logic of verification. Because its content is not directly observable, its logic of verification must be of the following indirect form: If *A* (what is affirmed), then *B* (specific, observable consequences). *B* is the case. Therefore *A* is the case. Such confirmation is not unique. Some other affirmation *C,* even one incompatible with *A,* might also imply the observable facts *B.* This entails that any such verified conception must be held with tentativeness and the mind open to other quite different possibilities.[51] Thus, whereas, the Far East, as Radhakrishnan has emphasized, locates the basis for toleration between different religions and philosophies in the identity of the object known, the West locates it in the method of knowing. Each basis is appropriate only for its particular type of knowledge.

It appears, therefore, that the contemporary task of relating Oriental and Occidental cultural values and resolving the ideological conflicts between different Western political and religious doctrines, with respect to which Professor Radhakrishnan has pioneered, is much more difficult than his analysis indicates and requires for its solution a method different from the one derived from the Oriental inductive type of knowledge and intuitive concept of the spiritual which he uses. Nonetheless there is a way, and the correct methods for this way are both specifiable and workable.

F. S. C. NORTHROP

DEPARTMENT OF PHILOSOPHY AND THE LAW SCHOOL
YALE UNIVERSITY

[51] See my "The Absolute and the Non-Absolute in Scientific Knowledge in Its Bearing on Toleration," in *Freedom and Reason,* edited by Salo W. Baron, Ernest Nagel and Koppel S. Pinson (Free Press Publishers, New York, 1951).

20

Dhirendra Mohan Datta

RADHAKRISHNAN AND COMPARATIVE
PHILOSOPHY

RADHAKRISHNAN AND COMPARATIVE PHILOSOPHY

I. COMPARATIVE PHILOSOPHY IN THE WEST

KNOWLEDGE of the categories of Reality, thinks Kaṇāda, the founder of the Indian school of atomism, can be perfected only by comparison and contrast. We often fail to realize the merits and defects of anything, as well as its basic principles, so long as our attention is confined to it alone. When Sanskrit became known to Western scholars the foundation of comparative philology was laid. The necessity of learning different kinds of language was keenly felt and the comparative study of such languages brought into prominence the peculiarities of each language and this latter fact helped in formulating the basic laws underlying human speech as a whole. Similarly, the growing acquaintance, in the West, with Indian literature and religion, stimulated the growth of Comparative Religion, of which the great Indologist, Max Müller, became a pioneer. We now have a host of comparative studies in different fields of science and other branches of knowledge.

But comparative philosophy is still in its relative infancy. The writers of the history of philosophy in the West have mostly been ignorant of Oriental philosophy. Some have even gone to the length of justifying this ignorance by inventing reasons why such thought should not find a place in the history of philosophy. The net result has been that the history of *Western* philosophy has all along passed for History of Philosophy. Bertrand Russell is perhaps the first to recognize this error, and to call his work frankly, *The History of Western Philosophy*. On the other hand, John Dewey realized long ago that "seen in the long perspective of the future, the whole of Western European history is a provincial episode." Whitehead similarly thought that contemporary Western philosophy was nothing more than a series of footnotes to Plato.

661

Systems of philosophy other than the Western came to be known to the West through the translations of philosophical treatises into European languages by a few generations of devoted scholars of the West during the second half of the nineteenth and the first part of the twentieth century. The East is indebted to such Orientalists not only for the dissemination of Oriental ideas in the West, but also for helping the East to realize the importance and value of its philosophical contributions in the estimation of the West. Thus Oriental scholars also became attracted to join in the work of the Western Orientalists, and their combined efforts produced a series of monographs and systematic histories in European languages. To this holy brotherhood belong such great scholars as Max Müller, Deussen, Winternitz, Keith, Woods, Stcherbatsky, Legge, Chan, Bodde, Hughes, Eliot, Jha, Radhakrishnan, Das Gupta, Hu Shih, Fung Yu-lan, Suzuki, Sogen, Takakusu, and many others.

The West was thus in possession of materials for a comparative study of its own philosophy with that of the East. But the opportunity was not utilized much by Western philosophers. Interest in Oriental philosophy remained the chief business of the Orientalists. The reason is quite obvious. Political power, economic progress, scientific knowledge, and the technical achievement of the West very naturally created an attitude of superiority towards those who were backward in these respects. This attitude stood, and still stands, in the way of thinking that there could be anything worth learning from the East. There have been a few exceptions to this general and natural state of things. Most noteworthy among them is the singular effort made by the University of Hawaii to organize the East-West Philosophers' Conference, once in 1939, and then on a bigger scale, in 1949. The latter Conference decided, moreover, to publish a journal on comparative philosophy. On the whole, Germany and America have shown perhaps greater interest in Eastern thought than other countries in the West. But still the average Western philosopher has remained largely unaffected.

II. COMPARATIVE PHILOSOPHY IN INDIA

The story of the comparative study of philosophy has been somewhat different in the East, particularly in India with which we are concerned here. Before the establishment of British rule in India and even long after it, the indigenous scholars conversant with the vast philosophical literature of India, but unacquainted with anything Western, were so proud of their heritage that they thought philosophy was the exclusive monopoly of India. When, however, the British established universities in India, instruction was imparted mostly by British teachers through the medium of English and on subjects taught in British universities. Consequently only European philosophy was taught thereafter in Indian universities and the students of philosophy who came out of these universities had read no Indian philosophy at all. Comparative study could therefore not flourish in the universities.

During the earlier part of the present century some of the talented Indian scholars of Western philosophy became teachers of philosophy, and a few of them privately studied Indian philosophy under the Pandits—indigenous scholars—and were impressed by the wealth of ancient and medieval Indian thought. They introduced Indian philosophy into the university courses, and since then the Indian student has gradually been studying Western and Indian philosophy side by side. Although it is true that Indian students still do read much more Western philosophy than Indian, they do have an opportunity to compare both.

One of the earliest teachers who initiated a number of young scholars into the comparative and critical study of Indian and Western thought was the great polymath, Sir Brajendra Nath Seal (George V Professor of Philosophy at the U. of Calcutta), who had a thorough grasp of both systems. Professor S. Radhakrishnan, who succeeded him in that chair, continued that noble tradition. Gradually, during the second quarter of the present century, comparative study has become the attractive and fruitful field of labour for all ambitious students of philosophy in India.

As a result of this a wider outlook has definitely been established in Indian thought. Any one who now desires to contribute something original to philosophy has to satisfy himself and his readers that he knows what Indian and Western thinkers have already thought and written about the subject. The works of Radhakrishnan, K. C. Bhattacharya, Aurobindo, and many others testify to this fact.

III. The Ideal of Comparative Philosophy

Comparative philosophy can, therefore, be said to have taken root in India. Her geographical position and her past history have made India a meeting place of many races, cultures, and religions. It is only natural, therefore, that India should offer a very favourable atmosphere for the comparative study of philosophy. But, unfortunately, during the British rule, while India adopted English and got into close touch with Western culture, she began to neglect and ignore, partly under the glamour of the West, the culture of her close neighbors. The policy of 'divide and rule' also encouraged fissiparous tendencies, accentuated and widened the differences which had been minimized by centuries of living together and by the cementing influence of the great saints, teachers, and rulers of the past. A modern Indian student of philosophy, therefore, knows almost nothing of Chinese and Japanese thought, and little of Islamic philosophy; what is worse, he is scarcely even conscious of his ignorance. The comparative study of philosophy has, therefore, remained confined to comparisons of Indian and Western systems only.

The ideal of comparative philosophy should, however, be to study, assimilate, and co-ordinate the philosophies of all countries, races, and cultures. This is one of the great needs of the modern world, which has been planning the integration of the entire human race and trying to evolve a global consciousness based on mutual understanding, common security, and common prosperity. This cultural and political task is constantly coming up against the great problem of understanding ideological backgrounds, the ultimate standard of values, and the ethical codes of the different peoples of the world. This problem largely falls within the scope of comparative philosophy.

Judged by this higher ideal, even India falls far short. But happily some of the greatest sons of India, like Ram Mohan Roy, Tagore, Gandhi, Nehru and Radhakrishnan, kept alive the ideal of international understanding even in the midst of opposing forces. Soon after independence Maulana Abul Kalam Azad, the Minister of Education of India, sponsored a comprehensive "History of Philosophy—Eastern and Western." This work has been completed with the help of over sixty writers and edited by a board, of which Radhakrishnan is Chairman. When published, it will constitute a momentous contribution towards the higher ideal of comparative philosophy.

It should be borne in mind that the ideal of comparative philosophy should also include the comparative study of ancient and modern thought, as well as of the ideas of different countries. For, in philosophy we can often discover ideas of great wisdom even in ancient thinkers which, like the ideas of other countries, will help us to realize that there are other possible problems, approaches, and conclusions than those offered by our contemporaries. Moreover, the comparative study of the ancient and the modern very often shows that what passes now as peculiarly Eastern or Western was not always so and that human thought is capable of remarkable adjustment. The comparative study of the ideas of different ages and countries thus gives us both vertical and horizontal perspectives and thereby widens our outlook and liberalizes our minds, enables us to realize our idiosyncrasies and shortcomings, as well as our merits and agreements, and thus prepares us as much for better adjustment in practical life as for a more comprehensive understanding of theoretical truths. Finally, it also promotes a fresh and more thorough speculative effort, supported by ampler evidence and endowed with a much wider appeal.

In the light of this preliminary discussion we shall now try to estimate the work done by Radhakrishnan in the sphere of comparative philosophy.

IV. THE BACKGROUND OF RADHAKRISHNAN'S THOUGHT

The already mentioned historical and geographical facts peculiar to India and the background of Radhakrishnan's personal life were all favourable to the comparative study of philosophy. He was born in South India which was, on the one hand, the citadel of orthodox Hindu culture (being comparatively free from Muslim invasion), but which, on the other hand, had already assimilated Dravidian culture with which the North was comparatively unacquainted. He was born in an orthodox Brahmin family, but was educated from his early days in Christian Missionary schools, which taught him the Christian scriptures and instilled into his young mind orthodox Christian ideas. These were later rationally fortified when he was admitted into a missionary college, where competent Christian teachers taught him Western philosophy for his degree course. It appears that there was no arrangement for the teaching of Indian philosophy, which latter, however, ran in his blood and filled, as well, the intellectual and religious atmosphere of South India, where the great founders of the different Vedānta schools were born and still lived in the lives of countless followers. He was also possessed of an innate religious sense which found itself challenged by an age of skepticism.

In such an intriguing atmosphere full of cultural conflicts, the Indian mind has usually taken one of three resultant paths: either (1) conversion to the Christian and Western outlook, or (2) a stronger adherence to everything Indian by a kind of dialectical antithesis, or (3) the accommodation of both kinds of ideas in two logic-tight compartments of the mind, developing a kind of divided personality. The last has been by far the most common phenomenon. For the average mind, the indigenous culture of hoary antiquity is too deeply rooted to be cast out, while the glamour and grandeur of Western culture, backed by the ruling classes and glorified by success, are also too great to be resisted. The latter is, therefore, simply allowed to rest on the former, and the heavy burden of both deadens all powers of spontaneous reaction.

Radhakrishnan's mind, however, proved to be an exception. Its extraordinary vitality enabled it to analyse both currents of thought and to assimilate from each what he thought was essential and valuable. At the same time, the conflict in his young mind was very great. In an autobiographical account, *My Search for Truth,* he says,

My pride as a Hindu, roused by the enterprise and eloquence of Swami Vivekananda, was deeply hurt by the treatment accorded to Hinduism in missionary institutions. It was difficult for me to concede that Hindu ascetics and teachers who preserved for our world a living contact with the classical culture of India, which is at the root of much that we know and almost all that we practice, were not truly religious.[1]

Also: "The challenge of Christian critics impelled me to make a study of Hinduism and find out what is living and what is dead in it."[2]

It was not, however, only the conflict among religious beliefs and semiconscious cultural trends—from which the average Indian mind also suffered—which perplexed Radhakrishnan's mind. As a brilliant student and teacher of Western philosophy he read, on the one hand, more and more of ancient and modern Western philosophers; and as a proud and inquisitive Indian, he also read, with the help of several very renowned orthodox Pandits, the original texts of Indian philosophy. He was faced, therefore, by the stupendous task of rationally understanding and re-orientating, on a critical philosophical level, all that he studied and learned from the two mighty thought-currents.

This, naturally, was a life-long task, which he tried to perform through the successive periods of his long academic career. The gradual evolution of his thought is reflected in his successive pub-

[1] MST (1946 separate offprint), 5.   [2] *Ibid.,* 9.

lished works, which may be regarded as constituting a series of persistent efforts in the different regions of comparative philosophy. A surpassing quickness of intellect, a wonderful selective memory, an innate and catholic religious heart, a keen absorption in all human affairs and a consequent interest in the history of human civilization, art, literature, society, and politics, in addition to philosophy and religion, and above all a keen sense of essential and ultimate values, characterize the inner constitution of Radhakrishnan. This rare combination of qualities enables him to grapple with his own problems and incidentally with those of his country and of the modern world.

His wide outlook, versatile interest in all human affairs, great powers of expression, and practical sagacity never allowed him to remain confined to the solitary sphere of metaphysical contemplation; although, he tells us, he is a great lover of solitude and loves to retire to his inner self to be in touch with the spirit. He believes that, "The civilization of India is an effort to embody philosophical wisdom in social life." [3] Even in his administrative and advisory work as the head of universities, as the chairman of the Indian University Commission, and as an ambassador, it is easy to observe the wide and far-reaching outlook, the stabilizing effort and harmonizing ability which characterize his work in comparative philosophy as well.

V. The Earlier Works of Radhakrishnan

While still a student he wrote a thesis on the *Ethics of the Vedānta,* for the M.A. degree of the University of Madras; this was, in fact, highly commended by his teacher, Professor A. G. Hogg of the Madras Christian College. Though in college he had been taught only Western philosophy, it seems that his interest in Indian philosophy was aroused because it was adversely criticized by the Christian teachers, apparently without much knowledge of it. He was actuated to read the Vedānta in order to be able to give "a reply to the charge that the Vedānta system had no room for ethics." [4] This may be regarded as his first attempt at comparative philosophy, inasmuch as he tried here to restate the Vedānta for the benefit of the Western mind and to justify it in terms of the Western conception of ethics. The praise he received for this early work even from his Christian professor encouraged him perhaps to adopt this comparative method later on. And this is the method

3 *Ibid.,* 12.   4 *Ibid.,* 9.

which has been very widely used by many of the later Indian writers also, who have produced monographs on different aspects and schools of Indian philosophy and have tried to interpret and evaluate Indian thought in terms of Western ideas.

By temperament, Radhakrishnan is a religious mystic. As he says, "I cannot account for the fact that from the time I knew myself I have had firm faith in the reality of the unseen world . . . and even when I was faced by grave difficulties, this faith remained unshaken." [5] This religious temperament was nourished by his long education in the religious and theological atmosphere of Christian institutions. The religious motive, therefore, became strong in his life and works, including even his philosophical studies and writings. But the direction his religious enthusiasm took was determined chiefly by "the criticisms levelled by Christian missionaries on Hindu beliefs and practices." [6] Like Vivekananda, but in a more scholarly and philosophical sphere, he gradually became a defender of the criticized faith and culture. This accounts for a series of contributions to learned philosophical magazines like the *International Journal of Ethics,* the *Monist, Quest,* etc., made by him soon after he became a teacher of philosophy.

The method and means adopted by him in such writings were partly taken from the Christian critics and teachers and partly were his own. He must have learned to appreciate from the Christian teachers of that age, the absolute idealism and monism of Hegel and his followers. Because it was this philosophy which was at the height of its popularity then and was, therefore, utilized by the enlightened fathers for the re-orientation of their faith and for capturing educated minds. For Radhakrishnan it also was the nearest approximation to the Vedānta, many aspects of which could better be cast into this modern Western mould and displayed to the West both for defence and appreciation. From the Western critics, he also learned to admire a dynamic and realistic outlook and imbibed the missionary zeal for social service and for the dissemination of religious ideas. His attitude of respect even for the faith of the critic, viz., defending his own without hurting that of the critic, this was his own typically Indian method. He attributes this to his own innate religious sense and Hindu tradition: "My religious sense did not allow me to speak a rash or a profane word of anything which the soul of man holds or has held

[5] *Ibid.,* 1f.   [6] *Ibid.,* 5.

sacred. This attitude . . . is bred into the marrow of one's bones by the Hindu tradition, by its experience of centuries." [7]

Even in his early articles he tried to show that the teachings of the Vedānta leave room for a practical and realistic attitude towards life and society. The doctrine of Māyā itself does not reduce the world to a baseless illusion, but it makes it dependent on an Absolute Reality. The Vedānta does not undermine morality. Though it places the absolute beyond good and evil, it makes moral discipline an indispensable preparation for the attainment of the knowledge of that Ultimate Reality and lays down a definite moral code which every aspirer to higher knowledge must obey. Moreover, the Vedantic recognition of the ideal of a perfect life in this very world is opposed to the ordinary acosmic interpretation of it. "To the truly religious, all life is a sacrament. Modern attempts to improve the general conditions of the community . . . are not inconsistent with the Hindu religion but are demanded by it." [8]

In India religion and philosophy have a history of about five thousand years. There have naturally been divergent creeds, practices and systems of thought, therefore, and even the persisting elements and principles have been differently emphasized and interpreted at different times to suit changing conditions. In all his writings Radhakrishnan takes this comparative historical view of Indian civilization and stresses those aspects which would be helpful to the progress of India in modern times and which he believes will be beneficial to other countries also. Such change of emphasis and re-interpretation, he points out, have taken place in India itself at different critical stages and are to be found in the history of other civilizations as well. This gradual evolution of thought and culture is a human necessity. Neither an individual nor a country, Radhakrishnan firmly believes, can jump out of its past history and traditions and make a completely new beginning. The traditions have to be moulded to suit social needs and to aid human progress.

Different traditional religions can continue along the lines of their respective basic principles and yet mutually adjust themselves to form a harmonious brotherhood. The philosophy underlying this conviction is drawn from the catholic teachings of the *Bhagavadgītā*. It teaches the possibility of different paths, varying according to different tastes and aptitudes but leading to the same God. "Doctrines about God are only guides to the seekers who have

7 *Ibid.*, 7.   8 *Ibid.*, 12.

not reached the end." [9] "God has not left Himself without witness among any people." [10] "The different religions are . . . but fellow labourers in the same great task." [11] In spite of apparent diversities, different religions have a wonderful unity as concerns essentials on which they can co-operate with one another. Radhakrishnan never tires of impressing this lesson on all humanity.

In Rabindranath Tagore Radhakrishnan found a kindred soul. Sir Sarvepalli was attracted by Tagore's deep spiritual outlook, by his theistic and realistic interpretation of Indian culture particularly as found in the *Upaniṣads,* the basis of the Vedānta, by his wide sympathies and patriotism as well as by his internationalism. Radhakrishnan's first major book was *The Philosophy of Rabindranath Tagore.* In this book Radhakrishnan was really (although probably unwittingly) rehearsing his future flights in the domain of international literature. Much of what he says there about Indian religion, philosophy, and civilization in general, forms the themes of his later works, and much of what he says in appreciation of Tagore is now being said or felt about himself at home and abroad. Take, for example, sentences like the following: "In his work, India finds the lost word she was seeking." [12] "We do not know whether it is Rabindranath's own heart or the heart of India that is beating here." [13] "The world-wide interest and popularity of his writings are due as much to the lofty idealism of his thoughts as to the literary grace and beauty of his writings." [14] And Radhakrishnan could say now about himself what Tagore says in the sentence, "To me the verses of the *Upaniṣads* and the teachings of Buddha have ever been things of the spirit, . . . I have used them, both in my own life and in my preaching . . ." [15] Apart from the interpretation of the philosophy of the Indian poet to the Western world, this book can be said to have attempted a bridge between poetry and philosophy, comparing and contrasting the two, and thus served the cause of comparative philosophy in still another way.

In *The Reign of Religion in Contemporary Philosophy* Radhakrishnan may be said to reverse his rôle. Instead of interpreting Indian thought in the light of Western ideas, he studies and examines Western thought from his own or Indian point of view. In a period when India, long subjugated by foreign rule, suffered from an inferiority complex and could at best only muster enough cour-

9 *Ibid.,* 7.   10 *Ibid.,* 8.   11 *Ibid.,* 9.
12 PRT, vii.   13 *Ibid.,* vii.   14 *Ibid.,* 2.
15 *Ibid.,* 3.

age for self-defence, it required exceptional boldness for a young Indian of about thirty years to measure by his own rod such a whole group of outstanding thinkers as Leibnitz, Ward, Bergson, James, Eucken, and Russell, and to assess their shortcomings. This courage sprang, no doubt, from his mystic feeling of being guided by an unseen principle, from his strong conviction of the greatness of Indian culture and particularly of the mystic literature of the *Upaniṣads* which embody this principle, and perhaps also from the success and popularity already attained by the messages of India, based mainly on the *Upaniṣads,* delivered to the Western world by both India's saint and by her poet, Vivekananda and Tagore.

In this work he tries to show how even the greatest of the modern Western philosophers are unconsciously pushed by 'religious prepossessions' to reject monism in favour of pluralistic and personalistic types of theories and to reject intellectualism and absolutism. Philosophy should obey the intellect and logic and follow their lead to discover truth, unperturbed by religious, emotional or political considerations. "It is my opinion that systems which play the game of philosophy squarely and fairly, with freedom from presuppositions and religious neutrality, naturally end in absolute idealism," [16] he confidently asserts.

Though Radhakrishnan, in his sixties, may now blush at the emphasis of his youthful assertions and may phrase his feelings more cautiously, the book still sums up his essential standpoint, viz., Absolute Idealism which he now prefers to call a spiritual view of the world. What he advocates there is based on the philosophy of the *Upaniṣads,* to the exposition of which he devotes the last chapter of the book.

From the point of view of comparative philosophy it will be of interest to note that the careful study of contemporary Western thinkers presupposed by this volume rounded out his knowledge of European philosophy (only the earlier periods of which were then generally taught in Indian universities). The philosophers criticized by him in this early volume from one point of view entered, however, from other points of view, into the very texture of his thought and exerted an abiding influence on his later growth. Bergson's dynamic and evolutionary outlook as well as his emphasis on intuition, James and Western science, and the value of the individual in the thought of these and other Christian thinkers gradually passed into his own thought as well. Only, he sought confirmation for these popular trends of Western thought in the

16 RR

long history of Indian culture and, by doing so, tried to bring them to the careful attention of the modern Indian mind. This shift of emphasis and remoulding of ancient tradition in the light of Western thought is, as we have previously noted, present in other modern Indian thinkers as well. Many competent Western critics, accustomed to the notion that everything great and good in human civilization must be of Greek, Roman, or Christian origin, have, consequently, been wondering whether Gandhi, Tagore, Radhakrishnan and others were not good Indian Christians, after all. Such suspicion, however ignorant, only proves that a synthesis of the Eastern and the Western mind is not only a possibility, but has already been accomplished in India, at least on the higher level. Incidentally it may be mentioned that repeated reinterpretation of past tradition and scriptures, in order to suit the temper of the changing times, is to be found in the history of Christianity also. Neo-Thomists, for example, now try to interpret and justify their ancient and medieval teachings in the light of even the latest developments in science.

These facts should be borne in mind also in evaluating Radhakrishnan's work in the two monumental volumes entitled *Indian Philosophy*. These volumes constituted the first attempt to give a connected account of the different phases of philosophical development in India, from approximately three thousand B.C. on. This work was the fruit of about twenty years' labour, Radhakrishnan having worked on it, more or less, ever since he passed the M.A. examination in 1908. What challenged this talented Indian to this sustained effort was, as already noted, chiefly the systematic misinterpretation of Indian philosophy and the consequent harmful propaganda carried on not only by missionaries in India, but also by Indologists abroad and by the latter's satellites in India—either from racial pride or in order to support the imperialistic doctrine of "the white man's burden" in Asia. Radhakrishnan's work serves the cause of comparative philosophy in different ways. In the first place, it presents Indian thought in an English the literary grace and beauty of which easily attracts the Western reader. Secondly, it does not merely reproduce translations of different Indian texts so as to create an impression of authenticity, while at the same time producing a repelling atmosphere of exploded antiquity. On the contrary, it brings Indian ideas within the focus of Western thought by profuse comparisons with the ideas of Western scriptures, poets, playwrights, philosophers, scientists, and the like. Thirdly, it gives a comparative analysis of Indian systems themselves and views Indian doctrines in their historical perspective. Fourthly, it refutes the many misrepresentations of Indian thought by previous Orientalists. Fifthly, his analysis is not confined to a comparison between Indian and Western thought only, but is extended to wide regions of ancient and modern philosophies of China, Japan, Palestine, Egypt, and other lands, in all of which his wide and catholic soul displays a profound interest.

The great service rendered by this work in behalf of the spread of the knowledge of Indian philosophy in the English-speaking world can partly be judged from the many editions the volumes have undergone. It has acted as a veritable bridge between India and the West as well as between India and other Eastern countries where English is understood. In India itself it has enabled the universities, whose teaching up till now has been done mostly through the medium of the English language, to introduce Indian philosophy along with Western, and comparative study thus became possible. *Indian Philosophy* has, therefore, come to be regarded as Radhakrishnan's *magnum opus*.

Evaluation of this work from other points of view lies outside the scope of this paper. The only additional relevant question which should, perhaps, be raised here is how far Radhakrishnan's rendering of the text in English is authentic; whether he does not read Western philosophy into the Indian. In general our own answer to this question has already been given. However, the question has often been raised by two types of persons. They have to be dealt with separately.

The first group of critics consists of those who propound (or support or derive satisfaction from) an interpretation of Indian philosophy which has helped to perpetuate the flattering belief in the superiority of Western philosophy and culture. Neither evidence nor arguments can convince these. However, the increasing number of monographs which—since the appearance of Radhakrishnan's *Indian Philosophy* (in 1923 and 1927, respectively)— have been written by other Indian scholars on different schools and aspects of Indian thought, backed by the gradual coming back of India onto the political map of the world, have slowly been eliminating this class of critics.

The other group of persons consists of those who find it difficult to believe that a scholar at home in Western philosophy, whose mind is steeped in Western ideas, can either penetrate into the mysteries of the abstruse philosophical texts written in Sanskrit or present them in their original purity. Such critics are mostly Indians who argue from their initial impression of Radhakrishnan as a fluent speaker and writer of English; these people suffer from, what the American neo-realists call, the fallacies of initial predication and exclusive particularity. I had the rare privilege of studying many original Sanskrit texts with some of India's renowned Pandits. In my ignorance and youthful vanity, therefore, I too was inclined to take such a view of Radhakrishnan before I came to know this philosopher and his work intimately and compared his work with other English works on Indian philosophy. The fact that, long before he attracted public attention, Radhakrishnan, under the guidance of some great Pandits in Madras, Mysore, and even later in Calcutta, worked for about twenty years in the field of original Indian texts is still unknown to many. If personal testimony be of any value, I may recall what I regard as two fool-proof demonstrations which dispelled any lingering doubts I might have had concerning Radhakrishnan's capacity for understanding the intricacies of both metaphysics and of Indian philosophical texts. In the University of Calcutta Professor Radhakrishnan once presided over a lecture delivered by the late Professor K. C. Bhattacharya, who was regarded as a very profound metaphysician whose abstruse and analytic writings yielded meaning only after repeated readings. On the conclusion of the lecture, all eyes were fixed on the presiding chairman who rose to comment on a lecture which had gone over the heads of most of the learned listeners. There was a tense moment of curiosity. However, when Radhakrishnan, in five minutes, summed up the one-hour lecture of the abstruse metaphysician, who repeatedly nodded assent to the accuracy of his exposition, all doubts disappeared. It was an acid test for the presiding officer, who stood revealed before the scholarly audience as a mind who was able quickly to grasp the most abstruse kind of metaphysics. The other incident which convinced me of Radhakrishnan's great powers of understanding abstruse Sanskrit texts was when, in Calcutta, we happened, on one occasion, to be discussing some intricate points of Jaina philosophy. He took up a very difficult Jaina work, *Prameya-kamala-mārtaṇḍa,* which is the despair of many Pandits, began to read it fluently with the tempo of his English elocution, and translated it off-hand into English. Spontaneous admiration removed any doubts I might still have had. I was convinced of his equal competence to write on both Western and Indian philosophical systems. He is not a superficial orator or a mere literary artist, but a really competent interpreter who can link up India and the West by his extraordinary talents.

But this eulogy does not mean that I accept all of Radhakrishnan's interpretations of Indian ideas. I have my difficulties with some of them; but I have similar, if not greater, difficulties in respect of the English works of such Indian writers as DasGupta, Hiriyanna, and even of such a paragon of Sanskrit scholarship as Kuppuswami Sastri. I am, to be frank, even dissatisfied with some of my own renderings and interpretations in this field. The truth is that philosophical discussion, more than anything else, is bound up with the idiom and genius of the language of the philosopher; its translation into foreign language is often impossible without breaking up the original texts into their component parts by logical analysis and then interpreting the elements in terms of the nearest foreign concepts and finally trying to reconstruct the original meaning, bearing in mind the spirit of the whole. What passes sometimes as very faithful translation or exposition is often nothing but a meaningless jumble of words and sentences which, when put together, may convey nothing more than a recognition of a very honest attempt, which, however, leads nowhere. It is such writings which often have created the impression in some foreign readers that Indian philosophy is all meaningless jargon. No expositor of good sense can help interpreting what *he thinks* would be fair to the original writer. There is thus room for honest difference.

In this connection it should particularly be borne in mind that a foreign treatise on mathematics, natural science, music, etc., cannot be translated into English unless the translator is conversant with the technical English literature and the terms of those particular subjects. This is even more true of philosophy. Were it not for the limitations of space, it could easily be shown how some of the reputed Orientalists of the West as well as in India have quite unknowingly wrought havoc with Indian philosophy in English translations and expositions, because of their lack of accurate knowledge of the exact connotations of English philosophical terms, such, for example, as genus, universal, *a priori, a posteriori*, mind, sense, empiricism, rationalism, etc. I have become increasingly convinced of the truth of the advice given me by an early teacher of mine, Professor Vanamali Vedānta-tirtha, who taught Sanskrit as well as European philosophy: "If you want to do any work in Indian philosophy read European philosophy first." It is for this reason that scholars like Radhakrishnan, who have a thorough grasp of both, are best fitted for an interpretation of Indian philosophy to the West.

VI. The Later Works

Radhakrishnan's career from 1908 to the completion of his *Indian Philosophy* in 1927 may be said to form one complete period. Even if he had done nothing thereafter, his name would have gone down in the history of comparative philosophy. But the final goal of such comparative study would have remained unattained. The study of original texts in different languages, assimilation, evaluation, interpretation and interrelation of Western and Eastern ideas should only be a means to a higher end, namely the evolution of philosophical speculation on a global scale. In such a philosophy the problems common to all peoples who have been brought together by political, economic, scientific and cultural forces must be dealt with in the light of the accumulated wisdom of all peoples. But this goal can be achieved only when scholars of different countries have co-operated to perfect the means, and when constructive geniuses work on the materials supplied by such scholars. The whole process demands the co-operation of hundreds of scholars and geniuses of all nations who feel called upon to evolve a world-philosophy. In so far as talented persons can be expected to perform such a task single-handedly, Radhakrishnan's contribution certainly ranks very high. There is in him that rare combination of scholarship and synthetic vision. The first period of his career, therefore, was only a period of preparation and the means for undertaking the constructive tasks which constitute the second period. The success and renown he achieved during his first period led the way to unusual opportunities in the second period which, it is to be hoped, will be a long one.

The two major works of this (second) period thus far, which we may briefly note here from the point of view of comparative philosophy, are *An Idealist View of Life* and *Eastern Religions and Western Thought*. The former represents Radhakrishnan's Hibbert Lectures delivered at the Universities of London and Manchester in 1929. The latter is based on his lectures delivered during 1936-38 in Oxford, where he had been appointed to the Spalding Professorship for Eastern Religions and Ethics. As the chief centre of his activities during this second period shifted from India to Europe, his previously broad international outlook is further strengthened. As a thinker of the contemporary world he addresses his thoughts to the many-sided cultural problems of this world and suggests solutions for the modern man in any country. His is no longer the voice of an offended India defending herself against misrepresentation and claiming due recognition. It is the voice, rather, of modern man up against serious problems but trying to solve them in the light of all that is great and worthy in the teachings of the best traditions of all ages. His work is thus done on a world platform and with a cosmopolitan spirit. If some of the basic idealistic principles he adopts for this purpose are taken from Indian philosophy, they are the principles which, with his wide scholarship, he shows to be present also in the teachings of the greatest philosophers, prophets, and saints of the world at large.

An Idealist View of Life tries to show the presence of a deep under-current of Idealism in the different Indian and European philosophical systems which, on the surface, appear to be so widely divergent. "The fountain-heads of the Vedas, including the *Upaniṣads* in the East and Socrates and Plato in the West, set forth this creed in broad and flexible terms." [17] "If we are not carried away by the noise of the controversy among the philosophical sects, but watch the deeper currents which are shaping them, we seem to find a strong tendency to insist on the insights of idealism, though, of course, the language and the style are different." [18] At the same time, however, Radhakrishnan is aware that mere restatements of such principles in old terms will be quite ineffectual in the modern world. "Idealism today has to reckon with our problems and help us to face them. The stage seems to be set for a fresh statement." [19]

With a profound interest and an alert mind Radhakrishnan tries to probe sympathetically into the many-sided problems of today arising from physics, astronomy, biology, psychology, psycho-analysis, and sociology, which seem to challenge the Idealist view, religion, and spiritual outlook. He also considers the many substitutes for religion which have their origin in the dissatisfied spirit of modern man, such as naturalism, atheism, agnosticism, scepticism, humanism, pragmatism, modernism, and the like. He finds, however, that these also fail to satisfy man just as the many prevailing forms of religion do. Man will never be able to rest until he recognises the spirit in him as the highest reality and value, and understands the deeper meaning of his restlessness as a mere blind groping for the spirit. Knowledge of the spirit, which underlies man and his universe, is obtainable only by intuition. Intuition is not, however, opposed to the intellect, but is rather its highest goal,

[17] IVL, 16.   [18] *Ibid.*, 17.   [19] *Ibid.*, 17.

perfection, consummation. It gives an internal view of life and reality. It is the ultimate source of all true and abiding religion. The founders of all great faiths as well as many saints and great philosophers, in the East as well as in the West—the Vedic seers, Buddha, Moses, Christ, St. John, Muhammad, Socrates, Plato, Plotinus, Porphyry, Augustine, Dante, Bunyan, Wesley, and the like— "testify to the felt reality of God. It is as old as humanity and is not confined to any one people. The evidence is too massive to run away from." [20] True religion is based on an integral view of life and the world. It helps man to integrate his life so as "to let the spirit in him permeate his whole being, his soul, flesh and affections." [21] It is such integration or spiritual life that can save man and society from unrest. "Integrated lives are the saved ones. They possess the unspeakable joy, the peace that passeth understanding." [22]

Radhakrishnan does not like to pose as a new "prophet" who "sets forth some new-fangled paradox." [23] He merely attempts to present a point of view which "constitutes the very essence of the great philosophic tradition of idealism." [24] The essence of all idealism and of all philosophy, in the sense of Hegel, is spirit. The basic categories which Radhakrishnan employs to depict the life of the spirit in its different phases are Absolute, God, Self, matter, life, intellect, intuition, and salvation. The way in which he weaves these concepts into a philosophical and theological theory is what can be claimed to be his original contribution.

This work of Radhakrishnan can be regarded as the first grand experiment on the constructive side of comparative philosophy. The technique adopted by him is the fluidity of the basic concepts and the flexibility of the structure secured with the help of pliable connections. This protean outline is amply filled in with wonderfully apt quotations from all great philosophers, poets, scientists, prophets, saints, preachers, politicians, atheists, and sceptics to make it applicable and attractive to many, scarcely boring to any, and offensive to none. The effect is that it can strike a sympathetic chord in a Christian, Hindu, Buddhist, Confucian, Taoist, Sufi, and even in one who is dissatisfied with all religious sects. It is a work of genuine spiritual sympathy for all who are regarded as treading by diverse paths, crooked or straight, to the one goal of spiritual recovery. The student of comparative philosophy might well wonder whether the author of this treatise is an Indian He-

20 *Ibid.*, 91.   21 MST (offprint 1948), 31.   22 MST (offprint 1948), 31.
23 *Ibid.*   24 *Ibid.*

gelian or a Bergsonian or a Mahāyāna Buddhist or a Neo-Platonist or a Vedantist. But an unsophisticated general reader, unacquainted with philosophical 'isms' and conforming to no church, in a word, an open modern mind will find in the work a reasonable and attractive view of life, perhaps the vision of a prophet for the new age. It has, therefore, won considerable applause from the philosophical press and from the intelligentsia and, when it was delivered in the form of public lectures in London, it attracted crowds from all strata of society.

Yet this very merit of the work, its fluid and plastic universality, will cause it to appear intolerably ambiguous to the analytic philosopher of today, engaged as this latter is in the narrow but useful field of an analysis of the meaning of words and finding out the logical connections and structures of sentences. He will search in vain for an exact and rigorous definition of the key words used in the volume and their exact interrelations, and miss a geometrical deduction of the conclusions from those logical elements. The intellectualist may, therefore, complain, "It can create a mystic atmosphere, rouse vague tendencies and emotions but lays down nothing tangible, concrete, logically verifiable." [25]

The reply to such an unappreciative attitude can, however, also be found in the book itself, particularly in Chapter IV, which discusses the relative spheres and uses of intellect and of intuition. Radhakrishnan recognises the utility of the intellect as well as of logical analysis. "Logical knowledge enables us to know the conditions of the world in which we live and to control them for our ends. But if we want to know things in their uniqueness, in their indefeasible reality, we must transcend discursive thinking." [26] Such non-discursive, but simple and direct knowledge or intuition alone can give us knowledge of our self, of our inner mental processes, and also enable us to have an integral knowledge of reality. Such knowledge is not only the source of religion, but also present in science, art, and philosophy, which could scarcely make any progress with the help of only sense and intellect. Life and philosophy would be much poorer and incomplete without intuitive apprehension. Intellectual analysis can only present materials or elements which fall apart unless interrelated in the light of some integral and synthetic view of reality. "Philosophy is not so much a conceptual reconstruction as an exhibition of insights." [27] "Absolute knowledge in its concreteness is more in the form of effortless insight or intuition." [28]

25 *Ibid.*   26 *Ibid.*, 146.   27 *Ibid.*, 152.   28 *Ibid.*

Philosophy as conceptual knowing is a preparation for intuitive insight, and an exposition of it when it arises. There is a need for logic and language; . . . Only we have to remember that rationalisation of experience is not its whole truth. The great truths of philosophy are not proved but seen.[29]

As regards the flexible and ambiguous nature of the outline of an intuitive view of life, Radhakrishnan's reply would probably take the line of the following statements found in another context in the same book: "The intuitive seers shrink from precise statements and clearcut definitions. They speak in picture and allegory, parable and miracle." [30] In still other contexts he also points out how the language of the founders of different religions as found, for example, in the Bible, in the Upaniṣads and Tripiṭakas, is pliable in form and has, therefore, lent itself to different kinds of interpretation and satisfied the lives of millions of followers in all kinds of situations.

From the point of view of comparative philosophy, it may be added that constructive work in this field requires a synthetic genius who, after analysing by comparative study the basic concepts of the different systems, can present a philosophy universally or at least largely acceptable to peoples of divergent traditions. One who aims at such a work can afford to speak only in broad and general terms and concepts which are capable of different kinds of concrete formulation in the light of different tastes and experiences. In fact, this is also essentially the process—though to a much more limited extent—by which we communicate our unique experiences in sentences composed of general terms, which are interpreted by the listeners in the concrete setting of their own experiences; we can, of course, never vouch for the identity between what is intended and what is understood. We need not, however, on this account, minimise the importance of precision in philosophical statements. But we must, at the same time, recognise the importance of universal pliable forms and symbols under which innumerable concrete cases can unite. To deny this would be to ignore the fact that modern science itself could not progress without algebra, which latter is based on the very principle of universal symbolism. In fact, the logical empiricists, who advocate most insistently the analytic use of intellect in philosophy, are themselves adopting this algebraic method of symbolic logic for the unification of all sciences in their ambitious scheme, The Encyclopedia

29 Ibid.   30 Ibid., 202f.

of Unified Science. Analysis and synthesis are the two legs necessary for the forward movement of philosophy. We may also mention here the example of Whitehead, whose masterly analysis of
mathematical and metaphysical complexes was followed by an
equally competent constructive work in his *Process and Reality.*
But some critics failed to appreciate his broad synthetic views, particularly his highly plastic and accommodating conception of God,
and accused Whitehead also of ambiguity and unclear thinking.

Before leaving our discussion of *An Idealist View of Life,* it
should probably be mentioned that a kind of nemesis overtakes
our philosopher in this constructive work. In *The Reign of Religion in Contemporary Philosophy* he had criticized many Western
philosophers for allowing their religious beliefs to influence their
philosophical search after truth. In *An Idealist View of Life* Radhakrishnan seems to expose himself to the same charge; for the religious motive behind his philosophical theory is certainly quite
evident here. The difference lies, perhaps, in the fact that, whereas
the philosophers criticized in *The Reign of Religion* were unconsciously influenced by religious biases, Radhakrishnan consciously
courts intuition—which, from his point of view, lies at the bottom
of true religion—for guidance in the formulation of a philosophical view of life. Or, perhaps, the difference lies in the fact that,
whereas those thinkers were influenced by religious dogmas, he
himself is moved by true religion which consists in true insight or
an integral view of reality, from which true philosophy also originates. Or, perhaps, he no longer holds his older views.

In *Eastern Religions and Western Thought* we find the same
philosophical outlook, but the subject-matter is different. It is not
so much comparative philosophy as comparative religion which is
discussed here in its historical perspective. But, inasmuch as true
religion and true philosophy are, for Radhakrishnan, only differences of emphasis between emotion and thought, it may be of some
interest briefly to consider the book here. Those who, misled by
Radhakrishnan's easy flowing expositions, are tempted to suppose
that he builds castles in the air and temples of international amity
on Utopian dreams, have only to glance through this book to realize their error. Its four hundred pages are packed with the sicken-
ing details of the political, cultural, and religious history of the
world from the dawn of civilisation. Exhausting catalogues of dates
and proper names and profuse quotations from original documents, opinions and confessions of unsuspected authorities are
marshalled, chapter after chapter, to convince even sceptical and

prejudiced readers that his idealism is firmly rooted in acknowledged facts. In striking contrast with the former book, this one has
a marble structure, even though it is sustained throughout by a
spiritual ideal.

The ground plan of this work is traceable in Lecture I ("Comparative Religion") of his earlier little book, entitled *East and West
in Religion*. What in the earlier little volume was contained in a
paragraph is in this later book substantiated in considerable detail,
as if it had been provoked by the challenging and scholarly atmosphere of Oxford, which also offered him the seclusion and the enormous library facilities necessary for this prodigious collection of
facts. The main theme of this book is that the meeting of the East
and of the West, which is a major problem for the modern mind,
is by no means merely the ideal of a few visionaries; there actually
have been such repeated meetings in the history of East and West.
Though the means of communication were much more difficult,
actual trade by land and sea, military expeditions, pilgrimages of
scholars and preachers had, many times in the past, overcome the
barriers of space and time and brought the different peoples together. As a consequence of such meetings throughout history,
what is now regarded as Western culture contains many elements
derived from the East, and *vice versa*. The different cultures are
not nearly so alien to each other, therefore, as they are now assumed
to be. On behalf of the East Radhakrishnan tries to show, from
historical documents, the Eastern, and more particularly the Indian, elements which had entered into early Greek thought as well
as into early and medieval Christian thought. On the other hand,
he also shows how the different races and religions of the world met
and fused together in India and also lived there side by side in
mutual toleration. History, therefore, repeatedly has proved the
union of Eastern and Western cultures to be a possibility.

Today "the supreme task of our generation is to give a soul to
the growing world-consciousness, to develop ideals and institutions
necessary for this creative expression of the world soul, to transmit
these loyalties and impulses to future generations and train them
into world citizens."[31] "The contributions of ancient Greece, of the
Roman Empire, of Renaissance Italy to the progress of humanity
do not concern only the inhabitants of modern Greece or modern
Italy. They are a part of the heritage of humanity."[32] Similarly, if
modern provincialism in thought can be overcome, it will be recognised that the East, particularly India which is typical of the

[31] ER, viii.   [32] *Ibid.*, viii.

East, can contribute today, as it did in the past, some lessons which will enable the modern world to live in peace and amity. Radhakrishnan's elaborate examination and analysis of the East and the West may be summed up as follows. Western civilization, dominated by the Graeco-Roman, "has for its chief elements rationalism, humanism, and the sovereignty of the state." [33] In spite of the acceptance of Christianity, its inner spirituality, its spirit of renunciation, tolerance, and meekness, which were the Eastern elements in that faith, did not make much impression on the West. Religion was subordinated to political ends for the consolidation of kingship, states, national pride, and imperial designs. There was absent, therefore, the power of real unity, which can not be built without the spiritual unity of man and the consequent power of toleration and renunciation. Internal strife and narrow nationalism destroyed the Greeks and the Romans within eight or nine hundred years. Indian and Chinese civilizations, on the other hand, marked as they are by an inner spirituality which inculcates a life of charity, tolerance, renunciation and contentment, have survived repeated political vicissitudes and lasted for five thousand years or more. "To be gentle is to be invincible," said the great Chinese sage, Lao Tze. "While the Western races crave for freedom even at the price of conflict, the Easterns stoop to peace even at the price of subjection." [34] The Eastern peoples "turn their limitations into virtues" [35] and adjust themselves to new conditions and live on. "The future is hidden from us, but the past warns us that the world in the end belongs to the unworldly." [36] But the "Eastern civilisations are by no means self-sufficient." [37] Their peoples are now unpractical and inefficient and suffer from weakness derived from age. "They require to be rejuvenated." [38] They can benefit by assimilating the best things from Western humanism, rationalism, and practical enthusiasm. Such a combination of the spiritual and the worldly will benefit both East and West. Such a life was the ideal of India in the days of its glory. It is found best reflected in the synthesis and gradation in individual and social life: (1) the fourfold object of life: wealth, enjoyment, morality, and spiritual freedom; (2) the fourfold order of society: the man of learning, of power, of skilled productivity, and of service; (3) the fourfold stages of life: student, householder, forest recluse, and the free supersocial man.

But Radhakrishnan does not plead for the revival of any one past

33 *Ibid.*, 260. 34 *Ibid.*, 257. 35 *Ibid.*, 257.
36 *Ibid.*, 258. 37 *Ibid.*, 258. 38 *Ibid.*, 258.

tradition which might have been good for its respective age, but does not suit us now. On the contrary, he asks: "May we not strive for a philosophy which will combine the best of European humanism and Asiatic religion, a philosophy profounder and more living than either, endowed with greater spiritual and ethical force, which will conquer the hearts of men and compel peoples to acknowledge its sway?" [39]

The answer to this question he gives partly by his own life-long labour in comparative philosophy and religion, the results of which we have so imperfectly tried to present in these pages. But the best minds of all nations must undertake this arduous but urgent task from their own respective points of view, must bring forward the best from their own systems for the development of a world-philosophy which can consolidate world-consciousness on a stable basis for the benefit of all mankind.

VII. CONCLUSION

This essay really should have ended here. But the well-conceived purpose of this series offers a unique opportunity for the clarification of difficulties and answering of questions by the philosopher himself. This tempts us to seek for more light on some basic issues of comparative philosophy.

1. We have seen that, in the long history of its philosophy, there are, in every country, divergent trends, sometimes differing as much as the two poles. Radhakrishnan has selected for constructive syntheses the Idealist point of view and, emphasizing the basic unity between the Idealistic traditions of India and the West, he conceives a reconciliation between the two. Although he has not overlooked other Western trends, which may profitably complement and counterbalance the acosmic and absolutist tendency of Idealism, nevertheless Idealism constitutes his fundamental viewpoint. Now the question is: Could not the attempt for a synthesis be based on other points of view also? In recent times Indian Marxists, for example, have been busy viewing both Eastern and Western thought from their point of view and emphasizing the value of materialist ideas already present in both. They are trying to build a bridge between the two on other, unexpected, foundations. Are there not, then, many alternative possible syntheses arising from a comparative study of philosophy conducted from the standpoint

39 *Ibid.*, 259.

of different conceptions of values, that is, of what is best in different countries and periods?

2. We have previously noted that, whereas in his earlier critical work, *The Reign of Religion,* Radhakrishnan thinks that the aim of philosophy should be a relentless logical pursuit of truth free from religious beliefs, in his later constructive works he seems to base his philosophy largely on intuition, which for him is also the basic spiritual or religious consciousness. How are we to resolve this conflict? What, in his mature thought now, is the relation between philosophy and religion? Is it necessary to harmonize religious ideas for securing harmony amongst philosophies?

3. Since the days of Darwin the West is increasingly thinking, in every sphere, in terms of the evolution of the human race and of human institutions, whereas the dominant idea in Indian thought is the possibility of the evolution or devolution of the individual in accordance with his own actions through successive births. How can the evolution of the race (and with it of the body through racial heredity) be harmonized with the evolution or devolution of the moral individual?

These are some of the basic difficulties which we also met with in the course of our long discussions in the last East-West Philosophers' Conference (in Hawaii) and which block the way to international understanding. There are hints here and there in Radhakrishnan's writings for the solution of these problems. But fuller light on them would be most helpful in the advancement of comparative philosophy.

DHIRENDRA MOHAN DATTA

DEPARTMENT OF PHILOSOPHY
UNIVERSITY OF PATNA
PATNA, BIHAR, INDIA

21

Humayun Kabir

RADHAKRISHNAN'S POLITICAL PHILOSOPHY

RADHAKRISHNAN'S POLITICAL PHILOSOPHY

RADHAKRISHNAN'S approach to politics is essentially that of a rationalist. This is not surprising; for, as a life-long student of philosophy, his interests have always been primarily intellectual. The practice of philosophy leads not only to the development of intellectual finesse but also to the growth of a spirit of disinterestedness. In spite of acute awareness of current problems, Radhakrishnan has, therefore, always brought to their analysis a dispassionate and detached view. This is characteristically a rationalist approach and has in Radhakrishnan's case proved more successful, because, following the traditions of Indian philosophy, he has given to rationalism a connotation wider than mere intellectualism. For him, philosophy has meant not mere logical thought nor the discursive use of the intellect, but a wider and more comprehensive view of reality in which thought and emotion, intellect and intuition have their proper place. His attitude towards politics has, therefore, been synoptic, not sectional or fragmentary.

It is necessary to stress this point since the enormous increase in human knowledge seems to make specialisation inevitable. It is evident that without specialisation the progress which has been achieved in different fields of knowledge and practice would not have been possible. Nevertheless, specialisation has at times led to a narrow and sectional point of view. Fragmentation of society into different groups and interests has led to a divergence in attitudes and outlooks that have concealed or distorted the identity of social values. It has also led to a sharp division of theory from practice to the detriment of both. Not only so, but divisions have manifested themselves within each field of theory and practice. Unreconciled oppositions have been the result; and, inasmuch as unreconciled oppositions inevitably lead to conflict, the result has been full of danger to man. There have been conflicts within and between individuals and societies. Divergence of interests has led to outward clashes; but still more dangerous has been the tendency to disintegration of personality. This has expressed itself not only in conflicting views on politics, society and morals, but also in the application of different standards to the same problem in different contexts. Radhakrishnan has refused to recognise such sharp divisions, and has identified himself with the political aspirations of his people while, at the same time, retaining his academic temper.

Radhakrishnan has not, however, attempted to develop a systematic political philosophy. His views on politics are scattered among his writings and speeches and form part of his general philosophical outlook. If we try to analyse the basis of his political thought, we find that it is derived from his attitude towards Reality. In philosophy he may perhaps be described as a qualified monist. Although he recognises the supreme Reality as one and unique, he is conscious of the individual's claim to identity and continuity. A consciousness of the value and uniqueness of the individual distinguishes his position from that of extreme monists, for whom the individuals are ultimately only moments in the being of Brahman.

Radhakrishnan's faith in democracy derives, therefore, from his recognition of the value and significance of the individual. For him, democracy is not a question of merely "a fine political arrangement, but it is the highest religion. The human individual is the highest, the most concrete embodiment of the Spirit on earth and anything which hurts his individuality or damages his dignity is undemocratic and irreligious." [1] Whenever he speaks of democracy, it is with almost a religious fervour. He interprets it as a spiritual achievement and insists that in advocating democracy he is

referring not so much to parliamentary institutions as to the dignity of man, the recognition of the fundamental right of all men to develop the possibilities in them. The common man is not common. He is precious, has in him the power to assert his nature against the iron web of necessity. To tear his texture, to trample him in blood and filth is an unspeakable crime.[2]

From this insistence on democracy follows Radhakrishnan's passionate advocacy of freedom in the fullest sense of the term. If each human individual is unique and valuable, it follows that no political arrangement in which individuality is suppressed can be justified. He, therefore, expresses himself against all forms of regimentation and totalitarianism. That is why, in spite of his recognition of the value of social security, he has never been able to

[1] EPW, 8.   [2] Ibid., 39.

adopt the Communist outlook, which prefers the claims of organisation to those of freedom. According to him—and here his thought is deeply influenced by the Liberal tradition of the 19th century—that State is best which governs least. Institutions and forms of government are merely meant to regulate the relations of individuals to one another. They can never be ends in themselves; and hence they are to be judged by the contribution they make to the development of the individual. Whatever is conducive to the self-realisation of the individual is good; whatever suppresses individuality is a bar to progress.

As against the views of Bryce, who held that "that which the mass of any people desires is not to govern itself but to be well governed," he quotes with approval the judgment of Mommsen:

According to the same law of nature in virtue of which the smallest organism infinitely surpasses the most artistic machine, every Constitution, however defective, which gives play to the free self-determination of a majority of the citizens infinitely surpasses the most brilliant and humane absolutism; for the former is capable of development and therefore living; the latter is what it is and therefore dead.[3]

He has no doubt that, taking all in all,

in this imperfect world democratic government is the most satisfactory. It is based on the fundamental principle that, in the long run, government should rest on the consent of the governed and that there should be freedom of expression for minority groups. Without such freedom, the principle of consent loses its value. In democratic institutions, there is protection against the abuse of power. Irresponsible power is bound to be used in the interests of the group which possesses it.[4]

Liberty is a condition for man's moral growth, and hence no State can claim men's allegiance unless it is based on their voluntary acceptance. If men are not free to express their views and feelings, there is no way of knowing whether acceptance is voluntary or otherwise. Without freedom of expression, truth may become subservient to the interests of a powerful group. Freedom of speech is therefore necessary both as evidence and expression of freedom of choice. Election, not compulsion, is the essence of democracy; for, "we cannot build a democratic State on the foundation of force. If once we develop a tradition of violence, it will become difficult to abandon it. Violence has for its effect counter-violence and produces an atmosphere of suspicion, resentment, and hatred."[5]

---

[3] *Ibid.*, 38.   [4] *Ibid.*, 40.   [5] *Ibid.*, 14.

There is no doubt in Radhakrishnan's mind that violence and democracy are incompatible. He has therefore condemned in unequivocal terms the use of violence for the solution of any human problem. He recognises that violence can take different forms, for "violence is either active or passive. The aggressive powers are now actively violent; the imperial powers who persist in the enjoyment of unjust advantages acquired from past violence are as much guilty of violence and are inimical to freedom and democracy." [6] This is the reason why Mahatma Gandhi's conception and practice of *Satyāgraha* has evoked his unstinted admiration. "*Satyāgraha* is rooted in the power of reality, in the inner strength of the soul" [7] and hence

it does not evade the issue but fearlessly faces the wrong-doer and resists his wrong with the overpowering force of love and suffering, for it is contrary to human nature to fight with force. Our conflicts are to be settled by the human means of intelligence and goodwill, of love and service.[8]

With Mahatma Gandhi he believes that "*satyāgraha* may seem to be an ineffectual answer to the gigantic displays of brute force; but there is something more formidable than force, the immortal spirit of man which will not be subdued by noise or numbers. It will break all fetters which tyrants seek to rivet on it." [9]

Radhakrishnan is, however, careful to draw a distinction between violence and force. "Violence, *hiṁsā*," he says,

is not to be confused with coercive force or *daṇḍa*. There is a difference between the use of force in a state and the use of force in wars between states. The use of force is permissible when it is ordered in accordance with law by a neutral authority in the general interest and not in the interest of one of the parties to the dispute. In a well-ordered state we have the rule of law, courts of justice and police and prisons. . . . Where there is no world government, where there is no impartial court to determine what is just, no one has a right to use force to make his cause prevail over that of his neighbour.[10]

Radhakrishnan elaborates the distinction further by defining it in terms of that between the functions of the teacher and the administrator, the Brahmin and the Kṣatriya, the dreamer and the organiser, or, as perhaps Koestler would express it, between the Yogi and the Commissar. According to Radhakrishnan,

---

6 MG, 27.   7 *Ibid.*, 32.   8 *Ibid.*, 32.
9 *Ibid.*, 38.   10 *Ibid.*, 357.

the distinctions of conduct, the complete abstention from force of the teacher who is educating us in ancient charity and disciplined co-operation and the use of force under just authority by the judges and the police, arises from the distinction of functions. Charity and justice have both a place in the imperfect human society.[11]

Radhakrishnan's repugnance to violence as an instrument for effecting changes in society is not, however, derived merely from a consideration of the evil consequences of such a course. He is also keenly aware that force simplifies things to the point of distortion. A human being is a complex entity, and suppression of one aspect has incalculable effects on other aspects of his mind and character. This is true not only of the individual but also of society. Suppression of any one element in society has consequences on other elements, which are not always seen immediately but are nevertheless real. Radhakrishnan is quite conscious of the fact that

human nature is not a matter of surfaces but of strata, of external experience, of reflective consciousness, of moral and aesthetic apprehension, of religious insight. Every stratum has its own life. We have diseases of the body as well as of the mind. If cold and catarrh are illnesses of physical nature, if error, prejudice and falsehood are defects of our mind, lust, anger and jealousy are deformations of our heart. However much we may progress in the conquest of natural forces or in the control of social injustices, a very important part of the human problem will consist in the disciplining of our wayward desires and the achievement of an attitude of poise toward the inevitable limitations of finite existence.[12]

Both by nature and temperament as well as by his reading of history, Radhakrishnan is, therefore, averse to violence. Not only must violence, in the nature of the case, defeat itself, but history shows that violence is not necessary. Steady pressure of public opinion has carried through greater reforms and changes than the most violent of revolutions. With the Liberals, he believes that "the progress of the consciousness of freedom is the essence of human history."[13] The influence of the Liberal tradition is in fact one of the strongest traits in his political thought. He shares the Liberals' suspicion of government and their faith in the possibility of progress through education and enlightenment. He points out that we do not realise sufficiently the progress which humanity has made in spite of setbacks, blind alleys and disasters.

---

11 *Ibid.*, 359.   12 EPW, 29.   13 MG, 20.

Through the continued effort of mankind "serfs are becoming free men, heretics are no longer burned; nobles are surrendering their privileges, slaves are being freed from a life of shame, rich men are apologizing for their wealth, militant empires are proclaiming the necessity of peace, and even dreams of the union of mankind are cherished." [14] Those who do not see the great tradition of democracy are, according to him, blind, for "unceasing is the toil of those who are labouring to build a world where the poorest have a right to sufficient food, to light, air and sunshine in their homes, to hope, dignity and beauty in their lives." [15]

Democracy is, therefore, for Radhakrishnan, based on the recognition of the value of the individual. In other forms of political organisation, the many are subject to the will or even to the whim of one or a few. It is only in democracy that all have equal opportunity of sharing in the shaping of a common life. The emphasis must, however, be as much on equality as on opportunity. Since democracy is a system of equal rights for all, it follows that there can be no encroachment on the rights of any. Or, in other words, democracy creates conditions for the free and full development of the individual, but does not permit individual license. The distinction between liberty and license is thus fundamental to democracy. Radhakrishnan points out that

it is easy to acquire the forms of democracy, but not so easy to get its spirit, that sensitive adjustment of the self to the infinitely varied demands of other persons. Essentially, a democrat is one who has that trait of humility, the power to put himself in the second place, to believe that he may possibly be mistaken and his opponent probably right.[16]

According to Radhakrishnan, the religious tradition of India also justifies democracy; although he is too much of a realist to deny that in practice India has often failed to carry out the implications of this principle. He also recognises that much of the suffering, subjection and degradation of India is due to her failure to be faithful to the principles of democracy. He points out that

the central fact of religion is the felt existence within us of an abounding inner life which transcends consciousness. In man alone does the Universal come to consciousness. . . . Faith in the one Supreme means that we, His offspring, are of one body, of one flesh—the Brahmin, the Harijan, the black, the yellow and the white whose prayers go up to one God under different names.[17]

14 *Ibid.*, 20.　　　15 *Ibid.*, 20.　　　16 EPW, 16.　　　17 *Ibid.*, 30-32.

With his insistence on the dignity of the individual, it is inevitable that Radhakrishnan should be sensitive to all failures of social justice. He says that such failures make a mockery of all our professions of loyalty to the ideal of democracy. He further says that, if democracy is to be realised in practice, it is necessary to extend its principles beyond the political field. He warns that "we cannot have an effective democracy so long as its material basis, which is its economy, is defective." [18] Any social order that is based on great inequalities in wealth must inevitably lead to inequalities in social status and political power. Similarly, inequalities in social or political relations result in inequalities in material wealth and in opportunities for progress and prosperity. Without equality of opportunity in matters of food, health and education, democracy may become a mockery. That is why Radhakrishnan has always been a critic of capitalism; for he sees that it is incompatible with democracy. He explains that

if one group or nation attempts to make itself secure at the expense of another, Germans at the expense of the Czechs, landlords at the expense of tenants, capitalists at the expense of workers, it is adopting an undemocratic method and can defend its injustice only by the force of arms. The dominant group has the fear of dispossession and the oppressed stores up just resentment.[19]

In his view capitalism is morally dangerous because it permits and encourages the growth of large disparities between the haves and the have-nots. Those who are privileged tend to develop habits of waste and luxury, while those who do not have the bare essentials for human living become frustrated and embittered.

So long as economic power is concentrated in a few hands, there can be no sense of security among the large masses of the people. Failure to recognise this fact has been the blind spot of Western democracy, while Communism has won the allegiance of dispossessed individuals and nations by highlighting it and promising early remedy. Radhakrishnan concedes the force of Communist criticism of democracy and insists that its appeal can be overcome only if democracy comes closer to satisfying the ideal. Ideas cannot be crushed by violence; hence to think of defeating Communism on the field of battle or suppressing it by force is sheer illusion. Speaking before the Fifth General Session of UNESCO, Radhakrishnan pointed out that "while more than half the population of the world in Asia and Africa lives under normal subsistence level,

18 *Ibid.*, 13.   19 MG, 19.

the other part is spending its time, wealth and energy in building armies, navies and air forces which will avert nothing, which will solve nothing." [20] He, therefore, warns that

if we do not provide opportunities to peoples of Asia and Africa to rehabilitate themselves, they will lend a receptive ear to the other pattern of life which offers a vision of human equality and brotherhood, which promises deliverance from poverty and insecurity, and supports liberation movements of colonial peoples. If democracy is to defeat it, it must become disciplined, purposeful and sacrificial.[21]

Communism can, according to Radhakrishnan, be overcome only if the imperfect democracy of to-day overcomes its own shortcomings and defects, and not only promises, but takes effective steps to ensure for the dispossessed a future of hope and security. If this is not done, the under-privileged will soon realise that their only strength lies in their numbers and will attempt to organise themselves in opposition to the powers-that-be and in seeking to overthrow the *status quo*. Hence, conflict is inevitable in a capitalist world. Within the country, capitalism leads to clashes between individuals and classes. Between countries, it leads to clashes between the producers of raw materials and the producers of finished goods. For, "people who live in the shadow of hunger, poverty and disease do not care for '*isms*'. They do not discuss abstract ideas, they want practical solutions to their problems. Millions spent in defence will not save us. Our ultimate security is in the contentment of the people." [22] Radhakrishnan warns that "Hitler and Stalin are the symptoms of the frustration of individuals in societies and of nations in the world." [23] The only way out, therefore, is the achievement of economic justice, which involves a reshaping of the economic order. According to Radhakrishnan, "an economic order based on social ownership of large sources of wealth and power would be far less dangerous to ethical life and more helpful to social fellowship." [24]

It is, therefore, not surprising that, with the Social Democrat, Radhakrishnan believes in state ownership of public utility services. He also holds that peasants and workers must have a right to the full fruits of their labour; but he has refused to accept a theory of value according to which all wealth is merely congealed labour. Nor is he against private property as such; for he recognises that "economic rewards should not be divorced from services." [25] He

---

[20] Address to UNESCO Conference—24th May, 1950.
[21] *Ibid.*   [22] *Ibid.*   [23] EPW, 69.
[24] *Ibid.*, 42.   [25] *Ibid.*, 42.

therefore urges that "while equalisation of rewards is impossible, the present disparities should be diminished." [26] The acquisition of wealth should be related to the discharge of social functions, and hence inequality of earnings can, within limits, be justified. In order, however, to prevent the growth of glaring inequalities, "huge incomes can be restricted by means of taxes." [27]

Radhakrishnan's attitude towards Communism brings out the essential characteristics of his political philosophy. He concedes the communist claim that real democracy cannot be achieved without social and economic justice, and agrees that "there is nothing wrong in the ideal which attempts to make the State the owner of all public utilities for the benefit of all." [28] He does not, however, believe that it is necessary to abolish all private property to ensure this end. Such a demand he regards as an instance of "the blind uncritical devotion to an idea or a cause which is so sure of its own rectitude that it refuses to argue or examine evidence . . ." [29] He holds that such fanaticism is opposed to the spirit of democracy, of which he finds a fine expression in the British "spirit of compromise, of adjustment to facts, of flexibility of mind, of no doctrinairism." [30] Further, he believes that changes in social and economic organisation can and ought to be brought about gradually through education of public opinion and by consent of all parties. Although he fully recognises the importance and value of the ideal of distributive justice advocated by Communism, he holds that the methods and instruments it proposes to use for achieving economic and social democracy create more problems than they solve. For these methods depend upon the imposition of the will of one section or class upon the whole of society through violent revolution and class warfare. Violence and class conflict are disvalues which Radhakrishnan repudiates; nor does he consider them as unavoidable, for "there is nothing inevitable in social phenomena." [31] Radhakrishnan points out that "Liberals failed because they were not sufficiently socialistic. Communists failed because they were not sufficiently democratic." [32] His faith is in the creation of a free world, a good society, in which both mind and spirit are free, and in which the right of the individual to be different is recognised. If this is done, the explosive appeal of Communism would disappear, for "people do not wish to exchange intellectual serfdom for economic security. We want not only better standards

---

[26] *Ibid.,* 44.   [27] *Ibid.,* 42.   [28] *Ibid.,* 13.
[29] Address to UNESCO Conference—24th May 1950.
[30] *Ibid.,* on 30th May, 1950.   [31] EPW, 14.   [32] *Ibid.,* 8.

of living but a better way of life." [33] His final criticism of Communism is that it interferes with the individual's freedom of thought and with his sturdy independence; for, all "the great achievements of art and religion, like those of science and philosophy, are the results of what a man does with his solitariness." [34]

One of the clearest expositions of Radhakrishnan's attitude to the theory and practice of Communism is to be found in *Religion and Society*. Elsewhere his criticism of Communism is directed mainly against some of its unattractive features. In *Religion and Society* he attacks its theoretical foundations as well. He is fully conscious of the great moral force behind Communism, and recognises that its plea for social justice and racial equality must appeal to all individuals and groups who suffer from a sense of disability. According to him, Communism—in spite of its ostentatious repudiation of religion—is essentially religious in spirit, and even the adverse comments of Marx and Lenin against religion "are not without the spirit of religion, of understanding, of compassion. . . . With a tremendous effort of religious imagination, Marx sees and feels that human society is a single, organic whole, and strives to oppose the supernatural, other-worldly religions." [35]

With all his sympathy for the social and economic programmes of Communism, Radhakrishnan holds that it cannot be accepted as a way of life. The chief reason for his rejection of Communism lies in the fact that he finds it intellectually inadequate. Not only is the materialist hypothesis, even in the revised version of dialectical materialism, unsatisfactory, but "Marx offers no proof for metaphysical materialism." [36] It is a hypothesis Marx accepts uncritically. Radhakrishnan also points out that nowhere has Marx proved that the validity of his metaphysical doctrine is a necessary condition for the acceptance of his economic programme. In fact, one may accept the metaphysical theory and reject the economic programme, and *vice versa*. Marx's derivation of the one from the other is thus an act of faith and not the result of logical insight. Marx's belief in the inevitability of progress is equally uncritical; for, "history is full of examples of decay and retrogression and cannot be regarded as a continuous development through conflict." [37] Nor can Marx explain why evolution must stop with the emergence of the Communist state.

[33] Address to UNESCO General Conference—24th May, 1950.
[34] *Ibid.*   [35] RS, 69.
[36] *Ibid.*, 26.   [37] *Ibid.*, 33.

If the evolution of human society is a perpetual play of materialist forces in which, through a series of conflicts and class wars, capitalism is ended and a classless and equalitarian state is established, why should this new society be exempt from the law of dialectical progress determined by materialist forces? [38]

The Marxist interpretation of history as a movement through a series of contradictions is an over-simplification; for the evidence of history is that "development proceeds at different paces and in varying fashions, now in a transition from one state to its opposite, now in an unbroken line." [39] Radhakrishnan points out also that, contrary to Communist beliefs, all wars are not caused by class struggles, for "there are class struggles and civil wars, but there are wars of religions and nations also. The latter have been more decisive for human evolution." [40] He concludes that the Communist "emphasis on the importance of economic conditions is correct; the suggestion that they are exclusively determinant of history is incorrect." [41]

Radhakrishnan holds that, on account of its preoccupation with economic factors, communism fails to appreciate the values of individuality. If, as Marx holds, the capitalist order will disappear from the stage of history by the inevitable processes of history, there is hardly any room for individual action or initiative. In fact, the individual tends to lose his individuality and becomes a mere moment in a universal historical process. Radhakrishnan pertinently asks, "How can we ask the individual to behave as a revolutionary if he has no reality at all? If the tendencies work out with an iron necessity towards an inevitable goal, there is no point in asking us to work for it." [42] The truth, however, is that "all progress is due to the initiation of new ideas by exceptionally endowed individuals. Without intellectual freedom, there would have been no Shakespeare or Goethe, no Newton or Faraday, no Pasteur or Lister." [43] And, one may add, no Marx or Lenin. Radhakrishnan's faith in the individual has in it the force of a mystic intuition, for "there is nothing final or eternal about states or nations which wax and wane. But the humblest individual has the spark of spirit in him which the mightiest empire cannot crush. Rooted in one life, we are all fragments of the divine, sons of immortality, amṛtasya putrāḥ." [44]

The Communist as well as the Liberal fallacy can be traced

[38] *Ibid.*, 34. [39] *Ibid.*, 32. [40] *Ibid.*, 38.
[41] *Ibid.*, 35. [42] *Ibid.*, 65. [43] *Ibid.*, 64.
[44] *Ibid.*, 66.

back to the uncritical belief in competition as the guiding force of human progress. This is, in Radhakrishnan's opinion, due to the adoption of a crude version of the Darwinian theory of the struggle for existence; but human as well as natural history is witness to the value of the co-operative principle. It is because this is not fully recognised that modern society suffers from so many ills. Conquest of the forces of nature has made it possible to eliminate hunger and disease and provide all the amenities of civilised existence to all, but "society is sick because the soul of man is infected with the germs of greed and selfishness. . . . Competitive pride is the root of the problem, the supreme evil," [45] for, "between man and society there exists such a deep, mysterious, primordial relationship, a concrete interdependence, that a divorce between them is impossible. This natural sympathy is countered by the unnatural selfishness of individuals and the egotism of collectivities." [46] Since "the spirit in man is one with the soul of all things," [47] separatism which follows from self-assertiveness "results in a disruption of the inner unity. The nature of man becomes a wild chaos. . . . Complete harmony can take place only when there is a return to unity." [48]

Radhakrishnan's belief in the dignity of the individual and in the value of co-operation as a principle of social organisation leads him to utter a warning against the increasing mechanisation of life. He is not against large scale production—his passion for securing abundance for all cannot be satisfied except through the use of the machine—, but he feels that men must remember that "in a highly industrialised society men's minds act like machines and not as living organisms. They are dependent on large and complicated forms of organisation, capitalist combines and labour unions . . ." [49] This, he recognises, is the real danger; for in such a society the individual cannot have much influence on the decisions of society. The more complex the social organisation, the more

natural creative impulses are suppressed in millions of human beings who do one little piece of work and not the whole. There is not the sense of satisfaction in the work we do when we do not act as responsible individuals in the society to which we belong; our lives become tiresome and meaningless and we take to wild forms of compensation for excitement and vital experience. The rich and the poor both seem to suffer in a mechanised society. The rich, men and women, seem as though

[45] EPW, 93.   [46] Ibid., 98.   [47] Ibid., 99.
[48] Ibid., 99.   [49] MG (1949 ed.), 347.

they have an almost physical sense of spiritual death with their souls still and rigid. Old men starve to death condemned to work until they can work no longer, and women are forced to undertake the most exhausting labours.[50]

For Radhakrishnan, therefore, freedom is not a mere political fact but a social reality. Its essence is the recognition that "in the last resort man lives by what cannot be regulated." [51] He, therefore, pleads that "the dignity of man requires, that he be not lost in an anonymous crowd." [52] Because "the eclipse of human rights by State compulsions, the debasing of ethical standards by demagogy in all spheres, politics and art, trade and international relations, the indoctrination by the press, radio and cinema, the bureaucratic control of education, information and publicity are dehumanising men and producing ant-hill society," [53] he repudiates Communism in spite of its plea for social justice and race equality, and is against totalitarianism of every type. Equally, his opposition to imperialism in the field of politics and capitalism in the field of economics is due to his realisation that in such systems the individual loses his freedom and initiative. According to him, "a collectivist society becomes tyrannical and spells great dangers to human life and freedom." [54] He thinks that the only solution lies in increasing decentralisation, both in the economic and the political fields. He, therefore, welcomes every step "towards decentralisation on territorial as well as administrative lines which is so marked in all progressive democracies." [55] In the economic field, he advocates "the ancient Indian ideal of distributive justice by which not only the labourers and the cultivators but the barbers and the washermen, sweepers and watchmen, were all allowed a share in the produce of the field." [56] Steps must, however, be taken to ensure that the different functional groups do not become classes which denote barriers and cleavages. "Class in the sense of a group which makes its own peculiar contribution to the general welfare is right and legitimate," [57] but it becomes inconsistent with social justice when such distinctions are made the basis of discrimination and disparity.

With all his insistence upon the need of social changes, Radhakrishnan has, however, little sympathy with revolutionaries. He is positive that there is "no justification for preserving the *status quo*," [58] and states that "I am all for equalitarian society and I be-

50 MG (1949 ed.), 347.   51 Address to UNESCO Conference—24th May 1950.
52 *Ibid.*   53 *Ibid.*   54 EPW, 42.   58 *Ibid.*, 42.
55 *Ibid.*, 21.   56 *Ibid.*, 43.   57 *Ibid.*, 43.

lieve that it is not only not inconsistent with but is actually demanded by the highest religion." [59] But, at the same time, he is convinced that "the programme of the future cannot be imposed on us by threats." [60] He is satisfied that "even revolutionary changes in the economic order can be brought about by means of persuasion," [61] and pleads that "in our anxiety to bring about a social revolution, we should not resort to force and thus destroy the democratic system." [62] For him, "to decide conflicts by force is to abandon the democratic method of reason, conciliation and conference." [63] At the same time he warns against dilatoriness, for "the world is in a hurry and gradual reform is not an answer to the demand for a social overhaul. The slowness of evolution is the cause of revolutions." [64]

Radhakrishnan's internationalism is a natural development of his insistence on democracy and equality. Democracy demands not only tolerance and goodwill among all members of a community but also among members of all communities of the world. Equality of man becomes meaningless if it is restricted to people of only the same pigmentation. To be real, democracy must apply to all members of the human family. This age-old truth has acquired new significance on account of the invention and spread of new means of rapid communication and transportation. They have converted the world into a single whole and brought about what may be called the first era of world civilisation. Radhakrishnan traces man's sufferings in recent decades to "the neglect of responsible thinking and the violation of the basic unity of mankind by nationalist vanity" [65] and rightly points out that "the root cause of our present trouble is an inter-dependent world worked on a particularist basis." [66]

The whole course of history is leading towards the growth of the world "into a moral community, a single commonwealth in which the human race will find ordered peace, settled government, material prosperity, the reign of law and freedom for all." [67] From this arises the supreme need of toleration as a principle of human intercourse. Even within the same family, different members have different likes and dislikes; and when the unit expands from family to the nation and from the nation to humanity, diversity of nature, temperament and preferences are bound to increase. It is because of fanaticism and the desire to impose one's own way

[59] Ibid., 14.   [60] Ibid., 43.   [61] Ibid., 44.   [62] Ibid., 44.
[63] Ibid., 44.   [64] Address to UNESCO Conference—24th May 1950.
[65] Ibid.   [66] EPW, 33.   [67] Ibid., 32.

of life, religion, and methods of social change on others that conflicts develop. Hence "toleration is the first condition of peace and intolerance its greatest enemy. Tolerance is not indifference but it is that most precious and difficult quality of impartiality that combines loyalty to one's own convictions with respect and fairness to the convictions of those who passionately adhere to other views." [68] The development of such an outlook is the central problem of the modern age, for

the political and economic tragedies of our generation are due to the conflict between the past and the future, the past international anarchy with its sixty and odd sovereign states, with its colonial imperialisms, economic injustices and racial inequalities, and the future, a world order based on freedom for all nations, great and small, strong and weak and respect for human dignity regardless of class, race or nation.[69]

Such a conception of world order demands the subordination of national interests to the common good, and Radhakrishnan is never tired of pointing out that "we must refine the spirit of patriotism so as to make it a pathway from man to mankind." [70]

Radhakrishnan accepted Mahatma Gandhi as his leader, as "in Gandhi we have that rarest kind of religious man who could face a fanatical, patriotic assembly and say that he would, if he had to, sacrifice even India to the Truth." [71] Only such recognition of universal values can secure the fate of civilisation and humanity on this earth, for "a civilised society is possible only in an ordered community, where there is a rule of law before which the poor man and the rich, the weak nation and the strong are equal, which believes that the world belongs to all." [72]

The basis of society is the individual's renunciation and self-limitation. The basis of world order is the acceptance of renunciation and self-imposed limits by nations and states. The balance between self-expression and social duty may be difficult to attain, but Radhakrishnan has no doubt in his mind that

a balance of liberties, an organised harmony of individual freedoms is the ideal. Unrestricted freedom, whether of the individual, or of a class or of even a nation, as we are slowly coming to recognise, is a danger for other individuals, for other classes, for other nations and so for the whole community. Here as elsewhere the truth lies in the union of opposites, in a reconciling synthesis. We should strive for a socialised individualism and a world community of free states.[73]

[68] Address to UNESCO Conference—24th May 1950.
[69] Speech broadcast by BBC—12th June 1950.   [70] EPW, 36.
[71] MG, 36.   [72] EPW, 83.   [73] Ibid., 97.

Radhakrishnan's introduction to politics has thus been due to two factors. On the one hand, he has been keenly sensitive to human misery, and, on the other, as a rationalist, he has felt that this misery is unnecessary. A dispassionate view of human affairs demonstrates that wars have rarely, if ever, led to a satisfactory solution of the problems they set out to solve. In most cases, the real causes of the conflict are concealed and the protagonists profess to fight for moral aims. In any case, once the war starts, the reasons are forgotten and the clash continues for almost its own sake. Besides, the resultant damage is invariably greater than the one it sets out to remedy. Radhakrishnan has seen into the folly of wars, and that is why he pleads so strongly for an intellectual approach to problems and their settlement by persuasion and the exercise of reasonableness. His rôle is, therefore, essentially that of a reconciler, who sees that there is an element of right on either side and seeks to bring together the antagonists on the basis of their common rationality.

As a believer in man's essential reasonableness, Radhakrishnan holds that wars were always unnecessary and irrelevant, but to-day they are a positive menace to the survival of man. Modern scientific and technical progress has created conditions in which men must either live together in peace or face common death and destruction. Peace is today a condition for survival and "we have to pay the price for world peace by setting up social democracies, by surrendering control over subject nations and by submitting national sovereignties to international control." [74]

Intellectual considerations have thus led Radhakrishnan to perceive the need of an international order in which individuals as well as nations can develop their latent abilities in an atmosphere of freedom and justice. Both freedom and justice are, according to him, expressions of man's innate rationality; for reason is itself only when it can pursue its methods without restraint or limitation. His response to the call for freedom was not, however, merely intellectual. It was also conditioned by the recognition that freedom alone can fulfil the emotional urge of sensitive men and women. He has expressed beautifully the sense of impersonal sorrow which is the lot of unfree people. Speaking in the days before India had attained freedom, he said,

if you watch closely and catch a face in repose of any intelligent young man or woman, you will see there is a shade which is not quite natural

[74] *Ibid.*, 11.

to youth, an undercurrent of sorrow that he belongs to a country vast, populous and ancient, that is still a subject nation. It is there, that impersonal detached shadow, and will be there so long as the present condition continues. The shame of subjection is written across the faces of young intelligent Indians and that is what gives meaning to the demand for independence.[75]

His deep sympathy with suffering is also derived from his recognition that insecurity, fear and unhappiness result from man's attempt to exploit his fellows. Where an individual, a group or a nation bases its wealth, pride and power on the shame, subjugation and poverty of others, it is living in a house built on sand. For such a society violates the moral law and "it is not safe to be immoral. Evil systems inevitably destroy themselves by their own greed and egotism. Against the rock of moral law, earth's conquerors and exploiters hurl themselves eventually to their own destruction." [76]

Radhakrishnan, therefore, holds that it is only on the basis of religion that different nations and countries can live together in peace. It is this faith which is one of the distinctive marks of his political thought, and differentiates it from Victorian Liberalism With the Liberals, he believes in human rationality and in progress through education. With them, he holds that government is only a means to peace and order and should not dominate human life. Unlike them, he does not, however, believe in the inevitability of progress, nor does he identify it with material prosperity. According to him,

we may acquire greater power over the universe, produce greater abundance of wealth, get rid of physical suffering and obtain more leisure, and yet the world will be a dull inhuman one until we recover contact with the sources of life and realise that unillumined knowledge is no knowledge at all.[77]

The intellectual approach or even considerations of enlightened self-interest are therefore not enough. Radhakrishnan confesses that in his younger days he "believed that we could use intelligence in our dealings with physical environment, our social institutions and our inmost selves—we assumed that it was all a question of technology or engineering like control of floods or improvement of communications;" [78] but with the growth of experience he has discovered that "the creation of ideal human rela-

[75] *Ibid.*, 5.   [76] *Ibid.*, 35.   [77] *Ibid.*, 97.   [78] *Ibid.*, 28.

tions is a different problem from the mastery of nature." [79] This
can be achieved only by religious faith, for

religion appeals to the inward man, a stranger who has no traffic with
this world. It is the core and centre of his being in which he strives to
set himself in direct relation to the All. To develop the spiritual dimension we may have to withdraw our souls from the flux of existence,
endure an agony of experience or travel barren and stony wastes of
despair. When once this recognition arises, pride, prejudice, and privilege fall away and a new humility is born in the soul.[80]

For Radhakrishnan, "religion includes faith in human brotherhood, and politics is the most effective means of rendering it into
visible form. Politics is but applied religion." [81]

We may now try to sum up briefly Radhakrishnan's attitude towards the problems of the individual, society, and the state. He
recognises the supreme value of the individual for, "man is a
spark of Spirit, a child of God." [82] The individual is not, however,
isolated, for "man is one with the whole world, we belong to each
other." [83] The individual must, therefore, have the liberty to develop to his fullest capacity, and this he can do only in an atmosphere of freedom. Freedom is not, however, alien to discipline; for
the freedom of individuals depends on their mutual consideration
for one another. This gives rise to the rule of law; for only under
the rule of law can there be justice for all. Equality in the eye of
law is possible only in a democratic society; but in order to ensure
true democracy, man must have not only political but also social
and economic rights. In the field of politics, individual initiative
must be subject to considerations of the common good. In the
sphere of economic affairs, the right to private property must be
equally subject to the demands of social justice.

What applies to individuals applies equally to societies and
states. States express themselves through governments; and Radhakrishnan whole-heartedly accepts "the well-known democratic
theory of the sovereignty of the people, the fact that Governments
are merely the mouthpiece, the voice so to say of the sovereign
people." [84] He has no doubt that only a government rooted in the
affections of the people, and commanding their respect and goodwill can be regarded as the expression of the General Will. Hence,
societies and nations must also be democratic, tolerant of one an-

[79] *Ibid.*, 29.   [80] *Ibid.*, 30.   [81] *Ibid.*, 2.
[82] *Ibid.*, 99.   [83] *Ibid.*, 98.
[84] Address to UNESCO Conference—30th May 1950.

other and free, and must in their dealings with one another exhibit goodwill and understanding. National selfishness and pride have always led to the downfall of nations; but never has the danger been so great as to-day. This is so because, under modern conditions, the fall of a nation will affect not only its own members, but the whole of mankind. Integration of the world has taken place through scientific and technical advance; but there has been no corresponding development in man's psychological and moral outlook. Consequently, "the greatest impediment to the advance of civilisation to-day is the old familiar institutions of race and class to which we are emotionally attached." [85] If, therefore, man is to survive, the world must be organised on the basis of an international state in which "the differences need not be fused, but they need not conflict." [86]

Radhakrishnan believes that such an international order based on considerations of justice, equality and liberty can be established through the operation of human reason. Violence cannot achieve it; for such world order can be based only on the voluntary co-operation of all. His faith in the possibility of progress derives directly from his belief in the rationality of man. From this it is but one step to recognise that "true religion affirms that the image of God is in each man, whatever may be his race, or sect. It is founded on self-knowledge. . . ." [87] When men attain to this knowledge, they realise the oneness of all life and can say in truth that "wherever men love reason, shun darkness, turn towards light, praise virtue, despise meanness, hate vulgarity, kindle sheer beauty, wherever minds are sensitive, hearts generous, spirits free, there is your country." [88]

Radhakrishnan's political philosophy may, therefore, be summed up in one phrase as 'Enlightened Humanism.' With Plato he believes that the world's future cannot be assured till philosophers are kings and kings become philosophers. A philosopher is one who picks out the fundamentals in the midst of the masses of detail and pursues truth for its own sake. As such, a philosopher must develop a disinterested spirit and look at reality objectively and without bias. A philosopher can, therefore, never be a partisan. His judgment is based on a total view, and not on sectional or fragmentary considerations. Unless statesmen develop a philosophical attitude and learn to analyse with clear vision and judge with dispassionate detachment the tangled issues of the

85 EPW, 49.   86 Ibid., 53.
87 Ibid., 110.   88 Ibid., 169.

modern world, one common convulsion may engulf the civilisation which man has built up through the efforts of centuries.

Honesty and integrity, insight and judgment, have been the basis of social stability and progress throughout the ages. Societies which exhibited these characteristics prospered, while societies which lacked them invariably languished. Never has it been so necessary to insist on this as to-day when conflicting ideologies claim the allegiance of man. The philosophy of Western democracy places a greater value on political liberty and individual initiative, and for their sake would minimise the demands of social security. That of Communism regards social welfare and security to be greater values whose achievement would justify restrictions on the liberty and enterprise of the individual. The difference may be intrinsically one of emphasis; but it has come to express itself in widely differing beliefs and institutions, and developed into two conflicting ideologies. Unless the claims of freedom and organisation can be reconciled, the outlook is dark for man.

Scientific and technical progress has achieved the factual unity of the world. There has, unfortunately, been no corresponding progress in the realm of moral values. A world united through the achievements of science is, therefore, administered by men and women divided emotionally and psychologically. In this world, divided against itself, man's knowledge may become a potent menace to his future. Radhakrishnan's political philosophy, by its insistence that the claims of individual enterprise and social security are not incompatible, indicates the lines on which the impasse can be resolved. He proclaims equal devotion to the ideals of political liberty, economic equality and racial tolerance; for to him they are merely different elements of one common good. The perception of unity in diversity is the philosopher's rôle. If the philosopher can communicate to the statesmen and to the masses his own sense of unity of the good, one chief obstacle to understanding and co-operation will have been removed. This requires a synoptic view. Never have statesmen needed so much the disinterested wisdom which a philosophic temper alone can give.

HUMAYUN KABIR

THE MINISTRY OF EDUCATION
GOVERNMENT OF INDIA
NEW DELHI, INDIA

22

B. K. Mallik

RADHAKRISHNAN AND PHILOSOPHY
OF THE STATE AND COMMUNITY

RADHAKRISHNAN AND PHILOSOPHY
OF THE STATE AND COMMUNITY

IT IS not exactly in his craftsmanship that we shall find the basis or staple of Radhakrishnan's political thought; indeed it was not in his nature that he should or could ever be what we call a politician. There is too much of the 'man of the spirit' in him to allow him even a sojourn in that world of moods and fancies in which the politicians have to carve out the fortunes of the modern man. Nor does the ancient glory, the mead of the statesman, seem to hold for him the acme of his aim in life, if by any chance the dim light of diplomacy, or the marshy blue haze from Machiavelli, shaded it. If still the crowded vicinity of the politician not unusually finds a place for him as does also the more sombre "close" of the heads of states, he moves in every sphere under the direct guidance of what he believes to be truth. He never swerves from it even in the name of holy patriotism, whether to charm secrets out of his foes, if any, or to distil falsehoods into them by strategic device. Indeed, there is not even a remote parallel to his political behaviour in contemporary Europe, and if Gandhi could by some stratagem be called a statesman or politician rather than a man of faith and ascetic morals, Radhakrishnan would easily find a place by his side. That perhaps was the reason why Nehru chose him as ambassador to Stalin. Such a choice may be taken either as a challenge to what Europe, whether in her classical or Christian mood, considered to be rational or divine or as an earnest of what the future may be holding in prospect as to the fulfilment of the Indian State. It is permissible to think that Radhakrishnan as a political thinker in his rôle as ambassador to Stalin is the first instalment of Indian wisdom in the field of the modern European.

It will be difficult, however, to assess his political merit unless one is conversant with what may be called the key-note of his life —the historic injunction in our ancestry to ameliorate suffering wherever it is found. It was perhaps the one theme which the

Buddha and Kṛṣṇa equally propounded. If it was a theme for a philosophic quest of supreme importance, it was equally noble or holy enough even to serve as a divine mission—if we follow the *Bhagavadgītā*. Perhaps it is here that the main clue to Radhakrishnan's acute political insight will be found. His political thought like all his contribution is definite and firm. But what held him was not the call of a mere theory, or the spirit which is academic, but the urgency of social existence which alone can test the theory or the capacity of a theory to renovate life.

What is called for, therefore, as a preliminary to a formulation of his political philosophy is a review of his activities in the political field. It may well be that we shall gather the essentials of his political thinking in his long, searching criticism of the modern shape of political life under the leadership of the European mind. Besides, Radhakrishnan is not a political philosopher *par excellence* like Hobbes or Chanakya. He is a metaphysician, with a distinct flair for the historical. His achievement in the political field, although it is bound to shed light on his political faith, will also indicate where exactly that faith lay, in mere academic practice or in a steadily burning emotion. His one aim in life has been to restore order and peace in the human family. Not unlike the great reformers in all ages, he has steadily set his face against oppression and corruption in whatever form they may appear. Never once, in his innumerable speeches and writings, does he doubt that human nature is essentially good and that it is spirit and not matter that holds the universe together. What is more, he firmly believes that a new age is on the eve of rebirth with the promise of a fresh advent of the spirit on earth, if not in the messianic style, at least in the prophetic form which the *Bhagavadgītā* long ago portrayed. It would be difficult indeed to account for his traversing the whole earth year in and year out, as if he had never had any domestic cares, unless one held that it was perhaps his duty to proclaim to the world the imminence of the advent of the spirit on earth. Perhaps in the end he has come to lay more stress on exposing the prevailing corruption in all life than on the sheer logical analysis of the political concepts which lie behind his incessant movement in the political field. To be fair to him and precise about his place in history, he is *par excellence* a man of peace and a reformer.

Radhakrishnan made his debut in the political field in the year 1931, when he came to Europe to serve the League of Nations on behalf of his country, where he remained in its International Committee on Intellectual Co-operation to the very end. Here began his first intimate acquaintance with the domineering structure of European civilisation. Through fellowship with the outstanding minds in Europe he soon learned the exact position of his own civilisation, with its age and sanctity, in relation to its chief modern antagonist, the European. The rest of his career in the political field, one might presume, was almost wholly derived from this, his maiden European experience as an orthodox Hindu of scholarship and faith.

An assessment of this experience and an account of his *locus standi* in the League, therefore, falls due. It is the only way by which we can give an historical date to the formulation of his political ideas in the ferment of practical politics, or trace the process which matured his political philosophy into a living political principle. It was the League which stimulated Radhakrishnan to give concrete shape to what had been but a faith or an academic belief.

I have to develop, therefore, as a preliminary to an analysis of Radhakrishnan's political principle, a brief account of the League, and that for two additional reasons. First, it was a strange political phenomenon in the career of modern Europe. Secondly, there is no account of it which appears to be either final or fair.

The League

If the League of Nations by common consent was a landmark in the political history of modern Europe, this outstanding claim accrued to it from the fact that it was the first representative European body to sound a note of warning in that long, eventful history. There had been no such note struck in the steadily progressing society of nations which had come into existence five to six centuries before. The long era that preceded the League's warning had staged the classical civilisation of Europe in a modern frame by a gradual replacement of the medieval culture. It seems that there was a turn of the tide as the twentieth century came in, and the note which was struck concerned the doubtful wisdom of European expansion without a plan or a common objective. It implied that a meteoric growth in any civilisation may have fatality lurking within its bosom. The League, by its constitution, was not merely a European League even as the peace and order that it stood for was not merely European, but world-wide in its scope. It included naturally nations outside Europe; yet at the same time it held that world opportunities for peace were possible only on the basis of the European view.

It was most acutely felt after the First World War that the society of nations had lost the cohesion which no healthy, progressive society can afford to lose. Some, especially those who still harked back to the medieval days, even doubted if there was any unity in the twentieth century as certainly there had been in Europe in the Roman and post-Roman ages. Behind the note that the League of Nations struck there was this implication that Europe must be a unity again if Europe was to survive, and as an immediate preliminary stage of that unity the League established itself as an assembly of nations for serious consultations and a constant exchange of views. If a supernational State should eventually arise as a result of this establishment, that would be just the thing devoutly prayed for. For the moment, the League stood as if it were a focus on which converged, like flocks of birds coming home at dusk, the scattered nation states, after centuries of unbridled political and economic expansion under the unparalleled stimulation of three distinct phenomena—scientific discoveries, industrial development, and "god-given access to well-stocked preserves of gold."

What was plainly hinted at was that the nation states, whatever their structural proportions in terms of wealth and power, might easily collapse like a house of cards, if they were determined to continue their course like the primeval atoms without a common objective or plan. The stakes at issue were as high as the survival of European civilisation. If Humanism, Renaissance, Reformation and Political Revolution succeeded in reviving Classical culture in a modern setting by firmly giving a quietus to the medieval, it did not follow that it would consolidate itself, unless it had a common objective or plan. It was not questioned whether the revival itself was altogether sound or whether any civilisation could last long, if it had to come into existence by submerging two such major civilisations as the medieval culture of Europe and the mystical culture of Asia. Apparently the faith in the secular culture of Europe was still dominant, with the sense of power and authority proportionate to its claim.

But, like a sign on the horizon, doubt arose after the First World War as to whether the nation states could possibly survive without an objective or plan. There was a widespread sense of crisis all over Europe.

Moreover, once doubt had infected the even flow of power and

faith which had continued for centuries, it could by an inner necessity only deepen steadily. Sooner or later it was bound to appear to
all that a secular civilisation with its oligarchic parliamentary states
and competitive economy could not escape two things: the corro-
sive process of internal disruption, and the fatality of external
attack. That nemesis followed from the law of social existence.
Even if the issue of a revival of medieval culture was a dead issue,
it was quite in the cards that the modern secular civilisation of
Europe might have to meet the challenge of the Asiatic group or
mystical civilisation which was still lying prostrate in its grip.

It is permissible to argue that, once the drama of conflict between
the European and the Asian civilisations began in real earnest, the
stage was set for a full and complete enactment of it. If the last
three centuries indisputably formed the European Age and held
the rest of the world, especially the ancient land of Asia, in its firm
and adamant grip, there could be no escape for Europe from the
inevitable reversal of the same grim process. There is such a thing
as historical adjustment. No civilisation has ruled for ever, nor
was any denied the chance of evolving its claim. If, still, none of
the civilisations of history ever reached truth or peace, every one
of them most punctiliously went through the dual process of masking and unmasking their claims in turn. There was sufficient
ground for holding that the modern secular civilisation of Europe
could not possibly escape the cosmic provision for internal decline
or an external challenge.

Perhaps even when the call for a halt was made in the planless,
meteoric expansion of Europe, a premonition with regard to that
dual threat might well have lain implicit in this call. If history
can but repeat a rhythm, at least in the broad outline of all life, it
was for the historian to expect a parallel between what happened
to the medieval culture when it was outflanked by a revival of
humanism and was at the same moment drawn into an internal
chaos by Protestant demand, and the changes so positively fore-
shadowed in the career of the secular age.

It is no part, however, of my thesis to suggest that the League
of Nations did explicitly formulate its objective in the terms in
which I have stated it. There is no evidence that even the founders
of the League envisaged what I have called this dual threat. They
had no qualms about what they called the indisputably superior
merit of the secular as distinguished from the mystical claim. The
view that they openly took of modern Europe was that it was the
centre of the most advanced phase of human civilisation, since they

all advocated the still popular evolutionary view. They were individualists, with faith in evolution, and would not tolerate the group civilisation, whether in its pristine form of Hindu mysticism or the less coherent form of medieval Catholicism. A threat to what was claimed to be the most advanced form of society from the undeveloped group form could mean to them only a retrogression, which neither reason nor the Law of Nature, which was supposed to deputise for reason in the raw world of matter, could possibly allow. Besides, had not the modern European testified in a hundred ways to his innate superiority by simply massing aids to the way of living comfortably, healthily, and with joy? Could any creative genius of the past stand up to the man of science, to modern technology, or even to the philosophic thought of the present age?

No European of the evolutionary school could be expected to see that modern Europe was no exception to the law of social processes, or that, if its classical ancestry had to submit to a decline and fall, there was no escape for it from either an internal chaos or an external challenge.

But the League atmosphere was full of the premonition about the dual threat I have referred to, and its frank attempt to rationalise warfare could not be accounted for by any other hypothesis.

But I do not suggest that there had never been a common objective in the whole history of the society of nations. How otherwise could it have achieved wonders, as they all believed that it had?

Moreover, without a doubt three distinct achievements lay to the credit of modern Europe:

First, it replaced the medieval by means of a fresh experiment with the classical.

Second, it suppressed the Asiatic group civilisation and put in its place some type of bureaucratic individualism.

Third, it created a scientific, industrial age under the aegis of the Parliamentary State.

These are enormous achievements on any computation and were never even dreamt of in the long past of the human species, if we judge by scale or proportion. Would any one of them have been possible if the society of nation states had in no conceivable sense ever been a unity? The answer is obvious. If even modern Europe had never been free from warfare, that fact was by no means the only one that determined the course of modern Europe. There was perfect agreement among the nation states to put an end to the long Dark Age of Europe and to shed at least some light on what they called the primeval darkness of Asia. A resolute will to eliminate both medievalism and mysticism was the sheet-anchor of their agreement; their very existence depended upon the achievement of that end. And so the wars that were fought were fought within that agreement and never at its cost. The faith in Reason never disappeared, however constant and fierce the warfare between nation states may have been: consequently science, technology, and industry grew to enormous proportions side by side with the devastation wrought by warfare.

The conclusion is irresistible that the nation states did form a compact society as they came into being, though not of the Roman type, Holy or otherwise. It was a secular society, *par excellence,* with no leaning to mysticism; it could not dissolve the individuality of the nation states in a unity, whether of the Platonic or mystical types.

The First World War and the appearance of the League of Nations which followed it was only an evidence that the society of nation states, since their rise in the fifteenth century, had already reached its peak. There was nothing of the medieval civilisation left which could be called a real challenge to its authority. The world of man in the twentieth century was almost wholly denuded of mysticism. The monk of medieval Europe was dead and gone and, as for the ascetics in India or any part of Asia, they had long ago retired to the mountains and forests.

No longer was it the spiritual that prevailed in all that vitally mattered in Europe; what ruled instead was its direct opposite, the bare moral claim. If there still was the monk of the modern age he was a working man and would be at any moment a proletarian, if the State so desired. He had committed spiritual suicide by choosing, under compulsion, work and action for its own sake.

Between the age of mystical prayer and that of barefaced morality there was an interval, since the latter scrupulously sanctioned action without objective and judged it in terms of abstractions like honesty, spontaneity, and consistency. In such an interval no line can be drawn between values or between truth and illusion, since morality gives the death-blow to mysticism and humanism alike. The notion that still survives is the concept of law without a source, or a state of nationhood which, because of its lack of objective, is either ruthless fiction, or sheer, cold abstraction. The League, to me, was a make-believe or a desperate refusal to meet the consequences of the past.

When the monk became a day-labourer in Europe, it became a steady cry among the new élite in India that the ascetic world should be conscripted for labour, since it was not right that the society should maintain them as workless drones. The ascetic claim of untold centuries was, as it were, by violence, ejected from the social code. Perhaps it was the only way for the new élite to consolidate the British statecraft which neutralised the religious issue and destroyed the immemorial village community.

In fact, not merely Asia and India but the world at large came under the domination of Europe in her modern garb; there was only one type of State, the Parliamentary, and one civilisation, the modern type of classical humanism. It was like a sea which washed away the two mainlands of medieval Europe and mystical Asia and stood facing the limitless sky above, with no boundaries to regulate its movement.

And this ubiquitous presence of the European State was evidence that the programme of the modern civilisation of Europe was worked out to the full. To its credit lay not only the stupendous negative achievement I have just noted, but the building up of a towering edifice in the shape of the Parliamentary State, which lived on gracious opulence, the joint gift from scientific discoveries and industrial might. How puny and small did the ancient races of history look by the side of the European giants!

But, by the inevitable stroke of destiny, decline set in after the peak was reached and it was the League of Nations which sounded the note of warning about this decline. Whatever the verdict of the historian on the League, it will never lose its credit as the most significant event in twentieth century Europe, if only for that lone achievement. It was in this profound diagnosis of the malady in European life that its significance lay.

I had to introduce all this European history, since the genesis of Radhakrishnan's political thought has to be traced to his impact with the Europe of the twentieth century as it appeared to him in the League of Nations. And the issue now is, what could that impact have meant to him?

There was no question of his being made familiar with the high policies and aims of the League. Even if by a mischance he had accepted in his youth the Christian faith, or had subscribed to the humanistic model, that would not have qualified him to sit at the same table with the leaders of Europe to discuss either the strictly European or world affairs. As the fates would have it the League of Nations was Janus-faced; it had one face for the Europeans whose culture and civilisation it was its main object to protect, and another for the non-Europeans who were expected by it to be thankful for what had been generously done for them.

To Radhakrishnan, who was firm like the Polar Star in his ancestral faith, his membership in the League of Nations meant nothing if not a baptism of fire. It could not but be the height of an ordeal for him to have to face such a direct or indirect challenge to his faith. Apparently, it was not peace, order, or progress in the human home, as he understood it, that his membership called upon him to consider; the membership was the result of a gracious gesture to an Asian to accept the supreme chance of collaborating with the European in planting the European tree where hitherto stunted vegetation for millennia had led to an aridity of soil almost pointing to a return of the glacial age.

And it was only natural that his reaction to the League should have coincided absolutely with that of Gandhi when he, in his turn, came into contact with the same European claim earlier in the day. Both of them, with rock-like faith in their ancestral stock, were anxious that the world some day should follow the *Bhagavadgītā* or the Buddha or Śaṁkara, since there must be peace in the world, in spite of the European. Whether Jesus should also serve as a model in the projected peaceful future of the human race on the same level as the Buddha or Kṛṣṇa, I forbear to say. Gandhi is gone, and, as I have made public, I did not take the same view of his deeds and sayings while he was alive as any of my contemporaries did. As regards Radhakrishnan, he does not hesitate to distinguish features in the life of Jesus which seem to him to be almost parallel to what is familiar in the Hindu figures of the same eminence. But I would much rather leave undecided whether he would place Jesus by the side of the Buddha or even hold that Jesus embodied the spirit of the Hindu scriptures. Besides, my own personal view of the Christian faith or the social technique which is traced to Jesus is altogether different from that of any of my contemporaries who stand rooted in some tradition or other. The point, however, is that Radhakrishnan's reaction to the League of Nations did not coincide with that of the other members, since he repudiated the claim that European culture was the most advanced ever known in human history. He stood by himself in the League as a keen protagonist of his faith and a downright critic of the European claim where it exceeded its bounds.

Here began the first scholarly and responsible attempt to orient an Asian challenge to Europe. The European from now on will be given full opportunity to revise his centuries-old judgment about Asia, and there will be no occasion for him to depend wholly upon what his fellow Europeans brought him from their varied experiences of Asia whether as administrators, traders, or missionaries. In fact, one of the distinct services which Radhakrishnan has rendered in the cause of peace in the human home lies in the fact that, from his works and teaching in the University of Oxford, the European experts and specialists on Hindu thought have had the rare opportunity of testing their judgments in the light of an original and comprehensive interpretation. The times that set in marked a change which to all appearance closed the age of Theosophy in Europe for good and paved the way, perhaps, for real peace in the world.

If Radhakrishnan stands, as on a rock, on his own civilisation as a Hindu, should it be at all difficult either to trace the source of his political thought or to assess its merit? It is inconceivable that it could be un-Hindu or deviate from the essential form of the Hindu political outlook even by a hair's breadth. It is possible, however, that the orthodox Hindu view might have undergone changes at his hands in view of the modern conditions of life. A reformulation of it might well be standing to his credit as a matter of shifting emphasis from one feature to another. It will soon be apparent what actually happened to Hindu political thought at the hands of this twentieth century, orthodox Hindu. In the meantime a review of political thought in its essentials falls due, if only to reinforce the basis on which he stood. What then is the State?

THE NATURE OF THE STATE

The issue is simple enough except for one or two urgent preliminary observations. The first of these refers to the necessity of relating the European view of the State to the Hindu conception, since the two conceptions, in the nature of things, imply one another. It is not possible, in the twentieth century, to discuss either of them as if the other never existed. What is more, judging by 'real politics' today, the world public has no use for a bare, abstract analysis of either the Hindu or the European view of the State. Since the chief interest of contemporary life centres in the settlement of conflicts which have divided the world, an enquiry into the nature of the Hindu or the European state means nothing more than determining what prospects are held out by them for that settlement. Finally, it is only by a contrast between the Hindu and European views of the State that their specific worth can be measured. The Hindu claim, which Radhakrishnan definitely holds, that the Hindu alone was responsible for peace in human society, since toleration, persuasion, and non-violence formed the very keynote of his civilisation, will have to be measured against the equally absolute European claim that it was the European who kept order both in the civilised and primitive worlds.

The second observation refers to the much deeper need of changing our usual approach to the technique of analysis. Personally I have no faith in merely restating historical controversies. I do feel that we have by now exhausted the possibilities of any yield from the familiar controversies of all tradition. Perhaps we may be heading for another of those periodic impasses which precipitate what is known as a Dark Age or the age of decadence in human society. I propose, therefore, to suggest a new technique of approach to an analysis of the conception of State on the basis of a fresh view of society, and the immediate issue for discussion refers to the nature of Organisation.

If we have to analyse such complicated organisations as Civilisation, Society, and State, it is essential that we should, if possible, begin that analysis with an indisputable notion about the nature of Organisation, as such. There need be no dissent from this claim, nor need there be any objection to my choosing the category of related multiplicity as the background of my analysis. If I am not mistaken, it is universally agreed that this category is the ultimate presupposition of all organisation. If by any chance the notion of multiplicity were inconceivable, the Universe would have to do without organisation altogether. The 'simple,' whether we call it 'one' or 'unity,' is by no means an organised entity or being. Even if it may be credited with having created the multiple, and therefore the very possibility of existence, it did not by that inscrutable function become itself organised. But it is not multiplicity alone which gives rise to the organised State. Organisation arises when the multiple stands related. In fact, the multiples by themselves— or the unrelated multiples in so far as they are absolute differents —cannot constitute any form of the universe that we can think of. The stuff of which the Universe is made is related multiplicity. So that even if one finds it necessary to trace its creation or emanation to God or the Ātman one will have to provide for at least the implicit creation of both multiplicity and relationship in Divine selection or 'sport.'

Can we now find out what Organisation is? Do the two notions of multiplicity and relationship give us a clue to its nature? The obvious answer is that Organisation can mean only related multiplicity since there is no third entity. It almost seems as if Organisation is only another name for related multiplicity.

But the question arises, do the notions of multiplicity and relationship necessarily cohere? Do the multiple entities with their uniqueness normally develop identicalness with one another, which they must if they are to be related to one another? If uniqueness means distinctness, can it cohere with relationship, which must mean identicalness?

The issue that I am raising is logically simple and historically familiar in all traditions. With rare exceptions, there will be universal agreement that entities as such have to be unique and distinct, and, if relationship is added on as a fresh feature or predicate to their identities, they have also to be non-unique and non-distinct which must be defined as common or identical. Related multiplicity, therefore, or Organisation, as such, implies the coherence of two such features or predicates as uniqueness and unity. The multiple entities, as they stand organised, are expected to be distinct from one another as well as perfectly identical.

But, except in esoteric and non-social attitudes of the human mind or when desperation in the experiences of life precipitates a loss of balance, nobody has found it possible to co-ordinate identicalness and distinctness in any entity or situation. By all the definitions, uniqueness and unity stand out as incompatibles. No entity could possibly embody them at the same time and yet remain coherent and integral. There could be no chance of developing any life of thought and action, if both of them were accepted as principles of equal standing and value. Finally, any attempt to hold them together or incorporate them on equal terms into any body politic was bound to produce tension which could only end in extinction.

The question, however, arises, if Organisation embodying both unity and individuality on equal terms could or did produce nothing but tension, how do we account for the existence of the Universe to which we belong, which certainly is not another name for tension? And we cannot possibly deny that we do exist as members of a Universe, even if we may be forced to admit that there has been nothing but illusion outside the Ātman. What type of Organisation, then, does our integral and coherent Universe imply? How did it come into existence?

There was one and only one way by which the Universe could possibly have come into being, and that was by dropping the valuation of unity and individuality on equal terms, even if that device meant falling into illusion. There was no other alternative, assuming that the universe had to come into existence. And there was no chance of dropping either of those terms, since relative multiplicity is the *sine qua non* of existence.

Indeed, the very core of existence lies in the dual necessity for unity and individuality; consequently, the only alternative for the Universe after it had gone through the fruitless experience of the state of tension was to drop the theory of equal valuation and accept its direct opposite, the notion of unequal valuation. Personally I hold that such a momentous step was actually taken in the economy of the Universe at a definite stage of its existence. Here in this cosmic decision lay the source and secret of all history. Indeed, the whole future of the Universe, after the state of tension, was laid out in this supreme moment, when equal valuation of unity and individuality was superseded by an unequal valuation of them: besides, there was no alternative to such a procedure, since the other possibility was absolute extinction of all existence. Indeed, no issue about the validity or rationality of our history or of our Universe on the basis of unequal valuation need or could possibly arise.

The question that arises instead refers to the type of organisations which unequal valuation of unity and individuality necessarily imply. Does unequal valuation imply only one single organisation of multiple entities? And if there have to be more than one, how would they stand one to another or what would be their internal economies when they are realising their own specific objectives?

All these are cardinal issues which bear directly on our enquiry into the nature of both the Hindu and European States. In fact, a complete answer to them may, for the first time, pave the way for tracing their nature and significance and yet escape the maze of insoluble controversies.

We cannot, however, determine the types of organisations without a clear grasp of what is meant by unequal valuation. We have, in fact, to discuss three distinct questions: what happens to unity and individuality when they are unequally valued, what bearing has unequal valuation on equal valuation, and, finally, in what relation do the two types of valuation stand to one another. These are central issues to our enquiry.

Clearly, the distinction between equal and unequal valuation must presuppose as its background the simple notion of valuation as such, and, if we have to define valuation as the process by which we distinguish the ultimate, existential feature of an entity, the categories which are relevant to it must be the two ultimate categories, the absolute and the relative. An entity has to be either absolute or relative, and it is only an existent entity that can be valued. The non-existent or the absolute negative does not admit of valuation.

Our concern in this enquiry, therefore, which deals with related multiplicity, should be wholly with the relative; we should not be called upon to raise any issue about the absolute, which excludes relationship altogether. If unity and individuality are features of the multiple world, if multiple entities have to undergo qualification by them, the issue as to whether they are absolute cannot legitimately arise. No entity in the realm of multiplicity is or can be absolute, and the features or predicates of those entities must, therefore, be relative. That seems to be straightforward and clear.

Curiously, however, there is no record in our history which would confirm the truth of this conclusion. The related multiple, though universally recognised, has been invariably associated with one or the other of the two forms of the absolute. Not only have both the conceptions, unity and individuality, been given proportions of the absolute; an eternal State has also been built up with a combination of the two. The instances of this universal practice are the Mystical, the Humanist and the Dualist accounts of reality.

An explanation, therefore, is necessary why such a discrepancy should have arisen.

The Multiple World

The multiple world, whatever its origin, had to provide for conflict—a grim necessity which stands on both logical and historical grounds. In fact, the only attempt to deny this ubiquitous fact in all history by the theory of differences ended in self-contradiction, since it could not escape negating the claim that there was conflict.

But once we accept the presence of conflict in the Universe it follows that the Universe has to have sufficient room for illusion, since truth, by definition, cannot account for conflict. Nor is it consistent to argue that conflict is an issue between truth on the one hand and falsehood or illusion on the other, since it can occur only between illusions or falsehoods which eliminate truth altogether. The Universe, in consequence, had to be full of illusions and nothing but illusions, since there has been no provision in it so far for anything but conflict.

Does it not follow then that, if unity and individuality were given the stature of absoluteness, this inadvertence took place as a matter of sheer illusion? There was no alternative. If conflict could not be kept out of the Universe and if, in consequence, illusions had to appear, if only to form its constituents, it could not possibly be that unity and individuality would at the very inception of our history appear in their relative proportions.

But how exactly did unity and individuality appear in the garb of the absolute as objectives rather than as predicates? If it was preordained that we should miss their relative proportions, in what exact form of the absolute was it decreed that we should take them?

To give an account of what actually happened in the universe in the stage of illusion is only another name for relating the cosmic story of Organisation. There was only one issue before the Universe on the eve of its appearance and that was to organise its multiple constituents; and this issue meant utilising unity and individuality as the prime movers of that process. Organisation, in other words, was the simple process of unifying and individualising the multiple entities. Its main purpose would naturally remain uncompleted so long as the multiple did not stand out as both unified and individualised.

And this is exactly what I meant by my claim that unity and individuality appeared as ends or objectives. There were two distinct possibilities: the possibility of the multiple entities for ever standing unorganised, and the possibility of their appearing in the form of complete Organisation. There was a chance before the Universe to choose between the state of absolute differents and that of the individualised and unified multiple. There was no third alternative. And if the state of absolute differents had to be scrapped for obvious reasons, the state of organised multiples meant in its turn more than one phase and stage.

The reason for the plurality of stages was that the first attempt to organise the multiple on the supposition that both unity and individuality were equally absolute could only lead to an impasse, and that for two reasons:

First, the Universe could not make room for two absolutes, nor could there be two eternities or totalities.

Second, since, by definition, unity and individuality were opposites, they could not be utilised for the same Organisation without producing an immediate tension.

And this is exactly what was implied by the phrase 'equal valuation.'

If, however, the attempt to organise the multiple on the basis of equal valuation led to an impasse, and therefore to the possibility of complete extinction, this impasse had to be resolved—the world of inaction had to be replaced by at least the world of action, since the Universe could not thrive on the absolute negative.

A second stage of organisation, therefore, had to follow; and the issue in it was to find an interpretation of unity and individuality which would replace the theory of dual absolutes without violating the law of contradiction.

Conceivably there were two distinct interpretations of unity and individuality, and both of them were equally capable of staging the universe of action, and thereby of putting an end to the universe of inaction and tension:

One interpretation accepted the meaning of ultimate reality in terms of the absolute, but implied a change in the respective claims of unity and individuality to that meaning.

The other interpretation accepted the claims of unity and individuality to reality, but suggested a complete change in the meaning of reality.

I have sufficient metaphysical grounds to hold that both interpretations had to be worked out in the economy of our Universe. What we call history is only the result of that supreme cosmic necessity to utilise both interpretations.

The Universe, whatever its proportion at the stage of inaction, gave rise to three fresh forms with three distinct organisations, which means that the universe of action, in replacing the universe of inaction, appeared with three distinct modes of behaviour.

By the first interpretation, in which reality was considered to be absolute, *either* unity *or* individuality was defined as real, but not both. The result was that two types of organisation came into existence:

The organisation with unity as the real and individuality as the unreal.

The organisation with individuality as the real and unity as the unreal.

These are the mystical and the humanistic organisations, which developed respectively the group and the individualistic civilisations of our history.

By the second interpretation unity and individuality came to be valued as equally real: but reality did not mean the absolute, which excluded relationship. On the contrary, it was relationship which came to be considered as ultimately real. Unity and individuality stood in eternal relationship and became actually relative.

The organisation which followed from this interpretation was necessarily simple: it did not give rise to a dual civilisation. But since the dualistic scheme stood on an unequal valuation of unity and individuality, it, too, like the other two schemes, provided for two stages in its organisation—eternal and temporal. It was the eternal in this scheme that took the place of the real, while the temporal embodied the unreal. We have between the two schemes, therefore, three organisations and two different sets of the real and the unreal:

1. The absolute or the unity with the unreal in the shape of individuality, and *vice versa.*

2. The eternal relationship with the unreal in the shape of temporal relationship.

The organisations are the Mystical, Humanistic and Dualistic.

But how do the multiple individuals who form the basic constituents of the three organisations appear with their identities and groupings?

The three organisations have three distinct types of individuals:

Individuals who or which have the sense of being at one with others.

Individuals who or which have the sense of being unique and distinct from others.

Individuals who or which have the sense of cohesion or solidarity with others.

The types are quite distinct, and it should not be difficult to trace them in history or contemporary life. The sense of being at one with others, or a desire for unity or identicalness, although it is the direct opposite of the sense of being distinct from others, is equally distinguishable from the sense of being related to others. Most certainly the state of identicalness annihilates relationship, which implies the existence of duality or distinction.

Like the types of individuals, the types of groupings, too, which these individuals are bound to form, can be traced in history. In fact, the individuals in each organisation form groups of such familiar types as family, clan, tribe, nation, or people. Equally do they all develop the religious, political, economic and cultural institutions. The groupings, again, take on a small or large shape according to the region or tradition or era in which they appear. There is nothing to choose between them, if we look at the essential features of their constitutions, in spite of vast differences in content or texture. But they certainly stand as not only different from but also opposed to one another. And these grim differences are the result solely of the determining factors in their career, the ideals or objectives which they profess. In so far as they profess identicalness, independence, or solidarity as their goal, all forms of grouping necessarily appear in competing forms. They live, in consequence, in three distinct types of families, belong to three unique types of States and worship God in three altogether distinct environments—and all in a state of perpetual conflict.

But how exactly do the organisations shape themselves? What forms do their constitutions assume?

Whatever their formations, the 'unity' and 'individuality' schemes differ from the dualist as to the numerical strength of the actual determining factor in their formations. The former, unlike the latter, will have one central determining factor, and it will consist either of unity or individuality, since they are both absolutist. It will be a clear sign of decadence in their career if they are found to be inspired or regulated by both unity and individuality. In their normal state, the individuals or groups which constitute them will profess one ideal or be subject to an attachment to or weakness for its opposite.

The dualist scheme, on the other hand, since it upholds cohesion rather than unity or individuality, will provide for two distinct factors instead of one, and so for two distinct types of institutions derived from those two distinct principles—that in line with unity and that in line with individuality. E.g., the Church and the State as unique and mutually interdependent.

But do these organisations pass through more than one phase or stage, or is it necessary that they should have only one phase to cover their whole career?

There are two main stages in the life history of each organisation:—

The phase in which it formulates and establishes its main objective.

The phase in which it realises the objective which has been formulated.

An organisation exists in two distinct forms and functions in two distinct ways. If it has to conceive or formulate its objective it has also equally to realise it.

Both stages as a matter of course appear in a milieu of conflict, and this rather gruesome complication is due to the fact that the objective which a community professes is not absolute but has to face its contrary. If the objective, for instance, of the mystical community is unity, it implies individuality as its direct opposite—so that the group cannot come into existence so long as it has not succeeded in suppressing the individualist claim, whatever form the latter may take. Here at the very inception of the group community is a conflict to dispose of, and this conflict is known as external for the obvious reason that the individualist claim forms no part of the group community.

The conflict in the second stage of the community, if it presupposes its existence as a continuous phenomenon, takes place in the internal economy of the community, when the community in question has no longer the care and burden of dealing with a hostile environment. And the reason why the community breaks out into conflict within itself is that the issue of realising the objective raises a dichotomy of modes in which its objective could be realised. In so far as unity and individuality admit of being realised in two incompatible modes, two fresh groupings arise inside the life of the community if only to realise them. Exactly the same applies to the dualistic scheme.

We shall now discuss three allied notions, Community, Law, and State, in order to complete our logical account of the Hindu State, which is the main theme of Radhakrishnan's political philosophy.

An organisation may be called a Community, if we emphasise its feature of harmony. And no organisation exists and functions except as a community, since the pre-communal stage is a logical abstraction. What we call the historical fact, naturally, is not organisation, as such, but community. History begins in the shape of community, and the individuals who form it do not come into existence except in a communal framework. This primary communal origin of individuals is a logical necessity, since no form or type of existence is conceivable in its origin except in the form of complete agreement and harmony among its constituent individuals. They are born full-fledged as communal beings—never as unrelated or discrete beings.

But the birth of a community is only a feature in its history. If it is the precondition of any possibility in its career, it need not preclude even disagreement and conflict in its later phases. In fact, if it is bound to be saturated with unanimity in its formative stage nothing but difference and disagreements can possibly constitute the stage that follows. So that a community appears in a dual form: a form in which the constituent individuals stand together as one mass and a form in which it stands split into two opposite sections. And the explanation of this apparent contradiction is that, whilst in its formative stage it is bound up with the formulation of its objective it becomes involved in conflict as it proceeds to realise that objective, since there are two competing modes of realising it.

The community, therefore, as I have already said, has a two-fold state which marks agreement and disagreement in its career with perfect consistency, and the origin of this strange career follows from the central need of the two separate functions of conceiving and realising the objective.

It follows, therefore, that the community has to make room for both Law and State in its economy. In so far as there has to be intuition and interpretation of the objective—the objective is a mystical and transcendent entity—there has to be Law which embodies that interpretation. The community, in other words, has to provide for a legislative body with the innate capacity to intuit the objective and formulate it in a way which can supply the technique and mode of living for the whole community.

And the State naturally becomes a necessity, since the objective of the community could not avoid a direct clash with its contrary in a rival community—a fact which means that there must be a body in the community capable of both overcoming resistance to its objective and of establishing it. No community can do without a State, since no community can escape being born in a state of conflict with its rival community. The strange thing is that it has to be knit together as if it were one mass, to be integrated as a community. If the legislature is the seat of the intuition of the mystical entity, the State is the seat of power or strength to defend and establish that entity in its historical shape.

And we may add that the rest of the body politic will be entrusted with the equally essential function of keeping, as it were, the whole community alive. Logically, the essence of this function lies in the fact of identity, the *sine qua non* of individuality, without which neither existence nor distinguishability is conceivable. The community in consequence has to provide for the Legislature, State and a productive body commonly known as the economic function.

The theories about State, Community, and Law that I have just outlined do not repeat any tradition. It will be a mistake to align my view with the Golden Age of the primeval societies, or try to prove that it is hostile to the Contract theories, or confuse it with the Dialectic interpretations of history. I depart from all tradition, and the chief reason is that my metaphysic leans against a different rampart from that of any school of thought in history.

The four notions I have just outlined: Community, State, Law, and the Economic, all of which refer to a mystical source—although in three distinct senses—are common to all organisations. The group, the individualist and the dualist organisations equally presuppose them, and in each case there is a dual form of them—one in which they enjoy unanimity of consent or agreement, and the other in which they stand supported only by the minority or the majority of the constituent individuals. It is in the latter case that the State is a sovereign power with coercive authority—and then it is by no means fully representative. In fact, the whole of civilisation as it is moulded in the second stage stands with power alone as its basis.

THE HINDU STATE

What now is the Hindu State? Is it mystical, humanistic or dualistic? We shall go straight to Radhakrishnan for an answer.

Radhakrishnan is perhaps more a statesman in his political thinking than a logician or a philosopher, inasmuch as his central aim is to establish peace in human society. It is even conceivable that he would, if it were possible, let the whole of his thought-mechanism lapse by attrition, provided he could get at the heart of truth by immediate vision. And perhaps his deep conviction that peace could be established by the simple expedient of developing a sense of unity among mankind derived from this vision of his ancestry more than from any mere logical thinking. It is indeed difficult for any but the Hindu to see how the issue of peace in the twentieth century could be simplified to the mere technique of regulating the conflicting States of the world by the Hindu way of life.

There can be no question that in Radhakrishnan's opinion the Hindu social scheme was built up in the course of long centuries as a scheme for the human species, or civilisation as such. The historical evidence for such a view is the fact that many races and varied faiths and cultures met and coalesced in India, as if to specialise in civilisation and peace. He is confident that, even though contacts on a large scale between races, cultures and faiths also took place on other continents, such contacts did not produce a society for peace but only for organisation and government.

It is another issue why the results from the same assemblage of factors differed so considerably; and even if Radhakrishnan has not yet had occasion to discuss the issue at length, the fact in his considered judgment remains that the Hindu concept of society, whatever its origin, could not by any chance be confused with, say, the European or Christian.

We have to discuss three distinct issues, which Radhakrishnan's account of the Hindu State implies:

The origin of the society or civilisation to which this state belongs.

The nature of the constitution of the society, which determines the exact shape of this state.

The reason why Radhakrishnan thinks that it is the only solution of the problems which the human race is facing today.

As I have already said, Radhakrishnan is convinced that a peaceful security for the whole human society is not only possible, but has fallen due, and the historical grounds which he adduces for such a hopeful prospect are two:

First, the nature of man is the same, whatever differentiation it may have undergone in the course of ages. "If we leave aside the fanatics . . ., the leaders of every historical civilization to-day are convinced that mankind in all its extent and history is a single organism." [1] He quotes Dante: " 'There is not one goal for this civilization and one for that, but for the civilization of all mankind there is a single goal.' " [2] "Though Asia and Europe are different, they are not so completely different as to disallow an interchange of goods, material and spiritual. This interchange has occurred throughout the centuries and points to the underlying unity of the human mind." [3] He repudiates Spengler's thesis. "Spengler's thesis . . . that different nations have different cultures expressive of distinctive ideals is rather damaging to any hope of the development of a common culture or civilization." [4] "When Spengler tells us . . . that all provincial civilizations are tending to pass away and we are about to make a new experiment in the art of life on a world-wide scale." [5] "Before we can build a stable civilization worthy of humanity as a whole, it is necessary

1 K, 12.   2 Ibid., 13.   3 ER, 115.
4 K, 10.   5 K, 11.

that each historical civilization should become conscious of its limitations and its unworthiness to become the ideal civilization of the world." [6] "Every spiritual or scientific advance which any branch of the human family achieves is achieved not for itself alone, but for all mankind." [7]

Second, if in the past maybe 6,000 years different civilisations arose with specific objectives, the present is the moment when the prospect of building up one family and society for our race has definitely arisen. "For the first time in the history of mankind, the consciousness of the unity of the world has dawned on us. Whether we like it or not, East and West have come together and can no more part." [8]

But the question arises, did the past ever embody civilisations which stood apart, as if they were altogether distinct and unique types? It is difficult to see that it did. If there had to be three, and only three, types of civilisation, in a state of conflict one with another, Radhakrishnan could not have meant that they remained discreetly at a distance from one another and indulged in merely internal conflicts. Besides, if human nature is organically one, this side of human nature becomes significant only when it is in conflict with animal nature—or, perhaps, the superhuman. The rest of the time it necessarily takes fundamentally three forms. Radhakrishnan's conviction, therefore, that a peaceful society is on the eve of appearance simply because we are in a special way conscious of the unity of the world may well be taken as an augury of the times that are coming. In other words, if the three civilisations in the course of centuries failed to establish one society for the whole species, it is conceivable that they are on the way to grow or mature into such a society. Personally, I do take Radhakrishnan's conviction as an augury, precisely because he is a man of peace and feels in his blood and bones that the mandate of his ancestry immemorially pointed to peace in the human family.

But what is Radhakrishnan's view about the origin of the Hindu scheme and the State which is bound up with it?

Radhakrishnan would, in the light of the excavations in the Indus Valley, rather shift the origin of the Hindu civilisation from the usually accepted age of the Aryan conquest of India to a much earlier date which marked the appearance of Mohenjo Daro and Harappa. There is no doubt a big gap to be filled in between the two dates and ages; but that need not create a barrier to legitimate sociological speculation. Moreover, fresh findings are gradual-

[6] *Ibid.*, 11-12.   [7] ER, 116.   [8] *Ibid.*, 115.

ly closing the gap—*vide* the pottery in Bihar. "Hindu civilization goes back to the period of the Indus Valley in which were found great cities of well-planned houses built with baths and sanitary arrangements." [9] "As Professor Childe puts it: 'The Indus civilisation represents a very perfect adjustment of human life to a specific environment that can only have resulted from years of patient effort. And it has endured; it is already specifically Indian and forms the basis of modern Indian culture.' " [10] "We can infer the presence of the Śiva cult, Śakti worship, and *yoga* method . . . the social order was not based on any racial or religious exclusiveness. It permitted the worship of more than one God, exalted yogic perfection, and tolerated different racial groups." [11]

If we look into the past history of India, we see how the country has been subjected to one race invasion after another. Even at the beginning of her history India was peopled by various racial groups, the dark aboriginal tribes, the sturdy Dravidians, the yellow-skinned Mongols and the blithe forceful Aryans. Very soon she developed intimate intercourse with the Persians, the Greeks and the Scythians, and some of these settled down in India. No other country in the world has had such racial problems as India.[12]

It may be difficult to make sure from the data so far collected whether the Indus Valley civilisation was a fully matured Hindu scheme or only partially so. But, as Radhakrishnan points out, at least three or four distinct features stand out in the collected data which leave no doubt as to its intimate connection with the Hindu idea. These are the Śiva cult, Śakti worship, Yogic practices and a non-exclusive social scheme. It would be stupid to deny that they are marks of the Hindu conception nor would it be correct to associate these features with the Sumerian scheme. Besides, one may argue, with reason, that the features under consideration go together; which means that it was only a non-exclusive social scheme which could evolve the Śiva cult, Yogic practices and Śakti worship. This necessity rules out the possibility that the Sumerians, if they did come over to India and built up the Indus Valley civilisation, could have brought these features with them, since there is no evidence that they are a group people. What, then, is the explanation of the fact that the Indus Valley civilisation did develop three or four features which could not be associated with any civilisation, Sumerian or Aryan, whose original home was not India? Exactly the same question arises when we come to analyse what

---

[9] ER, 117.   [10] *Ibid.*, 117-118.   [11] *Ibid.*, 118.   [12] HVL, 94.

is generally described as the period of Aryan conquest. The Aryans may by all accounts be closely related to the Iranians, and both of them, as our authorities hold, with the Greeks, Romans, Celts, Germans and Slavs in at least language, mythology, religious tradition, and social schemes. As a matter of fact, Radhakrishnan expounded all these race affinities with great lucidity in his Inaugural Lecture in the University of Oxford. But did any of these races in their homes of origin develop the Śiva cult, Yogic method, or the non-exclusive social scheme of the Indian civilisation? Have we any logical evidence to conclude that they were bound by their social schemes to develop them? It is universally agreed that the Aryans, near and close to the Indian frontier, in 3,000 B.C., had features peculiar to the Indo-Aryans of the *Ṛg-Veda* period and different from the Iranians. What exactly can account for this change in them which distinguished them from all other Aryans? And, if we look for an explanation in the regional conditions of the Indian continent which was their home after they had left their Iranian cousins, we shall have to conclude that the people whom the Aryans met in India must have already had these very features in a highly developed form. The issue thus will be unexpectedly simplified and the conclusion will have to be drawn that it was the Non-Aryans,—whoever they might have been—who assimilated the Aryans, and not the other way about. Besides, the 'special features' of the Indo-Aryans of the *Ṛg-Veda* period, as a result of their transformation in contact with the Non-Aryans, should at least include features like the Śiva cult, Yogic method, Śakti worship and non-exclusive social scheme, whether our authorities choose to mention that fact or not. And the conclusion will follow that, since these features were unmistakably Indian in their origin, they would characterise any race or people who ever came from outside to make their home in India. In other words, if India has been subject to invasions from the outside world since at least the authenticated ages of Mohenjo Daro and Harappa, the conflicts which invariably took place between the people of the land and the outsiders must have resulted in the "assimilation of the invaders," to quote an expression of Radhakrishnan's. Whether it was a Sumerian invasion, or Iranian, Persian, Greek, or Scythian, all invasion and conquest must have led to the Hinduisation of the invading races and peoples. This was the only possible consequence of an invasion of the Indian continent, the home of the group civilisation.

What happens, then, to the theory usually held that the Hindu

civilisation was the result of a 'synthesis' or 'amalgamation' between the Sumerians and the Non-Sumerians, or the Aryans and
the Non-Aryans, which Radhakrishnan would not reject offhand,
and which many of his Indian colleagues frankly espouse? Can
we account for the origin of the Hindu social scheme by the well-
worn hypothesis of 'synthesis' or 'amalgamation?'

There are great difficulties in accepting it, both on logical and
historical grounds. If synthesis does imply, according to those who
seriously uphold it, a conflict between opposites, its credit must
be bound up with at least two implications:

The opposites instead of running out as sheer contraries capable of
producing nothing but confusion, have to change into complementaries.

That change is possible if only the values or terms that clashed as opposites can be reinterpreted.

Even if we do not raise the issue as to the origin of the opposites
—there has been no account of it yet which is intelligible—, their
culmination in synthesis must presuppose their transformation into complementaries by a definite change in their meaning. Historically, no philosopher who ever subscribed to the idea of
synthesis had the good fortune to discover that change or a fresh
interpretation of the terms. The notion of synthesis, therefore,
however desirable in the economy of human existence, has stood
on our philosophic horizon only as a pious wish. There has been
no instance of 'synthesis' or 'amalgamation' in human history. Instead there have been instances of compromise which it would be
unpardonable to confuse with synthesis.

There is still a Dialectic in the Indian tradition to consider, and
it does give an account of the opposites in its own way. In fact,
Professor Murti, who was recently here in the University of Oxford as the deputy of Radhakrishnan, holds the view that, according to Madhyamecka, Gautama the Buddha is the father of
Dialectic.

But the dialectical conflict between Vedantism and Buddhism
does not end in a synthesis of the Hegelian type. On the contrary,
the whole dialectical process is dropped in the Indian tradition as
an evidence for the unreal and the conflict after that by sheer intuition terminates in the Absolute. This is the common ground
between the Vedānta and the Buddha and is furthest removed
from anything like a Hegelian synthesis.

The two conceptions of the dialectic evidently are quite distinct;

but neither of them will help us to conclude that the Sumerian and Non-Sumerian, or the Aryan and Non-Aryan, after they had faced each other as opposites on the continent of India, came to amalgamate their societies into one single society known as the Hindu civilisation. Whatever else may have happened to them, synthesis and amalgamation could not happen between their opposite positions. I do not think Radhakrishnan will accept such a hypothesis with regard to the origin of the Hindu scheme.

But it does not follow that, at this rate, one had to deny the clash between the Aryan and Non-Aryan, or any clash between the people of India and the outsiders, as historical facts. Radhakrishnan is perhaps more alive to this strenuous feature of our history with its grim consequences than any other historian. But, once we admit that our ancestors had had to put up with invasion from the outside world, it becomes imperative that we must define it in terms of cultures as distinct from mere races or regional conditions. No people, whatever their proportion, ever existed without belonging to some social scheme or other. Our ancestors, even while they were moving through the Stone and Bronze Ages, must have been matured social beings.

But what conclusion have we to draw as to the origin of the Hindu social scheme, if we have to believe that our ancestors, whether in Mohenjo Daro or Harappa or as Non-Aryans and Dravidians, were matured social beings? If there is no alternative to our thinking that the clashes between our ancestors and the outsiders were fundamentally clashes between social schemes, could we still hold that the group scheme, which appeared in the dawn of our history and never ceased to bless us right down to the moment when the latest occupation of our country took place in the eighteenth century, was but a gift of synthesis? Can the group scheme be regarded as a derivative, even if we assume that synthesis or amalgamation was a sociological process? It is not possible that I could accept such a hypothesis. The group scheme, as I have delineated it on grounds of indisputable evidence, is one of the three ultimate schemes of society. To put it emphatically, it was a gift from the cosmic order and by no means left for human ingenuity or what is called the prehistoric civilisation of our race to invent.

If, however, the group scheme was not a derivative, does it not follow that it must have been one of the schemes which were responsible for the clash between our ancestors and the invaders of their ancient land? Either the Aryans, or the Non-Aryans must be supposed to have professed it. The clash in India must have been between the group people and the people who were not group but individualist or dualist.

It will be bold indeed, if we prefer to call the Aryans group people. There is no evidence that the culture of the Aryans, whatever their racial feature, was group. On the other hand, there is ample evidence that it was individualist, even as there is evidence that our ancestors were not individualists. Should we not then conclude that the clash between the Aryans and the Non-Aryans was not only a clash between the group scheme and the individualist scheme, but that it was the Non-Aryan rather than the Aryan who must have professed the group culture in that clash? The Hindu social scheme, therefore, which is unmistakably a group scheme, has to be admitted as the scheme of the people whom we come across both in the dim and lighted regions in our history. Its origin truly must be shrouded in the mists of tradition, and, if still we claim on behalf of our ancestry the right of being its creator or originator, we do so only to follow historical precedent.

In any case, the hypothesis of 'amalgamation' and 'synthesis' goes by the board, and in its place we are justified in putting the other hypothesis, what Radhakrishnan calls 'assimilation.' It has to be granted that it was the group scheme, the indigenous scheme of the Indian people, which clashed with the non-group schemes of the invaders and periodically succeeded in assimilating them. And this meant that, from the Gods to the diverse cultures of the invaders, they all came to be accommodated in the Indian social scheme instead of being exterminated or completely suppressed. And nobody refers to the Hindu technique of preservation with such emotion and earnestness as does Radhakrishnan. There is, at any rate, no question about its specific character; but whether it means all that is claimed for it, it will soon be necessary for us to discuss.

If the Hindu social scheme may legitimately be taken as indigenous and wholly spontaneous in its origin, its main features must be simple and straightforward. It stands by itself without any complication, with a structure and constituents which it should be possible for any scientific enquiry to demarcate from that of the non-Hindu in the modern, medieval, and classical ages of human history.

The concept which Radhakrishnan has wisely chosen in order to bring out its strictly fundamental feature is the familiar concept of organism. And, if we follow his lead, it should be possible to derive from it all the other salient features which stand out in vivid contrast with what all the non-Hindu social systems emphasised.

The Hindu society, according to Radhakrishnan, is organic; and the evidence for this will technically be found in the four-fold classes definitely mentioned in the *Puruṣa Sūkta* of the *Ṛg Veda*. The four classes are the Brahmins, Kṣatriyas, Vaisyas and Sūdras. The belief is that these classes took their origins from the head, arms, thighs and feet respectively of the cosmic creator. "The earliest reference to the four classes is in the *Puruṣa Sūkta* of the *Ṛg Veda*, where they are described as having sprung from the body of the creative spirit, from his head, arms, thighs, and feet. This poetical image is intended to convey the organic character of society." [13]

Whatever the metaphysical value of this belief, it leaves no room for doubt that the cosmic creator had no weakness for what is called the atomistic or mechanistic view of creation. If the social scheme had to be constituted by the offspring of the head, arms, thighs, and feet of the cosmic creator, that scheme could not but be organic. Or, to put it in Radhakrishnan's language, the cosmic organisation or the social scheme was by "the ordinance of God and dispensation of Spirit," and had to be organic. The technical term for this social scheme that Radhakrishnan quotes is *loka-samgraha*, or the holding together of the human race. It is obvious that this theory of the creation of the organic scheme implies that it was the only legitimate social scheme and meant for the whole of the human species. "The fourfold classification is conceived in the interests of world progress. It is not intended specially for the Hindus, but applies to the whole human race, which has one destiny which it seeks and increasingly attains through the countless millenniums of history." [14]

The concept of organism, however, with universal consent, implies two distinct features which are equally fundamental.

An organism is constituted by organs which stand in precise and intimate relationship with one another.

The related organs presuppose a force or entity or principle which is outside them, and functions as the sole determinant of the changes which take place in the career of the organs. That force or entity or principle stands also as the common objective or end of the constituent organs.

[13] ER, 355.   [14] ER, 356.

There can be no question that in Radhakrishnan's account of the Hindu scheme both conceptions are equally provided for. The four classes, *i.e.* the Brahmin, Kṣatriyas, Vaisyas and Sūdras, are the four main organs, and the transcendent principle which determines their activity is unity, or the Absolute.

It has to be noted, however, that 'unity' should be clearly distinguished as well from 'individuality' as from 'community.' Radhakrishnan certainly can have no objection to this demarcation; although, in his anxiety to bring about *lokasamgraha,* he may be at times skipping, by an oversight, the interval between the Idea and the Universal of the Greeks and the Personal God of the Christians on the one hand, and the Unity or Absolute of his ancestors on the other. As a historian of great repute, he is fully alive to the historical fact that the Being of Parmenides was not the Being of Plato or Aristotle, since Parmenides kept Being apart and aloof from Non-Being, which neither Plato nor Aristotle did, whatever the reasons for that might have been. On no account, therefore, could the Unity, the untouched and immaculate Being of his ancestry, be brought down to the level of the Platonic Being or the Being of Judaism, Christianity, or Islam. If there was any similarity between the Hindu Unity and any of the conceptions of Ultimate Reality in human history, it lay in the Parmenidean conception of Being. And yet even there a line of departure divided the Being of Parmenides from the Hindu conception; it appeared in the bold Hindu theory of Illusion, which was claimed to be an additional category to Being and Non-Being. Indeed, the whole of Radhakrishnan's ancestry in its purity marked an orientation which was not anticipated anywhere else. And this consisted in the claim that the third category is neither Being nor Non-Being, to which Radhakrishnan had so many occasions to refer in his philosophical works, as did his forbears of classical fame.

The next point to note in this organic theory of society refers to the nature of the unit which embodies in a multiple form the constituents of the organic society. The issue is whether the individuals in it should appear in 'communities,' 'classes' or 'castes.' If it is in no case possible that the individuals should live a solitary existence, but must appear as members of a class, community or caste, do the individuals in an organic society form a caste, class or community?

If Radhakrishnan has not had occasion to go into this question at length, there is absolute evidence in his writings that he upheld the 'caste' form as the only suitable one for the organic society.

And this conclusion follows from the basal fact that the organic society was oriented on the notion of unity rather than on 'individuality' or 'relationship.' The unique or related individual as a legitimate unit drops out of the organic scheme altogether. It is the 'caste' individual instead that comes to constitute it. I have no hesitation in claiming that Radhakrishnan meant exactly the same thing as I mean by the caste individual.

The unit, therefore, in the organic society is the group or caste, especially as the main purpose of the organic society is to eliminate the illusion of individuality as such and bring about, in the end, the state of perfect unity. This is perhaps the most salient feature in Radhakrishnan's conception of organic society. Unless, indeed, one keeps in mind his persistent claim that Hindu society dealt with groups and not individuals and solved all problems of conflicts and disagreements by the one expedient of creating fresh castes, the main point of organic society—*varnasram dharma* is sure to be missed. One has to note that the Hindu scheme has been wholly an experiment in group or caste formations. It dealt with ever-increasing groups and castes and as such the individuals of the class or community scheme could not possibly have any place in it. In fact, the Hindu scheme existed to give the human individual a chance to reach the state of unity, which it regarded as the only desirable state, by setting the caste order against both the class and community schemes. The stand for individuality or community is to Radhakrishnan, as it was to Gandhi, Śaṁkara and the Buddha, the one besetting illusion or the source of ignorance which kept the individual constantly leaving the straight path of the universe.

What, then, is the State in the organic society, as Radhakrishnan formulates it? If the society is a society of organs or castes, can the State be anything but an organ or caste in the technical sense of the term, whatever its proportion?

The state is one of the four main organs: Brahmin, Kṣatriya, Vaisya, or Sūdra. It is indeed the second caste, and it has, therefore, a special function of its own, which it is entitled to discharge in complete independence of the others. That function is to preserve the social order based on Law as it is formulated by the first caste, the Brahmin, whose special function it is to intuit the nature of Unity, and to formulate on the basis of that intuition the main objective of the organic society.

. . . It is the business of the Brahmin to lay down the science of values, draw out the blueprints for social reconstruction, and persuade the world to accept the high ends of life, it is the business of the Kṣatriya to devise the means for gaining the ends. . . . The Kṣatriyas rule only as the guardians and servants of the law. They have an executive power over the community which is valid only so long as they carry out the law, which is placed under the control of the Brahmins and the seers and protected from interference by political or economic power.[15]

The State in the Hindu scheme does not create the Law unless it oversteps jurisdiction so clearly marked out for it. But it is the one supreme authority for either establishing the Law or overcoming resistance to it. The issue of power and force, therefore, is a political issue. No other organ in the body politic has a claim to it or charge of it; and the responsibility that goes with it centres in the State instead of being distributed in the other organs or in any sense shared with them.

The political is not the highest category. The State exists in order that its members may have a good life. It is a social convenience. It is not the judge of its own conduct. Though righteousness depends on force, "it is wrong to say that it is the will of the strong." The State is not above ethics. It exists essentially for the good of the individual and has therefore no right to demand the sacrifice of the individual, though it has every right to demand the conditions essential for the performance of its task. . . . Rama tells Laksmana: "I bear arms for the sake of truth. It is not difficult for me to gain this whole universe but I desire not even the suzerainty of the heavens if it is to be through unrighteousness." [16]

But the supreme authority of the State has to reckon with the autonomy of the groups and castes. "People were allowed to manage their affairs in accordance with the traditional rules and customs. They did not care who the rulers were so long as their lives were undisturbed. One flag was as good as another, if social life was carried on in the same way." [17] As each and every caste has its own function to discharge, it must be left free, according to the law, to discharge it by its own mechanism.

Village communities presided over by councils of elders chosen from all castes and representing all interests maintained peace and order, controlled taxation, settled disputes, and preserved intact the internal economy of the country. Trade-guilds were also managed on similar lines, protecting the professional interests and regulating working hours and wages. The peasant worked the land to maintain himself and the family and contribute a little to the community. The craftsman fashioned the tools and the clothing necessary for the community, and was

15 ER, 359, 362.   16 ER, 360.   17 Ibid., 362.

in turn provided with the food and shelter necessary. This system prevailed even after the British rule started. Sir William Hunter observed:
'The trade guilds in the cities, and the village community in the country, act, together with caste, as mutual assurance societies, and under
normal conditions allow none of their members to starve. Caste, and
the trading or agricultural guilds concurrent with it, take the place of
a poor law in India.' [18]

This follows from the ultimate fact that it is the group or caste
that forms the unit of the organic society. Whether the group is
the family, clan, tribe, village community or guild association or
any other special body, their autonomy is the first consideration
of the State. They are really subdivisions of the four main organs,
the Brahmin, Kṣatriya, Vaisya and Śūdra, with specialised capacities for performing the four main functions. It is for the State only
to give the varied groups and bodies help or sustenance when
needed to carry out their objectives, to set them back on to the
right path if they have deviated from it and, finally, to protect
them from dangers which may threaten them, whether from the
outside world, or the internal changes in the career of the groups.
And in all this it is supported by the legislator, the Brahmin.

A question, however, arises—if the main issue of the caste
scheme is to give the individual the full chance of realising the
ideal of unity by its fourfold scheme, how does the question of
authority of the State with an absolute right to power and control
arise? Why do not the castes function spontaneously and in perfect harmony with one another? Why should the State have to preserve internal order or defend the caste scheme from invasion or
attack from outside?

If Radhakrishnan is anxious for peace, it follows that he believes that there is such a thing as conflict between social schemes.
What then is his diagnosis of the social conflict?

The source of this conflict according to him is deficiency in human nature as a concrete phenomenon. It is another question
whether this deficiency is due to illusion as a cosmic fact or tied
up with the law of Karma. What is evident is that Radhakrishnan
does not confuse the historical nature of man with its ideal form,
which is necessarily perfect. He is fully justified in holding, therefore, that *varnasrama dharma* has to provide in its social economy
for an organ or function the object of which would be to deal
with the innate deficiency in man's nature. In other words, if the
scheme itself by its fourfold division does make it possible for man

[18] ER, 369.

to reach the goal of unity, it does not follow that mankind will normally follow the straight path without any resistance. It has to be compelled in its own interest not to deviate from that straight path. The second organ, the Kṣatriya, therefore, has to be there with sovereign authority to counteract this innate deficiency by any means conceivable. The means will normally be persuasion, education, and force of character, since the source of deficiency is illusion; but it may have to be changed into force, if the illusion in exceptional cases takes the proportion of a challenge to the *varnasrama dharma* itself.

The Hindu scheme permits the use of force for the maintenance of order and enforcement of law, occasionally even to the point of the destruction of human life. In a perfect society where every one is naturally unselfish and loving, there would be no need for government or force, but so perfect a condition is perhaps not suited to mere men.[19]

"The ideal is the Brahminic one of non-resistance, for the means are as important as the end."[20] " '. . . the only true conquest is the conquest won by piety' (Aśoka)."[21]

But what forms does this innate deficiency in man assume? In what different ways has the State to deal with this deficiency?

It has two forms:

The form in which the *varnasrama dharma* itself with its objective is challenged by a stand for individualism on the part of societies which do not believe in unity.

The form in which the *dharma* itself develops an internal conflict in its own economy as a result of the perfectly legitimate efforts on the part of its constituents to realise its main objective.

The State in the first instance has to suppress the social schemes which stand on individuality rather than on unity. Here the issue is between *varnasrama dharma* and what has been known as Humanism, for instance the Greco-Roman system; equally there is another issue of the same type in which the State has to negate the dualistic society, Judaism or its two offshoots, Christianity and Islam.

In this stage of *varnasrama dharma* the whole of the caste society stands together in perfect agreement, and it is this stage to which Radhakrishnan refers when he refers to *sanatan dharma*. No Hindu worth the name will disown this claim on behalf of Hindu civilisation; and I shall not be far wrong if I add that Radhakrishnan, consciously or unconsciously, has never ceased to

[19] ER, 361.	[20] *Ibid.*, 361.	[21] *Ibid.*, footnote 1, 361.

preach Hinduism in this form. Indeed, the right to eternal existence of Hinduism in this pristine form of pure being or mystical
reality will never lapse, whatever the changes in our universe may
be. To Radhakrishnan, as to all true Hindus, here is the original
and eternal contribution of Hindu civilisation.

But the State in the second instance, when it is not called upon
to meet any challenge to *varnasrama dharma,* has to cope with
an internal conflict between two competing modes of realising
unity, for instance, the Vedantic Ātman and the Buddhistic Un-
Ātman or Nirvāṇa or in strictly categorical language, between the
claims of Being and Becoming. The strange fact is that, whereas
the Vedantist and the Buddhist agree absolutely about their objective and goal, they differ sharply with regard to the modes and
methods of its realisation.

It is a fact that the State has to function in a dual capacity.

It has to be vigilant in its preservation of the *sanatan dharma*
with the unanimity and consent of the whole community.

It has to act on behalf of the Vedantist or the Buddhist as fortune favours them. The fact is that either an Aśoka or a Harsa
rules; the Buddhist and the Brahmin never could or did rule
together, since they believed, as we shall soon see, in hierarchic or
equalitarian schemes of realisation.

I see no reason why Radhakrishnan should object to this analysis of our ancestral history. If he is anxious that the Vedantist and
the Buddhist should live in peace together and preach *sanatan
dharma* to the world at large, he must be aware of the bitter
conflict that has taken place for centuries between them. It is
well known to him that all the other movements in our history
were but attempts to solve the ultimate conflict between Being
and Becoming, or between Ātman and Nirvāṇa by what is known
as synthesis, but which is really compromise. Even such an astute
and profound attempt as the *Bhagavadgītā* embodied is not quite
free from that ambition, not to speak of the frank endeavour of
many to establish monotheism on the plea that the religious folk
of India wanted a Personal God.

The State never represented the whole community except when
it was defending *sanatan dharma.* It was either a Brahminic or a
Buddhistic State.

But which of these two States of our tradition would Radhakrishnan be inclined to uphold? If it is not possible for him to
preserve both of them all the time, will he just accept the State as

it exists and functions, whether Brahminic or Buddhistic, or will he uphold the Brahminic State alone?

I find it extremely difficult to make sure what exactly Radhakrishnan's political position is, if it has to be assessed in terms of the Brahminic or Buddhistic test. It is indisputable that he has profound faith in the *sanatan dharma* and would not mean even in his dreams the slightest offence to the spirit of Vedānta or Buddha. But the evidence, it seems, is not equally strong as to his adherence to both the Vedantic and Buddhistic claims on equal terms.

It is not possible, however,—unless one is too much in a hurry to establish peace,—to escape the sharp distinction that divides the Vedantic and Buddhistic interpretations of unity, the common meeting ground of both. The interpretation of unity in terms of Being and Ātman is the direct opposite of the interpretation which replaces Being by Becoming and the Ātman by Un-Ātman. And if, in our anxiety to remove all suffering, we do not lose sight of this ultimate distinction, we shall have to draw a line between the hierarchic conception of the social scheme which was so firmly and conscientiously laid down by the Brahminic theory and the conception which the Buddhist espoused by flatly negating the innate superiority of the Brahmin as indicated by birth. The note struck in the second conception is distinctly equalitarian. There is no inclination in Buddhism to tie up the life of the individual in the different castes with any permanent transcendental reality, which alone can guarantee the hierarchic conception of society. The determining agency was in the caste-individuals themselves, and the issue of liberation was an issue of self-exertion to live up to the Eightfold Path. The Brahmin, therefore, was known by his deed and way of living and so it was inevitable that movements from caste to caste would take place, whether in one direction or another, and not by what may be called compromises, such as, for instance, Anulam and Pratilam forms of marriage.

But does Radhakrishnan accept this distinction between the hierarchic and equalitarian views of social schemes as final? I do not know. There are, however, some distinct claims which stand to the credit of Radhakrishnan which may help in clearing the ground.

The Sūdra, according to Radhakrishnan is a man of instinct, whereas the Brahmin is frankly a man of intuition, although there have been cases in which the Sūdra born was qualified to be a Brahmin, while the Brahmin born could function only like a

Sūdra. Radhakrishnan has cited at least the exceptional and well known instances. But there is no attempt by Radhakrishnan to disguise his conviction that instinct, thought, and intuition do form a graded series as capacities of man to grasp unity and live up to it.

He is frankly anxious that the Sūdra because of his deficiency should be helped, and there is such a thing, in his opinion, as dignity of labour or the inestimable value of service as such. What is more, he would certainly not deny to the Sūdra *Mokṣa* or liberation any more than he will reserve it only for the upper castes. In fact, the last *Asrama* as he points out removes the caste distinctions and builds up a community, the members of which are recruited from all the castes without discrimination.

But the man of instinct, the Sūdra, must remain as such and offer only service, since he is congenitally incapable of offering anything better or higher. In the last analysis, birth is the only criterion by which the Brahmin or Sūdra or the four Varnas can be traced. Radhakrishnan frankly holds that this is better than all other tests. "The Hindu assumed that birth in a family which had the traditions of the leisured class might offer the best solution." [22] It would be unfair to him after this to suggest that he was equally attached to both the hierarchic and equalitarian views.

But I do not mean to suggest that the Buddha himself, or Buddhism in the course of centuries, drew out the full implication of the equalitarian position, which was evidently the Buddhistic contribution to the Hindu scheme. Besides, a hostile critic, especially if he is an Orientalist, may quote even Buddha himself for evidence against the full equalitarian trend of Buddhism. I do not pretend to any scholarship in Buddhistic or Brahminic history worth the name. The point that I have raised with regard to the full implications of the Buddhistic position has to be dealt with by Buddhist scholars. But I do stand on an indisputable logical interpretation.

And my formulation makes it quite clear that the Buddha must, as a matter of course, have come to the same kind of conclusion in the group system as the empiricist did in the individualist scheme, or the Protestant did in the dualist scheme. If the Vedantic view was oriented on unity as the main feature of the organisation for realisation, to the detriment of individuality, the Buddhist view chose the direct opposite, individuality, and so had to undermine the cause of unity. There was no alternative: and this hap-

[22] ER, 359.

pened, even though both the Buddha and the Vedanta stood for unity or the pure mystical reality as the only ultimate reality, in opposition to the individuality of the humanist and the community of the dualist. The reason was that the issue of organisation arose twice in all the schemes: first, while the nature of ultimate reality was being formulated and the structure of the social scheme was being laid down. Second, while the attempt was being made to realise that ultimate reality in the structure that was laid down.

So that even after the choice of unity as the objective was made—on the hypothesis that ultimate reality was nothing but unity—by both the Vedantist and the Buddhist, the whole issue of unity and individuality had to be faced again the moment the issue of the realisation of the objective arose. And this time both unity and individuality had to be equally valued and preserved; and if, for obvious reasons, they could not be preserved in the same scheme, two schemes had to be built up—and that, necessarily, in a state of conflict one with the other. There is enough evidence in the history of all the three civilisations to bear testimony to this inevitable schism in their structure. Buddhism, therefore, which frankly chose individuality rather than unity, must be supposed to have stood for uniqueness of the group, exactly as the empiricist did for the uniqueness of the individual. It is here, in this selection of the uniqueness of the group, that the true democratic feature of the Hindu scheme appeared. It followed that the Buddhist had to stand not only against the hierarchy of Brahminism but also for the uniqueness and freedom of the group.

The point, still, is not whether the Buddha himself or the schools of Buddhism that followed him actually drew this implication and completely established their claim; the point is that the implication was there and remained to be drawn sometime or other. It was not open to the Buddhist to form a gradation of values in which intuition would appear at the top and instinct at the bottom, as was done in the Brahminic scheme. What was necessary was that instinct, thought, and intuition had to be related in a state of mutual interdependence on the ground that they were all equally unique. And the finality of this process would necessarily aim at making the multiple groups and castes transcendent, exactly as the empiricist in the humanistic scheme aimed at the completely self-sufficient and perfect individual. This, to me, incidentally, is the explanation of Nirvāṇa, whether the Buddha referred to it or not.

It is another issue whether this stand for the uniqueness of groups leading up to multiple mystical groups had a stronger claim to validity than the clearly opposite stand for the monistic Ātman. Historically, neither experiment succeeded in solving the problem of realisation. Perhaps the height of our racial misfortune was not reached till Buddhism had to 'stay put' in the lands of our neighbours, while Brahmanism had to lie prostrate under the pressure of the stranger who invaded its home.

Could we now claim on behalf of Radhakrishnan that he is attached equally to both the Brahminic and Buddhistic schemes of polity? Does his faith in the gradation of capacities and hierarchy of values leave any room for his acceptance of the firmly democratic stand of Buddhism, which denied the innate superiority of the Brahmin and necessarily implied the uniqueness of all values and capacities? It is for Radhakrishnan himself to give the answer.

What, then, is the solution of the problem of peace in the world today? If Radhakrishnan honestly finds it difficult to accept the true democratic position, will he satisfy either the democrat of the West or the Buddhist on his own continent with his stand for what seems to be only a regulated form of hierarchy? Could the intensity and earnestness of his stand for peace, about which there is no question, make up for his inability to recognise the true democratic claim?

Far be it from me to imply that he has openly or frankly stood against the democrat or his creed, whether in Asia or the West. There is indisputable evidence that nobody has espoused more consistently the cause of the people in any part of the globe, irrespective of race, tradition, and status, than he has done. The capitalist, the militarist, and the autocrat, all equally came in for even bitter denunciation at his hands. Besides, he has not only stood for the individual as individual but made a definite claim on behalf of Hinduism that it alone stood for true democracy. And when Radhakrishnan gives expression to his views, they come from the fullness of heart and are furthest removed from any political bias.

But democracy, as he understands it, is something very different from what democrats of all traditions could possibly have meant to imply by their creed. Democracy in the Hindu scheme, in his opinion, stands on the claim that it made room for all races, cultures, and faiths in its economy instead of either exterminating or suppressing them when they came into violent conflict with it. And the strength of this claim considerably increases when he robustly points out that in no other civilisation was such a remarkable feat achieved.

But the question arises, is the act of the preservation of races, cultures, and faiths as such necessarily a democratic achievement? Does it serve the purpose of the true democratic need? It would, provided the races, cultures, and faiths, if they were preserved, were preserved in their uniquenesses, exactly as they were in their origin and growth. But could the Hindu scheme, which is a group scheme, accommodate any race, culture, or faith in it which is not only not organic in its origin but is bound up with the individualist or dualist scheme? Did the Hindu, for instance, ever dare to preserve the Christianity of Christ, the creed of Islam or the Humanist individual in their historic proportions? If, nevertheless, Christ, Mahomet, and the Aryan gods found honoured and dignified places in the Hindu scheme, it would be unfair both to the Hindu and to the non-Hindu to forget that the accommodation was heavily conditioned by at least the acceptance of a group, or truly mystical, claim. Jesus or Mahomet, Moses or Jupiter could only play the rôles of Avatars in the Hindu scheme, or, more technically, survive as mere symbols, *i.e.*, conceptions of the mystical reality. So that even if they were given a high or medium status in the hierarchic system, that would not mitigate the rigour of the loss they had to undergo in their stentorian claims to divinity, direct or indirect. And yet no Hindu, however anxious for peace for all concerned, could achieve anything better or wiser exactly as no Greek or Christian could preserve the Hindu in the Greek empire or in the family of the one God respectively.

It would be death for the Hindu mystic to accept the Personal God of the Christian or citizenship in the empire of the Greek. No Roman, again, will sacrifice his individuality for the sake of preserving the group society of the Hindu in his far-flung empire, even as it would be planting heresy in the home of one God to mix up universal brotherhood with the Hindu stand for compassion and unity. There is nothing to choose between the Hindu and the Greek or the Hindu and the Christian, so far as the prospects they all offer towards building up a common human home are concerned. The sooner this truth is realised, the better it will be for the human species.

In any case Hindu preservation as such could not imply a satisfaction of the democratic need, even if its peculiarity lay in the fact that by it races, cultures, and faiths were assimilated as groups altogether rather than in a state in which the groups were split up into individuals.

Equally true it is that the individual Radhakrishnan referred to in the Hindu scheme is by no means the same individual as in any other tradition. Radhakrishnan's individual is a person who is detached from all social obligations in the sense that he has no longer any alignment with the objectives which the social structure enjoins on the first three castes to realise.

But what really is the state of detached personality? Evidently the more detached a person is, the more of a unity he must be. There is no third alternative to the state of unity and the state of multiplicity. Either one has to be attached to other individuals or to be detached from them. One can be either a social being or a being in a state of unity which excludes both multiplicity and relationship.

It is another matter whether the state of unity is or can be a historical fact, and if we have to conclude that it is not and cannot be, the conclusion is that the persons who appear to us to be detached must belong to a society which is beyond *varnasram dharma*, with provision for fresh attachments. Where then is the detached individual? In fact, if we follow our tradition, we have to keep in mind that individuality in any shape or form is the one and only source of illusion, since it is bound to create attachment. It was not for nothing that our ancestry perpetually warned us against the individual, and nobody knows that better than Radhakrishnan himself.

Radhakrishnan's conception of democracy and individuality, therefore, may not satisfy the individualist or democrat of the world today. How, then, is the problem of peace going to be solved, whether in the Western World or in the East?

If, again, his claim that the Hindu scheme can solve the problems of race, culture, and faith is not likely to satisfy the democrat, could he expect any better result by his further claim that all conflicts could be solved if only we took the varieties of races, cultures, and faiths as differences, rather than as contradictories or contraries? He cannot, since this is a very old plea and has been well tried. It is well known to Radhakrishnan that the theory of differences appeared in history as only a challenge to the dialectic in the same history. Only yesterday, Mahatma Gandhi had to pay with his life for preaching it as the doctrine of love. Still, there are many minds in the world who are exhausted by the rigour of the dialectic and would fain turn to the theory of differences. And at least in India all attempts to seek relief in the shape of theistic movements made an apotheosis of this view. But Radhakrishnan, as an authority on Hindu thought, is fully aware of the keen dialectic in our own ancestry. He knows that its recurrence, after repeated theistic attempts to drown it, was a sign of its eternal existence. There is no reason why Madhyamika should not appeal to a Vedantist like Radhakrishnan. Finally, if the Buddha was the first dialectician, it is inconceivable that the Personal God of the dualist, or the pagan god of the humanist will accept the rôle of being a symbol of the Vedantic Ātman. It is another story if otherwise there is any chance for their survival in the age that is coming. Nothing, not even the divine as human mind conceived it, escaped the fatal blow from the dialectic.

Finally, it is almost a calculated offence to human dignity to collect at this late hour the agreements on ways of life in the shape of moral principles from the *obiter dicta* of the prophets of all ages only to bolster up the strength of the theory of differences. And, if Radhakrishnan does not stoop to any such device, I may be pardoned if I add that he may not seriously object to my claim that there is a trichotomy on every moral principle that ever was formulated. After all, he never departed from the Vedantic claim that we are still in the realm of Māyā or illusion. How, then, could one see truth whole and steadily in such a predicament, if the claim is rigidly adhered to?

What, then, is the explanation of his insistence on the claim that the hour of peace for the human family is at hand, or that it will be the handicraft of the *sanatan dharma*?

The explanation will be found in the deep, historic source of the claim. Radhakrishnan has been for a quarter of a century talking as prophets and reformers do. And in all this talk he has perpetually reminded his fellow men that a fresh epoch in our history is due. I take it that this vision in him arises from his infinite faith in that immortal verse in the *Bhavagadgītā* in which Sri Kṛṣṇa as a token of divine gesture assures the afflicted and down-trodden of every age of his direct commiseration in the arrival of an Avatar. Millions of Hindus for long ages have gone through the tribulations of life with nothing but their faith in this divine assurance. In the baffling hour of gloom that shuts out all light it is the mystical assurance alone that holds men together. No civilisation ever went quite out of the mystical realm, and the issue in question never was as to its final form or significance. Proverbially it is open to a Hindu never to cease interpreting that realm. To me the verse in the *Bhavagadgītā* points to the *dharma* which has ruled the Universe till today, and its keynote is justice— not peace. It never fell due for the Avatar to appear till the cup was full to the brim, or the claims to readjustment had arisen. To the *Bhavagadgītā,* it is the field of battle that symbolises the universe, and the law that sanctifies it is the law of justice and not that of peace. The concrete, whatever its shape or form, has a nature of its own which inexorably decides for it as much a passage through the grim experience as a fulfilment in the shape of justice. The *Bhavagadgītā* is the final comment on what we call history or is an interpretation of it. Radhakrishnan indisputably follows its lead with faith and assurance, as one almost lost in a dream. What his heart so poignantly demands is justice, or an adjustment, after long centuries of privation and anguish of soul. There must be an end of domination and of the suppression of spirit that follows from it.

It is another issue whether this adjustment when it comes will come with peace—and that for the whole human family. There is no indication in the *Bhavagadgītā* that it will or will not—if the Buddha kept silent about Nirvāṇa, the Kṛṣṇa kept silent about Peace. But neither denied the future.

Like Radhakrishnan many are drawn to a horizon of peace. They feel it is almost time for another version of the *Bhavagadgītā,* in which the Kurus and Panchalas, if they have to fight again, will fight on the same front by what may be called mutual sacrifice and so finish the fight for good. And Sri Kṛṣṇa then in his new guise will preach an ethics which will fulfil the mission of this Universe, which came rushing along out of the deep and almost unfathomable cavern of illusion.

It is difficult for me to think that Radhakrishnan has not a vision of this coming change. The load of suffering has weighed heavily on him, as it has on some at least of his fellow-men. It was sufficiently heavy even 2,600 years ago, and our Saint in the twentieth century had no release from it till it culminated in the final blow to his long cherished hopes. But suffering, as Radhakrishnan knows, is not the final test of life. The final test, indisputably, is the comprehension of its final end, as all our seers held. If peace and not justice is that final end, there can be justice to herald the arrival of peace. May not one hope that justice may even give way to peace? It is indeed an issue for cosmic decision—whether the history of mankind will, for the sake of justice, begin again a fresh cycle with the mystical group system as the dominant factor in it or begin an altogether new cycle which will control the field of battle for the preservation of the species, and guarantee the arrival of peace. It is for Radhakrishnan himself to decide which way he will turn.

B. K. MALLIK

EXETER COLLEGE
OXFORD UNIVERSITY
ENGLAND

23

A. R. Wadia

THE SOCIAL PHILOSOPHY OF RADHAKRISHNAN

THE SOCIAL PHILOSOPHY OF RADHAKRISHNAN

IT SHOULD be a pleasant duty for an Indian to write on any aspect of Professor Radhakrishnan's philosophy, for his wide scholarship and deep human understanding have marked him out as a cementing link between the apparently widely differing cultures of the East and West. His mastery of the English language as well as the facility with which he can present even the most abstruse ideas in a strikingly picturesque manner have made him an attractive speaker and writer. *Prima facie* his writings are all simple and present straight-forward views on men and things; each sentence of his stands out in crystal clearness and with an emphasis that can leave no doubt about his meaning. But behind this apparent simplicity is a welter of thoughts, not easily or always reconcilable, and perhaps this is what gives zest to the essays in this volume. To understand these conflicts we have to know the man behind the thinker: the psychological approach he makes toward the problems of Hinduism; the historical background of his upbringing and the missionary zest with which he defends Hinduism, at other times criticizes it, and pleads for the right of all cultures to continue and yet pleads for an international culture, which would make our national patriotism a thing of the past.

It may not be out of place to trace the mental growth of Radhakrishnan. His birth almost synchronized with the birth of the Indian National Congress. Like most educated Indians he chafed under a sense of frustration inevitable under foreign domination, however benign it may have been. This was all the more inevitable because the system of education in vogue in India emphasized the superiority of Western culture and Western politics and made everything Indian look squalid and paltry. In the political climate of the country the tallest of Indians felt dwarfed, and the sense of humiliation stunted their mental growth. Countries in the West can afford to look upon their Nobel Laureates with a balanced pride and appreciation; they can hardly appreciate the mental revolution, therefore, that India underwent when Rabindranath Tagore was awarded a Nobel Prize for Literature. It gave a new pride to Indians, a new sense of life, a new hope for the future. Radhakrishnan too was affected by this. He set about conning Tagore's books and with the eye of a philosopher read more philosophy into Tagore than Tagore himself as a man of literature could have imagined. With his *Philosophy of Tagore* Radhakrishnan became famous overnight and started his brilliant career as a writer and as a philosopher. He was interested in picturing Tagore as a pure product of Indian culture, especially as envisaged in the *Upaniṣads*. The book was of importance inasmuch as its success encouraged him to dive deeper into the sources of Indian thought, culminating in the first volume of his *Indian Philosophy* five years later, in 1923. In the interval his studies in European philosophy took shape in his *The Reign of Religion in Contemporary Philosophy*. This appeared in 1920. It stands out by itself. As a devotee of pure philosophy, he found the reign of religion in much of the philosophy of that time as a disturbing factor, which did not make for true philosophy. It was not playing the game according to the rules, and he had to protest against "the interference of religious prejudice with the genuine spirit of speculation." [1] "A religious system, though the terminus of philosophic study, should not be its governing influence. It does not augur well for the future of either religion or philosophy, if religion becomes the starting point and dominating motive of philosophy." [2] The book as a whole left an impression on one's mind that Radhakrishnan looked upon religion as something cheap, not worthy of being taken seriously by any philosopher worth the name. A colleague of his in the University of Mysore felt impelled to ask: Is religion as bad as all that?

But this phase of his thought was only a passing mood. Every subsequent book from his pen has exalted religion as the most precious thing in life. The following quotations represent his crystallised view of religion, from which he has not swerved.

Religion is that knowledge of the essential nature of reality, that insight or penetration which satisfies not only a more or less powerful intellectual impulse in us, but that which gives to our very being the point of contact which it needs for its vital power, for the realisation of its true dignity, for its saving. [3]

[1] RR, vii.   [2] RR, 23.   [3] MST, 21 (1946 ed., 11).

"Religions attempt to satisfy this fundamental need of man by giving him a faith and a way of life, a creed and a community, and thus restore the relationship between him and the spiritual world above and the human world around." [4]

If, however, religion has had its full justification, it has left behind in Radhakrishnan's thought an unsolved conflict between intellect and intuition, or between logical reasoning and some deeper knowledge. With his deepening understanding of Hindu thought he had a certain revulsion of feeling against "intellectual ping-pong." "Unless we are illumined from the heights above, earth-born intellect cannot take us far." [5] "Religious experience is of a self-certifying character. It is *svatassiddha*." [6] But he immediately proceeds to say that a religious seer must have his convictions justified "in a way that satisfies the thought of the age. If there is not this intellectual confirmation, the seer's attitude is one of trust." [7] Similar see-saw statements are scattered throughout his works. It is the conflict between the man of thought and the man of religion. Nowhere has he been able to show a clear-cut method of confirming intuitions by logic. His final appeal is to the authority of prophets and mystics. There can be no harm in accepting this conflict as ultimate, if there is no means of overcoming it; but it is hardly justifiable to pour scorn on the effort of the philosopher to pierce through the mystery of life, as Radhakrishnan is tempted to do at times.

This emphasis on intuition has, however, helped him to be an effective expounder of Hinduism. The Indian in Radhakrishnan rebelled against the neglect into which the study of Indian philosophy had fallen, at least among the educated classes in India. Strong in his conviction that India has something to teach the world, even in the twentieth century, he displayed a missionary zeal to carry the message of India to the West. His erudition and eloquence found a place for Indian philosophy in the curricula of Western universities. I am here not concerned with the metaphysical aspect of Hinduism, except in so far as it bears on Radhakrishnan's social philosophy. The important point to note is that he accepts the supremacy of the spirit, and he envisages this spirit as God: "God is not the great silent sea of infinity in which the individuals lose themselves, but the Divine person who inspires the process first, last, and without ceasing. . . . God is a real symbol of the Absolute reality." [8] Radhakrishnan claims to be an

---

[4] ER, 39.   [5] EPW, 182.   [6] HVL, 15.
[7] HVL, 15f.   [8] MST, 40f (1946 ed., 31f).

Advaitin or a follower of Śaṁkara; but his theistic bias marks him out more as a follower of Rāmānuja, as has been noticed by many in India. In his presentation of Indian philosophy he was actuated by both a patriotic and a philosophic zeal. This comes out all the more clearly in his presentation of Hindu social philosophy, wherein he is apt in his earlier writings to gloss over the palpable shortcomings of Hindu society and over-emphasise several other aspects of it. His presentation of Hindu social philosophy has passed through three phases. The earliest phase is represented by his Upton Lectures, delivered at Oxford in 1926, and published as *The Hindu View of Life*. They have been extremely popular both in India and in the West. The popular vein in which they are composed may explain the naiveté of their assumptions. The book is more impressive than convincing. The second phase is more mature. For example, his *Eastern Religions and Western Thought*, where a philosophical justification of basic social ideas in Hinduism is attempted. This was in 1939. The third phase begins with his lectures in 1942, delivered at Calcutta and Banaras, and published under the title, *Religion and Society*. This latter publication is frank and outspoken in its showing up of various defects in Hindu social institutions. Whereas the previous works depicted an idealised Hindu society, existing neither on land nor sea, *Religion and Society* presents a realistic picture, and hence is of greater value; for the reformation of a society is of far greater significance than the attempt to make people believe that India had built up an ideal social organisation. It is, however, impossible to understand Hindu social philosophy without first understanding its background as presented by Hinduism.

WHAT IS HINDUISM?

This is not an easy question to answer. Nobody has quite succeeded in defining it, for it is not a creed associated with any particular prophet or teacher. It does not present a coherent or well-defined system of thought. As Radhakrishnan himself, with his usual felicity of language, puts it: it is "a name without a content." It is as indefinable as Europeanism or Occidentalism. "Hinduism has come to be a tapestry of the most variegated tissues and almost endless diversity of hues." [9] Within its spacious bosom Hinduism makes room for the highest philosophic thought as found in the Upaniṣads or the Gītā; it has a spiritual agnosticism

9 HVL, 20.

as in Advaita; it has pure theism as in Viśiṣṭadvaita or in Dvaita; it does not even repudiate animism or fetishism. "The deities of some men are in water (*i.e.*, bathing places), those of the more advanced are in the heavens, those of the children (in religion) are in images of wood and stone, but the sage finds his God in his deeper self." [10] It would be difficult indeed to get anything coherent out of such a heterogeneous mass of doctrines and practices. But Radhakrishnan does find in it certain basic ideas, the most prominent of them being the all-pervasiveness of spirit, an unaccountable feeling of "certain powers moving within us, we know not what, we know not why." [11] This very heterogeneity of content makes for tolerance. And Radhakrishnan spares no pains to emphasise this, especially for the benefit of countries which, in the name of religion, have not hesitated to torture, burn and kill so-called heretics. The history of Christian Churches and Islamic sects goes to bear this out. But Radhakrishnan does not seem to appreciate the fact that, where conversion is not permitted, toleration follows as a matter of course. On the other hand, when a Hindu has dared to go against his caste or creed, the spirit of tolerance has not always been exercised. No reformer in the long centuries of Hinduism has escaped the banter and the contempt of the orthodox or the tribulation which goes with an exquisitely organised excommunication. Radhakrishnan claims that Hinduism is a missionary religion, if not in the sense of individual proselytism, then at least in the sense that whole tribes or communities have been absorbed by Hinduism. He avers that the priests of such tribes were absorbed as Brahmins, and soldiers as Kshatriyas; only the rank and file were absorbed as Śūdras. It is, however, a matter of history that vast masses of the original non-Aryan population were absorbed by the Aryan fold as Śūdras, a class which was not included in the Vedic trivarṇikas (a threefold division of society, as contrasted with the later fourfold division). As against the old dogma of the Aryan superiority over the Dravidians, recent historical discoveries have gone to show that the Aryans were unable to resist the pressure of Dravidian ideas to such an extent that it has become a real riddle to determine with any definiteness whether the Hinduism of today is more Aryan or more Dravidian.

Another feature of Hinduism which Radhakrishnan emphasises is its democratic character. But this is a claim which is least defensible of all. If any society is organised on a definitely aristocratic basis, it is the Hindu society; and caste is inseparable from it. We

[10] HVL, 32.   [11] EPW, 98.

shall take up this subject more at length when we come to deal with Radhakrishnan's views on caste.

There is a marked difference between the earlier writings of Radhakrishnan and the later ones. In the former there is an emphasis on things Hindu. He does not care to conceal the pride he feels in his inheritance. "Half the world moves on independent foundations which Hinduism supplied." [12] "To obliterate every other religion than one's own is a sort of bolshevism in religion which we must try to prevent. We can do so *only*, if we accept something like the Hindu solution, which seeks the unity of religion not in a common creed but in a common quest." [13] "On the principle that the best is not the enemy of the good, Hinduism accepts all forms of belief and lifts them to a higher level." [14] This is certainly a questionable statement. For there has been a general tendency on the part of Hinduism to let sleeping dogs lie; and, on the plea that human beings are not all equal and are not all fit to achieve the highest truth, most of them have been left alone to go their own way. This explains why even in the twentieth century, after some millennia of Hindu Aryan contact with the non-Aryans, there are still some aboriginal tribes, the so-called "criminal tribes." The long train of untouchables, moreover, can hardly claim to have been lifted to a higher level.

Even at the time of his Upton Lectures (1926), from which we have quoted above, Radhakrishnan was not unconscious of the fact that everything was not all right "in the state of Denmark." He had to admit: "During the last few centuries Hinduism has not been faithful to its ideals, and the task of the uplift of the uncivilised has been sadly neglected." [15] And in his *Eastern Religions and Western Thought,* which may be said to be his most substantial work so far, he has a certain nostalgic feeling for the Hinduism of his dreams; he looks upon it as an open-sesame which could easily unlock the doors leading to happiness and provide a simple solution for all the social problems which afflict the world today. But if there is a conscious or unconscious emphasis on an idealised Hinduism in these works, in his *Religion and Society,* which contains lectures delivered in India, he comes forth as an outright critic of a Hinduism, which, if not exactly decadent, certainly does not live up to its highest teachings. We shall take due note of this in the proper place.

The Hindu view of the individual and his relation to society is

12 HVL, 12.   13 HVL, 58 (*italics* are ours).
14 HVL, 125.   15 HVL, 55.

presented by Radhakrishnan under the three main heads of (1) the four ends of life, (2) the fourfold order of society, and (3) the fourfold stages of life. We shall take up the first and third before dealing with the second, which latter is the most live aspect of current Hinduism.

THE FOUR ENDS OF LIFE

Radhakrishnan presents the four ends of life in the following order: *Mokṣa* (spiritual freedom), *Kāma* (desire and enjoyment), *Artha* (interest, wealth), *Dharma* (ethical living). Perhaps it would be more logical to deal with them in the following order: *Kāma, Artha, Dharma,* and *Mokṣa. Kāma* has to deal with our physical needs. It bears witness to the fact that a man must eat and drink before he can live, and he must satisfy his sex cravings if he is to maintain the continuity of his species. Similarly *Artha* makes for the material well-being of man. This is sound common sense. But Radhakrishnan cannot be said to be quite correct when he says: "There is little in Hindu thought to support the view that one has to attain spiritual freedom by means of a violent rupture with ordinary life;" [16] or "There was never in India a national ideal of poverty or squalor." [17] There is nothing to exalt in squalor as such; but there can be no denying that Hinduism has exalted the principle of poverty, closely associated with the stage of *saṁnyāsa* or renunciation. It is the claim of Hinduism, to which Radhakrishnan himself has given expression in another place, that the ideal of the Hindus is not the king or the knight or the merchant prince, but the wandering *saṁnyāsin*, whom the king comes down from the throne to welcome and willingly prostrates himself before him as a spiritual *guru* (teacher, preceptor). The names which Hindus adore are those of saints, recluses, and mystics who have lost themselves in the love of God. If Hindu social organisation has provided the pursuit of *Kāma* and *Artha*, this is only for the rank and file, a concession made to ordinary mortals, as contrasted with the spiritual elite. Rudyard Kipling, in his story of *The Miracle of Puran Bhagat*, shows a deep insight into Hindu psychology, the correctness of which most Hindus will readily admit. Gandhiji's appeal to the Indian masses lay in his half-nakedness, symbolic of poverty, a negation of wealth as a tribute to the life of the spirit.

Dharma stands for the moral government of life, which in practice is closely associated with the caste organization. *Mokṣa*, as the

[16] ER, 352.   [17] ER, 353.

pursuit of spiritual freedom from the cycle of births and deaths is the Hindu ideal *par excellence*. It gives meaning to the varied strands of Hindu life. It is generally conceived of as the reward which comes as the culmination of a series of lives, in which the soul has been fashioning and fitting itself for its ultimate destiny of *mokṣa*. Śaṁkara conceived this freedom as attainable in this life here and now and spoke of it as *jīvanmukti*. Radhakrishnan accepts this; he does not look upon this body or life as a hindrance to *mokṣa* but rather as the vehicle through which this freedom is to be achieved.

THE FOUR STAGES OF LIFE

This doctrine of the four stages of life is an interesting idea— in theory, at least. It divides a man's life into four stages. The first is that of *Brahmachārya,* when one is a student under a *guru* (preceptor), wholly devoted to his studies, away from his parents and untrammelled by any ties of wife or children. He serves the *guru* and receives knowledge. *Prima facie* this appears to be a universal feature for all Hindus; in actual practice, however, it was confined to the Brahmins or the Kshatriyas. Moreover, when infant marriages became the rule rather than the exception, the ideal of the Brahmachāri necessarily suffered. Yet, the ideal, whatever its practical limitations, was good in itself, emphasising as it did the importance of knowledge; even though this knowledge aimed at spiritual knowledge as found in the *Upaniṣads* or their Vedāntic offshoots. The other (lower) castes had to go through their apprenticeship in the arts and crafts within their own families, as handed down from generation to generation.

The student days, which went on till the early twenties, were followed by the householder stage, when a man married, reared a family, and earned his living. From the standpoint of society and social welfare this is the most valuable portion of a man's life. Galton deplored the loss that humanity suffered when monasticism in the Middle Ages took the best men and women in Europe away from family life. Radhakrishnan shares this view when he writes: "To withdraw the noblest elements of humanity from the married state to monkhood is biologically and socially unhealthy." [18] He goes on to say that "Hinduism does not demand withdrawal from life to mountain tops or gloomy caves as an essential condition for spiritual life. The way to a higher life is normally through the

18 ER, 379.

world." [19] I am afraid Radhakrishnan here goes beyond the normal facts which through the ages have been associated with Hinduism. We simply cannot deny the ascetic flavour of Hinduism. The third stage is that of the Forest Dweller, which represents really the stage of retirement from active life, when a man can meditate on life and death.

The fourth and last stage is that of the *Saṁnyāsin* or Monk. Though not every Hindu is expected to renounce "all possessions, distinctions of caste, and practices of religion," it is true that for every Hindu the *saṁnyāsin* represents the highest ideal of life. ". . . the life of the *saṁnyāsin* is the goal of man." He is Hinduism's "picture of the ideal man." "It is India's pride that she has clung fast to this ideal and produces in every generation and in every part of the country from the time of the Ṛṣis of the *Upaniṣads* and Buddha to Ramakrishna and Gandhi, men who strove successfully to realise this ideal." [20] All this eulogy is not quite consistent with what Radhakrishnan had to say about the importance of the householder, which latter certainly is more applicable to the requirements of life. But the ideal of renunciation has a great fascination for the Hindu mind. It would not be fair, therefore, to deny that *saṁnyāsins* have played a great part in the spiritual life of the Hindus. Although many of the *saṁnyāsins* really lead an idle life and sponge on the slender earnings of the masses, there have been quite a goodly number who have been great teachers, holding aloft the ideals of a high moral and spiritual life. However, most of them are wandering idlers, who have taken to *saṁnyās* as a cheap and easy profession.

It is clear, nonetheless, that in the end Radhakrishnan does not attach much importance to this doctrine of the four stages, for he looks upon them as just "helpful but not indispensable." [21] If *saṁnyās* comes at the end, it would imply that no Hindu can become a *saṁnyāsin*, unless he has passed through all the three preceding stages. Yet Śaṁkara himself did not think it necessary to be a householder; and countless others have thought it best to skip these intermediate stages and take *saṁnyās* straight off. Rightly conceived, as has been done by Tagore in his *Sadhana*, a *saṁnyāsin* can be a great active missionary of a noble life instead of merely one who has despaired of life and runs away from it to mountain tops or into the depths of forests to find a peace which he has failed to achieve in the rough and tumble of life. Although praising *saṁnyās* as the Hindu ideal of life, Radhakrishnan rightly

[19] ER, 380.   [20] ER, 381.   [21] ER, 382.

emphasises the point that "the world and its activities are no barriers to it but constitute the training ground." [22]

THE FOUR CASTES (OR: THE FOURFOLD ORDER OF SOCIETY)

No treatment of Hindu social philosophy can be complete without a more or less full account of what has come to be known as the Hindu caste system. In his *Eastern Religions and Western Thought* Radhakrishnan deliberately prefers to speak of classes rather than of castes. In fact, he even goes so far as to speak of caste as a degeneration of class. We shall have to see in how far this view is justifiable. In his treatment of castes Radhakrishnan does not present a consistent position. Very likely there is a consistency at the back of his mind, but his presentation of the subject differs according to the audiences he addresses, whether in the West or in India. One can note three strands in his treatment of caste. In his Upton Lectures, *The Hindu View of Life,* delivered at Oxford in 1926, he advances caste as a great achievement of the Hindu genius. This book is written in a rather popular vein. A decade later, in his *Eastern Religions and Western Thought,* he prefers to speak of class rather than caste and gives a valuable philosophical justification of it. Here he seems to be exalting the Brahmin and thus *prima facie* appears to justify a certain student's description of Radhakrishnan's philosophy as "the Brahmin philosophy." But this is, obviously, due to Radhakrishnan's use of common terms in rather uncommon ways. This becomes abundantly clear in his *Religion and Society* (1947), wherein he appears as a bitter critic of the traditional caste system and calls upon his countrymen to revise their ways of thinking or go under. In this book he emerges as a citizen of the world, looking with contempt upon the narrowness of castes or races or nations. In may be that, after painting the caste system in all its bright colours and rivetting upon it the admiration of Westerners, he could see more clearly how far short of his ideal the caste system of India has proved to be in its actual working. Even as early as 1926 he had already been conscious of the fact that the caste system had "now degenerated into an instrument of oppression and intolerance," and that it tended "to perpetuate inequality and develop the spirit of exclusiveness." [23]

The word *caste* itself is of Portuguese origin and has been used as a translation of the Sanskrit word *varṇa* which refers to colour.

[22] ER, 382.   [23] HVL, 93.

THE SOCIAL PHILOSOPHY OF RADHAKRISHNAN 767

In the days of the early Aryan settlements in India there was a clear-cut distinction between the fair Aryans and the dark non-Aryans, who were described as Dasyus. Hence came into being the fourth caste of the Śūdras, comprising the farmers and the artisans. But among the Aryans themselves there were only the three castes of the Brahmins, Kshatriyas and the Vaiśyas, representing the priests, the warriors, and the rest. However, when the farmers and the artisans came to be the Śūdras, the Vaiśyas came to comprise only the merchant or commercial section of the community. In the first place, then, this division was only a division of functions or occupations.

This racial distinction between the three major Aryan castes and the Dasyus as the Śūdras is looked upon by Radhakrishnan as a signal achievement of the Aryans in their then historical condition:

> The tribes were admitted into the larger life of Hinduism with the opportunities and the responsibilities which that life gave them, the opportunities to share in the intellectual and cultural life of the Hindus and the responsibilities of contributing to its thoughts, its moral advancement and its spiritual worth—in short to all that makes a nation's life. Each group dealt with the Hindu ideas in its own characteristic way. We need not overrate the stagnation of the aboriginal tribes. They were also raised above the welter of savagery and imbued with the spirit of gentleness.[24]

Radhakrishnan appreciatively quotes Sir Valentine Chirol's tribute to caste: "The supple and subtle forces of Hinduism had already in prehistoric times welded together the discordant beliefs and customs of a vast variety of races into a comprehensive fabric sufficiently elastic to shelter most of the indigenous populations of India, and sufficiently rigid to secure the Aryan Hindu ascendancy."[25] There have been other Englishmen who have more frankly stated that caste was the best ally of the English; for it effectually kept the Hindus disunited. It is also questionable whether Radhakrishnan's tribute to the ameliorative effects of caste can be taken at its face value. Thanks to the caste system scavengers have remained scavengers for centuries, and the savagery of the aboriginals has continued right down to the days of the British. Only very recently have the criminal tribes been reclaimed, thanks *not* to the caste system which gave them that so-called "freedom" to develop along their own lines, but due to the

24 HVL, 98.
25 HVL, 98, quoted from *India: Old and New* (1921: 42f) by Valentine Chirol.

strong British rule, which would not tolerate the continued depre-
dations of these tribes according to their own customs.

The fundamental characteristic of caste is its hereditary nature,
buttressed by the rules of marriage permissible only within a caste,
and only even within a sub-caste. In his *Hindu View of Life*
Radhakrishnan states the fact that "the Hindu theory of caste does
not favour the indiscriminate crossing of men and women," [26]
and holds up to scorn, as the result of indiscriminate crossing, "the
deplorable example of the Eurasians." [27] This is not fair to the
Eurasians, who are a well educated community and many of whom
have risen to high posts and distinguished themselves in various
directions, especially as contrasted with the generation-to-genera-
tion backwardness of millions and millions of Śūdras and untouchables, which has been so sedulously fostered by the caste system.
Radhakrishnan should not have failed to note the new cry of
Dravidistan, which may be political in its origin, but which is
nourished by the idea that after four thousand years Aryans and
Dravidas have not sufficiently mixed either in blood or in ideas
to constitute one people.

From the economic standpoint there is much to be said in
favour of caste, provided it is not indissolubly associated with the
principle of heredity. Radhakrishnan is quite conscious of this
limitation. Although, in *The Hindu View of Life*, this limitation
is kept more in the background, it is by no means repudiated. On
the contrary, Radhakrishnan finds the justification of heredity in
the law of Karma, according to which "individual life is not a
term, but a series. Fresh opportunities will be open to us until we
reach the end of the journey. The historical forms we assume will
depend on our work in the past." [28] If this is to be taken literally,
it would imply that Hinduism offers the reward of Brahminic
birth to millions of Śūdras and untouchables in the course of centuries and millennia of births and deaths. Until then the birth
into a particular caste is to be taken as a certificate of fitness to
continue only in that caste; and until then the thus born is to be
content with performing the *dharma* of that caste. This belief finds
a theoretical justification in the doctrine of *karma* and rebirth,
but is refuted by the facts of life. For there are many Brahmins in
whom there is nothing Brahminic, and many Śūdras in whom
there are many Brahminic qualities. But, to the orthodox Hindu,
the former do not cease to be Brahmins nor do the latter cease to
be Śūdras. Radhakrishnan is fully conscious of these facts, and in

[26] HVL, 99.   [27] HVL, 100.   [28] HVL, 126.

his later works he repudiates the principle of heredity. But he often talks and writes as if caste based on heredity were a divine dispensation and a monument to Hindu wisdom. Towards the end of his Upton Lectures he admits that

Today we seem to be afraid of ourselves, and are therefore clinging to the shell of our religion for self-preservation. The envelope by which we try to protect life checks its expansion. . . . An institution appropriate and wholesome for one stage of human development becomes inadequate and even dangerous when another stage has been reached.[29]

These wise remarks are most pertinent with reference to caste, and, very likely, Radhakrishnan had caste most in mind. But his general praise of the caste system has successfully, though unfortunately, created an impression in the minds of most people that he favours caste. Consequently the orthodox look up to him as the champion of Hinduism, of which the caste system is regarded as the basic principle; whereas heterodox Hindus have been looking upon his philosophy as "the Brahmin philosophy."

In his *Eastern Religions and Western Thought* Radhakrishnan becomes self-conscious, eschews the word *caste,* and prefers to speak of *classes.* The account that he gives of classes is indeed very good and applies universally to all human societies. In this universalised form of a society divided on the basis of occupational functions, the idea is, of course, found everywhere: in Plato's *Republic,* in the feudal societies of mediaeval Europe, as also in the most democratic states of today or even in Communistic Russia; except that in the latter priests have lost the supremacy which they enjoyed in the early societies. In all this there is nothing specifically Hindu. What differentiates a class from a caste is the extreme emphasis on heredity in the caste, which results in endogamy—every man must marry only a woman of his own caste or even sub-caste— and commensal restrictions, which latter prohibit a person of one caste from sitting at a meal with persons of other castes or eating food prepared by a person belonging to a lower caste or sub-caste. Radhakrishnan repudiates all these characteristics so fundamental to the very conception of caste in Hinduism. He argues that Vedic India did not know caste in its present rigidity. But he himself cites the authority of Megasthenes on the heredity of caste; and this goes back to some two or three centuries before Christ. Radhakrishnan also admits that "caste in its rigour became established

29 HVL, 128.

by the time of Manu and the Puranas, which belong to the period of the Gupta kings (330 to 450 A.D.)." [30] It is quite clear, therefore, that castes are not a degeneration of the classes brought about by the degeneracy of the present days or of the last two or three centuries. What has characterised Hinduism for weal or for woe during the last 2,500 years, long before the days of the Muslim or the European invasions of India, has a right to be called really Hindu; and it is therefore that caste, and *not* class, is the typically Hindu social organisation with its endogamy and commensal restrictions. In fact, Radhakrishnan himself seems to justify endogamy, at least as suited to those times, when he writes:

Caste was the Hindu answer to the challenge of society in which different races had to live together without merging into one. The difficulty of determining the psychological basis led to the acceptance of birth as the criterion. . . . Besides, as the types fix themselves, their maintenance by education and tradition becomes necessary and hereditary grooves are formed.[31]

Thus, after repudiating the principle of heredity, Radhakrishnan seeks to justify it; his treatment of the four "classes," therefore, is coloured by this justification.

The Brahmins as conceived by Radhakrishnan are "pre-eminently intellectual" and their function is

to seek and find knowledge, communicate it to others, and make it prevail in the world. . . . The true Brahmin is said to be one who has sensed the deepest self and acts out of that consciousness. . . . The Brahmins give moral guidance. They reveal but do not enforce. Practical administration is not their task. They keep clear of the love of power as well as the pressure of immediate needs.[32]

All this is in conflict with the facts of Indian history. For, while the kings ruled and fought, the power behind the throne was that of the Brahmin ministers; they loved and enjoyed power as much as any minister can. This has, in fact, characterised Indian history from the days of Chanakya of *Artha Śāstra* fame to the days of the Peshwas, the last Hindu rulers to fall before the British. There are passages in the epics and other writings which seek to emphasise the purely moral make-up of the true Brahmin, in whom honesty, truthfulness, and all conceivable virtues are pictured as finding their natural home. But in actual Hindu society a Brahmin remains a Brahmin and is honoured as a Brahmin, however im-

30 ER, 372.   31 ER, 373.   32 ER, 357.

moral he may be and however far removed from the "true Brahmin."

The second caste is that of the Kshatriyas, or soldiers and rulers. The Rajputs are usually looked upon as the cream of the Hindu Kshatriyas; so much so that when a Śūdra, by dint of his genius, carved out a kingdom for himself he would try to prove his Rajput descent. Though in strict theory the Kshatriyas are inferior to the Brahmins—and this inferiority has been willingly accepted even by the proudest Kshatriyas—it is pertinent to note that in the early history of caste there was a continuous struggle between the two castes for supremacy. In this connection the historic struggle between Vaśiṣṭha and Viśvāmitra is interesting. The latter was not a Brahmin; but by virtue of his ascetic practices he had attained a certain prestige and power; and he therefore claimed to be a Brahmin, a claim which was resisted by his antagonist. But ultimately Vaśiṣṭha had to yield. This story has a double implication. It establishes the superiority of the Brahmins; but it also proves that a non-Brahmin by means of his worth can rise to be recognised as a Brahmin. Whereas the former is a historic fact, the latter is an aspiration. It is an irony of Indian history that the greatest names even in the history of Indian philosophy are not those of Brahmins but of Kshatriyas. In the *Upaniṣads,* which constitute the very fountainhead of Indian philosophy, no names are more honoured than those of Janaka and Ajātaśatru, who were both Kshatriyas. Buddha, the greatest Indian ever born, and Mahāvīra, the founder of Jainism, were both Kshatriyas. These names constitute an effective refutation of the hereditary claims of Brahmin superiority. Coming to our own times, we have the case of Mahatma Gandhi, who was a Vaiśya, but rose to be a leader and teacher of all Indians, including Brahmins.

In the scheme of castes it was the duty of the Kshatriyas to fight for and defend their country. There is an interesting story narrated of Radhakrishnan himself. While talking to a Maharajah about the fall of the Hindu kingdoms and their inability to resist foreign invaders, Radhakrishnan is reported to have said: "We fell because the Kshatriyas failed the country." *Prima facie* this brings out the inherent weakness of the caste system with its exclusive emphasis on specialised functions. In actual history this specialisation failed again and again. Brahmins like the Peshwas had to fight as much as the Kshatriyas; and at two critical junctures in India's history, Chandragupta and Śivāji, both Śūdras, and Gandhi, a Vaiśya, had to come forth as the saviours of their country and their religion.

The very recognition of the warrior caste raises the question whether it is not against the ideal of *Ahiṁsā* or non-violence, which is claimed to be the distinctive Hindu ideal. Radhakrishnan adopts a common sense attitude in dealing with this contradiction. He waxes eloquent over *Ahiṁsā;* Buddha and Gandhi become his heroes, and even the teaching of the *Gītā* can be adroitly put forth as preaching *Ahiṁsā.* But he does not go so far as Gandhiji in his repudiation of force in "this imperfect world." He is content to preach *Ahiṁsā* as the grand ideal of life; but points out the limitation of non-violence as a weapon of political agitation, when he says: "In this imperfect world, however, the non-resisters are able to practise their convictions only because they owe their security to the maintenance by others of the principles which they repudiate." [33] He goes on to say that

The use of force is limited to occasions where it is the only alternative and is applied for the sake of creating a more suitable environment for the growth of moral values and not for activities which can hardly fail to result in social chaos. Force, when employed, must be employed in an ethical spirit. The use of force does not become permissible simply because it has an ethical aim. It must be employed in an ethical way.[34]

If this were all that Radhakrishnan has said for *Ahiṁsā,* no one could take issue with him; but, of course, such a qualified *Ahiṁsā* is not merely the teaching of *all* religions, but even the greatest warmongers could justify their misdeeds on the grounds of "creating a more suitable environment." How easily God can be invoked by warring parties has been beautifully caricatured by Sir John Squire:

> To God th' embattled nations sing and shout,
> "Gott strafe England" and "God save the King,"
> "God this" and "God that" and "God the other thing."
> "Good God," said God, "I've got my work cut out."

Radhakrishnan also recognises the weakness involved in the specialisation of functions:

People were allowed to manage their affairs in accordance with their traditional rules and customs. They did not care who the rulers were so long as their lives were undisturbed. One flag was as good as another, if social life was carried on in the same way. This attitude has made the country a prey to invaders.[35]

[33] ER, 361.   [34] ER, 362.   [35] ER, 362.

In this one sentence he brings out the real weakness of the caste system.

The third caste is that of the Vaiśyas or merchants. It is their *dharma* to make money and they have practised it with a vengeance. The worship of Lakshmi as the goddess of wealth tries to give a religious veneer to a naked materialism. Radhakrishnan, as a moralist, may say that "if they are keen on wealth for its own sake, they are to be detested." [36] But people who are conscious of their money-making functions are not deterred by moral considerations, especially when they know that the power of money makes the spiritual Brahmins and the knightly Kshatriyas bow to their will. This is, of course, true throughout the world; but in India the greed of the Vaiśyas stands out in lurid colours as a feature of caste.

Speaking of the fourth caste, the Śūdras, Radhakrishnan begins with the statement:

A fourth variety of human nature finds its outlet in work and service. Labour is the basis of all human relations. While the first three classes are said to be twice-born, the fourth is said to be once born and so inferior. It only means that the activities of the numbers of the fourth class are instinctive and not governed by ideals of knowledge, strength, or mutual service.[37]

This implies a plain recognition of the unfortunate fact that in the hierarchy of caste in India, the Śūdras do occupy an inferior position. Nor can this inferiority be glossed over by glibly speaking of "the dignity of labour." The truth is that in the orthodox Hindu economy this dignity of labour is not recognised. In fact, all honest labour, although used to the fullest extent, is looked down upon with more or less open contempt. In the *Gītā*, which is an attempt to break down the inequalities of caste, Krishna himself classes women and Śūdras together, but promises that "even" they can find refuge in Him! This attitude of the higher castes is all the more perplexing when we remember that this caste (the Śūdras) includes all the basic vocations which alone can guarantee the maintenance of a healthy society; for it includes farmers, peasants, weavers, potters, masons, carpenters, and a whole army of most useful, hardworking, and honest workers. The extreme emphasis on learning as the occupation of the Brahmins has given a strange twist to Hindu society. Even Radhakrishnan himself admits that it is only "as the result of the liberalising influence of Western civilisa-

36 ER, 363. 37 ER, 364.

tion" [38] that the dignity of labour has come to be recognised and
the non-Brahmin movement has come into being as a revolt against
all the pretensions of the Brahmins through the ages. In Romesh
Chandra Dutt of the last generation, one of the finest products of
modern India, we find an expression of the weaknesses of caste on
its debit side. According to him Yajnavalkya looks upon a large
number of professions as impure, so much so that the food cooked
by people of these professions cannot be touched by the pure. At
this point Romesh Dutt proceeds:

> It is with pain that the historian of the Hindus finds in this passage all
> mechanical arts, trades, and industries classed with prostitution and
> crime. For the list includes misers, men in fetters, thieves, eunuchs, ac-
> tors, workers in leather (Vainas), men who are cursed, Vardushis, pros-
> titutes, men who initiate indiscriminately, physicians, diseased men,
> ill-tempered men, faithless women, drunkards, envious men, cruel and
> violent men, outcasts, Vratyas, conceited men, impure eaters, unpro-
> tected women, goldsmiths, hen-pecked husbands, indiscriminate priests,
> . . . How many honest trades do we find in this list of despised pro-
> fessions? [39]

No wonder that Dutt speaks out bitterly, thus:

> The results were disastrous so far as the arts were concerned. Genius
> was impossible except among priests and kings. Men held in a perpetual
> moral bondage and servitude never learnt to aspire after greatness and
> glory. Men to whom honour was impossible never learnt to deserve
> honour and distinction. In other countries a Cincinnatus might leave
> his plough and wield the destinies of his nation, or a Robert Burns
> might give expression to a nation's sentiments in thoughts that breathe
> and words that burn; but in India the cultivator's fate was sealed; he
> could never break through the adamant wall of social rules. Among
> other people a sculptor, a painter or an architect, like Phoedias or
> Praxiteles, like Raphael or Michael Angelo, might by the force of his
> genius win the highest honour in his country. But in India that highest
> honour was the exclusive privilege of the Brahmin and the Kshatriya;
> honour to an architect, to a sculptor was simply out of the question. [40]

These are burning words. How true they are can be gauged by the
fact that, although we stand in mute admiration of the wonderful
specimens of Hindu artistic genius, we do not even know the names
of these geniuses.

Radhakrishnan gives a philosophical justification of castes as a
hierarchy.

38 RS, 133.   39 R. C. Dutt, *Civilization in Ancient India*, Vol. III, 318.
40 *Ibid.*, Vol. III, 146f.

Hierarchy is not a coercion but a law of nature. The four classes repre-sent four stages of development in our manhood. . . . Highest of all is the Brahmin, who brings a spiritual rule into life. Though something of all these four is found in all men in different degrees of development, one or the other tends to predominate in the dealings of the soul with its embodied nature, and that becomes the basis for future development. As he unfolds and grows man changes his status and class.[41]

In a footnote he quotes from the *Mahābhārata* to show how a Brahmin by his misdeeds falls into a lower caste and how a man of lower caste can rise to a higher caste. But, as already noted above, this is only a pious wish. In actual Hindu society a change of castes is left only to future births; in the present life a man has to remain in the caste into which he is born. But the effect of even this pious wish is lost when Radhakrishnan proceeds to say:

If one who is of a lower nature desires to perform the social tasks of a higher class, before he has attained the answering capacities, *social order will be disturbed.* To fight is a sin for a Brahmin but not for a Kshatriya, whose function is to fight without ill will for a righteous cause, when there is no other course. . . . To follow the law of an-other's nature is dangerous. . . . The fourfold classification is against modern notions of conscription where every one is obliged to take to military service, or universal suffrage where ruling power is distributed among all. In the natural hierarchy there cannot be one moral standard for all. . . . Every man had his place in society and fixed duties at-tached to it.[42]

All of this is intelligible in the context of the strict Hindu the-ory of caste. But it is difficult to admit, with Radhakrishnan, that "In a real sense the fourfold scheme is democratic." [43] Radhakrish-nan offers some five grounds for this view.[44] In the *first* place, he finds in it the spiritual equality of all men. But this has to be taken with a grain of salt; for *prima facie* only the Brahmin is born in a setting where he can proceed with his spiritual development. If others tried to hasten their spiritual development, there would arise the risk of "the social order being disturbed."

Secondly, it is claimed that the fourfold scheme "makes for indi-viduality in the positive sense. Individuality is attained not through an escape from limitations but through the willing acceptance of obligations." [45] But, if caste is determined by birth and birth deter-mines functions, then it should be clear that there is no room here for a "willing acceptance of obligations," except in the sense that

41 ER, 366.
43 ER, 367-9.
42 ER, 367 (*italics* not in original).
44 ER, 367f.
45 ER, 367f.

the average Hindu is a patient sufferer and, until lately, did not bother to break his head against the stone wall of caste.

"*Thirdly* it points out that all work is socially useful and from an economic standpoint equally important." [46] This can hardly be adduced as an argument for the democratic nature of caste; since it is equally, and perhaps even more, pertinent to an aristocratic organisation of society.

Fourthly, it is argued that "social justice is not a scheme of rights but of opportunities." [47] Every historic democracy in the West has been more insistent on rights than on duties, and this fact is cited as a weakness of democracy by its critics. On the other hand, it is most questionable whether caste in India has operated in favour of social justice.

Fifthly, Radhakrishnan tells us, "the essence of democracy is consideration for others." [48] It is quite dubious, however, whether the intellectual exclusiveness of the caste system, as displayed in its matrimonial or commensal restrictions and its appendage of untouchability and even unapproachability, can accept this compliment with a clear conscience. If Kautilya discusses the theory of social contract, his whole *Artha Śāstra,* like Machiavelli's *Prince,* is a glorification of the monarch. What else, moreover, can be expected of a minister of Chandragupta? Radhakrishnan cites the existence of old village communities and *panchayats* in ancient India as proofs of a living democracy in India. But such primitive democracy is to be found even today in the savage tribes of Africa and Australia. In the prevailing climate of such communities, built upon caste in ancient India, there was a tendency to perpetuate the inequalities rather than ameliorate the inequalities of the caste system. It is very strange that, with the history of caste for over 3,000 years before him—a system which has seen the supremacy of caste feeling asserting itself time and again against the real democratic movements of Buddha and Mahāvīra, Krishna and the Vaishnavites, Kabir and Guru Nānak, Raja Ram Mohun Roy and Tagore—Radhakrishnan should find it possible to say: "A strange impression prevails that in India caste prevented the development of democratic institutions." [49] There is nothing "strange" about this impression; for the whole history of political India stands witness to it. Did not Radhakrishnan himself attribute the political misfortunes of India to the failure of the Kshatriyas, as if they alone had to fight while others proceeded with their peaceful occupations? In fact, he himself quotes James Kerr, the Principal of

---

[46] ER, 368.   [47] ER, 368.   [48] ER, 368.   [49] ER, 369.

the Hindu College at Calcutta, who, as far back as 1865, wrote: "It may be doubted if the existence of caste is on the whole unfavourable to the permanence of our rule. It may even be considered favourable to it, provided we act with prudence and forbearance. Its spirit is opposed to national union." [50]

It is indeed possible to say a great many things in favour of caste, and many orthodox Hindus have done so. Aristocrats like Nietzsche and his ilk in Europe can certainly look upon caste as something divine. Radhakrishnan too could have taken this stand; but he has weakened his position by trying to see in caste a reconciliation of aristocracy and democracy. Mahatma Gandhi gave a reality to his political agitation not merely by abusing the British rule, but by recognising the iniquity of caste towards the untouchables and by converting, if not the whole of Hindu India, at least the vocal and influential sections of Hindus sufficiently so that, *on paper at least,* untouchability has become a crime. It is for the future to decide whether Gandiji has succeeded in his crusade against caste, or whether he will figure merely as one more of the heroic Indians who have battled for the right and paid for it with their lives.

It has been necessary to criticise Radhakrishnan's exaltation of caste as mere class. But we gladly admit that, in his *Religion and Society,* he emerges as a critic of caste (although even in his *Eastern Religions and Western Thought* he had tried to make out that the class that he eulogised was something different from the caste as found in actual Hindu society). Gandhiji and Radhakrishnan are both in the Indian tradition when they use old words with new connotations and thus present themselves as true (*i.e.,* orthodox) Hindus, although, in fact, they have risen far above the orthodoxy of traditional Hinduism. There is hardly a rule of caste which Gandhiji did not break; and almost the same could be said of Radhakrishnan. What they praise in caste is not what they practise; for the catholicity of both is far removed from the soul-killing aloofness of caste. Both have had to face an inner tussle between a wish to be true to Hindu traditions and a wish to be alive to the demands of the present. The result is a bewildering conflict of statements, rendered all the more bewildering in Radhakrishnan by his habit of putting a certain facet of thought as forcibly as possible, leaving it to others to make what they can out of these contradictions. This may explain why an orthodox Brahmin like Pandit Madan Mohun Malaviya, a thorough-going reformer like Gandhiji, and a secular Hindu like Pandit Jawaharlal Nehru, all

50 ER, 376.

feel equally attracted by him; for each can pick out of Radhakrishnan's writings whatever suits him. The same may be said of Western scholars who see in his presentation of Hinduism a real universalism; whereas in actual historical fact Hinduism has not been able to rise above the national level, in which the Himalayas and the rivers of India are the foci of worship.

After having done his best to give an air of respectability to caste, in his *Religion and Society* Radhakrishnan emerges as an enlightened critic of caste. He admits that in the days of the *Ṛg Veda* there was a certain mobility about caste, which was lost by the time of the *Brāhmaṇas*, when "the four classes became separated into rigid groups dependent on birth." [51] Now the *Brāhmaṇas* go back to some centuries before the birth of Christ; consequently, citing the mobility of castes as a feature of the system hardly carries conviction. Moreover, the rigidity of the groups was followed by certain characteristics of caste which even the patriotism of Radhakrishnan could not overlook. He is forced to admit that "Whatever the intentions were, caste developed a sense of false pride, and led to the humiliation of the lower classes." [52] And again: "Caste divisions have prevented the development of homogeneity among the Hindus. To develop a degree of organic wholeness and a sense of common obligation, the caste spirit must go. We have to get rid of the innumerable castes and outcasts, with their spirit of exclusiveness, jealousy, greed and fear." [53]

The sin of untouchability is degrading and the prejudice should be removed. . . . Any discrimination against the Harijans is unjustified. . . . Places of worship, public wells, and public utilities such as cremation grounds and bathing ghats, hotels and educational institutions, should be open to all. . . . What is being done today is a question not of justice or charity, but of atonement. Even when we have done all that is in our power, we shall not have atoned even for a small fraction of our guilt in this matter.[54]

It is refreshing to find that the philosopher in search of truth has triumphed over the mere patriot in Radhakrishnan. Whatever harm his former justification of caste may have done should now be effectually undone by so open and frank an admission of guilt perpetrated in the course of centuries in the name of religion by orthodox Hindus. The orthodox have not hesitated to cite the authority of the *Bhagavadgītā* in justification of castes by birth. But Radhakrishnan's comment on the verse, IV, 13, is suggestive:

51 RS, 130.   52 RS, 132.   53 RS, 133.   54 RS, 134f.

"cāturvarnyam: the fourfold order. The emphasis is on guna (aptitude) and karma (function) and not on jāti (birth)." [55]

WOMEN

We may now pass to the next important item in Radhakrishnan's social philosophy and that concerns the status of women. Here too the ideal as portrayed by Radhakrishnan is different from that represented in the current Hindu Law, for which latter the British Courts cannot be held wholly or even mainly responsible. That the marriage *ideal* among Hindus is very high must be conceded; but in practice this ideal loses much of its worth when, till only yesterday, polygamy was sanctioned, infant marriages were common, and women were left in ignorance and valued more as housewives than as human beings with inherent rights of their own. Not so many years ago a highly placed (though now deceased) Hindu, and a Western university graduate besides, married a second wife not merely while the first one was still living, and without having procured a divorce from her, but also without in any way providing for her support. Quite naturally this brought on adverse comments. When a Hindu savant deplored this in my presence, I replied sarcastically that it could not be wrong inasmuch as Hindu law allowed it. His answer was significant: "Law is alright," he said, "but what about the whole ideal of Rāmāyana?" When Hindus brag about the sanctity of marriage and its indissoluble character, it must be remembered that this means nothing to a man who can marry as many wives as his nature and purse will permit. It only means that the Hindu wife, however unhappy and miserable her marriage, has no way out of it; for Hindu sentiment has been against divorce and even against widow re-marriage. At this point too the ancient practice was more liberal.

Radhakrishnan offers a very plausible explanation for the later ideas. "The permission for separation and divorce was superseded by the doctrine of the indissolubility of the marriage bond, due perhaps to the fear of the fascination of the monastic life exalted by Buddhism." [56] There certainly can be no doubt that the Muslim conquest of India worked disastrously for Hindu women, for infant marriages became then the fashion. This naturally retarded women's education. The evils of polygamy, moreover, enhanced by the prohibition of widow re-marriage, have worked disastrously. No wonder that the modern educated Hindu woman has begun

55 BG, 160.   56 RS, 182.

to object to an unjust order which has nothing but the halo of time to give it a semblance of respectability. Radhakrishnan is in favour of monogamy, although he is not prepared to look upon it as "natural."

> We assume that monogamy is natural. It is not quite so simple. We have passions. Fidelity, though essential, is not easy. . . . The tribulations of love are admitted to be beautiful, but not moral. Unless we have tolerance for breakdowns we are not sufficiently human. Socrates was more significant than Miletus, who was only a moral person. Jesus had greater goodness than the Pharisee, who was only conventially correct. If love without marriage is illegal, marriage without love is immoral. . . . There are two kinds of morality, the absolute one of right and the relative one of social convention, which each society construes in its own way. Through the observance of moral rules we must approximate to the ideal, which is the holy more than the moral, the beautiful more than the correct, the perfect more than the adequate, love more than law.[57]

After this comment Radhakrishnan has a word in praise of self-restraint, for "civilisation is man's gradual mastery over savage nature." [58] This was in December 1942. In 1926, in his *Hindu View of Life,* he spoke in a more heroic, if less romantic, vein:

> Marriage is not the end of the struggle, it is but the beginning of a strenuous life where we attempt to realise a larger ideal by subordinating our private interests and inclinations. Service of a common ideal can bind together the most unlike individuals. Love demands its sacrifices. By restraint and endurance, we raise love to the likeness of the divine.[59]

This is a safer generalisation on marriage than the one based on the love of Abelard or of Anna Karenina.

Consistent with his human approach towards the problem of marriage, Radhakrishnan is not against divorce, although the average Hindu, man and woman alike, have looked upon it with horror and many still do.

> For two people to remain together in unhappiness, because they have entered into a bond which only death can break, is a sin against the best in us. It sometimes blasts the soul. It is better for the children that unhappy parents should not live together. Our laws make havoc of our domestic intimacies, in deference to dogmas we no longer respect.[60]

But in the very next sentence Radhakrishnan strikes a different note.

[57] RS, 192f.　　[58] RS, 197.　　[59] HVL, 85.　　[60] RS, 182.

To allow divorces freely would be to damage social stability. It is a question whether increased divorce facilities in the West have added appreciably to the sum of human happiness, or at any rate diminished human unhappiness. On the sanctity of marriage depend the practice of the domestic virtues, the integrity of the family, and the rearing of children.[61]

Radhakrishnan therefore advises people to approach marriage "in a sacramental spirit." On the whole he wants a change in the Hindu Law, which would permit divorce "where married life is absolutely impossible," [62] and he would permit re-marriage to the divorced. He wants monogamy established by law, for such a reform "is long overdue." [63] He is proud of the fact that "stable marriages are more numerous" [64] among Indians; and he attributes this "largely to the character of Indian women, who are miracles of dignity, graciousness, and peace." [65] It is a real question, however, whether this state of affairs can be attributed so easily to the superiority of Hindu women, or whether the utter helplessness of Indian women, uneducated, unfit to shoulder by themselves the burdens of life, and their complete dependence on fathers, husbands or sons, have not also been contributory factors. For in recent years, as women have begun at least to get an education, there has also come a greater degree of economic independence for women; the will to put up with the cruelty or whims of husbands has markedly declined, and divorce has lost its old evil odour. At the same time it must be admitted that Hindu women in the course of history have displayed an amazing capacity for suffering and a surprising ability to love even unlovable husbands. The average Hindu woman is markedly superior to the average Hindu man. Séta can claim superiority even over Rama. The pity of it is that Hindu men have not proved themselves worthy of such wonderful devotion.

With the emphasis on the ideal of saṁnyās that Hindu psychology has tended to foster, the day to day requirements of ordinary social life have also come to receive due recognition. It is odd that the country which has exalted asceticism has also produced a classic

in erotics like *Kāma Śāstra*. Radhakrishnan looks upon this as presenting "us with those stirrings of the human heart that make life so full and poignant." [66] But when he goes on to speak of its

61 *Ibid.*
63 RS, 184f.
65 *Ibid.*

62 RS, 184.
64 RS, 184.
66 RS, 149.

"passionate spiritual serenity" (*ibid.*), one is tempted to say with Hamlet's mother, "me thinks the lady protests too much."

There is no problem which confronts India today with greater difficulties than that of her steadily increasing population. Birth control is looked upon by many as irreligious; and some economists try to belittle the gravity of the situation by talking of the vast undeveloped resources of India. It would, of course, be far better if those resources were actually developed first before blessing an embarrassing increase in the population to the tune of five million per year. There are some eminent Indian leaders today, who, blessed with large families themselves, advise young couples to practise self-restraint. Mahatma Gandhi was fond of this advice. It is all the more refreshing to note, therefore, that, with all his enthusiasm for Gandhiji, Radhakrishnan deals with this problem in a far more human and scientific manner.

Here, as in other cases, what is ideal is different from what has to be permitted. The indissolubility of marriage is the ideal; but, in certain circumstances, divorces have to be permitted. So also control of births by abstinence is the ideal, and yet the use of contraceptives cannot be altogether forbidden. . . . It is wrong to think that sexual desire in itself is evil, and that virtue consists in dominating and suppressing it on principle. Marriage is not only for physical reproduction, but also for spiritual development. Men and women want each other as much as they want children. To remove from the lives of masses of men and women their one pleasure would be to produce an enormous amount of physical, mental and moral suffering.[67]

He quotes the authority of a great physician like Lord Dawson: ". . . birth control by abstention is either ineffective or, if effective, pernicious." [68] One feels in this treatment of a delicate problem the breath of fresh air, when ordinarily a good deal of nonsense comes to be passed off as moral or religious wisdom, and this in an age when psychoanalysis has laid bare the mischief that repression can play in the life of men and women. One cannot but appreciate the healthy sanity of Radhakrishnan's approach to problems which are apt to be fogged by old traditions and so-called "religious" prejudices.

RADHAKRISHNAN AS A SOCIAL PHILOSOPHER

In view of the great service Radhakrishnan has rendered to his country by his intensive study of Indian philosophy, metaphysical

67 RS, 189f.   68 RS, 190.

and social, and popularising it in the West, he can deservedly be called a philosopher of Hinduism. But there is abundant evidence in his writings to show that his studies have not been confined only to things Indian. In virtue of the English education in vogue in India, his familiarity with Western classics need not cause any surprise. His extensive reading and his remarkable memory are responsible for the endless quotations from authors from China to Peru and for the happy allusions which give such a charm to his writings. But the Hinduism which he has sought to teach the world is something distinctive to himself; not quite the same as the Hinduism of history. In this he was true to the Hindu tradition of using the same words but with a new connotation.[69] This explains the psychology behind the endless commentaries on the *Upaniṣads* and even more on the *Gītā*. But the Hinduism that Radhakrishnan expounds is so divested of the peculiarities which characterise the Hinduism of history that it comes to have a universal character; so that not merely a Hindu, but a Christian and a Muslim too can claim this Hinduism to be his own.[70] This universality makes Radhakrishnan a citizen of the world, equally at home in Banaras or at Oxford. He is prepared to accept whatsoever is beautiful and good and true and wheresoever found, so that for him "the varied cultures are but dialects of a single speech of the soul." [71] Out of these dialects he sees springing into being "a new humanism on the horizon," [72] which he finds embracing the whole of mankind.

Radhakrishnan's philosophy is fundamentally religious. But religion for him is not a matter of fasts and pilgrimages, of mumbling of prayers or worship in temples. "The religion of the truly religious . . . has for its practical expression the maxim: 'He that does good is of God.' " [73] Consistent with this dictum he suffuses his religious philosophy with a broad humanism in his very interesting autobiographical essay, entitled *My Search for Truth*, contained in the volume on *Religion in Transition* (edited by Vergilius Ferm). "God does not think less of people because they are poor or unintelligent. What matters is whether we have been

69 Vide my *Religion as a Quest for Values,* Lecture III, for a more detailed treatment.

70 "If what he describes in such masterly English and in such a scholarly and lucid way really be Hinduism, then there are many thousands of Friends who belong to that religion, though they call themselves Christians." In a review of Radhakrishnan's *The Hindu View of Life* in *Friend.*

71 ER, 350.   72 ER, vii.   73 RS, 47.

kind to others and honest and sincere with ourselves and in our intimate relations with others." [74]

There follows a beautiful word painting of sorrow-laden men, whose smiles cover only bleeding hearts, and who grow lonelier the older they become. "A nameless sadness weighs them down and they seem to grow indifferent to every feeling except a faint yearning to be at peace and dead. To the eye that has learnt to read the heart, their frivolous excitement, their gaiety and laughter is only a mask." [75] In all this the inherent sadness of the Indian heart finds expression, as it did in Buddha 2,500 years ago, and in the generations of Hindu mystic poets who have looked upon this world as a passing show of sad joys and frustrations, only to end, not merely with this life, but only with the end of the whole cycle of births and deaths. But behind this sorrow is a great experience and a great opportunity, for "the heart that aches is the heart which loves. The more tender it is, the more does it suffer." [76] In the midst of this sorrow arises the sense of the divine, a new yearning, which finds its realisation in friendship: "When the soul seems dead and all the world a wilderness, when our hearts are dry and brains barren, what brings us hope and solace is not analysis or criticism but love and friendship." [77]

It is easier to preach than to practise, but in Radhakrishnan's case practice keeps pace with preaching. He quotes a friend who criticised him for suffering "not only fools but the 'sinful'," and he pleads guilty to the charge; for, says he,

it is not easy to know the difference between good men and bad men. Ideas may be theoretically divided into good and bad, but not men and women, for each of us contains, in himself or herself, in varying degrees, the good and the bad, the high and the low, the true and the false.[78]

Many of us, who have had the privilege of knowing him intimately, can bear witness to the truth of what he says in the following: "It pleases me to know that to some lonely or enslaved souls I was perhaps the only or the first person to show any sympathy or understanding." [79]

Thus we find that the religion of Radhakrishnan, which is founded on the truth of spirit, manifests itself in a beautiful and invigorating humanism. The Upaniṣadic equation between *Brahman* and *Ātman,* which, in the course of Indian history, has often

74 MST, 46 (1946 offprint, 37).   75 MST, 47 (1946 offprint, 38).
76 *Ibid.*   77 MST, 49 (1946 offprint, 40f).
78 MST, 52 (1946 offprint, 43).   79 MST, 56 (1946 offprint, 47).

THE SOCIAL PHILOSOPHY OF RADHAKRISHNAN 785

tended to a deprecation of this world, comes to be visualised by him as the spirit asserting itself in man here and now. In him the East and the West meet in the essentials of life. It may be doubted whether Indian philosophy by itself would have led Radhakrishnan to the humanism he has been preaching. It is certain that the inspiration of Western thought has made him see more deeply into the truths of Vedānta. If the East invites him to a placid meditation, the West has infused in him the spirit of a fighter, so that he feels like Browning:

> One who never turned his back but marched breast forward,
> Never doubted clouds would break,
> Never dreamed, though right were worsted, wrong would triumph,
> Held we fall to rise, are baffled to fight better,
> Sleep to wake.[80]

Radhakrishnan battled first to prove the worth of Indian thought and Indian institutions. Having achieved this, he has been battling to convince his own fellow countrymen that all is not well in the State of Denmark, that India must awaken out of her complacency and remould her institutions in harmony with the age which has become democratic. India must remain on guard against a mechanisation of life, which is not alive to the supremacy of the spirit.

Twenty-five years ago Radhakrishnan concluded his Upton Lectures with these pregnant words: "Growth is slow when roots are deep. But those who light a little candle in the darkness will help to make the whole sky aflame." [81] If, after twenty-five years, the sky in India is overcast by the orthodox ranging themselves against the forces of liberalism operating in the world today, the fault is not Radhakrishnan's. He has done his duty, though he may feel with all the great souls who have worked and suffered: This is not enough; so much more remains to be done.

A. R. WADIA

PRO-VICE-CHANCELLERY
MAHARAJA SAYAJIRAO UNIVERSITY OF BARODA
BARODA, INDIA

80 Quoted in EPW, 90.
81 HVL, 130.

Sarvepalli Radhakrishnan

REPLY TO CRITICS

REPLY TO CRITICS

A LMOST all of those who have contributed to this volume are friendly interpreters and not harsh critics of my thought. Their statements are more appreciations than criticisms, and I am moved, very deeply moved, by their generous words of praise. There are, of course, some doubts raised, some questions asked and some clarifications called for. A detailed discussion of all the difficulties mentioned would require a volume. In the space at my disposal I can only suggest a few considerations which may help to elucidate my position. I wish to consider the main points raised under the four heads of Metaphysics, Religion, History of Philosophy, and Ethical, Social and Political Philosophy. The amount of space I give to the different commentators is, in no sense, a measure of the value and importance of their contributions.

I. METAPHYSICS

Philosophy and Religion. In several essays (Brightman, Conger, Datta, Wadia, Webb) a complaint is made that I make use of religion in the development of my thought, and yet object to the interference of religion in the pursuit of philosophy in an early work on *The Reign of Religion in Contemporary Philosophy.* In that work I tried to show how many writers there dealt with were biased in favour of Christian dogma and allowed their philosophic thought to be deflected by it. Philosophy is a sustained attempt to understand the universe as a whole, not some section of it as sciences do. It takes into account the reports of the scientists, the intuitions of the artists, and the insights of the saints. If philosophy is to co-ordinate and interpret all significant aspects of experience, it must reckon with religious experience also. This, however, does not mean that we should adopt any particular religious doctrine.

789

To defend a dogmatic tradition is not to discover philosophic truth. There does not seem to be any inconsistency between the criticism of the interference of religious *dogma* with the pursuit of philosophy and the recognition of the value of religious *experience* for philosophical interpretation.

Intuition and Intellect. Professor Conger is somewhat surprised that my account of Bergson's views in my *Reign of Religion in Contemporary Philosophy* has not been sufficiently cordial, in spite of the fact that there is much in common between us in regard to our views on religion and intuition.[1] My account was written in the years 1917-1919. Even then I attempted to set forth the religious implications of Bergson's thought which he himself developed with great brilliance in his later work on *The Two Sources of Morality and Religion.* At the time of writing (1917), this great work was not available for me.

In the development of my theory of intuition I took into account Bergson's views. Conger states in section X of his paper, that, if my theory of intuition as integral experience "were to be widely accepted, it would probably need to be freed from any implications of a superconsciousness, and rendered really integral as a total reaction or total adjustment of the whole man, physiologically as well as psychologically and/or spiritually to the total situation confronting him." Professors Wadia and Brightman and Dr. Bernard Phillips also refer to the problem of intuition, and Dr. Browning subjects my views to a detailed criticism. He has drawn attention to many of the obscurities and ambiguities in my treatment of the problem of Reason and Intuition.

Man's awareness is, broadly speaking, of three kinds, the perceptional, the logical, and the intuitive, *manas* or the sense-mind, *vijñāna,* or logical intelligence, and *ānanda,* which, for our present purposes, may be defined as spiritual intuition. All three belong to human consciousness. The human mind does not function in fractions. We need not assume that at the sense-level, there is no work of intuition or at the level of intuition there is not the work of intellect. When intuition is defined as integral insight, the sug-

---

[1] Professor J. H. Muirhead in a review of my *An Idealist View of Life* in the *Hibbert Journal* (October 1932) wrote: "What if in the religion which is being expounded, with certain doctrinal differences but with a singular unity of spirit, by two writers who occupy similar positions as leaders of thought in Europe and in India, we have just the vital faith for which they both think the world is waiting —one which, instead of dividing continents and sects within them, is capable of uniting them in a single allegiance, not to any material crown or empire, but to the values which are the crown of life and the empire of the spirit?" p. 153.

gestion is that the whole mind is at work in it. Any coherent philosophy should take into account observed data, rational reflection,
and intuitive insight. All these should be articulated in a systematic way.

Intuition, like the word *pratyakṣa*, in its original form *intuitus*,
implies the sense of sight. It is used to cover all cognitive processes
which have a directness or immediacy, i.e., all non-inferential cognition. What we know by inference or hearsay is not intuitive
knowledge. Intuition is of two kinds, perceptual knowledge and
integral insight. Personally, I use intuition for integral knowledge.

Even in intellectual work, there is scope for intuition. The
postulates of thought, the pervasive features of experience, number, causality, provide scope for the exercise of the intuitive functions. When Bradley says that "metaphysics is the finding of bad
reasons for what we believe upon instinct," [2] he makes out that our
vision of the real is not the result of intellectual co-ordination but
we start with it and justify it, if possible, to reason. Reason and
intuition are interdependent. Apart from sense perception, there
are intuitions of a logical and scientific, aesthetic and ethical, philosophical and religious type. With some straining these could be
correlated with the five types of intuition which Dr. Browning
mentions.

Intellectual consciousness is predominantly at work in scientific
procedure. It measures off, limits, divides. The scientist aims at objective knowledge and so is intent on eliminating personal prejudices or preferences. By eliminating what is peculiar to the individual, science helps us to achieve a standpoint from which we can
arrange and order the contents of experience in a way that it becomes common ground for all and makes possible common action.
The truth of science is independent of the person who holds it. It is
so impersonal that often observations are recorded by cameras and
measurements are taken by mechanical instruments like clocks.
For its purposes science assumes the separation of the mind from
the object. Particular things are not separate, though science treats
them as separate for the sake of convenience. It determines the
general characters with the utmost precision, enables us to obtain
mastery over nature.

All the same the knowledge obtained by science through the
intellectual processes of observation, experiment, and inference is
inadequate. It gives us the formal structure of existence, especially
physical existence, which can be represented by mathematical

2 *Appearance and Reality*, xii.

equations. Even with reference to physical nature, scientific knowledge does not give us the inner truth. The measurable aspects are
not the only ones. We may measure the current of electricity, but
we do not know what electricity is. The real being of physical nature does not consist in the abstract formal structure which science
succeeds in representing, but in its inner dynamism.[3]

The inadequacy of scientific knowledge becomes more apparent
when we proceed to living organisms and conscious processes. Scientific representations here fail to give us the essentially unitary
and dynamic characters of these processes. The development of
living organisms is controlled by certain aims. In conscious life
these aims are planned. History is the sphere of the unpredictable
and incalculable.

Science has not established that the world is a closed system in
which everything is determined in terms of cause and effect. This
assumption has worked successfully only in certain areas appropriate to it. Intellectual knowledge is inadequate, partial, fragmentary, but not false. It fails to reveal the truth in its fullness. It is,
however, an essential stage in the evolution of human consciousness. It can be trusted within limits.

In man's endeavour to comprehend reality we must find room
for creative vision and prophecy. The externality of the individual
consciousness to the object is transcended in the intuitive apprehension. In it there is a complete fusion of the subject and the
object. Even in scientific knowledge, it is not altogether absent.
The independence of the observer is only an ideal. Even when the
camera takes the place of the human observer, it is the observer
who has to fix it in position, who has to interpret the results of the
exposure. If, at any stage, the observer is careless or prejudiced, the
whole process becomes a failure.

In intuitive knowledge, man ceases to be an impartial spectator.
His whole being is at work, not merely the powers of observation
and inference. It is knowledge by coincidence. Being and knowing
are different aspects of one experience.

Intuitive knowledge is a self-subsistent mode of consciousness
different from the intellectual or the perceptual. Whereas perception gives us the outward properties of an object, and intellect

[3] Cp. A. N. Whitehead: Philosophy "seeks those generalities which characterise
the complete reality of fact, and apart from which any fact must sink into an
abstraction. But science makes the abstraction and is content to understand the
complete fact in respect to only some of its essential aspects." Adventures of
Ideas (1933), 187.

discerns the law of which the object is an instance, intuition gives depth, meaning, character to the object.

Knowledge of God is achieved not by intellect alone. Man's entire being—intellect and imagination, heart and will—is active. God is revealed through inner experience and not external observation. We gain this knowledge by a life of discipline and austerity, when we bring our personal will into accord with the divine will. "Everyone who loves is born of God and knows God."

There are many who argue that they have no experience of intuitive knowledge. This is due to a misapprehension. Intuitive knowledge is not limited to the highest knowledge of God.[4]

Wherever we have a knowledge of the individual, we have knowledge that is irreducible to intellectual specifications. In aesthetic experience we have a type of intuitive knowledge, a personal relationship with the object which is essentially different from what is found in intellectual cognition. The relation is direct, simple, intimate and personal. The artist's whole being responds to the object, his feeling is intensified and his imagination stimulated. Aesthetic perception or appreciation is different from intellectual discrimination and analysis. The object enters into the mind of the artist and unfolds its nature in his imagination. The consciousness of the artist enters into the object, sees, feels and vibrates with its truth. Here also, as in scientific procedure, there is disinterestedness, impersonality. The artist's experience is not limited by personal desires or petty cares. His enjoyment of the object is pure and disinterested. We intuit when we behold objects, freed from any context of fear or hope, prospect or regret, usefulness or injury, when we transcend every human bias. By the practice of vairāgya or detachment, the artist rises to the calm of the universal spirit. When Emerson says that all poetry is written in the heavens, he means that it is conceived by a self deeper than what appears in normal life. A poet is a seer, a revealer of hidden truths. The images used by him are not intended to please our fancy. They are symbols of the unrevealed. They convey truths which the precise intellectual word or logical concept cannot hope to manifest. The artist claims that his knowledge is significant of the universal character of reality. Works of art express significant individuality.

4 "It is characteristic of the learned mind to exalt words: Yet, mothers can ponder many things in their hearts which their lips cannot express. These many things, which are thus known, constitute the ultimate religious evidence beyond which there is no appeal." Whitehead: Religion in the Making (1926), 67.

Aesthetic satisfaction is akin to spiritual joy. Whereas pleasure is the result of the gratification of personal desires, joy is the fruit of the fulfilment of our inner being. It is not dependent on external circumstances and is superior to suffering or misfortune.

Intuitive knowledge is criticised as something private, subjective, incommunicable. It does not give universal truth and therefore is incapable of verification. Only those judgments can claim to affirm truth which relate to observed objective content and are stated in clear and distinct terms and are capable of empirical verification by further observations; others are said to be aimless chatter. So far as the intuitive insights are concerned, how are we to persuade those who are lacking in these insights or believe themselves to be possessed of insights which disclose something quite different about the ultimate nature of things? Some philosophers see; others do not. Some possess illumination of one type; others of a different type. Who is to decide?

Intuitive knowledge is verified by its capacity to bring coherence and harmony into systems framed by the intellect. The immediacy of intuitive knowledge can be mediated through intellectual definition and analysis. We use intellect to test the validity of intuition, and communicate them to others. Intuition and intellect are complementary. We have, of course, to recognise that intuition transcends the conceptual expressions as reality does not fit into categories. If intuition is not to be confused with vague sentiency below the level of relations, if it is wisdom which is sublimated knowledge, *jñānaṁ vijñāna sahitam,* it is direct experience, *aparokṣānubhūti.*

When the Vedic thinkers urge that *manana* or logical reflection is an essential preparation for direct insight, when the *Bhagavadgītā* urges us to adopt *paripraśna* or cross-examination as a step towards direct experience, they are insisting on a dialectical preparation fo; the direct experience. The immediacy of Eastern thinkers is not an unmediated one.

Just as we have both continuity and discontinuity between matter and life or life and mind, so also we have both continuity and discontinuity between intuitive wisdom and intellectual knowledge. Those who believe that wisdom negates knowledge are as onesided as those who believe that wisdom is nothing more than knowledge. As life appropriates and uses matter, as mind appropriates and uses life, so does spiritual wisdom appropriate and transform intellectual knowledge. Intellect is therefore an indispensable aid to support and clarify spiritual experience. The experience may be vitiated by error or impaired by emotions. There may be mistakes in the analysis and interpretation of the primary data of experience.

Intellect itself is an instrument of spirit and therefore should receive and accept direction from spirit. I will not quarrel with Professor Brightman's observation that "complete intuition is simply a name for complete reason." I would say that reason and sense are outgrowths or determinations of intuition. Intuition is open to all men who possess the capacity for its acquisition, and there are ways and methods by which we can prepare for its reception.

Intuitive insight assumes the essential unity of the human spirit which should never be disintegrated in its various activities. Our activities at their highest level draw their energy from the spiritual unity. We cannot be moral without the use of reason and imagination. We cannot be philosophical without a strain of poetry and strength of conscience. We cannot be artistic if we are not nourished by thought and sustained by moral ideals. Highest art, philosophy, and morality are manifestations of spiritual unity. There is in them a breath of sublimity which lifts us on its strong wing to the universal and eternal; an elevation and expansion which are not present in perceptual or intellectual life. Works of genius express our whole being and life. We should be whole men before we can be artists, philosophers, or heroes. The lives of such whole individuals are of world-wide significance. Their appeal crosses national frontiers and religious boundaries.

Mr. K. J. Spalding, in his essay, supports my general views of the relation of intuition to reason; his attractive account derives as much from technical philosophy as from general literature.

The Meaning of Idealism. Professor Hartshorne raises the question regarding the meaning of idealism, with special reference to the relation of subject and object. He observes "Radhakrishnan does not altogether approve of Whitehead's complete translation of physical concepts into terms of 'feeling,' 'satisfaction,' 'prehension,' and the like. He also seems to reject anything like the Berkeleyan type of subjectivism. Yet I, at least, am not able to discern any third possibility for idealism." I thought I had made my position clear. In the opening section of *An Idealist View of Life,* I said:

An idealist view finds that the universe has meaning, has value. Ideal values are the dynamic forces, the driving power of the universe. The world is intelligible only as a system of ends. Such a view has little to do with the problem whether a thing is only a particular image or a general relation. . . . Nor is it committed to the doctrine that the world is made of mind, an infinite mind or a society of minds. Idealism in the sense indicated concerns the ultimate nature of reality, whatever may be its relation to the knowing mind. It is an answer to the problem of the idea, the meaning or the purpose of it all. It has nothing in common with the view that makes reality an irrational blind striving or an irremediably miserable blunder. It finds life significant and purposeful. (Page 15)

This view of idealism does not require us to reduce matter to mind. To say that atoms have 'feeling' is confusing. Hartshorne seems to use the word 'feeling' in a wide sense to cover the *ways* in which different entities, atoms included, 'feel.' It seems to me quite legitimate to use the term 'idealism' in a sense that does not identify it with panpsychism.

God and the Absolute. Professors Hartshorne and Clement Webb raise the question of the relation of God and the Absolute. These are not to be regarded as exclusive of each other. The Supreme in its non-relational aspect is the Absolute; in its active aspect it is God. The Supreme, limited to its relation to the possibility which is actually accomplishing itself in the world, is the World Spirit. Professor Hartshorne says that the concrete and relative is more than the abstract and the absolute. This view assumes that the distinction of God and the Absolute is one of separation, which is not the case. The actual is more than the possible. The abstract possibility and the concrete realisation are both contained in the one reality, which is Absolute-God. The two aspects represent the absolute silence of the Spirit and its boundless movement. The silence is the basis of the movement, the condition of power. The distinction is only logical. The silence of the Spirit and its energising are complementary and inseparable. The infinite is both *amūrta*, formless, and *mūrta*, formed. The coexistence of the two is the very nature of Universal Being. It is not a mere juxtaposition of two opposites. The Divine is formless and nameless and yet capable of manifesting all forms and names.

The forms are not the objects of thought but creative conceptions in the mind of the Supreme, which is not restricted to any one form. But when we take up this universe, the Divine as working in it is said to be the World Spirit. The *Bhagavadgītā* says, "I support this entire universe pervading it with a single fraction of myself." [5] The World Spirit guides and controls the concretisation of one specific possibility. If we break up the Supreme into the Absolute which is the eternal home of all possibilities, God who is creative freedom and World Spirit which is the active principle of this cosmic process, then the question is relevant whether or not the World Spirit is more concrete, more full of content than either God or the Absolute. We may then say that the Absolute is deficient not only in actuality but also in any kind of activity, and God who is creative power is already related to the world. The Supreme has three simultaneous poises of being, the transcendent Absolute, *Brahman*, the creative freedom, *Īśvara*, and the wisdom, power, and love manifest in this world, *Hiraṇya-garbha*. These do not succeed each other in time. It is an order of arrangement and logical priority, not of temporal succession.

The tendency to regard *Īśvara* or God as phenomenal and Brahman or the Absolute as real is not correct. This is a distinction of great significance which we should preserve, if we are to have a balanced view of the Supreme. Professor Brightman's whole criticism about my vacillation between the non-dualism of Śaṁkara and the personal theism of Rāmānuja is based on the postulate that the Supreme must be either the one or the other, which I do not admit.

Hartshorne raises the question whether we can be certain that the possibility chosen for accomplishment in this world will be completely actualised. May it not be that the divine purpose with regard to the world is inexhaustible? I agree that the possibilities are inexhaustible, but not that any one specific possibility is inexhaustible. If we are not certain that the divine purpose with regard to this world will be realised, the cosmic process will turn out to be an unending pursuit of a goal which will for ever remain unaccomplished. There must be the assurance of the eventual triumph of this possibility, of the realisation of the ideal. Apart from this, life and effort would be meaningless. The gift of freedom to the human being is real and his abuse of it may conflict with the divine purpose. The wickedness of man may retard but cannot overpower the gracious purpose of the Divine. The accomplishment of the purpose of the world is contingent on the co-operation of human individuals with the divine will. If we feel certain that it will be accomplished, it is because we are certain of the power of divine love which will subdue man's obstinacy and

5 *ekāṁśena* X, 42.

selfishness. It may take infinite time; 'infinite' meaning indefinite or incalculable.

This view assumes the reality of human freedom, and therefore God does not impose his will but is perpetually giving Himself. He shares in the life of finite creatures. He bears in them and with them the whole burden of their finitude. A God who is indifferent to the fate of the world cannot be the God of love. There can be no love without sorrow and suffering. Either the love of God is a fiction or the sorrow of God is a reality. Through the conception of *avatāra* or descent of the Divine into the world, Hindu thought brings out how the Divine through suffering voluntarily accepted and endured brings the goal nearer.[6] His triumph in a universe of risks is certain.

Dr. Inge urges that the second law of thermodynamics suggests that the cosmic drama of the universe will end finally in universal death. How can God reveal himself through a world which is doomed to perish? The physicists now tell us that there is a counterbalancing process. May it not be that the end of the world will come when its purpose is consummated? Jesus and his early followers expected an imminent destruction of the world; but that did not for them affect in any way the integrity of the Divine. It is quite true that a God who is bound up with a universe which is doomed to decay and dissolution is not the perfect reality. Though the temporal world has an eternal significance, since souls evolve in and through it, the realm in which the true being of God resides cannot be temporal. If the unending temporal process were all, then the law of entropy would be ruinous. Time is not all, though the temporal world is the stage on which spiritual values are enacted. The eternal source of spiritual values and the final destiny of all who pursue them is God, the Absolute. Unending history, be it as progress or regress, is the essence of meaninglessness.

Even human beings have in their deepest nature an element to which temporal existents are irrelevant. It is because I have faith in the immanence of the eternal in the human that I believe in the eternal salvation of the human soul.

Dr. Inge remarks "Radhakrishnan thinks that in course of time every soul must win eternal salvation. But does he not here confound eternal life with never-ending salvation?" I do not. So long as we are immersed in time, opportunities will be available for us in the time series. Whatever we may do, the spirit in us cannot be

6 See my Introduction to the *Bhagavadgītā; Isaiah* XLVI, 3-4; *Hosea* XI, 8-9.

destroyed. It may be concealed or camouflaged, but it will catch us up one day and assert its superiority to the temporal.

Jesus sought and awaited the transfiguration of the world. He aims at not merely the conversion of the individual but the redemption of the world. "We, according to His promise look for a new heaven and a new earth, wherein dwelleth righteousness." [7] It has not occurred to me to think of the world as having no limits or finality. Limitation of the world is in contrast to the boundlessness and infinitude of Spirit. This world with its achievement or realisation reaches eternity. Attainment signifies eternity. There is no perfection in the finite. It can only be attained in the infinite. Every actualisation in the here and now is but a symbol of something, other and beyond. The meaning of history is beyond the confines of history. The historical process can be understood only in the light of its end, which is the end of history, victory over all objectification and alienation, a victory in which man ceases to be determined from without.

We have a tendency to imagine the end of history as taking place in history. What is beyond history cannot be related to history in simply historical terms. The Apocalyptic angel asserts that there would not be any time. Though we cannot dispense altogether with time in speaking of its end, the end cannot be a part of time. It belongs to another order of existence, where there is an end of time itself, however difficult it may be for us to think of something absolutely last. The flux of time is a symptom of the disrupted, fallen state of the world. The new heaven and the new earth represent victory over time.

The Status of the Individual. Brightman raises the question "of the value and destiny of the individual." Inge argues that the "I and Thou" relation is never transcended, and even when the mystics declare that there is "union of the knower and the known," it does not mean the extinction of personality. He asks, "is personal distinctness though not separation, preserved in the spiritual world?" There is no question in my scheme of the individual being included in and absorbed by the Divine. What is involved is unity in personal love. God and man remain distinct though they are bound together in love; so that we cannot speak of one apart from the other. God comes to self-expression through the regenerated individuals. Till the end of the cosmic process is achieved, the individuals retain their distinction though they possess universality of spirit. Even those who have freed themselves from subjection

[7] *Peter* III, 13.

to time, whose natures are indwelt by the Divine, work unceasingly for the service of the world, for its redemption. They retain their centres as individuals till the cosmic consummation is reached.

The Russian writer Vladimir Solovief (1853-1900) gave a fresh interpretation to the traditional doctrine of Christ as the God-man. "Christianity," he wrote,

is the revelation of a perfect God in a perfect man. This incarnation is not so much an event which took place at one stage in history but is something continually taking place. God is for ever becoming incarnate in the world. This is the meaning of the historical process that God becomes man so that man may one day become God.

When this universal incarnation is reached, the cosmic is taken over into the Absolute.

The status of the World and the Doctrine of Māyā. In my writings I have interpreted the doctrine of māyā so as to save the world and give to it a real meaning.

I. (i) The world is derived being. It is an expression of the Absolute and not the Absolute itself. To mark the distinction between Absolute Being and dependent being, we call the latter māyā. When the Absolute is taken as pure being, its relation to the world is inexplicable, *anirvacanīya*. We know that without the background of being there can be no world. The relation between the two cannot be logically explicated. This inexplicability of the logical relationship does not repudiate the existence of the world. It does not say that the world is not, though it appears to be.

To bring out that the changes of the world do not affect the nature of the Absolute, to indicate that the relationship is not one of organic inter-dependence, a distinction is made between *pariṇāma* or modification and *vivarta* or appearance. The one-sided dependence of the world on the Absolute is illustrated by the similes of the appearance of snake in the rope and of silver in the shell. The purpose of these analogies is not to suggest that the world is a dream or an illusion, but that the relationship is such that the world exists without any change in the being of the Absolute.

The world is not a modification of Absolute Being; for in that case Absolute Being would cease to be Absolute and become subject to modifications. We cannot say that a part of the Absolute is modified, whereas the remainder is intact. The Absolute is incapable of being divided into parts.

(ii) Although the Absolute is Eternal Being, the world is temporal being with limits to its existence. A time will come when it will be no more as a process. This essential temporality is indicated by the word *māyā*. This does not make the world into an illusion. To treat it as transitory is not to equate it with the nonexistent or the illusory.

II. (i) When the Supreme is viewed not merely as Absolute Being but as Eternal Creativity, the creative power is called māyā. In my account I distinguished Divine Being and Divine action, Absolute in itself, in repose, and the Absolute as active or energising, Brahman and Īśvara. The latter is said to be possessed of *māyā* or power of manifestation. It delights in manifesting.

(ii) As to why this specific possibility was chosen and not any other, one can only say that it is the free act of the Divine. Why did he choose this? is a question we cannot raise, for the simple reason that God is freedom. By calling creation a mystery, we mean no more than that it is an expression of his freedom, the mysterious working of his will, which is also called *māyā*.

III. In the world process itself, we have the divine interacting with primal matter, what Indian thinkers call the unmanifested *prakṛti*. This is also called *māyā*. The same duality is indicated in the passage of Genesis relating to the Spirit "moving on the face of the waters." [8] When the spirit of God brooded on the face of the waters, the original chaos was being shaped into order. As the dualities between the Divine and the matter, which is used as a means for the unfoldment of the Divine, are not ultimately two separate entities, māyā is not dissociated from the World Spirit. St. John's Gospel refers to light and darkness whose antagonism continues from the initial creation to the final consummation of the world. Two factors, the unbroken energy of light and darkness are affirmed. "And the light shineth in darkness and the darkness comprehended it not." [9] All things in the world participate in the characters of this duality. They are *sad-asad-ātmaka*. They are real as well as unreal. This dual character is sometimes indicated by the word *māyā*. The world and the World Spirit are both equally real.

IV. *Māyā* is also used for ignorance by which we do not recognise the principle of the universe. "He was in the world and the world was made by him and the world knew him not." This non-knowing is *avidyā*. It is also different from the real and the unreal. If it attains either reality or collapses into nothingness there would be no

8 *Genesis*, I, 1/2.   9 *John* I, 4.

tension, no process. So the world is said to be *sad-asad-vilakṣaṇa,* different from real and unreal.

Metaphysics and Ethics. Professor Moore has given a very understanding account of my views on the relation of metaphysics and ethics. This question has been with me from my student days. One of the chief criticisms raised against Indian philosophy, especially the Vedānta variety of it, is its non-ethical character. A somewhat jejune reply to this criticism is contained in my thesis on *The Ethics of the Vedānta,* submitted to the Madras University in the year 1908. That attempt evidently has not been successful, or perhaps prejudices die hard. Even so great a mind as Professor Schweitzer repeated this charge in his book, *Indian Thought and Its Development.*[10]

Bergson, in his *The Two Sources of Morality and Religion,* makes out that the Indian mystics are lost in contemplation or vision of God and fight shy of action which is said to be "a weakening of contemplation."[11] The Christian mystics, on the other hand, are complete mystics, who are absorbed in God not only in thought and feeling but also in will. In them there is a "superabundance of life. There is boundless impetus. There is an irresistible impulse which hurls it with vast enterprises."[12]

Moore quotes a passage from *The Hindu View of Life:* "The theist and the atheist, the sceptic and the agnostic may all be Hindus if they accept the Hindu system of culture and life. . . . In a very real sense practice precedes theory."[13] He points out that whereas the Hindu is expected to have "a religious and ethical outlook on life," it is difficult to understand "how this can include the sceptic and the atheist along with the theist as good Hindus." The passage quoted emphasises the infinite possibilities of the divine nature and the vast multiplicity of the aspirations of fallible human nature. Every type of human aspiration is admitted. Differences do not entail conflict or contradiction. Hinduism is not interested in confining the illimitable to one form or converting all souls to one type. It insists on the need for growth and rebukes sterile complacency. The famous *gāyatrī* prayer is a call for an unceasing and vigilant search for truth. Hinduism believes in intellectual freedom as an essential feature of the spiritual life. In the exercise of this freedom we may make mistakes. Wisdom is achieved through many errors. By examining the errors, we will

[10] Albert Schweitzer's book was published in 1936.
[11] Henri Bergson, *The Two Sources of Morality and Religion,* 188.
[12] *Ibid.,* 198.   [13] S. Radhakrishnan, HVL, 77.

find out the truth they aim at and thus disengage their significance. Spiritual life requires that no restrictions are imposed on the life of the intellect. We should not insist that the conclusions of science should square with the beliefs of religion. Intellect should be left free even to deny God, if its sincere observation and analysis of things lead it to such a conclusion. Conscientiousness is the essential requirement. We must act according to our conscience and not according to other people's conscience. Atheism has been, both for the individual and the society, a necessary means for the achievement of the larger truth. Sometimes we may have to deny God in order to find him. Though they may not be aware of it, even atheists revolt in the name of God. At the end of all earnest scepticism and denial, we will reach the truth.

Moore asks, whether it is not true that morality, on my scheme, has but a relative status and is not of absolute validity. It is true that the moral situation refers to the world of individuals and has validity in regard to it. As the world itself is rooted in the absolute reality, morality has also an ultimate significance.

The question whether value concepts apply to the Absolute or God or the World Spirit is answered in my essay with which this volume opens.

Contemplation and Action. The question of the relation of the contemplative to the active virtues raised by Professor Wadia is not a problem peculiar to Hindu or Buddhist thought. The difference between Martha and Mary recurs throughout the history of Christendom.

It is wrong to think that the great contemplative seers are deficient in practical sense. Though their lives are spent in prayer and contemplation, they endure persecutions and found new communities. There are some who go into periodical retreat for spiritual refreshment and return again to work in the world. Still others turn their work into prayer, their life into penance. If we survey the work accomplished in the field of action by the sages of India from the Buddha to Gandhi and by the great mystics in the West like St. Paul, St. Theresa, St. Francis, we will be struck by their capacity for action. They sink their roots in God and raise their branches in the world. If the Divine is ultimate reality, contemplation is not an escapism. Those who deal only with the transitory and the ephemeral, those who pride themselves on their realism and hardheadedness are the escapists. Philosophy is not an intellectual pastime. It is the pursuit of wisdom. It is intensely practical, being a way of life, an enterprise of the spirit.

The contemplative seers exercise great influence on society without deliberate calculation. Their gentle stillness is a rebuke to the noisy futility of our age, their restraint and renunciation a devastating criticism of its ambition and acquisitiveness. To assuage the bitterness and contradictions of our age we require men of detachment and dignity, of purposeful living and of abundant humanity.

To rest in the timeless Divine and to forget the world is wrong. We cannot divide eternity and time. The lowest details of existence are the channels of immortal life. The whole cosmic process is impregnated with the Divine down to the depths of hell.

I do believe that the great idealist tradition has in it the possibility of bringing East and West together in a closer union on the plane of mind and spirit. Professor D. M. Datta asks whether it is not possible to bring the world together on other bases. He writes: "In recent times Indian Marxists, for example, have been busy viewing both Eastern and Western thought from their point of view and emphasising the value of materialist ideas already present in both." May it not be, he asks, that the world unity can be achieved on other bases than those of spiritual idealism? Material unity has already been attained by the adventures of science and engineering. Economic and political unity is being built up by the United Nations Organisation. All these are external, and if the unity is to be sustained, it can only be by the development of cultural and spiritual unity. Even culturally the world is getting together. Scientific knowledge is available for the whole world though we may use it for mutual service or mutual destruction. It is my conviction that, if the achievements of science and criticism are to be harnessed for right ends, we should develop certain universal aims, and the idealist tradition of the world provides us with these goals for human endeavour and action.

II. RELIGION

Naturalism and Religion. Without religious vision human life is but a flash of occasional enjoyments lighting up a mass of pain and misery, a bagatelle of transient experience, as Whitehead says. Without some transcendent aim civilisation either wallows in pleasure or lapses into barren repetition.

Mr. M. N. Roy states that Indian philosophy has two tendencies, idealistic and naturalistic. The former represents reaction, the latter progress. Any one who stresses the idealist tradition is a reactionary. I am afraid that Mr. Roy's thesis is not the result of analysis but is an act of faith. An answer to his pleadings is contained in Dr. Bernard Phillips's essay.

Dr. Phillips refers to the striking absence in Indian philosophy of "any lasting form of philosophic naturalism." He traces it to the "insulation" of Indian philosophy "from the method and spirit of science." He refers to the possibility that India's spiritual outlook may disintegrate as it comes under the influence of modern science and technology, but believes that the spiritual view of life will assimilate whatever is of value in naturalist philosophies.

Man has the spark of spirit and is not a product of objective nature. He is an *aṁśa* or fragment of the Divine and is therefore a principle of light and power. So long as man's attention is limited to his surface-being and he takes himself to be a product of nature or a cell of the social organism, he is subject to the forces around him. When he becomes aware of his inner consciousness, his true being, he becomes superior to the forces around him. To use the Sāṁkhya expressions, so long as *puruṣa* is involved in the workings of *prakṛti*, he is subject to the laws of *prakṛti*, or objective nature, physical, vital, psychological and social. When he sees his distinction from *prakṛti*, he is able to see clearly and control his objective nature.

The end of human existence is perfection, which is not ascent to a heaven above but is ascent to the spirit within. The new birth for which humanity awaits as the crowning achievement of a long and painful process of evolution is not a post-mortem salvation but is a spiritualised humanity. "The Kingdom of God is not meat and drink, but righteousness and peace and joy in the Holy Spirit." [14]

Comparative Study of Religions and Christianity. Professor Joachim Wach is right in making out that the interpretation of the Vedānta by Śaṁkara is not the only expression of the spirit of Indian religion. There are other expressions of the Indian religious genius, of which the most notable is the spirit of devotion characteristic of mediaeval saints, Śaiva and Vaiṣṇava. The personal theism of the Ṛg Veda, of some of the *Upaniṣads* like the *Śvetāśvatara*, the *Bhagavadgītā*, of Rāmānuja and others is a dominant note of Indian religion. The Ineffable Absolute who dwelleth in the light which no man can approach is the God whom we approach in prayer. The two are not separate. For the theists, God

[14] *Romans*, XIV, 17.

is the Supreme Person, whose nature is absolute bliss and goodness,
. . . who is an ocean of kindness as it were for all who depend on
Him; who is all merciful; who is immeasurably raised above all possibility of any one being equal or superior to him; whose name is the
highest Brahman.[15]

Freedom, for Rāmānuja, is gained through the knowledge of God
who is possessed of all auspicious qualities. It comes through the
grace of God obtained through man's complete surrender to him.
Freedom consists in the enjoyment of communion with the living
personal God. The doctrines of the grace of the Supreme and
man's response to it through bhakti or devotion are common to
Vaiṣṇava, Śaiva and Śākta systems. The sense of sin and the need
for deliverance from it are to be found in many of the lives and
sayings of saints of these schools. Dādu, a sixteenth century saint,
cries:

> I have neglected God's service; a sinful servant am I;
> There is no other so foul as I am.
> I offend in every act, I fail in every duty,
> I sin against Thee every moment,
> Pardon my transgressions.[16]

Or take Tukārām, the Marāthā saint of the seventeenth century:

> Fallen of fallen; thrice fallen am I, but do Thou raise me by Thy
> power. I have neither purity of heart, nor a faith firmly set at Thy
> feet; I am created out of sin, how oft shall I repeat it? says Tuka.[17]

Professor Wach's criticisms about the presentation of Christianity to Indian youth by Christian missionaries are not altogether
fair to some of the great Christian teachers we had in India, not
at any rate to my teachers in the Madras Christian College. They
did not claim "that Hinduism whatever its form, was all darkness
and that Christianity, whatever its expression, is all light." They
were no doubt convinced about the uniqueness of Jesus's message
and India's need for it.[18] This, however, did not make them indif-

---

[15] Rāmānuja's Śrībhāṣya, IV. 4. 22.

[16] Orr: A Sixteenth Century Indian Mystic, 183.

[17] Fraser and Marāthe: The Poems of Tukārām, Vol. I, 124.

[18] One of the greatest Christian thinkers we had in India, Professor Alfred
G. Hogg, with whom I studied philosophy for four years 1905-1909, in his The
Christian Message to the Hindu (1947) writes: "The Incarnate Christ is a unique
intervention determinative once for all of the course of world-history, and
effected in a guise which is an unsurpassable revelation, within the temporal and
concrete, of the character and purpose of God." (p. 35.)

ferent to the spiritual aspirations and endeavours in non-Christian faiths.

Wach finds "a notable trace of bitterness in a great number of references to Christianity" in my writings. If he finds it so, there must be a basis for his statement and I am sincerely sorry for it. I am however heartened by what some other contributors have said about my treatment of the life and teachings of Jesus, as distinct from my views on doctrinal developments. Mr. A. N. Marlow says, "The personality of Jesus himself is treated with scrupulous reverence in *Eastern Religions and Western Thought*."

For me the person of Jesus is a historical fact. Christ is not a datum of history, but a judgment of history. Jesus' insight is expressive of a timeless spiritual fact; but what the theologians say of it are after-thoughts, interpretations of the fact, *viz.*, the life and death of Jesus. We interpret the facts in the light of our knowledge and against the background of history. Sometimes these interpretations act as drags on endeavour and we revise them. Many will not be happy if they are told that the only proofs of the reality of God and of the immortality of the human soul are found in the story of Jesus' resurrection. Miracles, faith in an infallible book or an infallible church, do not appeal to the modern mind steeped in the spirit of science.

'What do you think of Christ?' is undoubtedly a most important problem. To an educated Hindu, Jesus is a supreme illustration of the growth from human origins to divine destiny. As a mystic who believes in the inner light, Jesus ignores ritual and is indifferent to legalistic piety. He is contemptuous of the righteousness of the Scribes and the Pharisees. Being other-worldly in spirit, he is indifferent to the wealth of the world and exalts poverty as one of the greatest of goods. He wishes us to restrain not only our outward actions but our inner desires and carry the principle of non-attachment even into the sphere of family relationships. He is the great hero who exemplifies the noblest characteristics of manhood, the revealer of the profoundest depths in ourselves, one who brings home to us the ideal of human perfection by embodying it visibly in himself.

There is a difference, according to Wach, between the Indian conception of *avatāra* and the Christian view of the Son of God. With regard to the other great teachers, he would argue, on the basis of the distinction which he cites from William Temple "all therefore is alike revelation; but not all is equally revelatory of the divine character." There are certainly degrees of revelation;

they may be discovered in each of the living faiths of mankind. The Christians would regard Jesus Christ as the final and incomparably unique revelation of God. They see in Christ, "the supreme manifestation of the Divine love; which does not exclude other manifestations but supersedes them." No one can call himself a Christian, according to Wach, "if he does not hold his uniqueness to be true." There are many scholarly, and even saintly Christians who will support my general view of Jesus Christ. I need not refer to the great Christian mystics Erigena, Eckhart, Ruysbrock, and William Law, who, in the spirit of the Hindu and Buddhist thought, look upon Jesus as the expression of the timeless spirit which transcends the confines of churches and creeds.[19] To quote one or two contemporaries, Dr. W. R. Inge in the January (1951) number of the *Hibbert Journal* writes: "I believe that Jesus put himself in the succession of the later prophets, who helped to transform the crude religion of the nomad invaders of Palestine. He lived and taught and died as a prophet. The last thing that he wished to claim was to be the Messiah."[20] Dr. Albert Schweitzer observes: "Christian faith, under the influence of Greek metaphysics, was pleased to confer upon him [Jesus] a divinity and a divine inerrancy to which he made no claim."[21] Karl Jaspers says:

The religion of Christ contains the truth that God speaks to man through man. But God speaks through many men, in the Bible through the successive prophets of whom Jesus is the last. No man can be God; God speaks exclusively through no man, and what is more, His speech through every man has many meanings.[22]

Inge, Schweitzer, Jaspers, and many others are certainly aware of the statement which Wach quotes in defence of his theory of the exclusive and supreme saviourship of Jesus. "Neither is there salvation in any other name; for there is none other name under heaven given among men whereby we must be saved."[23] Jacques

---

[19] "Then the Blessed one spake and said: 'Know, Vasetha, that from time to time a Tathāgata is born into the world, a fully enlightened one, blessed and worthy, abounding in wisdom and goodness, happy with knowledge of the worlds, unsurpassed as a guide to erring mortals, a teacher of gods and men, a Blessed Buddha.'" (*Tevijja Sutta*)

[20] Wm. Ralph Inge, in *The Hibbert Journal*, January, 1951, 132.

[21] In the Epilogue to E. N. Mozley's *The Theology of Albert Schweitzer* (1950), 106.

[22] Karl Jaspers, in *The Perennial Scope of Philosophy* (1950), 103. "Why callest thou me good? There is none good but one, that is God."

[23] *Acts* IV, 12.

Maritain observes: "If the Catholics hold that there is no salvation outside the Church, all it means is that there is no salvation outside the Truth, which, explicitly or implicitly, is freely offered to all." [24] Maritain is here reverting to an ancient tradition in Christianity. In his *Apology*, Justin points out that Christ is spoken of by prophets who had lived centuries before him. To Clement and his fellow Alexandrians, the Logos or the Divine reason was the instructor of the Hebrew prophets and the Greek philosophers or rather of the whole race of men living before Jesus lived on earth. Clement said: "There is always a natural manifestation of the one Almighty God amongst all right thinking men." Origen, in reply to Celsus' criticism, said:

When God sent Jesus to the human race, it was not as though he had just awakened from a long sleep. Jesus has at all times been doing good to the human race. No noble deed amongst men has ever been done without the Divine Word visiting the souls of those who, even for a brief space, were able to receive its operations. [25]

"That which is called the Christian religion" said Augustine, "existed among the ancients, and never did not exist, from the beginning of the human race until Christ came in the flesh, at which time the true religion which already existed began to be called Christianity." [26] It is the eternal religion of which the *Bhagavadgītā* speaks. Islam regards God's revelation to the Jews and the Christians as part of the full revelation vouchsafed to the Prophet Muhammad.

Wach says: "To surrender all attempts of inviting and winning others to the cause of Christ, would actually be to deny him." Sincerity is the essential mark of religion. Each of us should express in word and in deed the springs of his action, "of hope, of joy, and of strength." A sincere Christian should hope, pray and work "for the acceptance of Christ by all men." Professor Wach gives the same freedom to a Buddhist or a Muslim and he holds that "Christ, the Buddha, Muhammad are universal options."

I have a vague fear that much of modern apologetics, which professes to combat atheism only serves to support it. Many of us do not seem to defend *faith in God*, but are concerned to defend our *ideas of God*. We seem to overlook the unfathomed and inexpressible depths of God's being and eternity and the limitations and imperfections of the human agency, through which all revela-

---

[24] Jacques Maritain, in *Redeeming the Time*, 105.
[25] Origen, in *Contra Celsum*, VI, 78.   [26] *Epis Retract.*, I.

tions are made known to us. The act of revelation is a twofold act; it issues from God, who cannot be reduced to any categories of this world; it is dependent on man, the recipient, limited and imperfect, historically conditioned though he be. Truth is eternal, but there are degrees and varieties in the disclosure of truth and in the way in which it is received.

The claim to the possession of a unique revealed truth, which declines to be classified as one among many, is ruinous for men.[27] It is dangerous both in its motive and in its consequences. The truth is claimed to be not only absolute but exclusive. Advocates of such a claim do not say "this is my way," but "this is the way and the only way." We deplore the evil consequences of the fanaticism of unbelief, which also springs from the sense of the possession of exclusive truth. The claim to exclusive absolutism has produced an aggressive profession of faith, the persecution of other beliefs, an inquisitorial attitude to other faiths, and an attempt to force it on others through schools, through courts of law, etc. History offers abundant evidence that believers in an absolute, whether it is an absolute economic system or an absolute political doctrine or an absolute religious faith, develop intolerance. St. Augustine interpreted the words, "Compel them to come in" so as to justify persecution, wars of religion, methods of the Inquisition, with results which we all deplore. Bertrand Russell states that "historically no great religion has been as persecuting as Christianity." [28]

Karl Jaspers writes:

Another danger is the tendency to imagine that God's will can be known with certainty; this becomes a source of fanaticism. Many of the horrible things done in the world have been justified by God's

[27] "Because Christians believed that there had been only one Avatār, Christian history has been disgraced by more and bloodier crusades, interdenominational wars, persecutions and proselytising imperialism than has the history of Hinduism and Buddhism. Absurd and idolatrous doctrines, affirming the quasi-divine nature of sovereign states and their rulers, have led Oriental, no less than Western, peoples into innumerable political wars; but because they have not believed in an exclusive revelation at one sole instant of time, or in the quasi-divinity of an ecclesiastical organization, Oriental peoples have kept remarkably clear of the mass murder for religion's sake which has been so dreadfully frequent in Christendom. And while, in this important respect, the level of public morality has been lower in the West than in the East, the levels of exceptional sanctity and of ordinary individual morality have not, so far as one can judge from the available evidence, been any higher. If the tree is indeed known by its fruits, Christianity's departure from the norm of the Perennial Philosophy would seem to be philosophically unjustifiable." Aldous Huxley, *The Perennial Philosophy* (1944), 50f.

[28] Bertrand Russell, in the *Listener*, 7 Oct. 1948.

will. Fanatics fail to hear the many meanings inherent in every experience of God's voice. Any one who knows for certain what God says and wants, makes God into a being in the world, over which he disposes, and is thus on the road to superstition. But no worldly claim or justification can be based on the voice of God. What is solid certainty in the individual and sometimes can become so for a community, cannot be concretely formulated in terms of universal validity.[29]

In these words Karl Jaspers is distinguishing between philosophical mysticism and rational theology.

All men are God's children and not merely a few. There are men of nobility of vision and purity of heart outside our communities, and not all who belong to us are lovable in any real sense. When in the Old Testament the Jews treated themselves as the chosen people, protests were uttered, and God becomes the universal God who loves all people and takes pity on the heathen of Nineveh as against Jonah. "Are ye not as the children of Ethiopians unto me, O children of Israel?" says Yahweh. "Have not I brought up Israel out of the land of Egypt and the Philistines from Caphtor and the Syrians from Kir?" [30]

In the Christian religion we discern a transition from the religion of the cult to the prophetic religion of pure morals, from the religion of law to the religion of love, from the religion of priests to the religion of individual prayer and inward life, from the national God to the universal God.

It is true that, when men feel the religious truth, it comes to them with absolute validity. What is absolutely true to us in our historical context need not be universally valid for all. The absoluteness of truth implies the relativity of all formulations of it. The perception or awareness of truth in realization is something fundamentally different from the comprehension of the universal validity of particular propositional formulations of it. Historical absoluteness does not carry with it the universal validity of its manifestations in cults and dogmas.

The possessors of spiritual knowledge in the East and in the West admit the possibility of salvation through other names. Truth wears many vestures and speaks in many tongues. The spirit of truth requires us to admit that others may also be in the right, as ourselves. To imagine that God's nature can be known with certainty and that our dogmas set them forth is the source

---

[29] Karl Jaspers, in *The Perennial Scope of Philosophy* (1950), 43f.
[30] *Amos*, IX, 7.

of all fanaticism. Even some of the most conservative theologians do not admit that the Christian scriptures are a verbally exact communication by supernatural authority of infallible and absolute knowledge. The spirit of Christianity is different from the formal statements through which it is communicated to others.

Besides, there has also been the development of dogma. Christian theologians are also attempting to come to terms with increasing knowledge and scriptural criticism. They are examining and restating their fundamental convictions, for the traditional doctrines have come down to us from ages "when the sun and the stars moved round the earth, when the meaning of natural law and evolution was only dimly apprehended, when the psychology of religion, the historical method and the critical study of ancient documents were yet unborn." [31] Jesus, in a number of his views, was restricted by the knowledge and outlook of his age and nation. For example, he seems to have believed in hosts of demons, who caused diseases which could be cured by exorcising the spirits.

When we talk about 'sharing' the insights of different religions, we do not suggest a mechanical addition or a world faith on a syncretistic basis. We are asking for the conscious development of a historical process which is not unfamiliar to Christian thought, which has profited greatly from the valuable insights of other faiths. The discoveries of ancient papyri has helped us to understand the growth of early Christianity in the setting of its Hellenistic environment. We there see the close relationship of Christianity to those mystery religions which also believed in a dying Saviour God, a ritual meal of fellowship, and rebirth out of death into a blessed immortality.

Christianity not only had a profound effect on Western culture, but Western culture had a profound influence on Christianity. It contributed as much to Christianity as Christianity did to the Western peoples.

Though Greek philosophy was essentially and originally foreign to the Christian faith, the whole philosophic development of Christianity from St. John shows a gradually increasing acceptance of Greek thought. In the Fourth Gospel, the Logos of Greek thought and the Logos of Christ seem to merge. St. Paul baptised into Christ elements of Jewish faith, Greek thought, and Roman Law. Justin, in his *Apology* and *Dialogue with the Jew Trypho*, develops the view that the word, the Logos of God who appeared in various forms to the heroes of the Old Testament, as a human

[31] *Foundations* (1912), Introduction.

being to Abraham, as fire in the bush to Moses, was born as a human being of the Virgin Mary, was crucified and rose again. In distinguishing the Word of God from the ultimate Invisible Creator, Justin took over the Greek conception of the Logos which provided a mediating principle between the Supreme God and the phenomenal world. For Clement the process of revelation was one in all stages. Jewish law and Greek philosophy were for him preparation for the truth of the Christian revelation.

Fourth century Christianity is not much different from Neo-Platonism. In the writings of the Greek and the Syrian fathers, the resemblances to Neo-Platonism are most marked. Hierotheus and Dionysius the Areopagite, who passed for the disciples of St. Paul, proclaimed a mystic absolutism. "God is the Being of all That is," and can only be described by negatives. The Cappadocian fathers, Basil and the two Gregorys, were Platonists at heart. They believed in the essential mystery of the Divine being, though they maintained that imperfection does not render human knowledge untrue. The wisdom manifested in the created universe helps us by analogy to grasp the divine wisdom.

Augustine was deeply affected by Plato and Plotinus. The ecstatic illumination recorded in the *Confessions* [32] is expressed in the very words of Plotinus. Augustine agrees with the Neo-Platonists in denying the possibility of describing God. "God is not even to be called ineffable, because to say this is to make an assertion about Him." [33] *Enneads* first impelled him "to enter into the inner chamber of his soul and there behold the light." [34]

Boethius, the last of the Roman philosophers and the first of the Scholastics, thought as a Neo-Platonist. Aristotle influenced the Mediaeval schoolmen and Plato the English Platonists.

Christianity, like every religion, gained in richness and adequacy by accepting the insights of faiths and cultures with which it came in contact. Today our cultural environment has expanded so much that another renaissance may well be on the horizon. The world is shrinking and the opportunities for a world perspective

[32] St. Augustine's *Confessions*, VII, 16, 23. [33] *De doctr. Christ*, I, 6.
[34] *Cambridge Mediaeval History*, Vol. I (1911), 579: "The appeal away from the illusion of things seen to the reality that belongs to God alone, the slight store set by him on institutions of time and place, in a word the philosophic idealism that underlies and colours all Augustine's utterance on doctrinal and even practical questions and forms the real basis of his thought, is Platonic. And, considering the vast effect of his mind and writings on succeeding generations, it is no exaggeration to say with Harnack that Neo-Platonism influenced the West under the cloak of Church doctrine and through the medium of Augustine."

of religion are available. The classics of religion, Jewish and Christian, Hindu and Buddhist, Zoroastrian and Confucian, Muslim and Sikh do not belong to any one denomination or religion but belong to all. There will be mutual teaching and learning consciously or unconsciously among the different living faiths of mankind.

A study of other religions will draw together all believers and help them to understand the beliefs of others. Mistakes due to misunderstanding will be removed such as that Catholics believe that all non-Catholics are damned. By understanding the emphases of other faiths, we enlarge our own. We contract and conciliate distant affections. We recognise the elements of truth and dignity, of values of spirit included in other faiths. Such a study helps us to break the spell of egotism in which we tend instinctively to enclose ourselves. Even a layman like Warren Hastings writing from Benares on 4th October 1784, in his introduction to Charles Wilkins' English translation of the *Bhagavadgītā* refers to the "sublimity of conception, reasoning and diction, almost unequalled; and a single exception, among all the known religions of mankind of a theology accurately corresponding with that of the Christian dispensation and most powerfully illustrating its fundamental doctrines." [35]

A study of comparative religion gives us insight into the values of the various faiths, values which transcend their differing symbols and creeds and in transcending penetrate to the depths of spiritual consciousness, where the symbols and the formulas shrink into insignificance. In the uplifted consciousness of the Eternal, in the felt indwelling of the great Spirit, we recognise the relativity of all symbols and definitions and know that the central principles of religion, principles which harmonise all religions are the communion of the individual with God and the law of love or charity or kindness.[36]

Philosophy and Theology. In an interesting paper, written with strong conviction, Swāmi Agehānanda Bhārati is at pains to

[35] A noted Indian Christian leader, Mr. P. Chenchiah writes: "There was a type of convert in the past who hated Hinduism and surrendered himself wholeheartedly to what he supposed to be Christianity. The convert of today regards Hinduism as his spiritual mother who has nurtured him in a sense of spiritual values in the past. He discovers the supreme value of Christ, not in spite of Hinduism but because Hinduism has taught him to discern spiritual greatness." "Jesus and Non-Christian Faith," in *Rethinking Christianity in India*, 2nd ed. (1939), 60.
[36] Cf. "Religion and World Unity," *Hibbert Journal*, April, 1951.

make out that Indian philosophy is still in the scholastic state and most Indian philosophers are Schoolmen. He "who has surrendered his mind to one particular tradition of philosophical thinking" is a "School philosopher." His statement of other systems of thought becomes biassed. He sees only their defects and is blind to their merits. "Scholasticism, Indian and Western alike, is the way of biassed philosophising." The comparative philosopher should adopt an attitude of neutrality. "In the process of mastering other schools each will have to sacrifice his agreeable conviction of being right." He must be a mere spectator of life, viewing things from outside. While, for the Schoolmen, doubt is "a kind of disease or a symptom of immaturity," for the comparative philosopher, "doubt is his method." In other words, the philosophical impartiality expected of a historian or a student of comparative philosophy is not possible for one who has strong convictions. Only a consistent sceptic who is uncommitted to any school can deal justly with all systems of thought. Anyone who has strong views will find it difficult to be fair to other systems.

My own point of view on this matter has been indicated in the Preface to the first volume of my *Indian Philosophy,* written thirty years ago.

The task of the historian is hard, especially in philosophy. However much he may try to assume the attitude of a mere chronicler and let the history in some fashion unfold its own inner meaning and continuity, furnish its own criticism of errors and partial insights, still the judgments and sympathies of the writer cannot long be hidden. Besides, Indian philosophy offers another difficulty. We have the commentaries which, being older, come nearer in time to the work commented upon. The presumption is that they will be more enlightening about the meaning of the texts. But when the commentators differ about their interpretations, one cannot stand silently by without offering some judgment on the conflict of views. Such personal expressions of opinion, however dangerous, can hardly be avoided. Effective exposition means criticism and evaluation, and I do not think it is necessary to abstain from criticism in order that I may give a fair and impartial statement.[37]

It is difficult but not very difficult for one to be sincere, broad-minded and imaginative in the consideration of views with which one is not in sympathy or agreement. It would be rather hard if only sceptics are to undertake comparative studies in philosophy and non-religious persons comparative studies in religion. Their

[37] P. 9.

very scepticism may be an impediment to proper understanding of non-sceptical systems.

Apparently the writer seems to have a good deal of sympathy with the new philosophical movement of logical positivism, though he may not agree with all its 'dogmas.' As all schools of the Vedānta lay great stress on ontology and metaphysics, he would classify them as theological. He says:

> Without hesitation I would call any philosophy a theology which puts its entire emphasis on ontology and metaphysics (apart from its stress on revelation in cruder cases) at the cost of the other philosophic disciplines, viz., logic, ethics and perhaps aesthetics, if the last be claimed as an essential discipline. All the schools of the Vedānta do this.

I admit that it is so. But ontology and metaphysics are not the special province of theology as the latter term is ordinarily understood. There is no generally accepted definition of philosophy; but a definition which is broad enough to cover most of the systems dealt with in histories of philosophy would be this, *a logical inquiry into the nature of reality.* The results of the cognitive encounter with reality include more than logic and ethics. Every theory of knowledge refers to an interpretation of being. Even logical positivism, which makes metaphysics irrelevant, does not escape from metaphysics. If it is based on an analysis of human knowledge, it is based on metaphysical assumptions. What is the relation of verbal signs or logical operations to reality? Any answer to this question expresses a view of the structure of being. It is ontological. Ethics deals with value judgments. We cannot escape the question, what is the logical foundation of the validity of these judgments? This problem takes us to metaphysics.

If the Swāmiji means that we should take more interest in ethics and aesthetics, he is quite right. We assess the worth and importance of things quite as much as we notice other points about them. Each process conditions the other. The task of philosophy is to connect these two ways of thinking, harmonise the various aspects under which reality appears.

Swāmiji tells us that: "Surety is for the theologian; doubt is for the philosopher." "The Schoolman is a theologian and little of a philosopher." "He who adopts the Vedānta philosophy, whatever its variants may be, he is a theologian." Swāmiji quotes my sentence, "Man cannot live on doubt," and comments "but the philosopher can, though the theologian may not be aware of it."

It is somewhat arbitrary to say that men of conviction are theologians and men who are in a state of doubt are philosophers. Scepticism as a method is valuable, but not scepticism as a metaphysics. Doubt has been a great stimulus to inquiry, but it is not an end in itself. Even after the scholastic period in European thought, there have been eminent philosophers who are not sceptics, Descartes, Spinoza, Leibniz, and in our own time, Alexander, Whitehead.

Many of those who are lost in a sea of doubt are now taking to totalitarian creeds, political and religious, to get armoured in certainties.

It is one thing to say that we should question beliefs, since many are very questionable, and another thing to say that we should not have any beliefs. We should not hold beliefs simply because an authority, Scripture, church, or dictator announces them. Philosophy is a rebuttal of dogmatic assertions. It should offer rational evidence in support of its conclusions. Whether a system is a philosophy or not depends on the methods employed and not on the conclusions reached. We cannot, for example, argue that all theistic systems are theological and that atheistic systems are philosophical.

Another argument which the author adduces to show philosophy is confused with theology is that a philosopher is expected to be a Swāmi, a monk, his home is a retreat, an āśram. The average Hindu does not look upon a married man as quite a philosopher. "This is the reason why Radhakrishnan is not known to the Hindu who knows and refers to the output of the Dayānandas, the Rāmatīrthas, and the Vivekānandas rather than to the genuine knower—to the man who actually masters all the issues of Hindu thought."

On this matter the judgment of the Hindus is perhaps right. Philosophy as logical reflection is different from philosophy as the love of wisdom. Sophia or wisdom is not mere knowledge. It is knowledge lived. It is a way of life where valid knowledge is the condition of just action. With the monks, the ascetics, ideals and achievements are said to coincide. They are expected to practice what they preach. The tapasvin is not only a glowing coal but a shining lamp. He is not only consumed, but he illumines. I agree that this is an ideal difficult of achievement. I would feel most uncomfortable among authentic monks who are, of course, very rare; for I am aware of my weaknesses. I am human, much too human, and I do not know whether I do not prefer to be human.

Swāmiji points out that whereas the Hindu tolerates all kinds of teaching, he insists on the final authority of the scriptures. Systems which repudiate the Veda are condemned and those which accept the Vedic authority are approved, even though their teaching may be reprehensible. This is so and it is wrong. My whole treatment of Buddhism indicates that it is as great a system of thought as any evolved in our country and its repudiation of Vedic authority is an irrelevant issue. Loyalty to the Vedic tradition is a legal fiction that has enabled us to preserve the continuity of thought. A philosophy becomes dogmatic, if the assertions of the Scripture are looked upon as superior to the evidence of the senses and the conclusions of reason. We have had our scholastics.

After the eighth century philosophical controversy became traditional and scholastic in character, and we miss the freedom of the earlier era. The founders of the schools are canonised and so questioning their opinions is little short of sacrilege and impiety. The fundamental propositions are settled once for all and the function of the teacher is only to transmit the beliefs of the school with such changes as his brain can command and the times require. . . . The treasure that is the tradition clogs us with its own burdensome wealth, and philosophy ceases to move and sometimes finds it hard to breathe at all.[38]

The great teachers are not scholastics. The difference between the scholastic and the genuine philosopher is not that the latter invents a complete new set of opinions for himself while the former repeats stereotyped forms of thinking, but that the philosopher persistently rethinks the old material and is not content merely to learn and to repeat. Whatever department of thought we may cultivate, in that we have to rethink the insights of the past, carry inquiry further and make our own contribution. It is a waste of time to try to be original by despising the past. Whitehead remarks that the whole course of European philosophy is a series of footnotes to Plato. We cannot therefore say that it is all scholasticism.

Another argument mentioned by the Swāmiji to illustrate the theological character of Indian philosophy is that the Sanskrit equivalent of Philosophy is *darśana*, derived from *dṛś*, to see. From it the writer argues that it is "some kind of supra-intellectual realization or intuition." This view is popular in the West which is now suffering from a radical dissatisfaction with discursive thinking

[38] Ind P, 51.

which leads nowhere, a sort of unanchored thought, and there are so-called Swāmis who exploit this craving. Our author writes: "There is also much agreeable emotion and melodrama in sitting at the feet of masters belonging to very exotic regions; and the mention of lotuses and seers, of sacred groves and mountains easily thrills the primitivity-starved Westerner." These words of warning are well taken. The corruption of the best is the worst. It is not merely in the West but in India also that there are many of these pseudo-saṁnyāsins who exploit the credulity of emotionally unstable men and women. In 1934 at Hardwar I addressed the assembled monks on the theme "Beware of Sādhus."

But all this has little to do with philosophy as darśana. This does not mean the conversion of philosophy into theology. Swāmiji writes, "Philosophy avoids a mediator between wisdom and itself, whereas for theology the scripture is the only source of mediation to wisdom." "Authority, which does not bother about logic, is consistently substituted for the ratio."

I am afraid that the author is hardly fair to the Indian philosophical tradition. The material for the philosopher is supplied by empirical research, the inspection of facts, logical investigation, or insight of the soul. The fact of the existence of elaborate discussions and commentaries shows that intuition is not accepted on its own authority. Religious intuitions, like aesthetic judgments or common-sense facts, are the perceptions without which, in Kant's words, conceptions are empty. Philosophy does not work in a vacuum. The facts are given and the interpretations are free. If our conclusions agree with this or that view, it is an extra-philosophical accident. Any system of thought derives its authority as a philosophy from its own rational evidence and not from agreement with this or that system of dogma.

Swāmiji suggests that any system of philosophy which accepts intuition as a separate source of knowledge is theology, metaphysics, dogma, scholasticism. These four words are used to indicate the non-philosophical frame of mind. But surely many philosophers in Swāmiji's sense find it necessary to use intuition as a source distinct from sense perception and logical reasoning. Swāmiji accepts the laws of thought as fundamental to all philosophical investigation. They are not exactly objects of observation or results of logical reasoning. If they are self-evident axioms, what is self-evidence? Descartes, who found the method of mathematics to be the clue to the activity of reason, points out that by intuition we discover certain self-evident truths which answer to the postulates and axioms of geometry and, by a rigorous deduction of their consequences, we obtain a conceptual scheme which will reflect the nature of the real.

The Vedānta does not repudiate logic or the laws of thought. Were it so, the whole doctrine would have been so much imbecile incoherence and not "among the most searching thought-patterns created in this country," as the Swāmiji says.

Swāmiji takes up a sentence where I say: "It is essentially a philosophical solution since Śaṁkara lifts us through the power of thought which alone can reconcile and ennoble the different sides of life," [39] and argues that joy and peace are not the criteria for a philosophical solution. If a philosophy relieves us of doubt and uncertainty, it gives us logical satisfaction. If it enables us to integrate our nature, it gives us joy and peace.

The other points raised in Swāmiji's paper, such as the question of māyā, the contradictory accounts of Brahman, are discussed elsewhere in this "Reply."

While the general spirit of Śaṁkara's philosophy is commended in my writings, on many essential points I have developed on independent lines. My endeavour has been to expound a philosophy, not to state a dogmatic theology, a philosophy which offers an interpretation of the universe, which is at once rational and spiritual, which depends on logical reflection and not on acts of faith.

It is refreshing to read Swāmiji's plea for the debunking of the tall claims put forward both in India and outside that "India and India alone can save the world from disaster." He thinks that the West, tired of doubt and uncertainty and seeking security, is attracted by Indian systems of thought. In my writings my main contention has been to make out that there is one perennial and universal philosophy which is found in all lands and cultures, in the seers of the *Upaniṣads* and the Buddha, Plato and Plotinus, in Hillel and Philo, Jesus and Paul and the mediaeval mystics of Islam. It is this spirit which binds continents and unites the ages that can save us from the meaninglessness of the present situation, and not any local variant of it which we find in the Indian tradition. It is absurd to speak of any Indian monopolies of philosophic wisdom.

[39] Ind P, II, 656.

III. History of Philosophy

Historical Interpretation. In the interpretation of history, although we should not take liberties with the texts, we should not be satisfied with a mere collection of data. History of philosophy requires the employment of sympathetic imagination and creative insight. Every act of judgment calls for a delicate balancing of the mind. If my historical work suggests occasionally a painting rather than a photograph, as Professor Conger says, it is because I do not regard the past as a fossil for the scientific curiosity of the excavator. Whereas we should avoid conjectural interpretations, we must assume that the thinkers of the past have profundity of mind and motive which we ourselves possess. Objectivity does not mean unimaginativeness. There are some histories of philosophy in the East as well as in the West which are content with bald summaries of textual material. Reading them is like visiting Madame Tussaud's wax-works. Everything is there except life.

East and West. A certain pre-eminence of religious interest has been characteristic of Asian peoples, though it is by no means peculiar to them. Greek science and humanism determined the development of the West, though they are not unknown to the peoples of the East. Those of the West are distinguished by a restless activity of mind, by boundless curiosity, by insatiable idealism. As the spirit of perpetual search and exploration dominates the Western mind, stability, serenity, certitude are somewhat alien to it. Christianity infused a new spirit into the West. In the Middle Ages, under the admirable discipline which brought together the lessons of Greek thought and the teachings of the Christian Church, a delicate balance was found and under its influence, great masterpieces in art and literature, philosophy and religion were produced.

The mediaeval outlook soon yielded to the fierce and confused enthusiasms of the Renaissance; and, in the age of enlightenment that followed, the audacities of speculative daring and doubt found expression in a succession of great thinkers. A profound dissatisfaction with absolute standards produced a moral and intellectual impressionism. Between the mediaeval tradition of the West and the modern irregular way of life there is as much difference as between the Eastern and the modern.

We live in an age of fanatical scepticism. In the history of the past, ages of scepticism were followed by those of faith and spiritual awakening. The intellectual ferment in India of the 6th century B.C. gave rise to the Buddha and Mahāvīra. The age of the Sophists in Greece was succeeded by that of Socrates and Plato, the scepticism of the Academy by the onrush of Christianity. The restlessness of our age may be a preparation for a worldwide spiritual renaissance. For this a clear understanding of the basic assumptions of the Eastern and Western cultural developments is essential.

In his essay on *Eastern and Western Cultural Values*, Professor Northrop refers to the attitude of positive appreciation of other faiths adopted by Hinduism and Buddhism and the negative rejection of other faiths which is the basic feature of Judaism, Christianity and Islam, which may be taken as representative of the spirit of the West. He traces this distinction to the "indeterminateness" of the highest religious state, *mokṣa* in the Hindu and *nirvāṇa* in the Buddhist religions. The non-dogmatic attitude of the Eastern religions is, for Northrop, the logical consequence of the "basic naturalistic and philosophical conception of Far Eastern Oriental culture, philosophy and religion." He argues that the

ultimate object of empirical intuitive knowledge and religious devotion has two characteristics. First, it is not inferred by logical methods; instead it is a factor within the totality of immediacy of experience which can be known only immediately by direct apprehension. Second, it is to be distinguished from other immediately apprehended factors in the totality of immediacy by the fact that it is indeterminate and undifferentiated.[40]

From this Northrop deduces that "propositionalised formulations of the object of knowledge and value do not matter much." He says: "It follows from the intuitive nature of the basic knowledge underlying Oriental culture and religion that there not only will be but must be, if men are empirically and scientifically honest, different formulations of the relativistic *esse est percipi* differentiated factors in experience." So for these religions, doctrinal differences are "a mere quibble over words."

[40] The Supreme for Eastern religions is not "a speculatively postulated, syntactically designated and only indirectly and experimentally unified entity such as the mathematical as opposed to the sensed space in Newton's physics or the Unseen God the Father in the traditional Christianity of the West. He [the Hindu or the Buddhist] means something which is not inferred, not speculatively arrived at by the logical, scientific method of hypothesis but which is immediately experienced, its 'transcendency' of the senses being due to the fact that the senses deliver specific, limited, determinate data within it, whereas it is indeterminate and all-embracing." *The Meeting of East and West* (1946), 377.

The essential points in Professor Northrop's statement are: In the East (1) the ultimate object of knowledge is not logically inferred. (2) It is immediately apprehended. (3) It is indeterminate in its character. (4) Toleration of other views becomes legitimate and even necessary on this scheme. In the West (1) the central object of religion and value is a logical construction. (2) It is not immediately apprehended. (3) It has a determinate character. (4) Toleration on such a scheme is not possible in the easy way in which it is adopted in the East.

Although the great religious teachers of the East tell us that religion is a matter of life and discipline and not merely a matter of belief, they do not set aside logical inference. There are many for whom the ultimate reality is not an immediately experienced fact; for them the reality of God is conveyed by proofs. The different systems of thought are at great pains to demonstrate the logical necessity of the Ultimate Reality of which we can have direct apprehension also. Almost all the main concepts of Indian thought, *Brahman* and *Īśvara, puruṣa* and *prakṛti, karma* and rebirth are more concepts by postulation than concepts by intuition. The Nyāya system was originally called *ānvīkṣikī,* a rational investigation of what is given to us in scripture.[41] The very name, Buddha, the enlightened, shows the insistence on philosophical knowledge. Śaṁkara refers to two sections of the *Bṛhadāraṇyaka Upaniṣad* and says that the earlier depends on scripture (*āgamapradhānam*) and the later on reasoning (*upapattipradhānam*). He says, "When the two, scripture and reasoning, demonstrate the unity of the self, it is seen clearly as a bael fruit in the palm of one's hand." Śaṁkara affirms that the Divine reality is something given and also inferred. God can be known directly and derivatively. If we exaggerate in either direction the balance of religious tradition is disturbed. The whole of mediaeval scholasticism is an attempt to prove by reason the truths of revelation.

Even scientific propositions proceed on immediate data of perception and laws of reasoning. They are not speculations in the air. They cannot legislate things into existence. If the scientist confines his attention to the immediate data of perception and introspection and builds his hypotheses on them, the philosopher takes also the immediate data of religious life and points out the legitimacy of his hypothesis even to those who have not had a direct knowledge.

All knowledge involves an element of intuition which is later

41 *īkṣitasya ānvīkṣaṇam anvīkṣā.*

completed by postulation or deduction. There is no opposition between these two factors of knowledge. Northrop admits as much when he says that postulational theories require to be verified by direct intuition. The sharp opposition between immediate apprehension and logical analysis does not seem to be justified.

Because of the impressive achievements of science in the West in recent centuries we should not conclude that the scientific method was unknown to the East. Till the period of the Renaissance, there was not any striking difference in the field of science between the East and the West. There were great scientific minds in ancient India; only their powers of observation were directed to the inner world. The Nyāya logic, the Sāṁkhya psychology, the Vaiśeṣika analysis of the nature of substances, qualities and relationships, and the works on grammar show careful observation, close thinking, and a drawing of fine distinctions.[42]

Besides, if we are careful we will notice that the great metaphysical systems which are worked out in a logical way are really points of view, darśanas as they are called in India, visions of reality for which we discover reasons. The systems of Plato and Aristotle, Descartes and Spinoza, of Kant and Hegel, Bradley and Bergson, Alexander and Whitehead are as much the results of demonstration as the working out of intuitions.

The second proposition is that the ultimate reality is immediately apprehended. This is, no doubt, a prominent feature of Eastern religions; but it is also to be found in what Northrop adopts as the typical religions of the West. The vision of God is the aim of religious life. "Yet in my flesh shall I see God."[43] Professor Northrop cannot slight the great tradition in Western thought from the time of the Orphic and Eleusinian mystery religions down to our own day, which subordinates propositional forms to intuitive apprehensions. The great seers of religious truth are "near to one another on mountains farthest apart."

God is not, for Western religions, a "theoretically designated, directly unobservable entity." The immense variety of Western thought cannot be reduced to a single pattern of "concepts of postulation." The significance of transcendental intuition in Western philosophy cannot be overlooked.[44] For Plato, the ascent of

---

[42] Of Pāṇini's Sanskrit grammar, which could be printed in about 35 pages of quarto size, the late Professor A. Macdonell of Oxford said: "And yet this grammar describes the entire Sanskrit language in all the details of its structure with a completeness which has never been equalled elsewhere. It is at once the shortest and fullest grammar in the world."

[43] Job, XIX, 26.   [44] See IVL, chap. IV.

knowledge is a gradual progression from the world of common experience to a realm of Ideas, where the philosopher achieves a vision of the meaning of existence, of the source of all life. Unless we are freed from the fetters that confine us like the prisoners in the cave, unless we turn our face to the light behind us, unless we are spiritually liberated, we cannot have the vision. All the dialectical preparation is for the intuitive vision.

Northrop contends that there are two types of mysticism, that of the empirical, denotative, particular reality, and that of the logical and intellectual reality. The former he calls the aesthetic or the existential or the concrete, and the latter the theoretic or the logical. In the discussion of the relation of intuition to intellect, I have referred to the intellectual character of intuition. The highest type of mysticism is most rational.

Professor Northrop's third point is that the Western mode of knowing gives us determinate knowledge and not knowledge of the "indeterminate undifferentiated formlessness which is the source of value in Oriental religion." *Brahman, nirvāṇa* are "states without any specific condition," whereas the Western conception of God is determinate.[45]

Simply because the Eastern thinkers stress that the Divine reality cannot be adequately grasped and expressed by logical categories, that its truth can only be conveyed negatively or analogically, it does not follow that the Eastern concept of the spiritual has no place for determinate logical knowledge. Even in Advaita Vedānta, to which alone Northrop's characterisation may be said to apply, we have the distinction between the indescribable Absolute Brahman knowable by direct experience and "a determinate being knowable only by means of postulated propositions indirectly verified." [46] Even in Western thought there is this confession of verbal and logical inadequacy. I need not refer to the well known mystics. St. Thomas Aquinas writes:

Although in God there is no privation, still, according to the mode of our apprehension, he is known to us only by way of privation and

45 From this Northrop argues that the Eastern religions are non-theistic. He says, "theism in religion is the thesis that the divine is identified with an immortal non-transitory factor in the nature of things which is determinate in character. A theistic God is one whose character can be conveyed positively by a determinate thesis. His nature is describable in terms of specific attributes. All of the Oriental religions which have been examined up to this point deny this characteristic of the divine . . . specific determinate properties designate what it is not, not what it is." *The Meeting of East and West* (1946), 401.

46 See Ind P, I, 35-41.

remotion. Thus there is no reason why certain privative terms should not be predicated of God, for instance that he is *incorporeal* and *infinite;* and in the same way it is said of God that he is one.[47]

These words are used to show the freedom from limitations and should not be used to support an indeterminate formlessness in the sense of utter vacuity.

The fourth point is in regard to the attitude of toleration. Northrop asks, "Why is it that contradictions are impossible within the Oriental mode of knowing and its concept of the spiritual, whereas contradictions between diverse doctrines are of the very essence of the Western type of knowledge and its attendantly different concept of the spiritual?" The doctrine of toleration is regarded as "appropriate to Oriental belief grounded in its mode of knowing" and inappropriate to "Western beliefs and spiritual values grounded in their different mode of knowing."

In the Western mode of knowing, the universal is the essential factor. "Moral man is not merely determinate man but also propositionalised man." Therefore, "when propositionalised conceptions turn out to be self-contradictory, then ideological conflict is the result." The believer in a dogma must burn the heretic!

Logical method knows no frontiers. The law of contradiction obtains in both East and West. Even in the East no one can hold at the same time the two principles of the reality of God and His unreality. The acceptance of one requires the rejection of the other.

Even if Northrop's view is correct, scientific hypotheses are arrived at by a process of trial and error and cannot therefore be regarded as possessing absoluteness or finality.[48] Freedom from the spirit of dogmatism is the chief characteristic of the scientific temper. Northrop himself cites how, in mathematical physics, we are adopting two contradictory hypotheses, the relativity theory and quantum mechanics.

Possibly many doctrines which seem to be opposites may, on closer examination, turn out to be distincts which are compatible with each other. It is by the method of free inquiry that we have

[47] *Summa Theologica,* 1 Q.11.a.3.

[48] Professor Northrop would be surprised to find Stalin ask for the spirit of free inquiry. In his article on *Linguistics,* Stalin writes about N. Y. Marr and his disciples: "It is generally recognised that no science can develop and flourish without a battle of opinions, without freedom of criticism. But this generally recognised rule was ignored and flaunted in the most unceremonious fashion. A group of infallible leaders, having ensured themselves against all possible criticism, began to act arbitrarily and highhandedly."

to find out whether two propositions or theories are logically opposed to each other or are only distinct propositions or theories which are not logically incompatible. But when these propositional forms are accepted as absolute and of universal validity from all frames of reference, further inquiry becomes taboo. In the interests of the progress of thought, which for Northrop is the central trend of Western culture, it is essential to treat propositional forms as working hypotheses and not as final truths.

The tendency to question and explore and not accept any proposition as final, to move forward, not to live in the old forms bequeathed to us, has made the Western world what it is. Luther attacking Rome, Columbus sailing westward to the East, ardent humanists canonising Plato and dethroning Aristotle who had presided over mediaeval thought, Copernicus questioning Ptolemy, all these are symbolic of the whole thought structure of the Western people. The Greeks had the scientific spirit, but their scientific life was shortlived. We need not pause to consider whether the arrest was due to Plato or to Jesus. The process was resumed roughly in the sixteenth century, but essentially not until then. The periods when the propositional forms were treated as of absolute authority were not the ages of progress.

The view which holds that the propositional forms are inadequate attempts at expressing what Northrop calls "undifferentiated immediacy" helps the progress of thought.[49] It is the aim of religious life to get at the ultimate Fact of the universe, and the symbols are the means by which we get access to the fact. They are working methods and not final theories.

To say that these formulations have instrumental or symbolic value and are to be tested in our lives is not to adopt an attitude of utter indifference to the different forms. The alternatives are not dogmatism and indifference. St. Thomas Aquinas, a characteristic Western thinker, says,

It is agreed that whatever is received into anything is therein after the mode of the recipient; and consequently the likeness of the divine essence impressed on our intellect will be according to the mode of our intellect; and the mode of our intellect falls short of a perfect

---

[49] Dewey, a typical American philosopher, argues that the world is 'indeterminate' and the determinate objects of knowledge are in some way constructed by the 'operations of knowing.' Construction is a working determinate of something which was originally formless and indeterminate. See his *Essays in Experimental Logic*, Chap. 11.

reception of the divine likeness; and the lack of perfect likeness may occur in as many ways as unlikeness may occur.[50]

Religious people, the world over, aim at a knowledge of God, enlightenment, *jñāna, bodhi*. Religion is outwardly a rite; inwardly it is a being born again. If we agree on principles, we may allow differences in the forms of worship. Every one must make use of the forms appropriate to his own psycho-physical constitution and develop contemplative disciplines suited to his temperament.

By introducing sharp distinctions and treating them as exclusive of each other Northrop suggests that the basic assumptions of the two streams of thought are opposed to each other. He, however, admits that they are only different but not incompatible. They are not identical, but can subsist together.

Philosophy in the East like science is rooted in experience. The validity of the theories is confirmed or falsified by immediately perceived data. "Within the method of Western scientific knowledge the relation between its immediately apprehended component, on which the Oriental concept of the spiritual rests, and the propositionalised, theoretically known, non-immediately apprehended component, from which the Western concept of the spiritual derives, must be contained." This is true not only of "Western scientific knowledge" but of all knowledge, either Western or Eastern. Kant's words that perceptions without conceptions are blind and conceptions without perceptions are empty are well known. Northrop paraphrases this principle when he says: "The important consequence is that this makes the immediately known aesthetic component of things upon which the Oriental concept of the spiritual rests as ultimate, irreducible, and real as the propositionalised theoretic component of things in which the Western concept of the spiritual has its roots."

The truth, which is somewhat exaggerated in Northrop's analysis, is that in the East there is a greater preoccupation with the richer and less determinate facts of existence than with the abstract and determinate facts of essence. There is a point in this distinction, if it is a question of more and less and not of either or. Therefore it is possible, as Northrop hopes, to achieve a truly world society in which the two sets of values derived from the two modes of knowing can be reconciled.

It is unfortunate that Northrop attributes the political weak-

50 *Summa Theologica*, iii, Q. 92, a. 1.

ness of India to this spirit of tolerance and makes out that it is "probably the major explanation of the historical fact that India through almost the entirety of her history has been under the domination of Western or Middle Eastern theistic peoples and powers." Professor Northrop is afraid that India, with her spirit of toleration, is not appreciating "the exceptionally dangerous character of contemporary world Communism." If India adopts the same "attitude of toleration appropriate for Oriental differences of beliefs," she will "have rid herself from the recent domination of the Western British only to welcome and find herself again under the yoke of the even more doctrinaire and dangerously intolerant Western Marxist Communists." Perhaps one may venture the hope that it is the acceptance on a larger scale of the principle of toleration which will make for the healing of the world's divisions. This end can be reached only by finding out the facts accounted for by the apparently incompatible doctrines and achieving a larger synthesis which takes note of all the considerations implied by the two opposed views.

Professor Northrop holds that there is "a logical and practical incompatibility of Marxist Communism and traditional French and Anglo-American democracy" and "an end cannot be put to the present cold war in the world after the manner suggested by Professor Radhakrishnan and the Quakers by appealing from the Foreign Secretaries and the militarists to ethics and to religion, nor by acting towards Communists as if they were Quakers or nondualistic Vedānta pacifists." Professor Northrop is evidently unhappy about my attitude in regard to this cold war. In these matters each one has to try to think for himself and act according to his conscience. This is the basic principle of democracy. The spirit of the United Nations Charter requires us to strive for a pacific settlement of the present conflict. To strive for a peaceful settlement is not to appease. I agree that the Communists are neither "Quakers nor nondualistic Vedānta pacifists." Nor are most of us Quakers or pacifists.

I do not plead for peace at any price or for nonviolence in all conditions of life. But I most emphatically affirm that, in this troubled and irrational world, our actions should be governed by right principles, if they are to lead to any improvement in international affairs. Conflicts within states are adjusted by laws; among states they are adjusted by agreements and treaties. If we shift and change our policies to suit our military strategy, if we scrap solemn agreements simply because they are inconvenient, we weaken respect for a code of right conduct among nations.

To resolve the present conflict it is not necessary to adopt either the method of negation which is war or the method of mergence which will lead to an indeterminate confusion. To destroy Soviet Russia or to submit to it are not the only alternatives. Wise statesmen all over the world are striving their utmost to prevent a third world war, for that would mean a general impoverishment and social desolation, just the soil for the breeding of subversive creeds. Mr. Lewis Douglas, former U. S. Ambassador to the United Kingdom, said on the 23rd of April, 1951, "The very desolation which it [a war] will leave in its trail will make the social soil in the Orient, in Europe, indeed, everywhere including here at home, more fertile and better watered for the seeds of Communism and revolution to take root in." [51] President Truman in an address to the National Civil Defence Conference (7th May, 1951) said: "The best defence against atomic bombing is to prevent the outbreak of another world war and achieve a real peace. We must bend all our energy to the job of keeping our free way of life and to doing it without another war." We cannot overestimate the gravity of the present time. The whole civilised world is in danger. This is not the moment for the display of fanaticism designed to disrupt or coerce governments or confuse the public mind. The business of statesmanship is not to sharpen existing dangers and hatreds, but to reconcile the apparent opposites and contain them within a peaceful world order and not impose by force any particular way of life on the whole world in the hope that all tensions will then be removed.

Never in human history has the universal in the soul of man burnt so dimly as today. It is for the philosophers to realise the human in all, Russian or American, Chinese or British. We have to give up the war mentality and the belief that we want peace while the others want war, to find out if the basic assumptions of the conflicting ways of life are so completely incompatible that the only relationship between the two is war to the knife.

Whereas some of us regard the leaders of Russia as gangsters who are ready to surge across Europe, Asia and Africa in search of fresh booty and far flung frontiers, there are others who are hypnotised by the alleged moral and religious appeal of Communism. The leaders of Soviet Russia and Peoples' China are treated as apostles of a new religion, crusaders for a new world order, who

[51] *Times* (London), April, 24, 1951.

strike terror into bourgeois society by the moral authority with which they speak to the masses about the brutalities of capitalist society. To look upon Communist leaders as fiends filled with greed, fraud, cruelty and savage ambition is as extreme as to idolise them as the heroes of a new world order. Their defiance of constitutional methods, their faith in the doctrine that the end justifies the means, their use of democratic liberties for attaining power and their suppression of them when they attain it,[52] the way in which they employ cunning and cruelty to reach their goal are often mentioned. I do not say that in the matter of civil liberties and political democracy, conditions are anything comparable to what these doctrines generally imply. The Communists do not believe in free speech. Where they are in power, they suppress it. They ban all other political parties. There is much resentment in regard to their interference in Eastern democracies. Apart from Tito in Yugoslavia, the cases of Gomulka in Poland, Clementis in Czechoslovakia, Rajk in Hungary, Patrashcanu in Rumania, Kostov in Bulgaria, Xoxe in Albania, point to the way in which nationalist sentiments are suppressed in Communist lands. Insistence on subservience to Soviet Russia in non-Russian Communist countries hurts the pride of the people. It is most prominent in Eastern democracies where, for security reasons and under cover of the Yalta Agreement, Russia is practically dominating. All these are points which are distinctly to the discredit of Communist theory and practice.

In spite of these obvious disadvantages, if Communist parties spring up and thrive in different parts of the world, it is because the doctrine satisfies certain basic human needs. Political ideologies which are committed to the maintenance of the existing economic structure, which propose to effect economic improvements for the large majority while retaining their present framework cannot wean peoples away from Communism. Communism spreads among people who are alienated from capitalist society, who are not held together by the bond of a shared moral principle, where a majority of people do not find a meaning and purpose to individual existence in the groups to which they belong. We need a new type of society whose basic concern will be the welfare of the people as a whole. We must transform the community so as to

52 Montalembert's description of the Catholic attitude applies to the Communist policy: "When I am the weaker I ask you for liberty because it is your principle, but when I am the stronger, I take it away from you because it is not my principle." Communist parties seek the aid of other leftist parties when they are weak and turn against them when they are strong.

give to it a new social vision. The economic security aimed at in a welfare state cannot be attained without a surrender of some democratic liberties. The planned economy of the United Kingdom and the Scandinavian States offers a middle course between totalitarian planning and unregulated private enterprise. All these attempts indicate that there is some justification for the Communist criticisms.

By fighting Communism in the battlefields of Europe and Asia, we attack only the symptoms, not the disease. We fight on a material terrain where boundaries are drawn between Communist and non-Communist countries, where victories are marked by triumphal arches built on waste land but not in the arena of the minds of men. It is not by pouring munitions into all parts of the world to arm every one against every one else, but by devoting a part of our wealth and attention to world betterment, that we can meet the challenge of Communism. In large parts of the world today we have suffering men, impatient, ready to revolt, with a smouldering rage against the existent order. We must demonstrate to them that democracy is a truly revolutionary force. America has the great opportunity of world leadership, moral and material. Her people are known for their idealism and generosity. Their anxiety to save the world from Communism is serious and genuine. They are prepared for extraordinary sacrifices in this cause. But the most effective way of overcoming the social and economic dangers which Communism threatens will be to set up a world reconstruction fund for the removal of social and economic ills in large parts of the world, for the speeding up of the struggle for world betterment. This is to make the world "safe for democracy." Again, while poverty and starvation predispose the suffering people to the acceptance of Communism, the intellectuals are attracted to it as it fills an emotional void caused by the loosening hold of traditional religion. Democracy must become an active faith working for freeing the peoples from colonial rule and establishing equal human rights for all racial minorities. So long as democracy compromises with its own foundations, it cannot stop the spread of Communism. A Communist may be tempted to say that the difference between Communism and democracy is not a question of difference of programmes but is essentially a difference between those who are honest and those who are not honest abou implementing the ideals of democracy, social justice, race equality, anti-imperialism, political or economic. From my slight acquaintance with the American people I know that the democratic ideology is not played out with them. There are vast, powerful sections of the American people at all levels, who, if they get a chance, will affirm their confidence in democracy and social progress, work for understanding with Russia and China and support every, where not narrow anti-Communism but progressive and demo, cratic forces.

It is wishful thinking to imagine that because we feel the lack of certain liberties in Soviet Russia, which we associate with parliamentary democracies, therefore the people of Russia are all disgruntled and ready to throw off the 'tyranny' when the first opportunity arises. It is true that standards are low compared to the American, that beggars are sometimes found in the streets of Moscow, that class distinctions have not disappeared altogether, etc., etc. But the standards have improved a great deal. There is a more equitable distribution of food and opportunity than ever before. Literacy is widespread and intellectual interests are fostered. Religion is tolerated; it is neither encouraged nor suppressed.[53] Art is not decadent. Literature and drama, painting and ballet have, in some ways, achieved perfection. The wordless beauties which are enacted before our eyes are the eternal protest of men and women of refined feeling against the glamour and falseness of so much tinsel that passes for life. The children are full of spontaneous life and gaiety and their interests are served with admirable care. Attendance at the theatre and at concerts is a part of organised education. The dramatic, musical and artistic life of the country is decentralised and in every province and town distinctive developments are to be noticed. As in some previous ages of communal civilised life the artist and the public each sustain and live on the other. There is an environment of art which breeds the free spirit of the individual. Great art is not merely a way of social living but is a sign of social health. It will eventually make for the removal of the coercive control over arts and education which now prevails. Even religion has been, for the Russian, a profound aesthetic experience. Russian Orthodoxy differs from the Greek

53 Stalin said to Roosevelt "that at the time of the revolution the Russian Communist party had proclaimed the right of freedom of religion as one of the points of their programme. The Russian Patriarch and the entire then existing Church had declared the Soviet Government an anathema and had called on all Church members not to pay taxes nor to work, etc. He said what could the Soviet Government do but to, in fact, declare war on the Church which assumed that attitude. He added that the present war had wiped out this antagonism and that now the freedom of religion, as promised, could be granted to the Church." *The White House Papers of Harry Hopkins*, p. 896.

Orthodoxy, Roman Catholicism and Western Protestantism, insofar as its interest is more in liturgy than in philosophy, theology
or dogma. Religion is a quality of life which binds together the
faithful who share a common experience in an invisible community. It is the sense of the community of men as comprising a single
congregation bound by a common ritual and liturgy and ultimately by a common sense of brotherhood. Above all there is an
atmosphere of hope and purpose. The eyes of Russia are turned
towards the future, towards the possibilities of things. The people
have a sense of pride that their country has become, through blood
and tears, one of the two great powers of the world. With all this
we cannot say that in Soviet Russia man's powers are decaying.
Not even the most hostile witness can affirm that any living Russian would prefer Tsarist Russia to Soviet Russia. If there are such
they only illustrate the triumph of unreasoning prejudice.

Like all historic institutions the Soviet system has elements of
evil as well as of good. It is wrong to assume that our world is the
only possible civilised world and beyond its frontiers is barbarism.
If we are patient and restrained, I am not without hope that peaceful adjustments and approximations may take place between the
Communist and non-Communist worlds. No tyranny can outlast
the unquenchable energy and adventures of the mind. Basic human nature in its impregnable majesty will triumph sooner or
later over every attempted tyranny.

Communist doctrine is not a fixed star. Marx and Engels did not
lay down a final doctrine. They had conceived of their theory as
dynamic and subject to development. 'Marxism' according to its
founders is 'no doctrine but a movement.' It is not dogmatic but
creative. Lenin and Stalin have continually reinterpreted and
adapted Marxist principles to the Russian Revolution and the
Soviet State. Communism in Russia is a blend of Marxism and the
Russian inheritance. It is a different thing in Yugoslavia. In China
the New Democracy has dropped certain principles of Marxism
and adapted others to local conditions. In the People's democracies
of Eastern Europe, when conditions of peace and stability obtain,
changes will occur, which will foster the growth of democratic
socialism.

We need not despair that the "police state" will be the permanent form of the Soviet State. In the words of the *Communist
Manifesto* (1848), "when in the course of development, class distinctions have disappeared and all production has been concentrated in the hands of a vast association of the whole nation, the

public power will lose its political character. In place of the old bourgeois society, with its classes and class antagonism we shall have an association in which the free development of each is the condition for the free development of all." This is the vision of the future, a true and universal humanism in which there will be a gradual superseding of law by a regime of free self-determination. The common people believe that this is the ideal for which they are working. "The logic of facts," even Stalin admits, "is stronger than any other logic." In compliance with this logic, the "International" was dropped as the national anthem and a new hymn beginning with the words "unbreakable union of free republics welded together by the great Rus" has replaced it. Bonds of family life, legal and economic, are restored and a judicial process of divorce was established in 1944 for the first time since the Revolution. In regard to the economic rights of the individual also there have been changes. The League of the Militant godless has disappeared. The 1936 Constitution enfranchised the clergy. In 1937 wage penalisation for attendance at religious festivals was discontinued.[54] In 1940 the seven-day week was restored with Sunday as a common day of rest. I give these illustrations to show that the Soviet system is capable of changes.

The Soviet State has two sides to it, the Police and the Welfare. When we criticise it we have in view the former. The Police State begins to function when persons are suspected of antagonism to the regime, when they are picked up by the secret police, tried secretly by administrative boards and condemned to hard labour. These methods are adopted to check counter-revolution from within and intervention from without. The Russian people and their leaders suffer, not unjustifiably, from the intervention complex. So long as there is encouragement of resistance movements to established governments either in Russia or in China, the police methods will continue. If we wish to help their removal, we must make these governments feel secure and not organise resistance movements or encourage associations of "Friends of fighters for freedom in Russia." It is essential that the Cominform should be

---

[54] "The rôle of the Church as having a legitimate part to play in the life of the people (but not of the Communist Party) has been recognised, anti-religious publications have been discontinued, a few Church Seminaries have been opened, many thousands of new Churches have been licensed, monasteries have been exempted from taxation, a religious periodical is published—not to satisfy American public opinion, but primarily to satisfy Soviet public opinion." Harold J. Benman, *Justice in Russia* (1950), 40. However, the six million party members and the sixteen million young Communists are not allowed to go to Church.

abolished, and Russia should make it clear that she will not interfere overtly or covertly with established governments of a non-
Communist character. If she has faith in her philosophy she should
leave peoples and governments to reform themselves. She may
feel that she has saved herself by her effort and may save the world
by her example. If she really believes in the coexistence of the two
systems, then non-interference with each other should be the
motto for both the Russians and the non-Russians. If we recognise
that the Chinese and the Russians are after all human beings, with
all their failings, we shall help them to improve the systems under
which they live. Communism as an economic system need not be
totalitarian or anti-democratic. The State may have the right to
control the means of production in the interests of the common
good; but it need not interfere with individual liberty in other
matters. We may help Russia to build a classless, co-operative,
cohesive society based on democratic principles. I wish to emphasise that the Soviet State is in flux and is changing as the result of
conflicting ideas and circumstances, intentions and realities. Our
duty is not to curse Communism but to regenerate it.

I regret to say that the way we are now going about with our
sharp distinctions of good and evil is the sure road to disaster. We
have become the victims of transient passions and are overlooking
the fundamental needs of humanity. History will hold us responsible if we throw the world into flames in our fanatic zeal for our
way of life.

Our enemy is the anonymous machine which brings about great
concentration of power and subjects the majority of people to a
state of monotonous automatism, encouraging the use of power
for unworthy ends. To abuse opportunities for improving the lot
of man and work for what we assume to be our self-interest and
security are the greatest dangers. The sense of the impotence of
the individual is not limited to any one country or ideology. We
had similar periods in human history when people believed that
their fortunes were controlled by distant stars or unseen spirits.
We must get out of the hypnotic influence of the inevitability of
history and realise that human intelligence can shape the future.
Democracy believes in freedom of the spirit, in the principle of
toleration which is not exclusively Indian. It is an eternal truth at
once a heritage of the past and an attraction of the future. It is
the demand of Eastern religions and the postulate of Western science. If the peoples of the world are humble and honest and
realise that neither side to the present conflict is absolutely right

or absolutely wrong, they may get together and resolve the conflict. The world is not to consist of all like-minded people; no state consists of such. A state is instituted by people who have to live together and who find it difficult to do so peacefully.

Let us heed the warning uttered more than a hundred years ago by Alexis de Tocqueville in the Preface to his *Democracy in America:*

The Christian nations of our age seem to me to present a most alarming spectacle; the impulse which is bearing them along is so strong that it cannot be stopped, but it is not yet so rapid that it cannot be guided; their fate is in their hands; yet a little while and it may be so no longer. The first duty which is at this time imposed upon those who direct our affairs is to educate the democracy; to warm its faith, if that be possible; to purify its morals; to direct its energies, to substitute a knowledge of business for its inexperience and an acquaintance with its true interests for its blind propensities; to adapt its government to time and place, and to modify it in compliance with the occurrences and the actors of the age. A new science of politics is indispensable to a new world. This, however, is what we think of least; launched in the middle of a rapid stream, we obstinately fix our eyes on the ruins which may still be described upon the shore we have left, while the current sweeps us along and drives us backward toward the gulf.

A "new science of politics" is "indispensable to a new world." Let us understand the historic forces which are shaping the future and not bury our heads in the sands of the past.

Buddhism. Professor T. R. V. Murti's account of my treatment of Buddhism raises one fundamental question. While he agrees that the Buddha repudiated the reality of the empirical world and the empirical ego, and admitted the reality of a Transcendent Principle, he feels that the Buddha stood out of the tradition of the *Upaniṣads* in rejecting the reality of the ātman. He says that "the Buddha's implicit acceptance of a transcendent Reality does not mean that he accepted the Upaniṣad tradition, for nowhere does he identify it with the ātman." The ātman for the *Upaniṣads,* is the universal self distinct from the empirical ego or the *jīva.* The question relates therefore to the views of the Buddha on the nature of the self. His *anattā* doctrine denies the reality of the mutable ego, the psycho-physical individual. That the mortals are devoid of self is an ancient Hindu view.[55]

The liberated realise the universal self which is non-empirical.

55 *Śatapatha Brāhmaṇa,* II.2.2.3.

In the passage which Murti quotes from the *Udāna* it is said that "there is an unborn, unbecome, unmade (akatam), incomposite (asaṁkhatam) and were there not, there would be no escape from the born, the become, the made and the composite." The knower of this, transcendent, what is never made is *akataññū*. The liberated individual is awake, *buddho*, immovable, *anejo;* he has done whatever has to be done by him, *kataṁ karaṇīyam.* What can this *bodhi* or enlightened consciousness be if it is not the universal self? The many passages in which the Buddha stresses that this or that "is not my self," that there is "a self that is the lord of self, that is the goal of self," [56] "that the self upbraids the self," [57] suggest the reality of the universal self, the ātman, that is transcendent to the empirical ego. The individual, whose self is liberated, is spoken of as one who is existent, altogether content, who knows that there is no more birth, no more becoming for him.[58] The difference between the views of the *Upaniṣads* and the Buddha is not one of acceptance or rejection of the theory of ātman but of emphasis or lack of emphasis on the reality of the ātman.

Sung Confucianism. Professor Hinman's article on this subject is an implicit criticism of the position that for Eastern religions ultimate reality is an indifferenced indeterminate formlessness. He argues that Neo-Confucianism is not to be confused with an abstract monism. Referring to Śaṁkara, Hinman observes: "There is no negativity within this abstract affirmation, therefore no difference or parts and that therefore it could not ground or engender anything whatever. And yet there exists the entire universe of fact, although its manifold of existence has just been denied." My own views on the nature of the Supreme Reality and māyā have already been given in the sections on "*Absolute and God*" and "*The Status of the World.*" An undifferenced *Brahman,* what Hinman calls an "Empty Absolute," negation as non-entity and the world of māyā are not to be left fused and confused. I am as keen as is Hinman to "defend the concreteness of the Supreme Ultimate," and save the world of appearances; though I doubt whether the philosophy of the Concrete Universal does this satisfactorily. My acquaintance with Sung Confucianism is slight and second hand; but I feel considerable sympathy with its criticism of abstractionism. Its insistence on relating "its unchangeable

---

[56] *Dhammapada*, 380.
[57] *attāpi attānam upavadati. Aṅguttara Nikāya* I, 57-58.
[58] *Samyutta Nikāya*, III, 55.

clear law" to "the business of life" is worthy of imitation by all systems of philosophy and religion.

The Neo-Confucian criticism of Buddhist philosophy is based on the idea that Buddhism leads to "the destruction of the social relations and the cardinal virtues." This is an estimate of Buddhist ethics which will not be generally accepted.

IV. ETHICAL, SOCIAL, AND POLITICAL PHILOSOPHY

Professor Wadia and Mr. Marlow refer to my views on caste and hold that, whereas I repudiate it in the form in which it has come down to us, I discern elements of value in that institution when it was established. The explanation of my "inconsistencies" may be given in the words which Wadia himself has quoted from my *Hindu View of Life*, which was published twenty-five years ago: "Today we are clinging to the shell of our religion for self-preservation. The envelope by which we try to protect life checks its expansion. An institution appropriate and wholesome for one stage of human development becomes inadequate and even dangerous when another stage has been reached." Like all historical institutions caste had its elements of good and of evil. Social conditions bring out certain institutions. They create themselves or are created. They seem to appear as the solid foundations of the social order; but they are not solid. They are continually changing. When the framework becomes cramping, it is exploded. If we look at the way in which the idea grew up in our history, it will appear a natural and even a necessary stage.

There are universal moral principles based on human nature as such; there are variations in our understanding of them from one period to another. A change of circumstances alters the manner of their application. Institutions as applications of certain fundamental principles to contingent circumstances are subject to alteration. The elements of good are brought out in Professor S. K. Chatterji's essay on "Dynamic Hinduism."

Mr. Mallik suggests that the caste scheme has something to teach us even today, that the individual is a feeble creature apart from the collective life from which he draws his strength.[59] Mr.

[59] The late Mr. K. Natarajan, an ardent social reformer, in a paper on *What is Caste?* wrote: "Other communities in India have moulded their social life on the caste pattern. The Parsis, not only according to judicial ruling but also by their own preference, are a caste. The Jews who settled in India many centuries ago are divided into two castes. The Syrian Christians, another anciently settled Indian community, are also split in several groups having the essential characteristics of

Mallik's closely reasoned and subtle exposition of the various problems, such as the achievements of European civilisation, the League
of Nations, the theory of the State, organization as related multiplicity, indicates his approach to the solution of outstanding questions,
such as the freedom of the individual and planning by the State.
He is right in stating that I have not developed any metaphysical
theory of the State.

I am afraid that I cannot agree with Mr. Mallik in thinking
that there is a fundamental difference between the Brahmanical
and the Buddhist views. Individualist egalitarianism is a modern
motive. The Buddha says that "men belittle the doctrine of caste
only when they are overcome by greed." [60] Both systems are opposed to a conception of society which makes it an inorganic
multiplicity where all are proletarians with no vocations but jobs.
The principle of society is not uniformity but unity in variety.
There is so much insistence today on individuality; but the modern machine has effectively suppressed it. I should like to make it
clear that any scheme based on heredity is not only undemocratic
but unspiritual. Our perception of the equality of human beings
is the result of the realisation that heaven and earth, life and
history are irradiated by a Spiritual Presence.

When the Hindu Scriptures, like the *Bhagavadgītā*, emphasise
the correlation of *svabhāva* and *svadharma*, one's nature and one's
duty, they refer to the special vocation of the individual, the way
in which, in a particular set of circumstances, he can best realise
his possibilities.[61] Each individual, according to this scheme, reflects
an element of the divine. His character, his ethical training, his
social occupation should be developed with reference to the conditions of that element. Plato defines justice as "doing one's work

caste. Roman Catholic Christians in Southern India maintain the distinction of
high caste and low caste. In Western India they cherish the memories of their
original castes and intermarriages between descendants of converts from different
castes are uncommon. There are Muslim castes also. The Khojas, the Bohras, the
Memons are Muslim castes. When an institution is so widely diffused, the obvious
inference is that it possesses some definite advantages to those who follow it. . . .
Brahmins are credited with having evolved the present day castes from machiavel-
lian motives. No one with a trace of sociological insight will credit this fantastic
notion of comparatively small groups imposing their selfish will on the mass of
mankind." *Indian Social Reformer*, Feb. 5, 1938. An institution good for its own
time becomes dangerous at a later age. The reforms of one age may easily become
the reactionary patterns of a later period.

[60] *jātivādaṁ niramkatva. Sutta Nipāta*, 314, 315.
[61] Whoe'er thou art, that to this work art born,
  A chosen task thou hast, howe'er the world may scorn.
          Jacob Böhme, *Signatura Rerum*.

according to nature," for in these conditions "more will be done and better done and more easily than in any other way." [62]

In its empirical variety human nature is not uniform. To make this variety work with efficiency is the aim of any social structure. The fourfold classification emphasised the principal functions of the search for knowledge, inner and outer, the exercise of power and rulership, the production of wealth, and the maintenance of the well-being of society. It is also natural that groups get formed, developing their own environment, association, and training. Human beings are not single-tracked, and there should, therefore, be scope for free movement. Freedom and harmony are the two principles of variation and oneness, freedom of the individual, community or nation, and co-ordinated harmony of all individuals in groups and all groups in humanity. The principle of all human action is *lokasaṁgraha*, the holding together of the human race in its evolution. *Ṛg Veda* speaks of the four classes; so does the *Bhagavadgītā*. In neither was heredity taken as the determining factor. In the Dharma Śāstras the principle of heredity became important, though they permitted transition from one caste to another in accordance with the character and aptitude of the individuals.

So long as caste is treated as hereditary, whatever the theory may be, in practice there is no way by which one can pass from one caste to another. Spiritual gifts, moral achievements, elicit respect and admiration, but do not involve a change of caste. This is rendered difficult, because the position in the social structure was determined by birth. Even if it were true that specialised capacity is hereditarily transmitted, there is no justification for caste rigidity.

Mr. Marlow asks why we should adopt certain parts of our heritage and reject the rest. History is the endless process of the education of the human spirit. It never ceases, though it may be halted. We take what we need of our inheritance and use it for our purposes. Doctrinal developments in all religions proceed on the same pattern. The way in which the doctrine of hell is interpreted in centuries of Christian thought is not different from the way in which the doctrines of karma and rebirth are viewed by me. An eternal hell means that God's purpose has been defeated for good by a part of his creation, and intelligent Christians do not accept it today. All progress in religious thought is due to

[62] *Republic*, 433 A-D. *Cp*. St. Paul "As God has distributed to every man, as the Lord hath called every one, let him walk." I. *Corinthians*, VII, 17.

interpretation in the light of increasing knowledge and growing conscience.

As for the Harijans, Professor Wadia quotes my words about the improvement of their status: "What is being done today is a question, not of justice or charity, but of atonement. Even when we have done all that is in our power, we shall not have atoned even for a small fraction of our guilt in this matter." In the early years of the social reform movement, the upper classes offered the Harijans hard advice to improve their position, instead of active help. We should ask for their forgiveness; for we have wronged them, not knowingly always, but still we have wronged them. The only way in which we can repay is by devoting our lives to their service. By acknowledging our mistakes, by wisdom and devotion, we will merit and gain their forgiveness.

Mr. Marlow's statement, that "active work for the poor in India coincided with the first full impact of Christianity," does not do full justice to the protestant movements in Hinduism from Gautama the Buddha to the Vaiṣṇava and Śaiva saints. There is, however, no doubt that an impetus was given to the democratic impulses of Hinduism by Western influence. What we need in our country today is a social revolution.

The common people of the world have never known freedom. The forces of privilege and oppression have kept the freedom for themselves, and the masses of people have had to work on conditions laid down for them or starve and die. In present-day India we find a few living in luxury, while the millions are terribly emaciated with nothing to cover their nakedness but a rag for the middle of their bodies, shivering in the cold of dawn and sweating in the heat of noon, toiling without cease for a scanty subsistence. When we look at the vast scale of human suffering, we feel that we are perhaps the most corrupt generation of the human race. We must, however, distinguish between the prosperity of a country and the happiness of its inhabitants. A society which is acquisitive in its nature, unhealthy in its pleasures, disillusioned in its ideals, is a murderous machine without a conscience. Those who are anxious to regulate our lives and make us 'happy' even against our wills have to remember that man does not live by bread alone. We must regain health, physical and spiritual. With this in mind let us proclaim our leadership towards the future.

ALL SOULS COLLEGE
OXFORD UNIVERSITY   *S. Radhakrishnan*

BIBLIOGRAPHY OF THE WRITINGS OF
SARVEPALLI RADHAKRISHNAN
To March 1952

Compiled by

T. R. V. MURTI

BIBLIOGRAPHICAL NOTE

I AM not conscious of even a modest competence to compile a bibliography of such proportions. It is in obedience to the command of my revered teacher, Professor Radhakrishnan, that I have undertaken this task. I have derived the greatest help from him: he started me on the work with an almost full list of his works, and from time to time supplied me particulars from his unfailing memory. I had only to check up and fill in the remaining entries. I have also received help from many friends. I am afraid that, in spite of all this co-operation, many items have eluded my search. The Bibliography represents a fairly complete record of the many-sided intellectual activities of Professor Radhakrishnan for over a period of four decades.

I have generally conformed to the method followed in the previous volumes of this series. I have however included his Lectures and Speeches, a few of which are not published. He is not only one of the foremost writers, but an eloquent and inspired speaker as well; and no bibliography could be considered complete without including these. Many of his books were first delivered as *extempore lectures* and later on prepared for the press from notes. Professor Radhakrishnan used to deliver, during the nine years that he was Vice-Chancellor of the Banaras Hindu University, inspiring discourses on the *Bhagavadgītā* to crowded audiences on Sundays. No permanent record has been kept of these spiritual sermons, and the Bibliography does not make any mention of them. I only hope that the substance of these has been incorporated in his abiding work on *Bhagavadgītā*. I am also aware of some other omissions, notably the Watumull Foundation Lectures delivered in American University centres. I would be happy if, in spite of the admitted defects, the Bibliography should prove of help to readers in following the thought development of the great Indian Philosopher.

T. R. V. MURTI

DEPARTMENT OF PHILOSOPHY
UNIVERSITY OF CEYLON
COLOMBO, CEYLON

845

WRITINGS OF SARVEPALLI RADHAKRISHNAN TO MARCH, 1952

NOTE: Items marked with an asterisk are books.

1908

* 1. THE ETHICS OF THE VEDĀNTA AND ITS METAPHYSICAL PRESUPPOSI-
TIONS. A Thesis submitted in partial fulfillment of the requirements for the M. A. Degree of the Madras University. Madras,
The Guardian Press. ii + 93 pp.
2. KARMA AND FREE WILL. *Modern Review,* Vol. III, May, 1908,
pp. 424-428.
3. INDIAN PHILOSOPHY—THE VEDAS AND THE SIX SYSTEMS. *Madras
Christian College Magazine,* Vol. VIII (N.S.), 1908, pp. 22-35.

1910

1. "NATURE" AND "CONVENTION" IN GREEK ETHICS. *Calcutta Review,*
Vol. CXXX, January 1910, pp. 9-23.
2. EGOISM AND ALTRUISM—THE VEDĀNTA SOLUTION. *East and West,*
Vol. IX (No. 105), July 1910, pp. 626-630.
3. MORALITY AND RELIGION IN EDUCATION. *Madras Christian College Magazine,* Vol. X (N.S.), 1910-11, pp. 233-239.

1911

1. THE ETHICS OF THE BHAGAVADGĪTĀ AND KANT. *International
Journal of Ethics,* Vol. XXI (No. 4), July 1911, pp. 465-475.

1912

* 1. THE ESSENTIALS OF PSYCHOLOGY. Oxford, The University Press.
75 pp. Contents: Introduction—Man and Brain—Consciousness
and Its Nature—Mental Growth—Sense-Perception—Space and
External Reality—Imagination—Conception—Feeling—Emotions—
Voluntary Action—Attention.

1914

1. THE ETHICS OF THE VEDĀNTA. *International Journal of Ethics,* Vol. XXIV (No. 2), January 1914, pp. 168-183.
2. THE VEDĀNTA PHILOSOPHY AND THE DOCTRINE OF MĀYĀ. *International Journal of Ethics,* Vol. XXIV (No. 4), July 1914, pp. 431-451.

1915

1. A VIEW FROM INDIA ON THE WAR—I. *Asiatic Review,* Vol. VI, May 1915, pp. 369-374. (The second part of the article was not published, as the Censor did not permit its publication.)

1916

1. THE VEDĀNTA APPROACH TO REALITY. *The Monist,* Vol. XXVI (No. 2), April 1916, pp. 200-231.
2. RELIGION AND LIFE. *International Journal of Ethics,* Vol. XXVII (No. 1), October 1916, pp. 91-106.
3. BERGSON'S IDEA OF GOD. *The Quest* (A Quarterly Review, Ed. by G. R. S. Mead), Vol. VIII (No. 1), October 1916, pp. 1-8.

1917

1. THE PHILOSOPHY OF RABINDRANATH TAGORE—I. *The Quest,* Vol. VIII (No. 3), April 1917, pp. 457-477.
2. THE PHILOSOPHY OF RABINDRANATH TAGORE—II. *The Quest,* Vol. VIII (No. 4), July 1917, pp. 592-612.
3. IS BERGSON'S PHILOSOPHY MONISTIC? *Mind,* Vol. XXVI (N.S.), July 1917, pp. 329-339.

1918

* 1. THE PHILOSOPHY OF RABINDRANATH TAGORE. Dedicated to Rabindranath Tagore. 1st Ed., London, Macmillan and Co., 1918. ix + 294 pp. Second impression. Contents: I. The Philosophy of Rabindranath Tagore—II. The Philosophy of Rabindranath Tagore—III. Poetry and Philosophy—IV. The Message of Rabindranath Tagore to India—V. The Message of Rabindranath Tagore to the World.
2. JAMES WARD'S PLURALISTIC THEISM—I. *Indian Philosophical Review,* Vol. II (No. 2), October 1918, pp. 97-118.
3. JAMES WARD'S PLURALISTIC THEISM—II. *Indian Philosophical Review,* Vol. II (No. 3), December 1918, pp. 210-232.

1919

1. BERGSON AND ABSOLUTE IDEALISM—I. *Mind,* Vol. XXVIII (N.S.), January 1919, pp. 41-53.
2. BERGSON AND ABSOLUTE IDEALISM—II. *Mind,* Vol. XXVIII (N.S.), July 1919, pp. 275-296.

1920

* 1. THE REIGN OF RELIGION IN CONTEMPORARY PHILOSOPHY. London, Macmillan and Co., 1920. xii + 463 pp. Contents: Science, Religion and Philosophy—Recent Tendencies in Philosophy—The Monadism of Leibniz—The Philosophy of Professor James Ward —M. Bergson and Absolute Idealism—Bergson's Idea of God— Pragmatism—The Pluralistic Universe of William James—The New Idealism of Rudolf Eucken—The New Realism of Bertrand Russell—Personal Idealism—Suggestions of an Approach to Reality Based on the Upaniṣads.
2. THE METAPHYSICS OF THE UPANISADS—I. *Indian Philosophical Review,* Vol. III (No. 3), July 1920, pp. 213-235.
3. THE METAPHYSICS OF THE UPANISADS—II. *Indian Philosophical Review,* Vol. III (No. 4), October 1920, pp. 346-362.
4. Review of: Bosanquet's IMPLICATION AND LINEAR INFERENCE. *Indian Philosophical Review,* Vol. III, p. 301.
5. THE FUTURE OF RELIGION. *Mysore University Magazine,* Vol. IV, 1920, pp. 148-157.

1921

1. GANDHI AND TAGORE. *Calcutta Review,* Third Series, Vol. I, October 1921, pp. 14-29.
2. RELIGION AND PHILOSOPHY. *Hibbert Journal,* Vol. XX, October 1921, pp. 35-45.
3. TILAK AS AN ORIENTALIST. *Indian Review,* Vol. XXII, 1921, p. 737.

1922

1. THE HEART OF HINDUISM. *Hibbert Journal,* Vol. XXI (No. 1), October 1922, pp. 5-19. Reprinted in: *Heart of Hindusthan,* pp. 1-22.
2. THE HINDU DHARMA. *International Journal of Ethics,* Vol. XXXII (No. 1), October 1922, pp. 1-22.
3. CONTEMPORARY PHILOSOPHY. *Indian Review,* Vol. XXIII, 1922, p. 440.

1923

* 1. INDIAN PHILOSOPHY. VOL. I. Published in the *Library of Philosophy,* London, Allen & Unwin, 1st Ed., 1923. 738 pp. Revised ed.,

1929, Indian ed., 1940. Partly translated into Bengali, 1928. Contents: Introduction–The Hymns of the Ṛg Veda–Transition to the Upaniṣads–The Philosophy of the Upaniṣads–Materialism –The Pluralistic Realism of the Jainas–The Ethical Idealism of Early Buddhism–Epic Philosophy–The Theism of the Bhagavad-Gītā–Buddhism as a Religion–The Schools of Buddhism–Appendix (Further Consideration of Some Problems)–Notes–Index.

2. ISLAM AND INDIAN THOUGHT. *Indian Review*, Vol. XXIV, p. 665. Reprinted in: *Heart of Hindusthan*, pp. 53-72.

3. RELIGIOUS UNITY. *Mysore University Magazine*, Vol. VII, 1923, pp. 187-198.

1924

* 1. THE PHILOSOPHY OF THE UPANISADS. Reprint from *Indian Philosophy*, Vol. I, with a Foreword by Rabindranath Tagore and an Introduction by Edmond Holmes. London, George Allen & Unwin, Ltd., 1924. xv + 143 pp. Revised 2nd Ed., 1935.

2. HINDU THOUGHT AND CHRISTIAN DOCTRINE. *Madras Christian College Magazine*, Quarterly Series, January 1924, pp. 18-24.

3. THE HINDU IDEA OF GOD. *The Quest*, Vol. XV (No. 3), April 1924, pp. 289-310.

1926

* 1. THE HINDU VIEW OF LIFE. Upton Lectures delivered at Manchester College, Oxford, 1926. London, George Allen & Unwin, Ltd., 1927. 133 pp. Second Impression (1928), Third (1931), Fourth (1936), Fifth (1939), Sixth (1941), Seventh (1948), Eighth (1950). Contents: I. Religious Experience: Its Nature and Content –II. Conflict of Religions: The Hindu Attitude–III. Hindu Dharma-I–IV. Hindu Dharma-II–Index. Translated into German (Leipzig), French (Felix Alcan, Paris), Telugu, Kannada, Hindi, and Gujarati.

2. INDIAN PHILOSOPHY–SOME PROBLEMS. *Mind*, Vol. XXXV (N.S.), April 1926, pp. 154-180.

3. HASKELL LECTURES delivered at the University of Chicago. August, 1926. Not published.

4. THE ROLE OF PHILOSOPHY IN THE HISTORY OF CIVILISATION. Address given at Sixth International Congress of Philosophy, held at Harvard, September 1926. Published in E. S. Brightman, Ed., *Proceedings of the Sixth International Congress of Philosophy*, New York, Longmans, Green & Co., 1927, pp. 543-550. Reprinted in D. S. Robinson, Ed., *Anthology of Recent Philosophy*, New York, Thomas Y. Crowell Co., 1929, pp. 55-63.

5. THE DOCTRINE OF MĀYĀ: SOME PROBLEMS. Address given at Sixth International Congress of Philosophy, held at Harvard, September

1926. Published in E. S. Brightman, Ed., *Proceedings of the Sixth International Congress of Philosophy*, New York, Longmans, Green & Co., 1927, pp. 683-689.

1927

* 1. INDIAN PHILOSOPHY. VOL. II. Published in the *Library of Philosophy*, London, George Allen & Unwin, Ltd., 1927. 807 pp. Revised 2nd Ed., with Notes, 1931. Contents: Introduction—The Logical Realism of the Nyāya—The Atomistic Pluralism of the Vaiśeṣika—The Sāṅkhya System—The Yoga System of Patañjali—The Pūrva Mīmāṁsā—The Vedānta Sūtra— The Advaita Vedānta of Śaṁkara —The Theism of Rāmānuja—The Śaiva, Śākta and the Later Vaiṣṇava Theism—Conclusion—Notes—Index.

2. UNIVERSITIES AND NATIONAL LIFE. Andhra University Convocation Address, Waltair, December 5, 1927. Included in *Freedom and Culture*, pp. 1-21.

3. PRESIDENTIAL ADDRESS given at Third Indian Philosophical Congress, Bombay University, December, 19-22, 1927. Published in *Proceedings of the III Indian Philosophical Congress*. Calcutta, University of Calcutta, pp. 19-30.

1928

* 1. THE RELIGION WE NEED. A Booklet in the Affirmation Series. London, Ernest Benn, 32 pp. Contents: The Tendencies of Modern Belief—The Evidence of Biology—Cosmic Evolution—The Quest for God—The True Religious Life—The Ideal of Universal Brotherhood.

* 2. THE VEDĀNTA ACCORDING TO ŚAṀKARA AND RĀMĀNUJA. Reprinted from *Indian Philosophy*, Vol. II. London, George Allen & Unwin, Ltd., 1928. 287 pp. Contents: The Advaita of Śaṁkara—The Theism of Rāmānuja.

3. INDIAN PHILOSOPHY—NOTES: A Reply to Dr. E. J. Thomas's review of *Indian Philosophy*, Vol. I, which appeared in *Mind*, October 1927. *Mind*, XXXVII (N.S.), January 1928, pp. 130-131.

4. EVOLUTION AND ITS IMPLICATIONS. *New Era*, November 1928, pp. 102-111.

1929

* 1. KALKI—OR THE FUTURE OF CIVILISATION. London, Kegan Paul & Co., 1929. 96 pp. Reprinted 1934. Second Ed., Bombay, Hind Kitabs, 1948. Contents: Introduction—The Negative Results—The Problem—Reconstruction.

* 2. AN IDEALIST VIEW OF LIFE. Being the Hibbert Lectures for 1929 (lectures given in the University of Manchester in December 1929

and the University College, London, in January 1930). London,
George Allen & Unwin, Ltd., 1932. 352 pp. Revised Second Ed.,
1937; Third Impression, 1947. Translated into Swedish, Stockholm, 1949. Contents: The Modern Challenge to Religion—Substitutes for Religion—Religious Experience and Its Affirmations—
Intellect and Intuition—The Spirit in Man—Matter, Life and Mind
—Human Personality and Its Destiny—Ultimate Reality—Notes
and Index.

3. INDIAN PHILOSOPHY. Article in the 12th Vol. of the *Encyclopaedia
Britannica*, 14th Ed., New York, 1929 and following years, pp.247-
253. Contents: The Vedic Period (Ṛg Veda, Upaniṣads)—The
Epic Period—The Six Systems; Nyāya, Vaiśesika, Sāṁkhya, Yoga—
Pūrva Mīmāṁsā, Vedānta (Śaṁkara's Non-dualism, Rāmānuja's
Theism and Madhva's Dualism).

4. COMPARATIVE RELIGION. First of a series of lectures on Comparative Religion, given at Manchester College, Oxford, on October
22, 1929. Included in *East and West in Religion*, Ch. I, pp. 13-40.

5. CHAOS AND CREATION. Sermon delivered at Manchester College,
Oxford, November 1929. Included in *East and West in Religion*,
Ch. III, pp. 73-98.

1930

1. EAST AND WEST IN RELIGION. The Jowett Lecture, given on
March 18, 1930, at the Mary Ward Settlement, London. Included
in *East and West in Religion*, Ch. II, pp. 43-70. Reprinted in
Indian Review, Vol. XXXI, p. 257ff.

2. REVOLUTION THROUGH SUFFERING. Sermon delivered at Manchester College Chapel, Oxford, June 8, 1930. Included in *East and
West in Religion*, Ch. IV, pp. 101-125.

3. Review of: John Baillie's INTERPRETATION OF RELIGION—AN IN-
TRODUCTORY STUDY OF THEOLOGICAL PRINCIPLES (Edinburgh, 1929).
Hibbert Journal, Vol. XXVIII, July 1930, pp. 740-742.

4. EDUCATION AND NATIONALISM. Mysore University Convocation
Address, Mysore, October 10, 1930. Included in *Freedom and
Culture*, pp. 22-35.

5. TRAINING FOR LEADERSHIP. Punjab University Convocation Address, Lahore, December 23, 1930. Included in *Freedom and
Culture*, pp. 36-47.

6. Third Krisnarajendra Silver Jubilee Lecture. Delivered in the
Mysore University, Mysore, October, 1930.

7. THE RESPONSIBILITY OF THE INTELLECTUALS. An address to the
Indian Students' Hostel, London, February 1930. Included in *Freedom and Culture*, 105-114.

8. Foreword to A. K. Majumdar's *The Sāṁkhya Conception of Personality*, Calcutta, pp. ix-xii.

1931

1. The Spirit in Man. The Principal Miller Lectures, Madras University, Madras, February, 1931.
2. The Hindu Idea of God. *The Spectator*, May 31, 1931. Reprinted in: *The Heart of Hindusthan*, pp. 47-52.
3. Intuition and Intellect. Contribution to *The Golden Book of Tagore*, Calcutta, pp. 310-313.
4. The Spirit of Youth. Lucknow University Convocation Address, December 5, 1931. Included in *Freedom and Culture*, pp. 48-60.
5. Rabindranath Tagore. Presidential Address at the General Conference in connection with the 70th Birthday of Rabindranath Tagore, Calcutta, December 1931. Included in *East and West in Religion*, Ch. V, pp. 129-143.

1932

1. Education and the New Democracy. Convocation Address given at Nagpur University, Nagpur, November 19, 1932. Included in *Freedom and Culture*, pp. 61-74.
2. Foreword to Dr. N. K. Brahma's The Philosophy of Hindu Sādhāna. London, Kegan Paul, 1932.
3. Presidential Address given at VIII (Mysore) Session of the Indian Philosophical Congress. Published in *Proceedings of the Indian Philosophical Congress*, Calcutta, pp. v-xvi.
4. Sarvamukti (Universal Salvation)—A Symposium. Published in *Proceedings of the Eighth Indian Philosophical Congress*, Calcutta, 1932, pp. 314-318.

1933

* 1. East and West in Religion. London, George Allen & Unwin, Ltd., 1933. 146 pp. Second impression, 1949. Contents: I. Comparative Religion—II. East and West in Religion—III. Chaos and Creation—IV. Revolution Through Suffering—V. Rabindranath Tagore, Index.
2. Intellect and Intuition in Śaṁkara's Philosophy. *Triveni*, Vol. VI (No. 1), July-August 1933.
3. The Teaching of the Buddha. Inaugural Lecture under the Don Alphina Ratnayaka Trust, delivered at Colombo, Ceylon, October 2, 1933. Published by the Public Trustee of Ceylon, Colombo, Ceylon, 1933. 23 pp.
4. An Appeal to Women. Address to the All India Women's Conference, Calcutta, December 1933. Included in *Freedom and Culture*, pp. 117-121.

5. INTELLECTUAL CO-OPERATION. Speech delivered at Geneva. Included in *Freedom and Culture*, pp. 115ff.

1934

1. THE TEACHING OF THE BUDDHA BY SPEECH AND BY SILENCE. *Hibbert Journal*, Vol. XXXII (No. 3), April 1934, pp. 342-356.
2. DEMOCRACY AND DICTATORSHIP. Allahabad University Convocation Address, Allahabad, November 13, 1934. Included in *Freedom and Culture*, pp. 75-87.
3. Foreword to THE HINDU ART IN ITS SOCIAL SETTING, by Miss P. N. P. Dubash. Madras, 1934.

1935

1. A NEW SOCIAL ORDER. An address to the Andhra University, Waltair, November 1935. Included in *Freedom and Culture*, pp. 88-92.
2. WESTERN EDUCATION IN INDIA. Address to the Jubilee Celebration of Morris College, Nagpur, December 1935. Included in *Freedom and Culture*, pp. 93-104.

1936

* 1. FREEDOM AND CULTURE; University Convocation and other Addresses. Madras, G. A. Natesan & Co., 1936. 158 pp. Fourth edition, 1946.
* 2. CONTEMPORARY INDIAN PHILOSOPHY, Edited jointly with Professor J. H. Muirhead. *Library of Philosophy*, London, George Allen & Unwin, Ltd., 1936. 375 pp. Contributions by Mahātmā Gāndhi, Rabindranath Tagore, Prof. K. C. Bhattacharya, Professor S. Radhakrishnan (See Item 9, below), Ananda K. Coomaraswami, M. Hiriyanna, and others.
* 3. THE HEART OF HINDUSTHAN. On Indian religions and philosophy. Madras, G. A. Natesan & Co., 1936. 151 pp. Reprinted several times. Eighth edition, April 1945.
4. THE SUPREME SPIRITUAL IDEAL—THE HINDU VIEW. An Address delivered before the World Congress of Faiths at Queen's Hall, London, July 6, 1936. Included in *Faith and Fellowship*, London, J. M. Watkins, pp. 422-430. Also printed in *Hibbert Journal*, Vol. XXXV (No. 1), October 1936, pp. 26-39. Reprinted in: *Eastern Religions and Western Thought*, Ch. II, pp. 35-57.
5. RELIGION AND RELIGIONS. A Lecture delivered before the World Congress of Faiths on July 8, 1936. Published in *Proceedings of the World Congress of Faiths*, pp. 104-115 (discussion on the

lecture, pp. 116-119, Professor Radhakrishnan's reply, pp. 119-121).
6. THE WORLD'S UNBORN SOUL. Inaugural Lecture as Spalding Professor of Eastern Religions and Ethics, delivered before the University of Oxford, October 20, 1936. Published by the Clarendon Press, Oxford. Reprinted in: *Eastern Religions and Western Thought*, pp. 1-34.
7. Foreword to THE PHILOSOPHY OF YOGA VĀŚISTHA, by Dr. B. L. Atreya. Madras, Adyar, 1936.
8. SPIRITUAL FREEDOM AND THE NEW EDUCATION. A lecture delivered on August 3, 1936, before the New Education Fellowship, 7th World Conference, held at Cheltenham, England, July 31-August 14, 1936. Published in the *New Era*, Vol. XVII, pp. 233f.
9. THE SPIRIT IN MAN. Professor Radhakrishnan's contribution in *Contemporary Indian Philosophy*, pp. 257-289.

1937

1. PROGRESS AND SPIRITUAL VALUES. A lecture delivered at the Evening Meeting of the British Institute of Philosophy, January 19, 1937. Published in *Philosophy*, Vol. XII, July 1937, pp. 259-275.
2. MYSTICISM AND HINDU THOUGHT. The Sir George Birdwood Memorial Lecture given at the Royal Society of Arts, London, April 30, 1937. Reprinted in *Eastern Religions and Western Thought*, Ch. III, pp. 58-114.
3. HINDUISM. An Article in G. T. Garrett, ed., *The Legacy of India*, pp. 256-286. Oxford, Clarendon Press, 1937.
4. MY SEARCH FOR TRUTH. Radhakrishnan's only actual Autobiography. Contributed to the volume, *Religion in Transition*, edited by Vergilius Ferm, New York, Macmillan & Co. (also: London, George Allen & Unwin, Ltd.), 1937, pp. 11-59. Reprinted as a separate offprint by Shiva Lal Agarwala & Co., Ltd., Agra, India (1st Indian edition, 1946), 49 pp.
5. THE INDIVIDUAL AND THE SOCIAL ORDER IN HINDUISM. A lecture delivered before the University of Oxford, 1936. Printed in *Eastern Religions and Western Thought*, Ch. IX, pp. 349-385.
6. THE FAILURE OF THE INTELLECTUALS. *Indian Review*, Vol. XXXVIII (1937), pp. 737ff.
7. STEPHANOS NIRMALENDU GHOSH LECTURES. Delivered under the above Foundation in the University of Calcutta. Not published.
8. EDUCATION AND SPIRITUAL FREEDOM. Based on a report of the World Education Conference at Cheltenham, 1937. *Triveni*, Vol. X (No. 3), (N.S.), September 1937. Also in: *Education, Politics and War*, pp. 91-110.
9. Introduction to: THE CULTURAL HERITAGE OF INDIA, Vol. I. Calcutta, The Ramakrishna Centenary Publication (3 vols.), 1937.

10. Foreword to Dr. S. K. Das's A STUDY OF THE VEDĀNTA. Calcutta University Press.

1938

* 1. GAUTAMA—THE BUDDHA. Annual Henriette Hertz Trust Lecture on a Master Mind, delivered at the British Academy on June 29, 1938. First published in *Proceedings of the British Academy*, London, 1938. Published separately by Humphrey Milford, London, Oxford University Press. 50 pp. Reprinted by Hind Kitabs, Bombay. Also in *The Dhammapada*, 1950.
2. RELIGION: A PLEA FOR SANITY. Broadcast Talk from the All-India Radio, Calcutta. Published in *Triveni*, Vol. XI (N.S.), November 1938. Also in: *Education, Politics and War*, pp. 157-164.
3. THE RENAISSANCE OF RELIGION—A HINDU VIEW. Lecture delivered July 24, 1938, before the World Congress of Faiths, Cambridge. Published in *Proceedings of the World Congress of Faiths*, London, A. Probsthain.
4. WHAT BRITISH PEOPLE OUGHT TO KNOW. Bombay, *The Indian World*. Included in *Education, Politics and War*, pp. 1-10.
5. RELIGION AND POLITICS. An address to the Convocation of the Benares Hindu University, Benares, December 17, 1938. Included in *Education, Politics and War*, pp. 26-46.
6. Foreword to Dr. T. M. P. Mahadevan's THE PHILOSOPHY OF THE ADVAITA. London, Luzac & Co., 1938.
7. DEMOCRACY: A HABIT OF MIND. Presidential Address to the Andhra Mahasabha, Madras Session. Included in *Education, Politics and War*, pp. 10-25.

1939

* 1. EASTERN RELIGIONS AND WESTERN THOUGHT. London, Humphrey Milford, Oxford University Press, 1939. xiii + 396 pp. Revised second edition, 1940. Translated into German, Amsterdam. Contents: I. The World's Unborn Soul—II. The Supreme Spiritual Ideal—The Hindu View—III. Mysticism and Ethics in Hindu Thought—IV. India and Western Religious Thought—Greece—V. India and Western Religious Thought—Christendom I—VI. India and Western Religious Thought—Christendom II—VII. Greece and Palestine and India—VIII. The Meeting of Religions—IX. The Individual and the Social Order in Hinduism—Appendix—Index.
* 2. Introduction to MAHATMA GANDHI, essays and reflections on Gandhi's life and work by Albert Einstein, Pearl Buck, Rabindranath Tagore, and many others, edited by Professor S. Radhakrishnan and presented to Gandhi on his 70th Birthday, October

2, 1939. London, George Allen & Unwin, Ltd., 1939. 557 pp. 2nd impression, 1940. Professor Radhakrishnan's Introduction, pp. 13-40. Second (enlarged) Edition, with a Memorial Section, 1949. INTRODUCTION to the Memorial Section by Professor Radhakrishnan, pp. 336-361.

3. THE RENAISSANCE IN RELIGION. The Lewis Fry Memorial Lectures delivered before the Bristol University, February 27-28, 1939.

4. THE FUTURE OF SOUTH AFRICA. Talk broadcast from Johannesburg, South Africa, April 1939.

5. CIVILISATION AND JUSTICE. Speech broadcast from the Durban Station, South Africa, April 19, 1939. Included in *Freedom and Culture*, pp. 134-139. Also printed in *Education, Politics and War*, pp. 47-53.

6. CULTURE NOT NATIONAL. Presidential Address given at the All-India Education Conference, December 27, 1939. Printed in *Education, Politics and War*, pp. 66-71.

7. Foreword to S. K. George's GANDHI'S CHALLENGE TO CHRISTIANITY. London, George Allen & Unwin.

8. INDIA AND CHINA. Speech broadcast from the All India Radio, Calcutta, on China Day Celebrations.

9. PRESIDENTIAL ADDRESS. Given at 15th Conference, All India Federation of Educational Associations, Lucknow, December 26-31, 1939. Printed in *Proceedings* of the Conference (Allahabad, Ram Narain Lal), pp. 100-105.

1940

1. EDUCATION, POLITICS AND WAR. Address to the Convocation of the University of Patna, November 29, 1940. Printed in *Education, Politics and War*, pp. 75-90.

1941

1. HINDUISM AND THE WEST. Contribution to: O'Malley, ed., *Modern India and the West* (Oxford, the University Press), Ch. IX, pp. 338-353.

2. HINDU MUSLIM RELATIONS. Address to the Convocation of the University of Dacca. Included in *Education, Politics and War*, pp. 136-151.

3. TRUTH ALONE CONQUERS, NOT FALSEHOOD. Presidential address delivered at the Inaugural Conference of the India Youth League, Lahore, February, 1941. Included in *Education, Politics and War*, pp. 129-135.

4. TRUE FREEDOM. Speech declaring open the Bharatiya Vidya Bhavan, delivered in Bombay, October 8, 1941. Included in *Education, Politics and War*, pp. 111-119.

5. PURPOSE OF EDUCATION. Address to the Convocation of the University of Agra, November 22, 1941. Included in *Education, Politics and War*, pp. 129-135.

1942

1. GĀNDHIJĪ AND MĀLAVĪYAJĪ. Concluding Speech at the Special Silver Jubilee Convocation of the Benares Hindu University, Benares, January 21, 1942. Included in *Education, Politics and War*, pp. 152-156.
2. GENERAL PREFACE to Dr. G. Jha's THE PŪRVA MĪMĀMSĀ IN ITS SOURCES. Benares, The University Press.
3. THE CULTURAL PROBLEM. Madras, Oxford University Press, *Oxford Pamphlets on Indian Affairs* (No. 1), pp. 41-50.
4. FREEDOM IS DEEP AND ELEMENTAL. Address to the Convocation of the Benares Hindu University, November 29, 1942. Included in *Education, Politics and War*, pp. 156-169.
5. UNIVERSITIES. Presidential Address at the Quinquennial Conference of Universities, Hyderabad, December 1942. Included in *Education, Politics and War*, pp. 170-178.

1943

1. INDIA'S HERITAGE. Welcome Address to the XII All India Oriental Conference, Benares, 1943-44. Published in *The Proceedings and Transactions of the XII Session of the All India Oriental Conference*, pp. 1-5. Included in *Education, Politics and War*, pp. 176-186.
2. SILVER JUBILEE ADDRESS to the Bhandarkar Oriental Research Institute on its completion of 25 years, January 4, 1943. Published in the *Annals of the Bhandarkar Oriental Research Institute*, Vol. XXIV, pp. 1-8.

1944

* 1. INDIA AND CHINA. Based on notes of lectures delivered in China in May (6-21), 1944. Bombay, Hind Kitabs. 168 pp. Contents: Preface–Introduction–China and India–Chinese Ideals of Education–Religion in China (Confucianism)–Religion in China (Taoism)–Gautama the Buddha and His Teaching–Buddhism in China–War and World Security–7 Appendices–Index.
* 2. EDUCATION, POLITICS AND WAR. Poona, International Book Service, 1944. 208 pp.
3. Foreword to THE RENAISSANCE OF HINDUISM, by Professor D. S. Sarma. Benares, The University Press.

4. Foreword to Swami Nirvedānanda's HINDUISM AT A GLANCE. Calcutta, Vidyā-Mandir.
5. BENGAL FAMINE AND INDIAN POLITICS. Convocation Address, University of Calcutta, March 11, 1944. Included in *Education, Politics and War,* pp. 199-208.
6. RELIGION AND SOCIAL SERVICE. Address delivered to the Sir Dorabji Tata Graduate School of Social Work, Bombay. Included in *Education, Politics and War,* pp. 199-208.

1945

* 1. IS THIS PEACE? Substance of two lectures delivered at the inauguration of the Benares Hindu University Parliament, September 10, 1945, and the Karachi Rotary Club on October 17, 1945. Bombay, Hind Kitabs, 70 pp. Contents: The Problem—The Defeated Powers—The Power of Veto—Conflicts Among Great Powers —Colonial Rivalries—International Force—Cultural Co-operation.
2. Foreword to the GĪTĀ LETTERS by Swāmi Avināsānanda. Bombay, Hind Kitabs.
3. MORAL VALUES IN LITERATURE. Lecture delivered at the P.E.N. Conference, Jaipur, September 1945. Published in *The Proceedings of the P.E.N. Conference* (Bombay, International Book House), pp. 86-105.
4. SPEECH, unveiling statue of Mahātmā Gāndhi in Karachi. Not published.
5. INTRODUCTION to Dilip Kumar Roy's AMONG THE GREAT. Bombay, Nalanda Publishing House.
6. ADDRESS at the Vidyālaṅkāra Pirivena, Kelaniya, Ceylon, on the occasion of Award of Distinction of 'Vidyāchakravarti.' Not published.
7. FOREWORD to THE MIND OF MAHATMA GANDHI by R. K. Prabhu and U. R. Rao. Bombay, Oxford University Press.

1946

1. P.E.N. DINNER SPEECH, February 6, 1946. Published in the *P.E.N. News,* No. 142, March 1946, pp. 8-11.
2. THE INDIAN DELEGATION TO THE UNESCO. A Talk from Paris, broadcast in the B.B.C's Overseas Service, December 4, 1946. Published in *Records of the General Conference, UNESCO,* 1946, p. 27f. Also in *UNESCO, 1946-48,* A Report issued by the Ministry of Education, Government of India, New Delhi.
3. BHAGAWĀN ŚRĪ RAMANA. An Article contributed to the *Golden Jubilee Souvenir,* Sri Ramanashram, Tiruvannamalai, S. India.

1947

* 1. RELIGION AND SOCIETY. Based on notes of lectures delivered in the Universities of Calcutta and Benares in the winter of 1942 under the Kamala Lectures Foundation. London, George Allen & Unwin, Ltd., 242 pp. 2nd Ed., 1948. Translated into Hindi, Agra (India), 1949. Contents: I. The Need for Religion—II. The Inspiration of Religion and the New World Order—III. Hindu Dharma—IV. Women in Hindu Society—V. War and Non-Violence. Also contains 3 portraits of Asutosh Mukkerji, Śrīmatī Kamalā Devi, and Professor Radhakrishnan.

2. INDIA'S INFLUENCE. A Talk in the Series, "The Kingdom of the Mind," given on the 27th of February, 1947, and broadcast by the B.B.C.

3. SCIENCE AND RELIGION. In: Art and Thought, A Volume in Honour of the late Dr. Ananda K. Coomaraswamy (London, Luzac & Co.), pp. 180-185.

4. THE SPIRIT OF ASIA. Opening Address to the Asian Relations Conference, broadcast on the All India Radio, March, 1947. Printed and distributed by the Government of India Information Service.

5. INDEPENDENCE DAY BROADCAST TALK. Delhi, All India Radio, August 15, 1947. Not published.

6. UNESCO ADDRESS. Delivered before the 2nd (Mexico) Session of the UNESCO, as leader of the Indian Delegation, November 8, 1947. Printed in: Records of the General Conference, 1947, pp. 58-62.

1948

* 1. THE BHAGAVADGĪTĀ. With an Introductory Essay, Sanskrit Text, English translation, and Notes. London, George Allen & Unwin, Ltd., 388 pp. American edition, New York, Harper & Brothers. Translated into French (Paris), Swedish (Stockholm), Hindi, Marathi, and Kannada (Bombay). Second edition, 1949. Contents: Introductory Essay—Text: Chapts. I-XVIII, translation and notes.

2. MAHĀTMĀ GĀNDHI. Address delivered in the All Souls College, Oxford, Sunday, February 1, 1948. Printed in Hibbert Journal, Vol. XLVI, pp. 193-197. Reprinted in Mahātmā Gāndhi, Memorial Section of second edition.

3. UNESCO ADDRESS. Delivered before the Third (Beirut) General Session of UNESCO. Published in Records of the General Session, 1948, pp. 56-59.

4. INDIAN CULTURE. Lecture delivered at the opening session of UNESCO at the Sorbonne University, Paris. Printed in The Reflections on Our Age (London, Allan Wingate), pp. 115-133.

5. GENERAL STATEMENT in: Clara Urquhart, ed. *Last Chance, Eleven Questions on Issues Determining Our Destiny Answered by 26 Leaders of Thought of 14 Nations* (Boston, The Beacon Press), pp. 46-54.
6. HINDUISM. Article in Hutchinson's *Twentieth Century Encyclopedia*, p. 522.

1949

* 1. GREAT INDIANS. With an introductory essay on the author by Prof. D. S. Sarma. Bombay, Hind Kitabs, 108 pp. Contents: Mahatma Gandhi—Bhagawan Sri Ramana—Sri Ramakrishna Paramahamsa—Rabindranath Tagore.
* 2. REPORT OF THE UNIVERSITY EDUCATION COMMISSION, VOL. I. Jointly with Sir James Duff, Dr. A. E. Morgan, Dr. Tigert, Dr. Tarachand, Dr. A. L. Mudaliayar, Professor M. Saha, Professor K. N. Bahl, Dr. Z. Hussain, and Professor N. K. Sidhanta. New Delhi, Govt. of India Manager of Publication, 747 pp. Contents: Introduction—Historical Retrospect—The Aims of University Education—Teaching Staff—Standards of Teaching—Courses of Study (Arts and Science)—Post-Graduate Training and Research—Professional Education—Religious Education—Medium of Instruction —Examinations—Students, Their Activities and Welfare—Women's Education—Constitution and Control—Finance—Benares, Aligarh and Delhi Universities—Other Universities—New Universities— Rural Universities—Conclusion—Appendices and Graphs.
3. SPEECH made at the Fourth (Paris) General Session of UNESCO. Published in *General Records of the UNESCO,* 1949, pp. 44-45 and 58-60.
4. Foreword to R. R. Diwakar, THE UPANIṢADS IN STORY AND DIALOGUE. Bombay, Hind Kitabs.
5. CONVOCATION ADDRESS. Delivered at Lucknow University Silver Jubilee Celebration, January 1949.
6. A CLEAN ADVOCATE OF GREAT IDEALS. Contribution to *The Nehru Birthday Book* (Delhi, Nehru Abhinandan Granth), pp. 93-96.
7. GOETHE. In: *Goethe,* UNESCO's Homage on the occasion of the two hundredth anniversary of his birth (Paris, UNESCO Publication No. 411), pp. 99-108.

1950

* 1. THE DHAMMAPADA. Translated into English with Introduction and notes. Oxford, the University Press. viii + 192 pp. Contents: Preface—Introductory Essays—Pali Text—English Translation and Notes—Pali Index—General Index.

2. SPEECH made at the Fifth (Florence) Session of the UNESCO. Published in *General Records of the UNESCO*, 1950.
3. UNESCO AND WORLD REVOLUTION. *The New Republic*, July 10, 1950, pp. 15-16.
4. SCIENCE AND PHILOSOPHY. Presidential Address at Silver Jubilee Session of the Indian Philosophical Congress, Calcutta, December 20, 1950.

1951

1. THE SPIRIT OF DEMOCRACY. Convocation Address to the University of Gauhati, India, January 3, 1951.
2. RELIGION AND WORLD UNITY. *Hibbert Journal*, April 1951, pp. 218-225.
3. VEDĀNTA: THE ADVAITA SCHOOL: ŚAṀKARA. Contributed to *History of Philosophy, Eastern and Western*, London, George Allen & Unwin, Vol. I, pp. 272-286.
4. EPILOGUE. Contributed to *History of Philosophy, Eastern and Western*, London, George Allen & Unwin, Vol. II.
5. THE NATURE OF MAN. An essay contributed to *Creators of the Modern Spirit*, edited by Barbara Waylen (London, Rocliff), 64-66.
6. RELIGION AND THE WORLD CRISES. An essay contributed to *Vedanta for Modern Man*, edited by Christopher Isherwood, pp. 338-341.

1952

1. THE RELIGION OF THE SPIRIT AND THE WORLD'S NEED. Introductory Autobiographical Essay in Paul Arthur Schilpp, ed., *The Philosophy of Sarvepalli Radhakrishnan*, in *The Library of Living Philosophers*. New York, Tudor Publishing Company, 1952.
2. REPLY TO CRITICS, also in *The Philosophy of Sarvepalli Radhakrishnan* (Paul A. Schilpp, ed.).

CHRONOLOGICAL LIST OF PRINCIPAL WORKS

NOTE: The number in brackets after each title refers to the num
ber of that work under the particular year, to which the
reader may refer for complete bibliographical data.

Year	Work	Number
1918	The Philosophy of Rabindranath Tagore	[1]
1920	The Reign of Religion in Contemporary Philosophy	[1]
1923	(& 1927) Indian Philosophy. Two Volumes. *Library of Philosophy*, 1923 [1] and 1927 [1].	
1926	The Hindu View of Life	[1]
1928	The Religion We Need	[1]
1929	Kalki, or The Future of Civilisation	[1]
1932	An Idealist View of Life (see 1929)	[2]
1933	East and West in Religion	[1]
1936	Freedom and Culture	[1]
1936	The Heart of Hindusthan	[3]
1937	My Search for Truth (Autobiography)	[4]
1938	Gautama—The Buddha	[1]
1939	Eastern Religions and Western Thought	[1]
1939	Mahātmā Gāndhi	[2]
1944	India and China	[1]
1944	Education, Politics and War	[2]
1945	Is This Peace?	[1]
1947	Religion and Society	[1]
1948	The Bhagavadgītā	[1]
1949	Great Indians	[1]
1950	The Dhammapada	[1]
1952	The Religion of the Spirit and the World's Need (Autobiographical)	[1]

INDEX

(Arranged by SURINDAR S. SURI)